T0136809

PERFORMANCE EVALUATION OF COMPUTER AND COMMUNICATION SYSTEMS

COMPUTER AND COMMUNICATION SCIENCES

PERFORMANCE EVALUATION OF COMPUTER AND COMMUNICATION SYSTEMS

Jean-Yves Le Boudec

EPFL Press
A Swiss academic publisher distributed by CRC Press

CRC Press
Taylor & Francis Group

Taylor and Francis Group, LLC
6000 Broken Sound Parkway, NW, Suite 300,
Boca Raton, FL 33487

Distribution and Customer Service
orders@crcpress.com

www.crcpress.com

Library of Congress Cataloging-in-Publication Data
A catalog record for this book is available from the Library of Congress.

This book is published under the editorial direction of
Professor Serge Vaudenay (EPFL).

The authors and publisher express their thanks to the Ecole polytechnique fédérale
de Lausanne (EPFL) for its generous support towards the publication of this book.

Cover artwork: Elias Le Boudec

EPFL Press

is an imprint owned by Presses polytechniques et universitaires romandes, a Swiss
academic publishing company whose main purpose is to publish the teaching and
research works of the Ecole polytechnique fédérale de Lausanne (EPFL) and other
universities and institutions of higher learning.

Presses polytechniques et universitaires romandes
EPFL – Rolex Learning Center
Post office box 119
CH-1015 Lausanne, Switzerland
E-mail: ppur@epfl.ch
Phone: 021 / 693 21 30
Fax: 021 / 693 40 27

www.epflpress.org

© 2010, First edition, EPFL Press, Lausanne (Switzerland)
ISBN 978-2-940222-40-7 (EPFL Press)
ISBN 978-1-4398-4992-7 (CRC Press)

Printed in Italy

Preface

Performance evaluation is often the critical part of evaluating the results of a research project. Many of us are familiar with simulations, but it is frequently difficult to address questions like: Should I eliminate the beginning of the simulation in order for the system to become stabilized? I simulate a random way-point model but the average speed in my simulation is not as expected. What happened? The reviewers of my study complained that I did not provide confidence intervals. How do I go about this? I would like to characterize the fairness of my protocol. Should I use Jain's Fairness Index or the Lorenz Curve Gap? I would like to fit a distribution to the flow sizes that I measured, but all my measurements are truncated to a maximum value; how do I account for the truncation?

This book groups a set of lecture notes for a course given at EPFL. It contains all the material needed by an engineer who wishes to evaluate the performance of a computer or communication system. More precisely, with this book and some accompanying practicals, you will be able to answer the above and other questions, evaluate the performance of computer and communication systems and master the theoretical foundations of performance evaluation and of the corresponding software packages.

In the past, many textbooks on performance evaluation have given the impression that this is a complex field, with large amounts of baroque queuing theory excursions, which can be exercised only by performance evaluation experts. This is not necessarily the case. In contrast, performance evaluation can and should be performed by any computer engineering specialist who designs a system. When a plumber installs pipes in our house, one expects her to properly size their diameters; the same holds for computer engineers.

This book is not intended for the performance evaluation specialist. It is adressed *to any computer engineer or scientist* who is active in the development or operation of software or hardware systems. The required background is an elementary course in probability and one in calculus.

The objective of this book is therefore to make performance evaluation usable by all computer engineers and scientists. The foundations of performance evaluation reside in statistics and queuing theory. Therefore, *some* mathematics are involved and the text cannot be overly simplified. However, it turns out that much of the complications are not in the general theories, but in the exact solution of specific models. For example, certain textbooks on statistics (but none of the ones cited in the reference list) develop various solution techniques for specific models, the vast majority of which are encapsulated in commercially or freely available software packages like Matlab, S-PLUS, Excel, Scilab or R.

To avoid this pitfall, we focus first on the *what* before the *how*. Indeed, the most difficult question in a performance analysis is often "what to do"; once you know what to do, it is less difficult to find a way with your usual software tools or by shopping the web. For example, what do we do when we fit a model to data using least square fitting (Chapter 3)? What is a confidence interval? What is a prediction interval (Chapter 2)? What is the congestion collapse pattern (Chapter 1)? What is the null hypothesis in a test and what does the result of a test *really* mean (Chapter 4)? What is an information criterion (Chapter 5)? If no failure appears out of n experiments, what confidence interval can I give for the failure probability (Chapter 2)?

Second, regarding the *how*, we looked for solution methods that are as universal as possible, i.e. that apply to many situations, whether simple or complex. There are several reasons for this. Firstly, one should use only methods and tools that one understands, and a good engineer should first invest some time in learning tools and methods that he/she will use more often. Secondly, brute force and a computer can do a lot more than one often seems to believe. This philosophy is in sharp contrast to some publications on performance evaluation. For example, computing confidence or prediction intervals can be made simple and systematic if we use the median and not the mean; if we have to employ the mean, the use of the likelihood ratio statistic is quite universal and requires little intellectual sophistication regarding the model. Thus, we focus on generic methods such as: the use of filters for forecasting (Chapter 5), bootstrap and Monte-Carlo simulations for evaluating averages or prediction intervals (Chapter 6), the likelihood ratio statistic for tests (Chapter 2, Chapter 4), importance sampling (Chapter 6), least-square and ℓ^1-norm minimization methods (Chapter 3).

When presenting solutions, we try *not* to hide their limitations and the cases where they do not work. Indeed, some frustrations experienced by young researchers can sometimes be attributed to false expectations about the power of various methods.

We give a coverage of queuing theory that attempts to strike a balance between depth and relevance. During a performance analysis, one is often confronted with the dilemma: should we use an approximate model for which exact solutions exist, or approximate solutions for a more exact model? We propose four topics (deterministic analysis, operational laws, single queues, queuing networks) which provide a good balance. We illustrate in a case study how the four topics can be utilized to provide different insights on a queuing question. For queuing networks, we give a unified treatment, which is perhaps the first of its kind at this level of synthesis. We show that complex topics such as queues with concurrency (MSCCC queues) or networks with bandwidth sharing (Whittle networks) all fit in the same framework of product form queuing networks. Results of this kind have been traditionally presented as separate; unifying them simplifies the student's job and provides new insights.

We develop the topic of Palm calculus, also called "the importance of the viewpoint", which is so central to queuing theory, as a topic of its own. Indeed, this topic has so many applications to simulation and to system analysis in general, that it is a very good time investment. Here too, we focus on general purpose methods and results, in particular the large-time heuristic for mapping various viewpoints (Chapter 7).

Chapter 1 gives a methodology and serves as an introduction to the rest of the book. Performance patterns are also described, i.e. facts that repeatedly appear in various situations, and the knowledge of which considerably helps the performance evaluation.

Chapter 2 demonstrates how to summarize experimental or simulation results, as well as how to quantify their accuracy. It also serves as an introduction to a scientific use of the statistical method, i.e. pose a model and verify its assumptions. In Chapter 3, we present general methods for fitting an explanatory model to data and the concept of heavy tail. Chapter 4 describes the techniques of tests, and Chapter 5 those of forecasting. These four chapters give a coverage of modern statistics useful to our field.

Chapter 6 discusses discrete event simulation and several important, though simple issues such as the need for transient removal, for confidence intervals, and classical simulation techniques. We also discuss importance sampling, which is very useful for computing estimates of rare events; we give a simple, though quite general and broadly applicable method.

Chapter 7 describes Palm calculus, which relates the varying viewpoints resulting from measurements done by different operators. Here, we discuss freezing simulations, a phenomenon which can be a problem for even simple simulations if one is not aware of it. We also present how to perform a perfect simulation of stochastic recurrences. Chapter 8 discusses patterns specific to queuing, classical solution methods for queuing networks, and, perhaps more important, operational analysis for rapid evaluation.

The appendix gives background information that cannot yet be easily found elsewhere, such as a Fourier-free quick crash course on digital filters (used in Chapter 5) and confidence intervals for quantiles.

Performance evaluation is primarily an art, and involves using sophisticated tools such as mathematical packages, measurement tools and simulation tools. See the web site of the EPFL lecture on Performance Evaluation for some examples of *practicals*, implemented in Matlab and designed around this book.

The text is intended for self-study. Proofs are not given when there are easily accessible references (these are indicated in the text); otherwise they can be found in appendixes at the end of the chapters.

The *Index* collects all terms and expressions that are highlighted in the text like **this** and also serves as a notation list.

Acknowledgements

I would like to thank Anthony Davison for allowing me to access a beta version of his book "Statistical Models" as well as Richard Weber, who made his lecture notes freely available on the web and allowed me to use them as constituent material in an early version of this course. I am grateful to François Baccelli and Pierre Brémaud who helped me obtain some understanding of their fields. Many thanks go to Mourad Kara for discussions and input, to Irina Baltcheva, Manuel Flury, Olivier Gallay, Assane Gueye, Paul Hurley, Ruben Merz, Boži-dar Radunović, Gianluca Rizzo, Slaviša Sarafijanović, Milan Vojnović, Utkarsh Upadhyay and Jonas Wagner for various input and comments. I thank Scouac, Pilou and their friends for visiting our pages here and there. Last but not least, I thank Elias for the artwork.

Jean-Yves Le Boudec, EPFL

Contents

Methodology

Perhaps the most difficult part when carrying out a performance evaluation is knowing where to start. In this chapter, we propose a methodology, i.e. a set of recommendations, that is valid for any performance evaluation study. We stress the importance of factors, in particular hidden ones, and the need to use the scientific method. We also discuss a few frequent performance patterns, as a means of quickly focusing on important issues.

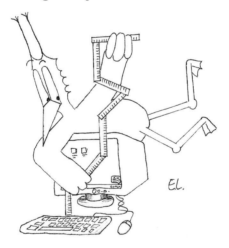

1.1   What is Performance Evaluation?

In the context of this book, performance evaluation involves quantifying the service delivered by a computer or a communication system. For example, we might be interested in: comparing the power consumption of several server farm configurations; knowing the response time experienced by a customer performing a reservation over the Internet; comparing compilers for a multiprocessor machine.

In all cases it is important to carefully define the *load* and the *metric*, and to be aware of the performance evaluation *goals*.

1.1.1   Load

An important feature of computer or communication systems is that their performance depends dramatically on the **workload** (or simply **load**) that they are subjected to. The load characterizes the quantity and the nature of requests submitted to the system. Consider for instance the problem of quantifying the performance of a web server. We could characterize the load by a simple concept such as the number of requests per second. This is called the ***intensity of the workload***. In general, the performance deteriorates when the intensity increases, but this deterioration is often sudden. The reason for this is the non-linearity of queuing systems – a ***performance pattern*** example that is discussed in Section 1.5 and Chapter 8.

The performance of a system depends not only on the intensity of the workload, but also on its nature. On a web server, for example, all requests are not equivalent: some web server softwares might perform well with *get* requests for frequently used objects, and less well with requests that require database access. For other web servers, things might be different. This issue is addressed by using standardized mixes of web server requests. These are generated by a ***benchmark***, defined as a load generation process that intends to mimic a typical user behavior. Chapter 3 presents a study of how such a benchmark can be constructed.

1.1.2   Metric

A performance ***metric*** is a measurable quantity that precisely captures what we want to measure – it can take on many forms. There is no general definition of a performance metric: it is system dependent, and its definition requires a good understanding of the system and its users. We will often mention examples where the metric corresponds to throughput (the number of tasks completed per unit of time), power consumption (the integral of the electrical energy consumed by the system, per time unit), or response time (i.e. the time elapsed between a start and an end event). For each performance metric, we may be interested in the average, 95-percentile, worst-case, etc., as explained in Chapter 2.

Example 1.1   Windows versus Linux

Chen and co-authors compare Windows to Linux in [25]. As metric, they use the number of CPU cycles, the number of instructions, the number of data read/write operations required by a typical job. The load was generated by various benchmarks: "syscall" generates elementary operations (system calls); "memory read" generates references to an array; an application benchmark runs a popular application.

It is also important to be aware of the experimental conditions under which the metric is measured, as illustrated by the following example.

Example 1.2 Power Consumption

The electrical power consumed by a computer or telecom equipment depends on how efficiently the equipment can take advantage of low activity periods to save energy. One operator proposes the following metric as a measure of power consumption [29]:

$$P_{\text{total}} = 0.35\, P_{\max} + 0.4\, P_{50} + 0.25\, P_{\text{sleep}}$$

where P_{total} is the power consumption when the equipment is running at full load, P_{50} is when it is submitted to a load equal to 50% of its capacity and P_{sleep} is when it is idle. The example uses weights (0.35, 0.4 and 0.25) that reflect our assumption of the proportion of time during which a given load condition typically occurs (for example, the full load condition is assumed to occur during 35% of the time).

In this example, **utilization** is a parameter of the operating conditions. The utilization of a resource is defined as the proportion of time during which the resource is busy. The example also illustrates that it may be important to define which *sampling method* is used, i.e. when the measurements are taken. This is an integral part of the definition of the metric and we discuss this point in more detail in Chapter 7.

A metric may be simple, i.e. expressed by a single number (e.g. the power consumption), or *multi-dimensional*, i.e. represented by a vector of several numbers (e.g. power consumption, response time and throughput). When comparing two vectors of multi-dimensional metric values, one should compare the corresponding components (e.g. the power consumption of A versus the power consumption of B, the response time of A versus the response time of B, etc.). As a result, it is possible that neither of the two vectors is better than the other. We say that the comparison of vectors is a **partial order**, as opposed to the comparison of numbers, which is a **complete order**. It is however useful to determine whether a vector is **non-dominated**, i.e. that no other vector (in the set of available results) is better. In a finite set of performance results expressed with a multi-dimensional metric, there is usually more than one non-dominated result. When comparing several configurations, only the non-dominated ones are of interest.

Example 1.3 Multi-dimensional Metric and Kiviat Diagram

We measure the performance of a web server submitted to the load of a standard workbench. We compare 5 configurations, and obtain the results below.

Config	Power [W]	Response [ms]	Throughput [tps]
A	23.5	3.78	42.2
B	40.8	5.30	29.1
C	92.7	4.03	22.6
D	53.1	2.19	73.1
E	54.7	5.92	24.3

We see, for example, that configuration A is better than B but that it is not better than D. There are two non-dominated configurations: A and D. A is better with regard to power consumption, whereas D is better when it comes to throughput and response time.

The numerical values can be visualized on a **Kiviat Diagram** (also called Radar graph or **Spider Plot**) as in Figure 1.1.

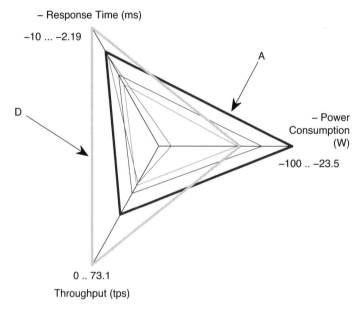

Figure 1.1 A visualization of the data in Example 1.3 by means of a Kiviat Diagram. Configurations A and D are non-dominated.

1.1.3   The Different Goals of Performance Evaluation

The goal of a performance evaluation may either be a **comparison** of design alternatives, i.e. quantifying the improvement due to some design option, or **system dimensioning**, i.e. determining the size of all system components for a given planned utilization. A comparison of designs requires a well-defined load model; however, the exact value of its intensity does not have to be identified. In contrast, system dimensioning requires a detailed estimation of the load intensity. As for all prediction exercises, this is very hazardous. For any performance evaluation, it is important to know whether the results depend on a workload prediction or not. Simple forecasting techniques are discussed in Chapter 5.

Example 1.4 Different Goals

QUESTION 1.1 Determine the nature of the goal for each of the following performance evaluations statements:[1]

(1) PC configuration 1 is 25% faster than PC configuration 2 when running Photoshop.

(2) For your video on demand application, the number of required servers is 35, and the number of disk units is 68.

(3) Using the new version of `sendfile()` increases the server throughput by 51%.

The benefit of a performance evaluation study has to be weighted against its cost as well as that of the system. In practice, detailed performance evaluations are carried out by product development units (system design). During system operation, it is not economical (except for huge systems such as public communication networks) to do so. Instead, manufacturers provide *engineering rules*, which capture the relation between the load intensity and performance. Example (2) of above Question 1.1 is probably best replaced by an engineering rule such as:

Example 1.5 Engineering Rule

For your video-on-demand application, the number of required servers is given by $N_1 = \lceil \frac{R}{59.3} + \frac{B}{3.6} \rceil$ and the number of disk units by $N_2 = \lceil \frac{R}{19.0} + \frac{B}{2.4} \rceil$, where R (resp. B) is the number of residential (resp. business) customers ($\lceil x \rceil$ is the floor of x, i.e. the smallest integer $\geq x$).

This book deals with the techniques of performance evaluation that apply to all such cases. However, how to implement a high performance system (e.g. how to efficiently code a real time application in Linux) or how to design bug-free systems are *beyond* its scope.

1.2 Factors

After defining the goal, load and metric, one needs to establish a list of *factors*. These are the system elements or the load affecting the performance. One is tempted to focus only on the factor of interest, however, it is important to know all factors that may impact the performance measure, whether they are desired or not.

Example 1.6 Windows versus Linux, Continued

In [25], Chen and co-authors consider the following external factors: background activity; multiple users; network activity. These were reduced to a minimum by shutting the network down and allowing only

---

[1](1), (3) are comparisons of design options; (2) involves dimensioning.

one user. They also consider: the various ways of handling idle periods in Windows and Linux, since they affect the interpretation of the
measurements.

1.2.1   The Hidden Factor Paradox

Ignoring various hidden factors may invalidate the result of the performance
evaluation, as demonstrated in the next example.

Example 1.7 TCP Throughput

Figure 1.2(a), plots the throughput achieved by a mobile node during
a file transfer as a function of its velocity (speed). It suggests that the
throughput increases with the mobility. (b) The plot shows the same
data, but now the mobiles are separated in two groups: one group ('s')
uses a small socket buffer (4 K Bytes), whereas the second ('L') em-

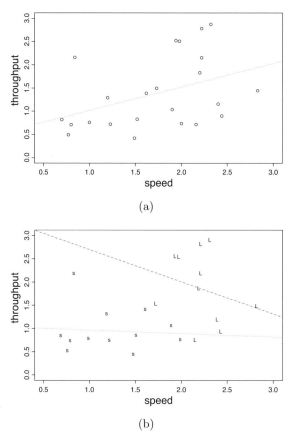

Figure 1.2 (a) A plot of the throughput (in Mb/s) versus speed (in m/s)
for a mobile node. (b) The same plot, but showing the socket buffer size;
s = small buffer, L = large buffer.

ploys a larger socket buffer (16 K Bytes). The conclusion thus becomes inverted: the throughput decreases with the mobility. The hidden factor influences the final result: all experiments with low speed are for small socket buffer sizes. The socket buffer size is a hidden factor.

Hidden factors may be avoided by a proper randomization of the experiments. In the example above, a proper design would have distributed the socket buffer sizes randomly with respect to the speed. However, this may not always be possible as certain experimental conditions may be imposed upon us; in such cases, all factors have to be incorporated in the analysis. In Figure 1.2, we fitted a linear regression to the two figures, using the method explained in Chapter 3. The slope of the linear regression is negative when we explicit the hidden factor, demonstrating that the mobility decreases the throughput.

The importance of hidden factors may be interpreted as our tendency to mix cause and correlation [77]. In Figure 1.2(a) the throughput is positively correlated with the speed, but this should not be interpreted as a causal relationship.

In conclusion at this point, knowing all factors is a tedious, but necessary task. In particular, all factors should be incorporated, whether they interest you or not (factors that you have no interest in are called *nuisance factors*). This implies that you have to know your system well, or be assisted by people who do.

1.2.2 Simpson's Paradox

Simpson's reversal, also denoted *Simpson's paradox*, is a well known case of the problem of hidden factors, when the performance metric is a success probability.

Example 1.8 TCP Throughput, continued

We revisit the previous example, but now limit our interest to determining whether a mobile can reach a throughput of at least 1.5 Mb/s, i.e. a mobile is said to be successful if its throughput is $\geq$ 1.5 Mb/s. We classify the mobiles as slow (speed $\leq$ 2 m/s) or fast (speed $>$ 2 m/s), and obtain the following result:

	failure	success	total	$\mathbb{P}(\text{success})$
slow	11	3	14	0.214
fast	5	4	9	0.444
total	16	7	23	

From this, we conclude that fast mobiles have a higher success probability than their slow counterparts. We now introduce the nuisance parameter "socket buffer size", i.e. we qualify the mobiles as 's' (small buffer size) or 'L' (large buffer size):

's' mobiles	failure	success	total	$\mathbb{P}$(success)
slow	10	1	11	0.091
fast	1	0	1	0.00
total	11	1	12	

'L' mobiles	failure	success	total	$\mathbb{P}$(success)
slow	1	2	3	0.667
fast	4	4	8	0.500
total	5	6	11	

For both cases, slow mobiles have a higher success probability than fast ones, which is the correct answer. The former answer was wrong as it ignored a hidden factor. This is known as Simpsons's reversal.

Simpsons' paradox can be formulated in a general manner as follows [65]. Let S denote the fact that the outcome of an experiment is a success, and let C be the factor of interest (in the above example: mobile speed). Let N_i, $i = 1, \ldots, k$, be binary hidden factors (nuisance factors; in the example, there is only one, i.e. the socket buffer size). Assume that the factor of interest has a positive influence on the success rate, i.e.

$$\mathbb{P}(S|C) > \mathbb{P}(S|\bar{C}) \tag{1.1}$$

This may occur while, at the same time, the combination of the factor of interest with the hidden factors N_i has the opposite effect:

$$\mathbb{P}(S|C \text{ and } N_i) < P(S|\bar{C} \text{ and } N_i) \tag{1.2}$$

for all $i = 1, \ldots, k$. As illustrated in Examples 1.8 and 1.2, the reversal takes place when the effect of hidden factors is large.

The fact that Simpson's reversal is a paradox is assumed to originate in our (false) intuition that an average of factors leads to an average of outcomes. In other words, we may (wrongly) assume that Equation (1.1) is a weighted sum of (1.2).

COMMENT: We do have weighted sums, but the weights are $\mathbb{P}(N_i|C)$ for the left-hand side in (1.1) versus $\mathbb{P}(N_i|\bar{C})$ for the right-hand side:

$$\mathbb{P}(S|C) = \sum_i \mathbb{P}(S|C \text{ and } N_i)\mathbb{P}(N_i|C)$$

$$\mathbb{P}(S|\bar{C}) = \sum_i \mathbb{P}(S|\bar{C} \text{ and } N_i)\mathbb{P}(N_i|\bar{C}) \qquad \square$$

1.3 Evaluation Methods

Once goal, load, metric and factors are well defined, the performance evaluation can then proceed with a solution method, which usually falls within one of the three cases below. Which method to use depends on the nature of the problem and the skills or taste of the evaluation team.

- *Measurement* of the real system. As in physics, it is hard to carry out a measurement without disturbing the system. Some special hardware devices (e.g. optical splitters in network links) sometimes prevent any disturbances. If, in contrast, measurements are taken by the system itself, the impact has to be analyzed with caution. Measurements are not always possible (for instance, if the system does not yet exist).

- Discrete Event *Simulation*: a simplified model of the system and its load are implemented in software. Time is simulated and often flows several orders of magnitude slower than real time. The performance of interest is measured as on a real system, but measurement side-effects are usually not present. It is often easier than a measurement study, but not always. It is the most widespread method and is the subject of Chapter 6.

- *Analytical* method: a mathematical model of the system is analyzed numerically. This is viewed by some as a special form of simulation. It is often much faster than a simulation, but sometimes requires wild assumptions to be made in order for the numerical procedures to be applicable. Analytical methods are frequently used to gain insight during a development phase, or also to learn fundamental facts about a system, which we call "patterns". We demonstrate in Chapter 8 how certain performance analyses can be solved approximately in a very simple way, by means of bottleneck analysis.

1.4 The Scientific Method

The scientific method can be applied to any technical work, not only to performance evaluation. However, in the author's experience, the lack of scientific methods is a prominent cause for failed performance studies. In short, the scientific method requires one not to believe in a conclusion unless it is thoroughly tested.

Example 1.9 Joe's kiosk

Joe's e-kiosk sells videos online to customers equipped with smartphones. The system comprises one server and one 802.11 base station. Before deployment, performance evaluation tests are carried out, as shown in Figure 1.3(a). We see that the throughput reaches a maximum at around 8 transactions per second.

Joe concludes that the bottleneck is the wireless LAN and decides to buy and install 2 more base stations. The results obtained after installation are presented in Figure 1.3(b). Surprisingly, there is no improvement. The conclusion that the wireless LAN was the bottleneck was thus wrong.

Joe scratches his head and decides to be more careful when drawing conclusions. Measurements are taken on the wireless LAN; the number of collisions is less than 0.1%, and the utilization is below 5%. This confirms that the wireless LAN is *not* a bottleneck. Joe makes the hypothesis that the bottleneck may be on the server side. After doubling the amount of real memory allocated to the server process, the results correspond to what is shown in Figure 1.3(c). This identifies the real memory as the limiting factor.

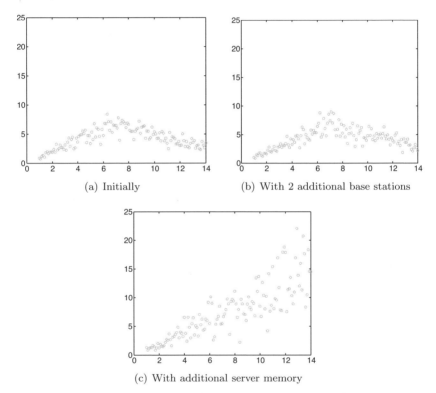

(a) Initially   (b) With 2 additional base stations

(c) With additional server memory

Figure 1.3 Performance results for Joe's server. X-axis: offered load; Y-axis: achieved throughput, both in transactions per second.

A common pitfall is to draw conclusions from an experiment that has not been explicitly designed to validate such conclusions. The risk is that hidden factors might interfere, as illustrated by the previous example. Indeed, Joe concluded from the first experiment that the LAN performance would be improved by adding a base station. This may have been *suggested* by the result of Figure 1.3(a), but these results are inconclusive. It is necessary to perform other experiments, designed to validate a potential conclusion, before making a final statement. Following Popper's philosophy of science [82], we claim that it is necessary for the performance analyst to take on two roles:

(1) to make tentative statements, and

(2) to design experiments attempting to invalidate them.

Example 1.10 ATM UBR better than ATM ABR

In [66], the authors evaluate whether the ATM-UBR protocol is better than ATM-ABR (both are alternative methods for managing switches used in communication networks). They employ a typical scientific method, by posing each potential conclusion as a hypothesis and designing experiments with the aim of invalidating them.

"ABSTRACT. We compare the performance of ABR and UBR for providing high-speed network interconnection services for TCP traffic. We test the hypothesis that UBR with adequate buffering in the ATM switches results in better overall goodput for TCP traffic than explicit rate ABR for LAN interconnection. This is shown to be true in a wide selection of scenarios. Four phenomena that may lead to bad ABR performance are identified and we test whether each of these has a significant impact on TCP goodput. This reveals that the extra delay incurred in the ABR end-systems and the overhead of RM cells account for the difference in performance. We test whether it is better to use ABR to push congestion to the end-systems in a parking-lot scenario or whether we can allow congestion to occur in the network. Finally, we test whether the presence of a "multiplexing loop" causes performance degradation for ABR and UBR. We find our original hypothesis to be true in all cases. We observe, however, that ABR is able to improve performance when the buffering inside the ABR part of the network is small compared to that available at the ABR end-systems. We also see that ABR allows the network to control fairness between end-systems."

Other aspects of the scientific method are to:

- Give an evaluation of the *accuracy* of your quantitative results. Consider the measured data in Example 1.11. There is much variability in them, and merely claiming that the average response time is better with B than A is not sufficient. It is necessary to give uncertainty margins, or confidence intervals. Techniques for this are discussed in Chapter 2.

- Make the results of your performance evaluation easily *reproducible*. This implies that all assumptions should be made explicit and documented.

- Remove what can be removed. Often, at the end of a performance evaluation study, many results are found uninteresting. The correct thing to do would be to remove such results, but this seems difficult in practice !

1.5 Performance Patterns

Performance evaluation is simpler if the evaluator is aware of performance *patterns*, i.e. traits that are common to numerous settings.

1.5.1 Bottlenecks

A prominent pattern is constituted by **bottlenecks**. In many systems, the overall performance is dictated by the behavior of the weakest components, called the bottlenecks.

Example 1.11 Bottlenecks

You are asked to evaluate the performance of an information system. An application server can be compiled with two options, A and B. An experiment is done: ten test users (remote or local) measure the time it takes to complete a complex transaction on four days. On day 1, option A is used; on day 2, option B is. The results are listed in the table below.

	remote	local			remote	local
A	123	43		B	107	62
	189	38			179	69
	99	49			199	56
	167	37			103	47
	177	44			178	71

The expert concludes that the performance for remote users is independent of the choice of the information system. We can criticize this finding and instead carry out a bottleneck analysis. For remote users, the bottleneck is the network access; the compiler option has little impact. When the bottleneck is removed, i.e. for local users, option A is slightly better.

Bottlenecks are friends to the performance analyst, in the sense that they may considerably *simplify the performance evaluation*, as illustrated next.

Example 1.12 CPU model

A detailed screening of a transaction system shows that the average cost of one transaction is $1,238,400$ CPU instructions; 102.3 disk accesses and 4 packets sent on the network. The processor can handle 10^9 instructions per second; the disk can support 10^4 accesses per second; the network can support 10^4 packets per second. We would like to know how many transactions per second the system can support.

The resource utilization per transaction per second is: CPU: 0.12% – disk: 1.02% – network: 0.04%; therefore, the disk is the bottleneck. The capacity of the system is determined by how many transactions per second the disk can support and a gross estimate is $\frac{100}{1.02} \approx 99$ transactions per second.

If we would like a higher accuracy, we need to model queuing at the disk, thereby determing at which number of transactions per second delays start to become large. A global queuing model of CPU, disk access and network is probably unnecessary.

In Section 8.2.4, we study bottleneck analysis for queuing systems in a systematic way.

However, one should not be fooled by the apparent simplicity of the previous example, as bottlenecks are moving targets. They depend on all parameters of the system as well as on the load: a component may be a bottleneck in certain conditions, but not in others. In particular, removing one bottleneck may cause some other bottleneck to appear.

Example 1.13   High Performance Web Sites

In [99], the author discusses how to design high-performance web sites. He takes the user's response time as the performance metric. He observes that modern web sites have highly optimized backends, for which reason their bottleneck is at the frontend. A common bottleneck is the DNS lookup. Entirely avoiding DNS lookups in web pages improves performances, but reveals another bottleneck, namely, script parsing. This, in turn, can be avoided by making scripts external to the web page parsing scripts, but doing so will reveal yet another bottleneck, etc. The author describes 14 possible components, any of which, if present, is a candidate for being the bottleneck, and suggests to remove them all. Subsequently, the system is left with the network access and the server CPU speed as bottlenecks, which is desirable.

1.5.2   Congestion Collapse

Congestion occurs when the intensity of the load exceeds the system capacity (as determined by the bottleneck). Any system, when subject to a high enough load, will become congested. The only way to prevent this is to limit the load, which is often difficult or impossible. Therefore, it is no easy task to avoid congestion entirely.

In contrast, it is possible, and desirable, to avoid ***congestion collapse***, which is defined as a reduction in system utility, or revenue when the load increases.

Example 1.14   Congestion Collapse

Consider a ring network as in Figure 1.4 (such a topology is common, as it is a simple way to provide resilience to single link or node failure). There are I nodes and links, and the sources are numbered $0, 1, \ldots,$ $I - 1$. At every node, there is one source, whose traffic uses the two next downstream links (i.e. source i uses links $\left[(i+1) \bmod I \right]$ and $\left[(i+2) \bmod I \right]$). All links and sources are identicals.

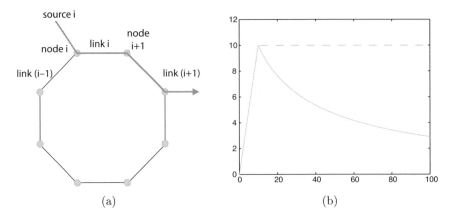

Figure 1.4 (a) A network exhibiting congestion collapse if sources are greedy. (b) The throughput per source λ'' versus the offered load per source λ, in Mb/s (plain line). Numbers are in Mb/s; the link capacity is $c = 20$ Mb/s for all links. Dotted line: The ideal throughput with congestion but without congestion collapse.

Every source sends at a rate λ and c corresponds to the useful capacity of a link (c and λ are in Mb/s). Let λ' be the rate achieved by one source on its first hop, and λ'' the rate on its second hop (λ'' is the throughput per source). Since a source uses two links, we can assume (in a simplified analysis) that, as long as $\lambda < \frac{c}{2}$, all traffic is carried by the network without loss, i.e.

$$\text{if } \lambda < \frac{c}{2} \quad \text{then } \lambda' = \lambda'' = \lambda$$

Assume now that the sources are greedy and send as much as they can, with a rate $\lambda > \frac{c}{2}$. The network capacity is exceeded, and there will thus be losses. We assume that packet dropping is fair, i.e. the proportion of dropped packets is the same for all flows at any given link. The proportion of packets lost by one source on its first hop is $\frac{\lambda - \lambda'}{\lambda}$, and on its second hop it is $\frac{\lambda' - \lambda''}{\lambda'}$. By the fair packet dropping assumption, these proportions are equal, which gives

$$\frac{\lambda'}{\lambda} = \frac{\lambda''}{\lambda'} \tag{1.3}$$

Furthermore, we assume that links are fully utilized when the capacity is reached, i.e.

$$\text{if } \lambda > \frac{c}{2} \quad \text{then } \lambda' + \lambda'' = c$$

We can solve for λ' (a polynomial equation of the 2nd degree) and substitute λ' in (1.3) to finally obtain the throughput per source:

$$\lambda'' = c - \frac{\lambda}{2}\left(\sqrt{1 + 4\frac{c}{\lambda}} - 1\right) \tag{1.4}$$

Figure 1.4 plots λ'' versus λ, suggesting that $\lambda'' \to 0$ as $\lambda \to \infty$. We can verify this by using a Taylor expansion of $\sqrt{1+u}$, for $u \to 0$ in (1.4). We obtain

$$\lambda'' = \frac{c^2}{\lambda}\left(1 + \epsilon(\lambda)\right)$$

with $\lim_{\lambda \to \infty} \epsilon(\lambda) = 0$. This shows that the limit of the achieved throughput, when the offered load goes to $+\infty$, is 0, and we thus have a clear case of *congestion collapse*.

Figure 1.4 also illustrates the difference between congestion and congestion collapse. The dotted line represents the ideal throughput per source assuming that there is congestion without congestion collapse. This could be achieved by employing a feedback mechanism to prevent sources from sending more than $\frac{c}{2}$ (for example by using TCP).

Two common causes for congestion collapse are:

(1) The system dedicates significant amounts of resources to jobs that cannot be completed. This is demonstrated in Figure 1.4, where packets are accepted on the first hop, and eventually become dropped on the second hop. This is also known to occur on busy web sites or call centers due to customer **impatience**: when the response time becomes long, impatient customers drop requests before they are satisfied.

(2) The service time per job increases as the load increases. An example of this is when memory is paged to the disk when the number of active processes increases.

Congestion collapse is very common in complex systems. It is a nuisance since it reduces the total system utility to below its capacity. Avoiding congestion collapse is part of a good system design. A common solution to the problem is **admission control**, which consists in rejecting jobs when there is a risk of exceeding the system capacity [50].

1.5.3   Competition Side Effect

In many systems, the performance of one user influences other users. This may cause an apparent paradox, where putting in more resources worsens the performance for some users. The root cause is as follows: increasing certain resources may allow some users to increase their load, which in turn can decrease the performance of competing users. From the point of view of the user for which the performance is decreased, there is an apparent paradox: the addition of resources to the system gives rise to an adverse effect.

Example 1.15 Competing Users with Ideal Congestion Control
Figure 1.5 shows a simple network with 2 users, 1 and 2, sending traffic to destinations D1 and D2, respectively. Both users share a common link $X - Y$.

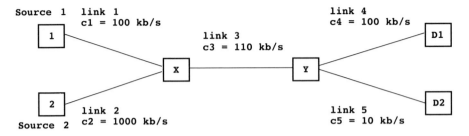

Figure 1.5 A simple 2-user network showing the pattern of the competition side effect. Increasing the capacity of link 5 worsens the performance of user 1.

Assume that the sources employ some form of congestion control, for example as a result of their using the TCP protocol. The goal of congestion control is to limit the source rates to the system capacity while maintaining a certain fairness objective. We do not discuss fairness in detail in this book, but refer to example [50] for a quick tutorial. For the sake of simplicity, we may here assume that congestion control has the effect of maximizing the logarithms of the rates of the sources, subject to the constraints that all link capacities are not exceeded (this is called **proportional fairness** and is approximately what TCP implements). Let x_1 and x_2 be the rates achieved by sources 1 and 2 respectively. With the numbers shown in the figure, the constraints are $x_1 \leq 100$ kb/s and $x_2 \leq 10$ kb/s (other constraints are redundant), which gives us $x_1 = 100$ kb/s and $x_2 = 10$ kb/s.

Assume now that we add resources to the system, by increasing the capacity of link 5 (the weakest link) from $c_5 = 10$ kb/s to $c_5 = 100$ kb/s. The constraints are now

$$x_1 \leq 100 \text{ kb/s}$$
$$x_2 \leq 100 \text{ kb/s}$$
$$x_1 + x_2 \leq 110 \text{ kb/s}$$

By symmetry, the rates allocated under proportional fairness are thus $x_1 = x_2 = 55$ kb/s. We see that increasing the capacity results in a decrease for source 1.

The pattern of the competition side effect in the previous example is a "good" case, in the sense that the decrease in performance for some users is compensated by an increase for others. But this is not always true; combined with the ingredients of congestion collapse, the competition side effect may result in a performance decrease without any benefit for any other user ("give more, get less"), as shown in the next example.

Example 1.16 Competing Users without Congestion Control

Consider Figure 1.5 again, but assume that there is no congestion control (for instance due to sources using UDP instead of TCP). Assume that the sources send as much as their access link allows, i.e. source 1 sends at the rate of link 1 and source 2 at the rate of link 2.

Assume that we keep all rates as shown in the figure, except for the rate of link 2, which we vary from $c_2 = 0$ to $c_2 = 1000$ kb/s. Now define the rates x_1 and x_2 as the amounts of traffic that reach the destinations. If $c_2 \leq 10$ kb/s, there is no loss and $x_1 = 100$ kb/s, $x_2 = c_2$. If $c_2 > 10$ kb/s, there are losses at X. Assume that the losses are in proportion to the offered traffic. Using the same analysis as in Example 1.14, we obtain, for $c_2 > 10$:

$$x_1 = 110 \times \frac{100}{c_2 + 100}$$

$$x_2 = \min\left(110 \times \frac{c_2}{c_2 + 100}, 10\right)$$

Figure 1.6 plots the rates versus c_2. We see that increasing c_2 beyond 10 kb/s renders things worse for source 1, with no benefit for source 2.

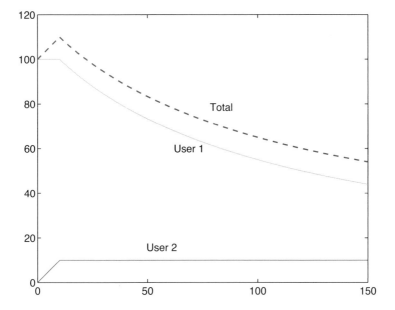

Figure 1.6 Achieved throughputs for the sources in Figure 1.5 versus c_2.

1.5.4 Latent Congestion Collapse

Many complex systems have several potential bottlenecks, and may be susceptible to congestion collapse. Removing a bottleneck (by adding more resources) may reveal a congestion collapse, resulting in a deteriorated performance. Before the addition of more resources, the system was protected from congestion

collapse by the bottleneck, which acted as an implicit admission control. This
results in the "give more, get less" paradox.

Example 1.17 Museum audio guides

A museum offers free audio guides to be downloaded on MP3 players.
Visitors plug their MP3 players into the docking devices, and the latter
connect via a wireless LAN to the museum server. Data transfer from
the docking device to the MP3 player goes through a USB connector.
The system was tested with different numbers of docking devices, and
Figure 1.7(a) shows the download time versus the number of docking
devices in use.

The museum later decides to buy better docking devices, with a faster
USB connection between the device and MP3 player (enabling the
transfer rate to be doubled). As can be expected, the download time is
smaller when the number n of docking devices is low, but, surprisingly,
it is larger when $n \geq 7$ (Figure 1.7(a)). What can have happened? It is
known that the wireless LAN access method is susceptible to congestion
collapse: when the offered load increases, packet collisions become frequent and the time to successfully transfer one packet becomes larger,
causing the throughput to be lowered. We may conjecture that improving the transfer speed between the docking device and the MP3
player increases the load on the wireless LAN. The congestion collapse
was not possible before due to the low speed docking devices acting as
an (involuntary) access control method.

We can verify this conjecture by plotting the throughput in the place
of the download time, and extending the first experiment to large values of n. We see in Figure 1.7(b) that there is indeed a reduction in
throughput, at a point that depends on the speed of the USB connection.

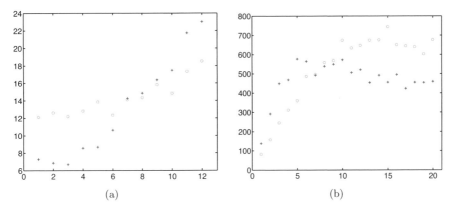

Figure 1.7 An illustration of latent congestion collapse. The download time (in sec.) and System throughput (in Mb/s) as functions of the number of docking devices, with lower speed USB connections (∘) and with higher speed USB connections (+).

1.6   Review

1.6.1   Check-List

Performance Evaluation Checklist

PE1 *Define your goal.* For example: dimension the system, find the overload behavior; evaluate alternatives. Do you need a performance evaluation study? Are the results not obvious? Are they too dependent on the input factors, which are arbitrary?

PE2 *Identify the factors.* What are all the factors? Are there external factors which need to be controlled?

PE3 *Define your metrics.* For example: response time, server occupancy, number of transactions per hour, Joule per Megabyte. Define not only what is measured but also under which condition or sampling method. If the metric is multi-dimensional, different metric values are not always comparable and there may not be a best metric value. However, we might have non-dominated metric values.

PE4 *Define the offered load.* How is it expressed: transactions per second, number of users, number of visits per hour? Is it measured on a real system? Artificial load generated by a simulator, by a synthetic load generator? Load model in a theoretical model?

PE5 *Know your bottlenecks.* The performance often depends only on a small number of factors, frequently those with a high utilization (= load/capacity). Make sure that you are indeed evaluating one of them.

PE6 *Know your system well.* Know the system you are evaluating and list all factors. Use evaluation tools that you are familiar with. Know common performance patterns for your system.

Scientific Method Checklist

S1 *Scientific Method*
   do { Define hypothesis; design experiments; validate } **until** validation is OK.

S2 Quantify the *accuracy* of your results.

S3 Make your findings *reproducible*; define your assumptions.

S4 *Remove* what can be removed.

1.6.2   Review Questions

1.1 For each of the following examples:

(1) Design a Web server code that is efficient and fast.

(2) Compare TCP-SACK versus TCP-new Reno for hand-held mobile devices.

(3) Compare Windows 2000 Professional to Linux.

(4) Design a rate control for an internet audio application.

(5) Compare various wireless MAC protocols.

(6) Determine how many servers a video-on-demand company needs to install.

(7) Compare various compilers.

(8) How many control processor blades should this Cisco router have?

(9) Compare various consensus algorithms.

(10) Design bug-free code.

(11) Design a server farm that will not crash when the load is high.

(12) Design call center software that generates guaranteed revenue.

(13) Size a hospital's information system.

(14) What capacity is needed for an international data link?

(15) How many new servers, if any, should I install next quarter for my business application?

State whether a detailed identification of the intensity of the workload is required.[2]

1.2 Consider the following scenarios.

(1) The web server used for online booking at the "Fête des Vignerons" was so popular that it collapsed under the load, and was unavailable for several hours.

(2) Buffers were added to an operating system task, but the overall performance was degraded (instead of improved, as expected).

---

[2]Examples (6), (8), (13), (14), (15) are dimensioning exercises and require identification of the predicted workload intensity. Examples (1) and (10) are beyond the scope of the book. Examples (11) and (12) concern about avoiding congestion collapse.

(3) The response time on a complex web server is determined primarily by the performance of the frontend.

(4) When too many users employ the international link, the response time is poor.

(5) When too many users are present on the wireless LAN, no one gets useful work done

(6) A traffic volume increase of 20% causes traffic jams.

(7) New parking facilities were created in the city center but the availability of free parking availability did not increase.

and the following patterns:

(a) non-linearity of response time with respect to load;

(b) congestion collapse (useful work decreases as load increases);

(c) performance is determined by bottleneck;

Determine which pattern is present in which scenario.[3]

1.3 Read [63] written by one of Akamai's founders. Which of the present chapter's topics does it illustrate?[4]

---

[3] (1b); (2) : perhaps a combination of (b) and (c); (3c); (4a); (5b); (6b); (7c).

[4] (1) The performance bottleneck in internet response time is the *middle mile*, i.e. the intermediate providers between web site provider and end-user ISP. (2) Performance metrics of interest are not only the response time but also the reliability.

Summarizing Performance Data and Confidence Intervals

In most measurements or simulations, we obtain large amounts of data. Displaying the data correctly is important, and implies utilizing various graphical packages, or math packages with graphical capabilities. (Different tools have varying capabilities, and produce graphics of different aesthetic value; but the most important is to use a tool that you are familiar with). Tools do not do everything and you need to know what to represent. Here, we discuss important and frequent summarizations that can be employed to display and compare data: the complete distribution; summarized quantities such as means, standard deviations, medians and tail quantiles; as well as fairness indices.

We discuss certain properties of these summarizations and indices; they are not all equivalent, and some, though less frequently used, are preferable if one has a choice.

2.1   Summarized Performance Data

2.1.1   Histograms and Empirical CDF

Assume that you have obtained a large set of results for the value of a performance metric. This can be fully described by the distribution of the data, and illustrated by a ***histogram***. A histogram uses bins for the data values and plots on the y axis the proportion of data samples that fall in the bin on the x axis, see Figure 2.1.

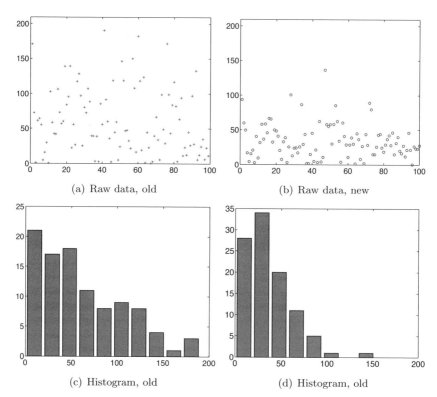

(a) Raw data, old   (b) Raw data, new

(c) Histogram, old   (d) Histogram, old

Figure 2.1 Data for Example 2.1. Measured execution times (in ms) for 100 transactions with the old and new code, with histograms.

     The ***empirical cumulative distribution function*** (ECDF) is an alternative to histograms, and sometimes facilitates comparisons. The ECDF of a data set $x_1, \ldots, x_n$ is the function F defined by

$$F(x) = \frac{1}{n} \sum_{i=1}^{n} 1_{\{x_i \leq x\}} \tag{2.1}$$

so that $F(x)$ is the proportion of data samples that do not exceed x.

Data sets may be compared by collecting their ECDFs. If one is consistently above the other, it may be considered to as superior, even though some data points in the first set may be less good. This is called ***stochastic majorization***. Figure 2.2 demonstrates that the new data set (left) clearly outperforms the old one. Note that the stochastic majorization is a partial order, as is the comparison of multi-dimensional metrics (Section 1.1.2).

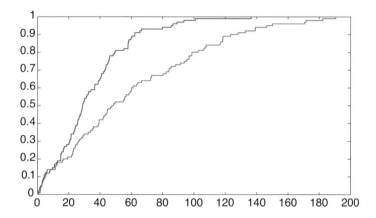

Figure 2.2 Data of Example 2.1. Empirical distribution functions for the old (right curve) and the new (left curve) code. The new outperforms the old; the improvement is significant at the tail of the distribution.

Assume that the data samples come from a well defined probability distribution; the histogram can then be viewed as an estimate of the PDF of the distribution, and the ECDF as an estimate of the CDF.[1]

2.1.2   Means, Medians and Quantiles

Instead of considering entire histograms or ECDFs, one would often like to summarize, i.e. compress, the histogram into one or several numbers representing both average and variability. This is commonly done by either of the following methods:

Median and Quantile

A median is a value that falls in the middle of the distribution, i.e. 50% of the data is below and 50% above. A $p\%$-quantile leaves $p\%$ of the observation below and $(100 - p)\%$ above. The median gives some information about the average, while extreme quantiles provide information about the dispersion. A commonly used plot is the ***box plot***. It shows the median, the 25% and 75% quantiles (called "quartiles") and the "outliers", defined as data points that are a fixed fraction away from the quartiles (Figure 2.3).

---

[1]The CDF of the random variable X is a function defined by $F(x) = \mathbb{P}(X \leq x)$.

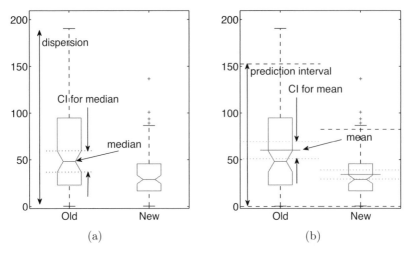

(a)   (b)

Figure 2.3 Box plots for the data of Example 2.1. (a) A standard box plot commonly used by statisticians showing the median (notch) and quartiles (top and bottom of boxes); "dispersion" is an ad-hoc measure, defined here as 1.5 times the interquartile distance; the notch width shows the confidence interval for the median. (b) The same, overlaid with quantities commonly used in signal processing: mean, confidence interval for the mean (= mean $\pm\ 1.96\,\sigma/\sqrt{n}$, where σ is the standard deviation and n is the number of samples) and prediction interval (= mean $\pm 1.96\,\sigma$).

COMMENT: The **sample median** of a data set is defined as follows. Assume there are n data points $x_1, \ldots, x_n$. Sort the points in increasing order and obtain $x_{(1)} \le \ldots \le x_{(n)}$. If n is odd, the median is $x_{(\frac{n+1}{2})}$, otherwise $\frac{1}{2}(x_{(\frac{n}{2})} + x_{(\frac{n}{2}+1)})$. More generally, the **sample q-quantile** is defined as

$$\frac{x_{(k')} + x_{(k'')}}{2} \qquad \text{with } k' = \lfloor qn + (1-q) \rfloor \text{ and } k' = \lceil qn + (1-q) \rceil$$

$\lfloor x \rfloor$ is the largest integer $\le x$ and $\lceil x \rceil$ is the smallest integer $\ge x$.   □

Mean and Standard Deviation

The **mean** m of a data set $x_1, \ldots, x_n$ is $m = \frac{1}{n} \sum_{i=1}^{n} x_i$, and gives information about the average. The **standard deviation** s *of a data set* is defined by $s^2 = \frac{1}{n} \sum_{i=1}^{n} (x_i - m)^2$ or $s^2 = \frac{1}{n-1} \sum_{i=1}^{n} (x_i - m)^2$ (either of the two conventions is used – see Section 2.2 for an explanation), and provides information about the variability. The utilization of standard deviation is rooted in the belief that data roughly follows a **normal distribution**, also called **Gaussian distribution**. It is characterized by a Bell-shaped histogram (see Wikipedia and Table 3.1); the CDF of the general normal distribution is denoted N_{μ,σ^2}, where μ is the mean and σ^2 is the variance. It is very frequently encountered because of the central limit theorem stating that an average of many things tends to be normal (but there are some exceptions, called heavy tail in Chapter 3). If such a hypothesis is true, and if we have $m \approx \mu$ and $\sigma \approx s$, then with 95% probability, the data sample would lie in the interval $m \pm 1.96\,s$ (see the normal distribution table in the appendix). This justifies the use of **mean-variance** plots, as in

Figure 2.3, which employ the interval $m \pm 1.96\,s$ (distance 3 in Figure 2.3) as a measure of variabillty. This is also called a **prediction interval** since it predicts a likely range for a future sample (Section 2.4).

Example 2.1 Comparison of two Options

An operating system vendor claims that the new version of the database management code significantly improves the performance. We measured the execution times of a series of commonly used programs with both options. The data are displayed in Figure 2.3. The raw displays and histograms demonstrate that both options have the same range, but it seems (graphically) that the new system more often provides a smaller execution time. The box plots are more suggestive; they show that the average and the range are about half for the new system.

In Section 2.5, we discuss the differences between these two modes of summarization.

2.1.3 Coefficient of Variation and Lorenz Curve Gap

The coefficient of variation and the Lorenz curve gap are frequently used measures of variation, rescaled to be invariant by change of scale. They apply to a positive data set $x_1, \ldots, x_n$.

Coefficient of Variation

It is defined by

$$\mathrm{CoV} = \frac{s}{m} \tag{2.2}$$

where m is the mean and s the standard deviation, i.e. it represents the standard deviation rescaled by the mean. It is also sometimes called the **signal to noise ratio**. For a data set with n values one always has[2]

$$0 \leq \mathrm{CoV} \leq \sqrt{n-1} \tag{2.3}$$

where the upper bound is obtained when all x_i have the same value except for one of them.

Lorenz Curve Gap

This is an alternative measure of dispersion, obtained when we replace the standard deviation by the **Mean Absolute Deviation** (**MAD**). The MAD is defined as

$$\mathrm{MAD} = \frac{1}{n} \sum_{i=1}^{n} |x_i - m|$$

i.e. we compute the mean distance to the mean, instead of the square root of the mean square distance. Compared to the standard deviation, the MAD is

---

[2]Consider the maximization problem: maximize $\sum_i (x_i - m)^2$ subject to $x_i \geq 0$ and $\sum x_i = mn$. Since $x \mapsto \sum_i (x_i - m)^2$ is convex, the maximum is at an extreme point $x_{i_0} = mn$, $x_i = 0$, $i \neq i_0$.

less sensitive to a few very large values. It follows from the Cauchy-Schwarz inequality that it is always less than the standard deviation, i.e.

$$0 \leq \text{MAD} \leq s \tag{2.4}$$

with equality only if x_i is constant, i.e. $x_i = m$ for all i.

If n is large and x_i is independent and identically distribued (**iid**) from a Gaussian distribution, then

$$\text{MAD} \approx \sqrt{\frac{2}{\pi}} s \approx 0.8 \, s \tag{2.5}$$

In contrast, if x_i comes from a heavy-tailed distribution with a finite mean m, then $s \to \infty$ as n becomes large, whereas MAD converges to a finite limit.

The **_Lorenz curve gap_** is a rescaled version of MAD, defined as

$$\text{gap} = \frac{\text{MAD}}{2m} \tag{2.6}$$

The factor 2 is explained in the next section. We always have

$$0 \leq \text{gap} \leq 1 - \frac{1}{n} \tag{2.7}$$

thus, contrary to CoV, gap is between 0 and 1. If n is large and x_i is iid from a Gaussian distribution, then gap $\approx 0.4 \, \text{CoV}$. If on the other hand it comes from an exponential distribution, gap ≈ 0.74 and CoV ≈ 1.

COMMENT: If x_i is iid and comes from a distribution with PDF $f(\cdot)$, then, for large n, CoV and MAD converge to their theoretical counterparts:

$$\text{CoV} \to \text{CoV}_{\text{th}} = \frac{\sqrt{\int_0^\infty (x - \mu)^2 f(x) \, dx}}{\mu}$$

$$\text{MAD} \to \text{gap}_{\text{th}} = \frac{\int_0^\infty |x - \mu| f(x) \, dx}{2\mu}$$

with $\mu = \int_0^\infty x f(x) \, dx$.

If the distribution is Gaussian N_{μ, σ^2} then $\text{CoV}_{\text{th}} = \frac{\sigma}{\mu}$ and $\text{gap}_{\text{th}} = \sqrt{\frac{2}{\pi}} \frac{\sigma}{\mu}$; if it is exponential then $\text{CoV}_{\text{th}} = 1$ and $\text{gap}_{\text{th}} = \frac{1}{e}$. □

2.1.4 Fairness Indices

Often one interprets variability as fairness, and several fairness indices have been proposed. We review here the two most prominent ones. We also show that they are in fact reformulations of variability measures, i.e. they are equivalent to CoV and gap, after proper mapping (and the use of these indices may thus appear superfluous). As in the previous section, the data set x_i is here assumed to be positive.

Jain's Fairness Index

It is defined as the square of the cosine of the angle between the data set x_i and the hypothetical equal allocation (Figure 2.4). It is given by

$$\text{JFI} = \frac{\left(\sum_{i=1}^{n} x_i\right)^2}{n \sum_{i=1}^{n} x_i^2} \tag{2.8}$$

A straightforward computation shows that the fairness measure JFI is a decreasing function of the variability measure CoV:

$$\text{JFI} = \frac{1}{1 + \text{CoV}^2} \tag{2.9}$$

so that, through (2.3), we conclude that JFI ranges from $\frac{1}{n}$ (maximum unfairness) to 1 (all x_i are equal).

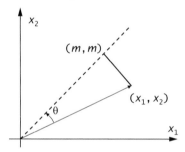

Figure 2.4 Jain's fairness index is $\cos^2 \theta$. $x_1, \ldots, x_n$ is the data set and m is the sample mean. The figure corresponds to $n = 2$.

Lorenz Curve

The **Lorenz curve** is defined as follows. A point (p, ℓ) on the curve, with p, $\ell \in [0, 1]$, signifies that the bottom fraction p of the distribution contributes to a fraction ℓ of the total $\sum_{i=1}^{n} x_i$.

More precisely, we are given a data set $x_i > 0$, $i = 1, \ldots, n$. We plot for all $i = 1, \ldots, n$ the points (p_i, ℓ_i) with

$$\begin{cases} p_i = \dfrac{i}{n} \\[2mm] \ell_i = \dfrac{\sum_{j=1}^{n} x_j \mathbf{1}_{\{x_j \leq x_i\}}}{\sum_{j=1}^{n} x_j} \end{cases} \tag{2.10}$$

See Figure 2.5 for examples. The Lorenz curve can be made into a continuous mapping $\ell = L(p)$ by linear interpolation and by setting $L(0) = 0$. The

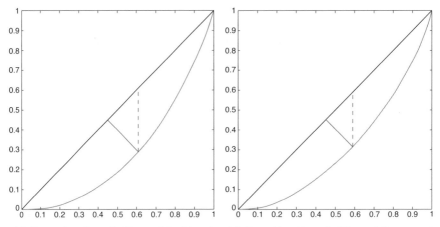

(a) Execution times in Figure 2.3, old code (b) Execution times in Figure 2.3, new code

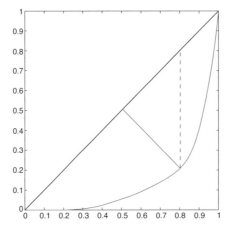

(c) Ethernet Byte Counts (x_n is the byte length of the nth packet of an Ethernet trace [64])

	CoV	JFI	gap	Gini	Gini-approx
Figure 2.3, old code	0.779	0.622	0.321	0.434	0.430
Figure 2.3, new code	0.720	0.658	0.275	0.386	0.375
Ethernet Byte Counts	1.84	0.228	0.594	0.730	0.715

Figure 2.5 Lorenz curves for three sets of data. The diagonal line corresponds to perfect equality. The maximum distance (plain line) is equal to $\sqrt{2}$ times the maximum vertical deviation (dashed line), which is called the Lorenz curve gap. The Gini coefficient is the area between the diagonal and the Lorenz curve, rescaled by its maximum value $\frac{1}{2}$. The table gives the values of coefficient of variation, Jain's fairness index, Lorenz curve gap, the Gini coefficient and the Gini coefficient approximation in (2.17).

resulting $L(\cdot)$ is a continuous mapping from $[0,1]$ onto $[0,1]$, monotone non-decreasing, convex, with $L(0) = 0$ and $L(1) = 1$.

The Lorenz curve $\ell = L(p)$ can be interpreted as a global measure of fairness (or variability). If all x_is are equal (maximum fairness), then $L(p) = p$ and $L(\cdot)$ is the diagonal of the square $[0,1] \times [0,1]$ (called the "line of perfect equality"). In the worst case, the Lorenz curve follows the bottom and right edges of the square (called the "line of perfect inequality") (Figure 2.6). In practice the Lorenz curve is computed by sorting x_i in increasing order ($x_{(1)} \leq x_{(2)} \leq \ldots \leq x_{(n)}$) and letting

$$l_i = \frac{x_{(1)} + \cdots + x_{(i)}}{nm} \tag{2.11}$$

where m is the sample mean. It follows that $0 \leq l_i \leq \frac{i}{n}$, i.e.

$$0 \leq L(p) \leq p$$

In other words, the Lorenz curve is always between the lines of perfect equality and perfect inequality.

Lorenz Curve Gap, again

A measure of fairness is the largest euclidian distance (the gap) from the Lorenz curve to the diagonal, rescaled by its maximum value ($\sqrt{2}$). It is also equal to the largest vertical distance, $\sup_{u \in [0,1]} (u - L(u))$ (Figure 2.5). The gap can easily be computed by observing that it is reached at index $i_0 = \max\{i : x_{(i)} \leq m\}$, i.e. at a value $p_0 = \frac{i_0}{n}$ such that the bottom fraction p_0 of the data has a value below the average. Thus

$$\text{gap} = \frac{i_0}{n} - \frac{x_{(1)} + \cdots + x_{(i_0)}}{mn} \tag{2.12}$$

We have already introduced the gap in (2.6), and we now need to demonstrate that the two definitions are equivalent. This follows from

$$\begin{aligned}
\text{MAD} &= \frac{1}{n} \sum_{i=1}^{n} |x_i - m| = \frac{1}{n} \sum_{i=1}^{n} |x_{(i)} - m| \\
&= \frac{1}{n} \left(\sum_{i=1}^{i_0} (m - x_{(i)}) + \sum_{i_0+1}^{n} (x_{(i)} - m) \right) \\
&= \frac{1}{n} \left(i_0 m - \sum_{i=1}^{i_0} x_{(i)} + nm - \sum_{i=1}^{i_0} x_{(i)} - (n - i_0)m \right) = 2m \text{ gap}
\end{aligned}$$

which is the same as (2.6).

COMMENT: The theoretical Lorenz curve is defined for a probability distribution with a cumulative distribution function CDF $F(\cdot)$ and finite mean μ by

$$L(p) = \frac{1}{\mu} \int_0^p F^{-1}(q)\, dq \tag{2.13}$$

where F^{-1} is the pseudo-inverse [51, Theorem 3.1.2]

$$F^{-1}(q) = \sup\{x : F(x) < p\} = \inf\{x : F(x) \geq q\}$$

If the CDF $F(\cdot)$ is continuous and increasing, then F^{-1} is the usual function inverse. In this case, the theoretical Lorenz curve gap is then equal to

$$\text{gap}_{\text{th}} = p_0 - L(p_0)$$

with $p_0 = F(\mu)$.

The theoretical Lorenz curve is the limit of the Lorenz curve for an iid data sample coming from $F(\cdot)$, when n is large. □

The Gini Coefficient

The **Gini coefficient** is yet another fairness index, very widespread in economy, and, by imitation, in computer and communication systems. Its definition is similar to that of the Lorenz curve gap, with the mean average deviation replaced by the **Mean Difference**:

$$\text{MD} = \frac{1}{n(n-1)} \sum_{i,j} |x_i - x_j| \tag{2.14}$$

The Gini coefficient is then defined as

$$\text{Gini} = \frac{\text{MD}}{2m} \tag{2.15}$$

where m is the empirical mean of the data set. It can be shown that it is equal to $2\times$ the area between the line of perfect equality and the Lorenz curve (the rescaling factor 2 causes it to lie between 0 and 1). In practice, the Gini coefficient can be computed with (2.11), which gives

$$\text{Gini} = \frac{2}{mn^2} \sum_{i=1}^n i x_{(i)} - 1 - \frac{1}{n} \tag{2.16}$$

COMMENT: The theoretical Gini coefficient for a probability distribution with CDF $F(\cdot)$ is defined by

$$\text{Gini}_{\text{th}} = 2 \int_0^\infty \left(q - L(q)\right) dq = 1 - 2 \int_0^\infty L(q)\, dq$$

where $L(\cdot)$ is the theoretical Lorenz curve defined in (2.13). □

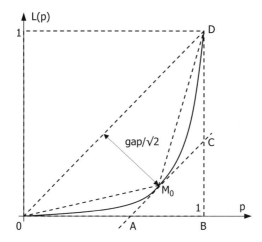

Figure 2.6 Lorenz curve (plain line). The line of perfect equality is OD, and that of perfect inequality is OBD. The Lorenz curve gap is the maximum distance to the line of perfect equality, re-scaled by $\sqrt{2}$. The Gini coefficient is the area between the line of perfect equality and the Lorenz curve, re-scaled by 2.

Since the Lorenz curve is convex, it is straightforward to bound the Gini coefficient by means of the Lorenz curve gap. In Figure 2.6, we see that the area between the Lorenz curve and the diagonal is lower bounded by the triangle OM_0D and upper bounded by the trapeze OACD. It follows from this and (2.16) that

$$0 \leq \text{gap} \leq \text{Gini} \leq 1 - \frac{1}{n}$$
$$\text{Gini} \leq \text{gap}\,(2 - \text{gap})$$

where the lower bound 0 is reached at maximum fairness.

Consequently, one can also approximate Gini by the arithmetic mean of the lower and upper bounds:

$$\text{Gini} \approx \text{gap}\,(1.5 - 0.5\,\text{gap}) \tag{2.17}$$

Summary

Since there are so many variability and fairness indices, we here give a summary with some recommendations.

First, since the Gini coefficient can be essentially predicted from the Lorenz curve gap, we do not use it further in this book. However, it may be useful to know the relationship between the two since you will find that it is employed in some performance evaluation results.

Second, Jain's fairness index and the Lorenz curve gap are fundamentally different and cannot be mapped to each other. The former is essentially the same as the coefficient of variation. If the data comes from a heavy-tailed distribution, the theoretical coefficient of variation is infinite, and CoV $\rightarrow \infty$

as the number of data points becomes large. Comparing different CoVs in such a case does not provide much information. In contrast, the Lorenz curve gap continues to be defined, as long as the distribution has a finite mean.

We recall the main inequalities and bounds in Table 2.1. See also Figure 2.5 for some examples.

Table 2.1 Relationships between different fairness indices of a data set with n samples and empirical mean m (MF = value when fairness is maximum, i.e. all data points are equal).

	Jain's Fairness Index (JFI)	Lorenz Curve Gap (gap)	Gini Coefficient (Gini)
Definition	$\dfrac{1}{1+\mathrm{CoV}^2}$	$\dfrac{\mathrm{MAD}}{2m}$	$\dfrac{\mathrm{MD}}{2m}$
	Eqs (2.2), (2.8)	Eq. (2.6)	Eq. (2.15)
Bounds	$\dfrac{1}{n} \leq \mathrm{JFI} \leq 1$ (MF)	(MF) $0 \leq \mathrm{gap} \leq 1 - \dfrac{1}{n}$	(MF) $0 \leq \mathrm{Gini} \leq 1 - \dfrac{1}{n}$
Relations	$\dfrac{1}{1+4\,\mathrm{gap}^2} \leq \mathrm{JFI}$		$\mathrm{gap} \leq \mathrm{Gini} \leq \mathrm{gap}\,(2-\mathrm{gap})$
	Equality only at MF		$\mathrm{Gini} \approx \mathrm{gap}\,(1.5 - 0.5\,\mathrm{gap})$
$\mathrm{Exp}(\lambda),\ \lambda > 0$	0.5	$\dfrac{1}{e} \approx 0.368$	0.5
$\mathrm{Unif}(a,b)$ $0 \leq a < b$	$\dfrac{1}{1+\dfrac{(b-a)^2}{3(b+a)^2}}$	$\dfrac{b-a}{4(a+b)}$	$\dfrac{b-a}{3(a+b)}$
Pareto (p,x_0) $x_0 > 0,\ p > 1$	$\dfrac{p(p-2)}{(p-1)^2}$ for $p>2$	$\dfrac{1}{p}\left(1-\dfrac{1}{p}\right)^{p-1}$	$\dfrac{1}{2p-1}$

2.2 Confidence Intervals

2.2.1 What is a Confidence Interval?

When we display numbers such as the median or the mean of a series of performance results, it is important to quantify their accuracy (as part of the scientific method, Chapter 1). **Confidence intervals** quantify the uncertainty regarding a summarized data set, which is due to the randomness of the measurements.

Example 2.2 Comparison of two Options, continued
We wish to quantify the improvement as obtained by the new system. To this end, we measure the reduction in run time for the same sequence of tasks as in Figure 2.3 (both data sets in Figure 2.3 come from the same transaction sequences – statisticians call this a *paired experiment*). The differences are displayed in Figure 2.7.
The last panel shows confidence intervals for the mean (horizontal lines) and for the median (notches in Box plot). For example, the mean of

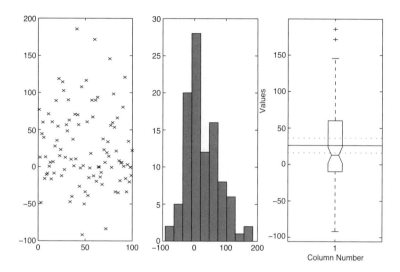

Figure 2.7 Data for Example 2.2: reduction in run time (in ms). Right: Box plot with mean and confidence interval for mean.

the reduction in run time is 26.1 ± 10.2. The uncertainty margin is designated the confidence interval for the mean. It is obtained by the method presented in this section. Here, the mean reduction is not negligible, but its uncertainty is large.

There exists a confidence interval for every summarized quantity: median, mean, quartile, standard deviation, fairness index, etc. In the remainder of this section, we explain *how* confidence intervals are computed.

2.2.2 Confidence Interval for the Median and Other Quantiles

We start with the median and other quantiles, as this is both the simplest and the most robust. This present section also serves as an illustration of the general method for computing confidence intervals.

The main idea (which underlies all classical statistics formulae) is to imagine that the data we have measured was in fact generated by a simulator, whose program is unknown to us. More precisely, we are given some data $x_1, \ldots, x_n$, and we imagine that there is a well defined probability distribution with CDF $F(\cdot)$ from which the data is sampled. In other words, we have received one sample from a sequence of independent and identically distributed (iid) random variables $X_1, \ldots, X_n$, each with a common CDF $F(\cdot)$. The assumption that the random variables are iid is capital; if it does not hold, the confidence intervals are wrong. We defer to Section 2.3 a discussion of when we may or may not make this assumption. For now we assume that it holds.

The distribution $F(\cdot)$ is non-random, but is unknown to us. It has a well-defined median m, defined by: for every i, $\mathbb{P}(X_i \leq m) = 0.5$. We can never know m exactly, but we *estimate* it by $\hat{m}(x_1,\ldots,x_n)$, equal to the sample median defined in Section 2.8.1. Note that the value of the estimated median depends on the data, and it is thus random: for different measurements, we obtain different estimated medians. The goal of a confidence interval is to bound this uncertainty. It is defined relative to a **confidence level** γ; typically $\gamma = 0.95$ or 0.99:

Definition 2.1

A *confidence interval* at level γ for the fixed but unknown parameter m is an interval $\big(u(X_1,\ldots,X_n),\, v(X_1,\ldots,X_n)\big)$ such that

$$\mathbb{P}\big(u(X_1,\ldots,X_n) < m < v(X_1,\ldots,X_n)\big) \geq \gamma \qquad (2.18)$$

In other words, the interval is constructed from the data, such that with at least 95% probability (for $\gamma = 0.95$), the true value of m falls within it. Note that *it is the confidence interval that is random, and not the unknown parameter m.*

A confidence interval for the median or any other quantile is very simple to compute, as demonstrated by the next theorem.

Theorem 2.1 (Confidence Interval for the Median and other Quantiles)

Let $X_1,\ldots,X_n$ be n iid random variables, with a common CDF $F(\cdot)$. Assume that $F(\cdot)$ has a density, and let m_p be a p-quantile of $F(\cdot)$, i.e. $F(m_p) = p$, for $0 < p < 1$.

*Let $X_{(1)} \leq X_{(2)} \leq \ldots \leq X_{(n)}$ be the **order statistic**, i.e. the set of values of X_i sorted in increasing order. Let $B_{n,p}$ be the CDF of the binomial distribution with n repetitions and probability of success p. A confidence interval for m_p at level γ is*

$$\big[X_{(j)}, X_{(k)}\big]$$

where j and k satisfy

$$B_{n,p}(k-1) - B_{n,p}(j-1) \geq \gamma$$

See the tables in Section A for practical values. For large n, we can use the approximation

$$j \approx \left\lfloor np - \eta\sqrt{np(1-p)} \right\rfloor$$

$$k \approx \left\lceil np + \eta\sqrt{np(1-p)} \right\rceil + 1$$

where η is defined by $N_{0,1}(\eta) = \frac{1+\gamma}{2}$ (e.g. $\eta = 1.96$ for $\gamma = 0.95$).

The **Binomial distribution** $B_{n,p}$, with n repetitions and a probability of success p, is the distribution of $Z = \sum_{i=1}^{n} Z_i$ where Z_i are iid random variables such that $Z_i = 0$ or 1 and $\mathbb{P}(Z_i = 1) = p$. It is in other words the distribution of the number of successes in an experiment with n trials and the individual success probability p. (The random variables Z_i are called **Bernoulli** random variables. $N_{0,1}$ is the CDF of the Gaussian distribution with the mean 0 and variance 1.)

For $n = 10$, the theorem and the table in Section A state that a 95%-confidence interval for the median (estimated as $\frac{X_{(5)}+X_{(6)}}{2}$) is $[X_{(2)}, X_{(9)}]$. In other words, we obtain a confidence interval for the median of 10 results by removing the smallest and the largest values. Could it be simpler?

Note that, for small values of n, no confidence interval is possible at the levels 0.95% or 0.99%. This is due to the probability that the true quantile is outside any of the observed data still being large.

For large n, the binomial distribution can be approximated by a Gaussian distribution, which explains the approximation in the theorem.

COMMENT: The assumption that the distribution has a density (also called PDF, probability density function) is for the simplicity of exposition. If $F(\cdot)$ does not have a density (e.g. due to the numbers X_i being integers) the theorem holds with the modification that the confidence interval is $[X_{(j)}, X_{(k)})$ (instead of $[X_{(j)}, X_{(k)}]$). □

2.2.3 Confidence Interval for the Mean

Also in this case there is a widely used result, given in the next theorem. The proof is standard and can by found in probability textbooks ([38], [76]).

Theorem 2.2

Let $X_1, \ldots, X_n$ be n iid random variables, the common distribution which is assumed to have a well-defined mean μ and a variance σ^2. Let $\hat{\mu}_n$ and s_n^2 be

$$\hat{\mu}_n = \frac{1}{n} \sum_{i=1}^{n} X_i \tag{2.19}$$

$$s_n^2 = \frac{1}{n} \sum_{i=1}^{n} (X_i - \hat{\mu}_n)^2 \tag{2.20}$$

The distribution of $\sqrt{n}\frac{\hat{\mu}_n - \mu}{s_n}$ converges to the normal distribution $N_{0,1}$ when $n \to +\infty$. An approximate confidence interval for the mean at level γ is

$$\hat{\mu}_n \pm \eta \frac{s_n}{\sqrt{n}} \tag{2.21}$$

where η is the $\frac{1+\gamma}{2}$ quantile of the normal distribution $N_{0,1}$, i.e. $N_{0,1}(\eta) = \frac{1+\gamma}{2}$. For example, $\eta = 1.96$ for $\gamma = 0.95$ and $\eta = 2.58$ for $\gamma = 0.99$.

Note that the amplitudes of the confidence interval decreases according to $\frac{1}{\sqrt{n}}$.

However, caution may be required when using the theorem, as it makes three assumptions:

(1) the data comes from an iid sequence,

(2) the common distribution has a finite variance,

(3) the number of samples is large.

It is worthwhile to screen each of these assumptions, as there are realistic cases where they do not hold. Assumption (1) is the same as for all confidence intervals in this chapter, and is discussed in Section 2.3. Assumption (2) is true provided that the distribution is not heavy-tailed, see Section 3.5. Assumption (3) generally holds even for small values of n, and can be verified using the method in Section 2.5.1.

Normal iid Case

The following theorem is a slight variant of Theorem 2.2. It applies only to cases where we know a priori that the distribution of the measured data follows a common Gaussian distribution N_{μ,σ^2}, with fixed but unknown μ and σ. It gives practically the same result as Theorem 2.2 for the confidence interval of the mean; in addition it gives a confidence interval of the standard deviation. This result is often used in practice, perhaps not rightfully, as the Gaussian assumptions are not frequently satisfied.

Theorem 2.3

Let $X_1, \ldots, X_n$ be a sequence of iid random variables with common distribution N_{μ,σ^2}. We have

$$\hat{\mu}_n = \frac{1}{n} \sum_{i=1}^{n} X_i \tag{2.22}$$

$$\hat{\sigma}_n^2 = \frac{1}{n-1} \sum_{i=1}^{n} (X_i - \hat{\mu}_n)^2 \tag{2.23}$$

Then

- *The distribution of $\sqrt{n}\frac{\hat{\mu}_n - \mu}{\hat{\sigma}_n}$ is Student's t_{n-1}; a confidence interval for the mean at level γ is*

$$\hat{\mu}_n \pm \eta \frac{\hat{\sigma}_n}{\sqrt{n}} \tag{2.24}$$

where η is the $\left(\frac{1+\gamma}{2}\right)$ quantile of the student distribution t_{n-1}.

- *The distribution of* $(n-1)\frac{\hat{\sigma}_n^2}{\sigma^2}$ *is* χ_{n-1}^2. *A confidence interval at level* γ *for the standard deviation is*

$$\left[\hat{\sigma}_n\sqrt{\frac{\zeta}{n-1}}, \hat{\sigma}_n\sqrt{\frac{\xi}{n-1}}\right] \tag{2.25}$$

where ζ *and* ξ *are quantiles of* χ_{n-1}^2: $\chi_{n-1}^2(\zeta) = \frac{1-\gamma}{2}$ *and* $\chi_{n-1}^2(\xi) = \frac{1+\gamma}{2}$.

The distributions χ^2 and t_n (Student) are defined as follows. **Chi-square** (χ_n^2) is the distribution of the sum of the squares of n independent random variables with distribution $N_{0,1}$ (its expectation is n and its variance $2n$). **Student** (t_n) is the distribution of

$$Z = \frac{X}{\sqrt{Y/n}}$$

where $X \sim N_{0,1}$, $Y \sim \chi_n^2$ and X and Y are independent.

Unlike in Theorem 2.2, the magic numbers η, ζ, ξ depend on the confidence level γ but also on the sample size n. For instance, with $n = 100$ and the confidence level 0.95, we have $\eta = 1.98$, $\zeta = 73.4$, and $\xi = 128.4$. This gives the confidence intervals for the mean and the standard deviation as

$$\left[\hat{\mu}_n - 0.198\,\hat{\sigma}_n\,, \hat{\mu}_n + 0.198\,\hat{\sigma}_n\right] \quad \text{and} \quad \left[0.86\,\hat{\sigma}_n\,, 1.14\,\hat{\sigma}_n\right]$$

QUESTION 2.1 Does the confidence interval for the mean in Theorem 2.3 depend on the estimator of the variance? Conversely?[3]

We can compare the confidence interval for the mean given by this theorem in (2.24) and by Theorem 2.2 in (2.21). The latter is only approximately true, so we may expect some small difference, vanishing with n. Indeed, the two formulas differ by two terms.

(1) The estimators of the variance

$$\hat{\sigma}_n^2 = \frac{1}{n-1}\sum_{i=1}^{n}(X_i - \hat{\mu}_n)^2 \quad \text{and} \quad s_n^2 = \frac{1}{n}\sum_{i=1}^{n}(X_i - \hat{\mu}_n)^2$$

differ by the factor $\frac{1}{n}$ versus $\frac{1}{n-1}$. The factor $\frac{1}{n-1}$ may seem unnatural, but it is required for Theorem 2.3 to hold. The factor $\frac{1}{n}$ appears naturally from the theory of maximum likelihood estimation (Section B.1). In practice, it is not a requisite to have an extreme accuracy for the estimator of σ^2 (since it is a second order parameter); thus using $\frac{1}{n-1}$ or $\frac{1}{n}$ makes little difference. Both $\hat{\sigma}_n$ and s_n are called **sample standard deviation**.

---

[3]Yes. No.

(2) η in (2.24) is defined by the student distribution, and by the normal distribution in (2.21). For large n, the student distribution is close to normal; for example, with $\gamma = 0.95$ and $n = 100$, we have $\eta = 1.98$ in (2.24) and $\eta = 1.96$ in (2.21).

See Figure 2.8 for an illustration.

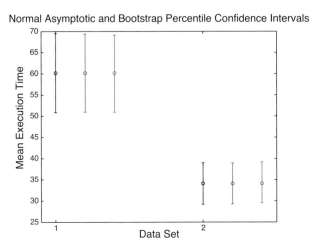

Figure 2.8 Confidence intervals for both compiler options of Example 2.1 computed with three different methods: assuming data would be normal (Theorem 2.3) (left); the general method in and with the bootstrap method (right).

2.2.4   Confidence Intervals for Fairness Indices and the Bootstrap Method

There is no analytical general method, even when n is large (but see [102] for some special cases, if the data is iid normal or log-normal). Instead, we use a generic, computational procedure, called the bootstrap method. It is general and can be used for any estimator, not just for fairness indices. It applies to all cases where data is iid.

The Bootstrap Method

Consider a sample $\vec{x} = (x_1, \ldots, x_n)$, which we assume to be a realization of an iid sequence $X_1, \ldots, X_n$. We know nothing about the common distribution $F(\cdot)$ of the X_is. We are interested in a certain quantity $t(\vec{x})$ derived from the data, for which we want to find a confidence interval (in this context $t(\vec{x})$ is called a **statistic**). For example, if the statistic of interest is the Lorenz curve gap, then according to Section 2.1.3:

$$t(\vec{x}) = \frac{1}{2\sum\limits_{i=1}^{n} x_i} \sum_{j=1}^{n} \left| x_j - \frac{1}{n}\sum_{i=1}^{n} x_i \right|$$

The **bootstrap method** uses the sample $\vec{x} = (x_1, \ldots, x_n)$ as an approximation of the true, unknown distribution. It is justified by the Glivenko-Cantelli theorem which claims that the ECDF converges with probability 1 to the true CDF $F(\cdot)$ when n becomes large.

The method is described formally in Algorithm 2.1.

Algorithm 2.1 The Bootstrap method, for computation of the confidence interval at level γ for the statistic $t(\vec{x})$. The data set $\vec{x} = (x_1, \ldots, x_n)$ is assumed to be a sample from an iid sequence, with unknown distribution. r_0 is the algorithm's accuracy parameter.

1: $R = \lceil 2\,r_0/(1 - \gamma) \rceil - 1$ ▷ For example $r_0 = 25$, $\gamma = 0.95$, $R = 999$

2: **for** $r = 1 : R$ **do**

3:     draw n numbers with replacement from the list $(x_1, \ldots, x_n)$

4:     and call them $X_1^r, \ldots, X_n^r$

5:     let $T^r = t(\vec{X^r})$

6: **end for**

7: $\left(T_{(1)}, \ldots, T_{(R)}\right) = \mathrm{sort}\left(T^1, \ldots, T^R\right)$

8: Prediction interval is $\left[T_{(r_0)}; T_{(R+1-r_0)}\right]$

The loop creates R ***bootstrap replicates*** $\vec{X}^r$, $r = 1, \ldots, R$. Each bootstrap replicate $\vec{X}^r = (X_1^r, \ldots, X_n^r)$ is a random vector of size n, like the original data. All X_i^r are independent copies of the same random variable, obtained by drawing from the list $(x_1, \ldots, x_n)$ *with replacement*. For example, if all x_k are distinct, we have $\mathbb{P}(X_i^r = x_k) = \frac{1}{n}$, $k = 1, \ldots, n$.

For each r, line 5 computes the value of the statistic obtained with the rth "replayed" experiment. The confidence interval in line 8 is the ***percentile bootstrap estimate*** at level γ. It is based on the order statistic $(T_{(r)})_{r=1,\ldots,R}$ of $(T^r)_{r=1,\ldots,R}$.

The value of R in line 1 needs to be chosen such that there are a sufficient number of points outside the interval, and depends on the confidence level. A good value is $R = \frac{50}{1-\gamma} - 1$. For example, with $\gamma = 0.95$, take $R = 999$ and the confidence interval in line 8 is $\left[T_{(25)}; T_{(975)}\right]$.

Example 2.3 Confidence Intervals for Fairness Indices
The confidence intervals for the left two cases on Figure 2.5 were obtained with the Bootstrap method, with a confidence level of 0.99, i.e. with $R = 4999$, bootstrap replicates (left and right: confidence interval; center: value of index computed in Figure 2.5).

	Jain's Fairness Index			Lorenz Curve Gap		
Old Code	0.5385	0.6223	0.7057	0.2631	0.3209	0.3809
New Code	0.5673	0.6584	0.7530	0.2222	0.2754	0.3311

For the third example, the bootstrap method cannot be applied directly. That is due to the data set not being iid and the bootstrap requiring iid data. Subsampling does not work as the data set is long-range dependent. A possible method would be is to fit a long-range dependent model, such as fractional arima, and then apply the bootstrap to the residuals.

The bootstrap method may be used for any metric, not just for fairness indices. Figure 2.8 gives a comparison of confidence intervals *for the mean* obtained with the bootstrap and with the classical methods (here $t(\vec{x}) = \frac{1}{n}\sum_{i=1}^{n} x_i$).

In general, the percentile estimate is an approximation that tends to be slightly on the small side. For a theoretical analysis of the bootstrap method, and other applications, see [33].

2.2.5   Confidence Interval for Success Probability

This is the frequent case where we carry out n independent experiments and are interested in a binary outcome (success or failure). Assume that we observe z successes (with $0 \leq z \leq n$). We would like to find a confidence interval for the probability p of success.

Mathematically, we can describe the situation as follows. We have a sequence $X_1, \ldots, X_n$ of independent Bernoulli random variables such that $\mathbb{P}(X_k = 0) = 1 - p$ and $\mathbb{P}(X_k = 1) = p$, and we observe $Z = \sum_{i=1}^{n} X_i$. The number n of experiments is known, but not the success probability p, which we want to estimate. A natural estimator of p is $\frac{1}{n}\sum_{k=1}^{n} X_i$, which correspond to the mean of the outcomes (this is the maximum likelihood estimator, see Section B.1). We can therefore apply the method for confidence intervals for the mean in Theorem 2.2. However, this method is valid only asymptotically, and does not work when z is very small as compared to n. A frequent case of interest is when we observe no success ($z = 0$) in any of the n experiments. In this case, Theorem 2.2 gives $[0, 0]$ as the confidence interval for p, which is incorrect. We can instead use the following result.

Theorem 2.4

See [43, p. 110]. Assume that we observe z successes out of n independent experiments. A confidence interval at level γ for the success probability p is $[L(z); U(z)]$ with

$$\begin{cases} L(0) = 0 \\ L(z) = \phi_{N,z-1}\left(\frac{1+\gamma}{2}\right), \quad z = 1, \ldots, n \\ U(z) = 1 - L(n - z) \end{cases} \qquad (2.26)$$

where $\phi_{n,z}(\alpha)$ is defined for $n = 2, 3, \ldots$, $z \in \{0, 1, \ldots, n\}$ and $\alpha \in (0; 1)$ by

$$
\begin{cases}
\phi_{n,z}(\alpha) = \dfrac{n_1 f}{n_2 + n_1 f} \\[2mm]
n_1 = 2(z+1), \quad n_2 = 2(n-z), \quad 1 - \alpha = F_{n_1, n_2}(f)
\end{cases}
\tag{2.27}
$$

($F_{n_1, n_2}(\cdot)$ is the CDF of the Fisher distribution with n_1, n_2 degrees of freedom). In particular, the confidence interval for p when we observe $z = 0$ successes is $[0; p_0(n)]$ with

$$
p_0(n) = 1 - \left(\frac{1-\gamma}{2}\right)^{\frac{1}{n}} = \frac{1}{n} \log\left(\frac{2}{1-\gamma}\right) + o\left(\frac{1}{n}\right) \qquad \text{for large } n \quad (2.28)
$$

Whenever $z \geq 6$ and $n - z \geq 6$, the normal approximation

$$
\begin{cases}
L(z) \approx \dfrac{z}{n} - \dfrac{\eta}{n}\sqrt{z\left(1 - \dfrac{z}{n}\right)} \\[3mm]
U(z) \approx \dfrac{z}{n} + \dfrac{\eta}{n}\sqrt{z\left(1 - \dfrac{z}{n}\right)}
\end{cases}
\tag{2.29}
$$

can be used instead, with $N_{0,1}(\eta) = \frac{1+\gamma}{2}$.

The confidence interval in the theorem is not the best, but it is perhaps the simplest. It is based on a symmetric coverage interval, i.e. the probability of being above (or below) is $< \frac{1-\gamma}{2}$ and it is the smallest interval with this property. Other non-symmetric intervals can be derived and are slightly smaller [12].

Note that the function $\phi_{N,z}(\cdot)$ is the reverse mapping of $p \mapsto B_{n,p}(z)$ where $B_{n,p}(\cdot)$ is the CDF of the binomial distribution (which explains (2.28)). Equation (2.27) is used in numerical implementations [43].

For $\gamma = 0.95$, Equation (2.28) gives $p_0(n) \approx \frac{3.689}{n}$ and this is accurate already with less than 10% relative error for $n \geq 20$. The confidence interval in (2.29) is obtained by applying the asymptotic confidence interval for the mean; indeed, a direct application of Theorem 2.2 gives $\hat{\mu}_n = \frac{z}{n}$ and $s_n^2 = \frac{z(n-z)}{n}$.

Example 2.4 Sensor Loss Ratio

We measure environmental data with a sensor network. There is reliable error detection, i.e. there is a coding system that declares whether a measurement is correct or not. In a calibration experiment with 10 independent replications, the system claims that all measurements are correct. What can we say about the probability p of finding an incorrect measurement?

Apply (2.28): we can state, with 95% confidence, that $p \leq 30.8\%$.

Later, in field experiments, we find that 32 out of 145 readings are declared incorrect. Assuming the measurements are independent, what can we say about p?

Apply (2.29) with $z = 32$, $n = 145$: with 95% confidence we can state that $L \leq p \leq U$ with

$$
\begin{cases}
L \approx \dfrac{z}{n} - \dfrac{1.96}{n}\sqrt{z\left(1 - \dfrac{z}{n}\right)} = 15.3\% \\[4mm]
U \approx \dfrac{z}{n} + \dfrac{1.96}{n}\sqrt{z\left(1 - \dfrac{z}{n}\right)} = 28.8\%
\end{cases}
$$

Instead of the normal approximation in (2.29), we could have used the exact formula in (2.26), which would give $L = 15.6\%, U = 29.7\%$.

Theorem 2.4 is frequently used in conjunction with Monte Carlo estimations of the p-value of a test, see Example 6.8 in Chapter 6.

2.3   The Independence Assumption

All results in the previous as well as the next section assume the data to be a sample of a sequence of independent and identically distributed random variables. We here present a detailed discussion of the meaning of this assumption (in Section 2.4.3 we also discuss the Gaussian assumption, required by Theorems 2.2 and 2.3).

2.3.1   What does iid mean?

Independent and identically distributed-ness is a property of a stochastic model, not of the data. When we say, by an abuse of language, that the collected data set is iid, we mean that we can do as if the collected data $x_1, \ldots, x_n$ is a sample (i.e. a simulation output) for a sequence of random variables $X_1, \ldots, X_n$, where $X_1, \ldots, X_n$ are independent and all have the same (usually unknown) distribution with CDF $F(\cdot)$.

To generate such an sample, we draw a random number from the distribution $F(\cdot)$, using a random number generator (see Section 6.6). Independence means that the random numbers generated at every step i are discarded and not re-used in the future steps $i+1, \ldots$ Another way to think of independence is with conditional probabilities: for any set of real numbers A

$$
\mathbb{P}(X_i \in A \mid X_1 = x_1, \ldots, X_{i-1} = x_{i-1}) = \mathbb{P}(X_i \in A) \tag{2.30}
$$

In other words, *if we know the distribution $F(x)$*, observing $X_1, \ldots, X_{i-1}$ does not give more information about X_i.

Note the importance of the "if" statement in the last sentence: remove it and the sentence is no longer true. To understand why, consider a sample $x_1, \ldots, x_n$ for which we assume to know that it is generated from a sequence of iid random variables $X_1, \ldots, X_n$ with normal distribution but with unknown parameters (μ, σ^2). If we observe, for example, that the average of $x_1, \ldots, x_{n-1}$ is 100 and all values are between 0 and 200, then we can imagine that it is very likely that x_n is also in the interval $[0, 200]$ and that it is unlikely that x_n exceeds 1000. Despite that the sequence is iid, we were able to gain information about the next element of the sequence by observing the past. There is no contradiction: if we know that the parameters of the random generator are $\mu = 100$ and $\sigma^2 = 10$, then observing $x_1, \ldots, x_{n-1}$ gives us no information about x_n.

2.3.2   How do I know in Practice if the iid Assumption is Valid?

If your performance data comes from a **_designed experiment_**, i.e. a set of simulation or tests that is entirely under your control, then it is up to you to design things in such a way that the collected data are iid. This is done as follows.

Every experiment has a number of factors, i.e. parameters that are likely to influence the outcome. Most of the factors are not really interesting, but you have to account for them in order to avoid hidden factor errors (see Section 1.2 for details). The experiment generates iid data if the values of the factors are chosen in an iid way, i.e. according to a random procedure that is the same for every measured point, and is memoriless. Consider Example 2.1, where the run time for a number of transactions is measured. One factor is the choice of the transaction. The data is made iid if, for every measurement, we choose one transactions _randomly with replacement_ in a list of transactions.

A special case of designed experiments is simulation. Here, the method is to generate _replications_ without resetting the random number generator, as explained in Section 6.3. Otherwise (i.e. if your data does not come from a designed experiment but from measurements on a running system), there is little chance that the complete sequence of measured data is iid. A simple fix is to _randomize the measurements_ in such a way that there is little dependence from one measurement point to the other. For example, assume that you are measuring the response time of an operational web server by data mining the log file. The response time to consecutive requests is highly correlated at the time scale of the minute (due to protocols like TCP); one common solution is to choose requests at random, for instance by selecting one request every two minutes in average.

When there is doubt, the following methods can be used to verify iid-ness:

(1) (Autocorrelation Plot): If the data appears to be stationary (no trend, no seasonal component), we can plot the sample autocorrelation coefficients, which are estimates of the true autocorrelation coefficients ρ_k (defined on Page 158). If the data is iid, then $\rho_k = 0$ for $k \geq 1$, and the sample autocorrelation coefficients fall within the values $\pm 1.96/\sqrt{n}$ (where n is the sample size) with 95% probability. An autocorrelation plot also displays

these bounds. A visual inspection can determine if this assumption is valid. For example, in Figure 2.9, we see that there is some autocorrelation in the first six diagrams but not in the last two. If visual inspection is not possible, a formal test can be used (the Ljung-Box test, Section 5.5.1). If the data is iid, any point transformation of the data (such as the Box Cox transformation for any exponent s, cf. Section 2.4.3) should also appear to be non-correlated.

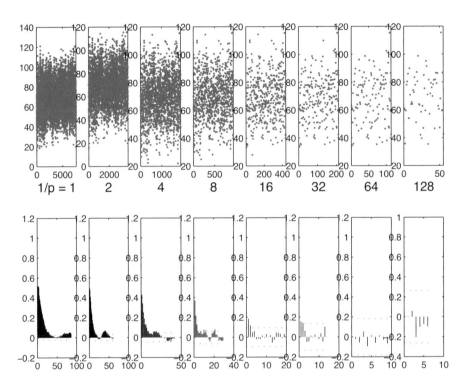

Figure 2.9 Execution times for $n = 7632$ requests (top left) and the autocorrelation function (bottom left), as well as for the data sub-sampled with probability $p = \frac{1}{2}$ to $\frac{1}{2^7} = \frac{1}{128}$. The data appears stationary and roughly normal, and the autocorrelation function can thus be used to test the independence. The original data is positively correlated, but the sub-sampled data loses correlation when the sampling probability is $p = \frac{1}{64}$. The turning point test for the sub-sampled data with $p = \frac{1}{64}$ has a p-value of 0.52648. Consequently, at confidence level 0.95, we accept the null hypothesis: the data is iid. The sub-sampled data has 116 points, and the confidence interval obtained from this for the median of the sub-sampled data is $[66.7, 75.2]$ (using Theorem 2.1). Compare with the confidence interval that would be obtained if we were to (wrongly) assume the data to be iid: $[69.0, 69.8]$. The iid assumption underestimates the confidence interval due to the data being positively correlated.

(2) (***Lag-Plot***): We can also plot the value of the data at time t versus at time $t + h$, for several values of h (lag plots). If the data is iid, the lag plots will not show any trend. Figure 2.10 diplays a negative trend at lag 1.

(3) (Turning Point Test): A test provides an automated answer, but is sometimes less sure than a visual inspection. A test usually has a null hypothesis
and returns a so called "p-value" (see Chapter 4 for an explanation). If the
p-value is smaller than $\alpha = 1 - \gamma$, then the test rejects the null hypothesis
at the confidence level γ. We refer to Section 4.5.2 for details.

2.3.3 What Happens if the iid Assumption does not hold?

If we compute a confidence interval (using a method that assumes iid data)
when in fact the iid assumption does not hold, we introduce bias. Data arising
from high resolution measurements are frequently positively correlated. In such
cases, the confidence interval is too small: there is not as much information in
the data as if it would have been iid. This is due to the data having a tendency
to repeat itself; see Figure 2.9 for an example.

Nevertheless, it may still be possible to obtain confidence intervals when
the data does not appear to be iid. Two possible methods are:

Sub-sampling. This involves selecting a fraction p of the measured data, and
verifying that the iid assumption can be made for this selection data. The hope
is that correlation disappears between data samples that are far apart.

A simple way would be to keep every pn data sample, where n is the
total number of points, but this is not recommended as such a strict periodic
sampling may introduce unwanted anomalies (called aliasing). A better method
is to decide independently for each data point, with probability p, whether it
is sub-sampled or not.

For example, in Figure 2.9, sub-sampling works for $p \leq \frac{1}{64}$; the confidence
interval for the median is much larger than if we were to (wrongly) assume the
original data to be iid.

Although sub-sampling is very simple and efficient, it does not always work.
For instance, it does not work if the data set is small, or for some large data
sets, which remain correlated after repeated sub-sampling (such data sets are
called long-range dependent).

Modeling. This is more complex but applies when sub sampling does not. It
consists in fitting a parametric model appropriate to the type of data, and computing confidence intervals for the model parameters (for example according to
Section B.1). We illustrate this method on the next example.

Example 2.5 Joe's Balance Data

Joe's shop sells online access to visitors who download electronic con-
tent on their smartphones. At the end of day $t - 1$, Joe's employee
counts the amount of cash c_{t-1} present in the cash register and puts
it into the safe. In the morning of day t, the cash amount c_{t-1} is
returned to the cash register. The total amount of service sold (according to bookkeeping data) during day t is s_t. During the day, some
amount of money b_t is sent to the bank. At the end of day t, we should

have $c_t = c_{t-1} + s_t - b_t$. However, there always occur small errors when counting the coins, in bookkeeping and in returning change. Joe computes the balance $Y_t = c_t - c_{t-1} - s_t + b_t$ and would like to know whether there is a systematic source of errors (i.e. Joe's employee is losing money, maybe as a result of being dishonest, or because certain customers are not paying for what they are taking). The data for Y_t is shown in Figure 2.10. The sample mean is -13.95, which is negative. However, we need a confidence interval for μ before risking any conclusion.

If we were to assume that the errors Y_t are iid, then a confidence interval would be given by Theorem 2.2 and we would find approximately $[-43, 15]$. Thus, with the iid model, we cannot conclude that there is a fraud.

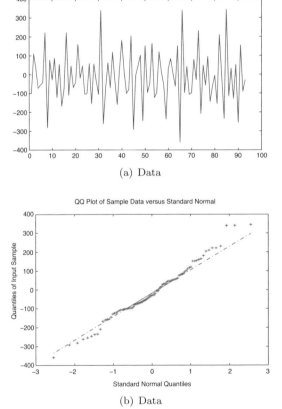

(a) Data

(b) Data

Figure 2.10 The daily balance at Joe's wireless access shop during 93 days. The lag plots show $y(t)$ versus $y(t + h)$ where $y(t)$ is the time series in (a). The data appears to have some correlation at lag 1 and is thus clearly not iid.

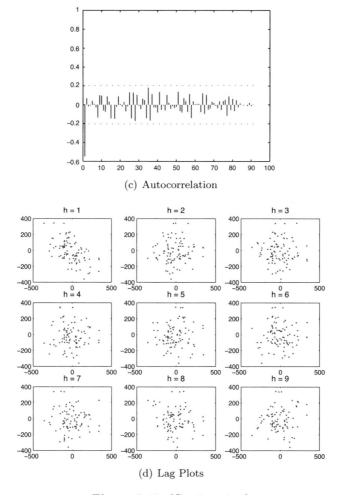

(c) Autocorrelation

(d) Lag Plots

Figure 2.10 (Continuation.)

However, the iid assumption is not valid, as Figure 2.10 shows (there is a strong correlation at lag 1, which is confirmed by the lag plot). We use a modeling approach. Y_t appears to be reasonably Gaussian (see also Section 2.4.3), and has correlation only at lag 1. (We study such processes in Chapter 5.) A Gaussian process that has correlation only at lag 1 is the moving average process, which satisfies

$$Y_t - \mu = \epsilon_t + \alpha\epsilon_{t-1}$$

where ϵ_t is iid N_{0,σ^2}. This is a parametric model, with parameters (μ, α, σ). We can fit it using a numerical package or the methods presented in Chapter 5. A confidence interval for μ can be obtained using Theorem B.2 and Theorem D.3. Here, it is plausible that the sample size is large enough. For any fixed μ, we compute the profile log-likelihood. It is obtained by fitting an MA(1) process to $W_t := Y_t - \mu$.

Good statistical packages give not only the MLE fit, but also the log-likelihood of the fitted model, which is exactly the profile log-likelihood $pl(\mu)$. The MLE $\hat{\mu}$ is the value of μ that maximizes $pl(\mu)$, and $-2(pl(\hat{\mu}) - pl(\mu))$ is approximately χ_1^2. Figure 2.11 shows a plot of $pl(\mu)$.

It follows that $\hat{\mu} = -13.2$ and an approximate 95%-confidence interval is $[-14.1, -12.2]$. Contrary to the iid model, this suggests that there *is* a loss of money, on average 13 € per day.

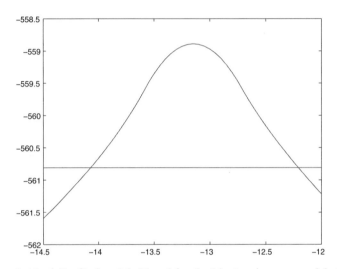

Figure 2.11 A Profile Log Likelihood for the Moving Average model of Joe's balance data. The horizontal line is at a value $\frac{\eta}{2} = 1.92$ below the maximum, with $\chi_1^2(\eta) = 0.95$: This gives an approximate confidence interval for the mean of the data on the x axis.

QUESTION 2.2 Give an example of identically distributed but dependent random variables.[4]

2.4 Prediction Interval

The previously studied confidence intervals quantify the accuracy of a mean or median. This is useful for diagnostic purposes: We can for example assert from the confidence intervals in Figure 2.7 that the new option reduces the run time, because the confidence intervals for the mean (or the median) are in the positive numbers.

---

[4] Here is a simple one: assume $X_1, X_3, X_5, \ldots$ are iid with CDF $F(\cdot)$ and let $X_2 = X_1$, $X_4 = X_3$, etc. The distribution of X_i is $F(\cdot)$ but the distribution of X_2 conditional to $X_1 = x_1$ is a dirac at x_1, thus depends on x_1. The random choices taken for X_1 influence (here deterministically) the value of X_2.

Sometimes we are interested in a different viewpoint and would like to characterize the *variability* of the data. We might for example like to summarize what can be expected for an arbitrary future (non-observed) transaction. Clearly, this run time is random. A **prediction interval** at level γ is an interval that we can compute by observing a realization of $X_1, \ldots, X_n$ and such that, with probability γ, a future transaction will have a run time in this interval. Intuitively, if the common CDF of all X_is would be known, a prediction interval would simply be an inter-quantile interval, e.g. $[m_{\alpha/2}, m_{1-\alpha/2}]$, with $\alpha = 1 - \gamma$. For instance, if the distribution is normal with known parameters, a prediction interval at level 0.95 would be $\mu \pm 1.96\,\sigma$. However, there is some additional uncertainty, due to the fact that we do not know the distribution, or its parameters a priori, and thus need to estimate it. The prediction interval captures both uncertainties. Formally, the definition is as follows.

Definition 2.2

Let $X_1, \ldots, X_n, X_{n+1}$ be a sequence of random variables. A prediction interval at level γ is an interval of the form $\big[u(X_1, \ldots, X_n), v(X_1, \ldots, X_n) \big]$ such that

$$\mathbb{P}\big(u(X_1, \ldots, X_n) \le X_{n+1} \le v(X_1, \ldots, X_n) \big) \ge \gamma \qquad (2.31)$$

Note that the definition does not assume that X_i is iid, however we focus in this chapter on the iid case (but see Section 2.4.1 for a discussion of the more general case). The trick is now to find functions u and v that are **pivots**, i.e. their distribution is known even if the common distribution of the X_is is not (or is not entirely known).

There is one general result, which in practice applies to sample sizes that are not too small ($n \ge 39$). It is given next.

2.4.1 Prediction for an iid Sample based on Order Statistic

Theorem 2.5 (General Independent and Identically Distributed Case)

Let $X_1, \ldots, X_n, X_{n+1}$ be an iid sequence and assume that the common distribution has a density. Let $X_{(1)}^n, \ldots, X_{(n)}^n$ be the order statistic of $X_1, \ldots, X_n$. For $1 \le j \le k \le n$:

$$\mathbb{P}\big(X_{(j)}^n \le X_{n+1} \le X_{(k)}^n \big) = \frac{k - j}{n + 1} \qquad (2.32)$$

thus for $\alpha \ge \frac{2}{n+1}$, $\big[X_{(\lfloor (n+1)\frac{\alpha}{2} \rfloor)}^n, X_{(\lceil (n+1)(1-\frac{\alpha}{2}) \rceil)}^n \big]$ is a prediction interval at a level of at least $\gamma = 1 - \alpha$.

For example, with $n = 999$, a prediction interval at the level 0.95 ($\alpha = 0.05$) is $[X_{(25)}, X_{(975)}]$. This theorem is similar to the bootstrap result in Section 2.2.4, but is exact and much simpler.

QUESTION 2.3 We have obtained n simulation results and use the prediction interval $[m, M]$ where m is the smallest result and M the largest. For which values of n is this a prediction interval at level at least 95%?[5]

For very small n, this result gives poor prediction intervals with values of γ that may be far from 100%. For example, with $n = 10$, the best prediction we can make is $[x_{\min}, x_{\max}]$, at the level $\gamma = 81\%$. If we can assume that the data is normal, we have a stronger result, as shown next.

2.4.2 Prediction for a Normal iid Sample

Theorem 2.6 (Normal Independent and Identically Distributed Case)
Let $X_1, \ldots, X_n, X_{n+1}$ be an iid sequence with common distribution N_{μ,σ^2}. Let $\hat{\mu}_n$ and $\hat{\sigma}_n^2$ be as in Theorem 2.3. The distribution of $\sqrt{\frac{n}{n+1}} \frac{X_{n+1} - \hat{\mu}_n}{\hat{\sigma}_n}$ is Student's t_{n-1}; a prediction interval at level $1 - \alpha$ is

$$\hat{\mu}_n \pm \eta' \sqrt{1 + \frac{1}{n}} \, \hat{\sigma}_n \tag{2.33}$$

where η' is the $(1 - \frac{\alpha}{2})$ quantile of the student distribution t_{n-1}. For large n, an approximate prediction interval is

$$\hat{\mu}_n \pm \eta \hat{\sigma}_n \tag{2.34}$$

where η is the $(1 - \frac{\alpha}{2})$ quantile of the normal distribution $N_{0,1}$.

For example, for $n = 100$ and $\alpha = 0.05$ we obtain the following prediction interval (we drop the index n): $[\hat{\mu} - 1.99\,\hat{\sigma}, \hat{\mu} + 1.99\,\hat{\sigma}]$. Compare this to the confidence interval for the mean given by Theorem 2.3 where the width of the interval is $\approx 10 = \sqrt{n}$ times smaller. For a large n, the prediction interval is approximately equal to $\hat{\mu}_n \pm \eta \hat{\sigma}_n$, which is the interval we would have if we ignore the uncertainty due to the fact that the parameters μ and σ are estimated from the data. For n as small as 26, the difference between the two is 7% and can be neglected in most cases.

The normal case is also convenient in that it requires the knowledge of only two statistics, the mean $\hat{\mu}_n$ and the mean of squares (from which $\hat{\sigma}_n$ is derived).

Comment

Compare the prediction interval in (2.34) to the confidence interval for the mean in (2.24): there is a difference of $\frac{1}{\sqrt{n}}$. Confusion between the two is frequent: when comparing confidence intervals, verify that the standard deviation is indeed divided by $\sqrt{n}$!

---

[5] The interval is $[X_{(1)}, X_{(n)}]$, thus the level is $\frac{n-1}{n+1}$. It is ≥ 0.95 for $n \geq 39$. In other words, we need at least 39 samples to provide a 95% prediction interval.

Example 2.6 File Transfer Times

Figure 2.12 shows the file transfer times obtained in 100 independent simulation runs, displayed in natural and log scales. The last panel shows 95%-prediction intervals. The left interval is obtained with the method of order statistic (Theorem 2.5); the middle one by (wrongly) assuming that the distribution is normal and applying Theorem 2.5 – it differs largely.

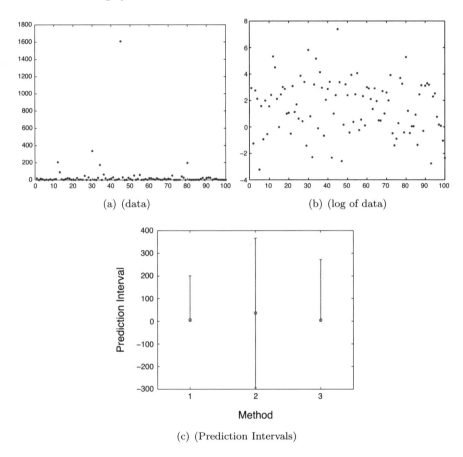

(a) (data)   (b) (log of data)

(c) (Prediction Intervals)

Figure 2.12 File transfer times for 100 independent simulation runs, with prediction intervals computed with the order statistic (1), assuming the data is normal (2), and assuming the log of data is normal (3).

The right interval is obtained with a log transformation. First, a prediction interval $[u(Y_1, \ldots, Y_n), v(Y_1, \ldots, Y_n)]$ is computed for the transformed data $Y_i = \ln(X_i)$; the prediction interval is mapped back to the original scale to obtain the prediction interval

$$\left[\exp\Big(u\big(\ln(X_1), \ldots, \ln(X_n)\big) \Big), \exp\Big(v\big(\ln(X_1), \ldots, \ln(X_n)\big) \Big) \right]$$

We leave it to the alert reader to verify that this reverse mapping is indeed valid. The left and right intervals are in good agreement, but the middle one is obviously wrong.

The prediction intervals also show the central values (with small circles). For the first one, it is the median. For the second one, the mean. For the last one, it is $\exp\left(\frac{\sum_{i=1}^{n} Y_i}{n}\right)$, i.e. the back transform of the mean of the transformed data.

QUESTION 2.4 The prediction intervals in Figure 2.12 are not all symmetric around the central values. Explain why.[6]

There is no "large n" result for a prediction interval, as there is in Theorem 2.2: a prediction interval depends on the original distribution of the X_is, unlike confidence intervals for the mean, which depend only on first and second moments thanks to the central limit theorem. Theorem 2.6 justifies the common practice of using the standard deviation as a measure of dispersion; however it provides useful prediction intervals only if the data appears to be iid *and* normal. In the next section, we discuss how to verify normality.

2.4.3 The Normal Assumption

qq-plots

This is a simple method for verifying the normal assumption, based on visual inspection. A **probability plot**, also called **qq-plot**, compares two samples X_i, Y_i, $i = 1, \ldots, n$ in order to determine whether they come from the same distribution. Call $X_{(i)}$ the **order statistic**, obtained by sorting X_i in increasing order. Thus $X_{(1)} \leq X_{(2)} \leq \ldots$ The qq-plot displays the points $(X_{(i)}, Y_{(i)})$. If the points are approximately along a straight line, then the distributions of X_i and Y_i can be assumed to be the same, modulo a change of scale and location.

Most often, we use qq-plots to verify the distribution of Y_i against a probability distribution F. To do so, we plot $(x_i, Y_{(i)})$, where x_i is an estimation of the expected value of $\mathbb{E}(Y_{(i)})$, assuming that the marginal of Y_i is F. The exact value of $\mathbb{E}(Y_{(i)})$ is hard to obtain, but a simple approximation (provided that F is strictly increasing) is [32]:

$$x_i := F^{-1}\left(\frac{i}{n+1}\right)$$

A **normal qq-plot** is a qq-plot such that $F = N_{0,1}$, and is often used to visually test for normality (Figure 2.13). More formal tests are the Jarque Bera test (Section 4.5.1) and the goodness of fit tests in Section 4.4.

---

[6] First interval: the distribution of the data is obviously not symmetric. Consequently, the median has no reason to be in the middle of the extreme quantiles. Second interval: By nature, it is strictly symmetric. Third interval: It is the exponential of a symmetric interval. The exponential is not an affine transformation, so we should not expect the transformed interval to be symmetric.

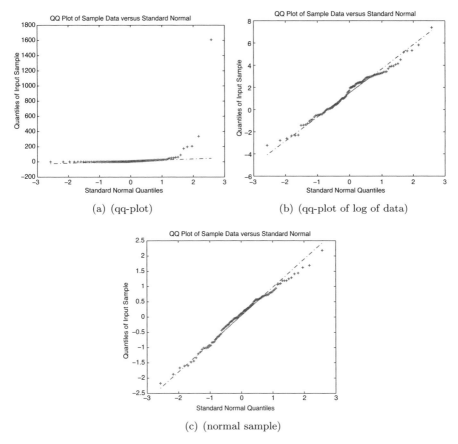

(a) (qq-plot) (b) (qq-plot of log of data)

(c) (normal sample)

Figure 2.13 Normal qq-plots of file transfer times in Figure 2.12 and of an artificially generated sample from the normal distribution with the same number of points. The first plot shows large deviation from normality, whereas the second does not.

Rescaling, Harmonic, Geometric and other Means

Figure 2.12 illustrates that the use of the standard deviation as a basis for a prediction interval may be better if we re-scale the data, using a point tranformation. For this the ***Box-Cox transformation*** is commonly employed. It has one shape parameter s and is given, for positive x, by

$$b_s(x) = \begin{cases} \dfrac{x^s - 1}{s} & s \neq 0 \\ \ln x & s = 0 \end{cases} \qquad (2.35)$$

Frequently utilized parameters include $s = 0$ (log transformation), $s = -1$ (inverse), $s = 0.5$ and $s = 2$. It presents this specific form in order to be continuous in s.

It is easy to see (as in Example 2.6) that a *prediction interval* for the original data can be obtained by reverse-transforming a prediction interval for the transformed data. In contrast, this does not hold for *confidence intervals*. Indeed, by reverse-transforming a confidence interval for the mean of the transformed data, we obtain a confidence interval for another type of mean (harmonic, etc.). More precisely, assume that we transform a data set $x_1, \ldots, x_n$ by an invertible (thus strictly monotonic) mapping $b(\cdot)$ into $y_1, \ldots, y_n$, i.e. $y_i = b(x_i)$ and $x_i = b^{-1}(y_i)$ for $i = 1, \ldots, n$. We designated **transformed sample mean** the quantity $b^{-1}(\frac{1}{n} \sum_{i=1}^{n} y_i)$, i.e. the back-transform of the mean of the transformed data. Similarly, the **transformed distribution mean** of the distribution of a random variable X is $b^{-1}(\mathbb{E}(b(X)))$. When $b(\cdot)$ is a Box-Cox transformation with index $s = -1, 0$ or 2, we obtain the classical following definitions, valid for a positive data set $x_i, i = 1 \ldots, n$ or a positive random variable X:

	Transformation	Transformed Sample Mean	Transformed Distribution Mean
Harmonic	$b(x) = \dfrac{1}{x}$	$\dfrac{1}{\dfrac{1}{n} \sum\limits_{i=1}^{n} \dfrac{1}{x_i}}$	$\dfrac{1}{\mathbb{E}\left(\dfrac{1}{X}\right)}$
Geometric	$b(x) = \ln(x)$	$\left(\prod\limits_{i=1}^{n} x_i\right)^{\frac{1}{n}}$	$e^{\mathbb{E}(\ln X)}$
Quadratic	$b(x) = x^2$	$\sqrt{\dfrac{1}{n} \sum\limits_{i=1}^{n} x_i^2}$	$\sqrt{\mathbb{E}(X^2)}$

Theorem 2.7

A confidence interval for a transformed mean is obtained by the inverse transformation of a confidence interval for the mean of the transformed data.

For example, a confidence interval for the geometric mean is the exponential of a confidence interval for the mean of the logarithms of the data.

2.5   Which Summarization to use?

The previous sections have presented various summarization methods. In this section, we discuss the use of these different methods. The methods differ in their objectives: *confidence intervals* for central value versus *prediction intervals*. The former quantify the accuracy of the estimated central value, the latter reflect how variable the data is. Both aspects are related (the more variable the data is, the less accurate is the estimated central value) but they are not the same.

The methods also differ in the techniques used, and overlap to a large extent. They fall into two methods: approches based on the order statistic (confidence interval for median or other quantiles, Theorem 2.1; prediction interval computed with the order statistic, Theorem 2.5) or based on means and standard deviations (Theorems 2.3, 2.2, 2.6). The two types of methods differ in their *robustness versus compactness*.

2.5.1 Robustness

Erroneous Distributional Hypotheses

The confidence interval for the mean given by Theorem 2.2 requires that the central limit theorem applies, i.e.

(1) that the common distribution has a finite variance, and

(2) that the sample size n is large enough.

While these two assumptions very often hold, it is important to detect cases where they do not.

Ideally, we would like to test whether the distribution of $T = \sum_{i=1}^{n} X_i$ is normal or not, but we cannot do this directly, since we have only one value of T. The bootstrap method can be used to solve this problem, as explained in the following example.

Example 2.7 Pareto Distribution

This is a toy example where we generate artificial data, iid, from a Pareto distribution on $[1, +\infty)$. It is defined by its CDF equal to $F(c) := \mathbb{P}(X > c) = \frac{1}{c^p}$ with $p = 1.25$; its mean is $= 5$, its variance is infinite (i.e. it is heavy-tailed) and its median is 1.74.

Assume that we do not know that it comes from a heavy-tailed distribution and would like to use the asymptotic result in Theorem 2.2 to compute a confidence interval for the mean. We use the bootstrap method to verify convergence to the normal distribution, as follows. We are given a data sample $x_1, \ldots, x_n$ from the Pareto distribution. We generate R replay experiments: for each r between 1 and R, we draw n samples X_i^r $i = 1, \ldots, n$ with replacement from the list $(x_1, \ldots, x_n)$ and let $T^r = \frac{i=1}{n} X_i^r$. T^r is the rth bootstrap replicate of T; we obtain a qq-plot of the T^r, $r = 1, \ldots, R$.

If the distribution of T is normal, the qq-plot should look normal as well. However, we see that this is not the case, which is an indication that the central limit theorem might not hold. Indeed, the confidence interval for the mean is not very good.

The previous example shows a case where the confidence interval for the mean is not good. This is due to a distributional assumption being made, which is incorrect. In contrast, the confidence interval for the median *is* correct (Figure 2.14), as it does not require any distributional assumption (other than the iid hypothesis).

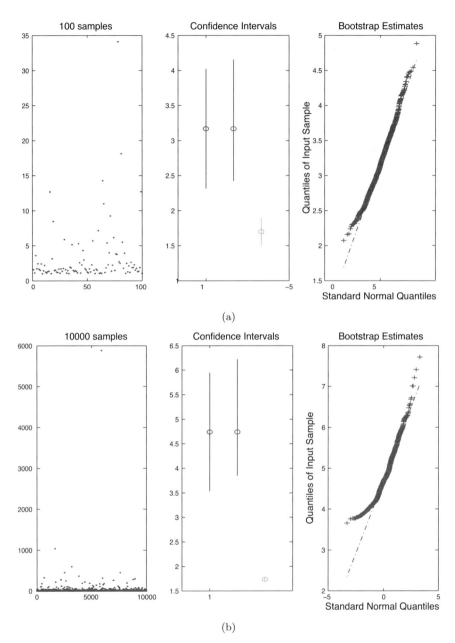

(a)

(b)

Figure 2.14 (a) Left: An artificially generated sample of 100 values from the Pareto distribution with exponent $p = 1.25$. Center: Confidence intervals for the mean computed from Theorem 2.2 (left) and the bootstrap percentile estimate (center), as well as the confidence interval for the median (right). Right: A qq-plot of 999 bootstrap replicates of the mean. The qq-plot deviates from normality, thus the confidence interval given by Theorem 2.2 is incorrect. Note that, in this case, the bootstrap percentile interval is not very good either, since it fails to capture the true value of the mean ($= 5$). In contrast, the confidence interval for the median captures the true value ($= 1.74$). (b) Same with $10,000$ samples. The true mean is now within the confidence interval, but there is still no convergence to normality.

Outliers

Methods based on the order statistic are more robust to outliers. An ***outlier*** is a value that significantly differs from the average. The median and the prediction interval based on order statistic are not affected by a few outliers, contrary to the mean and the prediction interval based on a mean and the standard deviation, as illustrated by the following example.

Example 2.8 File Transfer with one Outlier

In the data of Example 2.8, there is in fact one very large value, 5 times larger than the next largest value. One might be tempted to remove it, on the basis that such a large value might be due to measurement

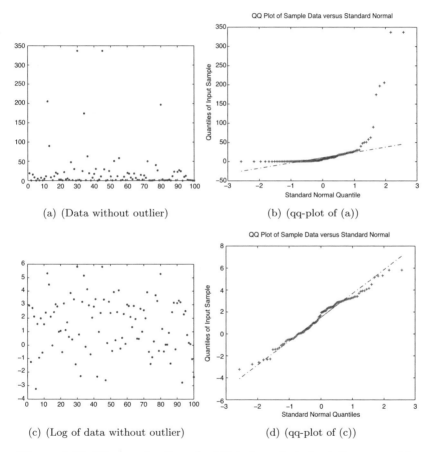

(a) (Data without outlier) (b) (qq-plot of (a))

(c) (Log of data without outlier) (d) (qq-plot of (c))

Figure 2.15 File transfer times for 100 independent simulation runs with the outlier removed. Confidence intervals without (left) and with (right) the outlier, and with (1) median (2) mean and (3) geometric mean methods. Prediction intervals without (left) and with (right) the outlier, computed with the three alternative methods discussed in Example 2.8: (1) order statistics (2) based on mean and standard deviation (3) based on mean and standard deviation after re-scaling.

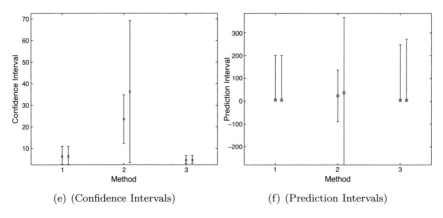

(e) (Confidence Intervals)   (f) (Prediction Intervals)

Figure 2.15 (Continuation.)

error. A qq-plot of the data without this "outlier" is shown in Figure 2.15, and can be compared to the corresponding qq-plot with the outlier in Figure 2.13(a). The prediction intervals based on order statistics are not affected, but the one based on mean and standard deviation is completely different.

Table 2.2 shows that the values of Jain's fairness index and the Lorenz curve gap are very sensitive to the presence of a single outlier, which is consistent with the previous observation. This is due to Jain's fairness index being defined by the coefficient of variation. The Lorenz curve gap is less sensitive.

Table 2.2 Fairness indices with and without the outlier.

		Index	Lower Bound, CI	Index	Upper Bound, CI
Without Outlier	JFI		0.1012	0.1477	0.3079
	gap		0.4681	0.5930	0.6903
With Outlier	JFI		0.0293	0.0462	0.3419
	gap		0.4691	0.6858	0.8116

The outlier is less so on the re-scaled data (with the log transformation). The qq-plot of the rescaled data is not affected very much, neither is the prediction interval based on the mean and standard deviation of the rescaled data. Similarly, the confidence intervals for a median and geometric mean are unaffected, as opposed to that for the mean. We do not show fairness indices for the re-scaled data since re-scaling changes their meaning.

Care should be taken to screen the data collection procedure for *true outliers*, namely values that are faulty because of measurement errors or problems. In the previous example, the outlier should not be removed. In practice, it may be difficult to differentiate between true and spurious outliers. The example illustrates the following facts:

- Outliers may affect the prediction and confidence intervals based on mean and standard deviation, as well as the values of fairness indices. Jain's fairness index is more sensitive to outliers than the Lorenz curve gap.
- This may go away if the data is properly rescaled. An outlier at a certain scale may not be an outlier at another scale.
- In contrast, confidence intervals for the median and prediction intervals based on order statistics are more robust to outliers. They are not affected by re-scaling.

2.5.2 Compactness

Assume that we wish to obtain both a central value with confidence interval and a prediction interval for a given data set. If we use methods based on order statistics, we will obtain a confidence interval for the median, and, say, a prediction interval at the level 95%. Variability and accuracy are given by different sample quantiles, and cannot be deduced from one another. Furthermore, if later we are interested in 99% prediction intervals rather than 95%, we need to recompute new estimates of the quantiles. The same argument speaks in favor of quantifying the variability by means of the Lorenz curve gap.

In contrast, if we employ methods based on mean and standard deviation, we obtain both confidence intervals and prediction intervals at any level with just 2 parameters (the sample mean and the sample standard deviation). In particular, the sample standard deviation gives an indication of both the accuracy of the estimator and the variability of the data. However, as we saw earlier, these estimators are meaningful only at a scale where the data is roughly normal.

Also, the mean and the standard deviation are less complex to compute than estimators based on order statistics, which require sorting of the data. In particular, the mean and the standard deviation can be computed incrementally online, by keeping only 2 counters (sum of values and sum of squares). This reason is less valid today as opposed to some years ago, since there are sorting algorithms with complexity $n \ln(n)$.

2.6   Other Aspects of Confidence Prediction Intervals

2.6.1 Intersection of Confidence, Prediction Intervals

In some cases, we have several confidence or prediction intervals for the same quantity of interest. For instance, we can have a prediction interval I based on a mean and standard deviation or I' based on order statistics. A natural deduction would be to consider that the intersection $I \cap I'$ is a better confidence interval. This is almost true:

> **Theorem 2.8**
>
> *If the random intervals I, I' are confidence intervals at the levels $\gamma = 1 - \alpha$, $\gamma' = 1 - \alpha'$ then the intersection $I \cap I'$ is a confidence interval at the level of at least $1 - \alpha - \alpha'$. The same holds for prediction intervals.*

Example 2.9 File Transfer Times

(Continuation of Example 2.8.) We can compute two prediction intervals at the level 0.975, using the order statistic method as well as the mean and standard deviation after rescaling (the prediction obtained without rescaling is not valid since the data is not normal). We get $[0.0394, 336.9]$ and $[0.0464, 392.7]$. We thus conclude that the prediction interval at the level 0.95 is $[0.0464, 336.9]$, which is better than the other.

Compare this interval to the prediction intervals at the level 95% for each of the two methods; these are $[0.0624, 205.6]$ and $[0.0828, 219.9]$. Both are thus better.

Thus, if we for example combine two confidence intervals at the level 97.5%, we obtain a confidence interval at the level 95%. As the example shows, this may give poorer results than an original confidence interval at the level 95%.

2.6.2 The Meaning of Confidence

When we claim that an interval I is a confidence interval at the level 0.95 for a certain parameter θ, we mean the following. Repeating the experiment many times would lead to, in about 95% of the cases, the interval I indeed containing the true value θ.

QUESTION 2.5 Assume that 1000 students independently perform a simulation of an M/M/1 queue with a load factor $\rho = 0.9$ and find a 95% confidence interval for the result. The true result, unknown to these (unsophisticated) students is 9. Although the students are unsophisticated, they are conscientious, and all of them performed the correct simulations. How many of the 1000 students would you expect to find a wrong confidence interval, i.e. one that does *not* contain the true value?[7]

2.7 Proofs

Theorem 2.1

Let $Z = \sum_{k=1}^{n} 1_{\{X_k \leq m_p\}}$ be the number of samples that lie below or at m_p. The CDF of Z is $B_{n,p}$ since the events $\{X_k \leq m_p\}$ are independent and

---

[7] Approximately 50 students should find a wrong interval.

$\mathbb{P}(X_k \leq m_p) = p$ by definition of the quantile m_p. Further:

$$j \leq Z \iff X_{(j)} \leq m_p$$
$$k \geq Z + 1 \iff X_{(k)} > m_p$$

thus we have the event equalities

$$\{X_{(j)} \leq m_p < X_{(k)}\} = \{j \leq Z \leq k - 1\} = \{j - 1 < Z \leq k - 1\}$$

and

$$\mathbb{P}(X_{(j)} \leq m_p < X_{(k)}) = B_{n,p}(k - 1) - B_{n,p}(j - 1)$$

It follows that $[X_{(j)}, X_{(k)})$ is a confidence interval for m_p at the level γ as soon as $B_{n,p}(k - 1) - B_{n,p}(j - 1) \geq \gamma$.

The distribution of the X_is has a density, thus so does $(X_{(j)}, X_{(k)})$. Moreover, $\mathbb{P}(X_{(j)} < m_p \leq X_{(k)}) = \mathbb{P}(X_{(j)} < m_p < X_{(k)})$, thus $[X_{(j)}, X_{(k)}]$ is also a confidence interval at the same level.

For large n, we approximate the binomial CDF by N_{μ,σ^2} with $\mu = np$ and $\sigma^2 = np(1 - p)$, as follows:

$$\mathbb{P}(j - 1 < Z \leq k - 1) = \mathbb{P}(j \leq Z \leq k - 1) \approx N_{\mu,\sigma^2}(k - 1) - N_{\mu,\sigma^2}(j)$$

and we pick j and k such that

$$N_{\mu,\sigma^2}(k - 1) \geq 0.5 + \frac{\gamma}{2}$$
$$N_{\mu,\sigma^2}(j) \leq 0.5 - \frac{\gamma}{2}$$

which guarantees that $N_{\mu,\sigma^2}(k - 1) - N_{\mu,\sigma^2}(j) \geq \gamma$. It follows that we need to have

$$k - 1 \geq \eta\sigma + \mu$$
$$j \leq -\eta\sigma + \mu$$

We take the smallest k and the largest j which satisfy these constraints, which gives the formulas in the theorem.

Theorem 2.5

Transform X_i into $U_i = F(X_i)$ which is iid uniform. For uniform RVs, use the fact that $\mathbb{E}(U_{(j)}) = \frac{j}{n+1}$. Then

$$\mathbb{P}(U_{(j)}^n \leq U_{n+1} \leq U_{(k)}^n \mid U_{(1)}^n = u_{(1)}, \ldots, U_{(n)}^n = u_{(n)}) = \mathbb{P}(u_{(j)} \leq U_{n+1} \leq u_{(k)})$$
$$= u_{(k)} - u_{(j)}$$

Since U_{n+1}, the former is independent of $(U_1, \ldots, U_n)$ and the latter shas a uniform distribution on $[0, 1]$. Thus

$$\mathbb{P}(U_{(j)}^n \leq U_{n+1} \leq U_{(k)}^n) = \mathbb{E}(U_{(k)}^n - U_{(j)}^n) = \frac{k - j}{n + 1}$$

Theorem 2.6

First note that X_{n+1} is independent of $\hat{\mu}_n, \hat{\sigma}_n$. Thus $X_{n+1} - \hat{\mu}_n$ is normal with the mean 0 and the variance

$$\text{var}(X_{n+1}) + \text{var}(\hat{\mu}_n) = \sigma^2 + \frac{1}{n}\sigma^2$$

Further, $\hat{\sigma}_n/\sigma^2$ has a χ^2_{n-1} distribution and is independent of $X_{n+1} - \hat{\mu}_n$. By definition of Student's t, the theorem follows.

Theorem 2.7

Let m' be the distribution mean of $b(X)$. By definition of a confidence interval, we have $\mathbb{P}\big(u(Y_1, \dots, Y_n) < m' < v(Y_1, \dots, Y_n)\big) \geq \gamma$ where the confidence interval is $[u, v]$. If $b(\cdot)$ is increasing (like the Box-Cox transformation with $s \geq 0$) then so is $b^{-1}(\cdot)$ and this is equivalent to

$$\mathbb{P}\big(b^{-1}\big(u(Y_1, \dots, Y_n)\big) < b^{-1}(m') < b^{-1}\big(v(Y_1, \dots, Y_n)\big)\big) \geq \gamma$$

Now $b^{-1}(m')$ is the transformed mean, which shows the statement in this case. If $b(\cdot)$ is decreasing (like the Box-Cox transformation with $s < 0$), the result is similar to an inversion of u and v.

Theorem 2.8

We carry out the proof for a confidence interval for a certain quantity θ. The proof is the same for a prediction interval. By definition, $\mathbb{P}(\theta \notin I) \leq \alpha$ and $\mathbb{P}(\theta \notin I') \leq \alpha'$. Thus

$$\mathbb{P}(\theta \notin I \cap I') = \mathbb{P}\big((\theta \notin I) \text{ or } (\theta \notin I')\big) \leq \mathbb{P}(\theta \notin I) + \mathbb{P}(\theta \notin I') \leq \alpha + \alpha'$$

2.8 Review

2.8.1 Summary

(1) A *confidence* interval is used to quantify the *accuracy* of a parameter estimated from the data.

(2) For computing the central value of a data set, you can use either the mean or the median. Unless you have special reasons (see below) for not doing so, the median is the preferred choice as it is more robust. You should compute not only the median but also a confidence interval for it, using Table A.1.

(3) A *prediction* interval reflects the *variability* of the data. For small data sets ($n < 38$), it is not meaningful. For larger data sets, it can be obtained by Theorem 2.5. The Lorenz curve gap also gives a scale free representation of the variability of the data.

(4) A confidence interval for the mean characterizes both the *variability* of the data and the *accuracy* of the measured average. In contrast, a confidence interval for the median does not give a good reflection of the variability of the data. Therefore, if we use the median, we need both a confidence interval for the median and a certain measure of the variability (the quantiles, as in a Box Plot). Mean and standard deviation give an accurate idea of the *variability* of the data, but only if the data is roughly normal. Otherwise, it should be re-scaled through for example a Box-Cox transformation. Normality can be verified with a qq-plot.

(5) The standard deviation gives an accurate idea of the *accuracy* of the mean if the data is normal, but also if the data set is large. The latter can be verified with a bootstrap method.

(6) The geometric (resp. harmonic) mean is meaningful if the data is roughly normal in log (resp. $\frac{1}{x}$) scale. A confidence interval for the geometric (resp. harmonic) mean is obtained as the exponential (resp. inverse) of the mean in log (resp. $\frac{1}{x}$) scale.

(7) All estimators in this chapter are valid only if the data points are independent (non-correlated). This assumption must be verified, either by designing the experiments in a randomized way, (as is the case with independent simulation runs), or by formal correlation analysis.

(8) If you have a choice, use median and quantiles rather than mean and standard deviation, as the former are more robust to distributional hypotheses and to outliers. Use prediction intervals based on order statistic rather than the classical mean and standard deviation. Use the Lorenz curve gap rather than Jain's fairness index.

2.8.2   Review Questions

2.1 Compare

(1) the confidence interval for the median of a sample of n data values, at the level 95% and

(2) a prediction interval at a level of at least of 95%, for $n = 9, 39, 99$.[8]

2.2 Denote $L = \min\{X_1, X_2\}$ and $U = \max\{X_1, X_2\}$. We perform an experiment and find $L = 7.4$, $U = 8.0$. Which of the following two statements is correct (θ is the median of the distribution):

---

[8] From the tables in Chapter A and Theorem 2.5 we obtain (confidence interval for median, prediction interval):
$n = 9$: $[x_{(2)}, x_{(9)}]$, impossible;
$n = 39$: $[x_{(13)}, x_{(27)}]$, $[x_{(1)}, x_{(39)}]$;
$n = 99$: $[x_{(39)}, x_{(61)}]$, $[x_{(2)}, x_{(97)}]$.
The confidence interval is always smaller than the prediction interval.

(a) the probability of the event $\{L \leq \theta \leq U\}$ is 0.5,

(b) the probability of the event $\{7.4 \leq \theta \leq 8.0\}$ is 0.5.[9]

2.3 How do we expect a 90% confidence interval to compare to a 95% one? Verify this on the tables in Section A[10]

2.4 A data set has 70 points. Give the formulae for confidence intervals at the level 0.95 for the median and the mean.[11]

2.5 A data set has 70 points. Give formulae for a prediction intervals at the level 95%.[12]

2.6 A data set $x_1, \ldots, x_n$ is such that $y_i = \ln x_i$ looks normal. We obtain a confidence interval $[\ell, u]$ for the mean of y_i. Can we obtain a confidence interval for the mean of x_i by a transformation of $[\ell, u]$?[13]

2.7 Assume that a set of measurements is corrupted by an error term that is normal, but positively correlated. If we were to compute a confidence interval for the mean using the iid hypothesis, would the confidence interval be too small or too large?[14]

2.8 We estimate the mean of an iid data set by two different methods and obtain two confidence intervals at the level 95%: $I_1 = [2.01, 3.87]$, and $I_2 = [2.45, 2.47]$. Since the second interval is smaller, we discard the first and keep only the second. Is this a correct 95% confidence interval?[15]

---

[9] In the classical (non-Bayesian) framework, (1) is correct and (2) is wrong. There is nothing random in the event $\{7.4 \leq \theta \leq 8.0\}$, since θ is a fixed (though unknown) parameter. The probability of this event is either 0 or 1, here it happens to be 1. Be careful with the ambiguity of a statement such as "the probability that θ lies between L and U is 0.5". In case of doubt, come back to a probability space. The probability of an event can be interpreted as the ideal proportion of simulations that would produce the event.

[10] It should be smaller. If we take more risk, we can accept a smaller interval. We can check that the values of j (resp. k) in the tables of confidence intervals at level $\gamma = 0.95$ are larger (resp. smaller) than at the confidence level $\gamma = 0.99$.

[11] Median: from the table in Section A $[x_{(27)}, x_{(44)}]$. Mean: from Theorem 2.2: $\hat{\mu} \pm 0.2343S$ where $\hat{\mu}$ is the sample mean and S the sample standard deviation. The latter assumes the normal approximation to hold, and should be verified by either a qq-plot or the bootstrap method.

[12] From Theorem 2.5: $[\min_i x_i, \max_i x_i]$.

[13] No, we know that $[e^\ell, e^u]$ is a confidence interval for the geometric mean, not the mean of x_i. In fact x_i comes from a log-normal distribution, for which the mean is $e^{\mu + \sigma^2/2}$. There μ is the mean of the distribution of y_i, and σ^2 its variance.

[14] Too small: we underestimate the error. This phenomenon is known in physics under the term **personal equation**: if the errors are linked to the experimenter, they are positively correlated.

[15] No, by doing so we keep the interval $I = I_1 \cap I_2$, which is a 90% confidence interval, not a 95% confidence interval.

CHAPTER 3

Model Fitting

In this chapter, we study how to derive a model from data, e.g. fitting a curve to a series of measurements. The method of least squares is widely used, and gives simple, often linear algorithms. However, it should be employed with care, as it leads to the hidden assumption that error terms are Gaussian with equal variance. We also discuss a less known alternative called ℓ^1 norm minimization, which implicitly assumes that error terms have a Laplace instead of Gaussian distribution. The resulting algorithms may be less simple, but are often tractable, as they correspond to convex (rather than linear) optimizations, and the method is more robust to outliers or wrong distributional assumptions.

We deal in detail with the so-called "linear models"; here it is the dependence on the hidden parameters that is linear, not the model itself. This is a very rich family of models with a wide applicability. We discuss both least square and ℓ^1 norm minimization in this context.

Subsequently, we bring up the issue of fitting a distribution to a data set; we describe commonly used features that are helpful when selection an appropriate distribution: distribution shape, power laws, fat tail and heavy tail. The latter property is often encountered in practice and provides interesting (or annoying) properties. We illustrate the use of such features in a load generation tool.

3.1   Model Fitting Criteria

3.1.1   What is Model Fitting?

We start with a simple example.

Example 3.1   Virus Spread Data

The number of hosts infected by a virus is plotted versus the time in hours.

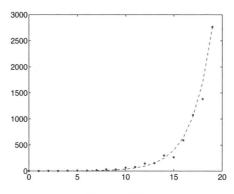

Figure 3.1

The plot suggests an exponential growth, and we are therefore we are inclined to fit these data to a model of the form

$$Y(t) = a\,e^{\alpha t} \tag{3.1}$$

where $Y(t)$ is the number of infected hosts at time t. We are particulary interested in the parameter α, which can be interpreted as the growth rate; the **doubling time** (time for the number of infected hosts to double) is $\frac{\ln 2}{\alpha}$. On the plot, the dashed line is the curve fitted by the method of least squares explained later. We find $\alpha = 0.4837$ per hour and the doubling time is 1.43 hours. We can use the model to predict that, 6 hours after the end of the measurement period, the number of infected hosts would be ca. $82,000$.

In general, **model fitting** can be defined as the problem of finding an **explanatory model** for the data, i.e. a mathematical relation of the form

$$y_i = f_i(\vec{\beta}) \tag{3.2}$$

that "explains the data well", in some sense. Here, y_i is the collection of measured data, i is the index of a measurement, f_i is an array of functions, and $\vec{\beta}$ is the parameter that we would like to obtain. In the previous example, the parameter is $\vec{\beta} = (a, \alpha)$ and $f_i(\vec{\beta}) = f_i(a, \alpha) = a\,e^{\alpha t_i}$ where t_i is the time of the ith measurement, assumed here to be known.

What does it mean to "explain the data well"? It is generally not possible to require that (3.2) holds *exactly* for all data points. Therefore, a common answer is to require that the model minimizes some metric of the discrepancy between the explanatory model and the data. A very common metric is the mean square distance $\sum_i \left(y_i - f_i(\vec{\beta})\right)^2$. The value of the growth rate α in the previous example was obtained in this way, namely, by computing a and α to minimize $\sum_i \left(y_i - a\, e^{\alpha t_i}\right)^2$.

But this raises another question. What metric should one use? What is so magical about least squares? Why not use other measures of discrepancy, for example $\sum_i \left|y_i - f_i(\vec{\beta})\right|$ or $\sum_i \left(\ln(y_i) - \ln(f_i(\vec{\beta}))\right)^2$? The following example shows the importance of the issue.

Example 3.2 Virus Spread Data, Ambiguity in the Optimization

Preceding example continued. We also plotted the number of infected hosts in log scale:

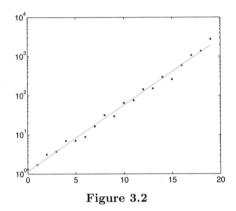

Figure 3.2

and then computed the least square fit of (3.2) in log scale (plain line). In other words, we calculted the a and α that minimize $\sum_i \big(\ln(y_i) - \ln(a) - \alpha t_i\big)^2$. We found for α the value 0.39 per hour, which gives a doubling time of 1.77 hours and a prediction at time $+6$ hours equal to ca. $39,000$ infected hosts (instead of the previously $82,000$). The two models are compared below (in linear and log scales).

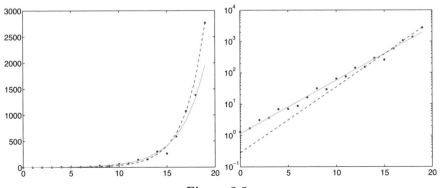

Figure 3.3

Both figures show that what visually appears to be a good fit in one scale is not so good in the other. Which one should we use?

An answer to the question can be obtained from statistics. The idea is to add to the explanatory model a description of the "noise" (informally defined as the deviation between the explanatory model and the data), which gives us a **statistical model**. We can also think of the statistical model as a description of a simulator that was used to produce the data we have. Its parameters are well defined, but not known to us.

The statistical model usually has a few more parameters than the explanatory model. The parameters of the statistical model are estimated using the classical approach of maximum likelihood. If we believe in the statistical model, this answers the previous question by stating that the criterion to be optimized is the likelihood. The belief in the model can be verified by examining residuals.

Example 3.3 Virus Spread Data, a Statistical Model

Preceding exemple continued.   One *statistical model* for the virus spread data is

$$Y_i = a\,e^{\alpha t_i} + \epsilon_i \qquad \text{with } \epsilon_i \text{ iid} \sim N_{0,\sigma^2} \qquad (3.3)$$

In other words, we assume that the measured data y_i is equal to the ideal value given by the explanatory model, plus a noise term ϵ_i. Further, we assume that all noises are independent, Gaussian, and with equal variance. The parameter is $\theta = (a, \alpha, \sigma)$.
In (3.3), we write Y_i instead of y_i to express that Y_i is a random variable. We think of our data y_i as being *one* sample produced by a simulator that implements (3.3).
We will see in Section 3.1.2 that the maximum likelihood estimator for this model is the one that minimizes the mean square distance. Thus, with this model, we obtain for α the value in Example 3.1.
A second statistical model could be:

$$\ln(Y_i) = \ln\!\big(a\,e^{\alpha t_i}\big) + \epsilon_i \qquad \text{with } \epsilon_i \text{ iid} \sim N_{0,\sigma^2} \qquad (3.4)$$

In this case, we assume that the noise terms in log-scale have the same variance, i.e. that the noise is proportional to the measured value. Here too, the maximum likelihood estimator is obtained by minimizing the least square distance, and we thus obtain for α the value in Example 3.2.
We can validate either model by plotting the residuals (Figure 3.4).
We clearly see that the residuals for the former model do not appear to be normally distributed, and the inverse is true for the latter model, which is the one we should adopt. Therefore, an acceptable fitting is obtained by minimizing least squares in log-scale.

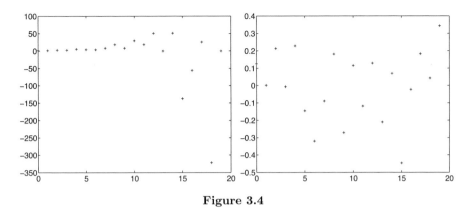

Figure 3.4

We summarize what we have learned so far as follows.

Fitting a Model to Data

(1) Define a statistical model that contains *both* the deterministic part (the one we are interested in) and a model of the noise.

(2) Estimate the parameters of the statistical model using maximum likelihood. If the number of data points is small, use a brute force approach (e.g `fminsearch`). If the number of data points is large, you may need to search the literature for efficient, possibly heuristic, optimization methods.

(3) Validate the model fit by screening the residuals, either visually, or through tests (Chapter 4). In practice, you will seldom obtain a perfect fit; however, large deviations indicate that the model might not be appropriate.

3.1.2 Least Squares Correspond to Gaussian, Equal Variance

A very frequent case is when the statistical model has the form

$$Y_i = f_i(\vec{\beta}) + \epsilon_i \qquad \text{for } i = 1, \ldots, I \text{ with } \epsilon_i \text{ iid} \sim N_{0,\sigma^2} \qquad (3.5)$$

as in the previous examples (Models in Equations (3.3) and (3.4)). The discrepancy between the explanatory model and the data is assumed to be Gaussian with *equal variance*. In some examples in the literature, the "equal variance" assumption is called ***homoscedasticity***.

The next theorem explains how to fit the explanatory model $y_i = f_i(\vec{\beta})$ to our data using least squares: we implicitly assume that the error terms in our data are independent, Gaussian, and of equal amplitude. We have seen in the examples above that care must be taken when validating this assumption. In particular, some rescaling may be needed for an improved validation.

Theorem 3.1 (Least Squares)

For the model in (3.5) :

(1) The maximum likelihood estimator of the parameter $(\vec{\beta}, \sigma)$ is given by:

(a) $\hat{\beta} = \arg\min\limits_{\vec{\beta}} \sum\limits_i \big(y_i - f_i(\vec{\beta})\big)^2$;

(b) $\hat{\sigma}^2 = \dfrac{1}{I} \sum\limits_i \big(y_i - f_i(\hat{\beta})\big)^2.$

(2) Let K be the square matrix of second derivatives (assumed to exist), defined by

$$K_{j,k} = \frac{1}{\sigma^2} \sum_i \frac{\partial f_i}{\partial \beta_j} \frac{\partial f_i}{\partial \beta_k}$$

If K is invertible and if the number I of data points is large, $\hat{\beta} - \vec{\beta}$ is approximately Gaussian with 0 mean and covariance matrix K^{-1}.

Alternatively, for large I, an approximate confidence set at level γ for the jth component β_j of $\vec{\beta}$ is implicitly defined by

$$-2I \ln(\hat{\sigma}) + 2I \ln\big(\hat{\sigma}(\hat{\beta}_1, \ldots, \hat{\beta}_{j-1}, \beta_j, \hat{\beta}_{j+1}, \ldots, \hat{\beta}_p)\big) \geq \xi_1$$

where $\hat{\sigma}(\vec{\beta})^2 = \frac{1}{I} \sum_i \big(y_i - f_i(\vec{\beta})\big)^2$ and ξ_1 is the γ quantile of the χ^2 distribution with one degree of freedom (e.g. for $\gamma = 0.95$, $\xi_1 = 3.92$).

The set of points in $\mathbb{R}^I$ that have coordinates of the form $f_i(\vec{\beta})$ constitutes a "manifold" (for $p = 2$, it is a surface). Item (1a) claims that $\vec{\beta}$ is the parameter of the point $\hat{y}$ on this manifold that is the nearest to the data point $\vec{y}$, in euclidian distance. The point $\hat{y}$ is called the **predicted response**; it is an estimate of the value that $\vec{y}$ would take if there was no noise. It is equal to the orthogonal projection of the data $\vec{y}$ onto the manifold.

The rest of the theorem can be used to obtain accuracy bounds for the estimation. A slight variant of the theorem can be used to make predictions with accuracy bounds, see Theorem 5.1.

3.1.3 ℓ^1 Norm Minimization Corresponds to Laplace Noise

Although less traditional than least square, one can also utilize minimization of the absolute deviation of the error. The absolute deviation is the ℓ^1 norm of the error,[1] and this method is consequently also called ℓ^1 **norm minimization**. Since it gives less weight to outliers, it is expected to be more robust. As we see now, it corresponds to assuming that errors follow a Laplace distribution (i.e. a bilateral exponential).

The **Laplace distribution** with 0 mean and rate λ is a two-sided exponential distribution, or, in other words, $X \sim \text{Laplace}(\lambda)$ if and only if

---

[1]The ℓ^1 norm of a sequence $z = (z_1, \ldots, z_n)$ is $\|z\|_1 = \sum_{i=1}^n |z_i|$.

$|X| \sim \text{Exp}(\lambda)$. It can be used to model error terms that have a heavier tail than the normal distribution. Its PDF is defined for $x \in \mathbb{R}$ by

$$f(x) = \frac{\lambda}{2} e^{-\lambda|x|} \tag{3.6}$$

The next theorem explains what we do when we fit the explanatory model $y_i = f_i(\vec{\beta})$ to our data by minimizing the ℓ^1 norm of the error: we implicitly assume that the error terms in our data are independent, Laplace with the same parameter, i.e., the data y_i is a sample generated by the model

$$Y_i = f_i(\vec{\beta}) + \epsilon_i \qquad \text{with } \epsilon_i \text{ iid} \sim \text{Laplace}(\lambda) \tag{3.7}$$

Theorem 3.2 (Least Deviation)
For the model in (3.7), the maximum likelihood estimator of the parameter $(\vec{\beta}, \lambda)$ is given by:

(1) $\hat{\beta} = \arg\min_{\vec{\beta}} \sum_i |y_i - f_i(\vec{\beta})|$;

(2) $\dfrac{1}{\hat{\lambda}} = \dfrac{1}{I} \sum_i |y_i - f_i(\hat{\beta})|$.

Example 3.4 Virus Propagation with one Outlier

Assume that the data in the virus propagation example (Example 3.1) is modified by changing the value of the second data point. Further assume that we fit the data in log scale. The modified data is an outlier,

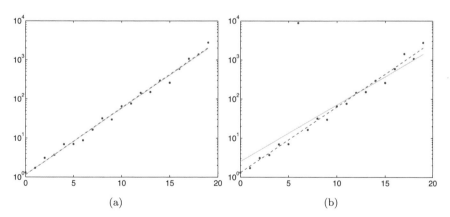

(a)   (b)

Figure 3.5 The fitting of an exponential growth model to the data in Example 3.1, demonstrating the fits obtained with least square (plain) and with ℓ^1 norm minimization (dashed). First panel: original data; both fits are the same; second panel: data corrupted by one outlier; the fit with ℓ^1 norm minimization is not affected, whereas the least square fit is.

and one could be tempted to remove it. An alternative is to fit the log of the data to Laplace noise instead of Gaussian noise (i.e. carry out ℓ^1 norm minimization instead of least squares), as this is known to be more robust. Figure 3.5, and the table below show the results (the prediction in the table is a 6-hour ahead point prediction).

	Least Square		ℓ^1 Norm Minimization	
	rate	prediction	rate	prediction
no outlier	0.3914	30, 300	0.3938	32, 300
with one outlier	0.3325	14, 500	0.3868	30, 500

We see that one single outlier completely modifies the result of least square fitting, whereas ℓ^1 norm minimization fitting is not impacted much.

The following example is important for understanding the difference between least square and ℓ^1 norm minimization.

Example 3.5 Mean versus Median

Assume that we want to fit a data set y_i, $i = 1, \ldots, I$ against a constant μ.

With least square fitting, we are looking for μ that minimizes $\sum_{i=1}^{I}(y_i - \mu)^2$. The solution is easily found to be $\mu = \frac{1}{I}\sum_{i=1}^{I} y_i$, i.e. μ is the sample mean.

With ℓ^1 norm minimization, we are looking for μ that minimizes $\sum_{i=1}^{I}|y_i - \mu|$. The solution is the median of y_i.

To see why, consider the mapping $f : \mu \mapsto \sum_{i=1}^{I}|y_i - \mu|$. To simplify, consider the case where all values y_i are distinct and written in increasing order ($y_i < y_{i+1}$). The derivative f' of f is defined everywhere except at points y_i, and for $y_i < \mu < y_{i+1}$, $f'(\mu) = i - (I - i) = 2 - I$. By continuity, if I is odd, f decreases on $(-\infty, y_{(2I+1)/2}]$ and increases on $[y_{(2I+1)/2}, +\infty)$. It thus has a minimum for $\mu = y_{(2I+1)/2}$, which is the sample median. If I is even, f is at a minimum for values in the interval $[y_{I/2}, y_{I/2+1}]$ and thus reaches the minimum at the sample median $\frac{y_{I/2}+y_{I/2+1}}{2}$.

In terms of computation, ℓ^1 norm minimization is more complex than least squares, though both are usually tractable. For instance, if the dependency on the parameter is linear, least square fitting consists in solving a linear system of equations whereas ℓ^1 norm minimization uses linear programming (as shown in the next section).

3.2   Linear Regression

Linear regression is a special case of least square fitting, where the explanatory model depends linearly on its parameter $\vec{\beta}$. This is called the **linear regression** model. The main fact here is that everything can be computed easily, using linear algebra. Be careful that the term "linear regression" implicitly assumes least square fitting. The popular fitting method called "ANOVA" is a special case of linear regression.

Assume that the *statistical model* of our experiment has the form:

Definition 3.1 (Linear Regression Model)

$$Y_i = (X\vec{\beta})_i + \epsilon_i \qquad \text{for } i = 1, \dots, I \text{ with } \epsilon_i \text{ iid} \sim N_{0,\sigma^2} \qquad (3.8)$$

where the unknown parameter $\vec{\beta}$ is in $\mathbb{R}^p$ and X is an $I \times p$ matrix. The matrix X is supposed to be exactly known in advance. We also assume that

$$X \text{ has rank } p \qquad\qquad\qquad (H)$$

Assumption (H) signifies that different values of $\vec{\beta}$ give varying values of the explanatory model $X\vec{\beta}$, i.e. the explanatory model is identifiable.

The elements of the known matrix X are sometimes called **explanatory variables**, and then the y_is are denoted the **response variables**.

Example 3.6   Joe's Shop again

See figure 1.3(b). We assume that there is a threshold ξ beyond which the throughput collapses (we take $\xi = 70$). The statistical model is

$$Y_i = (a + bx_i)1_{x_i \leq \xi} + (c + dx_i)1_{\{x_i > \xi\}} + \epsilon_i \qquad (3.9)$$

where we impose

$$a + b\xi = c + d\xi \qquad (3.10)$$

In other words, we assume the throughput response curve to be piecewise linear. Equation (3.10) expresses that the curve is continuous. Recall that x_i is the offered load and Y_i is the actual throughput. Here, we take $\vec{\beta} = (a, b, d)$ (we can derive $c = a + (b - d)\xi$ from (3.10)). The dependency of Y_i on $\vec{\beta}$ is indeed linear. Note that we assume ξ to be known (how to handle the case where ξ is to be identified is presented in Exemple 3.8).
Assume that we sort the x_is in increasing order and let i^* be the largest index i such that $x_i \leq \xi$. Re-write (3.9) as

$$Y_i = a + bx_i + \epsilon_i \qquad \text{for } i = 1, \dots, i^*$$
$$Y_i = a + b\xi + d(x_i - \xi) + \epsilon_i \qquad \text{for } i = i^* + 1, \dots, I$$

thus the matrix X is given by

$$
\begin{pmatrix}
1 & x_1 & 0 \\
1 & x_2 & 0 \\
\vdots & \ddots & \vdots \\
1 & x_{i^*} & 0 \\
1 & \xi & x_{i^*+1} - \xi \\
\vdots & \ddots & \vdots \\
1 & \xi & x_I - \xi
\end{pmatrix}
$$

It is simple to see that a *sufficient* condition for (H) is that there are at least two distinct values of $x_i \le \xi$ and at least one value $> \xi$.
QUESTION 3.1 Show this.[2]

A model as in this example is sometimes called ***intervention analysis***.

With the linear regression model, the manifold mentioned in the discussion after Theorem 3.1 is a linear manifold (for $p = 2$, a plane). It is equal to the linear sub-space spanned by the columns of matrix X. The nearest point is given by an orthogonal projection, which can be exactly computed. The details are given in the following theorem, the proof of which is contained in [32, Section 2.3].

Theorem 3.3 (Linear Regression)
Consider the model in Definition 3.1; let $\vec{y}$ be the $I \times 1$ column vector of the data.

(1) The $p \times p$ matrix $(X^T X)$ is invertible.

(2) (Estimation) The maximum likelihood estimator of $\vec{\beta}$ is $\hat{\beta} = K\vec{y}$ with

$$ K = \left(X^T X \right)^{-1} X^T $$

(3) (Standardized Residuals) Define the ith residual as $e_i = \left(\vec{y} - X\hat{\beta} \right)_i$. The residuals are zero-mean Gaussian but are correlated, with covariance

---

[2] We need to show, if the condition is true, that the matrix X has the rank $p = 3$. This is equivalent to saying that the equation

$$ X \begin{pmatrix} a \\ b \\ d \end{pmatrix} = 0 $$

has only the solution $a = b = d = 0$. Consider first a and b. If there are two distinct values of x_i, $i \le i^*$, say x_1 and x_2, then $a + bx_1 = a + bx_2 = 0$ thus $a = b = 0$. Since there is a value $x_i > \xi$, it follows that $i^* + 1 \le I$ and $d(x_I - \xi) = 0$ thus $d = 0$.

matrix $\sigma^2(Id_I - H)$, where $H = X(X^TX)^{-1}X^T$. Let

$$s^2 = \frac{1}{I-p}\|e\|^2 = \frac{1}{I-p}\sum_i e_i^2 \qquad \text{(rescaled sum of squared residuals)}$$

s^2 is an unbiased estimator of σ^2. The standardized residuals defined by $r_i := \frac{e_i}{s\sqrt{1-H_{i,i}}}$ have unit variance and $r_i \sim t_{I-p-1}$. This can be used to test the model by verifying that r_i are approximately normal with unit variance.

(4) (Confidence Intervals) Let $\gamma = \sum_{j=1}^p u_j\beta_j$ be a (non-random) linear combination of the parameter $\vec{\beta}$; $\hat{\gamma} = \sum_j u_j\hat{\beta}_j$ is our estimator of γ. Let

$$G = (X^TX)^{-1} \quad \text{and} \quad g = \sum_{j,k} u_j G_{j,k} u_k^2 = \sum_k \left(\sum_j u_j K_{j,k}\right)^2$$

(g is called the **variance bias**). Then $\frac{\hat{\gamma}-\gamma}{\sqrt{gs}} \sim t_{I-p}$. This can be used to obtain a confidence interval for γ.

Comments

Item (3) states that the residuals are (slightly) biased, and it is thus better to use standardized residuals.

The matrix H is the projection onto the subspace spanned by the columns of X.

The predicted response is $\hat{y} = X\hat{\beta}$. It is equal to the orthogonal projection of $\vec{y}$, and is given by

$$\hat{y} = H\vec{y} \qquad (3.11)$$

The scaled sum of squared residuals s^2 is also equal to $\frac{1}{I-p}(\|\vec{y}\|^2 - \|\hat{y}\|^2)$. Its distribution is $\frac{1}{I-p}\chi^2_{I-p}$. This can be used to compute a confidence interval for σ.

The proof of the theorem shows a slightly stronger result than item (4): the joint distribution of $\hat{\beta}$ is Gaussian with the mean $\vec{\beta}$ and the covariance matrix $\sigma^2 KK^T$. Moreover $\hat{\beta}$ is independent of e.

Example 3.7 Joe's Shop again. Continuation of Example 3.6

We can thus apply matrix computations given in Theorem 3.3; item (2) gives an estimate of (a, b, d) and thus of c. Item (4) gives confidence intervals. The values and the fitted linear regression model are shown in the table and figure below.

We also compute the residuals e_i (crosses) and standardized residuals r_i (circles). There is little difference between these two types. They appear reasonably normal, but one might criticize the model in that

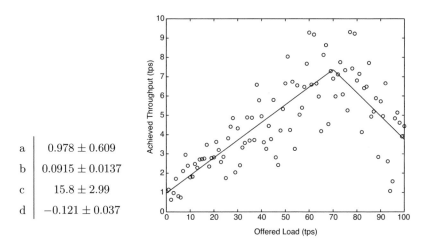

a	0.978 ± 0.609
b	0.0915 ± 0.0137
c	15.8 ± 2.99
d	-0.121 ± 0.037

Figure 3.6

the variance appears smaller for smaller values of x. The normal qq-plot of the residuals also shows approximate normality (the qq-plot of standardized residuals is similar and is not shown).

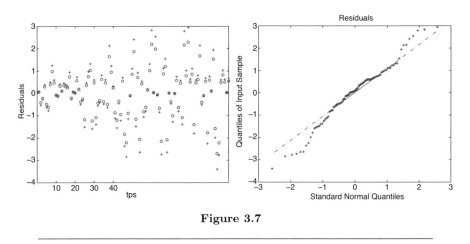

Figure 3.7

QUESTION 3.2 Can we conclude that there is congestion collapse?[3]

Where is Linearity?

In the previous example, we see that that y_i is a linear function of $\vec{\beta}$, but *not of* x_i. This is quite general, and we should avoid a widespread confusion: linear regression is not restricted to models where the data y_i is linear with the explanatory variables x_i.

---

[3] Yes, since the confidence interval for d is entirely positive (resp. negative).

Beyond the Linear Case

Example 3.8 Joe's Shop. Estimation of ξ

In Example 3.6, we assumed that the value ξ after which congestion collapse occurs is known in advance. Now, we relax this assumption. Our model is now the same as (3.9), except that ξ is also a parameter to be estimated.

To do this, we apply the maximum likelihood estimation. We have to maximize the log-likelihood $l_{\vec{y}}(a, b, d, \xi, \sigma)$, where $\vec{y}$, the data, is fixed. For a fixed ξ, we know the value of (a, b, d, σ) that achieves the maximum, as we have a linear regression model. We plot the value of this maximum versus ξ (Figure 3.8) and numerically find the maximum: it occurs for $\xi = 77$.

To find a confidence interval, we use the asymptotic result in Theorem B.2. It states that a 95% confidence interval is obtained by solving $l(\hat{\xi}) - l(\xi) \leq 1.9207$, which gives $\xi \in [73, 80]$.

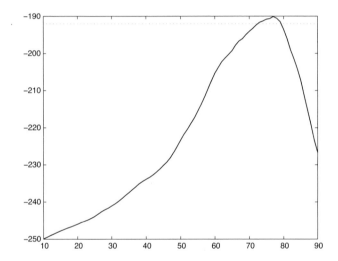

Figure 3.8 Log likelihood for Joes' shop as a function of ξ.

3.3 Linear Regression with ℓ^1 Norm Minimization

This is a variant of the linear regression model, but with Laplace instead of Gaussian noise. The theory is less simple, as we do not have explicit linear expressions. Nonetheless, it employs linear programming and is thus often tractable, with the benefit of an increased robustness to outliers.

The *statistical model* of our experiment has the form:

Definition 3.2 (Linear Regression Model with Laplace Noise)

$$Y_i = \left(X\vec{\beta}\right)_i + \epsilon_i \qquad \text{for } i = 1,\ldots,I \text{ with } \epsilon_i \text{ iid} \sim \text{Laplace}(\lambda) \qquad (3.12)$$

where the unknown parameter $\vec{\beta}$ is in $\mathbb{R}^p$ and X is a $I \times p$ matrix. The matrix X is supposedly exactly known in advance. As in Section 3.2, we assume that X has the rank p, otherwise the model is non-identifiable.

The following is an almost immediate consequence of Theorem 3.2.

Theorem 3.4

Consider the model in Definition 3.1; let $\vec{y}$ be the $I \times 1$ column vector of the data. The maximum likelihood estimator of $\vec{\beta}$ is obtained by solving the linear program:

$$minimize \qquad \sum_{i=1}^{I} u_i$$

$$over \qquad \vec{\beta} \in \mathbb{R}^p,\ u \in \mathbb{R}^I$$

$$subject\ to\ the\ constraints \qquad u_i \geq y_i - \left(X\vec{\beta}\right)_i$$
$$u_i \geq -y_i + \left(X\vec{\beta}\right)_i$$

The maximum likelihood estimator of the noise parameter λ is

$$\left(\frac{1}{I}\sum_{i=1}^{I}\left|y_i - \left(X\vec{\beta}\right)_i\right|\right)^{-1}$$

In view of Example 3.5, there is little hope of obtaining nice closed form formulas for confidence intervals. This is contrary to what happens with the least square method in Theorem 3.3, and indeed the theorem does not give any. To compute confidence intervals, we can use the bootstrap method, with re-sampling from residuals, as described in Algorithm 3.1.

Algorithm 3.1 The Bootstrap method with Re-Sampling From Residuals. The goal is to compute a confidence interval for some function $\varphi(\vec{\beta})$ of the parameter of the model in Definition 3.1. r_0 is the algorithm's accuracy parameter.

1: $R = \left\lceil 2\, r_0/(1 - \gamma)\right\rceil - 1$ ▷ For example $r_0 = 25$, $\gamma = 0.95$, $R = 999$

2: estimate $\vec{\beta}$ using Theorem 3.4; obtain $\hat{\beta}$

3: compute the residuals $e_i = y_i - \left(X\hat{\beta}\right)_i$

Algorithm 3.1 (Continued.)

5: **for** $r = 1 : R$ **do**   ▷ Re-sample from residuals

6:     draw I numbers with replacement from the list $(e_1, \ldots, e_I)$

7:     and call them $E_1^r, \ldots, E_I^r$

8:     generate the bootstrap replicate $Y_1^r, \ldots, Y_I^r$ from the estimated model:

9:         $Y_i^r = \left(X\hat{\beta}\right)_i + E_i^r$ for $i = 1, \ldots, I$

10:     re-estimate $\vec{\beta}$, using Y_i^r as data, using Theorem 3.4; obtain $\vec{\beta}^r$

11: **end for**

12: $\left(\varphi_{(1)}, \ldots, \varphi_{(R)}\right) = \text{sort}\left(\varphi(\vec{\beta}^1), \ldots, \varphi(\vec{\beta}^R)\right)$

13: confidence interval for $\varphi(\vec{\beta})$ is $[\varphi_{(r_0)} \; ; \; \varphi_{(R+1-r_0)}]$

Note that the algorithm applies to any model fitting method, not only to models fitted with Theorem 3.4. As always with the bootstrap approach, it provides approximate confidence intervals, with a tendency to underestimate.

Example 3.9 Joe's shop with ℓ^1 norm minimization

We revisit Example 3.6 and estimate a piecewise linear throughput response (as in (3.9)) with ℓ^1 norm minimization, i.e. assuming the error terms ϵ_i come from a Laplace distribution.

The problem is linear and has full rank if we, as parameter, take for example (a, b, c). However, it is not linear with respect to ξ. To overcome this issue, we first estimate the model, considering ξ as fixed, using linear programming. We then vary ξ and look for the value of ξ that maximizes the likelihood.

In Figure 3.9(b), we plot ξ versus the score (ℓ^1 norm of the error). According to Theorem 3.2, maximizing the likelihood is the same as minimizing the score. The optimal is obtained for $\xi = 69$ (but notice that the score curve is very flat, so any value around 70 would be just as good). For this value of ξ, the estimated parameters are: $\hat{a} = 1.35$, $\hat{b} = 0.0841$, $\hat{c} = 13.1$, $\hat{d} = -0.0858$. We compute the residuals (Figure 3.9(c)) and perform a Laplace qq-plot to verify the model assumption.

As explained in Section 2.4.3, a **Laplace qq-plot** of the residuals r_i, $i = 1, \ldots, I$, is obtained by plotting $F^{-1}(\frac{i}{I+1})$ versus the residuals $r_{(i)}$ sorted in increasing order. Here, F is the CDF of the Laplace distribution with rate $\lambda = 1$. A direct computation gives

$$F^{-1}(q) = \ln(2q) \qquad \text{if } 0 \leq q \leq 0.5$$
$$= -\ln(2(1-q)) \qquad \text{if } 0.5 \leq q \leq 1$$

Figure 3.9(d) shows the Laplace qq-plot of the residuals; we obtain a better fit than with least squares (Example 3.2).

We compute 95% confidence intervals for the parameters using the bootstrap approach (Algorithm 3.1) and obtain:

a	1.32 ± 0.675
b	0.0791 ± 0.0149
c	11.7 ± 3.24
d	-0.0685 ± 0.0398

The parameter of interest is d, for which the confidence interval is entirely negative. There is thus congestion collapse.

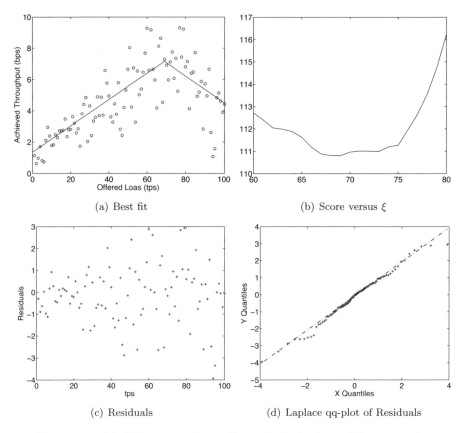

(a) Best fit   (b) Score versus ξ

(c) Residuals   (d) Laplace qq-plot of Residuals

Figure 3.9 Modeling congestion collapse in Joe's shop with a piecewise linear function and ℓ^1 norm minimization of the errors.

3.4 Choosing a Distribution

Assume that we are given a data set in the form of a sequence of numbers and would like to fit it to a distribution. Often, the data set is iid, but not always.

In this section and the next, we review a number of simple guidelines that are useful for finding the right distribution. We illustrate in the following section how this can be used to build a load generator (SURGE).

In this section and the next, a distribution signifies a probability distribution on the set of real numbers.

3.4.1   Shape

Perhaps the first attribute of interest is the shape of the distribution, or more precisely, of its PDF. We say that two distributions on $\mathbb{R}$, with CDFs $F(\cdot)$ and $G(\cdot)$, have the same **distribution shape** if they differ by a change of scale and location, i.e., there exist some $m \in \mathbb{R}$ and $s > 0$ such that $G(sx + m) = F(x)$ for all $x \in \mathbb{R}$. This is equivalent to saying that there are some random variables X, Y with distribution functions $F(\cdot), G(\cdot)$ respectively, and with $Y = sX + m$.

For example, the normal distribution N_{μ,σ^2} and the standard normal distribution $N_{0,1}$ have the same shape, in other words, all normal distributions are essentially identical.

When looking for a distribution, one may get a first feeling by plotting a histogram, which is a rough estimate of the PDF. Since most plotting tools automatically adapt the scales and origins on both axes, what one really obtains is a coarse estimate of the distribution shape.

A distribution is usually defined with a number of parameters. When browsing a distribution catalog (e.g. on Wikipedia), it is important to distinguish among the parameters that influence the shape and those that are simply location and scale parameters. For example, with the normal distribution N_{μ,σ^2}, μ is a location parameter and σ a scale parameter; if a random variable X has distribution N_{μ,σ^2}, one can write $X = \sigma Z + \mu$, where $Z \sim N_{0,1}$.

In Tables 3.1 and 3.2, we give a small catalog of distributions that are often used in the context of this book. For each distribution, we give only the set of parameters that influences the shape. Other distributions can be derived by a change of location and scale. The effect of this on various formulas is straightforward. Nevertheless, it is indicated in the table, for completeness.

The **log-normal distribution** with parameters $\mu, \sigma > 0$ is defined as the distribution of $X = e^Z$ where Z is Gaussian with the mean μ and variance σ^2. It is often used as a result of rescaling in log scale, as was done in (3.2). Note that

$$X = e^{\sigma Z_0 + \mu} = e^\mu \left(e^{Z_0}\right)^\sigma \qquad \text{with } Z_0 \sim N_{0,1}$$

Consequently μ corresponds to a scale parameter $s = e^\mu$. In contrast (unlike for the normal distribution), σ is a shape parameter. Table 3.1 gives properties of the standard log-normal distribution (i.e. for $\mu = 0$; other values of μ can be obtained by re-scaling). Figure 3.10 shows the shape of the log-normal distribution for various values of σ, rescaled such that the mean is consistently equal to 1.

Table 3.1 The catalog of distributions used in this chapter (continued in Table 3.2). The characteristic function is defined as $\mathbb{E}\!\left(e^{j\omega X}\right)$ and is given only when tractable. The notation $a(x) \sim b(x)$ means $\lim_{x\to\infty} \frac{a(x)}{b(x)} = 1$. Only parameters that affect the shape of the distribution are considered in the table. Other distributions in the same families can be derived by a change of scale and location, using the formulas given at the bottom of the table.

Distribution	Standard Normal $N_{0,1}$	Standard Laplace	Standard Log-normal
Parameters	none	none	$\sigma > 0$
Comment	Page 26	Page 72	Page 83
PDF	$\dfrac{1}{\sqrt{2\pi}}\,e^{-\frac{x^2}{2}}$	$\dfrac{1}{2}\,e^{-|x|}$	$\dfrac{1}{\sqrt{2\pi}\,\sigma x}\,e^{-\frac{(\ln x)^2}{2\sigma^2}}\,1_{\{x>0\}}$
Support	$\mathbb{R}$	$\mathbb{R}$	$[0,+\infty)$
CDF	$1 - Q(x)$ (by definition of $Q(\cdot)$)	$0.5\,e^{-|x|}$ for $x \le 0$ $1 - 0.5\,e^{-|x|}$ for $x \ge 0$	$\left(1 - Q\!\left(\dfrac{\ln x}{\sigma}\right)\right)1_{\{x>0\}}$
Characteristic function	$e^{-\frac{\omega^2}{2}}$	$\dfrac{1}{1+\omega^2}$	
Mean	0	0	$e^{\frac{\sigma^2}{2}}$
Variance	1	2	$\left(e^{\sigma^2}-1\right)e^{\sigma^2}$
Median	0	0	1
Skewness index	0	0	$\sqrt{e^{\sigma^2}-1}\left(e^{\sigma^2}+2\right)$
Kurtosis index	0	3	$e^{4\sigma^2}+2e^{3\sigma^2}+3e^{2\sigma^2}-6$
Hazard rate	$\sim x$	$=1$	$\sim \dfrac{\ln x}{\sigma^2 x}$

Effect of change of scale and location

	Original Distribution Distribution of X	Shifted and Re-scaled Distribution of $Y = sX + m$
Parameters		same plus $m \in \mathbb{R}$ (location), $s > 0$ (scale)
PDF	$f_X(x)$	$\dfrac{1}{s} f_X\!\left(\dfrac{x-m}{s}\right)$
CDF	$F_X(x)$	$F_X\!\left(\dfrac{x-m}{s}\right)$
Characteristic function	$\Phi_X(\omega)$	$e^{j\omega m}\Phi_X(s\omega)$
Mean	μ	$s\mu + m$
Variance	σ^2	$s^2\sigma^2$
Median	ν	$s\nu + m$
Sewness index		same
Kurtosis index		same
Hazard rate	$\lambda_X(x)$	$\dfrac{1}{s}\lambda_X\!\left(\dfrac{x-m}{s}\right)$

Table 3.2 Continuation of Table 3.1. $\Gamma()$ is the gamma function, defined as $\Gamma(x) = \int_0^\infty t^{x-1}\,dt$; if $x \in \mathbb{N}$ and $x > 0$, $\Gamma(x) = (x-1)!$

Distribution	Standard Weibull	Standard Pareto	Standard Stable with index $p < 2$
Parameters	$c > 0$	$0 < p$	$0 < p < 2$, $-1 \le \beta \le 1$
Comment	Page 91; called exponential for $c = 1$	Page 87	The stable definition is also defined for $p = 2$, in which case it is equal to the normal distribution $N_{0,2}$. See Page 97
PDF	$cx^{c-1}e^{-(x^c)}1_{\{x \ge 0\}}$	$\dfrac{p}{x^{p+1}}1_{\{x \ge 1\}}$	well defined but usually not tractable
support	$[0, +\infty)$	$[1, +\infty)$	$\mathbb{R}$ except when $\beta = \pm 1$
CDF	$\left(1 - e^{-(x^c)}\right)1_{\{x \ge 0\}}$	$\left(1 - \dfrac{1}{x^p}\right)1_{\{x \ge 1\}}$	well defined but usually not tractable
Characteristic function	$\dfrac{1}{1 - j\omega}$ for $c = 1$		$\exp\left[-|\omega|^p(1 + A)\right]$ with $A = -j\beta\mathrm{sgn}(\omega)\tan\dfrac{p\pi}{2}$ for $p \ne 1$ $\dfrac{2j\beta}{\pi}\mathrm{sgn}(\omega)\ln|\omega|$ for $p = 1$
mean μ	$\Gamma\left(\dfrac{c+1}{c}\right)$	$\dfrac{p}{p-1}$ for $p > 1$	0 for $p > 1$ else undefined
variance σ^2	$\Gamma\left(\dfrac{c+2}{c}\right) - \mu^2$	$\dfrac{1}{(p-1)^2(p-2)}$ for $p > 2$	undefined
median	$(\ln(2))^{\frac{1}{c}}$	$2^{1/p}$	0 when $\beta = 0$ else not tractable
skewness index γ_1	$\dfrac{\Gamma(\frac{c+3}{c}) - 3\mu\sigma^2 - \mu^3}{\sigma^3}$	$\dfrac{2(1+p)}{p-3}\sqrt{\dfrac{p-2}{p}}$ for $p > 3$	undefined
Kurtosis index	$\dfrac{G - 4\gamma_1\mu\sigma^3 - 6\mu^2\sigma^2 - \mu^4}{\sigma^4} - 3$ with $G = \Gamma(\frac{c+4}{c})$	$\dfrac{6(p^3 + p^2 - 6p - 2)}{p(p-3)(p-4)}$ for $p > 4$	undefined
hazard rate	$= cx^{c-1}$	$= \dfrac{p}{x}$	$= \dfrac{p}{x}$

QUESTION 3.3 What are the parameters μ, σ of the lognormal distributions in Figure 3.10?[4]

---

[4] According to Table 3.1, the mean is $e^{\sigma^2/2}$ when $\mu = 0$; other values of μ correspond to re-scaling by e^μ and therefore the mean is $e^{\sigma^2/2 + \mu}$. In the figure, we take the mean as 1, and we thus have $\mu = -\frac{\sigma^2}{2}$.

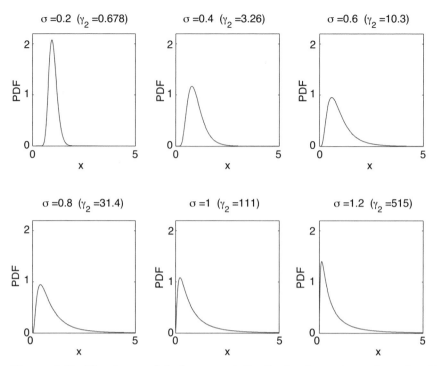

Figure 3.10 The shapes of the log-normal distribution for various values of σ. The shape is independent of μ, which is chosen such that the mean is 1 for all plots. γ_2 is the Kurtosis index.

3.4.2   Skewness and Kurtosis

These are indices that may be used to characterize a distribution shape. They are defined for a distribution that has finite moments up to order 4. The definition employs the **cumulant generating function** (cgf) of the distribution of a real random variable X: defined by

$$\mathrm{cgf}(s) := \ln \mathbb{E}\big(e^{sX}\big)$$

Assume that $\mathbb{E}(e^{s_0|X|}) < \infty$ for some s_0 so that the above is well-defined for real s around $s = 0$. This also implies that all moments are finite. Then, by a Taylor expansion:

$$\mathrm{cgf}(s) = \kappa_1 s + \kappa_2 \frac{s^2}{2} + \kappa_3 \frac{s^3}{3!} + \cdots + \kappa_k \frac{s^k}{k!} + \cdots$$

where $\kappa_k = \frac{d^k}{ds^k}\,\mathrm{cgf}(0)$ is called the **cumulant of order** k. The first four cumulants are:

$$\begin{cases} \kappa_1 = \mathbb{E}(X) \\ \kappa_2 = \mathbb{E}\big(X - \mathbb{E}(X)\big)^2 = \mathrm{var}(X) \\ \kappa_3 = \mathbb{E}\big(X - \mathbb{E}(X)\big)^3 \\ \kappa_4 = \mathbb{E}\big(X - \mathbb{E}(X)\big)^4 - 3\mathrm{var}(X)^2 \end{cases} \tag{3.13}$$

For the normal distribution N_{μ,σ^2}, $\text{cgf}(s) = \mu s + \frac{\sigma^2}{2}s^2$ thus all cumulants of order $k \geq 3$ are 0.

QUESTION 3.4 Show that the kth cumulant of the convolution of n distributions is the sum of the kth cumulants.[5]

Skewness Index

κ_3 is called **skewness**. The **skewness index** (sometimes also called skewness) is

$$\gamma_1 := \frac{\kappa_3}{\kappa_2^{3/2}} = \frac{\kappa_3}{\sigma^3}$$

The skewness index is insensitive to changes in scale (by a positive factor) or location. For a density that is symmetric around its mean, $\kappa_{2k+1} = 0$; γ_1 can be taken as a measure of asymmetry of the distribution. When $\gamma_1 > 0$, the distribution is right-skewed, and vice-versa. If ϕ is convex, then $\phi(X)$ has a greater skewness index than X.

Kurtosis Index

κ_4 is called Kurtosis. The **Kurtosis index**, also called **excess Kurtosis**, is

$$\gamma_2 := \frac{\kappa_4}{\kappa_2^2} = \frac{\kappa_4}{\sigma^4}$$

The Kurtosis index is insensitive to changes in scale or location. It is used to measure departure from the normal distribution. When $\gamma_2 > 0$, the distribution has a sharper peak around the mean and heavier tail; when $\gamma_2 < 0$, it has a flatter top and decays more abruptly. Note that $\gamma_2 \geq -2$, with equality only if the distribution is degenerate, i.e. equal to a constant.

The Kurtosis index gives some information concerning the distribution tail. When it is large and positive it indicates that the contribution of the tail is large. We see for example in Figure 3.10 and in Table 3.1 that the log-normal distribution has a larger tail for larger σ.

3.4.3 Power Laws, Pareto Distribution and Zipf's Law

Power laws are often invoked in the context of workload generation. Generally speaking, a power law is any relation of the form $y = ax^b$ between variables x and y, where a and b are constants. In log scales, this gives a linear relationship: $\ln y = b \ln x + \ln a$. Power laws have often been found to hold, at least approximately, for the **complementary CDFs**[6] of some variables such as file sizes or popularity of objects. They are discovered by plotting the empirical complementary CDF in log-log scales and verifying whether a linear relationship exists. Depending on whether the distribution is continuous or discrete, we obtain the Pareto and Zeta distributions.

---

[5] By independence: $\ln \mathbb{E}\big(e^{s(X_1+\cdots+X_n)}\big) = \sum_i \ln \mathbb{E}\big(e^{sX_i}\big)$.
[6] The complementary CDF is $1 - F(\cdot)$ where $F(\cdot)$ is the CDF.

The standard **Pareto** distribution with index $p > 0$ has CDF and PDF

$$F(x) = \left(1 - \frac{1}{x^p}\right) 1_{\{x \geq 1\}}$$

$$f(x) = \frac{p}{x^{p+1}} 1_{\{x \geq 1\}}$$

i.e. the complementary CDF and the PDF follow a power law for $x \geq 1$ (see Table 3.2). The general Pareto distribution is derived by a change of scale and has CDF $\left(1 - \frac{s^p}{x^p}\right) 1_{\{x \geq s\}}$ and PDF $\frac{ps^p}{x^{p+1}} 1_{\{x \geq s\}}$ for some $s > 0$.

For $p \leq 2$, the Pareto distribution has infinite variance and for $p \leq 1$ it has an infinite mean. The Kurtosis index is not defined unless $p > 4$ and tends towards ∞ when $p \to 4$: its tail is called "heavy", (see Section 3.5). Figure 3.11 shows the CDF of a Pareto distribution together with normal and log-normal distributions. The **Zeta** distribution is the integer analog of Pareto. It is defined for $n \in \mathbb{N}$, $n \geq 1$, by

$$\mathbb{P}(X = n) = \frac{1}{n^{p+1} \zeta(p+1)}$$

where $\zeta(n+1)$ is a normalizing constant (Riemann's zeta function).

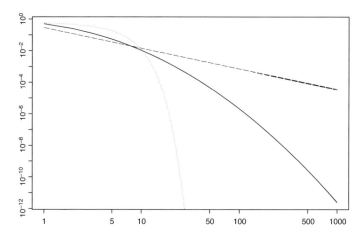

Figure 3.11 $P(x > x)$ versus x on log-log scales, when X is normal (dots), log-normal (solid) or Pareto (dashs). The three distributions have the same mean and 99%-quantile.

Zipf's law is not a probability distribution, but is related to the Pareto distribution. It states that the popularity of objects is inversely proportional to rank, or more generally, to a power of rank. This can be interpreted as follows.

We have a collection of N objects. We choose an object from the collection atrandom, according to a certain stationary process. We refer to θ_j as the probability that object j is chosen; this is our interpretation of the popularity of object j.

Let $\theta_{(1)} \geq \theta_{(2)} \geq \dots$ be the collection of θs in decreasing order. Zipf's law means

$$\theta_{(j)} \approx \frac{C}{j^\alpha}$$

where C is some constant and $\alpha > 0$. In Zipf's original formulation, $\alpha = 1$.

We now show the relation to a Pareto distribution. Assume that we draw the θs at random (as we do in a load generator) by obtaining a certain random value X_i for object i, and letting $\theta_i = \frac{X_i}{\sum_{i=1}^{N} X_i}$. Assume that the number of objects is large and X_i's marginal distribution is some fixed distribution on $\mathbb{R}^+$, with complementary distribution function $G(x)$. Let $X_{(n)}$ be the reverse order statistic, i.e. $X_{(1)} \geq X_{(2)} \geq \dots$ We would like to follow Zip's law, i.e. for some constant C:

$$X_{(j)} \approx \frac{C}{j^\alpha} \qquad (3.14)$$

Let us now consider the empirical complementary distribution $\hat{G}$, which is obtained by putting a point at each X_i, with probability $\frac{1}{N}$, where N is the number of objects. More precisely:

$$\hat{G}(x) = \frac{1}{N} \sum_{i=1}^{N} 1_{\{X_i \geq x\}}$$

Thus, $\hat{G}(X_{(j)}) = \frac{j}{N}$. Combined with (3.14); we find that, whenever $x = X_{(j)}$, we have $\hat{G}(x) \approx \frac{K}{x^p}$, with $p = \frac{1}{\alpha}$ and $K = c^p/N$. If we take the empirical complementaty CDF as an approximation of the true complementary CDF, this means that the distribution of X_i is Pareto with index $p = \frac{1}{\alpha}$.

In other words, Zipf's law can be interpreted as follows. The probability of choosing object i is itself a random variable, obtained by drawing from a Pareto distribution with tail index $p = \frac{1}{\alpha}$, then re-scaling to make the sum of the probabilities 1.

3.4.4 Hazard Rate

The hazard rate provides another means of deciding whether a distribution is well suited. Consider a distribution with support that includes $[a, +\infty)$ for some a, with a PDF $f(\cdot)$ and with CDF $F(\cdot)$. The **hazard rate** is defined for $x > a$ by

$$\lambda(x) = \frac{f(x)}{1 - F(x)}$$

It can be interpreted as follows. Let X be a random variable with distribution $F(\cdot)$. Then, for $x > a$

$$\lambda(x) = \lim_{dx \to 0} \frac{1}{dx} \mathbb{P}\big(X \leq x + dx \mid X > x\big)$$

If X is interpreted as a flow duration or a file size, $\lambda(x)\,dx$ is the probability that the flow ends in the next dx time units given that it survived until now. See Tables 3.1 and 3.2 for the hazard rates of several distributions.

The behavior of the hazard rate $\lambda(x)$ when x is large can be used as a characteristic of a distribution. Qualitatively, one may distinguish between the following three types of behavior:

(1) (Aging Property) $\lim_{x\to\infty} \lambda(x) = \infty$: the hazard rate becomes large for large x. This is very often expected, e.g. when one has reasons to believe that a file or flow is unlikely to be arbitrarily large. If X is interpreted as the system lifetime, this is the property of aging. The Gaussian distribution resides in this case.

(2) (Memoriless Property) $\lim_{x\to\infty} \lambda(x) = c > 0$: the hazard rate tends to become constant for large x. This is particularly true if the system is memoriless, i.e. when $\lambda(x)$ is a constant. The exponential distribution resides here (as does the Laplace distribution).

(3) (**Fat Tail**) $\lim_{x\to\infty} \lambda(x) = 0$: the hazard rate vanishes for large x. This may appear surprising: for a flow duration, it means that, given that we waited a significant amount of time for completion of the flow, we are likely to continue waiting for a very long time. The Pareto distribution with index p resides in this case for all values of p, as do all log-normal distributions. We may, informally, call this property a "fat tail". Heavy tail distributions (defined in Section 3.5) occur here, but there are also some non-heavy tail distributions.

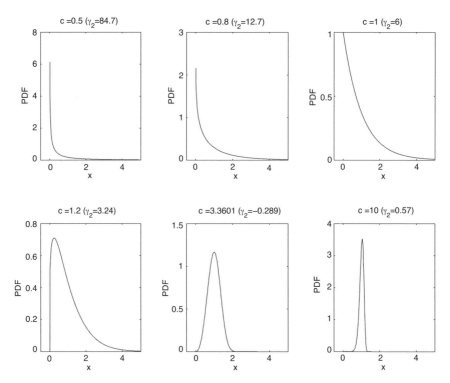

Figure 3.12 Shapes of the Weibull distribution for various values of the exponent c. The distribution is re-scaled to have mean $= 1$. γ_2 is the Kurtosis index.

The **Weibull distribution** is often used in this context, as it spans the three cases, depending on its parameters. The standard Weibull distribution with exponent c has support on $[0, \infty)$ and is defined by its CDF equal to $1 - e^{(x^c)}$. The general Weibull distribution is derived by a change of scale and location; see also Tables 3.1 and 3.2. For $c = 1$ it is the exponential distribution; for $c > 1$ it has the aging property; and for $c < 1$ it is fat-tailed. Figure 3.12 shows the shape of the Weibull distributions. The Kurtosis is minimum at $c \approx 3.360128$ and approaches ∞ as $c \to 0$ [87].

3.4.5   Fitting a Distribution

Fitting a distribution to a dataset is often a two-step process. First, a qualitative analysis is performed, where one attempts to get a feeling for the distribution shape, using a histogram. Here, one tries to make statements about the distribution shape, the hazard rate or the existence of power laws. These are obtained by appropriate plots (histograms, qq-plots, empirical CDFs, etc). One can also try to determine whether a heavy-tailed distribution is the right model, using for example the aest tool described in Section 3.5. The goal is to obtain a set of candidate families of distributions.

The second step is to fit the parameters of the distribution. If the data set can be assumed to come from an iid sequence, the method of choice is the maximum likelihood estimation (MLE), as explained in Section B.1.2, and illustrated in the next example. In particular, MLE is invariant by re-parametrization and change of scale.

If, as is frequent in practice, the data set may not be assumed to come from an iid sequence, then there is no simple method. The maximum likelihood estimation is often used in practice, but no confidence interval for the estimated parameters can be obtained.

3.4.6   Censored Data

When fitting the distribution parameters, it may be important to account for the fact that some very large or very small data values are not present, due to impossibilities of the measurement system (e.g. flow size durations may not measure very long flows). In statistics, this is called **censoring**.

A technique for accounting for censoring is as follows. Assume that we know that the data is truncated to a certain unknown maximum, called a. The distribution for the data can be described by the PDF

$$f_X(x) = \frac{1}{F_0(a)} f_0(x) 1_{\{x \le a\}} \tag{3.15}$$

where f_0 (resp. F_0) is the PDF (resp. CDF) of the non-truncated distribution. The explaination behing (3.15) lies in the theory of rejection sampling (Section 6.6.2) which states that when one rejects the data samples that do not satisfy a condition (here $X \le a$), one obtains a random variable with PDF proportional to the non censored PDF, restricted to the set of values given by the condition. The term $\frac{1}{F_0(a)}$ is the normalizing constant.

Assume that the non-truncated distribution F_0 depends on a certain parameter θ. The log likelihood of the data $x_1, \ldots, x_n$ is

$$\ell(\theta, a) = \sum_{i=1}^{n} \log f_0(x_i \mid \theta) - n \log F_0(a \mid \theta) \tag{3.16}$$

We obtain an estimate of θ and a by maximizing (3.16). Note that we must have $a \geq \max_i x_i$ and for any θ, the likelihood does not increase with a. Thus the optimum is obtained for $\hat{a} = \max_i x_i$.

We still need to optimize $\ell(\theta, \hat{a})$ over θ. This can be done by brute force when the dimensionality of the parameter θ is small, or by using other methods, as illustrated in the next example.

Example 3.10 Censored Log-normal Distribution

Figure 3.13(a) shows an artificial data set, obtained by sampling a log-normal distribution with parameters $\mu = 9.357$ and $\sigma = 1.318$,

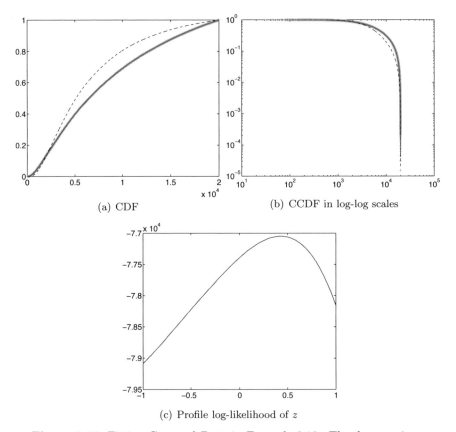

(a) CDF

(b) CCDF in log-log scales

(c) Profile log-likelihood of z

Figure 3.13 Fitting Censored Data in Example 3.10. The data set is an iid sample of a truncated log-normal distribution. Thick lines: data set; plain lines: fit obtained with a technique for censored data; dashed lines: fit obtained when ignoring the censored data.

truncated to $20,000$ (i.e. all data points larger than this value are removed from the data set).

Here, F_0 is the log-normal distribution with parameters μ and σ. Instead of brute force optimization, we can gain more insight in the following manner. We have to maximize $\ell(\mu, \sigma)$ over $\mu \in \mathbb{R}$, $\sigma > 0$, with

$$\ell(\mu, \sigma) = -n \ln(\sigma) - \frac{1}{2\sigma^2} \sum_{i=1}^{n} (\ln x_i - \mu)^2 - n \ln N_{0,1}(\mu + \sigma \ln a)$$

$$- \frac{n}{2} \ln(2\pi) - \sum_{i=1}^{n} \ln x_i$$

$$(3.17)$$

We can ignore the last two terms, which do not depend on (μ, σ). We can also do a change of variables by taking σ, z as parameters instead of σ, μ, with

$$z = \frac{\ln a - \mu}{\sigma} \tag{3.18}$$

For a fixed z, the optimization problem has a closed form solution (obtained by computing the derivative with respect to σ); the maximum likelihood is obtained for $\sigma = \hat{\sigma}(z)$ with

$$\hat{\sigma}(z) = \frac{-\beta z + \sqrt{4s^2 + \beta^2 (4 + z^2)}}{2} \tag{3.19}$$

with

$$\beta = \ln a - y_1 \qquad y_1 = \frac{1}{n} \sum_{i=1}^{n} \ln x_i \qquad s^2 = \frac{1}{n} \sum_{i=1}^{n} (\ln x_i - y_1)^2$$

and the corresponding value of the likelihood (called "profile log-likelihood") is (we omit the constant terms in (3.17)):

$$pl(z) = -n \left[\ln(\hat{\sigma}(z)) - \frac{1}{2\hat{\sigma}^2(z)} \left((\hat{\sigma}(z)z - \beta)^2 + s^2 \right) - \ln N_{0,1}(z) \right]$$

$$(3.20)$$

We now need to minimize the square bracket as a function of $z \in \mathbb{R}$. This cannot be done in closed form, but it is numerically simple as it is a function of only one variable. Figure 3.13(c) shows $pl(z)$. There is a unique maximum at $z = 0.4276$, which, with (3.19) and (3.18), gives

$$\hat{\mu} = 9.3428 \qquad \hat{\sigma} = 1.3114$$

Compare this to the method that would ignore the truncation. Since MLE is invariant by change of scale, we can use the log of the data; we would estimate μ by the sample mean of the log of the data, and σ by the standard deviation, and would obtain

$$\hat{\mu}_n = 8.6253 \qquad \hat{\sigma}_n = 0.8960$$

3.4.7   Combinations of Distributions

It is often difficult to find a distribution that fits both the tail and the body of the data. In such a case, one may use a combination of distributions, also called **compound distribution**.

Given two distributions with CDFs F_1 and F_2 (resp. PDFs f_1 and f_2), a mixture distribution of F_1 and F_2 is a distribution with PDF

$$f(x) = pf_1(x) + (1-p)f_2(x)$$

with $p \in [0,1]$. A mixture is interpreted by saying that a sample is drawn with probability p from F_1 and with probability $1-p$ from F_2.

We are more often interested in a **combination of mixture and truncation**, i.e. in a combination for which the PDF has the form

$$f(x) = \alpha_1 1_{\{x \le a\}} f_1(x) + \alpha_2 1_{\{x > a\}} f_2(x) \tag{3.21}$$

where $\alpha_1, \alpha_2 \ge 0$ and $a \in \mathbb{R}$. This is useful for fitting a distribution separately to the tail and the body of the data set.

Note that we do not necessarily have $\alpha_1 + \alpha_2 = 1$ as in a pure mixture. Instead, one must have the normalizing condition

$$\alpha_1 F_1(a) + \alpha_2 (1 - F_2(a)) = 1 \tag{3.22}$$

thus (by letting $p = \alpha_1 F_1(a)$) we may rewrite (3.21) as

$$f(x) = \frac{p}{F_1(a)} 1_{\{x \le a\}} f_1(x) + \frac{1-p}{1 - F_2(a)} 1_{\{x > a\}} f_2(x) \tag{3.23}$$

with $p \in [0,1]$.

Assume that the distributions F_1, F_2 depend on various parameters, which are independent of p, and which need to be fitted. Note that p and a need to be fitted as well. When utilizing MLE, one can somewhat simplify the fitting by observing that the maximum likelihood estimate must satisfy

$$\hat{p} = \frac{n_1(a)}{n} \tag{3.24}$$

where $n_1(a)$ is the number of data points $\le a$.

To see why, assume that we are given a data set x_i of n data points, sorted in increasing order, so that $n_1(a) = \sum_{i=1}^{n} 1_{\{x_i \le a\}}$. The log-likelihood of the data is

$$\ell = \sum_{i=1}^{n_1(a)} \ln f_1(x_i) + \sum_{i=n_1(a)+1}^{n} \ln f_2(x_i) + n_1(a)(\ln p - \ln F_1(a))$$
$$+ (n - n_1(a))(\ln(1-p) - \ln(1 - F_2(a)))$$

and maximizing ℓ with respect to p shows (3.24).

Example 3.11 Combination of Log-Normal and Pareto

Figure 3.14(a) shows an empirical complementary CDF in log-log scales for a set of 10^5 data points representing file sizes. The plot shows an asymptotic power law, but not over the entire body of the distribution. We wish to fit a combination mixture of a truncated log-normal distribution for the body of the distribution (left of dashed line) and of a Pareto distribution for the tail, truncated on $[0, a)$ and Pareto rescaled to have support on $[a, +\infty)$. The model is thus

$$f_X(x) = q \frac{f_1(x)}{F_1(a)} 1_{\{x \le a\}} + (1 - q) \frac{f_2(x)}{1 - F_2(a)} 1_{\{x > a\}}$$

where F_1 is a log-normal distribution, F_2 is Pareto with exponent p, and breakpoint a. Note that $F_2(a) = 0$, and PDF is thus

$$f_X(x) = \frac{q}{N_{0,1}(\mu + \sigma \ln a)} \frac{1}{\sqrt{2\pi}\sigma x} e^{-\frac{(\ln x - \mu)^2}{2\sigma^2}} 1_{\{0 < x \le a\}} \tag{3.25}$$

$$+ (1 - q)p \frac{a^p}{x^{p+1}} 1_{\{x \ge a\}}$$

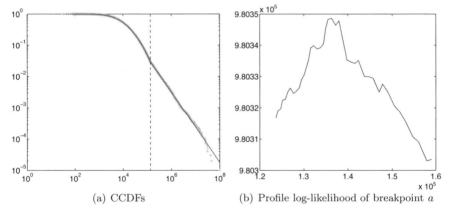

(a) CCDFs   (b) Profile log-likelihood of breakpoint a

Figure 3.14 Fitting a combination of log-normal for the body and Pareto for the tail. Dashed vertical line: breakpoint.

The parameters to be fitted are q, μ, σ, p and the breakpoint a. We first fix a to any arbitrary value and fit the other parameters. By (3.24), $q = \frac{n_1(a)}{n}$ where $n_1(a)$ is the number of data points $\le a$. The log-likelihood is thus

$$\ell(\mu, \sigma, p, a) = n_1(a) \ln n_1(a) + n_2(a) \ln n_2(a) - n \ln n$$
$$+ \ell_1(\mu, \sigma, a) + \ell_2(p, a)$$

where $n_2(a) = n - n_1(a)$, ℓ_1 is as in (3.17) (with $n_1(a)$ instead of n) and

$$\ell_2(a, p) = n_2(a)(\ln p + p \ln a) - (p + 1) \sum_{i=n_1(a)+1}^{n} \ln x_i$$

where we assume that the data x_i is sorted in increasing order. For a fixed a, the optimization of μ, σ on the one hand, and p on the other, are separated. The optimal $\hat{\mu}(a), \hat{\sigma}(a)$ are obtained as in Example 3.10 using techniques for censored data.
The optimal $\hat{p}$ is obtained directly:

$$\max_p l_2(a, p) = n_2(a)\big(\ln \hat{p}\big) - 1\big) - \sum_{i=n_1(a)+1}^{n} \ln x_i \qquad (3.26)$$

with

$$\hat{p}(a) = \frac{1}{-\ln a + \dfrac{1}{n_2(a)} \displaystyle\sum_{i=n_1(a)+1}^{n} \ln x_i}$$

Putting things together, we obtain the profile log-likelihood of a

$$pl(a) = \max_{\mu,\sigma>0,p>0} \ell(\mu, \sigma, p, a)$$

$$= -n_1(a)\left[\frac{\ln(2\pi)}{2} + \ln\big(\hat{\sigma}(a)\big) + \frac{1}{2\hat{\sigma}(a)^2}\Big(\big(\hat{\sigma}(a)\hat{z}(a) - \beta(a)\big)^2\right.$$

$$\left. + s^2(a)\Big) + \ln N_{0,1}\big(\hat{z}(a)\big)\right] + n_2(a)\big(\ln \hat{p}(a) - 1\big) - \sum_{i=1}^{n} \ln x_i$$

where $\beta(a)$, $\hat{\sigma}(a)$, $s^2(a)$ and $\hat{\mu}(a)$ are as in Example 3.10 and $\hat{z}(a)$ maximizes (3.20). We determine the maximum of $pl(a)$ numerically Figure 3.14(b) shows that there is a large uncertainty for the value of a, which can be explained by the fact that, in this region, the log-normal distribution locally follows a power law. We find $\hat{a} = 136300$, $\hat{\mu} = 9.3565$, $\hat{\sigma} = 1.3176$ and $\hat{p} = 1.1245$.

3.5 Heavy Tail

3.5.1 Definition

In Section 3.4.4, we have seen the definition of a fat tail, i.e. a distribution that has a vanishing hazard rate. In this section, we discuss an extreme case of a fat tail, called "heavy tail", which has unique, non intuitive features. It is frequently found in models of file sizes and flow durations.

We use the following definition (which is the simplest). We say that the distribution on $[a, \infty)$, with CDF F, is **heavy-tailed** with index $0 < p < 2$ if there is some constant k such that, for large x:

$$1 - F(x) \sim \frac{k}{x^p} \qquad (3.27)$$

Here, $f(x) \sim g(x)$ means that $f(x) = g(x)\big(1 + \epsilon(x)\big)$, with $\lim_{x\to\infty} \epsilon(x) = 0$.

A heavy-tailed distribution has an infinite variance, and for $p \leq 1$ an infinite mean.

- The Pareto distribution with exponent p is heavy-tailed with index p if $0 < p < 2$.

- The log-normal distribution is not heavy-tailed (its variance is always finite).

- The Cauchy distribution (density $\frac{1}{\pi(1+x^2)}$) is heavy-tailed with index 1.

3.5.2 Heavy Tail and Stable Distributions

Perhaps the most striking feature of heavy-tailed distributions is that the central limit theorem does not hold, i.e. the aggregation of many heavy-tailed quantities does *not* produce a Gaussian distribution.

Indeed, if X_i are idd with a finite variance σ^2 and with a mean μ, then $\frac{1}{n^{1/2}} \sum_{i=1}^n (X_i - \mu)$ tends in distribution to the normal distribution N_{0,σ^2}. In contrast, if X_i are iid, heavy-tailed with index p, then there exist constants d_n such that

$$\frac{1}{n^{\frac{1}{p}}} \sum_{i=1}^n X_i + d_n \xrightarrow[n \to \infty]{\text{distrib}} S_p$$

where S_p has a **stable distribution** with index p. Stable distributions are defined for $0 < p \leq 2$, for $p = 2$ they are the normal distributions. For $p < 2$, they are either constant or heavy-tailed with index p. Furthermore, they have a property of closure under aggregation: if X_i are iid and stable with index p, then $\frac{1}{n^{1/p}}(X_1 + \cdots + X_n)$ has the same distribution as the X_is, shifted by some number d_n.

The shape of a stable distribution with $p < 2$ is defined by one skewness parameter $\beta \in [-1, 1]$ (but the skewness index in the sense of Section 3.4.2 does not exist). The *standard* stable distribution is defined by its index p, and by β when $p < 2$. The general stable distribution is derived by a change of scale and location. When $\beta = 0$, the standard stable distribution is symmetric, otherwise not. The standard stable distribution with skewness parameter $-\beta$ is the symmetric (by change of sign) of the standard stable distribution with parameter β. When $p < 2$ and $\beta = 1$, the support of the stable distribution is $[0, +\infty)$ (and thus when $\beta = -1$ the support is $(-\infty, 0]$), otherwise the support is $\mathbb{R}$.

In general, stable distributions that are not constant have a continuous density, which it is not explicitly known. In contrast, their characteristic functions are explicitly known ([93], [73]), see Table 3.2. Note that the Pareto distribution is not stable.

Figure 3.15 illustrates the convergence of a sum of iid Pareto random variables to a stable distribution. In practice, stable distributions may be difficult to work with, and are sometimes replaced by heavy-tailed combinations, as in Example 3.11.

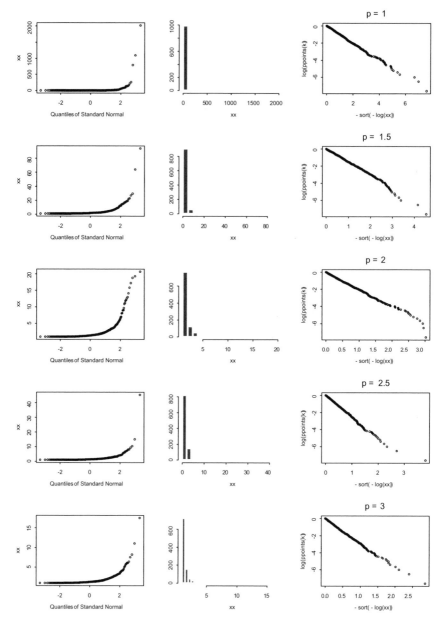

Figure 3.15 Aggregation of a sum of iid Pareto random variables ($a = 1$, $p \in \{1, 1.5, 2, 2.5, 3\}$). On every row: The first three diagrams show the empirical distribution (normal qq-plot, histogram, complementary CDF in log-log scale) of one sample of $n_1 = 10^4$ iid Pareto random variables. The last three show similar diagrams for a sample $(Y_j)_{1 \leq j \leq n}$ of $n = 10^3$ aggregated random variables: $Y_j = \frac{1}{n_1} \sum_{i=1}^{n_1} X_j^i$, where $X_j^i \sim$ iid Pareto. The figure illustrates that, for $p < 2$, there is no convergence to a normal distribution, whereas for $p \geq 2$ there is. It also shows that, for $p \geq 2$, the power law behavior disappears by aggregation, unlike for $p < 2$. Note that for $p = 2$, X_i has infinite variance, though there is convergence to a normal distribution.

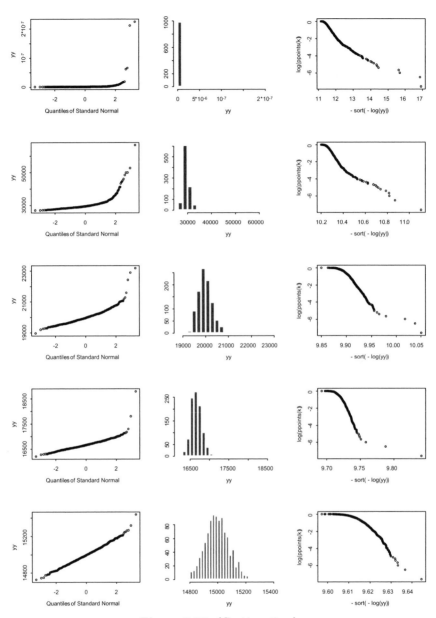

Figure 3.15 (Continuation.)

3.5.3 Heavy Tail in Practice

Concretely, a heavy tail signifies that very large outliers are possible. We illustrate this by two examples.

Example 3.12 Random Waypoint with Heavy-Tailed Trip Duration
Consider the following variant of the random waypoint mobility model as in Figure 6.3. A mobile moves in a certain area from one point to

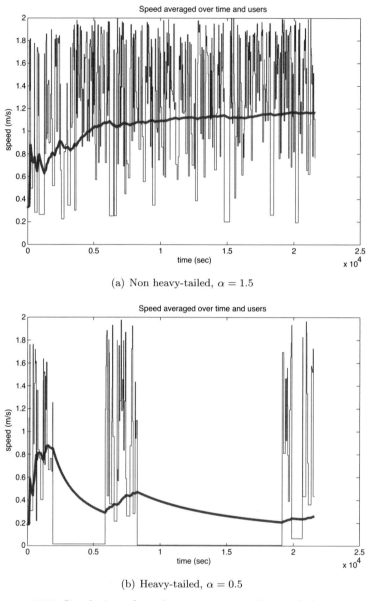

(a) Non heavy-tailed, $\alpha = 1.5$

(b) Heavy-tailed, $\alpha = 0.5$

Figure 3.16 Simulation of random waypoint with speed density equal to $f_V^0(v) = K_\alpha v^\alpha 1_{\{0 \le v \le v_{\max}\}}$, showing instant speed and average speed (smoother line) for one user.

from one point to the next (we designate *trip* the movement from one point to another). The velocity on one trip is sampled from the distribution with PDF $f_V^0(v) = K_\alpha v^\alpha 1_{\{0 \le v \le v_{\max}\}}$, with $\alpha > 0$ and where

K_α is a normalizing constant. It follows that the complementary CDF of trip duration is equal to

$$1 - F_T^0(x) = \frac{K_\alpha \bar{D}}{\alpha + 1} \frac{1}{x^{\alpha+1}} \tag{3.28}$$

where $\bar{D}$ is the average length (in meters) of a trip.

For $\alpha = 0.5$ the trip duration is heavy-tailed, whereas for $\alpha = 1.5$, it has a finite variance and is thus not heavy-tailed. Figure 3.16 shows a sample simulation of both cases. In the heavy-tailed case, we see that most trip durations are very short, but once in a while, the trip duration is extraordinarily large.

Example 3.13 Queuing System

Consider a server that receives requests for downloading files. Assume that the arrival times of the requests form a Poisson process, and the requested file sizes are iid $\sim F$, where F is some distribution. This is a simplified model, but it is sufficient for making the point.

We assume that the server has a unit capacity, and that the time to serve a request is equal to the requested file size. This again is a simplifying assumption, which is valid if the bottleneck is a single, FIFO I/O device. As demonstrated in Chapter 8, the mean response time of a request is given by the Pollaczek-Khintchine formula

$$R = \rho + \frac{\rho^2 \left(1 + \frac{\sigma^2}{\mu^2}\right)}{2(1 - \rho)}$$

where μ is the mean and σ^2 the variance, of F (assuming both are finite), and ρ is the utilization factor ($=$ request arrival rate $\times \mu$). The response time thus depends not only on the utilization and the mean size of the requests, but also on the coefficient of variation $C := \frac{\sigma}{\mu}$. As C grows, the response times goes to infinity. If the real data supports the hypothesis that F is heavy-tailed, the average response time is likely to be high and the estimators of it are unstable.

3.5.4 Testing for a Heavy Tail

There are several methods for deciding whether a data set is heavy-tailed or not. One of these consists in fitting a Pareto distribution to the tail, as in Example 3.11.

A more general method is the tool by Crovella and Taqqu called aest [31]. It uses the scaling properties and convergence to stable distributions. Consider X_i that are iid and heavy-tailed, with index p. Call $X_i^{(m)}$ the aggregate sequence, where observations are grouped in bulks of m:

$$X_i^{(m)} := \sum_{j=(i-1)m+1}^{im} X_j$$

For large m_1, m_2, by the convergence result mentioned earlier, we should have approximately the distribution equalities according to

$$\frac{1}{m_1^{1/p}} X_i^{(m_1)} \sim \frac{1}{m_2^{1/p}} X_j^{(m_2)} \tag{3.29}$$

The idea is now to plot the empirical complementary distributions of $X_i^{(m)}$ for various values of m. Further, the deviation between two curves of the plot is analyzed by means of horizontal and vertical deviations δ and τ as shown in Figure 3.17. We have $\delta = \log x_2 - \log x_1$. By using (3.29), we get $x_2 = (\frac{m_2}{m_1})^{1/p} x_1$ and thus

$$\delta = \frac{1}{p} \log \frac{m_2}{m_1}$$

Also, if X_i is heavy-tailed, and m is large, then $X_i^{(m)}$ is approximately stable. Consequently, if $\frac{m_2}{m_1}$ is an integer, the distribution of $X_j^{(m_2)}$ (which is a sum of $X_i^{(m_1)}$) is the same as that of $(\frac{m_2}{m_1})^{1/p} X_i^{(m_1)}$. We should thus have

$$\tau = \log \mathbb{P}\big(X_i^{(m_2)} > x_1\big) - \log \mathbb{P}\big(X_i^{(m_1)} > x_1\big) \approx \log \frac{m_2}{m_1}$$

The method in aest consists in using only the points x_1 where the above holds, and subsequently, at such points, estimating p by

$$\hat{p} = \frac{1}{\delta} \log \frac{m_2}{m_1}$$

The average of these estimates is then used. See Figure 3.17 for an illustration.

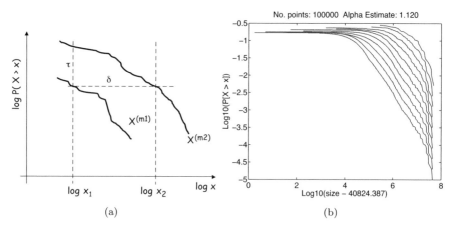

(a)   (b)

Figure 3.17 (a) : Deviations used in the aest tool. (b) Application to the dataset in Example 3.11. There is an heavy tail, with an estimated index $p = 1.12$ (the same as that obtained by the direct method in Example 3.11).

3.5.5 Application Example: The Workload Generator SURGE

Many of the concepts illustrated in this chapter are used in the tool SURGE [9], which is a load generator for web servers.

The load *intensity* is determined by the number of **user equivalents** (UEs), each implemented as an independent thread of execution, on one or several machines The *nature* of the load is defined by a set of constraints on the arrival process, the distribution of request sizes and the correlation of successive requests to the same object, as described below. The parameters of the distributions were obtained by fitting measured values (Table 3.3).

Table 3.3 Distributions and parameters used in SURGE.

	Model	Density $f(x)$	Value of Parameters
Inactive OFF time	Pareto	$\frac{ps^p}{x^{p+1}} 1_{\{x \geq s\}}$	$s = 1,\ p = 1.5$
No of embedded references	Pareto	$\frac{ps^p}{x^{p+1}} 1_{\{x \geq s\}}$	$s = 1,\ p = 2.43$
Active OFF time	Weibull	$\frac{c}{s}\left(\frac{x}{s}\right)^{c-1} e^{-(x/s)^c}$	$s = 1.46,\ c = 0.382$
File Size	Log-normal comb. Pareto	Eq. (3.25)	$\mu = 9.357,\ \sigma = 1.318$ $a = 133\,K,\ p = 1.1$ $q = N_{0,1}(\mu + \sigma \ln a)$
File Request Size	Pareto	$\frac{ps^p}{x^{p+1}} 1_{\{x \geq s\}}$	$s = 1000,\ p = 1.0$ (see footnote on Page 104)
Temporal Locality	Log-normal	$\frac{e^{-\frac{(\ln x - \mu)^2}{2\sigma^2}}}{\sqrt{2\pi}\sigma x} 1_{\{x > 0\}}$	$\mu = 1.5,\ \sigma = 0.80$

(1) One UE alternates between ON-object periods and "Inactive OFF periods". Inactive OFF periods are iid with a Pareto distribution .

(2) During an ON-object period, a UE sends a request with embedded references. Once the first reference is received, there is an "Active OFF period", after which the request for the second reference is sent, and so on, until all embedded references are received. There is only one TCP connection at a time per UE, and one TCP connection for each reference (an assumption that made sense with early versions of HTTP).

(3) The active OFF times are iid random variables with Weibull distributions.

(4) The number of embedded references is modeled as a set of iid random variables, with a Pareto distribution.

The references are viewed as requests for downloading files. The model assumes that there is a set of files labeled $i = 1, \ldots, I$, stored on the server. File i has two attributes: the size x_i and the request probability θ_i. The distribution of attributes needs to satisfy the following conditions.

(5) The distribution $H(x)$ of file sizes is a combination of truncated Log-normal and Pareto.

(6) θ_i satisfy Zipf's law with exponent $\alpha = 1$

(7) The distribution $F(x)$ of requested file sizes is Pareto.[7]

The distributions H and F are both file size distributions, sampled according to varying viewpoints. Consequently (as we discuss in Chapter 7), there must be a relation between these two distributions, which we now derive. Let $I(t)$ be the random variable that gives the index i of the tth file requested. Thus $F(x) = \mathbb{P}(x_{I(t)} = x)$. We can assume that the allocation of file sizes and popularities is done in a preliminary phase, and that it is independent of $I(t)$. Thus

$$F(x) = \sum_j \mathbb{P}\big(I(t) = j\big)1_{\{x_j \leq x\}} = \sum_j \theta_j 1_{\{x_j \leq x\}} \tag{3.30}$$

Let $x_{(1)} = x_{(2)} = \cdots$ be the file sizes sorted in increasing order, and let $z(n)$ be the index of the nth file in that order. z is a permutation of the set of indices, such that $x_{(n)} = x_{z(n)}$. By specializing (3.30) to the actual values $x_{(m)}$, we find, after a change of variable $j = z(n)$

$$F(x_{(m)}) = \sum_j \theta_j 1_{\{x_j \leq x_{(m)}\}} = \sum_n \theta_{z(n)} 1_{\{x_{(n)} \leq x_{(m)}\}}$$

and thus

$$F(x_{(m)}) = \sum_{n=1}^m \theta_{z(n)} \tag{3.31}$$

which gives a constraint between the θ_is and x_is.

The file request references $I(t)$, $t = 1, 2, \ldots$ are constrained by their marginal distribution (defined by θ_i). The authors find that there is some correlation in the series, and model the dependency as follows:

(8) For any file index i, define $T_1(i) < T_2(i) < \ldots$ the successive values of $t \in \{1, 2, \ldots\}$ such that $i = I(t)$. Assume that $T_{k+1}(i) - T_k(i)$ come from a common distribution, called "temporal locality". The authors find it log-normal (more precisely, it is a discretized log-normal distribution, since the values are integers).

Building a Process that Satisfies all Constraints

We are left with building a generator that produces a random output conformant to all constraints. Constraints (1) through (4) are straightforward to implement, with a proper random number generator, and by using the techniques described in Section 6.6. The inactive OFF periods, active OFF periods and number of embedded references are implemented as mutually independent iid sequences.

---

[7] The original paper [9] takes an index $p = 1$ for this Pareto distribution, which implies that the mean request file size is infinite, and thus the process of file size requests is not stationary (this is a freezing simulation problem as in Section 7.4). A value of p larger than 1 would be preferable.

Constraints (5) through (7) require more care. First, the x_i are drawn from H. Second, the θ_is are drawn (as explained in Section 3.4.3) but not yet bound to the file indexes. Instead, the values are put in a set Θ. In view of (3.31), define

$$\hat{\theta}_{z(m)} = F(x_{(m)}) - \sum_{n=1}^{m-1} \theta_{z(m)}$$

so that we should have $\hat{\theta}_{z(m)} = \theta_{z(m)}$ for all m. If this were true, it would be easy to see that all constraints are satisfied. However, this can only be done approximately in [9]. Here is one way of doing so. Assume that $z(m) =$, i.e. that we have sorted the file indices according to an increasing file size. For $m = 1$, we set θ_1 to the value in Θ that is closest to $\hat{\theta}_1 = F(x_1)$. This value is then renoved from Θ, and θ_2 is set to the value in Θ closest to $\hat{\theta}_2 = F(x_2) - \theta_1$, etc.

Lastly, we need to generate a time series of file requests $I(t)$ such that the marginal distribution is given by the θ_is and the temporal locality in condition (8) is satisfied. This can be formulated as a discrete optimization problem, as follows. First, a trace size T is arbitrarily chosen; it reflects the length of the load generation campaign. Then, for each file i, the number of references N_i is drawn, so as to satisfy Zipf's law (with $\mathbb{E}(N_i) = \theta_i$). Last, a sequence $S_1, , S_2, \ldots$ is drawn from the distribution in in condition (8).

The problem is now to create a sequence of file indices $\big(I(1), I(2), \ldots I(T)\big)$ such that i appears N_i times and the distances between successive repetitions of file references is as close as possible to the sequence $S_1, , S_2, \ldots$. Any heuristic for discrete optimization can be used (such as simulated annealing or tabu search). By [9]. an ad-hoc heuristic is employed.

3.6   Proofs

Theorem 3.1

The log likelihood of the data is

$$l_{\vec{y}}(\vec{\beta}, \sigma) = -\frac{I}{2} \ln(2\pi) - I \ln(\sigma) - \frac{1}{2\sigma^2} \sum_{i=1}^{I} \big(y_i - f_i(\vec{\beta})\big)^2 \qquad (3.32)$$

For any fixed σ, it is at a maximum when $\sum_{i=1}^{I} \big(y_i - f_i(\vec{\beta})\big)^2$ is at a minimum, which shows item 1(a). Take the derivative with respect to σ and find, that for any fixed $\vec{\beta}$, it is as a maximum for $\sigma = \frac{1}{I} \sum_i \big(y_i - f_i(\vec{\beta})\big)^2$, which shows item 1(b). The rest follows from Theorem B.1 and Theorem B.2.

Theorem 3.2

The log likelihood of the data is

$$l_{\vec{y}} = -I \ln(2) + I \ln(\lambda) - \lambda \sum_{i=1}^{I} \big| y_i - f_i(\vec{\beta}) \big| \qquad (3.33)$$

For any fixed $\vec{\beta}$, it is at a maximum when $\frac{1}{\lambda} = \frac{1}{I}\sum_i |y_i - f_i(\vec{\beta})|$ and the corresponding value is

$$-I \ln\left(\sum_{i=1}^{I} |y_i - f_i(\vec{\beta})|\right) + I \ln I - I - I \ln 2$$

which is at a maximum when $\vec{\beta}$ minimizes $\sum_{i=1}^{I} |y_i - f_i(\vec{\beta})|$.

Theorem 3.4

In view of Theorem 3.2, the MLE of $\vec{\beta}$ is obtained by minimizing $\sum_{i=1}^{I} |y_i - (X\vec{\beta})_i|$. This is equivalent to minimizing $\sum_{i=1}^{I} u_i$ over $(\vec{\beta}, u)$ with the constraints $u_i \geq |y_i - (X\vec{\beta})_i|$, which is equivalent to the constraints in the theorem.

3.7   Review

3.7.1   Review Questions

3.1 How would you compute a and α in Example 3.1?[8]

3.2 How would you compute the residuals in Example 3.3?[9]

3.3 How would you compute confidence intervals for the component β_j of $\vec{\beta}$ in Theorem 3.1 using the bootstrap method? In Theorem 3.2?[10]

3.4 Can you name distributions that are fat tailed but not heavy-tailed?[11]

3.5 If the tail of the distribution of X follows a power law, can you conclude that X is heavy-tailed?[12]

3.6 Which of the distributions used in SURGE are heavy-tailed? Fat-tailed?[13]

3.7.2   Useful Matlab Commands

- regress solves the general linear regression model as in Theorem 3.3.
- linprog solves the linear program in Theorem 3.4.

---

[8] By minimizing $\sum_i (y_i - ae^{\alpha t_i})^2$. This is an unconstrained optimization problem in two variables; use for example a generic solver such as fminsearch in matlab.

[9] The residuals are estimates of the noise terms ϵ_i. Let $\hat{a}$ and $\hat{\alpha}$ be the values estimated by maximum likelihood, for either model. The residuals are $r_i = y_i - \hat{a}\,e^{\hat{\alpha}t_i}$ for the former model, and $r_i = \ln y_i - \ln(\hat{a}\,e^{\hat{\alpha}t_i})$ for the latter.

[10] Draw R bootstrap replicates of $\vec{Y}$ and obtain R estimates $\vec{\beta}^1, \ldots, \vec{\beta}^R$ of $\vec{\beta}$, using the theorems. At level 95%, take $R = 999$ and use the order statistics of the jth component of the bootstrap estimates: $\beta_j^{(1)} \leq \ldots \leq \beta_j^{(R)}$; obtain as confidence interval $[\beta_j^{(25)}, \beta_j^{(975)}]$.

[11] The Pareto distributions with $p > 2$, the log-normal distributions, the Weibull distributions with $c < 1$.

[12] No, only if the exponent of the tail is < 2.

[13] Inactive OFF time, File size, File request size. The number of embedded references is Pareto with $p > 2$ it is thus fat-tailed but not heavy-tailed. The active OFF time and temporal locality are fat-tailed but not heavy-tailed.

CHAPTER 4

Tests

We use tests to decide whether a certain assertion on a model is true or not, for example whether the particular data set comes from a normal distribution. We have seen in Chapter 2 that visual tests may be used for such a purpose. Tests are meant to be a more objective way to reach the same goal.

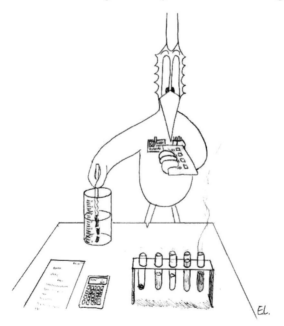

Tests are often used in empirical sciences to draw conclusions from noisy experiments. Though we use the same theories, our setting is somewhat different; we are concerned with the nested model setting, i.e. we want to decide whether a simpler model is good enough, or whether we need a more sophisticated one. Here, the question is asymmetric; if in doubt, we give preference to the simpler model – this is the principle of parsimony. The Neyman Pearson framework is well suited for such a setting, and we thus restrict ourselves to it.

There exists a large number of tests, and everyone can invent their own (this is perhaps a symptom of the absence of a simple, nonequivocal optimality criterion). In practice though, likelihood ratio tests are asymptotically optimal, in some sense, under very large sets of assumptions. They are very general, easy to use and even to develop; therefore, it is worth knowing them. We often make use of Monte Carlo simulations to compute the p-value of a test. This can sometimes be likened to brute force, but it avoids spending too much time solving for analytical formulae. We discuss ANOVA, as it is very simple when it applies. Finally, we also study robust tests, i.e. tests that make very few assumptions about the distribution of the data.

4.1   The Neyman Pearson Framework

4.1.1   The Null Hypothesis and the Alternative

We are given a data sample x_i, $i = 1, \ldots, n$, and we assume that the sample is the output generated by some unknown model. We consider two possible hypotheses about the model, H_0 and H_1, and we would like to infer from the data which of the two hypotheses is true. In the Neyman-Pearson framework, the two hypotheses play different roles: H_0, the **null hypothesis**, is the conservative one. We do not want to reject it unless we are fairly sure. H_1 is the **alternative** hypothesis.

We are most often interested in the **nested model** setting: the model is parameterized by a certain θ in some space Θ, and $H_0 \overset{\text{def}}{=}$ "$\theta \in \Theta_0$" whereas $H_1 \overset{\text{def}}{=}$ "$\theta \in \Theta \setminus \Theta_0$", where Θ_0 is a subset of Θ.

In Example 4.1, the model could be: all data points for compiler option 0 (resp. 1) are generated as iid random variables with some distribution F_0 (resp. F_1). Then, H_0 is "$F_0 = F_1$" and H_1 is "F_0 and F_1 differ by a shift in location". This is the model used by the Wilcoxon Rank Sum test (see Example 4.20 for more details). Here $\Theta_0 = \{(F_0, F_0), F_0 \text{ is a CDF}\}$ and $\Theta = \{(F_0, F_1), F_0 \text{ is a CDF and } F_1(x) = F_0(x - m), m \in \mathbb{R}\}$.

Another, commonly used model, for the same example could be: all data points for compiler option 0 (resp. 1) are generated as iid random variables with some normal distribution N_{μ_0, σ^2} (resp. N_{μ_1, σ^2}). Then, H_0 is "$\mu_0 = \mu_1$" and H_1 is "$\mu_0 \neq \mu_1$". This is the model used by the so-called "Analysis of variance" (see Example 4.10 for more details). Here, $\Theta_0 = \{(\mu_0, \mu_0, \sigma > 0)\}$ and $\Theta = \{(\mu_0, \mu_1, \sigma > 0)\}$. Clearly, this second model makes more assumptions, and is to be employed with more care.

Example 4.1   Nonpaired Data

A simulation study compares the execution time, on a log scale, with two compiler options. See Figure 4.1 for some data. We would like to test the hypothesis that compiler option 0 is better than 1. For one parameter set, the two series of data come from different experiments.

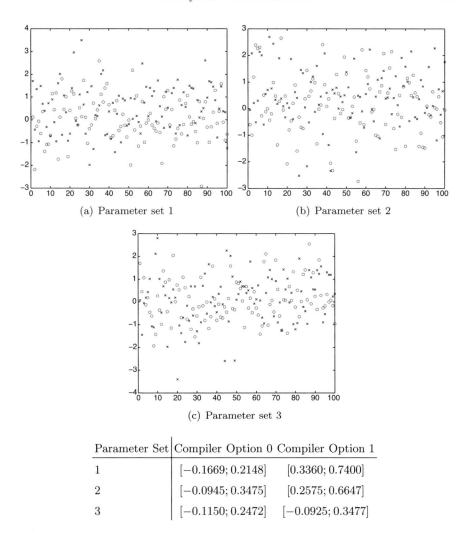

(a) Parameter set 1   (b) Parameter set 2

(c) Parameter set 3

Parameter Set	Compiler Option 0	Compiler Option 1
1	$[-0.1669; 0.2148]$	$[0.3360; 0.7400]$
2	$[-0.0945; 0.3475]$	$[0.2575; 0.6647]$
3	$[-0.1150; 0.2472]$	$[-0.0925; 0.3477]$

Figure 4.1 Data for Example 4.1. Top: The logarithm of the execution time, with two compiler options (o=option 0, x=option 1) for three different parameter sets. Bottom: 95% confidence intervals for the means.

We can compute a confidence interval for each of the compiler options. The data looks normal, so we apply the student statistic and find the confidence intervals shown in the figure.

For parameter set 1, the confidence intervals are disjoint, so it is clear that option 0 performs better. For parameter sets 2 and 3, the intervals are overlapping, and we thus cannot draw any conclusions at this point. We see here that confidence intervals may be used for hypothesis testing in some cases, but not always. The present chapter presents how tests can be used to disambiguate such cases.

4.1.2   Critical Region, Size and Power

The **critical region**, also called the **rejection region** C, of a test is a set of values of the tuple $(x_1, \ldots, x_n)$ such that if $(x_1, \ldots, x_n) \in C$, we reject H_0, and otherwise we accept H_0. The critical region entirely defines the test.[1]

The output of a test is thus a binary decision: "accept H_0", or "reject H_0". The output depends on the data, which is random, and may be wrong with some (hopefully small) probability. We distinguish between two types of errors.

- A **type-1** error occurs if we reject H_0 when H_0 is true.

- Conversely, a **type-2** error occurs if we accept H_0 when H_1 is true.

The art of test development consists in minimizing both error types. However, it is usually difficult to minimize two objectives at a time. The maximum probability of a type-1 error, taken over all $\theta \in \Theta_0$ is called the **size** of the test. The **power** function of the test is the probability of rejection of H_0 as a function of $\theta \in \Theta \setminus \Theta_0$. Neyman-Pearson tests are designed such that the size has a fixed, small value (typically 5%, or 1%). Good tests (i.e. those in these lecture notes and those used in Matlab) are designed so as to maximize, exactly or approximately, the power, subject to a fixed size. A test is said to be uniformly more powerful (UMP) if, among all tests of equal size, it maximizes the power for every value of $\theta \in \Theta \setminus \Theta_0$. UMP tests exist for few models, for which reason less restrictive requirements have been developed (the reference for these issues is [62]).

It is important to be aware of the two types of errors, and of the fact that the size of a test is just one facet. Assume that we use a UMP test of size 0.05; this does not mean that the risk of error is indeed 0.05, or even that it is small. This simply means that all other tests that have a risk of a type-1 error bounded by 0.05 must have a risk of a type-2 error which is the same or larger. Thus, we may need to verify whether, for the data at hand, the power is indeed large enough, though this is seldom done in practice.

Example 4.2   Comparison of two Options, Reduction in Run Time

The reduction in run time due to a new compiler option is given in Figure 2.7. Assume that we know that the data comes from some iid $X_i \sim N_{\mu,\sigma^2}$. This may be argued and will be discussed again, but it is convenient to simplify the discussion here. We do not know μ or σ. We want to test H_0: $\mu = 0$ against H_1: $\mu > 0$. Here, $\theta = (\mu, \sigma)$, $\Theta = [0, \infty) \times (0, \infty)$ and $\Theta_0 = \{0\} \times (0, \infty)$. An intuitive definition of a test is to reject H_0 if the sample mean is large enough; if we rescale

---

[1] In all generality, one should also consider randomized tests, whose output may be a random function of $(x_1, \ldots, x_n)$. See [81] for further details. We do not use such tests in our setting

the sample mean by its estimated standard deviation, this gives the rejection region

$$C = \left\{ (x_1, \ldots, x_n) \text{ such that } \frac{\bar{x}}{\frac{s_n}{\sqrt{n}}} > c \right\} \tag{4.1}$$

for some value of c to be defined later and with, as usual, $\bar{x} = \frac{1}{n} \sum_{i=1}^{n} X_i$ and $s_n^2 = \frac{1}{n} \sum_{i=1}^{n} (X_i - \bar{x})^2$.

The size of the test is the maximum probability of C for $\theta \in \Theta_0$. We have

$$\mathbb{P} \left(\sqrt{n} \frac{\bar{x}}{s_n} > c \,\Big|\, \mu = 0, \sigma \right) \approx 1 - N_{0,1}(c)$$

where $N_{0,1}$ is the CDF of the standard Gaussian distribution. Note that this is independent of σ and therefore

$$\alpha = \sup_{\sigma > 0} (1 - N_{0,1}(c)) = 1 - N_{0,1}(c)$$

If we want a test size equal to 0.05, we need to take $c = 1.645$. For the data at hand the value of the test statistic is $\sqrt{n} \frac{\bar{x}}{n} = 5.05 > c$, and we therefore reject H_0 and decide that the mean is positive.

The power function is

$$\beta(\mu, \sigma) \stackrel{\text{def}}{=} \mathbb{P} \left(\sqrt{n} \frac{\bar{x}}{s_n} > c \,\Big|\, \mu, \sigma \right) = \mathbb{P} \left(\sqrt{n} \frac{\bar{x} - \mu}{s_n} > c - \sqrt{n} \frac{\mu}{s_n} \,\Big|\, \mu, \sigma \right)$$

$$\approx 1 - N_{0,1} \left(c - \sqrt{n} \frac{\mu}{\sigma} \right) \tag{4.2}$$

Figure 4.2 plots the power as a function of μ when $c = 1.645$ and for σ replaced by its estimator value s_n. For μ close to 0, the power is poor (i.e. the probability of deciding H_1 is very small). This is unavoidable as $\lim_{\mu \to 0} \beta(\mu, \sigma) = \alpha$.

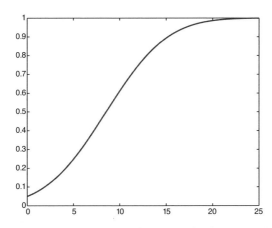

Figure 4.2 The power as a function of μ for Example 4.2.

For the present data, we estimate the power by setting $\mu = \bar{x}$ and $\sigma = s_n$ in (4.2). For a test size equal to 0.05 (i.e. for $c = 1.645$), we find 0.9997. The probability of a type-2 error (deciding for H_0 when H_1 is true) is thus approximately 0.0003, a very small value. If we select $\alpha = 0.1\%$ as test size, we find that the type-2 error probability is 2.5%.

The previous example shows that the test size does not say everything. In Figure 4.2, we see that there is a "grey zone" (values of μ below, say, 15) where the power of the test is not large. If the true parameter is in the grey zone, the probability of a type-2 error may be large, i.e. it is not improbable that the test will accept H_0 even when H_1 is true. It is important to keep the following in mind: a test may accept H_0 because it truly holds, but also because it is unable to reject it. This is the fundamental asymmetry of the Neyman-Pearson framework.

The power function can be used to decide on the size α of the test, at least in theory, as illustrated below.

Example 4.3 Optimal Test Size

Continuation of Example 4.2. Assume that we consider a reduction in run time to be negligible if it is below μ^*. We want the probability of deciding H_0 when the true value is equal to μ^* or more to be similar to the size α, i.e. we want to balance the two types of errors. This gives the equations

$$1 - N_{0,1}\left(c^*\right) = \alpha$$

$$1 - N_{0,1}\left(c^* - \sqrt{n}\,\frac{\mu^*}{s_n}\right) = 1 - \alpha$$

and thus

$$N_{0,1}\left(c^*\right) + N_{0,1}\left(c^* - \sqrt{n}\,\frac{\mu^*}{s_n}\right) = 1$$

By symmetry of the Gaussian PDF around its mean, we have

$$\text{if } N_{0,1}(x) + N_{0,1}(y) = 1 \text{ then } x + y = 0$$

from where we derive

$$c^* = \sqrt{n}\,\frac{\mu^*}{2s_n}$$

The table below gives a few numerical examples, together with the corresponding test size $\alpha^* = 1 - N_{0,1}\left(c^*\right)$.

resolution μ^*	optimal threshold c^*	size α^*
10	0.97	0.17
20	1.93	0.02
40	3.87	$5.38\,e - 005$

We see that if we take care to validly detect reductions in run time as small as $\mu^* = 10$ ms, we should have a test size of 17% or more. In contrast, if the resolution μ^* is 20 ms, then a test size of 2% is appropriate.

4.1.3 p-value of a Test

For many tests, the rejection region has the form $\{T(\vec{x}) > m_0\}$, where $\vec{x}$ is the observation, $T(\cdot)$ is a certain mapping, and m_0 is a parameter that depends on the size α of the test. In Example 4.2, we can take $T(\vec{x}) = \sqrt{n}\frac{\bar{x}}{s_n}$.

Definition 4.1

The p-value of an observation $\vec{x}$ is

$$p^*(\vec{x}) = \sup_{\theta \in \Theta_0} \mathbb{P}\big(T(\vec{X}) > T(\vec{x}) \mid \theta\big)$$

In this formula, $\vec{X}$ is a random vector that represents a hypothetical replication of the experiment, whereas $\vec{x}$ is the data that we have observed.

The mapping $m \mapsto \sup_{\theta \in \Theta_0} \mathbb{P}\big(T(\vec{X}) > m \mid \theta\big)$ is monotonic nonincreasing, and usually decreasing. Assuming the latter, we have the equivalence

$$p^*(\vec{x}) < \alpha \iff T(\vec{x}) > m_0$$

In other words, instead of comparing the test statistic $T(\vec{x})$ against the threshold m_0, we can compare the p-value to the test size α:

The test rejects H_0 when the p-value is smaller than the test size α.

The interest of the p-value is that it gives more information than just a binary answer. It is in fact the minimum test size required to reject H_0. Very often, software packages return p-values rather than hard decisions (H_0 or H_1).

Example 4.4 (Continuation of Example 4.2)

The p-value is $p^* = 1 - N_{0,1}\big(\frac{\sqrt{n}\bar{x}}{s_n}\big)$. We find $p^* = 2.2476\,e - 007$ which is small, therefore we reject H_0.

4.1.4 Tests are just Tests

When using a test, it is important to make the distinction between statistical significance and practical relevance. Consider for example a situation, as in Example 4.2, where we want to test whether a mean μ satisfies $\mu = \mu_0 = 0$ or $\mu > \mu_0$. We estimate the theoretical mean μ by the sample mean $\bar{x}$. It is never the case that $\mu = \bar{x}$ exactly. A test concerns deciding whether the distance between μ_0 and $\bar{x}$ can be explained by the randomness of the data alone (in which case we should decide that $\mu = \mu_0$), or by the fact that we truly have $\mu > \mu_0$. Statistical significance means that, in a case where we find $\bar{x} > \mu_0$, it is possible to conclude that there is a real difference, i.e. $\mu > \mu_0$.

Practical relevance means that the difference $\mu - \mu_0$ is important for the system under consideration. It may well be the case that a difference is statistically significant (e.g. with a very large data set) but practically irrelevant, and vice versa (e.g. when the data set is small).

In some cases, tests can be avoided by employing confidence intervals. This applies to matching pairs as in Example 4.2: a confidence interval for the mean can be readily obtained by Theorem 2.2. At the level 0.05, the confidence interval is $[15.9, 36.2]$, and we can thus conclude that $\mu > 0$ (and further that we have a lower bound on μ).

More generally, consider a generic model parameterized with some $\theta \in \Theta \subset \mathbb{R}$. For testing

$$\theta = \theta_0 \text{ against } H_1 \colon \theta \neq \theta_0$$

we can take as the rejection region

$$\left| \hat{\theta} - \theta_0 \right| > c$$

If $\hat{\theta} \pm c$ is a confidence interval at level $1 - \alpha$, then the size of this test is precisely α. For such cases, we do not need to use tests, since we can simply use confidence intervals as discussed in Chapter 2. However, it is often difficult, even impossible, to reduce a test to the computation of confidence intervals, as for instance with unpaired data in Example 4.1 (though it is possible to use confidence *sets* rather than confidence intervals).

4.2   Likelihood Ratio Tests

In this section we introduce a generic framework, very frequently used for constructing tests. It does not give UMP tests (as this is, in general, not possible), but the tests are asymptotically UMP (under the conditions of Theorem 4.3). We give the application to simple tests for paired data and for goodness of fit. Note that deciding which test is best is sometimes controversial, and the best tests, in the sense of UMP, are not always the likelihood ratio tests [61]. Note also that the issue of which criterion to use in order to decide that a test is best is disputed [79]. In our context, likelihood ratio tests are appealing as they are simple and generic.

4.2.1   Definition of Likelihood Ratio Tests

Assumptions and Notations

We assume a nested model setting, with $H_0 \stackrel{\text{def}}{=}$ "$\theta \in \Theta_0$" whereas $H_1 \stackrel{\text{def}}{=}$ "$\theta \in \Theta \setminus \Theta_0$". For a given statistic (random variable) $\vec{X}$ and value $\vec{x}$ of $\vec{X}$, we define:

- $l_{\vec{x}}(\theta) \stackrel{\text{def}}{=} f_{\vec{X}}(\vec{x} \mid \theta)$ where $f_{\vec{X}}(\cdot \mid \theta)$ is the probability density of the model, when the parameter is θ.

- $l_{\vec{x}}(H_0) = \sup_{\theta \in \Theta_0} l_{\vec{x}}(\theta)$.
- $l_{\vec{x}}(H_1) = \sup_{\theta \in \Theta} l_{\vec{x}}(\theta)$.

For example, we assume that some data comes from an iid sequence of normal RVs $\sim N(\mu, \sigma)$, and we want to test $\mu = 0$ versus $\mu \neq 0$. Here $\Theta = \{(\mu, \sigma > 0)\}$ and $\Theta_0 = \{(0, \sigma > 0)\}$.

If H_0 is true, then, the likelihood is approximately, at a maximum for $\theta \in \Theta_0$ and thus $l_{\vec{x}}(H_0) = l_{\vec{x}}(H_1)$. In the opposite case, the maximum likelihood is probably reached at some $\theta \notin \Theta_0$ and thus $l_{\vec{x}}(H_1) > l_{\vec{x}}(H_0)$. This gives the idea for a generic family of tests:

Definition 4.2

The likelihood ratio test is defined by the rejection region

$$C = \{l_{\vec{x}}(H_1) - l_{\vec{x}}(H_0) > k\}$$

where k is chosen based on the required size of the test.

The test statistic $l_{\vec{x}}(H_1) - l_{\vec{x}}(H_0)$ is called **likelihood ratio** for the two hypotheses H_0 and H_1.

We thus reject $\theta \in \Theta_0$ when the likelihood ratio statistic is large. The Neyman-Pearson lemma [104, Section 6.3] tells us that, in the simple case where Θ_0 and Θ_1 contain only one value each, the likelihood ratio test minimizes the probability of a type-2 error. Many tests used in this lecture are actually likelihood ratio tests. As we will see later, for a large sample size, there are simple, generic results for such tests.

There exists a link to the theory of the maximum likelihood estimation. Under the conditions in Definition B.1, we define

- $\hat{\theta}_0$: the maximum likelihood estimator of θ when we restrict θ to be in Θ_0
- $\hat{\theta}$: the unrestricted maximum likelihood estimator of θ

Consequently, $l_{\vec{x}}(H_0) = l_{\vec{x}}(\hat{\theta}_0)$ and $l_{\vec{x}}(H_1) = l_{\vec{x}}(\hat{\theta})$. In the rest of this section and in the following two, we show applications to various settings.

QUESTION 4.1 Why can we be sure that $l_{\vec{x}}(\hat{\theta}) - l_{\vec{x}}(\hat{\theta}_0) \geq 0$?[2]

Example 4.5 Continuation of Example 4.2, Compiler Options

We want to test H_0: $\mu = 0$ against H_1: $\mu > 0$. The log-likelihood of an observation is

$$l_{\vec{x}}(\mu, \sigma) = \frac{-n}{2} \ln(2\pi\sigma^2) - \frac{1}{2\sigma^2} \sum_i (x_i - \mu)^2$$

and the likelihood ratio statistic is

$$l_{\vec{x}}(H_1) - l_{\vec{x}}(H_0) = \sup_{\mu \geq 0, \sigma > 0} l_{\vec{x}}(\mu, \sigma) - \sup_{\sigma > 0} l_{\vec{x}}(0, \sigma) = -n \ln \frac{\hat{\sigma}_1}{\hat{\sigma}_0}$$

---

[2] As long as the MLEs exist: by definition, $l_{\vec{x}}(\hat{\theta}) \geq l_{\vec{x}}(\theta)$ for any θ.

with

$$\hat{\sigma}_0^2 = \frac{1}{n} \sum_i x_i^2$$

$$\hat{\sigma}_1^2 = \frac{1}{n} \sum_i (x_i^2 - \hat{\mu}_n^+)^2$$

$$\hat{\mu}_n^+ = \max(\bar{x}, 0)$$

The likelihood ratio test has a rejection region of the form $l_{\vec{x}}(H_1) - l_{\vec{x}}(H_0) > k$, which is equivalent to

$$\hat{\sigma}_1 < k\hat{\sigma}_0 \qquad (4.3)$$

In other words, we reject H_0 if the estimated variance under H_1 is small. Such a test is called "Analysis of Variance".

We can simplify the definition of the rejection region by first noting that $\hat{\sigma}_1 \leq \hat{\sigma}_0$, and that we consequently must have $k \leq 1$. Second, if $\bar{x} \geq 0$, then (4.3) is equivalent to $\sqrt{n} \frac{\bar{x}}{s_n} > c$ for some c. Third, if $\bar{x} \leq 0$, then (4.3) is never true. In summary, we have shown that this test is the same as the ad-hoc test developed in Example 4.2.

4.2.2 Student Test for Single Sample (or Paired Data)

This test applies to a single sample of data, assumed to be normal with an unknown mean and variance. It can also be applied to two paired samples, after computing the differences. It is thus the two-sided variant of Example 4.5. The model is: $X_1, \ldots, X_n \sim$ iid N_{μ,σ^2} where μ and σ are not known. The hypotheses are

H_0: $\mu = \mu_0$ against H_1: $\mu \neq \mu_0$

where μ_0 is a fixed value. We compute the likelihood ratio statistic and find after some algebra

$$l_{\vec{x}}(H_1) - l_{\vec{x}}(H_0) = \frac{n}{2} \ln \left(1 + \frac{n(\bar{x} - \mu_0)^2}{\sum_i (x_i - \bar{x})^2} \right)$$

Let $T(\vec{x}) = \sqrt{n} \frac{\bar{x} - \mu_0}{\hat{\sigma}}$ be the student statistic (Theorem 2.3), with $\hat{\sigma}^2 = \frac{1}{n-1} \sum_i (x_i - \bar{x})^2$. We can write the likelihood ratio statistic as

$$l_{\vec{x}}(H_1) - l_{\vec{x}}(H_0) = \frac{n}{2} \ln \left(1 + \frac{T(\vec{x})^2}{n - 1} \right) \qquad (4.4)$$

which is an increasing function of $|T(\vec{x})|$. The rejection region thus has the form

$$C = \left\{ \left| T(\vec{x}) \right| > \eta \right\}$$

We compute η from the condition that the size of the test is α. Under H_0, $T(\vec{X})$ has a student distribution t_{n-1} (Theorem 2.3). Thus

$$\eta = t_{n-1}^{-1}\left(1 - \frac{\alpha}{2}\right) \tag{4.5}$$

For example, for $\alpha = 0.05$ and $n = 100$, $\eta = 1.98$.

The p-value is

$$p^* = 2\left(1 - t_{n-1}\left(T(\vec{x})\right)\right) \tag{4.6}$$

Example 4.6 Paired Data

This is a variant of Example 4.2. Consider again the reduction in run time due to a new compiler option, as given in Figure 2.7 on Page 35. We want to test whether the reduction is significant. We assume the data to be iid normal and use the Student test:

H_0: $\mu = 0$ against H_1:$\mu \neq 0$

The test statistic is $T(\vec{x}) = 5.05$, which is larger than 1.98, so we reject H_0. Alternatively, we can compute the p-value and obtain $p^* = 1.80\,e - 006$, which is small, leading use to reject H_0.

As argued in Section 4.1.4, the Student test is equivalent to the confidence interval, and there is thus no need to use it. However, it is very commonly used by others, so it is important to understand what it does and when it is valid.

4.2.3 The Simple Goodness of Fit Test

Assume that we are given n data points $x_1, \ldots, x_n$, considered to be generated from an iid sequence, and we want to verify whether their common distribution is a given distribution $F(\cdot)$. A traditional method is to compare the empirical histogram to the theoretical one. Applying this idea gives the following likelihood ratio test, known as the *simple goodness of fit test* as the null hypothesis applies for a given, fixed distribution $F(\cdot)$ (as opposed to a family of distributions, which would give a *composite* goodness of fit test).

To compute the empirical histogram, we partition the set of values of $\vec{X}$ into *bins* B_i. Let $N_i = \sum_{k=1}^{n} 1_{\{B_i\}}(X_k)$ (number of observations that falls in bin B_i) and $q_i = \mathbb{P}\{X_1 \in B_i\}$. If the data comes from the distribution $F(\cdot)$, the distribution of N is *multinomial* $M_{n,\vec{q}}$, i.e.

$$\mathbb{P}\{N_1 = n_1, \ldots, N_k = n_k\} = \left(\frac{n!}{n_1! \cdots n_k!}\right) q_1^{n_1} \cdots q_k^{n_k} \tag{4.7}$$

The test is

H_0: N_i comes from the multinomial distribution $M_{n,\vec{q}}$

against

H_1: N_i comes from a multinomial distribution $M_{n,\vec{p}}$ for some arbitrary $\vec{p}$

We now compute the likelihood ratio statistic. The parameter is $\theta = \vec{p}$. Under H_0, there is only one possible value so $\hat{\theta}_0 = \vec{q}$. From (4.7), the likelihood is

$$l_{\vec{x}}(\vec{p}) = C + \sum_{i=1}^{k} n_i \ln(p_i) \qquad (4.8)$$

where $n_i = \sum_{k=1}^{n} 1_{\{B_i\}}(x_k)$ and $C = \ln(n!) - \sum_{i=1}^{k} \ln(n_i!)$. C is a constant and can be ignored from here on. To find $\hat{\theta}$, we have to maximize (4.8), subject to the constraint $\sum_{i=1}^{k} p_i = 1$. The function to maximize is concave in p_i, so we can find the maximum by the Lagrangian technique. The Lagrangian is

$$L(\vec{p}, \lambda) = \sum_{i=1}^{k} n_i \ln(p_i) + \lambda \left(1 - \sum_{i=1}^{k} p_i \right) \qquad (4.9)$$

The equations $\frac{\partial L}{\partial p_i} = 0$ give $n_i = \lambda p_i$. Consider first the case $n_i \neq 0$ for all i. We find λ by the constraint $\sum_{i=1}^{k} p_i = 1$, which gives $\lambda = n$ and thus $\hat{p}_i = \frac{n_i}{n}$. Finally, the likelihood ratio statistic is

$$l_{\vec{x}}(H_1) - l_{\vec{x}}(H_0) = \sum_{i=1}^{k} n_i \ln \frac{n_i}{nq_i} \qquad (4.10)$$

In the case where $n_i = 0$ for some i, the formula is the same if we adopt the convention that, in (4.10), the term $n_i \ln \frac{n_i}{nq_i}$ is replaced by 0 whenever $n_i = 0$.

We now compute the p-value, which is equal to

$$\mathbb{P} \left(\sum_{i=1}^{k} N_i \ln \frac{N_i}{nq_i} > \sum_{i=1}^{k} n_i \ln \frac{n_i}{nq_i} \right) \qquad (4.11)$$

where $\vec{N}$ has the multinomial distribution $M_{n,\vec{q}}$.

For large n, Section 4.4 provides a simple approximation for the p-value. If n is not large, there is no known closed form, but we can use the Monte Carlo simulation as discussed in Section 6.4.

Example 4.7 Mendel [104]

Mendel crossed peas and classified the results into 4 classes $i = 1, 2, 3, 4$. If his genetic theory is true, the probability that a pea belongs to class i is $q_1 = \frac{9}{16}$, $q_2 = q_3 = \frac{3}{16}$, $q_4 = \frac{1}{16}$. In one experiment, Mendel obtained $n = 556$ peas, with $n_1 = 315$, $n_2 = 108$, $n_3 = 102$ and $n_4 = 31$. The test is

H_0: "$\vec{q} = \vec{p}$" against H_1 : "$\vec{p}$ is arbitrary"

The test statistic is

$$\sum_{i=1}^{k} n_i \ln \frac{n_i}{nq_i} = 0.3092 \qquad (4.12)$$

We find the p-value by Monte Carlo simulation (Example 6.8) and find $p = 0.9191 \pm 0.0458$. The p-value is (very) large, and we thus accept H_0.

QUESTION 4.2 Assume that we compute the p-value of a test by Monte Carlo simulation with 100 replicates and find an estimated p equal to 0. Can we say that the p-value is small enough to reject H_0?[3]

4.3 ANOVA

In this section, we cover a family of exact tests for when we can assume that the data is normal. The tests apply primarily to cases with multiple, unpaired samples.

4.3.1 Analysis of Variance (ANOVA) and F-tests

Analysis of variance (*ANOVA*) is used when we can assume that the data is a family of independent normal variables, with an arbitrary family of means, but with a common variance. The goal is to test a certain property of the mean. The name ANOVA is explained by Theorem 4.1.

ANOVA is found under many variants, and the basis is often obscured by complex computations. All variants of ANOVA are based on a single result, which we give next; they differ only in the details of the linear operators Π_M and Π_{M_0} introduced below.

Assumptions and Notations for ANOVA

- The data is a collection of *independent, normal* random variables X_r, where the index r is in some finite set R (with $|R| =$ number of elements in R).
- $X_r \sim N_{\mu_r, \sigma^2}$, i.e. all variables have the *same variance* (this is pompously called "homoscedasticity"). The common variance is fixed but unknown.
- The means μ_r satisfy some linear constraints, i.e. we assume that $\vec{\mu} \overset{\text{def}}{=} (\mu_r)_{r \in R} \in M$, where M is a linear subspace of $\mathbb{R}^R$. Let $k = \dim M$. The parameter of the model is $\theta = (\vec{\mu}, \sigma)$ and the parameter space is $\Theta = M \times (0, +\infty)$
- We want to test the nested model $\vec{\mu} \in M_0$, where M_0 is a linear sub-space of M. Let $k_0 = \dim M_0$. We have $\Theta_0 = M_0 \times (0, +\infty)$.
- Π_M (resp. Π_{M_0}) is the orthogonal projector on M (resp. M_0)

Example 4.8 Nonpaired Data

(Continuation of Example 4.1.) Consider the data for one parameter set. The model is

$$X_i = \mu_1 + \epsilon_{1,i} \qquad Y_j = \mu_2 + \epsilon_{2,j} \qquad (4.13)$$

with $\epsilon_{i,j} \sim$ iid N_{0,σ^2}. We can model the collection of variables as $X_1, \ldots, X_m, Y_1, \ldots, Y_n$ thus $R = \{1, \ldots, m+n\}$. We then have

---

[3] A confidence interval for the p-value at level γ is given by Theorem 2.4 and is equal to $[0, \frac{3.689}{R}]$ where R is the number of replicates. We obtain $p \leq 0.037$ at confidence $\gamma = 0.95$, and we thus reject H_0.

- $M = \{(\mu_1, \ldots \mu_1, \mu_2, \ldots \mu_2), \ \mu_1 \in \mathbb{R}, \ \mu_2 \in \mathbb{R}\}$ and $k = 2$;
- $M_0 = \{(\mu, \ldots \mu, \mu, \ldots \mu), \ \mu \in \mathbb{R}\}$ and $k_0 = 1$;
- $\Pi_M(x_1, \ldots, x_m, y_1, \ldots, y_n) = (\bar{x}, \ldots, \bar{x}, \bar{y}, \ldots, \bar{y})$, where

$$\bar{x} = \frac{\sum_{i=1}^{m} x_i}{m} \quad \text{and} \quad \bar{y} = \frac{\sum_{j=1}^{n} y_j)}{n}$$

- $\Pi_{M_0}(x_1, \ldots, x_m, y_1, \ldots, y_n) = (\bar{z}, \ldots, \bar{z}, \bar{z}, \ldots, \bar{z})$, where

$$\bar{z} = \frac{\sum_{i=1}^{m} x_i + \sum_{j=1}^{n} y_j}{m + n}$$

This model is an instance of what is called "one way ANOVA".

Example 4.9 Network Monitoring

A network monitoring experiment tries to detect changes in user behavior by measuring the number of servers inside the intranet accessed by users. Three groups were measured, with 16 measurements in each group. Only the average and standard deviations of the numbers of accessed servers are available:

Group	Mean number of remote servers	Standard deviation
1	15.0625	3.2346
2	14.9375	3.5491
3	17.3125	3.5349

(Here, the **standard deviation** is $\sqrt{\frac{1}{n-1} \sum_{i=1}^{n}(x_i - \bar{x})^2}$). The model is

$$X_{i,j} = \mu_i + \epsilon_{i,j} \qquad 1 \le n_i \ i = 1, \ldots, k \qquad (4.14)$$

with $\epsilon_{i,j} \sim$ iid N_{0,σ^2}. It is also called the one-way ANOVA model (one way because there is one "factor", index i). Here i represents the group, and j is one measurement for one member of the group. The collection is $X_r = X_{i,j}$ so $R = \{(i,j), i = 1, \ldots, k = 3 \text{ and } j = 1, \ldots, n_i\}$ and $|R| = \sum_i n_i$. We have

- $M = \{(\mu_{i,j}), \text{ such that } \mu_{i,j} = \mu_i, \ \forall i, j\}$; the dimension of M is $k = 3$.
- $M_0 = \{(\mu_{i,j}) \text{ such that } \mu_{i,j} = \mu, \ \forall i, j\}$ and $k_0 = 1$.
- $\Pi_M(\vec{x})$ is the vector whose (i,j)th coordinate is independent of j and is equal to $\bar{x}_{i\cdot} \overset{\text{def}}{=} \frac{\sum_{j=1}^{n_i} x_{i,j}}{n_i}$.
- $\Pi_{M_0}(\vec{x})$ is the vector whose coordinates are all identical and equal to the overall mean $\bar{x}_{\cdot\cdot} \overset{\text{def}}{=} \frac{\sum_{i,j} x_{i,j}}{|R|}$.

Theorem 4.1 (ANOVA)

Consider an ANOVA model as defined above. The p-value of the likelihood ratio test of H_0: "$\vec{\mu} \in M_0, \sigma > 0$" against H_1: "$\vec{\mu} \in M \setminus M_0, \sigma > 0$" is $p^* = 1 - F_{k-k_0,|R|-k}(f)$, where $F_{m,n}(\cdot)$ is the Fisher distribution with degrees of freedom m, n, and $\vec{x}$ is the dataset. Moreover,

$$f = \frac{SS2/(k-k_0)}{SS1/(|R|-k)} \tag{4.15}$$

$$SS2 = \left\| \hat{\mu} - \hat{\mu}_0 \right\|^2 \tag{4.16}$$

$$SS1 = \left\| \vec{x} - \hat{\mu} \right\|^2 \tag{4.17}$$

$$\hat{\mu}_0 = \Pi_{M_0}(\vec{x}) \tag{4.18}$$

$$\hat{\mu} = \Pi_M(\vec{x}) \tag{4.19}$$

(The norm is euclidian, i.e. $\left\| \vec{x} \right\|^2 = \sum_r x_r^2$.)

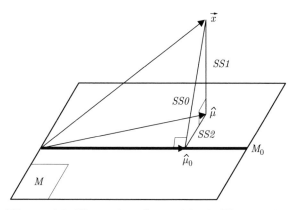

Figure 4.3 Illustration of quantities in Theorem 4.1.

The theorem, the proof of which is a direct application of the general ANOVA theorem C.7, can be understood as follows. The maximum likelihood estimators under H_0 and H_1 are obtained by orthogonal projection:

$$\hat{\mu}_0 = \Pi_{M_0}(\vec{x}) \qquad \hat{\sigma}_0^2 = \frac{1}{|R|} \left\| \vec{x} - \hat{\mu}_0 \right\|^2$$

$$\hat{\mu} = \Pi_M(\vec{x}) \qquad \hat{\sigma}^2 = \frac{1}{|R|} \left\| \vec{x} - \hat{\mu} \right\|^2$$

The likelihood ratio statistic can be computed explicitly and is equal to $-\frac{|R|}{2} \ln \frac{SS1}{SS0} = \frac{|R|}{2} \ln(1 + \frac{SS2}{SS1})$, where $SS0 \stackrel{\text{def}}{=} \left\| \vec{x} - \hat{\mu}_0 \right\|^2 = |R|\,\hat{\sigma}_0^2 = SS1 + SS2$. Under H_0, the distribution of f, given by (4.15), is Fisher $F_{k-k_0,|R|-k}$. Consequently we can compute the p-value exactly. The equality $SS0 = SS1 + SS2$ can be interpreted as a decomposition of a sum of squares, as follows. Consider Θ_0 as the base model, with k_0 dimensions for the mean; we ask ourselves whether it is worth considering the more complex model Θ, which has $k > k_0$ dimensions for the mean. From its definition, we can interpret those sums of squares according to the following.

- $SS2$ is the sum of squares explained by the model Θ, or explained variation.

- $SS1$ is the residual sum of squares.

- $SS0$ is the total sum of squares.

The likelihood ratio test accepts Θ when $SS2/SS1$ is large, i.e. when the percentage of the sum of squares $SS2/SS1$ (also called percentage of variation), explained by the model Θ, is high.

The dimensions are interpreted as degrees of freedom: $SS2$ (explained variation) is in the orthogonal of M_0 in M, with dimension $k - k_0$ and the number of degrees of freedom for $SS2$ is $k - k_0$; $SS1$ (residual variation) is the square of the norm of a vector that is orthogonal to M and the number of degrees of freedom for $SS1$ is $|R| - k$. This explains the name "ANOVA": the likelihood ratio statistic depends only on estimators of variance. Note that this is very specific for homoscedasticity.

Table 4.1 ANOVA Tests for Example 4.1 (nonpaired data).

Parameter Set 1	SS	df	MS	F	Prob>F
Columns	13.2120	1	13.2120	13.4705	0.0003116
Errors	194.2003	198	0.9808		
Total	207.4123	199			

Parameter Set 2	SS	df	MS	F	Prob>F
Columns	5.5975	1	5.5975	4.8813	0.0283
Errors	227.0525	198	1.1467		
Total	232.6500	199			

Parameter Set 3	SS	df	MS	F	Prob>F
columns	0.1892	1	0.1892	0.1835	0.6689
Errors	204.2256	198	1.0314		
Total	204.4148	199			

Example 4.10 Application to Example 4.1, Compiler Options

We assume homoscedasticity. We verify this hypothesis later by applying the test in Section 4.3.2. The theorem gives the following computations:

- $\hat{\mu} = (\bar{X}, \ldots, \bar{X}, \bar{Y}, \ldots, \bar{Y})$ and

$$\hat{\sigma} = \frac{1}{m+n} \left(\sum_i (X_i - \bar{X})^2 + \sum_j (Y_j - \bar{Y})^2 \right)$$

- $\hat{\mu}_0 = (\bar{Z}, \ldots, \bar{Z}, \bar{Z}, \ldots, \bar{Z})$ with $\bar{Z} = \frac{m\bar{X}+n\bar{Y}}{m+n}$ and

$$\hat{\sigma}_0 = \frac{1}{m+n} \left(\sum_i (X_i - \bar{Z})^2 + \sum_j (Y_j - \bar{Z})^2 \right)$$

- $SS1 = \sum_i (X_i - \bar{X})^2 + \sum_j (Y_j - \bar{Y})^2 = S_{XX} + S_{YY}$;
- $SS2 = m(\bar{Z} - \bar{X})^2 + n(\bar{Z} - \bar{Y})^2 = \frac{(\bar{X}-\bar{Y})^2}{1/m+1/n}$;
- the f value is $\frac{SS2}{SS1/(m+n-2)}$.

The ANOVA tables for parameter sets 1 to 3 are given in Table 4.1. The F-test rejects the hypothesis of the same mean for parameter sets 1 and 2, and accepts it for parameter set 3. The software employed to produce this example uses the following terminology:

- SS2: "Columns" (explained variation, variation between columns, or between groups).
- SS1: "Error" (residual variation, unexplained variation).
- SS0: "Total" (total variation).

QUESTION 4.3 Compare to the confidence intervals given in the introduction.[4]

QUESTION 4.4 What are $SS0$, $SS1$ and $SS2$ for parameter set 1?[5]

Example 4.11 Network Monitoring
The numerical solution of Example 4.9 is shown in the table below. We thus accept H_0, i.e. the three measured groups are similar, though the evidence is not strong.

Source	SS	df	MS	F	Prob>F
Columns	57.1667	2	28.5833	2.4118	0.1012
Errors	533.3140	45	11.8514		
Total	590.4807	47			

---

[4] For parameter set 1, the conclusion is the same as with the confidence interval. For parameter sets 2 and 3, confidence intervals did not render it possible to draw any conclusions. ANOVA disambiguates these two cases.

[5] The column "SS" gives, from top to bottom: $SS2$, $SS1$ and $SS0$.

QUESTION 4.5 Write down the expressions of MLEs, $SS1$, $SS2$ and the F-value.[6]

The Student test as a special case of ANOVA

In the special case where $k - k_0 = 1$ (as in Example 4.1), the F-statistic is the square of a student statistic, and a student test could be used instead. This is employed by certain statistics packages.

Testing for specific Values

By an additive change of variable, we can extend the ANOVA framework to the case where $M_0 \subset M$ are affine (instead of linear) varieties of $\mathbb{R}^R$. This includes testing for a specific value. For example, assume we that have the model

$$X_{i,j} = \mu_i + \epsilon_{i,j} \tag{4.20}$$

with $\epsilon_{i,j} \sim$ iid N_{0,σ^2}. We want to test

H_0: "$\mu_i = \mu_0$ for all i" against H_1: "μ_i unconstrained"

We change models by letting $X'_{i,j} = X_{i,j} - \mu_0$ and we are back to the ANOVA framework.

4.3.2   Testing for a Common Variance

We often need to verify that the common variance assumption holds. Here too, a likelihood ratio test gives the answer. In the general case, the p-value of the test cannot be computed in closed form, so we use either Monte Carlo simulation or an asymptotic approximation. When the number of groups is 2, there is a closed form using the Fisher distribution.

We are given a data set with I groups $x_{i,j}$, $i = 1, \ldots, I$, $j = 1, \ldots, n_i$; the total number of samples is $n = \sum_{j=1}^{I} n_j$. We assume that it is a realization of the model $X_{i,j} \sim$ iid N_{μ_i,σ_i^2}. We assume that the normal assumption holds and wish to test

H_0: $\sigma_i = \sigma > 0$ for all i against H_1: $\sigma_i > 0$

Theorem 4.2 (Testing for Common Variance)
The likelihood ratio statistic ℓ of the test of common variance under the

---

[6] $\hat{\mu}$ is the vector whose (i,j)th coordinate is independent of j and is equal to $\bar{X}_{i\cdot} \overset{\text{def}}{=} \sum_{j=1}^{n_i} \frac{X_{i,j}}{n_i}$.

$SS1 = \sum_{i,j}(X_{i,j} - \bar{X}_{i\cdot})^2$; $\hat{\sigma}^2 = \frac{1}{|R|} SS1$.

$\hat{\mu}_0$ is the vector whose coordinates are all identical and equal to the overall mean $\bar{X}.. \overset{\text{def}}{=} \frac{\sum_{i,j} X_{i,j}}{|R|}$

$SS2 = \sum_i n_i(\bar{X}_{i\cdot} - \bar{X}..)^2$; $SS0 = SS1 + SS2$; $\hat{\sigma}_0^2 = \frac{1}{|R|} SS0$; $F = SS2 \frac{|R|-k}{[SS1(k-1)]}$.

hypothesis above is given by

$$2\ell = n\ln(s^2) - \sum_{i=1}^{I} n_i \ln(s_i^2) \tag{4.21}$$

with

$$\hat{\mu}_i \stackrel{\text{def}}{=} \frac{1}{n_i}\sum_{j=1}^{I} x_{i,j} \qquad s_i^2 \stackrel{\text{def}}{=} \frac{1}{n_i}\sum_{j=1}^{I}\left(x_{i,j}-\hat{\mu}_i\right)^2$$

$$s^2 \stackrel{\text{def}}{=} \frac{1}{n}\sum_{i=1}^{I}\sum_{j=1}^{n_i}\left(x_{i,j}-\hat{\mu}_i\right)^2 = \sum_{i=1}^{I}\frac{n_i}{n}s_i^2$$

The test rejects H_0 when ℓ is large. The p-value is

$$p = \mathbb{P}\left(n\log\sum_{i=1}^{I}Z_i - \sum_{i=1}^{I}n_i\log Z_i > 2\ell + n\log n - \sum_{i=1}^{I}n_i\log n_i\right) \tag{4.22}$$

where Z_i are independent random variables, $Z_i \sim \chi^2_{n_i-1}$ and $Z = \sum_{i=1}^{I}\frac{n_i}{n}Z_i$. The p-value can be computed by Monte Carlo simulation. When n is large, we have

$$p \approx 1 - \chi^2_{I-1}(2\ell) \tag{4.23}$$

In the special case $I = 2$, we can replace the statistic ℓ by

$$f \stackrel{\text{def}}{=} \frac{\hat{\sigma}_1^2}{\hat{\sigma}_2^2} \qquad \text{with } \hat{\sigma}_i^2 \stackrel{\text{def}}{=} \frac{1}{n_i-1}\sum_{j=1}^{I}\left(x_{i,j}-\hat{\mu}_i\right)^2$$

and the distribution of f under H_0 is Fisher F_{n_1-1,n_2-1}. The test at size α rejects H_0 when $f < \eta$ or $f > \xi$ with $F_{n_1-1,n_2-1}(\eta) = \frac{\alpha}{2}$, $F_{n_1-1,n_2-1}(\xi) = 1 - \frac{\alpha}{2}$. The p-value is

$$p = F_{n_1-1,n_2-1}\left(\min\left(f,\frac{1}{f}\right) - F_{n_1-1,n_2-1}\left(\max\left(f,\frac{1}{f}\right)\right) + 1\right) \tag{4.24}$$

Example 4.12 Network Monitoring again

We want to test whether the data in groups 1 and 2 in Example 4.9 have the same variance. We have $\eta = 0.3494$, $\xi = 2.862$; the F statistic is 0.8306 so we accept H_0, i.e. the fact that the variance is the same. Alternatively, we can use (4.24) and find $p = 0.7239$, which is large leading us to accept H_0.

Of course, we are more interested in comparing the 3 groups together. We apply (4.21) and find as the likelihood ratio statistic $\ell = 0.0862$. The asymptotic approximation gives $p \approx 0.9174$, but since the number of samples n is not large we do not trust it. We evaluate (4.22) by

Monte Carlo simulation; with $R = 10^4$ replicates we find a confidence interval for the estimated p-value of $[0.9247; 0.9347]$. We conclude that the p-value is very large, and we thus accept that the variance is the same.

4.4   Asymptotic Results

In many cases it is hard to find the exact distribution of a test statistic. An interesting feature of likelihood ratio tests is that we have a simple asymptotic result. We used this result already in the test for equal variance in Section 4.3.2.

4.4.1   Likelihood Ratio Statistic

The following theorem derives immediately from Theorem B.2.

Theorem 4.3 ([32])
Consider a likelihood ratio test (Section 4.2) with $\Theta = \Theta_1 \times \Theta_2$, where Θ_1, Θ_2 are open subsets of $\mathbb{R}^{q_1}, \mathbb{R}^{q_2}$ and denote $\theta = (\theta_1, \theta_2)$. Consider the likelihood ratio test of $H_0 : \theta_2 = 0$ against $H_1 : \theta_2 \neq 0$. Assume that the conditions in Definition B.1 hold. Then, approximately, for large sample sizes, under H_0, $2lrs \sim \chi^2_{q_2}$, where lrs is the likelihood ratio statistic.

It follows that the p-value of the likelihood ratio test can be approximated for large sample sizes by

$$p^* \approx 1 - \chi^2_{q_2}(2lrs) \qquad (4.25)$$

where q_2 is the number of degrees of freedom that H_1 adds to H_0.

Example 4.13   Application to Example 4.1 (Compiler Options)
Using Theorem 4.1 and Theorem 4.3, we find that

$$2lrs \stackrel{\text{def}}{=} N \ln\left(1 + \frac{SS2}{SS1}\right) \sim \chi_1^2$$

The corresponding p-values are

```
Parameter Set 1   pchi2 = 0.0002854
Parameter Set 1   pchi2 = 0.02731
Parameter Set 1   pchi2 = 0.6669
```

They are all very close to the exact values (given by ANOVA in Table 4.1).

4.4.2   Pearson Chi-squared Statistic and Goodness of Fit

We can apply the large sample asymptotic to goodness of fit tests as defined in Section 4.2.3. This gives a simpler means of computing the p-value, and renders it possible to extend the test to the **composite goodness of fit** test, defined as follows.

Composite Goodness of Fit

As in Section 4.2.3, assume that we are given n data points $x_1, \ldots, x_n$, generated from an iid sequence, and that we want to verify whether their common distribution comes from a given family of distributions $F(\cdot \mid \theta)$, where the parameter θ is in some set Θ_0. We say that the test is composite because the null hypothesis has several possible values of θ. We compare the empirical histograms: we partition the set of values of $\vec{X}$ into **bins** B_i, $i = 1, \ldots, I$. Let $N_i = \sum_{k=1}^{n} 1_{\{B_i\}}(X_k)$ (number of observation that fall in bin B_i) and $q_i = \mathbb{P}_\theta\{X_1 \in B_i\}$. If the data comes from a distribution $F(\cdot \mid \theta)$ the distribution of N_i is multinomial $M_{n,\vec{q}(\theta)}$. The likelihood ratio statistic test is

H_0: N_i comes from a multinomial distribution $M_{n,\vec{q}(\theta)}$, with $\theta \in \Theta_0$

against

H_1: N_i comes from a multinomial distribution $M_{n,\vec{p}}$ for some arbitrary $\vec{p}$

We now compute the likelihood ratio statistic. The maximum likelihood estimator of the parameter under H_1 is the same as in Section 4.2.3. Let $\hat{\theta}$ be the maximum likelihood estimator of θ under H_0. The likelihood ratio statistic is thus

$$lrs = \sum_{i=1}^{k} n_i \ln \frac{n_i}{nq_i(\hat{\theta})} \tag{4.26}$$

The p-value is

$$\sup_{\theta \in \Theta_0} \mathbb{P}\left(\sum_{i=1}^{k} N_i \ln \frac{N_i}{nq_i} > \sum_{i=1}^{k} n_i \ln \frac{n_i}{nq_i(\hat{\theta})} \right) \tag{4.27}$$

where $\vec{N}$ has the multinomial distribution $M_{n,\vec{q}(\hat{\theta})}$. It can be computed by Monte Carlo simulation as in the case of a simple test, but this may be difficult because of the supremum.

An alternative for large n is to use the asymptotic result in Theorem 4.3. It says that, for large n, under H_0, the distribution of $2lrs$ is approximately $\chi^2_{q_2}$, with $q_2 =$ the number of degrees of freedom that H_1 adds to H_0. Here H_0 has k_0 degrees of freedom (where k_0 is the dimension of Θ_0) and H_1 has $I - 1$ degrees of freedom (where I is the number of bins). Thus the p-value of the test is approximately

$$1 - \chi^2_{I-k_0-1}(2lrs) \tag{4.28}$$

Example 4.14 Impact of Estimation of (μ, σ)

We want to test whether the data set to the right in Figure 4.4 has a normal distribution. We use a histogram with 10 bins, but we first need to estimate $\hat{\theta} = (\hat{\mu}, \hat{\sigma})$.

(1) Assume that we do this by fitting a line to the qq-plot. We obtain $\hat{\mu} = -0.2652$, $\hat{\sigma} = 0.8709$. The values of $nq_i(\hat{\theta})$ and n_i are

7.9297	7.0000
11.4034	9.0000
18.0564	17.0000
21.4172	21.0000
19.0305	14.0000
12.6672	17.0000
6.3156	6.0000
2.3583	4.0000
0.6594	3.0000
0.1624	2.0000

The likelihood ratio statistic as in (4.26) is $lrs = 7.6352$. The p-value is obtained using a χ_7^2 distribution ($q_2 = 10 - 2 - 1$): $p_1 = 0.0327$, and we would thus reject normality at size 0.05.

(2) It might not be a good idea to simply fit (μ, σ) on the qq-plot. A better way would be to use estimation theory, which suggests determining (μ, σ) in order to maximize the log likelihood of the model. This is equivalent to minimizing the likelihood ratio statistic $l_{H_1}(\vec{x}) - l_{\mu,\sigma}(\vec{x})$ (note that the value of $l_{H_1}(\vec{x})$ is easy to compute). This is done with a numerical optimization procedure and we now find $\hat{\mu} = -0.0725$, $\hat{\sigma} = 1.0269$. The corresponding values of $nq_i(\hat{\theta})$ and n_i are thus:

8.3309	7.0000
9.5028	9.0000
14.4317	17.0000
17.7801	21.0000
17.7709	14.0000
14.4093	17.0000
9.4783	6.0000
5.0577	4.0000
2.1892	3.0000
1.0491	2.0000

Note how the true value of $\hat{\mu}, \hat{\sigma}$ provides a better fit to the tail of the histogram. The likelihood ratio statistic is now $lrs = 2.5973$, which also presents a much better fit. The p-value, obtained using a χ_7^2 distribution is now $p_1 = 0.6362$, and we thus accept that the data is normal.

(3) Assume that we were to ignore that (μ, σ) is estimated from the data, but go ahead as if the test were a simple goodness of fit test, with H_0: "The distribution is $N_{-0.0725,1.0269}$" instead of H_0: "The distribution is normal". We would compute the p-value using a χ_9^2 distribution ($q_2 = 10 - 1$) and would obtain: $p_2 = 0.8170$, a value larger than the true p-value. This is quite general: if we estimate some parameter and pretend it is known a priori, we consequently overestimate the p-value.

Pearson Chi-Squared Statistic

In the case where n is large, $2\times$ the likelihood ratio statistic can be replaced by the *Pearson chi-squared statistic*, which has the same asymptotic distribution. It is defined by

$$pcs = \sum_{i=1}^{I} \frac{\left(n_i - nq_i(\hat{\theta})\right)^2}{nq_i(\hat{\theta})} \tag{4.29}$$

Indeed, when n is large we expect, under H_0 that $n_i - nq_i(\hat{\theta})$ is relatively small, i.e. that $\epsilon_i = \frac{n_i}{nq_i(\hat{\theta})} - 1$ is small. An approximation of $2lrs$ is found from the second order development around $\epsilon = 0$: $\ln(1 + \epsilon) = \epsilon - \frac{1}{2}\epsilon^2 + o(\epsilon^2)$ and thus

$$lrs = \sum_i n_i \frac{n_i}{nq_i(\hat{\theta})} n \sum_i (1 + \epsilon_i)q_i(\hat{\theta}) \ln(1 + \epsilon_i)$$

$$= n \sum_i \left(\epsilon_i - \frac{1}{2}\epsilon_i^2 + o(\epsilon_i^2)(1 + \epsilon_i)q_i(\hat{\theta}) \right)$$

$$= n \sum_i q_i(\hat{\theta})\epsilon_i \left(1 - \frac{1}{2}\epsilon_i + o(\epsilon_i)(1 + \epsilon_i) \right)$$

$$= n \sum_i q_i(\hat{\theta})\epsilon_i \left(1 + \frac{1}{2}\epsilon_i + o(\epsilon_i) \right)$$

$$= n \sum_i q_i(\hat{\theta})\epsilon_i + n \sum_i q_i(\hat{\theta})\frac{1}{2}\epsilon_i^2 + n \sum_i o(\epsilon_i^2)$$

Note that $\sum_i q_i(\hat{\theta})\epsilon_i = 0$, thus

$$lrs \approx \frac{1}{2}pcs \tag{4.30}$$

The Pearson Chi-squared statistic was historically developed before the theory of likelihood ratio tests, which explains why it is commonly used.

In summary, for large n, the composite goodness of fit test is solved by computing either $2lrs$ or pcs. The p-value is $1 - \chi^2_{n-k_0-1}(2lrs)$ or $1 - \chi^2_{I-k_0-1}(pcs)$. If either is small, we reject H_0, i.e. we reject that the distribution of X_i comes from the family of distributions $F(\cdot \mid \theta)$.

Simple Goodness of Fit Test

This is a special case of the composite test. In this case, $q_2 = I - 1$ and thus the p-value of the test (given in (4.11)) can be approximated for large n by $1 - \chi^2_{I-1}(2lrs)$ or $1 - \chi^2_{I-1}(pcs)$. Also, the likelihood ratio statistic $\sum_{i=1}^{k} n_i \ln \frac{n_i}{nq_i}$ can be replaced by the Pearson-Chi-Squared statistic, equal to

$$\sum_{i=1}^{I} \frac{(n_i - nq_i)^2}{nq_i} \tag{4.31}$$

Example 4.15 Mendel's peas, continuation of Example 4.7

The likelihood ratio statistic is $lrs = 0.3092$ and we found by Monte Carlo simulation a p-value $p^* = 0.9191 \pm 0.0458$. By the asymptotic result, we can approximate the p-value by $1 - \chi_3^2(2lrs) = 0.8922$.
The Pearson Chi-squared statistic is $pcs = 0.6043$, very close to $2lrs = 0.618$. The corresponding p-value is 0.8954.

4.4.3 Test of Independence

Ideas equivalent to those in Section 4.4.2 can be applied to a **test of independence**. We are given a sequence (x_k, y_k), which we interpret as a sample of the sequence (X_k, Y_k), $k = 1, \ldots, n$. The sequence is iid ((X_k, Y_k) is independent of $(X_k, Y_{k'})$ and has the same distribution).

We are interested in knowing whether X_k is independent of Y_k. To this end, we compute an empirical histogram of (X, Y), as follows. We partition the set of values of X (resp. Y) into I (resp. J) bins B_i (resp. C_j). Let $N_{i,j} = \sum_{k=1}^n 1_{\{B_i\}}(X_k) 1_{\{C_j\}}(Y_k)$ (number of observation that fall into bin (B_i, C_j)) and $p_{i,j} = \mathbb{P}\{X_1 \in B_i \text{ and } Y_1 \in C_j\}$. The distribution of N is multinomial. The test of independence is

H_0: "$p_{i,j} = q_i r_j$ for some q and r such that $\sum_i q_i = \sum_j r_j = 1$"
against
H_1: "$p_{i,j}$ is arbitrary"

The maximum likelihood estimator under H_0 is $\hat{p}_{i,j}^0 = \frac{n_{i\cdot}}{n}\frac{n_{\cdot j}}{n}$, where $n_{i,j} = \sum_{k=1}^n 1_{\{B_i\}}(x_k) 1_{\{C_j\}}(y_k)$ and

$$\begin{cases} n_{i\cdot} = \sum_j n_{i,j} \\ n_{\cdot j} = \sum_i n_{i,j} \end{cases} \tag{4.32}$$

The maximum likelihood estimator under H_1 is $\hat{p}_{i,j}^1 = \frac{n_{i,j}}{n}$. The likelihood ratio statistic is thus

$$lrs = \sum_{i,j} n_{i,j} \ln \frac{n n_{i,j}}{n_{i\cdot} n_{\cdot j}} \tag{4.33}$$

To compute the p-value, we use, for large n, a $\chi_{q_2}^2$ distribution. The number of degrees of freedom under H_1 is $IJ - 1$, and under H_0 it is $(I - 1) + (J - 1)$. As a result, $q_2 = (IJ - 1) - (I - 1) - (J - 1) = (I - 1)(J - 1)$. The p-value beomes thus

$$p^* = \left(1 - \chi_{(I-1)(J-1)}^2\right)(2lrs) \tag{4.34}$$

As in Section 4.4.2, $2lrs$ can be replaced, for large n, by the Pearson Chi-squared statistic:

$$pcs = \sum_{i,j} \frac{\left(n_{i,j} - \frac{n_{i\cdot} n_{\cdot j}}{n}\right)^2}{\frac{n_{i\cdot} n_{\cdot j}}{n}} \tag{4.35}$$

Example 4.16 Brassica Oleracea Gemmifera

A survey was conducted at the campus cafeteria, where customers were asked whether they like Brussels sprouts. The answers were

$i\backslash j$	Male	Female	Total
Like	454 44.69%	251 48.08%	705 45.84%
Dislike	295 29.04%	123 23.56%	418 27.18%
No Answer/Neutral	267 26.28%	148 28.35%	415 26.98%
Total	1016 100%	522 100%	1538 100%

We wish to test whether the affinity to Brussels sprouts is independent of customer's gender. Here we have $I = 3$ and $J = 2$, so we use a χ^2 distribution with $q_2 = 2$ degrees of freedom. The likelihood ratio statistic and the p-value are

$$lrs = 2.6489 \qquad p = 0.0707 \qquad (4.36)$$

We thus accept H_0, i.e. the affinity to Brussels sprouts is independent of gender. Note that the Pearson Chi-squared statistic is

$$pcs = 5.2178 \qquad (4.37)$$

which is very close to $2lrs$.

4.5   Other Tests

4.5.1   Goodness of Fit Tests based on Ad-Hoc Pivots

In addition to the Pearson χ^2 test, the following two tests are often used. They apply to a continuous distribution, thus do not require the observations to be quantized. Assume that X_i, $i = 1, \ldots, n$, are iid samples. We want to test H_0: the distribution of X_i is F against non H_0.

We define the empirical distribution $\hat{F}$ by

$$\hat{F}(x) \stackrel{\text{def}}{=} \frac{1}{n} \sum_{i=1}^{n} 1_{\{X_i \leq x\}} \qquad (4.38)$$

Kolmogorov-Smirnov

The pivot is

$$T = \sup_x \left| \hat{F}(x) - F(x) \right|$$

It is not entirely obvious that the distribution of this random variable is independent of F, but it can be easily derived in the case where F is continuous and strictly increasing, as follows. The idea is to change the scale on the x-axis by $u = F(x)$. Formally, we define

$$U_i = F(X_i)$$

so that $U_i \sim U(0,1)$. Also

$$\hat{F}(x) = \frac{1}{n}\sum_i 1_{\{X_i \le x\}} = \frac{1}{n}\sum_i 1_{\{U_i \le F(x)\}} = \hat{G}\big(F(x)\big)$$

where $\hat{G}$ is the empirical distribution of the sample U_i, $i = 1, \ldots, n$. By a change of variable $u = F(x)$, we have

$$T = \sup_{u \in [0,1]} \big|\hat{G}(u) - u\big|$$

which shows that the distribution of T is independent of F. Its distribution is tabulated in statistical software packages. For a large n, its tail can be approximated by $\tau \approx \frac{\sqrt{-(\ln \alpha)}}{2}$ where $\mathbb{P}(T > \tau) = \alpha$.

Anderson-Darling

Here the pivot is

$$A = n \int_{\mathbb{R}} \frac{\big(\hat{F}(x) - F(x)\big)^2}{F(x)\big(1 - F(x)\big)} \, dF(x)$$

The test is similar to that of K-S but is less sensitive to outliers.

QUESTION 4.6 Demonstrate that A is indeed a pivot.[7]

Example 4.17 File Transfer Data

We would like to test whether the data in Figure 4.4 and its log are normal. We cannot directly apply Kolmogorov Smirnov since we do not know exactly in advance the parameters of the normal distribution to be tested against. An approximate method is to estimate the slope and intercept of the straight line in the qq-plot. We obtain

```
Original Data
slope     =    0.8155
intercept =    1.0421

Transformed Data
slope     =    0.8709
intercept =   -0.2652
```

For example, this means that for the original data we take for H_0: "the distribution is $N(\mu = 1.0421, \sigma^2 = 0.8155^2)$". We can now use the Kolmogorov-Smirnov test and obtain

```
Original Data      h = 1      p = 0.0493
Transformed Data   h = 0      p = 0.2415
```

---

[7] Use the fact that $\hat{F}(x) = \hat{G}\big(F(x)\big)$ and perform the change of variable $u = F(x)$ in the integral.

The test thus rejects the normality assumption for the original data and accepts it for the transformed data.

Such an approach is approximate in that we use estimated parameters for H_0. This introduces a certain bias, similar to when using the normal statistic instead of Student when we have a normal sample. The bias should be small when the data sample is large, which is the case here. A fix to this problem is to perform a variant of KS, for example the Lilliefors test, or to use different normality tests such as Jarque Bera (see Example 4.18) or Shapiro-Wilk. The Lilliefors test is a heuristic that corrects the p-value of the KS to account for the uncertainty due to estimation. In this specific example, with the Lilliefors test, we obtain the same results.

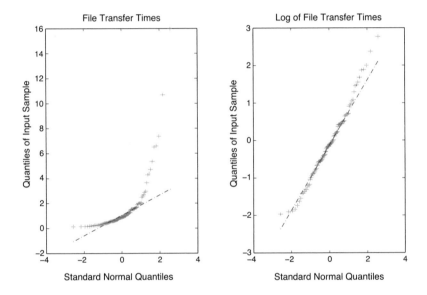

Figure 4.4 Normal qq-plots of file transfer data and its logarithm.

Jarque-Bera

The **_Jarque-Bera_** statistic is used to test whether an iid sample comes from a normal distribution. It uses the skewness and kurtosis indices γ_1 and γ_2 defined in Section 3.4.2. The test statistic is equal to $\frac{n}{6}(\hat{\gamma}_1^2 + \frac{\hat{\gamma}_2^2}{4})$, the distribution of which is asymptotically χ_2^2 for a large sample size n. In the formula, $\hat{\gamma}_1$ and $\hat{\gamma}_2$ are the sample indices of skewness and kurtosis, obtained by replacing expectations by sample averages in (3.13).

Example 4.18 Application to Example 4.17

We would like to test whether the data in Example 4.17 and its transform are normal.

```
Original Data      h = 1        p =    0.0010
Transformed Data   h = 0        p =    0.1913
```

The conclusions are the same as in Example 4.17. Nevertheless, for the original data, the normality assumption could be clearly rejected, whereas it was borderline in Example 4.17.

4.5.2 Robust Tests

We give two examples of tests that make no assumption regarding the distribution of the sample (but do nonetheless assume it to be iid). They are **non-parametric** in the sense that they do not assume a parameterized family of densities.

Median Test

The model is $X_i \sim$ iid with some distribution $F()$ with a density. We want to test

H_0: "the median of F is 0" against H_1: "unspecified"

A simple test is based on confidence interval, as mentioned in Section 4.1.4. Let $I(\vec{x})$ be a confidence interval for the median (Theorem 2.1). We reject H_0 if

$$0 \notin I(\vec{x}) \tag{4.39}$$

This test is robust in the sense that it makes no assumptions other than independence.

Wilcoxon Signed Rank Test

It is used for testing equality of distribution in paired experiments. It tests

H_0: $X_1, \ldots, X_n$ is iid with a common symmetric, continuous distribution, the median of which is 0

against

H_1: $X_1, \ldots, X_n$ is iid with a common symmetric, continuous distribution

The **Wilcoxon signed rank** statistic is

$$W = \sum_{j=1}^{n} \text{rank}\big(|X_j|\big) \, \text{sign}(X_j)$$

where $\text{rank}\big(|X_j|\big)$ is the rank in increasing order (the smallest value has rank 1) and $\text{sign}(X_j)$ is -1 for negative data, $+1$ for positive data, and 0 for null data. If the median is positive, then many values with high rank will be positive and

W will tend to be positive and large. We reject the null hypothesis when $|W|$ is large.

It can be shown that the distribution of W under H_0 is always the same. It is tabulated and contained in software packages. For non-small data samples, it can easily be approximated by a normal distribution. The mean and variance under H_0 can easily be computed:

$$\mathbb{E}_{H_0}(W) = \sum_{j=1}^{n} \mathbb{E}_{H_0}\left(\text{rank}(|X_j|)\mathbb{E}_{H_0}\left(\text{sign}(X_j)\right)\right)$$

since, under H_0, $\text{rank}(|X_j|)$ is independent of $\text{sign}(X_j)$. Thus, $\mathbb{E}_{H_0}(W) = 0$. The variance is

$$\mathbb{E}_{H_0}(W^2) = \sum_{j=1}^{n} \mathbb{E}_{H_0}\left(\text{rank}(|X_j|)^2\text{sign}(X_j)^2\right) = \sum_{j=1}^{n} \mathbb{E}_{H_0}\left(\text{rank}(|X_j|)^2\right)$$

since $\text{sign}(X_j)^2 = 1$. Now, $\sum_j \text{rank}(|X_j|)^2 = \sum_j j^2$ is non-random and thus

$$\text{var}_{H_0}(W) = \sum_{j=1}^{n} \mathbb{E}_{H_0}\left(\text{rank}(|X_j|)^2\right)$$

$$= \mathbb{E}_{H_0}\left(\sum_j \text{rank}(|X_j|)^2\right) = \sum_{j=1}^{n} j^2 = \frac{n(n+1)(2n+1)}{6}$$

For large n, the test at size α rejects H_0 if $|W| > \eta\sqrt{\frac{n(n+1)(2n+1)}{6}}$ with $N_{0,1}(\eta) = 1 - \frac{\alpha}{2}$ (e.g. $\eta = 1.96$ at size 0.05). The p-value is

$$p = 2\left(1 - N_{0,1}\left(\frac{|W|}{\sqrt{\frac{n(n+1)(2n+1)}{6}}}\right)\right) \tag{4.40}$$

Example 4.19 Paired Data
This is a variant of Example 4.2. Consider again the reduction in run time due to a new compiler option, as given in Figure 2.7. We want to test whether the reduction is significant. We assume that the data is iid, but not necessarily normal. The median test gives a confidence interval

$$I(\vec{x}) = [2.9127; 33.7597]$$

which does not contain 0. Consequently, we reject H_0.
Alternatively, let us use the Wilcoxon signed rank test. We obtain the p-value

$$p = 2.3103\,e - 005$$

and thus also rejects H_0 with this test.

Wilcoxon Rank Sum Test and Kruskal-Wallis

The **Wilcoxon rank sum** test is used for testing equality of distribution in non-paired experiments. It tests

H_0: the two samples come from the same continuous distribution

against

H_1: the distributions of the two samples are continuous and differ by a location shift

Let X_i^1, $i = 1 \ldots, n_1$, and X_i^2, $i = 1 \ldots, n_2$, be the two iid sequences that the data is assumed to be a sample of. The **Wilcoxon rank sum statistic** R is the sum of the ranks of the first sample in the concatenated sample.

As for the Wilcoxon signed rank test, its distribution under the null hypothesis depends only on the sample sizes and can be tabulated or, for a large sample size, approximated by a normal distribution. The mean and variance under H_0 are

$$m_{n_1,n_2} = \frac{n_1(n_1 + n_2 + 1)}{2} \tag{4.41}$$

$$v_{n_1,n_2} = \frac{n_1 n_2(n_1 + n_2 + 1)}{12} \tag{4.42}$$

We reject H_0 when the rank sum statistic deviates largely from its expectation under H_0. For large n_1 and n_2, the p-value is

$$p = 2\left(1 - N_{0,1}\left(\frac{|R - m_{n_1,n_2}|}{\sqrt{v_{n_1,n_2}}}\right)\right) \tag{4.43}$$

Example 4.20 Nonpaired Data

The Wilcoxon rank sum test applied to Example 4.1 gives the following p-values:

```
Parameter Set 1     p = 0.0002854
Parameter Set 2     p = 0.02731
Parameter Set 3     p = 0.6669
```

The results are the same as with ANOVA. H_0 (same distribution) is accepted for the 3rd data set only, at size= 0.05.

The **Kruskal-Wallis** test is a generalization of Wilcoxon Rank Sum to more than 2 nonpaired data series. It tests (H_0): the samples come from the same distribution against (H_1): the distributions may differ by a location shift.

Turning Point Test

This is a test of iid-ness. It tests

H_0: $X_1, \ldots, X_n$ is iid against H_1: $X_1, \ldots, X_n$ is not iid

We say that the vector $X_1, \ldots, X_n$ is monotonic at index i ($i \in \{2, \ldots, n-1\}$) if

$$X_{i-1} \le X_i \le X_{i+1} \quad \text{or} \quad X_{i-1} \ge X_i \ge X_{i+1}$$

and we further say that there is a **turning point** at i if the vector $X_1, \ldots, X_n$ is not monotonic at i. Under H_0, the probability of a turning point at i is $\frac{2}{3}$. (To see why, list all possible cases for the relative orderings of X_{i-1}, X_i, X_{i+1}.)

More precisely, let T be the number of turning points in $X_1, \ldots, X_n$. It can be shown [18, 105] that, for large n, T is approximately $N_{\frac{2n-4}{3}, \frac{16n-29}{90}}$. Thus, the p-value for large n is approximatively

$$p = 2 \left(1 - N_{0,1} \left(\frac{\left| T - \frac{2n-4}{3} \right|}{\sqrt{\frac{16n-29}{90}}} \right) \right) \tag{4.44}$$

4.6 Proofs

Proof of Theorem 4.2

We make a likelihood ratio test and compute the likelihood ratio statistic. We need to first compute the maximum likelihood under H_1. The log-likelihood of the model is

$$l_{\vec{x}}(\vec{\mu}, \vec{\sigma}) = -\frac{1}{2} \left[\ln(2\pi) + \sum_{i=1}^{I} \left(2n_i \ln(\sigma_i) + \sum_{j=1}^{n_i} \frac{(\vec{x}_{i,j} - \mu_i)^2}{\sigma_i^2} \right) \right] \tag{4.45}$$

To find the maximum under H_1, observe that the terms in the summation do not have cross dependencies. We can thus maximize each of the I terms separately. The maximum of the ith term is for $\mu_i = \hat{\mu}_i$ and $\sigma_i^2 = s_i^2$, and thus

$$l_{\vec{x}}(H_1) = -\frac{1}{2} \left[\ln(2\pi) + \sum_{i=1}^{I} n_i \left(2 \ln(s_i) + 1 \right) \right] = -\frac{1}{2} \left[\ln(2\pi) + n + 2 \sum_{i=1}^{I} n_i \ln(s_i) \right] \tag{4.46}$$

Under H_0, the likelihood is as in (4.45) but with σ_i replaced by the common value σ. To find the maximum, we use the ANOVA Theorem C.7. The maximum is obtained for $\mu_i = \hat{\mu}_i$ and $\sigma^2 = s^2$ and thus

$$l_{\vec{x}}(H_0) = -\frac{1}{2} \left[\ln(2\pi) + \sum_{i=1}^{I} n_i \frac{s_i^2}{s^2} + 2n \ln(s) \right] = -\frac{1}{2} \left[\ln(2\pi) + n + 2n \ln(s) \right] \tag{4.47}$$

The test statistic is the likelihood ratio statistic $\ell = l_{\vec{x}}(H_1) - l_{\vec{x}}(H_0)$: and thus

$$2\ell = n \ln(s^2) - \sum_{i=1}^{I} n_i \ln(s_i^2) \tag{4.48}$$

The test has the following form: reject H_0 when $lrs > K$ for some constant K. The p-value can be obtained using Monte Carlo simulation. The problem is now to compute $\mathbb{P}(T > 2\ell)$ where T is a random variable distributed according to

$$n \ln(s^2) - \sum_{i=1}^{I} n_i \ln(s_i^2) \tag{4.49}$$

and assuming that H_0 holds. Observe that all we need is to generate the random variables s_i^2. They are independent, and $Z_i = n_i s_i$ is distributed as $\sigma^2 \chi^2_{n_i-1}$ (Corollary C.3). Note that T is independent of the specific value of the unknown but fixed parameter σ, and we can thus let $\sigma = 1$ in the Monte Carlo simulation, which proves (4.22). Alternatively, one can use the large sample asymptotic in Theorem 4.3, which gives (4.23).

When $I = 2$, we can rewrite the likelihood ratio statistic as

$$\ell = \frac{1}{2}\left[n \ln(n_1 F + n_2) - n_1 \ln(F)\right] + C \tag{4.50}$$

where C is a constant term (assuming n_1 and n_2 are fixed) and $F = \frac{s_1^2}{s_2^2}$. The derivative of ℓ with respect to F is

$$\frac{\partial \ell}{\partial F} = \frac{n_1 n_2 (F - 1)}{2F(n_1 F + n_2)} \tag{4.51}$$

thus ℓ decreases with F for $F < 1$ and increases for $F > 1$. Consequently, the rejection region, defined as $\{\ell > K\}$, is also of the form $\{F < K_1 \text{ or } F > K_2\}$. Now define

$$f = \frac{\hat{\sigma}_1^2}{\hat{\sigma}_2^2} \tag{4.52}$$

Note that $f = FC'$, where C' is a constant, so the set $\{F < K_1 \text{ or } F > K_2\}$ is equal to the set $\{f\eta \text{ or } f > \xi\}$ with $\eta = C'K_1$ and $\xi = C'K_2$. Under H_0, the distribution of F is Fisher with parameters $(n_1 - 1, n_2 - 1)$ (Theorem C.7), so we have a Fisher test. The bounds η and ξ are classically computed by the conditions $F_{n_1-1,n_2-1}(\eta) = \frac{\alpha}{2}$, $F_{n_1-1,n_2-1}(\xi) = 1 - \frac{\alpha}{2}$.

Last, note that, by the properties of the Fisher distribution, the particular choice of η and ξ above is such that $\xi = \frac{1}{\eta}$, so the rejection region is also defined by $\{f > \xi \text{ or } f < \frac{1}{\xi}\}$. This is the same as $\{\max(f, \frac{1}{f}) > \xi\}$, a form suitable to define a p-value (Section 4.1.3). Let $g = \max(f, \frac{1}{f})$ and $X \sim F_{m,n}$. We then have

$$p \stackrel{\text{def}}{=} P\left(\max\left(X, \frac{1}{X1}\right) > g\right) = P\left(X < \frac{1}{g}\right) + P(X > g)$$

$$= F_{n_1-1,n_2-1}\left(\frac{1}{g}\right) + 1 - F_{n_1-1,n_2-1}(g)$$

which, together with $\frac{1}{g} = \min(f, \frac{1}{f})$, gives (4.24).

4.7 Review

4.7.1 Tests are just Tests

(1) The first test to perform on any data is a visual exploration. In most cases, this is sufficient.

(2) Testing for a 0 mean or 0 median is the same as computing a confidence interval for the mean or the median.

(3) Tests work only if the underlying assumptions are verified (in particular, practically all tests, even robust ones, assume that the data comes from an iid sample).

(4) Some tests work under a larger spectrum of assumptions (e.g. even if the data is not normal). These are called robust tests, and should be preferred whenever possible.

(5) Test whether the same variance assumption holds, otherwise, use robust tests or asymptotic results.

(6) If you perform a large number of different tests on the same data, the probability of rejecting H_0 is larger than for any single test. So, contrary to non-statistical tests, increasing the number of tests does not always improve the decision.

4.7.2 Review Questions

4.1 What is the critical region of a test?[8]

4.2 What is a type-1 error? A type-2 error? The size of a test?[9]

4.3 What is the p-value of a test?[10]

4.4 What are the hypotheses for ANOVA?[11]

4.5 How do you compute a p-value by Monte Carlo simulation?[12]

---

[8] Call $\vec{x}$ the data used for the test. The critical region C is a set of possible values of $\vec{x}$ such that, when $\vec{x} \in C$, we reject H_0.

[9] A type-1 error occurs when the test says "do not accept H_0" whereas the truth is H_0. A type-2 error occurs when the test says "accept H_0" whereas the truth is H_1. The size of a test is $\sup_\theta$ such that H_0 is true $\mathbb{P}_\theta(C)$ (= the worst case probability of a type 1 error).

[10] It applies to tests where the critical region is of the form $T(\vec{x}) > m$ where $T(\vec{x})$ is the test statistic and $\vec{x}$ is the data. The p-value is the probability that $T(\vec{X}) > T(\vec{x})$, where $\vec{X}$ is a hypothetical data set, generated under the hypothesis H_0. We reject H_0 at size α if $p > \alpha$.

[11] The data is iid, Gaussian, perhaps with different means but with the same variance.

[12] Generate R iid samples T^r from the distribution of $T(\vec{X})$ under H_0 and compute $\hat{p}$ as the fraction of times that $T^r > T(\vec{x})$. We need R large enough (typically on the order of $10,000$) and compute a confidence interval for $\hat{p}$ using Theorem 2.4.

4.6 A Monte Carlo simulation returns $\hat{p} = 0$ as an estimate of the p-value. Can we reject H_0?[13]

4.7 What is the likelihood ratio statistic test in a nested model? What can we say in general about its p-value?[14]

---

[13] We need to know the number R of Monte Carlo replicates. A confidence interval for p is $[0; 3.869/R]$ at level 95%; if R is on the order of 100 or more, we can reject H_0 at size 0.05.

[14] The test statistic is lrs, the log of the likelihood ratios under H_1 and H_0, and the test rejects H_0 if lrs is large. The nested model means that the model is parametric, with some sets $\Theta_0 \subset \Theta$ such that H_0 means $\theta \in \Theta_0$ and H_1 means $\theta \in \Theta \setminus \Theta_0$. If the data sample is large, the p-value is obtained by saying that, under H_0, $2lrs \sim \chi_{q_2}^2$, where q_2 is the number of degrees of freedom that H_1 adds to H_0.

CHAPTER 5

Forecasting

Forecasting is a risky exercise, and involves many aspects that are well beyond the scope of this book. However, it is the engineer's responsibility to *forecast what can be forecast*. For example, if the demand on a communication line is multiplied by 2 every 6 months, it is wise to provision a sufficient capacity to accommodate this exponential growth. We present a simple framework to understand *what* forecasting is. We emphasize the need to quantify the accuracy of a forecast with a prediction interval. For the *how*, there are many methods (perhaps because an exact forecast is essentially impossible). We focus on simple, generic methods that have been found to work well in a large variety of cases. A first method is linear regression; it is very simple to use (with a computer) and of quite general application. It gives decent forecasts as long as the data does not vary too widly.

Better predictions may be obtained by a combination of differencing, de-seasonalizing filters and linear time series models (ARMA and ARIMA pro-cesses - this is also called the Box-Jenkins method). We discuss how to avoid model overfitting and present a set of simple models that have few parameters. We show that accounting for growth and seasonal effects is very simple and may be very effective. The necessary background on digital filters can be found in Chapter D in the Appendix.

5.1   What is Forecasting?

A classical forecasting example is capacity planning, where a communication or data center manager needs to decide when to buy additional capacity. Other examples concern the optimal use of resources: if a data center is able to predict that certain customers send less traffic at night, this may be used to save power or to resell the capacity to customers in other time zones.

As in any performance related activity, it is important to follow a clean methodology, in particular, define appropriate metrics relevant to the problem area, define measurement methods, and gather time series of data. The techniques seen in this chapter start at this point, i.e. we assume that we have gathered some past measurement data, and would like to establish a forecast.

Informally, one can say that a forecast consists in extracting all information about the future that is already present in the past. Mathematically, this can be done as follows. To avoid complex mathematical constructions, we assume time to be discrete. We are interested in a certain quantity $Y(t)$, where $t = 1, 2, \ldots$ We assume that there is *some* randomness in $Y(t)$, and it is thus modeled as a stochastic process. Assume that we have observed $Y_1, \ldots, Y_t$ and would like to say something about $Y_{t+\ell}$ for a certain $\ell > 0$.

Forecasting can be viewed as computing the conditional distribution of $Y_{t+\ell}$, given $Y_1, \ldots, Y_t$.

In particular, the *point prediction* or *predicted value* is

$$\hat{Y}_t(\ell) = \mathbb{E}\big(Y_{t+\ell} \mid Y_1 = y_1, \ldots, Y_t = y_t\big)$$

and a *prediction interval* at level $1 - \alpha$ is an interval $[A, B]$ such that

$$\mathbb{P}\big(A \leq Y_{t+\ell} \leq B \mid Y_1 = y_1, \ldots, Y_t = y_t\big) = 1 - \alpha$$

The forecasting problem thus becomes (1) to find and fit a good model, and (2) to compute conditional distributions.

5.2   Linear Regression

A simple and frequently used method is linear regression. It gives simple forecasting formulas, which are often sufficient. Linear regression models are defined in Chapter 3. In the context of forecasting, a linear regression model takes the form

$$Y_t = \sum_{j=1}^{p} \beta_j f_j(t) + \epsilon_t \tag{5.1}$$

where $f_j(t)$ are known, non-random functions and ϵ_t is iid N_{0,σ^2}. Recall that the model is linear with respect to $\vec{\beta}$, whereas the functions f_j need not be linear with respect to t.

Example 5.1 Internet Traffic
Figure 5.1 shows a prediction of the total amount of traffic on a coast-to-coast link of an American internet service provider. The traffic is periodic with period 16 (one time unit is 90 mn), and we therefore fit a simple sine function, i.e. we use a linear regression model with $p = 3$, $f_0(t) = 1$, $f_2(t) = \cos(\frac{\pi}{8}t)$ and $f_3(t) = \sin(\frac{\pi}{8}t)$. Using techniques presented in Section 3.2, we fit the parameters to the past data and obtain

$$Y_t = \sum_{j=1}^{3} \beta_j f_j(t) + \epsilon_t$$

$$= 238.2475 - 87.1876 \cos\left(\frac{\pi}{8}t\right) - 4.2961 \sin\left(\frac{\pi}{8}t\right) + \epsilon_t$$

with ϵ_t iid N_{0,σ^2} and $\sigma = 38.2667$.
A point prediction is

$$\hat{Y}_t(\ell) = \sum_{j=1}^{3} \beta_j f_j(t+\ell) \tag{5.2}$$

$$= 238.2475 - 87.1876 \cos\left(\frac{\pi}{8}(t+\ell)\right) - 4.2961 \sin\left(\frac{\pi}{8}(t+\ell)\right)$$

and a 95%-prediction interval can be approximated by $\hat{Y}_t(\ell) \pm 1.96\,\sigma$.

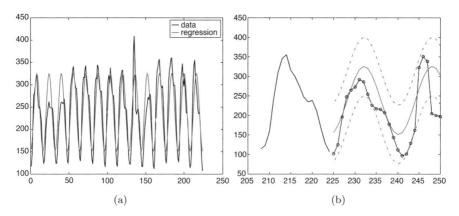

(a)   (b)

Figure 5.1 Internet traffic on a coast-to-coast link of an American internet service provider. One data point every 90 mn; the y-axis shows the amount of traffic in Mb/s, averaged over 90 mn. (a) Data for $t = 1$ to 224 and a sine function fitted to the data ; (b) zoom on the time interval from 205 to 250, showing the point prediction for the interval 225 to 250, the prediction interval and the true value (circles), not known when the prediction was done.

The computations in Example 5.1 are based on the following theorem and the formula after it; they result from the general theory of linear regression in Chapter 3 [32, Section 8.3]:

Theorem 5.1

Consider a linear regression model as in (5.1) with p degrees of freedom for $\vec{\beta}$. Assume that we have observed the data at n time points $t_1, \ldots, t_n$, and that we fit the model to these n observations using Theorem 3.3. Assume that the model is regular, i.e. that the matrix X defined by $X_{i,j} = f_j(t_i)$, $i = 1, \ldots, n$, $j = 1, \ldots, p$, has full rank. Let $\hat{\beta}_j$ be the estimator of β_j and s^2 the estimator of the variance, as in Theorem 3.3.

(1) The point prediction at time $t_n + \ell$ is

$$\hat{Y}_{t_n}(\ell) = \sum_{j=1}^{p} \hat{\beta}_j f_j(t_n + \ell)$$

(2) An exact prediction interval at level $1 - \alpha$ is

$$\hat{Y}_{t_n}(\ell) \pm \xi \sqrt{1 + g}\, s \tag{5.3}$$

with

$$g = \sum_{j=1}^{p} \sum_{k=1}^{p} f_j(t_n + \ell) G_{j,k} f_k(t_n + \ell)$$

where $G = (X^T X)^{-1}$ and ξ is the $(1 - \frac{\alpha}{2})$ quantile of the student distribution with $n - p$ degrees of freedom, or, for large n, of the standard normal distribution.

(3) An approximate prediction interval that ignores estimation uncertainty is

$$\hat{Y}_{t_n}(\ell) \pm \eta s \tag{5.4}$$

where η is the $1 - \alpha$ quantile of the standard normal distribution.

We now explain the difference between the last two items in the theorem. Item 2 gives an exact result for a prediction interval. It captures two effects:

(1) the *estimation error*, i.e. the uncertainty with regard to the model parameters due to the estimation procedure (term g in $\sqrt{1 + g}$) ;

(2) the *model forecast uncertainty*, due to the model being a random process.

In practice, we often expect the estimation error to be much smaller than the model forecast uncertainty, i.e. g is much smaller than 1. This occurs in the rule when the number n of points used for the estimation is large, so we can also replace student by standard normal. This explains (5.4).

Figure 5.2 shows the prediction intervals computed by Theorem 5.1 and (5.4) (they are indistinguishable). With Theorem 3.3, one can also see that a confidence interval for the point prediction is given by $\pm\xi\sqrt{g}\,s$ (versus $\pm\xi\sqrt{1+g}\,s$ for the prediction interval). The figure shows that the confidence interval for the point prediction is small but not negligible. However, its effect on the prediction interval *is* negligible. Figure 5.4 displays what might happen when the problem is ill posed.

In the simple case where the data is assumed to be iid, we can see from Theorem 2.6 that g decreases like $\frac{1}{n}$, so in this case the approximation in (5.4) is always valid for large n.

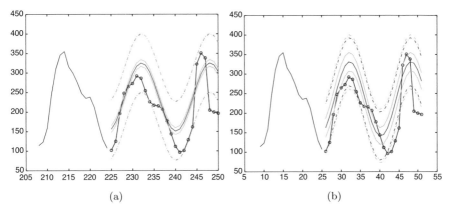

(a)   (b)

Figure 5.2 (a) The same example as in Figure 5.1, showing the prediction interval computed by Theorem 5.1 (dot-dashed lines) and the confidence interval for the point prediction (plain lines around center values). The prediction intervals computed by Theorem 5.1 and (5.4) are indistinguishable. (b) The same, but with only the last 24 points of the past data used to fit the model (instead of 224). The confidence interval for the point prediction is slightly larger than in panel (a); the exact prediction interval computed from Theorem 5.1 is only slightly larger than the approximate one computed from (5.4).

Verification

We cannot verify a prediction until the future comes. However, one can verify how well the model fits by screening the residuals, as explained in Theorem 3.3. The standardized residuals should look grossly normal, and not show any large trends or correlations. Figure 5.3 displays the standardized residuals for the model in Example 5.1. Although the residuals fit the normal assumption well, they do appear to have some correlation and some periodic behavior. Models that are able to better capture these effects are discussed in Section 5.5.

5.3   The Overfitting Problem

Perhaps contrary to intuition, a parametric model should not have too many parameters. To understand why, consider the model in Figure 5.1. Instead of a simple sine function, we now fit a more general model, where we add a

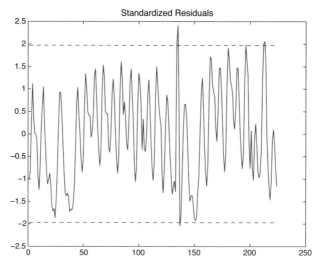

Figure 5.3 Residuals for the model fitted in Figure 5.1.

polynomial component and a more general periodic function (with harmonics), with the hope of improving the fit, and thus the prediction. The new model has the form

$$Y_t = \sum_{i=0}^{d} a_i t^i + \sum_{j=1}^{h} \left(b_j \cos \frac{j\pi t}{8} + c_j \sin \frac{j\pi t}{8} \right) \qquad (5.5)$$

Figure 5.4 shows the resulting fit for a polynomial of degree $d = 10$ and with $h-1 = 2$ harmonics. The fit is better ($\sigma = 25.4375$ instead of 38.2667), however,

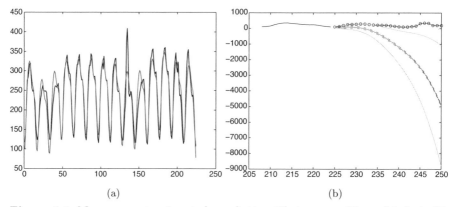

(a)   (b)

Figure 5.4 More parameters is not always better. That same as Figure 5.1, but with a more general model. (b) Prediction intervals computed with the simple formula 5.4 (dot-dashed lines) do not coincide with the exact prediction intervals (plain lines). The line with small circles is the exact values.

the prediction power is ridiculous. This displays the **overfitting problem**. At the extreme, a model with the absolute best fit has 0 residual error – but it is no longer an explanatory model. There are two classical solutions for avoiding overfitting: the use of test data or of information criteria.

5.3.1 Use of Test Data

The idea is to reserve a small fraction of the data set to test the model prediction. Consider for example Figure 5.5. We fitted the model in (5.5) with $h - 1 = 2$ harmonics and a polynomial of degree $d = 0$ to 10. The prediction error is here defined as the mean square error between the true values of the data at $t = 225$ to 250 and the point predictions given by Theorem 5.1. The estimation error is the estimator s of σ. The smallest prediction error is for $d = 4$. The fitting error decreases with d, whereas the prediction error is minimal for $d = 4$. This method is quite general but has the drawback of "burning" some of the data, as the test data cannot be used for fitting the model.

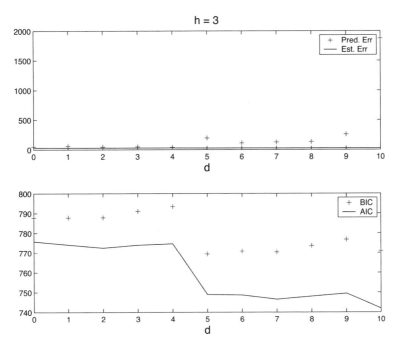

Figure 5.5 Model in (5.5) with $h - 1 = 2$ harmonics and a polynomial of degree $d = 0$ to 10. Top Panel: Use of test data: estimation and prediction errors. Bottom panel: Information criteria. The test data finds that the best model is for $d = 4$, but the information criteria find that the best model is for $d = 10$, which is an aberrant model. Information criteria should be used only for models that match the type of data.

5.3.2   Information Criterion

An alternative is to use an **information criterion**, which strikes a balance between model accuracy and the number of parameters.

Akaike's information criterion (AIC) is defined for any parametric model by

$$\text{AIC} = -2l(\hat{\theta}) + 2k \tag{5.6}$$

where k is the dimension of the parameter θ and $l(\hat{\theta})$ is the estimated log-likelihood. It can be interpreted in an information theoretic sense as follows [105, Section 7.3]. Consider an independent replication X_t of the sequence Y_t; AIC is an estimate of the number of bits needed by an optimal code to describe the sequence X_t, when the optimal code estimates the distribution of X_t from the sample Y_t. AIC thus measures the efficiency of our model to describe the data. The preferred model is the one with the *smallest* information criterion.

For the linear regression model with n data points and p degrees of freedom for $\vec{\beta}$, the parameter is $\theta = (\vec{\beta}, \sigma)$, thus $k = p + 1$. AIC can easily be computed and one obtains

$$\text{AIC} = 2\left(p + n \ln \hat{\sigma}\right) + C \tag{5.7}$$

where $C = 2 + n\left(1 + \ln(2\pi)\right)$ and $\hat{\sigma}$ is the MLE of σ, i.e.

$$\hat{\sigma}^2 = \left(1 - \frac{p}{n}\right) s^2$$

In practice, the AIC had a tendency to overestimate the model order k. An alternative criterion is the **Bayesian information criterion** (BIC) [19, 97], which is defined for a linear regression model by

$$\text{BIC} = -2l(\hat{\theta}) + k \ln n$$

where n is the number of observations. One thus finds

$$\text{BIC} = p \ln n + 2n \ln \hat{\sigma} + C' \tag{5.8}$$

with $C' = n(1 + \ln(2\pi)) + \ln n$ and p is the number of degrees of freedom for the parameter of the linear regression model.

Example 5.2 Internet Traffic, continued

We want to determine the best fit for the model in (5.5). It seems little appropriate to fit the growth in Figure 5.1 by a polynomial of high degree, and we therefore limit d to either $0, 1$ or 2. We utilise three methods: test data, AIC and BIC, and search for all values of $d \in \{0, 1, 2\}$ and $h \in \{0, \ldots, 10\}$. The results are

```
Test Data: d=2, h=2, prediction error = 44.6006
Best AIC : d=2, h=3, prediction error = 46.1003
Best BIC : d=0, h=2, prediction error = 48.7169
```

The test data method finds the smallest prediction error, by definition. All methods find a small number of harmonics, but there are some minor differences. Figure 5.6 shows the values for $d = 1$.

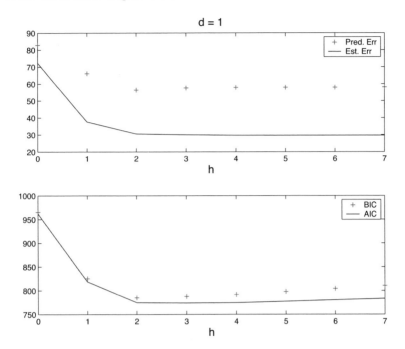

Figure 5.6 Choice of best model for (5.5) with degree $d = 1$ and various values of h. Top panel: The use of test data; estimation and prediction errors. Bottom panel: Information criteria. The prediction error is approximately the same for $h \geq 2$, which implies that the most adequate model is obtained for $h = 2$. The information criteria also find here that the best model is for $h = 2$.

5.4   Differencing the Data

A slightly more sophisticated alternative to the regression method is to combine two approaches: to first capture trends and periodic behavior by application of differencing or de-seasonalizing filters, and then to fit the filtered data to a time series stationary model that allows correlation, as we explain in this and the next section.

5.4.1   Differencing and De-seasonalizing Filters

Consider a time series $Y = (Y_1, \ldots, Y_n)$. Contrary to linear regression modeling, we require here that the indices are contiguous integers, $t = 1, \ldots, n$. The

differencing filter at lag 1 is the mapping, denoted with Δ_1, which transforms a times series Y of finite length into a time series $X = \Delta_1 Y$ of *equal length* such that

$$X_t = \left(\Delta_1 Y\right)_t = Y_t - Y_{t-1} \qquad t = 1, \ldots, n \qquad (5.9)$$

where by convention $Y_j = 0$ for $j \le 0$. Note that this convention is not the best possible, but it simplifies the theory to a large extent. In practice, the implication is that the first term of the filtered series is not meaningful and should not be used for fitting a model (these terms are removed from the plots in Figure 5.7). Formally, we consider Δ_1 to be a mapping from $\bigcup_{n=1}^{\infty} \mathbb{R}^n$ onto itself, i.e. it acts on the time series of any finite length.

The differencing filter Δ_1 is a discrete time equivalent of a derivative. If the data has a polynomial trend of degree $d \ge 1$, then $\Delta_1 Y$ has a trend of degree $d - 1$. Thus, d iterated applications of Δ_1 to the data remove any polynomial trend of degree up to d.

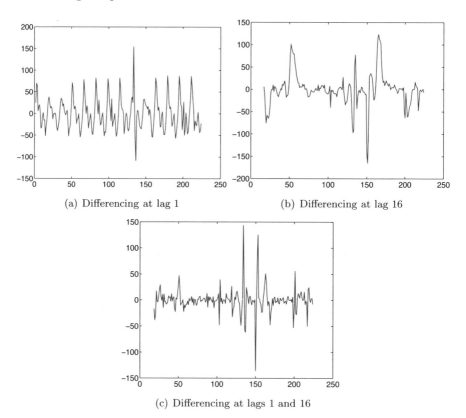

(a) Differencing at lag 1   (b) Differencing at lag 16

(c) Differencing at lags 1 and 16

Figure 5.7 Differencing filters Δ_1 and Δ_{16} applied to Example 5.1 (first terms removed). The forecasts are made under the assumption that the differenced data is iid Gaussian with 0 mean. $\circ$ =actual value of the future (not used for fitting the model).

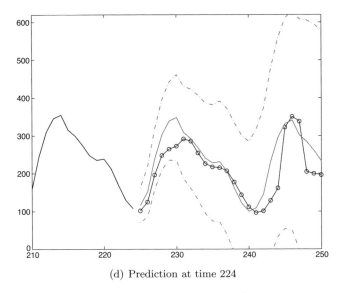

(d) Prediction at time 224

Figure 5.7 (Continuation.)

Similarly, if the data Y is periodic with period s, we can use the **de-seasonalizing** filter R_s (proposed by S.A. Roberts in [89]). It maps a times series Y of finite length into a time series $X = R_s Y$ of *equal length* such that we have

$$X_t = \sum_{j=0}^{s-1} Y_{t-j} \qquad t = 1, \ldots, n \qquad (5.10)$$

again with the convention that $Y_j = 0$ if $j \le 0$. One application of R_s removes a periodic component, in the sense that if Y_t is periodic of period s, then $R_s Y$ is equal to a constant.

The differencing filter at lag s, Δ_s, is defined in a similar manner by

$$\left(\Delta_s X\right)_t = Y_t - Y_{t-s} \qquad (5.11)$$

It can be easily seen that

$$\Delta_s = R_s \, \Delta_1 \qquad (5.12)$$

i.e. combining de-seasonalizing and differencing at lag 1 is the same as differencing at lag s.

Filters *commute*, e.g. $R_{s'} R_s Y = R_s R_{s'} Y$ for all s, s' and $Y \in \mathbb{R}^n$ (see Section D). It follows that the differencing filter and de-seasonalizing filter may be used to remove polynomial growth, non-zero mean and periodicities, and that one can apply them in any order. In practice, one tries to apply R_s once for any identified period d, and Δ_1 as many times as required for the data to appear stationary.

Example 5.3 Internet Traffic

In Figure 5.7, we apply the differencing filter Δ_1 to the time series in Example 5.1 and obtain a strong seasonal component with the period $s = 16$. We then apply the de-seasonalizing filter R_{16}; this is the same as applying Δ_{16} to the original data. The result does not appear to be stationary; for which reason an additional application of Δ_1 is performed.

Also note that if $Y_t = \mu + Z_t$, where Z_t is stationary, then $\Delta_s Y$ has a zero mean.[1] Thus, if after enough differencing we have obtained a stationary but non-zero mean sequence, an additional differencing operation produces a zero mean sequence.

5.4.2 Computing Point Prediction

With many time series, differencing and de-seasonalizing produces a data set that has neither growth nor periodicity. It is thus a good candidate for being fitted to a simple stochastic model. The present section illustrates a straightforward application of this idea. The method used here is also used in Section 5.5 with more elaborate models for the differenced data.

Assume that we have a model for the differenced data X_t that we can employ to obtain predictions for X_t. How can this information be used to derive a prediction for the original data Y_t? There is a very simple solution, based on the properties of filters given in the appendix.

We write compactly $X = LY$, i.e L is the combination of filters that are used (possibly several times each) for differencing and de-seasonalizing. For example, in Figure 5.7, $L = \Delta_{16}\Delta_1$. Δ_s is an invertible filter for all $s \geq 1$, and L is consequently also an invertible filter (see Section D for more details). We can use the AR(∞) representation of L^{-1} and write, using (D.16) in the appendix:

$$Y_t = X_t - g_1 Y_{t-1} - \cdots - g_q Y_{t-q} \qquad (5.13)$$

where $(g_0 = 1, g_1, \ldots, g_q)$ is the impulse response of the filter L. See the next example and Section D for more details on how to obtain the impulse response of L. The following result derives immediately from this and from Theorem D.2:

Proposition 5.2 *Assume that $X = LY$, where L is a differencing or de-seasonalizing filter with impulse response $g_0 = 1, g_1, \ldots, g_q$. Assume that we are able to produce a point prediction $\hat{X}_t(\ell)$ for $X_{t+\ell}$ given that we have observed X_1 to X_t. For example, if the differenced data can be assumed to be iid with a mean of μ, then $\hat{X}_t(\ell) = \mu$.*

---

[1] More precisely $\mathbb{E}(\Delta_s Y_t) = 0$ for $t \geq s + 1$. In other words the first s elements of the differenced time series may not be 0 mean.

A point prediction for $Y_{t+\ell}$ can be obtained iteratively by:

$$\hat{Y}_t(\ell) = \hat{X}_t(\ell) - g_1 \hat{Y}_t(\ell-1) - \cdots$$

$$- g_{\ell-1}\hat{Y}_t(1) - g_\ell y_t - \cdots - g_q y_{t-q+\ell} \qquad \text{for } 1 \le \ell \le q \qquad (5.14)$$

$$\hat{Y}_t(\ell) = \hat{X}_t(\ell) - g_1 \hat{Y}_t(\ell-1) - \cdots - g_q \hat{Y}_t(\ell-q) \qquad \text{for } \ell > q \qquad (5.15)$$

Note that by differencing enough times we are able to remove any non-zero means from the data. Consequently we often assume that $\mu = 0$.

Example 5.4 Internet Traffic, continued

For Figure 5.7, we have

$$L = \Delta_1^2 R_{16} = \Delta_1 \Delta_{16} = (1-B)(1-B^{16}) = 1 - B - B^{16} + B^{17}$$

thus the impulse response g of L is given by

$$g_0 = g_{17} = 1 \qquad g_1 = g_{16} = -1 \qquad g_m = 0 \quad \text{otherwise}$$

If we can assume that the differenced data is iid with 0 mean, the prediction formulae for Y are

$$\hat{Y}_t(1) = Y_t + Y_{t-15} - Y_{t-16}$$

$$\hat{Y}_t(\ell) = \hat{Y}_t(\ell-1) + Y_{t+\ell-16} - Y_{t+\ell-17} \qquad \text{for } 2 \le \ell \le 16$$

$$\hat{Y}_t(17) = \hat{Y}_t(16) + \hat{Y}_t(1) - Y_t$$

$$\hat{Y}_t(\ell) = \hat{Y}_t(\ell-1) + \hat{Y}_t(\ell-16) - \hat{Y}_t(\ell-17) \qquad \text{for } \ell \ge 18$$

5.4.3 Computing Prediction Intervals

If we want not only to obtain point predictions but also to quantify the prediction uncertainty, we need to compute prediction intervals. We consider a special, but frequent case. More general cases can be handled by Monte Carlo methods as explained in Section 5.5.4. The following result derives from Theorem D.2.

Proposition 5.3 *Assume that the differenced data is iid Gaussian, i.e. that $X_t = (LY)_t \sim iid\ N(\mu, \sigma^2)$.*

The conditional distribution of $Y_{t+\ell}$ given that $Y_1 = y_1, \ldots, Y_t = y_t$ is Gaussian with the mean $\hat{Y}_t(\ell)$ obtained from (5.14) and the variance

$$MSE_t^2(\ell) = \sigma^2 \left(h_0^2 + \cdots + h_{\ell-1}^2 \right) \qquad (5.16)$$

where $h_0, h_1, h_2, \ldots$ is the impulse response of L^{-1}. A prediction interval at level 0.95 is thus

$$\hat{Y}_t(\ell) \pm 1.96 \sqrt{MSE_t^2(\ell)} \tag{5.17}$$

Alternatively, one can compute $\hat{Y}_t(\ell)$ using

$$\hat{Y}_t(\ell) = \mu\big(h_0 + \cdots + h_{\ell-1}\big) + h_\ell x_t + \cdots h_{t+\ell-1} x_1 \tag{5.18}$$

The impulse response of L^{-1} can be obtained numerically (for example using the `filter` command), as explained in Section D. If L is not too complicated, it can be obtained in a simple closed form. For example, for $s = 1$, the reverse filter Δ_1^{-1} is defined by

$$\big(\Delta_1^{-1} X\big)_t = X_1 + X_2 + \ldots + X_t \qquad t = 1, \ldots, n$$

i.e. its impulse response is $h_m = 1$ for all $m \geq 0$. It is a discrete time equivalent of integration.

The impulse response of $L = \big(\Delta_1 \Delta_s\big)^{-1}$ used in Figure 5.7 is

$$h_m = 1 + \left\lfloor \frac{m}{16} \right\rfloor \tag{5.19}$$

where the notation $\lfloor x \rfloor$ means the largest integer $\leq x$.

Note that μ and σ need to be estimated from the differenced data.[2] In many cases, differencing produces 0 mean data, so we often assume that $\mu = 0$.

Example 5.5 Internet Traffic, continued

Figure 5.7 shows the prediction obtained assuming the differenced data is iid Gaussian with 0 mean. It is obtained by applying (5.18) with $\mu = 0$, (5.17) and (5.19).

The point prediction is good, but the confidence interval appears to be larger than necessary. Note that the model we use here is extremely simple; we only need to fil one parameter (namely σ), which is estimated as the sample standard deviation of the differenced data.

Compare to Figure 5.1: the point prediction seems to be more exact. Also, it starts just from the previous value. The point prediction with differencing filters is more adaptive than a regression model.

The prediction intervals are large and grow with the prediction horizon. This is a symptom suggesting that the iid Gaussian model for the differenced data may not be appropriate. In fact, there are two deviations from this model: when the distribution does not appear to be Gaussian, and when the differenced data appears to be correlated (large values are not isolated). Addressing these issues requires the fitting of a more complex model to the differenced time series: this is the topic of Section 5.5

---

[2] Here too, the prediction interval does not account for the estimation uncertainty.

5.5   Fitting Differenced Data to an ARMA Model

The method in this section is inspired by the original method of Box and Jenkins in [15] and can be called the **Box-Jenkins** method, although some of the details differ slightly. It applies to cases where the differenced data X appears to be stationary but not iid. In essence, the method provides a method to *whiten* the differenced data, i.e. it computes a filter F such that FX can be assumed to be iid. We first discuss how to recognize whether data can be assumed to be iid.

5.5.1   Stationary but non iid Differenced Data

After pre-processing with differencing and de-seasonalizing filters we have obtained a data set appearing to be *stationary*. We see in Chapter 6 that a stationary model is such that it is statistically impossible to recognize at which time a particular sample was taken. The time series in panel (c) of Figure 5.7 appear to have this property, whereas the original data set in panel (a) does not. In the context of time series, lack of stationarity is due to growth or periodicity: if a data set increases (or decreases), then by observing a sample we can have an idea of whether it is old or young; if there is a daily pattern, we can guess whether a sample is at night or at daytime.

Sample ACF

A means of testing whether a data series that appears to be stationary is iid or not is the **sample autocovariance** function. In analogy with the autocovariance of a process, it is defined, for $t \geq 0$ as

$$\hat{\gamma}_t = \frac{1}{n}\sum_{s=1}^{n-t}\left(X_{n+t} - \bar{X}\right)\left(X_n - \bar{X}\right) \tag{5.20}$$

where $\bar{X}$ is the sample mean. The **sample ACF** is defined as $\hat{\rho}_t = \hat{\gamma}_t / \hat{\gamma}_0$.

The sample PACF is also defined as an estimator of the true PACF (Section C.6)

If $X_1, \ldots, X_n$ are iid with finite variance, then the sample ACF and PACF are asymptotically centered normal with variance $1/n$. ACF and PACF plots usually display the bounds $\pm 1.96/\sqrt{n}$. If the sequence is iid with finite variance, then roughly 95% of the points should fall within the bounds. This provides a method for assessing whether X_t is iid or not. If it is, then no further modeling is required, and we are back to the case in Section 5.4.2. See Figure 5.10 for an example.

The ACF can be tested formally by means of the **Ljung-Box** test. It tests H_0: "the data is iid" versus H_1: "the data is stationary". The test statistic is $L = n(n+2)\sum_{s=1}^{t}\frac{\hat{\rho}_s^2}{n-s}$, where t is a parameter of the test (number of coefficients), typically $\sqrt{n}$. The distribution of L under H_0 is χ_t^2, which can be used to compute the p-value.

5.5.2 ARMA and ARIMA Processes

Once a data set appears to be stationary, but not iid (as in panel (c) of Figure 5.7), we can model it with an **Auto-Regressive Moving Average** (ARMA) process.

Definition 5.1

A 0-mean ARMA(p, q) process X_t is a process that satisfies for $t = 1, 2, \cdots$ a difference equation such as:

$$X_t + A_1 X_{t-1} + \cdots + A_p X_{t-p} = \epsilon_t + C_1 \epsilon_{t-1} + \cdots + C_q \epsilon_{t-q} \qquad \epsilon_t \text{ iid} \sim N_{0,\sigma^2} \tag{5.21}$$

Unless otherwise specified, we assume that $X_{-p+1} = \ldots = X_0 = 0$.

An ARMA(p, q) process with mean the μ is a process X_t such that $X_t - \mu$ is a 0-mean ARMA process and, unless otherwise specified, $X_{-p+1} = \ldots = X_0 = \mu$.

The parameters of the process are $A_1, \ldots, A_p$ (**auto-regressive coefficients**), $C_1, \ldots, C_q$ (**moving average coefficients**) and σ^2 (**white noise variance**). The iid sequence ϵ_t is called the noise sequence, or **innovation**.

An ARMA$(p, 0)$ process is also called an **auto-regressive** process, AR(p); and an ARMA$(0, q)$ process is also referred to as a **Moving Average** process, MA(q).

Since a difference equation, as the one in (5.21), defines a filter with rational transfer function (Section D), one can also define an ARMA process by

$$X = \mu + F\epsilon \tag{5.22}$$

ϵ is an iid Gaussian sequence and

$$F = \frac{1 + C_1 B + \cdots + C_q B^q}{1 + A_1 B + \cdots + A_p B^p} \tag{5.23}$$

B is the backshift operator, see Section D.

In order for an ARMA process to be practically useful, we need the following:

HYPOTHESIS 5.1 *The filter in (5.23) and its inverse are stable.*

In practice, this means that the zeroes of $1 + A_1 z^{-1} + \cdots + A_p z^{-p}$ and of $1 + C_1 z^{-1} + \cdots + C_q z^{-q}$ are within the unit disk.

Equation (5.22) can be used to simulate ARMA processes, as in Figure 5.8.

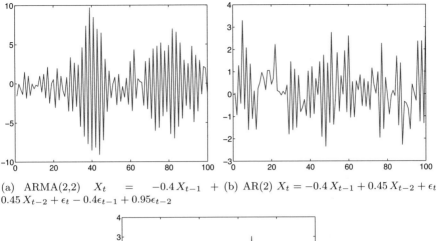

(a) ARMA(2,2) $X_t = -0.4\,X_{t-1} + 0.45\,X_{t-2} + \epsilon_t - 0.4\epsilon_{t-1} + 0.95\epsilon_{t-2}$

(b) AR(2) $X_t = -0.4\,X_{t-1} + 0.45\,X_{t-2} + \epsilon_t$

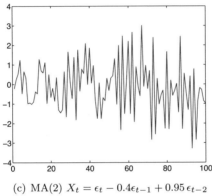

(c) MA(2) $X_t = \epsilon_t - 0.4\epsilon_{t-1} + 0.95\,\epsilon_{t-2}$

Figure 5.8 Simulated ARMA processes with 0 mean and noise variance $\sigma^2 = 1$. The first one, for example, is obtained by the matlab commands `Z=randn(1,n)` and `X=filter([1 -0.4 +0.95],[1 0.4 -0.45],Z)`.

ARMA Process as a Gaussian Process

Since an ARMA process is defined by linear transformation of a Gaussian process ϵ_t, it is itself a Gaussian process. Consequently it is entirely defined by its mean $\mathbb{E}(X_t) = \mu$ and its covariance. The latter can be computed in a number of ways, of which the simplest is perhaps obtained by noticing that

$$X_t = \mu + h_0\epsilon_t + \cdots + h_{t-1}\epsilon_1 \tag{5.24}$$

where h is the impulse response of the filter in (5.23). Note that, with our convention, $h_0 = 1$. It follows that, for $t \geq 1$ and $s \geq 0$, we have

$$\mathrm{cov}(X_t, X_{t+s}) = \sigma^2 \sum_{j=0}^{t-1} h_j h_{j+s} \tag{5.25}$$

For large t

$$\mathrm{cov}(X_t, X_{t+s}) \approx \gamma_s = \sigma^2 \sum_{j=0}^{\infty} h_j h_{j+s} \tag{5.26}$$

The convergence of the latter series follows from the assumption that the filter is stable. Thus, for large t, the covariance does not depend on t. More formally, one can show that an ARMA process with Hypothesis 5.1 is asymptotically stationary ([19], [97]), as required since we want to model stationary data.[3]

Note in particular that

$$\operatorname{var}(X_t) \approx \sigma^2 \sum_{j=0}^{\infty} h_j^2 = \sigma^2 \left(1 + \sum_{j=1}^{\infty} h_j^2 \right) \geq \sigma^2 \qquad (5.27)$$

thus the variance of the ARMA process is larger than that of the noise.[4]

For an MA(q) process, we have $h_j = C_j$ for $j = 1, \ldots, q$, and $h_j = 0$ for $j \geq q$, thus the ACF is 0 at lags $\geq q$.

The **Auto-Correlation Function** (ACF) is defined by $\rho_t = \gamma_t/\gamma_0$.[5] The ACF quantifies departure from an iid model; indeed, for an iid sequence (i.e. $h_1 = h_2 = \ldots = 0$), $\rho_t = 0$ for $t \geq 1$. The ACF can be computed from (5.26) but in practice there are more efficient methods that exploit (5.23), see [105], and which are implemented in standard packages. One also sometimes uses the **Partial Auto-Correlation Function** (PACF), which is defined in Section C.6 as the residual correlation of X_{t+s} and X_t, provided that $X_{t+1}, \ldots, X_{t+s-1}$ are known.[6]

Figure 5.9 shows the ACF and PACF of a few ARMA processes. They all decay exponentially. For an AR(p) process, the PACF is exactly 0 at lags $t > p$.[7]

ARIMA Process

By definition, the random sequence $Y = (Y_1, Y_2, \ldots)$ is an ARIMA(p, d, q) (Auto-Regressive Integrated Moving Average) process if differencing Y d times gives an ARMA(p, q) process (i.e. $X = \Delta_1^d Y$ is an ARMA process, where Δ_1 is the differencing filter at lag 1). For $d \geq 1$, an ARIMA process is not stationary.

---

[3]Furthermore, it can easily be shown that if the initial conditions $X_0, \ldots, X_{-p}$ are not set to 0 as we do for the sake of simplicity, but are drawn from the Gaussian process with mean μ and covariance γ_s, then X_t is (exactly) stationary. We ignore this subtlety in this chapter and consider only asymptotically stationary processes.

[4]Equality occurs only when $h_1 = h_2 = \ldots = 0$, i.e. for the trivial case where $X_t = \epsilon_t$.

[5]Some authors call autocorrelation the quantity γ_t instead of ρ_t.

[6]The PACF is well defined if the covariance matrix of $(X_t, \ldots, X_{t+s})$ is invertible. For an ARMA process, this is always true, according to Corollary C.2.

[7]This follows from the definition of PACF and the fact that X_{t+s} is entirely determined by $X_{t+s-p}, \ldots, X_{t+s-1}$.

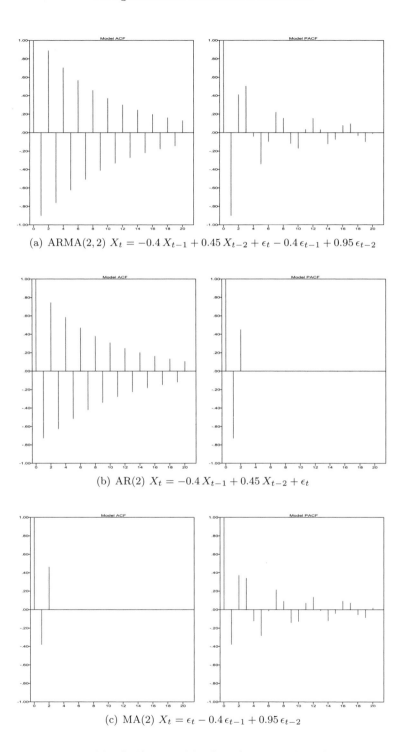

(a) ARMA$(2, 2)$ $X_t = -0.4\, X_{t-1} + 0.45\, X_{t-2} + \epsilon_t - 0.4\, \epsilon_{t-1} + 0.95\, \epsilon_{t-2}$

(b) AR(2) $X_t = -0.4\, X_{t-1} + 0.45\, X_{t-2} + \epsilon_t$

(c) MA(2) $X_t = \epsilon_t - 0.4\, \epsilon_{t-1} + 0.95\, \epsilon_{t-2}$

Figure 5.9 ACF (left) and PACF (right) of some ARMA processes.

In the statistics literature, it is customary to describe an ARIMA(p, d, q) process Y_t by writing

$$(1 - B)^d (1 + A_1 B + \cdots + A_p B^p) Y = (1 + C_1 B + \cdots + C_q B^q) \epsilon \qquad (5.28)$$

which is the same as saying that $\Delta^d Y$ is a zero mean ARMA(p, q) process.

By extension, we also call an ARIMA process a process Y_t such that LY is an ARMA process where L is a combination of differencing and de-seasonalizing filters.

5.5.3   Fitting an ARMA Model

Assume that we have a time series which, after differencing and de-seasonalizing (and possible re-scaling), produces a time series X_t that appears to be stationary and close to Gaussian (i.e it does not have too wild dynamics), but is not iid. We may now think of fitting an ARMA model to X_t.

The ACF and PACF plots can offer some bound of the orders p and q of the model, as there tend to be exponential decay at lags larger than p and q. Note that the samples ACF and PACF make sense only if the data appears to be generated from a *stationary* process. If the data comes from a non-stationary process, this may be grossly misleading (Figure 5.10).

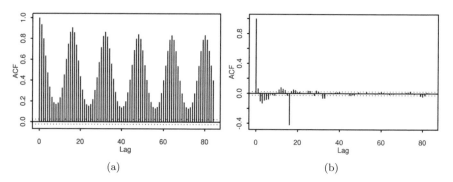

(a)   (b)

Figure 5.10 (a) Sample ACF of the internet traffic of Figure 5.1. The data does not appear to come from a stationary process so the sample ACF cannot be interpreted as an estimation of a true ACF (which does not exist). (b) Sample ACF of data differenced at lags 1 and 16. The sampled data appears to be stationary and the sample ACF decays rapidly. The differenced data appears to be suitable for modeling by an ARMA process.

Maximum Likelihood Estimation of an ARMA or ARIMA Model

Once we have decided on orders p and q, we need to estimate the parameters μ, σ, $A_1, \ldots, A_p$, $C_1, \ldots, C_q$. As usual, this is done by maximum likelihood, which is simplified by the following result.

Theorem 5.4

Consider an ARMA or ARIMA model with parameters as in Definition 5.1. The parameters are constrained to be in a certain set S. Assume that we are given some observed data $x_1, \ldots, x_N$.

(1) The log likelihood of the data is $-\frac{N}{2} \ln\left(2\pi\hat{\sigma}^2\right)$ where

$$\hat{\sigma}^2 = \frac{1}{N} \sum_{t=2}^{N} \left(x_t - \hat{X}_{t-1}(1)\right)^2 \tag{5.29}$$

and $\hat{X}_{t-1}(1)$ is the one step ahead forecast at time $t - 1$.

(2) The maximum likelihood estimation is equivalent to minimizing the mean square one step ahead forecast error $\hat{\sigma}$, subject to the model parameters being in S.

The one step forecasts $\hat{X}_{t-1}(1)$ are computed using Proposition 5.6. Care should be taken to remove the initial values if differencing is performed. Contrary to linear regression, the optimization involved here is non-linear, even if the constraints on the parameter set is linear. The optimizer usually requires some initial guess to run efficiently. For MA(q) or AR(p), there exist estimation procedures (called **moment heuristics**) that do not involve maximum likelihood but are numerically fast [105]. These are based on the observation that for MA(q) or AR(p) processes, if we know the autocovariance function exactly, then we can compute the coefficients numerically.[8] In such cases, we use the sample autocovariance as an estimate of the autocovariance function, whence we deduce an estimate of the parameters of the process. This is less accurate than the maximum likelihood, but is typically used as an initial guess. For example, if we want to compute the maximum likelihood estimate of a general ARMA(p, q) model, we may estimate the parameters μ, σ, $C_1, \ldots, C_q$ of an MA(q) model, using a moment fitting heuristic. As an initial estimate, we then give the same values plus $A_1 = \ldots = A_p = 0$.

It is necessary to verify that the obtained ARMA model corresponds to a stable filter with stable inverse. Good software packages automatically do so, but at times, it may be impossible to obtain both a stable filter and a stable inverse. It is generally admitted that this may be fixed by changing the differencing filter: too little differencing may make it impossible to obtain a stable filter (as the differenced data is not stationary). Conversely, too much differencing may render it impossible to obtain a stable inverse [19].

Determination of Best Model Order

Deciding on the correct order may be done with the help of an information criterion (Section 5.3.2), such as the AIC. For example, assume that we would like to fit the differenced data X_t to a general ARMA(p, q) model, without any

---

[8] For AR(p) processes, the AR coefficients are obtained by solving the "Yule-Walker" equations, using the "Levinson-Durbin" algorithm [105].

constraint on the parameters. We then have $p + q$ coefficients, plus the mean μ and the variance σ^2. Consequently, up to the constant $-N \ln(2\pi)$, which can be ignored, we have

$$\text{AIC} = -N \ln \hat{\sigma}^2 + 2(p + q + 2) \tag{5.30}$$

Note that the AIC counts as degrees of freedom only for continuous parameters, and does thus not count the number of times we applied differencing or de-seasonalizing to the original data. Among all the possible values of p, q and possibly among several applications of differencing or de-seasonalizing filters, we choose the one than minimizes AIC.

Verification of Residuals

The sequence of residuals $e = (e_1, e_2, \ldots)$ is an estimation of the non-observed innovation sequence ϵ. It is obtained by

$$(e_1, e_2, \ldots, e_t) = F^{-1}(x_1 - \mu, x_2 - \mu, \ldots, x_t - \mu) \tag{5.31}$$

where $(x_1, x_2, \ldots)$ is the differenced data and F is the ARMA filter in (5.23). If the model fit is good, the residuals should be roughly independent, therefore the ACF and PACF of the residuals should be close to 0 at all lags.

Note that the residuals can also be obtained from the following proposition (the proof of which easily follows from Corollary D.2, applied to X_t and ϵ_t instead of Y_t and X_t)

Proposition 5.5 (*Innovation Formula*)

$$\epsilon_t = X_t - \hat{X}_{t-1}(1) \tag{5.32}$$

where $\hat{X}_{t-1}(1)$ is the one step ahead prediction at time $t - 1$.

Thus, to estimate the residuals, one can compute the one step ahead predictions for the available data $\hat{x}_{t-1}(1)$, using the forecasting formulae given next. The residuals are then

$$e_t = x_t - \hat{x}_{t-1}(1) \tag{5.33}$$

5.5.4   Forecasting

Once a model is fitted to the differenced data, forecasting is easily derived from Theorem D.2, given in appendix, and its corollaries. Essentially, Theorem D.2 stater that predictions for X and Y are obtained by mapping predictions for ϵ by means of the reverse filters. Since ϵ is iid, predictions for ϵ are trivial: e.g. the point prediction $\hat{\epsilon}_t(h)$ is equal to the mean. One needs to be careful, though, since the first terms of the differenced time series X_t are not exactly known, and one should use recursive formulas that avoid the propagation of errors. This gives the following:

Proposition 5.6 *Assume that the differenced data $X = LY$ is fitted to an ARMA(p, q) model with the mean μ as in Definition 5.1.*

(1) The ℓ-step ahead predictions at time t, $\hat{X}_t(\ell)$, of the differenced data can be obtained for $t \geq 1$ from the recursion

$$\hat{X}_t(\ell) - \mu + A_1\big(\hat{X}_t(\ell - 1) - \mu\big) + \cdots + A_p\big(\hat{X}_t(\ell - p) - \mu\big)$$
$$= C_1\hat{e}_t(\ell - 1) + \cdots + C_q\hat{e}_t(\ell - q)$$

$$\hat{X}_t(\ell) = \begin{cases} X_{t+\ell} & \text{if } \ell \leq 0 \text{ and } 1 \leq t + \ell \\ \mu & \text{if } t + \ell \leq 0 \end{cases}$$

$$\hat{e}_t(\ell) = \begin{cases} 0 & \text{if } \ell \geq 1 \text{ or } t + \ell \leq 0 \\ X_{t+\ell} - \hat{X}_{t+\ell-1}(1) & \text{if } \ell \leq 0 \text{ and } t + \ell \geq 2 \\ X_1 - \mu & \text{if } t + \ell = 1 \text{ and } \ell \leq 0 \end{cases}$$

In the recursion, we allow $\ell \leq 0$ even though we are eventually interested only in $\ell \geq 1$.

(2) Alternatively, $\hat{X}_t(\ell)$ can be computed as follows. Let $(c_0 = 1, c_1, c_2, \ldots)$ be the impulse response of F^{-1}. In such a case,

$$\hat{X}_t(\ell) - \mu = -c_1\big(\hat{X}_t(\ell - 1) - \mu\big) - \cdots - c_{\ell-1}\big(\hat{X}_t(1) - \mu\big) - c_\ell(x_t - \mu) - \cdots$$
$$- c_{t+\ell-t_0}(x_{t_0} - \mu) \qquad \ell \geq 1 \tag{5.34}$$

where $(x_{t_0}, \ldots, x_t)$ is the differenced data observed up to time t, and where t_0 is the length of the impulse response of the differencing and de-seasonalizing filter L.

(3) The ℓ-step ahead predictions at time t, $\hat{Y}_t(\ell)$, of the non-differenced data follow, using Proposition 5.2.

(4) Let $(d_0, d_1, d_2, \ldots)$ be the impulse response of the filter $L^{-1}F$ and

$$\mathrm{MSE}_t^2(\ell) = \sigma^2\big(d_0^2 + \cdots + d_{\ell-1}^2\big) \tag{5.35}$$

A 95% prediction interval for $Y_{t+\ell}$ is

$$\hat{Y}_t(\ell) \pm 1.96 \sqrt{\mathrm{MSE}_t^2(\ell)} \tag{5.36}$$

We now use two steps for computing the point predictions: first for X_t, then for Y_t. One can wonder why, since is possible to utilize a single step, based on the fact that $Y = L^{-1}F\epsilon$. The reason is numerical stability: since the initial values of X_t (or equivalently, the past values Y_s for $s \leq 0$) are not known exactly, there is some numerical error in items 1 and 2. Since we assume that F^{-1} is stable, $c_m \to 0$ for large m, and consequently the values of x_t for small t do not influence the final value of (5.34). Indeed, the non-differenced data x_t for small values of t is not exactly known, as we made the simplifying assumption that $y_s = 0$ for $s \leq 0$. This is also why we remove the first t_0 data points of x in (5.34).

The problem does not exist for the computation of prediction intervals, for which reason we can directly use a single step in item (4). This is due to the variance of the forecast $\mathrm{MSE}_t^2(\ell)$ being independent of the past data (Theorem C.8).

If one insists on using a model such that F is, but not F^{-1}, stable the theorem is still formally true, but may be numerically wrong. It is then preferable to employ the formulae in of [19, Section 3.3] (however, in practice one should avoid using such models).

Point Predictions for an AR(p) 0 Mean Process

The formulae have simple closed forms when there is no differencing or de-seasonalizing and the ARMA process is AR(p) with 0 mean. In such a case, $Y_t = X_t$ and (5.34) becomes (with the usual convention $y_s = 0$ for $s \leq 0$):

$$\hat{Y}_t(\ell) = -\sum_{j=1}^{\ell-1} A_j \hat{Y}_t(\ell - j) - \sum_{j=\ell}^{p} A_j y_{t-j+\ell} \quad \text{for } 1 \leq \ell \leq p$$

$$\hat{Y}_t(\ell) = -\sum_{j=1}^{p} A_j \hat{Y}_t(\ell - j) \quad \text{for } \ell > p$$

where $A_1, A_2, \ldots, A_p$ are the auto-regressive coefficients as in (5.21). As a result of this simplicity, AR processes are often used, e.g. when real time predictions are required.

Example 5.6 Internet Traffic, continued

The differenced data in Figure 5.10 appears to be stationary and has decaying ACF. We model it as a 0 mean ARMA(p, q) process with $p, q \leq 20$ and fit the models to the data. The resulting models have very small coefficients A_m and C_m except for m close to 0 or above 16. Therefore we re-fit the model by forcing the parameters such that

$$A = (1, A_1, \ldots, A_p, 0, \ldots, 0, A_{16}, \ldots, A_{16+p})$$
$$C = (1, C_1, \ldots, C_p, 0, \ldots, 0, C_{16}, \ldots, C_{16+q})$$

for some p and q. The model with smallest AIC in this class is obtained for $p = 1$ and $q = 3$.

Figure 5.11 shows the point predictions and the prediction intervals for the original data. They were obtained by first computing point predictions for the differenced data (using Matlab's `predict` routine) and applying Proposition 5.2. The prediction intervals are made using Proposition 5.6. Compare to Figure 5.7: the point predictions are only marginally different, but the confidence intervals are much better.

We also plot the residuals and see that they appear uncorrelated. Nevertheless, there are some large values that do not appear to be compatible with the Gaussian assumption. Therefore the prediction intervals might be pessimistic. We compute point predictions and prediction intervals by re-sampling from residuals. Figure 5.12 shows that the confidence intervals are indeed smaller.

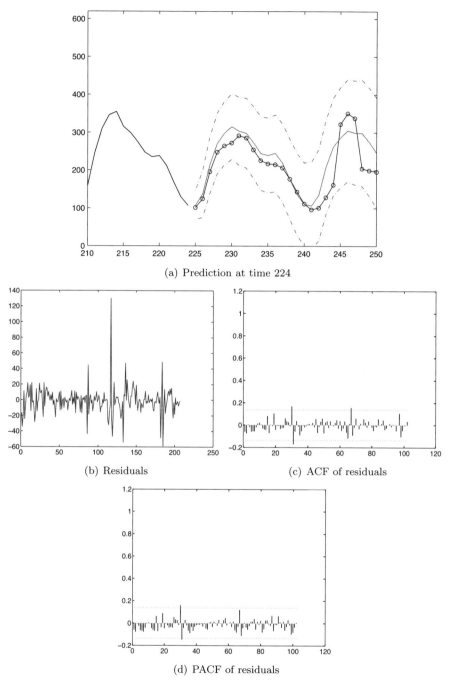

(a) Prediction at time 224

(b) Residuals

(c) ACF of residuals

(d) PACF of residuals

Figure 5.11 Prediction for internet traffic of Figure 5.1, using an ARMA model for the differenced data (○ = actual value of the future, not known at the time of prediction). Compare to Figure 5.7: the point predictions are almost identical, but the prediction intervals are more accurate (smaller).

Use of Bootstrap Replicates

When the residuals appear to be uncorrelated but non-Gaussian, the prediction intervals may be either over- or under-estimated. It is possible to avoid the problem by using a Monte Carlo method (Section 6.4), as explained in the following.

The idea is to draw many independent predictions for the residuals, from which we can derive predictions for the original data (by using reverse filters). There are several possibilities for generating independent predictions for the residuals: one can fit a distribution, or use Bootstrap replicates (i.e. re-sample from the residuals with replacement). We give an algorithm using this latter solution.

Algorithm 5.1 A Monte Carlo computation of prediction intervals at level $1 - \alpha$ for time series Y_t using re-samplig from residuals. We are given: a data set Y_t, a differencing and de-seasonalizing filter L, and an ARMA filter F such that the residual $\epsilon = F^{-1}LY_t$ appears to be iid; the current time t, the prediction lag ℓ and the confidence level α. r_0 is the algorithm's accuracy parameter.

1: $R = \lceil 2\, r_0/\alpha \rceil - 1$ ▷ For example $r_0 = 25$, $R = 999$

2: compute the differenced data $(x_1, \ldots, x_t) = L(y_1, \ldots, y_t)$

3: compute the residuals $(e_q, \ldots, e_t) = F^{-1}(x_q, \ldots, x_t)$ where q is an initial value chosen to remove initial inaccuracies due to differencing or de-seasonalizing (e.g. $q = $ length of impulse response of L)

4: **for** $r = 1 : R$ **do**

5:     draw ℓ numbers with replacement from the sequence $(e_q, \ldots, e_t)$ and call them $\epsilon^r_{t+1}, \ldots, \epsilon^r_{t+\ell}$

6:     let $e^r = (e_q, \ldots, e_t, \epsilon^r_{t+1}, \ldots, \epsilon^r_{t+\ell})$

7:     compute $X^r_{t+1}, \ldots, X^r_{t+\ell}$ using $(x_q, \ldots, x_t, X^r_{t+1}, \ldots, X^r_{t+\ell}) = F(e^r)$

8:     compute $Y^r_{t+1}, \ldots, Y^r_{t+\ell}$ using Proposition 5.2 (with X^r_{t+s} and Y^r_{t+s} in lieu of $\hat{X}_t(s)$ and $\hat{Y}_t(s)$)

9: **end for**

10: $\left(Y_{(1)}, \ldots, Y_{(R)}\right) = \text{sort}\left(Y^1_{t+\ell}, \ldots, Y^R_{t+\ell}\right)$

11: Prediction interval is $[Y_{(r_0)}\,;\, Y_{(R+1-r_0)}]$

The algorithm is basic in that in provides no information of its accuracy. A larger r_0 produces a better accuracy; a more sophisticated algorithm would set r_0 to give less accuracy is small. Also note that, as any bootstrap method, it will likely fail if the distribution of the residuals is heavy-tailed.

An alternative to the bootstrap is to fit a parametric distribution to the residuals; the algorithm is the same as Algorithm 5.1 except that line 5 is changed by the generation of a sample residual from its distribution.

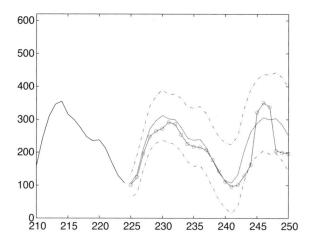

Figure 5.12 Prediction at time 224, with the same model as in Figure 5.11, but obtained with the bootstrap method (re-sampling from residuals).

5.6   Sparse ARMA and ARIMA Models

In order to avoid overfitting, it is desirable to use ARMA models that have as few parameters as possible. Such models are called *sparse*. The use of an information criterion is a means for obtaining sparse models, but it involves a complex non-linear optimization problem. An alternative is to impose constraints on the model, based on various sensible heuristics.

5.6.1   Constrained ARMA Models

A simple method consists in forcing some of the auto-regressive and moving average coefficients to 0, as in Example 5.6. Another approach, more adapted to models with periodicity, is called **seasonal ARIMA**. It assumes that the data has a period s; a seasonal ARMA model is thus an ARMA model where we force the filter F defined in (5.23) to have the form

$$
F = \frac{\left(1 + \sum_{i=1}^{q} c_i B^i\right)\left(1 + \sum_{i=1}^{Q} C_i B^{si}\right)}{\left(1 + \sum_{i=1}^{p} a_i B^i\right)\left(1 + \sum_{i=1}^{P} A_i B^{si}\right)} \tag{5.37}
$$

Y_t is a seasonal ARIMA model and $\Delta_1^d R_s^D Y$ is a seasonal ARMA model, for various non-negative integers d, D. This model is also called **multiplicative ARIMA** model, as the filter polynomials are products of polynomials.

The only difference with the rest of this section when using a seasonal ARIMA model is the fitting procedure, which optimizes the model parameters subject to the constraints (using Theorem 5.4). The forecasting formulae are the same as for any ARIMA or ARMA model.

5.6.2   Holt-Winters Models

Holt-Winters models are very simple, with few parameters. They have emerged empirically, but can be explained as ARIMA models with few parameters. Their interest lies in the simplicity of both fitting and forecasting. Holt-Winters models were originally introduced by Holt and Winters in [41] and [107], and later refined by Roberts in [89]. The presentation below follows that of the latter reference.

Exponentially Weighted Moving Average

This was originally defined as an ad-hoc forecasting formula. The idea is to keep a running estimate estimate $\hat{m}_t$ of the mean of the data, and to update it using the **exponentially weighted moving average** mechanism with parameter a, defined by

$$\hat{m}_t = (1-a)\hat{m}_{t-1} + aY_t \tag{5.38}$$

with initial condition $\hat{m}_t = Y_1$. The point forecast is then simply

$$\hat{Y}_t(\ell) = \hat{m}_t \tag{5.39}$$

Proposition 5.7 ([89])   *EWMA with parameter a is equivalent to modeling of the non-differenced time series with the $ARIMA(0,1,1)$ model defined by*

$$(1-B)Y = \big(1-(1-a)B\big)\epsilon \tag{5.40}$$

with $\epsilon_t \sim iid\ N_{0,\sigma^2}$.

The parameter a can be found by fitting the ARIMA model as usual, using Theorem 5.4, i.e. by minimizing the one step ahead forecast error. There is no constraint on a, though it is classically taken to be between 0 and 1.

The noise variance σ^2 can be estimated using (5.29), which, together with Proposition 5.6, can be used to find prediction intervals. EWMA works well only when the data has no trend or periodicity, see Figure 5.13.

QUESTION 5.1   What is EWMA for $a = 0$? $a = 1$?[9]

Double Exponential Smoothing with Regression

This is another simple model that can be used for data with trend but without season. Just as the simple EWMA, it is based on ad-hoc forecasting formulae that happen to correspond to ARIMA models. The idea is to keep a running estimate of both the mean level $\hat{m}_t$ and the trend $\hat{r}_t$. Further, a discounting

---

[9]$a = 0$: a constant, equal to the initial value; $a = 1$: no smoothing, $\hat{m}_t = Y_t$.

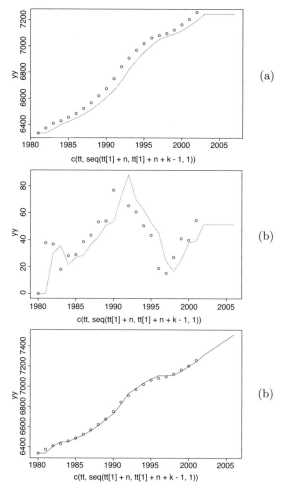

Figure 5.13 (a) A simple EWMA applied to the Swiss population data Y_t with $a = 0.9$. The EWMA is lagging behind the trend. (b) A simple EWMA applied to the differenced series ΔY_t. (c) A prediction reconstructed from the previous graph.

factor ϕ is applied in order to model practical cases where the growth is not linear.

The forecasting equation is

$$\hat{Y}_t(\ell) = \hat{m}_t + \hat{r}_t \sum_{i=1}^{\ell} \phi^i \qquad (5.41)$$

and the update equations are, for $t \geq 3$:

$$\hat{m}_t = (1 - a)\big(\hat{m}_{t-1} + \phi\hat{r}_{t-1}\big) + aY_t \qquad (5.42)$$

$$\hat{r}_t = (1 - b)\phi\hat{r}_{t-1} + b\big(\hat{m}_t - \hat{m}_{t-1}\big) \qquad (5.43)$$

with the initial conditions $\hat{m}_2 = Y_2$ and $\hat{r}_2 = Y_2 - Y_1$. We assume that $0 < \phi \leq 1$; there is no constraint on a and b, although they are generally taken between 0 and 1.

For $\phi = 1$ we have the classical Holt-Winters model, also called **double exponential weighted moving average**; for $0 < \phi < 1$ the model is said "with regression".

Proposition 5.8 ([89])   *Double EWMA with regression is equivalent to modeling the non-differenced data as the zero mean $ARIMA(1, 1, 2)$ process defined by*

$$(1 - B)(1 - \phi B)Y = \left(1 - \theta_1 B - \theta_2 B^2\right)\epsilon \tag{5.44}$$

with

$$\theta_1 = 1 + \phi - a - \phi ab \tag{5.45}$$
$$\theta_2 = -\phi(1 - a) \tag{5.46}$$

where $\epsilon_t \sim iid \; N_{0,\sigma^2}$.

Double EWMA is equivalent to the zero mean $ARIMA(0, 2, 2)$ model

$$(1 - B)^2 Y = \left(1 - \theta_1 B - \theta_2 B^2\right)\epsilon \tag{5.47}$$

with

$$\theta_1 = 2 - a - ab \tag{5.48}$$
$$\theta_2 = -(1 - a) \tag{5.49}$$

The maximum likelihood estimate of a, b and ϕ is obtained as usual by minimizing the one step ahead forecast error. Figure 5.14 shows an example of double EWMA.

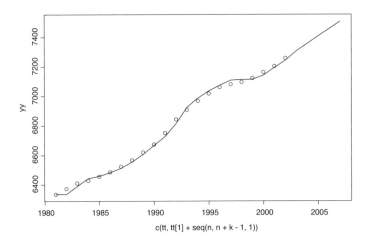

Figure 5.14 Double EWMA with $a = 0.8$, $b = 0.8$. It is a good predictor; it underestimates the trend in convex parts, and overestimates it in concave parts.

Seasonal Models

For time series with a periodic behavior, there exist extensions of the Holt-Winters model, which maintain the same simplicity, and can be explained as ARIMA models. There are several variants, which differ in the choice of certain coefficients.

Assume that we know that the non-differenced data has a period s. The idea is to keep the level and trend estimates $\hat{m}_t$ and $\hat{r}_t$, and to introduce corrections for seasonality $\hat{s}_t(i)$, for $i = 0, \ldots, s-1$. The forecasting formula is [89]:

$$\hat{Y}_t(\ell) = \hat{m}_t + \sum_{i=1}^{\ell} \phi^i \hat{r}_t + w^\ell \hat{s}_t(\ell \bmod s) \tag{5.50}$$

where ϕ and w are discounting factors. The estimates are updated according to (for $t \geq s+2$):

$$\hat{m}_t = a\big(Y_t - w\hat{s}_{t-1}(1)\big) + (1-a)\big(\hat{m}_{t-1} + \phi\hat{r}_{t-1}\big) \tag{5.51}$$

$$\hat{r}_t = b\big(\hat{m}_t - \hat{m}_{t-1}\big) + (1-b)\phi\hat{r}_t \tag{5.52}$$

$$\hat{s}_t(i) = w\hat{s}_{t-1}\big((i+1) \bmod s\big) + D_i e_t \quad \text{for } i = 0, \ldots, s-1 \tag{5.53}$$

where D_i are coefficients to be specified next and $e_t = Y_t - \hat{Y}_{t-1}(1)$.

Initial values of $\hat{m}$, $\hat{r}$, $\hat{s}$ are obtained by using the forecast equations from 1 to j. More precisely, we set $\hat{m}_t = Y_t$ for $t = 1, \ldots, s+1$, $\hat{r}_1 = r$, $\hat{s}_1(j) = s_j$ for $j = 0, \ldots, s-1$ and solve for $r, s_0, \ldots, s_{s-1}$ in

$$Y_{j+1} = Y_1 + r\sum_{i=1}^{j} \phi^i + w^j s_{j \bmod s} \qquad \text{for } j = 1 \ldots s$$

$$0 = \sum_{j=0}^{s-1} s_j$$

After some algebra, this gives the *initial conditions*

$$\hat{m}_{s+1} = Y_{s+1} \tag{5.54}$$

$$\hat{r}_{s+1} = \frac{\displaystyle\sum_{j=1}^{s} (Y_{j+1} - Y_1) w^{s-j}}{\displaystyle\sum_{j=1}^{s} \sum_{i=1}^{j} \phi^{i-s} w^{s-j}} \tag{5.55}$$

$$\hat{s}_{s+1}(0) = Y_{s+1} - Y_1 - \hat{r}_{s+1} \sum_{i=1}^{s} \phi^{i-s} \tag{5.56}$$

$$\hat{s}_{s+1}(j) = \left(Y_{j+1} - Y_1 - \hat{r}_{s+1} \sum_{i=1}^{j} \phi^{i-s}\right) w^{s-j} \qquad \text{for } j = 1, \ldots, s-1 \tag{5.57}$$

Roberts argues that we should impose $\sum_{i=0}^{s} D_i = 0$. **Roberts' seasonal model** is obtained by using an exponential family, i.e.

$$D_0 = 1 - c^{s-1} \tag{5.58}$$

$$D_i = -c^{i-1}(1-c) \qquad \text{for } i = 1, \ldots, s \tag{5.59}$$

for some parameter c.

Proposition 5.9 ([89])   *The Roberts seasonal model with parameters a, b, c, ϕ, w is equivalent to the zero mean ARIMA model*

$$(1 - \phi B)(1 - B)\left(1 + \sum_{i=1}^{s-1} w^i B^i\right) Y = \left(1 - \sum_{i=1}^{s+1} \theta_i B^i\right) \epsilon \tag{5.60}$$

with $\epsilon_t \sim iid\ N_{0,\sigma^2}$ and

$$\theta_1 = 1 + \phi - wc - a(1 + \phi b)$$
$$\theta_i = w^{i-2}\left\{c^{i-2}\left[(1+\phi)wc - \phi - w^2 c^2\right] - (w - \phi)a - w\phi ab\right\}$$
$$\text{for } i = 2, \ldots, s-1$$
$$\theta_s = w^{s-2}\left\{c^{s-2}\left[(1+\phi)wc - \phi\right] - (w-\phi)a - w\phi ab\right\}$$
$$\theta_{s+1} = -\phi w^{s-1}\left(c^{s-1} - a\right)$$

The **Holt-Winters additive seasonal model** is also commonly used. It corresponds to $\phi = 1, w = 1$ (no discounting) and

$$D_0 = c(1 - a) \tag{5.61}$$

$$D_i = 0 \qquad \text{for } i = 1, \ldots, s-1 \tag{5.62}$$

It seems more reasonable to impose $\sum_{i=0}^{s-1} D_i = 0$, and Roberts proposes a variant, the **Corrected Holt-Winters additive seasonal model**, for which $\phi = 1, w = 1$ and

$$D_0 = c(1 - a) \tag{5.63}$$

$$D_i = -\frac{c(1-a)}{s-1} \qquad \text{for } i = 1, \ldots, s \tag{5.64}$$

Proposition 5.10 ([89])   *The Holt-Winters additive seasonal models with parameters a, b, c are equivalent to the zero mean ARIMA models*

$$(1 - B)(1 - B^s)Y = \left(1 - \sum_{i=1}^{s+1} \theta_i B^i\right) \epsilon \tag{5.65}$$

with $\epsilon_t \sim iid\ N_{0,\sigma^2}$ and

$$\theta_1 = (1 - a)(1 + ch) - ab$$
$$\theta_i = -ab \qquad \text{for } i = 2, \ldots, s-1$$
$$\theta_s = 1 - ab - (1 - a)c(1 + h)$$
$$\theta_{s+1} = -(1 - a)(1 - c)$$

with $h = \frac{1}{s-1}$ *(Corrected Holt-Winters additive seasonal model) and $h = 0$ (Holt-Winters additive seasonal model)*.

For all of these models, the parameters can be estimated by minimizing the mean square one step ahead forecast error. Prediction intervals can be obtained from the ARIMA model representations.

There exist many variants of the Holt-Winters seasonal model; see for example [48] for the multiplicative model and other variants.

Example 5.7 Internet Traffic with Roberts Model

We applied the seasonal models in this section to the data set of Figure 5.1. We fitted the models by maximum likelihood, i.e. we minimized the one step ahead forecast error. We obtained prediction intervals by using the ARIMA representation and Proposition 5.6.

The best Roberts seasonal model was obtained for $a = 1$, $b = 0.99$, $c = 0.90$, $\phi = 0.050$ and $w = 1$. The best Holt-Winters additive seasonal model was for $a = 0.090$, $b = 0.037$ and $c = 0.64$. Both corrected and non-corrected Holt-Winters additive seasonal models gave practically the same results.

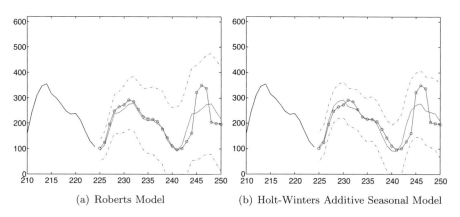

(a) Roberts Model   (b) Holt-Winters Additive Seasonal Model

Figure 5.15 Prediction of the internet traffic of Figure 5.1, using additive seasonal models. ($\circ$ = actual value of the future, not known at the time of prediction). The predictions are less accurate than in Figure 5.11, but the models are much simpler.

5.7   Proofs

Theorem 5.4

Let $X_t - \mu = F\epsilon_t$ where F is the ARMA filter and $\epsilon_t \sim$ iid N_{0,σ^2}. We identify F with an $N \times N$ invertible matrix as in (D.6). Y_t is a Gaussian vector with the mean μ and the covariance matrix $\Omega = \sigma^2 F F^T$. Thus, the log-likelihood of the data $x_1, \ldots, x_N$ is

$$-\frac{N}{2} \ln(2\pi) - N \ln \sigma - \frac{1}{2\sigma^2} \left((x^T - \mu \vec{1}^T) F^{-T} F^{-1} (x - \mu \vec{1}) \right)$$

where x is the column vector of the data and $\vec{1}$ is the column vector with N rows equal to 1. For a given x and F the log-likelihood is at a maximum for

$$\hat{\sigma}^2 = \frac{1}{N} \left((x^T - \mu \vec{1}^T) F^{-T} F^{-1} (x - \mu \vec{1}) \right)^2$$

and is equal to $-\frac{N}{2} \ln(2\pi \hat{\sigma}^2)$. Now

$$\hat{\sigma}^2 = \frac{1}{N} \left\| F^{-1} (x - \mu \vec{1}) \right\|^2$$

and, by definition of the model, $F^{-1}(x - \mu \vec{1})$ is the vector of residuals (i.e. the value of ϵ_t that correspond to the observed data $x_1, \ldots, x_N$). We now employ the innovation formula, (5.32), to conclude the proof.

Proposition 5.7

Assume that EWMA corresponds to an ARIMA model. Let $\epsilon_t = Y_t - \hat{Y}_{t-1}(1)$ be the innovation sequence. Re-write (5.38) as

$$\hat{m}_t = \hat{m}_{t-1} + a\epsilon_t$$

Using filters, this can be written as $\hat{m} = B\hat{m} + a\epsilon$. Combine with $Y = Bm + \epsilon$ and obtain $(1 - B)Y = (1 - (1 - a)B)\epsilon$, which is the required ARIMA model. Conversely, use the forecasting equations in Proposition 5.6) to show that we obtain the desired forecasting equations.

The proofs of Propositions 5.8, 5.9 and 5.10 are similar.

Chapter 6

Discrete Event Simulation

Simulations are often regarded as the simplest, though the most time-consuming, performance evaluation method. However, even a simple simulation program may cause problems, for instance if one is not aware of what stationarity means, or if one is unware of the potential problems that arise when a simulation does not have a stationary regime. We start by discussing this simple but important issue; the related topic of freezing simulations is presented in another chapter (Section 7.4).

Subsequently, we describe two commonly used techniques for implementing a simulation, namely, discrete events and stochastic recurrences, and discuss how confidence intervals can be applied to such settings. Next, we bring up Monte Carlo simulations, viewed here as a method for computing integrals or probabilities, and potential pitfalls regarding random number generators. Finally, we present practical techniques for sampling from a distribution (CDF inversion, rejection sampling).

Importance sampling is an efficient technique for computing estimates of rare events, such as a failure rate or a bit error rate. The main difficulty lies in the choice of an importance sampling distribution. Here too, we propose a very general approach that is widely applicable and does not require heavy developments.

6.1   What is a Simulation?

A simulation is an experiment in a computer (biologists say "in silico") where the real environment is replaced by the execution of a program.

Example 6.1 Mobile Sensors
You want to build an algorithm A for a system of n wireless sensors, carried by mobile users, sending information to a central database. A simulation of the algorithm consists in implementing the essential features of the program in the computer, with one instance of A per simulated sensor. The main difference between a simulation and a real implementation is that the real, physical world (here, the radio channel, with measurements performed by sensors) is replaced by events in the execution of a program.

6.1.1   Simulated Time and Real Time

In a simulation, the flow of time is controlled by the computer. A first task of a simulation program is to simulate parallelism: several parallel actions can take place in the real system, and in the program, they are serialized. Serializing is done by maintaining a *simulated time*, which is that at which an event in the real system is supposed to take place. Every action is then decomposed into instantaneous events (e.g. the beginning of a transmission), and we assume that it is impossible for two instantaneous events to take place at exactly the same time.

Assume for example that every sensor in Example 6.1 should send a message whenever there is a sudden change in its reading, and at most every 10 minutes. It may happen in a simulation program that two or more sensors decide to send a message simultaneously, say within a window of 10 μs. The program may take much more than 10 μs of *real time* to execute these events. In contrast, if no event occurs in the system during 5 minutes, the simulation program may jump to the next event and take just of few ms to execute 5 mn of simulated time. The real time depends on the performance of the computer (processor speed, amount of memory) and of the simulation program.

6.1.2   Simulation Types

There are many different types of simulations, and the following classification can be used.

Deterministic / Stochastic

A deterministic simulation has no random components. It is employed when we want to verify a system where the environment is entirely known, maybe to determine the feasibility of a schedule, or to test the feasibility of an implementation. In most cases however, this is not sufficient. The environment of the system is better modeled with a random component, causing the output of the simulation to also be random.

Terminating / Non-terminating

A terminating simulation ends when specific conditions occurs. For example, if we wish to evaluate the execution time of one sequence of operations in a well defined environment, we can run the sequence in the simulator and count the simulated time. A terminating simulation is typically used when

- we are interested in the lifetime of a certain system
- or when the inputs are time-dependent

Example 6.2 Joe's Computer Shop

We are interested in evaluating the time it takes to serve n customers who request a file together at time 0. We run a simulation program that terminates at time T_1 when all users have had their request satisfied. This is a terminating simulation; its output is the time T_1.

Asymptotically Stationary / Non-stationary

This applies only to a non-terminating, stochastic simulation. Stationarity is a property of the stochastic model being simulated. For an in-depth discussion of stationarity, see Chapter 7.

Very often, the state of the simulation depends on the *initial conditions* and it is difficult to find good initial conditions. For instance, if you simulate an information server and start with empty buffers, you are probably too optimistic, since a real server system that has been running for some time has many data structures that are not empty. Stationarity is a solution to this problem: if the simulator has a unique stationary regime, its distribution of state becomes independent of the initial condition.

A stationary simulation is such that you gain no information of its age by analyzing it. For example, if you run a stationary simulation and take a snapshot of the state of the system at times 10 and 10,000 seconds, there is no way to tell which of the two snapshots is at which time.

In practice, a non-terminating simulation is rarely exactly stationary, but can be *asymptotically stationary*. This means that the simulation becomes stationary after some simulated time.

More precisely, a simulation program with time independent inputs can always be thought of as the simulation of a Markov chain. A Markov chain is a generic stochastic process such that, in order to simulate the future after time t, the only information required is the state of the system at time t.

This is usually what happens in a simulation program. The theory of Markov chains (see Chapter 7) states that the simulation will either converge to some stationary behavior, or diverge. If we wish to measure the performance of the system being studied, it is most likely that we are interested in its stationary behavior.

Example 6.3 Information Server

An information server is modeled as a queue. The simulation program starts with an empty queue. Assume that the arrival rate of requests is smaller than the server can handle. Due to the fluctuations in the arrival process, we expect some requests to be held in the queue, from time to time. After some simulated time, the queue starts to oscillate between busy and idle periods. At the beginning of the simulation, the behavior is not typical of the stationary regime, but after a short time it becomes so (Figure 6.1(a)).

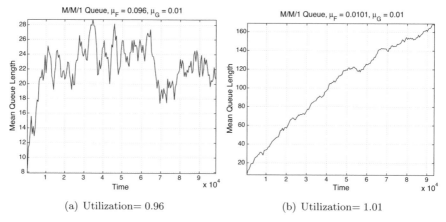

            (a) Utilization= 0.96   (b) Utilization= 1.01

Figure 6.1 A simulation of the information server in Example 6.3, with exponential service and interarrival times. The graphs show the number of requests in the queue as a function of time, for two values of the utilization factor.

If, in contrast, the model is unstable, the simulation output may show a non-converging behavior (Figure 6.1(b)).

In practice, the main reasons for non asymptotic stationarity are the following.

(1) *Unstable* models: In a queuing system where the input rate is larger than the service capacity, the buffer occupancy grows unbounded. The longer the simulation is run, the larger is the mean queue length.

(2) *Freezing* simulation: this is a more subtle form of non-stationarity, where the system does not converge to a steady state but, instead, freezes (becomes slower and slower). This is typically due to the occurrence of rare events of large impact. The longer the simulation, the more likely it is that a rare, but important, event occurs, and the larger the impact of this event

may be. If the simulation has regeneration points (points at which a clean state is reached, for example when the system becomes empty), then the simulation freezes if the time interval between regeneration points has an infinite mean. We study this topic in Section 7.4, where we see an example with the random waypoint.

(3) Models with *seasonal or growth* components, or more generally, time-dependent inputs; e.g. internet traffic grows month after month and is more intense at some times of the day.

In most cases, when you perform a non-terminating simulation, *you should make sure that it is in the stationary regime*. Otherwise, the output of the simulation depends on the initial condition and the length of the simulation, and it is often impossible to decide what are realistic initial conditions may be. It is not always easy, though, to know in advance whether a given simulation model is asymptotically stationary. Chapter 7 provides some examples.

QUESTION 6.1 Among the following sequences X_n, determine which ones are stationary:[1]

(1) X_n, $n \geq 1$ is iid.

(2) X_n $n \geq 1$ is drawn as follows. X_1 is sampled from a given distribution $F(\cdot)$. To obtain X_n, $n \geq 2$ we first flip a coin (and obtain 0 with probability $1 - p$, 1 with probability p). If the coin returns 0, we let $X_n = X_{n-1}$; else, we let $X_n = $ a new sample from the distribution $F(\cdot)$.

(3) $X_n = \sum_{i=1}^{n} Z_i$, $n \geq 1$, where Z_n, $n \geq 1$ is an iid sequence.

6.2   Simulation Techniques

There are numerous ways to implement a simulation program. We here describe two techniques that are commonly used in our context.

6.2.1   Discrete Event Simulation

A large number of computer and communication systems are simulated by means of *discrete event simulation*, for instance with the ns2 or ns3 simulator [1]. It works as follows. The core of the method is to use a global time `currentTime` and an *event scheduler*. Events are objects that represent different transitions; all events have an associated firing time. The event scheduler is a list of events, sorted by increasing firing times. The simulation program

---

[1] (1) Yes.

(2) Yes: (X_1, X_2) has the same joint distribution as for example (X_{10}, X_{11}). In general, $(X_n, X_{n+1}, \ldots, X_{n+k})$ has the same distribution for all n. This is an example of a non-iid, but stationary sequence.

(3) No, in general. For instance, if the common distribution $F(\cdot)$ has a finite variance σ^2, the variance of X_n is $n\sigma^2$, and grows with n, which is contradictory with stationarity.

picks the first event in the event scheduler, advances `currentTime` to the firing time of this event, and executes the event. The execution of an event may schedule new events with firing times $\geq$`currentTime`, and may change or delete events that were previously listed in the event scheduler. The global simulation time `currentTime` *cannot* be modified by an event. Thus, the simulation time jumps from one event firing time to the next – hence the name discrete event simulation. In addition to simulating the logic of the system being modeled, events have to update the counters used for statistics.

Example 6.4 Discrete Event Simulation of a Simple Server

A server receives requests and serves them one by one in order of arrival. The times between request arrivals and the service times are independent of each other. The distribution of the time between arrivals has CDF $F(\cdot)$ and the service time has CDF $G(\cdot)$. The model is in fact a $GI/GI/1$ queue, which stands for general independent inter-arrival and service times. An outline of the program is given below. The program computes the mean response time and the mean queue length.

Classes and Objects. We describe this example using an object-oriented terminology, close to that of the Java programming language. All you need to know about object-oriented programming in order to understand this example is the following. An object is a variable and a class is a type. For example, `arrival23` is the name of the variable that contains all of the information about the 23rd arrival; it is of the class `Arrival`. Classes can be nested, e.g. the class `Arrival` is a sub-class of `Event`. A method is a function for which the definition depends on the class of the object. For instance, the method `execute` is defined for all objects of the class `Event`, and is inherited by all subclasses such as `Arrival`. When the method `execute` is applied to the object `arrival23`, the actions that implement the simulation of an arrival are executed (e.g. the counter of the number of requests in the system is incremented).

Global Variables and Classes.

- `currentTime` is the global simulated time; it can be modified only by the main program.
- `eventScheduler` is the list of events, in order of increasing time.
- An event is an object of the class `Event`. It has an attribute `firingTime` which is the time at which it is to be executed. An event can be executed (i.e. the `Event` class has a method called `execute`), as described later.

  There are three `Event` subclasses: an event of the class `Arrival` represents the actions that occur when a request arrives; `Service` is when a request enters service; `Departure` is when a request leaves the system. The event classes are described in detail later.
- The object `buffer` is the FIFO queue of Requests. The queue length (in number of requests) is `buffer.length`. The number of requests

served so far is contained in the global variable `nbRequests`. The class `Request` is used to describe the requests arriving at the server. At a given point in time, there is one object of the class `Request` for every request present in the system being modeled. An object of the class `Request` has an arrival time attribute.

- Statistics Counters: `queueLengthCtr` is $\int_0^t q(s)ds$ where $q(s)$ is the value of `buffer.length` at time s and t is the current time. At the end of the simulation, the mean queue length is `queueLengthCtr`/T where T is the simulation finish time.

  The counter `responseTimeCtr` holds $\sum_{m=1}^n R_m$, where R_m is the response time for the mth request and n is the value of `nbRequests` at the current time. At the end of the simulation, the mean response time is `responseTimeCtr`/N where N is the value of `nbRequests`.

Event Classes. For each of the three event classes, we now describe the actions taken when an event of this class is "executed".

- `Arrival`: *Execute Event's Actions.* Create a new object of class `Request`, with an arrival time equal to `currentTime`. Queue it at the tail of `buffer`.

  Schedule Follow-Up Events. If `buffer` was empty before the insertion, create a new event of class `Service`, with the same `firingTime` as this event, and insert it into `eventScheduler`.

  Draw a random number Δ from the distribution $F(\cdot)$. Create a new event of class `Arrival`, with `firingTime` equal to this event `firingTime`+Δ, and insert it into `eventScheduler`.

- `Service`: *Schedule Follow-Up Events.* Draw a random number Δ from the distribution $G(\cdot)$. Create a new event of class `Departure`, with `firingTime` equal to this event's `firingTime`+Δ, and insert it into `eventScheduler`.

- `Departure`: *Update Event Based Counters.* Let c be the request at the head of `buffer`. Increment `responseTimeCtr` by $d - a$, where d is this event's `firingTime` and a is the arrival time of the request c. Increment `nbRequests` by 1.

  Execute Event's Actions. Remove the request c from `buffer` and delete it.

  Schedule Follow-Up Events. If `buffer` is not empty after the removal, create a new event of class `Service`, with `firingTime` equal to this event's `firingTime`, and insert it into `eventScheduler`.

Main Program
- *Bootstrapping.* Create a new event of class `Arrival` with `firingTime` equal to 0 and insert it into `eventScheduler`.
- *Execute Events.* While the simulation stopping condition is not fulfilled, do the following.

– *Increment Time Based Counters.* Let `e` be the first event in `eventScheduler`. Increment `queueLengthCtr` by $q(t_{\text{new}} - t_{\text{old}})$ where $q = \texttt{buffer.length}$, $t_{\text{new}} = \texttt{e.firingTime}$ and $t_{\text{old}} = \texttt{currentTime}$
– Execute `e`
– Set `currentTime` to `e.firingTime`
– Delete `e`

• *Termination.* Compute the final statistics:
`meanQueueLength=queueLengthCtr/currentTime`
`meanResponseTime=responseTimeCtr/nbRequests`

Figure 6.2 illustrates the program.

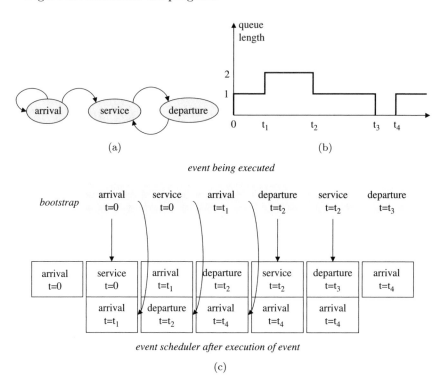

(a)   (b)

(c)

Figure 6.2 (a) Events and their dependencies for Example 6.4. An arrow indicates that an event may schedule another one, (b) a possible realization of the simulation and (c) the corresponding sequence of event execution. The arrows indicate that the execution of the event resulted in one or several new events being inserted into the scheduler.

QUESTION 6.2 Can consecutive events have the same firing time?[2]

---

[2]Yes. In Example 6.4, a `Departure` event when the queue is not empty is followed by a `Service` event with the same firing time.

QUESTION 6.3 What are the generic actions that are executed when an event is executed?[(3)]

QUESTION 6.4 Is the model in Example 6.4 stationary?[(4)]

QUESTION 6.5 Is the mean queue length an event-based or a time-based statistic? The mean response time?[(5)]

6.2.2 Stochastic Recurrence

This is another simulation method; it is usually a much more efficient than discrete event simulation, but requires more work on the model. A **stochastic recurrence** is a recurrence of the form

$$\begin{cases} X_0 = x_0 \\ X_{n+1} = f(X_n, Z_n) \end{cases} \tag{6.1}$$

where X_n is the state of the system at the nth transition (X_n is in some arbitrary state space $\mathcal{X}$), x_0 is a fixed, given state in $\mathcal{X}$, Z_n is some stochastic process that can be simulated (e.g. a sequence of iid random variables, or a Markov chain), and f is a deterministic mapping. The simulated time T_n at which the nth transition occurs is assumed to be included in the state variable X_n.

Example 6.5 Random Waypoint
The **random waypoint** is a model for a mobile point, and can be used to simulate the mobility pattern in Example 6.1. It is defined as follows. The state variable is $X_n = (M_n, T_n)$ where M_n is the position of the mobile at the nth transition (the nth "waypoint") and T_n is the time at which this destination is reached. The point M_n is chosen at random, uniformly in a given convex area $\mathcal{A}$. The speed at which the mobile travels to the next waypoint is also chosen at random uniformly in $[v_{\min}, v_{\max}]$.
The random waypoint model can be cast as a stochastic recurrence by letting $Z_n = (M_{n+1}, V_{n+1})$, where M_{n+1}, V_{n+1} are independent iid sequences, such that M_{n+1} is uniformly distributed in $\mathcal{A}$ and V_{n+1} in $[v_{\min}, v_{\max}]$. We then have the stochastic recurrence

$$X_{n+1} := (M_{n+1}, T_{n+1}) = \left(M_{n+1}, T_n + \frac{\|M_{n+1} - M_n\|}{V_n} \right)$$

[(3)] (1) Update Event-Based Counters.
      (2) Execute Event's Actions.
      (3) Schedule Follow-Up Events.
[(4)] It depends on the parameters. Let a (resp. b) be the mean of $F(\cdot)$ (resp. $G(\cdot)$). The utilization factor of the queue is $\rho = \frac{b}{a}$. If $\rho < 1$ the system is stable and thus asymptotically stationary, else not (see Chapter 8).
[(5)] Mean queue length: time-based. Mean response time: event-based.

See Figure 6.3 for an illustration.

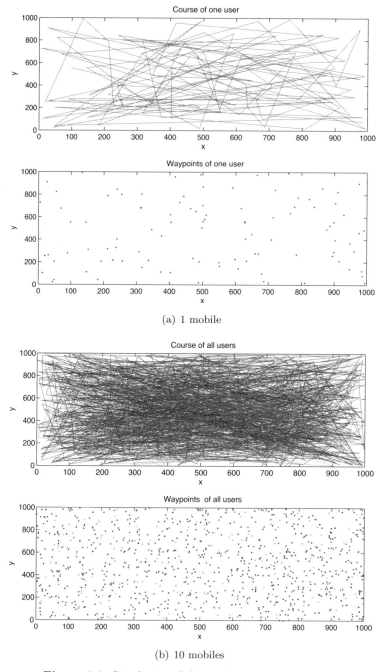

Figure 6.3 Simulation of the random waypoint model.

Once a system is cast as a stochastic recurrence, it can be simply simulated as a direct implementation of (6.1), for example in Matlab.

QUESTION 6.6 Is the random waypoint model asymptotically stationary?[6]

Stochastic Recurrence Versus Discrete Event Simulation

It is always possible to express a stochastic simulation as a stochastic recurrence, as illustrated by the next example. Both representations may have very different memory and CPU requirements; which of the representations that is best depends on the problem at hand.

Example 6.6 Simple Server as a Stochastic Recurrence

(Continuation of Example 6.4). Consider implementing the simple server in Example 6.4 as a stochastic recurrence. To simplify, assume that we are interested only in the mean queue length and not in the mean response time. This can be implemented as a stochastic recurrence as follows. Let $X_n = (t_n, b_n, q_n, a_n, d_n)$ represent the state of the simulator just *after* an arrival or a departure, t_n = the simulated time at which this transition occurs, b_n = `buffer.length`, q_n = `queueLengthCtr` (both just after the transition), a_n = the time interval from this transition to the next arrival and d_n = the time interval from this transition to the next departure.

Let Z_n be a couple of random numbers, drawn independently of anything else, with a distribution that is uniform in $(0, 1)$.
The initial state is

$$t_0 = 0, \quad b_0 = 0, \quad q_0 = 0, \quad a_0 = F^{-1}(u), \quad d_0 = \infty$$

where u is a sample of the uniform distribution on $(0, 1)$. The reason for the formula $a_0 = F^{-1}(u)$ is explained in Section 6.6: a_0 is a sample of the distribution with CDF $F(\cdot)$.
The recurrence is defined by $f\big((t, b, q, a, d), (z_1, z_2)\big) = (t', b', q', a', d')$ with,

> if $a < d$ // this transition is an arrival
> $\quad \Delta = a$
> $\quad t' = t + a$
> $\quad b' = b + 1$
> $\quad q' = q + b\,\Delta$
> $\quad a' = F^{-1}(z_1)$
> $\quad$ if $b == 0$ then $d' = G^{-1}(z_2)$ else $d' = d - \Delta$

---

[6] For $v_{\min} > 0$ it is asymptotically stationary. For $v_{\min} = 0$ it is not: the model "freezes" (the number of waypoints per time unit tends to 0). See Chapter 7 for a justification.

$$\text{else } // \text{ this transition is a departure}$$
$$\Delta = d$$
$$t' = t + d$$
$$b' = b - 1$$
$$q' = q + b\,\Delta$$
$$a' = a - \Delta$$
$$\text{if } b' > 0 \text{ then } d' = G^{-1}(z_1) \text{ else } d' = \infty$$

6.3   Computing the Accuracy of Stochastic Simulations

A simulation program is expected to output certain quantities of interest. For example, for a simulation of the algorithm A it may be the average number of lost messages. The output of a stochastic simulation is random: two different simulation runs produce different outputs. Therefore, it is not sufficient to give a single simulation result; in addition, we need to provide the accuracy of our results.

6.3.1   Independent Replications

A simple and very efficient method for obtaining confidence intervals is to use **replication**. Perform n independent replications of the simulation, each producing an output $x_1, \ldots, x_n$. *Be careful to have truly random seeds* for the random number generators, for example by accessing the computer time (Section 6.5).

6.3.2   Computing Confidence Intervals

We have to choose whether we want a confidence interval for the median or for the mean. The former is straightforward to compute, and should thus be preferred in general.

Methods for computing confidence intervals for medians and means are summarized in Section 2.2.

> **Example 6.7   Application to Example 6.2**
> Figure 6.4 shows the time it takes to transfer all files as a function of the number of customers. The simulation outputs do not appear to be normal, therefore we test whether n is large, by looking at the qq-plot of the the bootstrap replicates. We find that it looks normal, and we can therefore use the Student statistic. Out of curiosity, we also compute the bootstrap percentile estimate and find that both confidence intervals are very close, the bootstrap percentile estimate being slightly smaller.

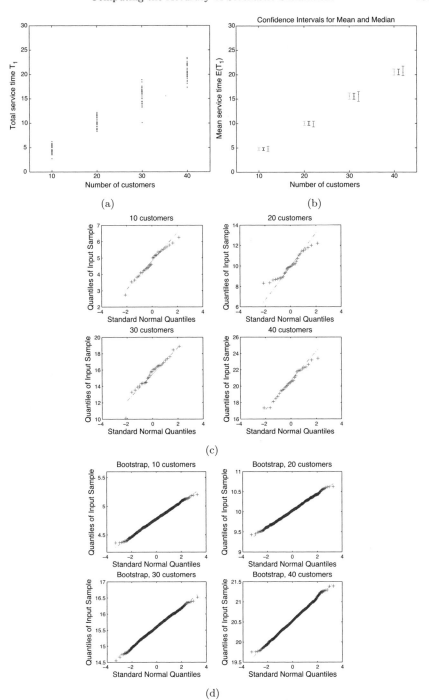

Figure 6.4 The time to serve n files in Joe's computer shop (Example 6.2):
(a) results of 30 independent replications, versus the number of customers;
(b) 95%confidence intervals for the mean obtained with the normal approximation
(left), with the bootstrap percentile estimate (middle); 95% confidence interval for
the median (right); (c) qq-plot of simulation outputs, showing the deviation from
normality; (d) qq-plots of the bootstrap replicates, displaying normality.

There are other methods for obtaining confidence intervals, but they involve specific assumptions of the model and require some care; see for example [49].

6.3.3   Non-Terminating Simulations

Non-terminating simulations should be asymptotically stationary (Section 6.1.2). When you simulate such a model, you should be careful to perform ***transient removal***. This involves determining:

- when to start measuring the output (i.e. the time at which we consider that the simulation has converged to its stationary regime) and
- when to stop the simulation.

Unfortunately, there is no simple, bullet-proof method to determine these two times. In theory, convergence to the stationary regime is governed by the value of the second eigenvalue modulus of the transition matrix of the Markov chain that represents your simulation. In all but very special cases, it is impossible to estimate this value. A practical method for removing transients is to look at the data produced by the simulation, and visually determine a time after which the simulation output does not seem to exhibit a clear trend behavior. For example, in Figure 6.1(a), the measurements could safely start at time $t = 1$. This is the same stationarity test as with time series (Chapter 5).

Determining when to stop a simulation is more tricky. The simulation should be large enough for transients to be removable. After that, you need to estimate whether running the simulation for a long time reduces the variance of the quantities that you are measuring. In practice, this is hard to predict a priori. A rule of thumb is to run the simulation long enough so that the output variable looks Gaussian across several replications, but not longer.

6.4   Monte Carlo Simulation

A ***Monte Carlo simulation*** is a method for computing probabilities, expectations, or, in general, integrals when direct evaluations are impossible or too complex. It simply consists in estimating the expectation as the mean of a number of independent replications.

Formally, assume that we are given a model for generating a data sequence $\vec{X}$. The sequence may be iid or not. Further assume that we want to compute $\beta = \mathbb{E}(\varphi(\vec{X}))$. Note that this covers the case where we wish to compute a probability: if $\varphi(\vec{x}) = 1_{\{\vec{x} \in A\}}$ for some set A, then $\beta = \mathbb{P}(\vec{X} \in A)$.

A Monte Carlo simulation consists in generating R iid replicates $\vec{X}^r$, $r = 1, \ldots, R$. The Monte Carlo estimate of β is

$$\hat{\beta} = \frac{1}{R} \sum_{r=1}^{R} \varphi(\vec{X}^r) \tag{6.2}$$

A confidence interval for β can then be computed using the methods in Chapter 2 (Theorems 2.2 and 2.4). By adjusting R, the number of replications, we can control the accuracy of the method, i.e. the width of the confidence interval.

In particular, the theorem for confidence intervals of success probabilities (Theorem 2.4) should be used when the goal is to find an upper bound on a rare probability and the Monte Carlo estimate returns 0, as illustrated in the example below.

Example 6.8 *p*-value of a test

Let $X_1, \ldots, X_n$ be a sequence of iid random variables that take on values in the discrete set $\{1, 2, \ldots, I\}$. Let $q_i = \mathbb{P}(X_k = i)$, and $N_i = \sum_{k=1}^{n} 1_{\{X_k = i\}}$ (number of observations equal to i). Assume that we want to compute

$$p = \mathbb{P}\left(\sum_{i=1}^{k} N_i \ln \frac{N_i}{nq_i} > a \right) \tag{6.3}$$

where $a > 0$ is given. This computation arises in the theory of goodness of fit tests, when we want to test whether X_i does indeed come from the model defined above (a is then equal to $\sum_{i=1}^{k} n_i \ln \frac{n_i}{nq_i}$ where n_i is our data set). For large values of the sample size n we can approximate β by a χ^2 distribution (see Section 4.4). For small values on the other hand, there is no analytic result.

We use a Monte Carlo simulation to compute p. We generate R iid replicates $X_1^r, \ldots, X_n^r$ of the sequence ($r = 1, \ldots, R$). This can be done by employing the inversion method described in the present chapter. For each replicate r, let

$$N_i^r = \sum_{k=1}^{n} 1_{\{X_k^r = i\}} \tag{6.4}$$

The Monte Carlo estimate of p is

$$\hat{p} = \frac{1}{R} \sum_{r=1}^{R} 1_{\{\sum_{i=1}^{k} N_i \ln \frac{N_i}{nq_i} > a\}} \tag{6.5}$$

Assuming that $\hat{p}R \geq 6$, we compute a confidence interval by using the normal approximation in (2.29). The sample variance is estimated by

$$\hat{\sigma} = \sqrt{\frac{\hat{p}(1 - \hat{p})}{R}} \tag{6.6}$$

and a confidence interval at level 0.95 is $\hat{p} \pm 1.96\hat{\sigma}$. Assume that we want a *relative* accuracy at least equal to some fixed value ϵ (for example $\epsilon = 0.05$). This is achieved if

$$\frac{1.96\,\hat{\sigma}}{\hat{p}} \leq \epsilon \tag{6.7}$$

which is equivalent to

$$R \geq \frac{3.92}{\epsilon^2} \left(\frac{1}{\hat{p}} - 1 \right) \tag{6.8}$$

For every value of R, we can test whether (6.8) is verified and stop the simulation when this is the case. Table 6.1 shows some results with $n = 100$ and $a = 2.4$; we see that p is equal to 0.19 with an accuracy of 5%; the number of Monte Carlo replicates is proportional to the relative accuracy to the power -2.

Table 6.1 Computation of p in Example 6.8 by Monte Carlo simulation. The parameters of the model are $I = 4$, $q_1 = \frac{9}{16}$, $q_2 = q_3 = \frac{3}{16}$, $q_4 = \frac{1}{16}$, $n = 100$ and $a = 2.4$. The table shows the estimate $\hat{p}$ of p with its 95% confidence margin versus the number of Monte Carlo replicates R. With 7680 replicates the relative accuracy (margin/$\hat{p}$) is below 5%.

R	$\hat{p}$	margin
30	0.2667	0.1582
60	0.2500	0.1096
120	0.2333	0.0757
240	0.1917	0.0498
480	0.1979	0.0356
960	0.2010	0.0254
1920	0.1865	0.0174
3840	0.1893	0.0124
7680	0.1931	0.0088

If $\hat{p}R < 6$, we cannot apply the normal approximation. This occurs when the p-value to be estimated is very small. In such cases, typically, we are not interested in an exact estimate of the p-value, but wish to know whether it is smaller than a certain threshold α (for example $\alpha = 0.05$). (2.26) and (2.27) can be used in this case. For example, assume the same data as in Table 6.1, except for $a = 18.2$. We do $R = 10^4$ Monte Carlo replicates and find $\hat{p}R = 0$. We can conclude, with 95% confidence, that $p \leq 1 - (0.025)^{1/R} = 3.7\,E{-}4$ (Theorem 2.4).

QUESTION 6.7 In the first case of Example 6.8 (Table 6.1), what is the conclusion of the test? In the second case?[7]

---

[7] In the first case we accept the null hypothesis, i.e. we believe that the probability of case i is q_i. In the second case, the p-value is smaller than 0.95, and we thus reject the null hypothesis.

6.5   Random Number Generators

The simulation of any random process uses a basic function (such as `rand` in Matlab) that is assumed to return independent uniform random variables. Arbitrary distributions can be derived from there, as explained in Section 6.6.

In fact, `rand` is a ***pseudo-random number generator***. It produces a sequence of numbers that appearing to be random, but which is in fact perfectly deterministic, depending only on one initialization value of its internal states, called the ***seed***. There are several methods to implement pseudo random number generators; all based on chaotic sequences, i.e. iterative processes where a small difference in the seed produces very different outputs.

Simple random number generators are based on ***linear congruences*** of the type $x_n = ax_{n-1} \bmod m$. Here, the internal state after n calls to `rand` is the last output x_n; the seed is x_0. As for any iterative algorithm, the sequence is periodic, but for appropriate choices of a and m, the period may be very large.

Example 6.9   Linear Congruence

A widespread but obsolete generator (for example the default in ns2) has $a = 16,807$ and $m = 2^{31} - 1$. The sequence is $x_n = \frac{sa^n \bmod m}{m}$ where s is the seed. m is a prime number, and the smallest exponent h such that $a^h = 1 \bmod m$ is $m - 1$. It follows that for any value of the seed s, the period of x_n is exactly $m - 1$. Figure 6.5 shows that the sequence x_n indeed looks random.

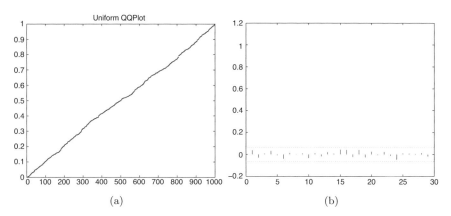

(a)   (b)

Figure 6.5 1000 successive numbers for the generator in Example 6.9. (a) A qq-plot against the uniform distribution in $(0,1)$, showing a perfect match, (b) an autocorrelation function, displaying no significant correlation at any lag, (c) lag plots at various lags, showing independence. Note that there is hovever correlation in dimensions higher than 2, see Example 6.10.

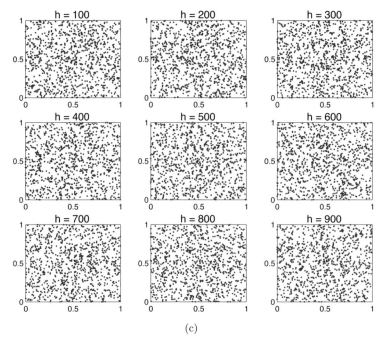

(c)

Figure 6.5 (Continuation.)

The period of a random number generator should be much smaller than the number of times it is called in a simulation. The generator in Example 6.9 has a period of ca. 2×10^9, which may be too small for very large simulations. There

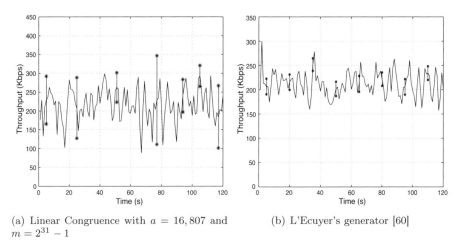

(a) Linear Congruence with $a = 16,807$ and $m = 2^{31} - 1$

(b) L'Ecuyer's generator [60]

Figure 6.6 Simulation outputs for the throughput of TCP connections over a wireless ad-hoc network. The wireless LAN protocol uses random numbers for its operation. This simulation consumes a very large number of calls to `rand`. The simulation results obtained with both generators are different: Lecuyer's generator produces consistently smaller confidence intervals.

are other generators with much longer periods, for example the "Mersenne Twister" [67] with a period of $2^{19,937} - 1$. Such generators use other chaotic sequences and combinations of them.

There is no such thing as a perfect pseudo-random number generator; only truly random generators can be perfect. Such generators exist: for example, a quantum mechanics generator is based on the fact that the state of a photon is believed to be truly random. For a general text on random numbers, see [59]; for software implementing good generators, see [60] and L'Ecuyer's home page. For a general discussion of generators in the framework of simulation, see [40]. Figure 6.6 illustrates a potential problem where the random number generator does not have a long enough period.

Using a Random Number Generator in Parallel Streams

For some (obsolete) generators, as in Example 6.9, the selection of small seed values in parallel streams may introduce a strong correlation (when in fact we would like the streams to be independent).

Example 6.10 Parallel Streams with Incorrect Seeds

Assume that we need to generate two parallel streams of random numbers. This is very frequent in discrete event simulations; we may want to have one stream for the arrival process, and a second one for the service process. Assume that we use the linear congruential generator of Example 6.9, and generate two streams x_n and x'_n with seeds $s = 1$ and $s' = 2$. Figure 6.7 shows the results: the two streams are strongly correlated. In contrast, taking $s' =$ the last value x_N of the first stream does not give rise to this problem.

As mentioned above, more modern generators do not have this problem either.

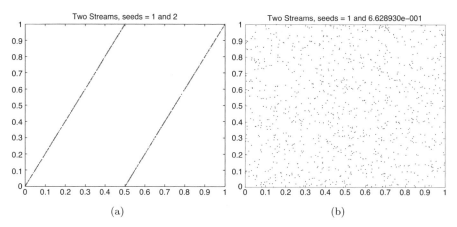

Figure 6.7 x_n versus x'_n for two streams generated with the linear congruential in Example 6.9. (a) Seed values are 1 and 2, (b) seed values are (1, last value of first stream).

Seeding the Random Number Generator

A safe way to make sure that replications are reasonably independent is to use the internal state of the generator at the end of the 1st replication as the seed for the second replication and so one. This way, if the generator has a long enough sequence, the different replications have non overlapping sequences.

In practice, though, we often want independent replications to be run in parallel, so this mode of operation is not possible. A common practice is to take a truly random number as the seed, for example derived from the computer clock or user input with the mouse, see for example random.org.

6.6 How to Sample from a Distribution

In this section, we discuss methods for producing a sample X for a random variable that has a known distribution. We assume that we have a random number generator, providing us with independent samples of the uniform distribution on $(0, 1)$. We focus on two methods of general applicability: CDF inversion and rejection sampling.

6.6.1 CDF Inversion

The method of **CDF inversion**, also called the **percentile inversion method**, applies to real or integer valued random variables, when the CDF is easy to invert.

Theorem 6.1

*Let F be the CDF of a random variable X with values in $\mathbb{R}$. Define the **pseudo-inverse**, F^{-1} of F, by*

$$F^{-1}(p) = \sup\{x : F(x) \le p\}$$

Let U be a sample of a random variable with a uniform distribution on $(0, 1)$; $F^{-1}(U)$ is a sample of X.

Application to real random variables

In the case where X has a positive density over some interval I, F is continuous and strictly increasing on I, and the pseudo-inverse is the inverse of F, as in the next example. It is obtained by solving for x in the equation $F(x) = p$, $x \in $ Id.

Example 6.11 Exponential Random Variable

The CDF of the **exponential distribution** with parameter λ is $F(x) = 1 - e^{-\lambda x}$. The pseudo-inverse (which in this case is the plain inverse) is obtained by solving the equation

$$1 - e^{-\lambda x} = p$$

where x is the unknown. The solution is $x = -\frac{\ln(1-p)}{\lambda}$. Thus a sample X of the exponential distribution is obtained by letting $X = -\frac{\ln(1-U)}{\lambda}$, or, since U and $1-U$ have the same distribution:

$$X = -\frac{\ln(U)}{\lambda} \qquad (6.9)$$

where U is the output of the random number generator.

Application to integer random variables

Assume that N is a random variable with values in $\mathbb{N}$. Let $p_k = \mathbb{P}(N = k)$, then for $n \in \mathbb{N}$

$$F(n) = \sum_{k=0}^{n} p_k$$

and for $x \in \mathbb{R}$

$$\begin{cases} \text{if } x < 0, \text{ then } F(x) = 0 \\ \text{else } F(x) = \mathbb{P}(N \le x) = \mathbb{P}\big(N \le \lfloor x \rfloor\big) = F\big(\lfloor x \rfloor\big) \end{cases}$$

We now compute $F^{-1}(p)$, for $0 < p < 1$. Let n be the smallest integer such that $p < F(n)$. The set $\{x : F(x) \le p\}$ is equal to $(-\infty, n)$ (Figure 6.8); the supremum of this set is n, thus $F^{-1}(p) = n$. In other words, the pseudo inverse is given by

$$F^{-1}(p) = n \iff F(n-1) \le p < F(n) \qquad (6.10)$$

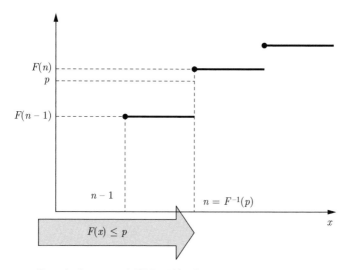

Figure 6.8 Pseudo-Inverse of CDF $F(\cdot)$ of an integer-valued random variable.

We have thus shown the following statement.

Corollary 6.1 *Let N be a random variable with values in $\mathbb{N}$ and let $p_k = \mathbb{P}(N = k)$, for $k \in \mathbb{N}$. A sample of N is obtained by setting N to the unique index n such that $\sum_{k=0}^{n-1} p_k \leq U < \sum_{k=0}^{n} p_k$, where U is the output of the random number generator.*

Example 6.12 Geometric Random Variable

Here, X takes on integer values $0, 1, 2, \ldots$ The **geometric distribution** with parameter θ satisfies $\mathbb{P}(X = k) = \theta(1 - \theta)^k$. Consequently, $n \in \mathbb{N}$

$$F(n) = \sum_{k=0}^{n} \theta(1 - \theta)^k = 1 - (1 - \theta)^{n+1}$$

By application of (6.10)

$$F^{-1}(p) = n \iff n \leq \frac{\ln(1 - p)}{\ln(1 - \theta)} < n + 1$$

hence

$$F^{-1}(p) = \left\lfloor \frac{\ln(1 - p)}{\ln(1 - \theta)} \right\rfloor$$

and, since U and $1 - U$ have the same distribution, a sample X of the geometric distribution is

$$X = \left\lfloor \frac{\ln(U)}{\ln(1 - \theta)} \right\rfloor \tag{6.11}$$

QUESTION 6.8 Consider the function defined by `COIN(p)= if rand()<p 0 else 1`. What does it compute?[8]

QUESTION 6.9 Compare (6.9) and (6.11).[9]

6.6.2 Rejection Sampling

The method of **rejection sampling** is widely applicable. It can be used to generate samples of random variables when the inversion method does not work easily. It applies to random vectors of any dimension.

The method is based on the following result, which is of independent interest. It allows to sample from a distribution given in conditional form.

---

[8] It generates a sample of the Bernoulli random variable that takes on the value 0 with p and the value 1 with probability $1 - p$.

[9] They are similar, in fact we have $N = \lfloor X \rfloor$ if we let $\lambda = \ln(1 - \theta)$. This follows from the fact that if $X \sim \exp(\lambda)$, then $\lfloor X \rfloor$ is geometric with parameter $\theta = 1 - e^{-\lambda}$.

Theorem 6.2 (Rejection Sampling for a Conditional Distribution)

Let X be a random variable in some space S such that the distribution of X is the conditional distribution of $\tilde{X}$, given that $\tilde{Y} \in \mathcal{A}$. Here, $(\tilde{X}, \tilde{Y})$ is a random variable in $S \times S'$ and $\mathcal{A}$ is a measurable subset of S.

A sample of X is obtained by the following algorithm:

> **do**
>> *draw a sample of* $(\tilde{X}, \tilde{Y})$
>> **until** $\tilde{Y} \in \mathcal{A}$
>> **return**$(\tilde{X})$

The expected number of iterations of the algorithm is $\frac{1}{\mathbb{P}(\tilde{Y} \in \mathcal{A})}$.

Example 6.13 Density Restricted to Arbitrary Subset

Consider a random variable in some space $(\mathbb{R}, \mathbb{R}^n, \mathbb{Z}, \ldots)$ that has a density $f_Y(y)$. Let $\mathcal{A}$ be a set such that $\mathbb{P}(Y \in \mathcal{A}) > 0$. We are interested in the distribution of a random variable X for which the density is that of Y, restricted to $\mathcal{A}$:

$$f_X(y) = K f_Y(y) 1_{\{y \in \mathcal{A}\}} \tag{6.12}$$

where $K^{-1} = \mathbb{P}(Y \in \mathcal{A}) > 0$ is a normalizing constant. This distribution is the conditional distribution of Y, given that $Y \in \mathcal{A}$.

QUESTION 6.10 Show this.[10]

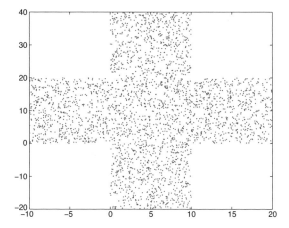

Figure 6.9 1000 independent samples of the uniform distribution over $\mathcal{A} =$ the interior of the cross. Samples are obtained by generating uniform samples in the bounding rectangle and rejecting those samples that do not fall in $\mathcal{A}$.

---

[10] For any (measurable) subset $\mathcal{B}$ of the space, $\mathbb{P}(X \in \mathcal{B}) = K \int_{\mathcal{B}} f_Y(y) 1_{\{y \in \mathcal{A}\}} \, dy = K \mathbb{P}(Y \in \mathcal{A} \text{ and } Y \in \mathcal{B}) = \mathbb{P}(Y \in \mathcal{B} \mid Y \in \mathcal{A})$.

Thus, a sampling method for the distribution with density in (6.12) is to draw samples of the distribution with density f_Y until a sample that belongs to $\mathcal{A}$ is found. The expected number of iterations is $\frac{1}{\mathbb{P}(Y \in \mathcal{A})}$.

For example, consider the sampling of a random point X, uniformly distributed on some bounded area $\mathcal{A} \subset \mathbb{R}^2$. We can consider this density as the restriction of the uniform density on some rectangle $\mathcal{R} = [x_{\min}, x_{\max}] \times [y_{\min}, y_{\max}]$ that contains the area $\mathcal{A}$. Thus, a sampling method is to draw points uniformly in $\mathcal{R}$, until we find one in $\mathcal{A}$. The expected numbers of iterations is the ratio of the area of $\mathcal{R}$ to that of $\mathcal{A}$; one should thus be careful to pick a rectangle that is close to $\mathcal{A}$. Figure 6.9 shows a sample of the uniform distribution over a non-convex area.

QUESTION 6.11 How can one generate a sample of the uniform distribution over $\mathcal{R}$?[11]

Now we come to a very general result, for all distributions that have a density.

Theorem 6.3 (Rejection Sampling for Distribution with Density)
Consider two random variables X, Y with values in the same space, that both have densities. Assume that:

- *we know a method for drawing a sample of X*
- *the density of Y is known up to a normalization constant K: $f_Y(y) = K f_Y^n(y)$, where f_Y^n is a known function*
- *there exist some $c > 0$ such that*

$$\frac{f_Y^n(x)}{f_X(x)} \leq c$$

A sample of Y is obtained by the following algorithm:

> **do**
> > draw independent samples of X and U, where $U \sim \text{Unif}(0, c)$
> **until** $U \leq \frac{f_Y^n(X)}{f_X(X)}$
> **return**(X)

The expected number of iterations of the algorithm is $\frac{c}{K}$.

A frequent application of Theorem 6.3 is the following.

Arbitrary Distribution with Density

Assume that we want a sample of Y, which takes on values in the bounded interval $[a, b]$ and has a density $f_Y = K f_Y^n(y)$. Assume that $f_Y^n(y)$ (non-normalized density) can be easily computed, but not the normalization constant K, which is unknown. Also assume that we know an upper bound M on f_Y^n.

---

[11]The coordinates are independent and uniform: generate two independent samples $U, V \sim \text{Unif}(0, 1)$; the sample is $\big((1 - U)x_{\min} + U x_{\max}, (1 - V)y_{\min} + V y_{\max}\big)$.

We take X uniformly distributed over $[a, b]$ and obtain the sampling method

> **do**
> > draw $X \sim \text{Unif}(a, b)$ and $U \sim \text{Unif}(0, M)$
> **until** $U \leq f_Y^n(X)$
> **return**(X)

Note that we do *not* need to know the multiplicative constant K. For example, consider the distribution with density

$$f_Y(y) = K \frac{\sin^2(y)}{y^2} 1_{\{-a \leq y \leq a\}} \tag{6.13}$$

K is hard to compute, but a bound M on f_Y^n is easy to find ($M = 1$) (Figure 6.10).

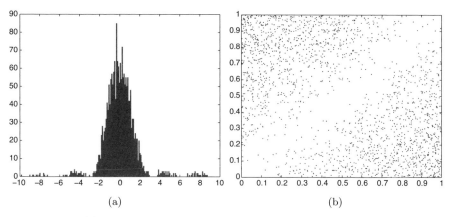

(a)   (b)

Figure 6.10 (a) An empirical histogram of 2000 samples of the distribution with density $f_X(x)$ proportional to $\frac{\sin^2(x)}{x^2} 1_{\{-a \leq y \leq a\}}$ with $a = 10$. (b) 2000 independent samples of the distribution on the rectangle with density $f_{X_1, X_2}(x_1, x_2)$ proportional to $|x_1 - x_2|$.

Example 6.14 A Stochastic Geometry Example

We want to sample the random vector (X_1, X_2) that takes on values in the rectangle $[0, 1] \times [0, 1]$ and whose distribution has a density proportional to $|X_1 - X_2|$. We take f_X = the uniform density over $[0, 1] \times [0, 1]$ and $f_Y^n(x_1, x_2) = |x_1 - x_2|$. An upper bound on the ratio $\frac{f_Y^n(x_1, x_2)}{f_X(x_1, x_2)}$ is 1. The sampling algorithm is thus

> **do**
> > draw X_1, X_2 and $U \sim \text{Unif}(0, 1)$
> **until** $U \leq |X_1 - X_2|$
> **return**(X_1, X_2)

Figure 6.10(b) shows an example. Note that we do not need to know the normalizing constant to apply the sampling algorithm.

6.6.3   Ad-Hoc Methods

The methods of inversion and rejection sampling may be improved in some special cases. We mention in detail the case of the normal distribution, which is important to optimize because of its frequent use.

Sampling a Normal Random Variable

The method of inversion cannot be directly used, as the CDF is hard to compute. An alternative is based on the method of *change of variables*, as given in the next proposition, the proof of which is by direct calculus.

Proposition 6.4   *Let (X, Y) be independent, standard normal random variables. Let*

$$\begin{cases} R = \sqrt{X^2 + Y^2} \\ \Theta = \arg(X + jY) \end{cases}$$

R *and* Θ *are independent,* R *has a Rayleigh distribution (i.e it is positive with the density* $r\,e^{-r^2/2}$*) and* Θ *is uniformly distributed on* $[0, 2\pi]$*.*

The CDF of the Rayleigh distribution can easily be inverted: $F(r) = \mathbb{P}(R \leq r) = 1 - e^{-r^2/2}$ and $F^{-1}(p) = \sqrt{-2\ln(1-p)}$. A sampling method for a couple of independent standard normal variables is thus (***Box-Müller method***)

> draw $U \sim \text{Unif}(0, 1)$ and $\Theta \sim \text{Unif}(0, 2\pi)$
> $R = \sqrt{-2\ln(U)}$
> $X = R\cos(\Theta), \; Y = R\sin(\Theta)$
> **return**(X, Y)

Correlated Normal Random Vectors

We want to sample $(X_1, \ldots, X_n)$ as a normal random vector with a zero mean and a covariance matrix Ω (Section C.2). If the covariance matrix is diagonal (i.e. $\Omega_{i,j} = 0$ for $i \neq j$), then X_is are independent and we can sample them one by one (or better, two by two). We are interested here in the case where there is some correlation.

The method we show here is again based on a change of variable. There always exists a change of basis in $\mathbb{R}^n$ such that, in the new basis, the random vector has a diagonal covariance matrix. In fact, there are many such bases (one of them is orthonormal and can be obtained by diagonalization of Ω, but is much more expensive than the method we discuss next). An inexpensive and stable algorithm to obtain one such basis is called Choleski's factorization method. It finds a triangular matrix L such that $\Omega = LL^T$. Let Y be a standard normal vector (i.e. an iid sequence of n standard normal random variables). Further, let $X = LY$. The covariance matrix of X is

$$\mathbb{E}(XX^T) = \mathbb{E}\big(LY(LY)^T\big) = \mathbb{E}\big(L(YY^T)L^T\big) = L\mathbb{E}(YY^T)L^T = LL^T = \Omega$$

Thus, a sample of X can be obtained by sampling Y first and computing LY. Figure 6.11 shows an example.

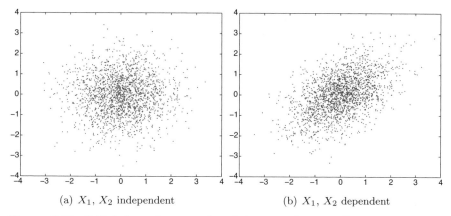

(a) X_1, X_2 independent   (b) X_1, X_2 dependent

Figure 6.11 1000 independent samples of the normal vector X_1, X_2 with 0 mean and covariance $\Omega_{1,1} = \sigma_1^2 = 1$, $\Omega_{2,2} = \sigma_2^2 = 1$ and $\Omega_{1,2} = \Omega_{2,1} = 0$ (left), $\Omega_{1,2} = \Omega_{2,1} = \frac{1}{2}$ (right). The right sample is obtained by the transformation $X = LY$ with Y iid $\sim N_{0,1}$ and $L = (1, 0; \frac{1}{2}, \frac{\sqrt{3}}{2})$.

There are many ways to optimize the generation of samples. Good references are [108] and [90]

6.7   Importance Sampling

6.7.1   Motivation

It is occassionaly desirable to estimate by simulation the probability of a **rare event**, e.g. a failure probability or a bit error rate. In such cases, straightforward Monte Carlo simulation is not efficient, as it requires a large number of runs to provide a reliable estimate. As an example, assume that the failure probability to be estimated is 10^{-5}. With R independent replications of a Monte Carlo simulation, the expected number or runs producing one failure is $\frac{N}{10^{-5}}$, and we consequently need 10^7 runs to be able to observe 100 failures. In fact, we require on the order of $4 \cdot 10^7$ runs to obtain a 95% confidence interval with a margin on the failure probability around 10%, as we show next.

Assume that we want to estimate a failure probability p, by performing R replications. A naive Monte Carlo estimate is $\hat{p} = \frac{N}{R}$ where N is the number of runs producing a failure. A $1 - \alpha$ confidence interval for p has a length of of η times the standard deviation of $\hat{p}$, where $N_{0,1}(\eta) = 1 - \frac{\alpha}{2}$. The relative accuracy of the estimator is ηc, where c is the coefficient of variation of $\hat{p}$. Now

$$c = \frac{\sqrt{\dfrac{p(1-p)}{R}}}{p} = \frac{\sqrt{1-p}}{\sqrt{Rp}} \approx \frac{1}{\sqrt{Rp}}$$

where the approximation is for very small p. Assume that we want a relative accuracy on our estimation of p equal to β. We should take $\frac{\eta}{\sqrt{Rp}} = \beta$, i.e.

$$R = \frac{\eta^2}{\beta^2 p} \tag{6.14}$$

For instance, for $\alpha = 0.05$, we have $\eta = 1.96$ and thus for $\beta = 0.10$, we should take $R \approx \frac{400}{p}$.

6.7.2 The Importance Sampling Framework

Importance sampling is a method that can be used to reduce the number of required runs in a Monte Carlo simulation, when the events of interest (e.g. the failures) are rare. The idea is to modify the distribution of the random variable to be simulated, in a way such that the impact of the modification can be exactly compensated, and such that, for the modified random variable, the events of interest are not rare.

Formally, assume that we simulate a random variable X in $\mathbb{R}^d$, with PDF $f_X(\cdot)$. Our goal is to estimate $p = \mathbb{E}\big(\phi(X)\big)$, where ϕ is the metric of interest.

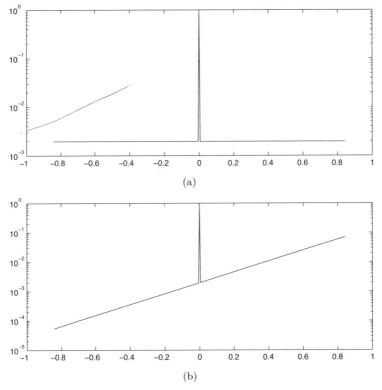

Figure 6.12 (a) Log of the PDF of X_1 in Example 6.15. (b) log of the PDF of the twisted distribution (i.e. the distribution of $\hat{X}_1$) when $\theta = 4.2$.

Frequently, $\phi(x)$ is the indicator function, equal to 1 if the value x corresponds to a failure of the system, and 0 otherwise. We replace the original PDF $f_X(\cdot)$ by another one, $f_{\hat{X}}(\cdot)$, called the PDF of the *importance sampling distribution*, on the same space $\mathbb{R}^d$. We assume that

$$\text{if } f_X(x) > 0, \text{ then } f_{\hat{X}}(x) > 0$$

i.e. the support of the importance sampling distribution contains that of the original one. For x in the support of $f_X(\cdot)$, define the *weighting function*

$$w(x) = \frac{f_X(x)}{f_{\hat{X}}(x)} \tag{6.15}$$

We assume that $w(x)$ can be easily evaluated. Let $\hat{X}$ be a random variable for which the distribution is that of the importance sampling. We also assume that it is easy to draw a sample of $\hat{X}$.

It comes immediately that

$$\mathbb{E}\big(\phi(\hat{X})w(\hat{X})\big) = \mathbb{E}\big(\phi(X)\big) = p \tag{6.16}$$

which is the fundamental equation of importance sampling. An estimate of p is thus given by

$$p_{\text{est}} = \frac{1}{R} \sum_{r=1}^{R} \phi(\hat{X}_r)w(\hat{X}_r) \tag{6.17}$$

where $\hat{X}_r$ are R independent replicates of $\hat{X}$.

Why would this be easier than the original problem? Assume that we have found a sampling distribution for which the events of interest are not rare. It follows that $w(x)$ is very small, but $\phi(\hat{X})$ is not. So the events $\phi(\hat{X}) = 1$ are not rare, and can be reproduced many times in a short simulation. The final result, p, is small because we weight the outputs $\phi(\hat{X})$ by small numbers.

Example 6.15 Bit Error Rate and Exponential Twisting

The Bit Error Rate on a communication channel with impulsive interferers can be expressed as [68]

$$p = \mathbb{P}\left(X_0 + X_1 + \cdots + X_d > a\right) \tag{6.18}$$

where $X_0 \sim N_{0,\sigma^2}$ is the thermal noise and X_j, $j = 1, \ldots, d$, represents impulsive interferers. The distribution of X_j is discrete, with support in $\{\pm x_{j,k}, \ k = 1, \ldots, n\} \cup \{0\}$ and

$$\mathbb{P}(X_j = \pm x_{j,k}) = q$$
$$\mathbb{P}(X_j = 0) = 1 - 2nq$$

where $n = 40$, $q = \frac{1}{512}$ and the array $\{\pm x_{j,k}, \ k = 1, \ldots, n\}$ are given numerically by channel estimation (Table 6.2 shows a few examples, for $d = 9$). The variables X_j, $j = 0, \ldots, d$, are independent. For large values of d, we could approximate p by a Gaussian approximation, but it can easily be verified that, for d on the order of 10 or less, this does not hold [68].

Table 6.2 Sample numerical values of $x_{j,k}$ for Example 6.15; the complete list of values is available at the book's web site.

k	$j=1$	$j=2$	$j=3$	$j=4$	$j=5$	$j=6$	$j=7$	$j=8$	$j=9$
1	0.4706	0.0547	0.0806	0.0944	0.4884	0.3324	0.4822	0.3794	0.2047
2	0.8429	0.0683	0.2684	0.2608	0.0630	0.1022	0.1224	0.0100	0.0282
$\vdots$				$\vdots$					

A direct Monte Carlo estimation (without importance sampling) gives the following results (R is the number of Monte Carlo runs required to reach 10% accuracy with confidence 95%, as of (6.14)):

σ	a	BER estimate	R
0.1	3	$(6.45 \pm 0.6) \times 10^{-6}$	6.2×10^7

We now apply importance sampling in order to reduce the required number of simulation runs R. We consider importance sampling distributions derived by **exponential twisting**, i.e. we define the distribution of $\hat{X}_j$, $j = 0, \ldots, d$ by

$$\begin{cases} \hat{X}_j \text{ has the same support as } X_j \\ \mathbb{P}(\hat{X}_j = x) = \eta_j(\theta) e^{\theta x} \mathbb{P}(X_j = x) \end{cases}$$

where $\eta_j(\theta)$ is a normalizing constant. This gives

$$\mathbb{P}(X_j = -x_{j,k}) = \eta_j(\theta) q \, e^{-\theta x_{j,k}}$$
$$\mathbb{P}(X_j = x_{j,k}) = \eta_j(\theta) q \, e^{\theta x_{j,k}}$$
$$\mathbb{P}(X_j = 0) = \eta_j(\theta)(1 - 2nq)$$
$$\eta_j(\theta)^{-1} = q \sum_{k=1}^{n} \left(e^{-\theta x_{j,k}} + e^{\theta x_{j,k}} \right) + 1 - 2nq$$

Similarly, the distribution of the Gaussian noise $\hat{X}_0$ is obtained by multiplying the PDF of the standard normal distribution by $e^{\theta x}$ and normalizing according to

$$f_{\hat{X}_0}(x) = \eta_0 \frac{1}{\sqrt{2\pi}\sigma} e^{-x^2/2\sigma^2} e^{\theta x}$$
$$= \eta_1 e^{\theta^2 \sigma^2/2} \frac{1}{\sqrt{2\pi}\sigma} e^{-(x-\theta\sigma^2)^2/2\sigma^2}$$

Thus, $\eta_0 = e^{-\theta^2 \sigma^2 / 2}$ and $\hat{X}_0$ is normally distributed with same variance as X_0 but with the mean $\sigma^2 \theta$ instead of 0. Note that for $\theta > 0$, $\hat{X}_j$ is more likely to take on large values than X_j. The weighting function is

$$w(x_0, \ldots, x_d) = e^{-\theta \sum_{j=0}^{d} x_j} \frac{1}{\prod_{j=0}^{d} \eta_j} \qquad (6.19)$$

We perform R Monte Carlo simulations with $\hat{X}_j$ in lieu of X_j; the estimate of p is

$$p_{\text{est}} = \frac{1}{R} \sum_{r=1}^{R} w\left(\hat{X}_0^r, \ldots, \hat{X}_d^r\right) 1_{\{\hat{X}_0^r + \cdots + \hat{X}_d^r > a\}} \qquad (6.20)$$

Note that $\theta = 0$ corresponds to a direct Monte Carlo simulation (without importance sampling). All simulations give the same estimated value $p \approx 0.645 \, E - 05$, but the required number of simulation runs in order to reach the same accuracy varies by more than 3 orders of magnitude (Figure 6.13(a)).

6.7.3 Selecting An Importance Sampling Distribution

The previous example shows that importance sampling can dramatically reduce the number of Monte Carlo runs for estimating rare events, but also that it is important to carefully choose the importance sampling distribution, as a wrong choice might offer no improvement (or might even be worse).

A first observation can be derived from the analysis of Figure 6.13: the best choice is when the probability of the event of interest, under the importance sampling distribution, is close to 0.5 (i.e. $\mathbb{E}(\phi(\hat{X})) \approx 0.5$). Note that, perhaps contrary to intuition, selecting $\mathbb{E}(\phi(\hat{X})) \approx 1$ is a very bad choice. In other words, we need to make the events of interest less rare, but not too certain. This can be explained as follows. If we take $\mathbb{E}(\phi(\hat{X})) \approx 1$, the simulator has a hard time producing samples where the event of interest does *not* occur, which is as bad as the initial problem.

A second observation is that we can evaluate the efficiency of an importance sampling estimator of p by its variance

$$\hat{v} = \text{var}\left(\phi(\hat{X}) w(\hat{X})\right) = \mathbb{E}\left(\phi(\hat{X})^2 w(\hat{X})^2\right) - p^2$$

Assume that we want a $1 - \alpha$ confidence interval of relative accuracy β. With a reasoning similar to that in (6.14), the required number of Monte Carlo estimates is

$$R = \hat{v} \frac{\eta^2}{\beta^2 p^2} \qquad (6.21)$$

Thus, it is proportional to $\hat{v}$. In the formula, η is defined by $N_{0,1}(\eta) = 1 - \frac{\alpha}{2}$; e.g. with $\alpha = 0.05, \beta = 0.1$, we need $R \approx \frac{400 \, \hat{v}}{p^2}$.

The problem is consequently to find a sampling distribution that minimizes $\hat{v}$, or, equivalently, $\mathbb{E}\big(\phi(\hat{X})^2 w(\hat{X})^2\big)$. The theoretical solution can be obtained by calculus of variation; it can be shown that the optimal sampling distribution $f_{\hat{X}}(x)$ is proportional to $|\phi(x)| f_X(x)$. In practice, however, it is impossible to compute, since we assume in the first place that it is hard to compute $\phi(x)$.

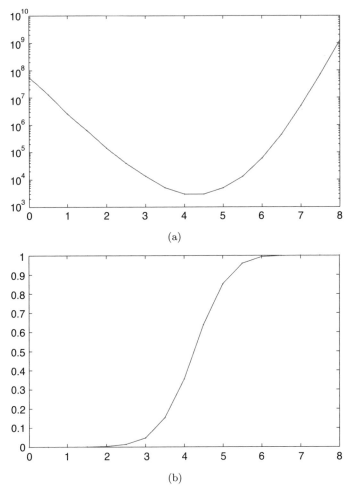

(a)

(b)

Figure 6.13 (a) The required number of simulation runs to estimate the bit error rate in Example 6.15 with 10% of relative accuracy, using an importance sampling distribution with parameter θ (on x-axis). All simulation estimates give the same estimated value of $p = 0.645\,E - 05$, but the required number of simulation runs R is proportional to the variance. (b) All simulations estimate p by the formula $p = \mathbb{E}\big(\phi(\hat{X})w(\hat{X})\big)$; the panel shows $\mathbb{E}\big(\phi(\hat{X})\big)$, i.e. the probability that there is a bit error when $\hat{X}$ is drawn from the importance sampling distribution with parameter θ. For $\theta = 0$ we have the true value $p = 0.645\,E - 05$. The smallest number of runs, i.e. the smallest variance, is obtained when $\mathbb{E}\big(\phi(\hat{X})\big) \approx 0.5$.

In Algorithm 6.1, we give a heuristic method, which combines these two observations. Assume that we have at our disposal a family of candidate importance sampling distributions, indexed by a parameter[12] $\theta \in \Theta$. The function varEst($\cdot$) estimates, by Monte Carlo, whether a given θ satisfies $\mathbb{E}(\phi(\hat{X})) \approx 0.5$. If so, it returns an estimate of $\mathbb{E}(\phi(\hat{X})^2 w(\hat{X})^2)$, otherwise it returns ∞. Note that the number of Monte Carlo runs required by varEst($\cdot$) is small, since we

---

Algorithm 6.1 The determination of a good Importance Sampling distribution. We wish to estimate $p = \mathbb{E}(\phi(X))$, where X is a random variable with values in $\mathbb{R}^d$ and $\phi(x) \in [0; 1]$; $\hat{X}$ is drawn from the importance sampling distribution with parameter θ; $w(\cdot)$ is the weighting function (6.15).

1: **function** MAIN
2: $\quad \eta = 1.96; \beta = 0.1; \text{pCountMin} = 10;$ ▷ β is the relative accuracy
3:   ▷ of the final result
4: $\quad$ GLOBAL $R_0 = 2\frac{\eta^2}{\beta^2};$ ▷ Typical number of iterations
5:                        ▷ R_0 chosen by (6.14) with $p = 0.5$
6: $\quad R_{\max} = 1E + 9;$ ▷ Maximum number of iterations
7: $\quad c = \frac{\beta^2}{\eta^2};$
8:
9: $\quad$ Find $\theta_0 \in \Theta$ which minimizes varest(θ);
10:
11: $\quad$ pCount0$= 0$; pCount$= 0$; $m_2 = 0$;
12: $\quad$ **for** $r = 1 : R_{\max}$ **do**
13: $\quad\quad$ draw a sample x of $\hat{X}$ using parameter θ_0;
14: $\quad\quad$ pCount0=pCount0+$\phi(x)$;
15: $\quad\quad$ pCount=pCount+$\phi(x)w(x)$;
16: $\quad\quad m_2 = m_2 + (\phi(x)w(x))^2;$
17: $\quad\quad$ **if** $r \geq R_0$ and pCountMin $<$ pCount $< r-$ pCountMin **then**
18: $\quad\quad\quad p = \dfrac{\text{pCount}}{r};$
19: $\quad\quad\quad v = \frac{m_2}{r} - p^2;$
20: $\quad\quad\quad$ **if** $v \leq cp^2 r$ **then break**
21: $\quad\quad\quad$ **end if**
22: $\quad\quad$ **end if**
23: $\quad$ **end for**
24: $\quad$ **return** p, r
25: **end function**

---

[12] For simplicity, we do not show the dependency on θ in expressions such as $\mathbb{E}(\phi(\hat{X}))$, which could be more accurately described as $\mathbb{E}(\phi(\hat{X}) \mid \theta)$.

Algorithm 6.1 (Continued.)

26: **function** VAREST(θ) $\triangleright$ Test if $\mathbb{E}\big(\phi(\hat{X})\big) \approx 0.5$

27: $\triangleright$ and if so estimate $\mathbb{E}\big(\phi(\hat{X})^2 w(\hat{X})^2\big)$

28:       CONST $\hat{p}_{\min} = 0.3$, $\hat{p}_{\max} = 0.7$;

29:       GLOBAL R_0;

30:       $\hat{p} = 0$; $m_2 = 0$;

31:       **for** $r = 1 : R_0$ **do**

32:            draw a sample x of $\hat{X}$ using parameter θ;

33:            $\hat{p} = \hat{p} + \phi(x)$;

34:            $m_2 = m_2 + \big(\phi(x)w(x)\big)^2$;

35:       **end for**

36:       $\hat{p} = \frac{\hat{p}}{R}$;

37:       $m_2 = \frac{m_2}{R}$;

38:       **if** $\hat{p}_{\min} \leq \hat{p} \leq \hat{p}_{\max}$ **then**

39:            **return** m_2;

40:       **else**

41:            **return** ∞;

42:       **end if**

43: **end function**

---

are interested only in returning results in the cases where $\mathbb{E}\big(\phi(\hat{X})\big) \approx 0.5$. In other words, we are not in the case of rare events.

The first part of the algorithm (line 9) consists in selecting one value of θ minimizing varEst(θ). This can be done by random exploration of the set Θ, or by any heuristic optimization method (such as Matlab's `fminsearch`).

The second part (lines 11 to 24) uses the best θ and importance sampling as explained earlier. The algorithms perform as many Monte Carlo samples as required to obtain a given accuracy level, using (6.21) (line 20).

Example 6.16 Bit Error Rate, re-visited

We can apply Algorithm 6.1 directly. With the same notation as in Example 6.15, an estimate of $\hat{v}$, the variance of the importance sampling estimator, is

$$\hat{v}_{\text{est}} = \frac{1}{R}\sum_{r=1}^{R} w\big(\hat{X}_0^r, \ldots, \hat{X}_d^r\big)^2 1_{\{\hat{X}_0^r + \cdots + \hat{X}_d^r > a\}} - p_{\text{est}}^2 \qquad (6.22)$$

We computed $\hat{v}_{\text{est}}$ for several values of θ; Figure 6.13 shows the corresponding values of the required number of simulation runs R (to reach 10% accuracy with confidence 95%), as given by (6.21)).

Alternatively, one could use the following optimization. We can avoid the simulation of a normal random variable by noticing that (6.18) can be replaced by

$$
\begin{aligned}
p &:= \mathbb{P}\big(X_0 + X_1 + \ldots + X_d > a\big) \\
&= \mathbb{P}\big(X_0 > a - (X_1 + \cdots + X_d)\big) \\
&= \mathbb{E}\Big(\mathbb{P}\big(X_0 > a - (X_1 + \cdots + X_d) \mid X_1, \ldots, X_d\big)\Big) \\
&= \mathbb{E}\left(1 - N_{0,1}\left(\frac{a - (X_1 + \cdots + X_d)}{\sigma}\right)\right) := \mathbb{E}\big(\phi(X_1 + \cdots + X_d)\big)
\end{aligned}
$$

where, as usual, $N_{0,1}(\cdot)$ is the cdf of the standard normal distribution and $\phi(x) = 1 - N_{0,1}(x)$. The problem is thus to compute $\mathbb{E}\big(\phi(X_1 + \cdots + X_d)\big)$.

We applied Algorithm 6.1 with the same numerical values as in Example 6.15 and with exponential twisting. Note the difference with Example 6.15: we modified the distributions of $X_1, \ldots, X_d$ but not of the normal variable X_0. The best θ is now obtained for $\mathbb{E}\big(\phi(\hat{X})\big) \approx 0.55$ (instead of 0.5) and the number of simulation runs required to achieve the same level of accuracy is slightly reduced.

In the above example, we restricted the choice of the importance sampling distribution to an exponential twist, with the same parameter θ for all random variables $X_1, \ldots, X_d$. There are of course many possible variants; one might for instance use a different θ for each X_j, or employ various methods of twisting the distribution (for example re-scaling). Note however that the complexity of the choice of an importance sampling distribution should not outweigh its final benefits. So, in general, we should aim for simple solutions. The interested reader will find a general discussion and overview of other methods in [98].

6.8   Proofs

Theorem 6.1

The pseudo-inverse has the property that [51, Thm 3.1.2]

$$
F(x) \geq p \Longleftrightarrow F^{-1}(p) \leq x
$$

Let $Y = F^{-1}(U)$. Consequently, $\mathbb{P}(Y \leq y) = \mathbb{P}\big(F(y) \leq U\big) = F(y)$ and the CDF of Y is $F(\cdot)$.

Theorem 6.2

Let N be the (random) number of iterations of the algorithm, and let $(\tilde{X}_k, \tilde{Y}_k)$ be the sample drawn at the kth iteration. (These samples are independent, but in general, $\tilde{X}_k$ and $\tilde{Y}_k$ are *not* independent.) Let $\theta = \mathbb{P}(\tilde{Y} \in \mathcal{A})$. We assume $\theta > 0$, otherwise the conditional distribution of $\tilde{X}$ is not defined. The output of the algorithm is $X = \tilde{X}_N$.

For some arbitrary measurable $\mathcal{B}$ in S, we compute $\mathbb{P}(\tilde{X}_N \in \mathcal{B})$:

$$\mathbb{P}(\tilde{X}_N \in \mathcal{B}) = \sum_{k \geq 1} \mathbb{P}(\tilde{X}_k \in \mathcal{B} \text{ and } N = k)$$

$$= \sum_{k \geq 1} \mathbb{P}(\tilde{X}_k \in \mathcal{B} \text{ and } \tilde{Y}_1 \notin \mathcal{A}, \dots, \tilde{Y}_{k-1} \notin \mathcal{A}, \tilde{Y}_k \in \mathcal{A})$$

$$= \sum_{k \geq 1} \mathbb{P}(\tilde{X}_k \in \mathcal{B} \text{ and } \tilde{Y}_k \in \mathcal{A}) \mathbb{P}(\tilde{Y}_1 \notin \mathcal{A}) \cdots \mathbb{P}(\tilde{Y}_{k-1} \notin \mathcal{A})$$

$$= \sum_{k \geq 1} \mathbb{P}(\tilde{X}_k \in \mathcal{B} \mid \tilde{Y}_k \in \mathcal{A}) \theta (1 - \theta)^{k-1}$$

$$= \sum_{k \geq 1} \mathbb{P}(\tilde{X}_1 \in \mathcal{B} \mid \tilde{Y}_1 \in \mathcal{A}) \theta (1 - \theta)^{k-1}$$

$$= \mathbb{P}(\tilde{X}_1 \in \mathcal{B} \mid \tilde{Y}_1 \in \mathcal{A}) \sum_{k \geq 1} \theta (1 - \theta)^{k-1}$$

$$= \mathbb{P}(\tilde{X}_1 \in \mathcal{B} \mid \tilde{Y}_1 \in \mathcal{A})$$

The second equality is by definition of N. The third is by the independence of $(\tilde{X}_k, \tilde{Y}_k)$ and $(\tilde{X}_{k'}, \tilde{Y}_{k'})$ for $k \neq k'$. The last equality is because $\theta > 0$. This shows that the distribution of X is as required.

$N - 1$ is geometric with parameter θ, and thus the expectation of N is $\frac{1}{\theta}$.

Theorem 6.3

Apply Theorem 6.2 with $\tilde{X} = X$ and $\tilde{Y} = (X, U)$. All we need to show is that the conditional density of X, given that $U \leq \frac{f_Y^n(X)}{f_X(X)}$ is f_Y.

To this end, pick some arbitrary function ϕ. We have

$$\mathbb{E}\left(\phi(X) \mid U \leq \frac{f_Y^n(X)}{f_X(X)}\right) = K_1 \mathbb{E}\left(\phi(X) 1_{\{U \leq \frac{f_Y^n(X)}{f_X(X)}\}}\right)$$

$$= K_1 \int \mathbb{E}\left(\phi(x) 1_{\{U \leq \frac{f_Y^n(x)}{f_X(x)}\}} \mid X = x\right) f_X(x) \, dx$$

$$= K_1 \int \phi(x) \frac{f_Y^n(x)}{f_X(x)} f_X(x) \, dx$$

$$= \frac{K_1}{K} \int \phi(x) f_Y(x) \, dx = \frac{K_1}{K} \mathbb{E}(\phi(Y))$$

where K_1 is some constant. This is true for all ϕ, and thus, necessarily, $\frac{K_1}{K} = 1$ (take $\phi = 1$).

6.9   Review

6.1 How do you generate a sample of a real random variable with PDF $f(\cdot)$ and CDF $F(\cdot)$?[13]

6.2 Why do we care about stationarity?[14]

6.3 What is rejection sampling?[15]

6.4 How do you generate a sample of a discrete random variable?[16]

6.5 What is importance sampling?[17]

6.6 Why do we need to run independent replications of a simulation? How are they obtained?[18]

6.7 Consider the sampling method: Draw `COIN(p)` until it returns 0. The value of the sample N is the number of iterations. Which distribution is that a sample from? Is this a good method?[19]

6.8 If we do a direct Monte Carlo simulation (i.e without importance sampling) of a rare event, the theorem for confidence intervals of success probabilities (Theorem 2.4) gives a confidence interval. So why do we need importance sampling?[20]

---

[13] In many cases matlab does it. If not, and if $F(\cdot)$ is easily invertible, use CDF inversion. Otherwise, if $f(\cdot)$ has a bounded support, use rejection sampling.

[14] Non-terminating simulations depend on the initial conditions, and on the length of the simulation. If the simulator has a stationary regime, we can eliminate the impact of the simulation length (in simulated time) and of the initial conditions.

[15] Drawing independent samples of an object with some probability distribution $p(\cdot)$, leads to a certain condition C being met. The result is a sample of the conditional probability $p(\cdot \mid C)$.

[16] With the method of CDF inversion. Let p_k be the probability of outcome k, $k = 1, \ldots, n$, and $F_k = p_1 + \cdots + p_k$ (with $F_0 = 0$). Draw $U \sim \text{Unif}(0,1)$; if $F_k \le U < F_k$, then let $N = k$.

[17] A method for computing probabilities of rare events. It consists in changing the initial probability distribution in order to make rare events less rare (but not certain).

[18] To obtain confidence intervals. By running multiple instances of the simulation program; if done sequentially, the seed of the random generator can be carried over from one run to the next. If replications are done in parallel on several machines, the seeds should be chosen independently by truly random sources.

[19] The distribution of N is geometric with $\theta = 1 - p$, so this method produces a sample from a geometric distribution. However, it draws in average $\frac{1}{\theta}$ random numbers from the generator, and the random number generator is usually considered an expensive computation compared to a floating point operation. If θ is small, the procedure in Example 6.12 (by CDF inversion) is much more efficient.

[20] Assume that we simulate a rare event, without importance sampling, and that we find 0 success out of R Monte Carlo replicates. Theorem 2.4 gives a confidence interval for the probability of success equal to $[0, \frac{3.869}{R}]$ at confidence level 0.95. For instance, if $R = 10^4$, we can say that $p < 4 \cdot 10^{-4}$. Importance sampling will give more, it will provide an estimate of, for example $5.33 \cdot 10^{-5} \pm 0.4 \cdot 10^{-5}$. In many cases (such as when computing p-values of tests), all we care about is whether p is smaller than some threshold. We may then not need importance sampling. Importance sampling is useful if we require the magnitude of the rare event.

CHAPTER 7

Palm Calculus, or the Importance of the Viewpoint

When computing or measuring a performance metric (as defined in Chapter 1), one should specify which observer's *viewpoint* that is taken. For example, in a simulation study of an information server, one may be interested in the metric "worst case backlog", defined as the 95-percentile of the number of pending requests.

One way to obtain this is to measure the queue of pending requests at request arrival epochs over a large number of arriving requests, and compute the 95-percentile of the resulting empirical distribution. An alternative is to measure the queue of pending requests at periodic intervals (say every second) over a long period of time and compute the 95-percentile of the resulting empirical distribution. The former method reflects the viewpoint of an arriving request, and the latter that of an observer at an arbitrary point in time. The former method evaluates the metric using a clock that ticks at every request arrival, whereas the latter uses a standard clock. Both methods will usually provide different values of the metric. Therefore, a metric definition should specify which clock, or viewpoint that is used, and the choice should be relevant for the specific issues being addressed.

In Section 7.1, we give an intuitive definition of event clocks and of event versus time averages; we show that subtle, but possibly large, sampling biases are unavoidable. We also show how to use the large time heuristic to derive Palm calculus formulas, i.e. formulas relating metrics obtained with various clocks.

In the rest of the chapter, we formally present Palm calculus, i.e. we give a formal treatment of these intuitive definitions and formulas. This is a branch of probability that is not well known, though it is quite important for any measurement or simulation study, and can be presented quite simply. In essence, the Palm probability of an event is the conditional probability, given that some specific point process has a point. Making sense of this is simple in discrete time, but very complex in continuous time, as is often the case in the theory of stochastic processes. We do not dwell on formal mathematical constructions, but we do give formulas and exact conditions under which they apply.

We introduce Feller's paradox, an apparent contradiction in waiting times that can be explained by a difference in viewpoints. We provide useful formulas such as the Rate Conservation Law and some of its many consequences such as Little's, Campbell's shot noise, Neveu's exchange and Palm's inversion formulas. We discuss simulations defined as stochastic recurrences, show how this can explain when simulations freeze and how to completely avoid transient removals (perfect simulation). Finally, we give practical formulas for computing Palm probabilities with Markov models observed along a subchain, and use these to derive the PASTA property.

7.1   An Informal Introduction

In this section, we present an intuitive treatment of event-versus-time averages and explain the use of event clocks. A formal treatment involving Palm calculus is given in Section 7.2.

7.1.1   Event-versus-Time Averages

Consider a discrete event simulation that runs for a long period of time, and let $T_0, T_1, \ldots, T_N$ be a sequence of **selected events**, for example, the request arrival times at an information server. Assume that we associate to the stream of selected events a clock that ticks at times $T_0, T_1, \ldots, T_N$ (the **event clock**). An **event average** statistic is any performance metric that his computed based on sampling of the simulation state at times T_n, i.e. using the event clock. For instance, the average queue length at the information server upon a request arrival can be defined as

$$\bar{Q}^0 := \frac{1}{N+1} \sum_{n=0}^{N} Q(T_n^-)$$

where $Q(t^-)$ – an event-average statistic – is the queue size just before time t.

In contrast, a **time-average** statistic is obtained using the standard clock, assumed to have infinite accuracy (i.e. the standard clock ticks every δ time units, where δ is "infinitely small"). For example, the average queue length, defined by

$$\bar{Q} := \frac{1}{T_N - T_0} \int_{T_0}^{T_N} Q(s)\, ds$$

is a time-average statistic.

In signal processing parlance, event averages correspond to **adaptive sampling**.

Example 7.1 Gatekeeper

A multitasking system receives jobs. Any arriving job is first processed by a "gatekeeper task", which allocates the job to an available "application processor". Due to power saving, the gatekeeper is available only at times, $0, 90, 100, 190, 200, \ldots$ (in milliseconds). For example, a job that arrives at the time 20 ms is processed by the gatekeeper at the time 90 ms.

A job that is processed by the gatekeeper at times $0, 100, 200 \ldots$ is allocated to an application processor with an execution time of 1000 ms. In contrast, a job that is processed by the gatekeeper at times $90, 190, \ldots$ has an execution time of 5000 ms (Figure 7.1). We assume that there is neither queuing nor any additional delay. We are interested in the average job execution time, excluding the time waiting for the gatekeeper to wake up to process the job.

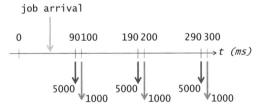

Figure 7.1 Gatekeeper: jobs are dispatched to a processor with processing times equal to 5000 or 1000 ms.

The system designer thinks that the average job execution time is

$$W_s = \frac{1000 + 5000}{2} = 3000 \text{ ms}$$

since there are two application processors and this is the average of their execution times.

A customer may have a different viewpoint. If she sends a job to the system at a random instant, she will be allocated to an application processor depending on the time of arrival. The customer computes her performance metric assuming that she picks a millisecond at random, uniformly in an interval $[0, T]$, where T is large, and obtains

$$W_c = \frac{90}{100} \times 5000 + \frac{10}{100} \times 1000 = 4600 \text{ ms}$$

The metric W_s is an event average; it can be measured using the event clock that ticks whenever the gatekeeper wakes up. The metric W_c is a time-average; it can be measured using a clock that ticks every millisecond.

This example shows that event averages may be very different from time averages. In other words, *sampling bias* may be a real issue. It is therefore necessary, when defining a metric, to specify the clock (i.e which viewpoint) that is adopted. Further, one should discuss which viewpoint makes sense for the performance of interest. In the previous example, the time-average viewpoint is a better metric as it directly reflects customer experience.

7.1.2   The Large Time Heuristic

Palm calculus is a set of formulas for relating event and time averages. They form the topic of the other sections in this chapter. However, it may be useful to know that most of these formulas can be derived heuristically using the *large time heuristic*, which can be described as follows.

(1) Formulate each performance metric as a long run ratio, as you would do in order to evaluate the metric in a discrete event simulation;

(2) take the formula for the time-average viewpoint and break it down into pieces, where each piece corresponds to a time interval between two selected events;

(3) compare the two formulations.

We explain this in the following example.

Example 7.2   Gatekeeper, Continued

We can formalize Example 7.1 as follows. The two metrics are W_s (event average, system designer's viewpoint) and W_c (time-average, customer's viewpoint).

(1) In a simulation, we would estimate W_s and W_c according to the following. Let $T_0, T_1, \ldots, T_N$ be the selected event times (times at which the gatekeeper wakes up) and let $S_n = T_n - T_{n-1}$ for $n = 1, \ldots, N$. Let X_n be the execution time for a job that is

processed by the gatekeeper at time T_n

$$W_s := \frac{1}{N} \sum_{n=1}^{N} X_n \tag{7.1}$$

$$W_c := \frac{1}{T_N - T_0} \int_{T_0}^{T_N} X_{N^+(t)} \, dt \tag{7.2}$$

where $N^+(t)$ is the index of the next event clock tick after t, i.e. a job arriving at time t is processed by the gatekeeper at time T_n with $n = N^+(t)$.

(2) We break the integral in (7.2) into pieces corresponding to the intervals $[T_n, T_{n+1})$:

$$W_c = \frac{1}{T_N - T_0} \sum_{n=1}^{N} \int_{T_{n-1}}^{T_n} X_{N^+(t)} \, dt = \frac{1}{T_N - T_0} \sum_{n=1}^{N} \int_{T_{n-1}}^{T_n} X_n \, dt$$

$$= \frac{1}{T_N - T_0} \sum_{n=1}^{N} S_n X_n \tag{7.3}$$

(3) We now compare (7.1) and (7.3). Define the sample average sleep time $\bar{S} := \frac{1}{N} \sum_{n=1}^{N} S_n$, the sample average execution time $\bar{X} := \frac{1}{N} \sum_{n=1}^{N} X_n$, and the sample cross-covariance

$$\hat{C} := \frac{1}{N} \sum_{n=1}^{N} (S_n - \bar{S})(X_n - \bar{X}) = \frac{1}{N} \sum_{n=1}^{N} S_n X_n - \bar{S}\bar{X}$$

We can re-write (7.1) and (7.3) as

$$W_s = \bar{X}$$

$$W_c = \frac{1}{N\bar{S}} \sum_{n=1}^{N} S_n X_n = \frac{1}{\bar{S}}(\hat{C} + \bar{S}\bar{X}) = \bar{X} + \frac{\hat{C}}{\bar{S}}$$

In other words, we have shown that

$$W_c = W_s + \frac{\hat{C}}{\bar{S}} \tag{7.4}$$

Numerically, we find $\frac{\hat{C}}{\bar{S}} = 1600$ and (7.4) is verified.

Equation (7.4) is our first example of a Palm calculus formula; it relates the time-average W_c to the event average W_s. Note that it holds quite generally, not only for the system in Example 7.1. We do not need any specific assumptions on the distribution of sleep or execution times, nor do we assume any form of independence. The only required assumption is that the metrics W_s and W_c can be measured using (7.1) and (7.2). In the next section, we give a formal framework where such assumptions hold.

Equation (7.4) shows that, for this example, the difference in viewpoints is attributed to the cross-covariance between sleep time and execution time. A positive (resp. negative) cross-covariance implies that the time-average is larger (resp. smaller) than the event average. In Example 7.1, the cross-covariance is positive and we find a larger time-average. If the sleep time and execution times are non-correlated, the two viewpoints happen to produce the same metric.

7.1.3 Two Event Clocks

There exist formulas not only for relating time and event averages, but also for relating various event averages (see Theorem 7.7). We show in this section how such formulas can be derived, using the following variant of the large time heuristic:

(1) formulate each performance metric as a long run ratio, as you would do if you were evaluating the metric in a discrete event simulation;

(2) take the formula for one event average viewpoint and break it down into pieces, where each piece corresponds to the time interval between two selected events of the second viewpoint;

(3) compare the two formulations.

Example 7.3 Stop and Go Protocol

A source sends packets to a destination. Error recovery is done by the stop and go protocol, as follows. When a packet is sent, a timer, with a fixed value t_1, is set. If the packet is acknowledged before t_1, transmission is successful. Otherwise, the packet is re-transmitted. The packet plus acknowledgement transmission and processing have a constant duration equal to $t_0 < t_1$. The proportion of successful transmissions (fresh or not) is $1 - \alpha$. We assume that the source is greedy, i.e. that it always has a packet ready for transmission. Can we compute the throughput θ of this protocol without making any further assumptions? The answer is yes, using the large time heuristic.

To this end, we compare the average transmission times sampled with the two different event clocks. The former (clock "a") ticks at every transmission or re-transmission attempt; the latter (clock "0") ticks at fresh arrivals. Accordingly, let τ_a be the average time between transmission or retransmission attempts, and let τ_0 be the average time between fresh arrivals (Figure 7.2).

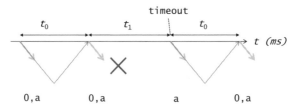

Figure 7.2 The Stop and Go protocol.

(1) Consider a simulation such that there are $N + 1$ fresh arrivals, at times $T_0, T_1, \ldots, T_N$, where N is large. T_n are the ticks of clock 0. The estimates of τ_a and τ_0 are

$$\tau_a = \frac{T_N - T_0}{N_a}$$

$$\tau_0 = \frac{T_N - T_0}{N} \tag{7.5}$$

where N_a is the number of transmission or retransmission attempts generated by packets 1 through N. The estimate of the throughput θ is

$$\theta = \frac{N}{T_N - T_0} = \frac{1}{\tau_0}$$

Also, by definition of the error ratio α: $N_a(1 - \alpha) = N$, thus

$$\tau_a = (1 - \alpha)\tau_0$$

(2) We focus on τ_a and break it down into pieces corresponding to the ticks of clock 0:

$$\tau_a = \frac{T_N - T_0}{N_a} = \frac{1}{N_a} \sum_{n=1}^{N} X_n$$

Here, X_n is the total transmission and retransmission time for the nth packet, i.e. the time interval between two ticks of clock 0. Let A_n be the number of unsuccessful transmission attempts for the nth packet (possibly 0). This gives us

$$X_n = A_n t_1 + t_0$$

$$\tau_a = \frac{1}{N_a} \left(t_1 \sum_{n=1}^{N} A_n + t_0 N \right) = \frac{1}{N_a} \left(t_1 (N_a - N) + t_0 N \right)$$

$$= \alpha t_1 + (1 - \alpha) t_0 \tag{7.6}$$

(3) Compare (7.5) and (7.6) and obtain $\tau_0 = \frac{\alpha}{1-\alpha} t_1 + t_0$; the throughput is thus

$$\theta = \frac{1}{\frac{\alpha}{1 - \alpha} t_1 + t_0} \tag{7.7}$$

In this example, as is generally the case with Palm calculus formulas, the validity of a formula such as (7.7) does not depend on any distributional or independence assumption. We did not make any particular assumption about the arrival and failure processes; they may thus be correlated, non-Poisson, etc.

7.1.4   Arbitrary Sampling Methods

To conclude this section we describe how different viewpoints occur in various situations, with clocks that may not be related to time. Here too, the large "time" heuristic provides useful relationships.

Example 7.4   Flow versus Packet Clock

Packets arriving at a router are classified in "flows" [96]. We would like to plot the empirical distribution of flow sizes, counted in packets. We measure all traffic at the router for some extended period of time. Our metric of interest is the probability distribution of flow sizes. We can take a flow "clock", or viewpoint, i.e. we ask: pick an arbitrary flow, what is its size? Or we could take a packet viewpoint and ask: take an arbitrary packet, what is the magnitude of its flow? We thus have two possible metrics (Figure 7.3):

Per flow. $f_F(s) = \frac{1}{N} \times$ number of flows with length s, where N is the number of flows in the dataset;

Per packet. $f_P(s) = \frac{1}{P} \times$ number of packets that belong to a flow of length s, where P is the number of packets in the dataset.

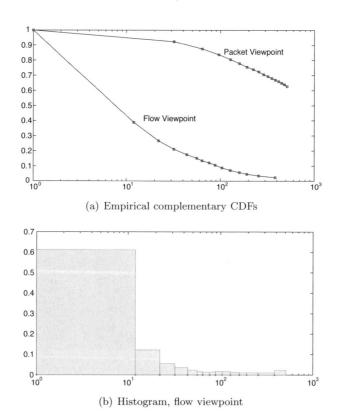

(a) Empirical complementary CDFs

(b) Histogram, flow viewpoint

Figure 7.3 Distribution of flow sizes, viewed by an arbitrary flow and an arbitrary packet, measured by an internet service provider.

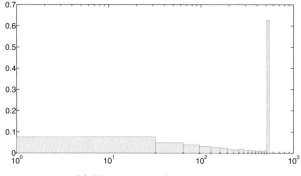

(c) Histogram, packet viewpoint

Figure 7.3 (Continuation.)

The large time heuristic helps us find a relation between the two metrics.

(1) For s spanning the set of observed flow sizes

$$f_F(s) = \frac{1}{N} \sum_{n=1}^{N} 1_{\{S_n=s\}} \qquad (7.8)$$

$$f_P(s) = \frac{1}{P} \sum_{p=1}^{P} 1_{\{S_{F(p)}=s\}} \qquad (7.9)$$

where S_n is the size in bytes of flow n, for $n = 1, \ldots, N$, and $F(p)$ is the index of the flow to which packet number p belongs.

(2) We can break the sum in (7.9) into pieces corresponding to ticks of the flow clock:

$$f_P(s) = \frac{1}{P} \sum_{n=1}^{N} \sum_{p:F(p)=n} 1_{\{S_n=s\}} = \frac{1}{P} \sum_{n=1}^{N} \sum_{p=1}^{P} 1_{\{F(p)=n\}} 1_{\{S_n=s\}}$$

$$= \frac{1}{P} \sum_{n=1}^{N} 1_{\{S_n=s\}} \sum_{p=1}^{P} 1_{\{F(p)=n\}} = \frac{1}{P} \sum_{n=1}^{N} 1_{\{S_n=s\}} s$$

$$= \frac{s}{P} \sum_{n=1}^{N} 1_{\{S_n=s\}} \qquad (7.10)$$

(3) Compare (7.8) and (7.10) and obtain the following expression for all flow sizes s:

$$f_P(s) = \eta s f_F(s) \qquad (7.11)$$

where η is a normalizing constant ($\eta = \frac{N}{P}$).

Equation (7.11) relates the two ways of computing the distribution of flow sizes. Note that they differ by one exponent, so it is possible that the flow size is heavy-tailed when sampled with a packet clock, but light-tailed when sampled with a flow clock.

Example 7.5 Kilometer versus Time Clock: Cyclist's Paradox

A cyclist rides Swiss mountains; his speed is 10 km/h uphill and 50 km/h downhill. A journey is comprised of 50% uphill slopes and 50% downhill slopes. At the end of the journey, the cyclist is disappointed to read on his speedometer an average speed of only 16.7 km/h, as he was expecting an average of $\frac{10+50}{2} = 30$ km/h. Here, we have two ways of measuring the average speed: with the standard clock (speedometer), or with the kilometer clock (cyclist's intuition). Let us apply the large time heuristic.

(1) Pick a unit of length (perhaps smaller than the kilometer) such that the cyclist's speed is constant on a section of the trip of length 1, and let v_l be the speed at the lth section of the trip, $l = 1, \ldots, L$, where L is the trip length. The average speeds measured with the standard clock, S_t and with the kilometer clock, S_k are

$$S_t = \frac{L}{T}$$

$$S_k = \frac{1}{L} \sum_{l=1}^{L} v_l \qquad (7.12)$$

where T is the trip duration.

(2) Break T into pieces corresponding to the km clock:

$$T = \sum_{l=1}^{L} \frac{1}{v_l}$$

$$S_t = \frac{L}{\sum_{l=1}^{L} \frac{1}{v_l}} \qquad (7.13)$$

(3) Thus, S_t (Eq. (7.13)) is the harmonic mean of v_l whereas S_k (Eq. (7.12)) is the arithmetic mean (Section 2.4.3). The harmonic mean is the inverse of the mean of the inverses. If the speed is not constant throughout the whole trip, the harmonic mean is smaller than the arithmetic mean [106], thus the cyclist's intuition will always have a positive bias (leading to frustration).

In this case, the large time heuristic does not give a closed-form relationship between the two averages; however, a closed-form relationship can be obtained for the two distributions of speeds. Using the same method as in Example 7.4, one obtains

$$f_t(v) = \eta \frac{1}{v} f_k(v) \qquad (7.14)$$

where $f_t(v)$ (resp. $f_k(v)$) is the PDF of the speed, sampled with the standard clock (resp. km clock) and η is a normalizing constant; f_t puts more mass on the small values of the speed v. This is another explanation to the cyclist's paradox.

7.2   Palm Calculus

Palm calculus is a branch of probability that applies to stationary point processes. We give an intuitive, but rigorous, treatment. A complete mathematical treatment can be found for example in [4] and [88] or in [95] in the context of continuous time Markov chains.

7.2.1   Hypotheses

Stationarity

We assume that we are observing the output of a simulation, which we interpret as a sample of a stochastic process $S(t)$. The time t is either discrete or continuous. This process is **stationary** if, for any any n, any sequence of times $t_1 < t_2 < \ldots < t_n$ and any time shift u, the joint distribution of $\big(S(t_1 + u), S(t_2 + u), \ldots, S(t_n + u)\big)$ is independent of u. In other words, the process does not change statistically as it gets older. In practice, stationarity occurs if the system has a stationary regime and we let the simulation run long enough (Chapter 6).

   We also assume that, at every time t, we are able to make an observation $X(t)$ from the simulation output. The value of $X(t)$ may be in any space. We assume that the process $X(t)$ is **jointly stationary** with the simulation state process $S(t)$ (i.e. $\big(X(t), S(t)\big)$ is a stationary process). Note that even if the simulation is stationary, one might easily define outputs that are not jointly stationary (such as: $X(t) =$ the most recent request arrival time at an information server). A sufficient condition for $X(t)$ to be jointly stationary with $S(t)$ is that

(1) at every time t, $X(t)$ can be computed from the present, the past and/or the future of the simulation state $S(t)$, and

(2) $X(t)$ is invariant under a change of the origin of times.

For example, if an information server can be assumed to be stationary, then $X(t) =$ time elapsed since the last request arrival time and $X(t) =$ the queue size at time t satisfy the conditions.

7.2.2   Definitions

Point Process

We introduce now the definition of a **stationary point process**. Intuitively, this is the sequence of times at which the simulation performs a transition in some specified set.

   Formally, a stationary point process in our setting is associated with a subset $\mathcal{F}_0$ of the set of all possible state transitions of the simulation. It is made of all time instants t at which the simulation carries out a transition in $\mathcal{F}_0$, i.e. such that $\big(S(t^-), S(t^+)\big) \in \mathcal{F}_0$.

   In practice, we do not need to specify $\mathcal{F}_0$ explicitly. In contrast, we have a simulation in steady state and we consider times at which something of a certain kind happens; the only important criterion is to make sure that the firing of a point can be entirely determined by observing only the simulation. For example, we can consider as point process the request arrival times at an information server.

Technically, we also need to assume that the simulation process is such that the point process is simple, i.e. that, with probability 1, two instants of the point process cannot be equal (this is true in practice if the simulation cannot have several transitions at the same time), and non explosive, i.e. the expected number of time instants over any finite interval is finite. The above implies that the instants of the point process can be enumerated and described as an increasing sequence of (random) times T_n, where n is an integer, and $T_n < T_{n+1}$.

In continuous time, to avoid ambiguities, we assume that all processes are right continuous, so that if there is a transition at time t, $S(t)$ corresponds to the state of the simulation just after the transition.

The sequence T_n is (as a thought experiment) assumed to be infinite both in the present and the past, i.e. the index n spans $\mathbb{Z}$. With the terminology of Section 7.1, $(T_n)_{n \in \mathbb{Z}}$ is the sequence of ticks of the event clock.

The Arbitrary Point in Time

Since the simulation is in the stationary regime, we imagine that, at time 0, it has been running for quite some time. Since the point process is defined in terms of transitions of the simulation state $S(t)$, it is also stationary. It is convenient, and customary, to denote the time instants of the point process T_n such that

$$\ldots < T_{-2} < T_{-1} < T_0 \leq 0 < T_1 < T_2 < \ldots \qquad (7.15)$$

In other words, T_0 is the last instant of the point process before time 0, and T_1 the next instant starting from time 0. This convention is the one used by mathematicians to give a meaning to "an arbitrary point in time": we regard $t = 0$ as our "random" time instant. Thus, in some sense, we fix the time origin arbitrarily.

This differs from the convention used in many simulations, where $t = 0$ is the beginning of the simulation. Our convention, in this chapter, is that $t = 0$ is the beginning of the observation period for a simulation that has a stationary regime and has run long enough to be in steady state.

Intensity

The *intensity* λ of the point process is defined as the expected number of points per time unit. We have assumed that there cannot be two points at the same instant. In discrete or continuous time, the intensity λ is defined as the unique number such that the number $N(t, t + \tau)$ of points during any interval $[t, t + \tau]$ satisfies [4]

$$\mathbb{E}\big(N(t, t + \tau)\big) = \lambda \tau \qquad (7.16)$$

In discrete time, λ is also simply equal to the probability that there is a point at an arbitrary time

$$\lambda = \mathbb{P}(T_0 = 0) = \mathbb{P}(N(0) = 1) = \mathbb{P}(N(t) = 1) \qquad (7.17)$$

where the latter is valid for any t, by stationarity.

One can think of λ as the (average) rate of the event clock.

Palm Expectation and Palm Probability

Let Y be a one time output of the simulation, assumed to be integrable (for example because it is bounded). We define the expectation $\mathbb{E}^t(Y)$ as the conditional expectation of Y given that a point occurs at time t

$$\mathbb{E}^t(Y) = \mathbb{E}(Y \mid \exists n \in \mathbb{Z}, \ T_n = t) \qquad (7.18)$$

If $Y = X(t)$, where $X(t)$ and the simulation are jointly stationary, $\mathbb{E}^t(X(t))$ does not depend on t. For $t = 0$, it is called

---

Definition 7.1 (Palm expectation)

$$\mathbb{E}^0(X(0)) = \mathbb{E}(X(0) \mid \text{a point of the process } T_n \text{ occurs at time } 0) \quad (7.19)$$

According to the labeling convention in (7.15), if there is a point of the process T_n at 0, it must be T_0, i.e.

$$\mathbb{E}^0(X(0)) = \mathbb{E}(X(0) \mid T_0 = 0)$$

Note that there is some ambiguity in the notation, as the process T_n is not explicitly mentioned (in Section 7.3.3 we will need to remove this ambiguity).

The Palm *probability* is defined similarly, namely as

$$\mathbb{P}^0(X(0) \in W) = \mathbb{P}(X(0) \in W \mid \text{a point of the process } T_n \text{ occurs at time } 0)$$

for any measurable subset W of the set of values of $X(t)$. In particular, we can write $\mathbb{P}^0(T_0 = 0) = 1$.

The interpretation of the definition is easy in discrete time, if, as is the case, we assume that the point process is "simple". In other words, there cannot be more than one point at any instant t. In this case, (7.18) has to be taken in the usual sense of conditional probabilities:

$$\mathbb{E}^t(Y) = \mathbb{E}(Y \mid N(t) = 1) = \frac{\mathbb{E}(YN(t))}{\mathbb{E}(N(t))} = \frac{\mathbb{E}(YN(t))}{\mathbb{P}(N(t) = 1)} = \frac{\mathbb{E}(YN(t))}{\lambda}$$

where $N(t) = 1$ if there is a point at time t, and 0 otherwise.

COMMENT: In continuous time, "there is a point at time t" has the probability 0 and cannot be conditioned upon. However, it is possible to give a meaning to such a conditional expectation, similarly to the way one can define the conditional probability density function of a continuous random variable:

$$E^t(Y) = \lim_{\tau \to 0} \frac{E(YN(t, t+\tau))}{E(N(t, t+\tau))} = \lim_{\tau \to 0} \frac{E(YN(t, t+\tau))}{\lambda\tau} \tag{7.20}$$

Here, the limit is in the Radon-Nykodim sense, defined as follows. For a given random variable Y, consider the measure μ defined for any measurable subset B of $\mathbb{R}$ by

$$\mu(B) = \frac{1}{\lambda} E\left(Y \sum_{n \in \mathbb{Z}} 1_{\{T_n \in B\}}\right) \tag{7.21}$$

where λ is the intensity of the point process T_n. If B is negligible (i.e. its Lebesgue measure, or length, is 0) then, with probability 1, there is no event in B and $\mu(B) = 0$. By the Radon-Nykodim theorem [91], there exists some function g defined on $\mathbb{R}$ such that for any B: $\mu(B) = \int_B g(t)\, dt$. The Palm expectation $E^t(Y)$ is defined as $g(t)$. In other words, for a given random variable Y, $E^t(Y)$ is defined as the function of t that, for any B, satisfies,

$$E\left(Y \sum_{n \in \mathbb{Z}} 1_{\{T_n \in B\}}\right) = \lambda \int_B E^t(Y)\, dt \tag{7.22}$$

□

7.2.3 Interpretation as Time and Event Averages

In this section, we make the link with the intuitive treatment in Section 7.1.

Time Averages

If $X(t)$ is jointly stationary with the simulation, it follows that the distribution of $X(t)$ is independent of t; it is called the *time stationary* distribution of X.

Assume that, in addition, $X(t)$ is ergodic, i.e. that time averages tend to expectations (which, is true for example on a discrete state space if any state can be reached from any other state), for any bounded function ϕ, we can estimate $E\left(\phi(X(t))\right)$ by (in discrete time)

$$E\left(\phi(X(t))\right) \approx \frac{1}{T} \sum_{t=1}^{T} \phi(X(t))$$

when T is large. An equivalent statement is that for any (measurable) subset W of the set of values of $X(t)$

$$P\left(X(t) \in W\right) \approx \text{fraction of time that } X(t) \text{ is in the set } W$$

In other words, the time stationary distribution of $X(t)$ can be estimated by a time-average.

Event Averages

We can interpret the Palm expectation and Palm probability as event averages if the process $X(t)$ is ergodic (note however that Palm calculus does not require ergodicity). Indeed, it follows from the definition of the Palm expectation that

$$\mathbb{E}^0\left(\phi(X(0))\right) \approx \frac{1}{N}\sum_{n=1}^{N}\phi(X(T_n))$$

for large N.

It can be shown [4] that if the process $X(t)$ is ergodic and integrable, then

$$\lim_{N\to\infty}\frac{1}{N}\sum_{n=1}^{N}\phi(X(T_n)) = \mathbb{E}^0\left(\phi(X^0)\right)$$

An equivalent statement is that, for any (measurable) subset W of the set of values of $X(t)$

$$\mathbb{P}^t\left(X(t)\in W\right) = \mathbb{P}^0\left(X(0)\in W\right)$$
$$\approx \text{fraction of points of the point process at which } X(t) \text{ is in } W$$

Thus the Palm expectation and the Palm probability can be interpreted as event averages. In other words, they are ideal quantities, which can be estimated by observing $X(t)$ sampled with the event clock.

7.2.4   The Inversion and Intensity Formulas

These are formulas that relate time and event averages. Also known under the name of Ryll-Nardzewski and Slivnyak's formula, the inversion formula relates the time stationary and Palm probabilities. The proof of discrete time, a direct application of the definition of conditional probability, is given in Section 7.7.

Theorem 7.1 (Inversion Formula)
- *In discrete time:*

$$\mathbb{E}\left(X(t)\right) = \mathbb{E}\left(X(0)\right) = \lambda\mathbb{E}^0\left(\sum_{s=1}^{T_1}X(s)\right) = \lambda\mathbb{E}^0\left(\sum_{s=0}^{T_1-1}X(s)\right) \qquad (7.23)$$

- *In continuous time*

$$\mathbb{E}\left(X(t)\right) = \mathbb{E}\left(X(0)\right) = \lambda\mathbb{E}^0\left(\int_0^{T_1}X(s)\,ds\right) \qquad (7.24)$$

By applying the inversion to $X(t) = 1$, we obtain the following formula, which states that the intensity of a point process is the inverse of the average time between points.

Theorem 7.2 (Intensity Formula)

$$\frac{1}{\lambda} = \mathbb{E}^0(T_1 - T_0) = \mathbb{E}^0(T_1) \tag{7.25}$$

Recall that the only assumption required is stationarity. There is no need for independence or Poisson assumptions.

Example 7.6 Gatekeeper, continued

Assume that we model the gatekeeper example as a discrete event simulation, and consider as point process the waking-up of the gatekeeper. Let $X(t)$ be the execution time of a hypothetical job that would arrive at time t. The average job execution time, sampled with the standard clock (customer viewpoint) is

$$W_c = \mathbb{E}\big(X(t)\big) = \mathbb{E}\big(X(0)\big)$$

whereas the average execution time, sampled with the event clock (system designer viewpoint), is

$$W_s = \mathbb{E}^t\big(X(t)\big) = \mathbb{E}^0\big(X(0)\big)$$

The inversion formula gives

$$W_c = \lambda \mathbb{E}^0\left(\int_0^{T_1} X(t)\, dt\right) = \lambda \mathbb{E}^0\big(X(0)T_1\big)$$

(recall that $T_0 = 0$ under the Palm probability and $X(0)$ is the execution time for a job that arrives just after time 0). Let C be the cross-covariance between sleep time and execution time:

$$C := \mathbb{E}^0\big(T_1 X(0)\big) - \mathbb{E}^0(T_1)\mathbb{E}^0\big(X(0)\big)$$

This gives

$$W_c = \lambda\left[C + \mathbb{E}^0\big(X(0)\big)\mathbb{E}^0(T_1)\right]$$

By the inversion formula $\lambda = \frac{1}{\mathbb{E}^0(T_1)}$, we thus have

$$W_c = W_s + \lambda C$$

which is the formula derived using the heuristic in Section 7.1.

To be rigorous, we need to make sure that the process being simulated is stationary. With the data in Example 7.1, this appears to be false, as the wake-up times are periodic, starting at time 0. This is not a problem for such cases: when the simulation state is periodic, say with period θ, then it is customary to consider the simulation as a realization of the stochastic process obtained by uniformly drawing the origin of times in $[0, \theta]$. This produces a stochastic process that is formally stationary, and which in practical terms, amounts to uniformly choosing the arbitrary point in time at random in $[0, \theta]$.

Example 7.7 Stationary Distribution of Random Waypoint

The random waypoint model is defined in Example 6.5, but we repeat the definitions here [52]. A mobile moves from one waypoint to the next in some bounded space $\mathcal{S}$. After having arrived at a waypoint, say M_n, it picks a new one, e.g. M_{n+1}, randomly and uniformly in $\mathcal{S}$, picks a speed V_n uniformly at random between $v_{\min}$ and $v_{\max}$ and proceeds to the next waypoint M_{n+1} at this constant speed.

Figure 7.4 shows that the distribution of *speed*, sampled at waypoints, is uniform between $v_{\min}$ and $v_{\max}$, as expected. In contrast, the distribution, sampled at an arbitrary point in time, is different. We can explain this by Palm's inversion formula.

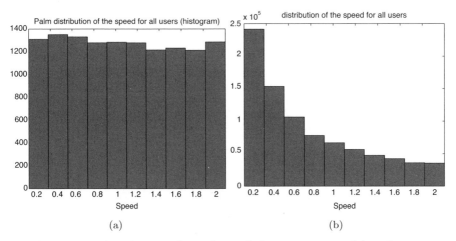

Figure 7.4 Distribution of speed sampled at a waypoint (a) and at an arbitrary time instant (b). $v_{\min} = 0.2$, $v_{\max} = 2$ m/s.

We assume that this model has a stationary regime, i.e. that $v_{\min} > 0$ (see Section 7.4). The stationary distribution of $V(t)$ is obtained if we know $\mathbb{E}\left(\phi\big(V(t)\big)\right)$ for any bounded, test function ϕ of the speed. Let $f_V^0(v)$ be the PDF of the speed chosen at a waypoint, i.e. $f_V^0(v) = \frac{1}{v_{\max} - v_{\min}} 1_{\{v_{\min} \le v \le v_{\max}\}}$. We have

$$
\mathbb{E}\big(\phi(V(t)) = \lambda \mathbb{E}^0\left(\int_0^{T_1} \phi\big(V(t)\big)\, dt\right)
$$

$$
= \lambda \mathbb{E}^0\big(T_1 \phi(V_0)\big) = \lambda \mathbb{E}^0\left(\frac{\|M_1 - M_0\|}{V_0}\phi(V_0)\right)
$$

$$
= \lambda \mathbb{E}^0\big(\|M_1 - M_0\|\big)\, \mathbb{E}^0\left(\frac{1}{V_0}\phi(V_0)\right)
$$

$$
= K_1 \int \frac{1}{v}\phi(v) f_V^0(v)\, dv \qquad\qquad (7.26)
$$

where T_n is the time at which the mobile arrives at the waypoint M_n and K_1 is a certain constant. This shows that the distribution of speed sampled at an arbitrary point in time has PDF

$$f(v) = K_1 \frac{1}{v} f_V^0(v) \qquad (7.27)$$

This explains the shape in $\frac{1}{v}$ of the second histogram in Figure 7.4.
A similar argument can be made for the distribution of location. At
a waypoint, it is uniformly distributed, by construction. Figure 7.5
shows that, at an arbitrary time instant, it is no longer so. Palm's
inversion formula can also be used to derive the PDF of location, but it
is very complex [57]. It is simpler to use the perfect simulation formula
explained in Section 7.4.3.

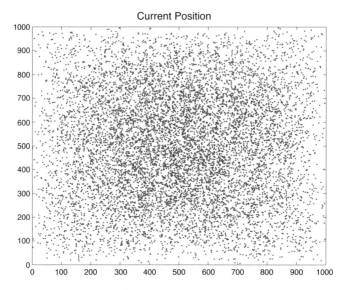

Figure 7.5 A sample of 10^4 points drawn from the stationary distribution
of the random waypoint. The distribution is not uniform, even though waypoints are picked uniformly in the area.

7.3   Other Useful Palm Calculus Results

In this section, we consider a stationary simulation and a point process following
the assumptions in the previous section.

7.3.1   Residual Time and Feller's Paradox

We are here interested in the **residual time**, i.e. the time from now to the
next point. More precisely, let $T^+(t)$ (resp. $T^-(t)$) be the first point after

(resp. before or at) t. Thus, for example, $T^+(0) = T_1$ and $T^-(0) = T_0$. The following theorem is an immediate consequence of the inversion formula.

Theorem 7.3
Let $X(t) = T^+(t) - t$ (time until next point, also called residual time), $Y(t) = t - T^-(t)$ (time since last point), $Z(t) = T^+(t) - T^-(t)$ (duration of current interval). For any t, the distributions of $X(t)$ and $Y(t)$ are equal, with PDF:

$$f_X(s) = f_Y(s) = \lambda \mathbb{P}^0(T_1 > s) = \lambda \int_s^{+\infty} f_T^0(u)\, du \qquad (7.28)$$

where f_T^0 is the Palm PDF of $T_1 - T_0$ (PDF of inter-arrival times) and λ is the intensity of the point process. The PDF of $Z(t)$ is

$$f_Z(s) = \lambda s f_T^0(s) \qquad (7.29)$$

In particular, it follows that

$$\mathbb{E}\big(X(t)\big) = \mathbb{E}\big(Y(t)\big) = \frac{\lambda}{2}\, \mathbb{E}^0(T_1^2) \quad \text{in continuous time} \qquad (7.30)$$

$$\mathbb{E}\big(X(t)\big) = \mathbb{E}\big(Y(t)\big) = \frac{\lambda}{2}\, \mathbb{E}^0(T_1(T_1+1)) \quad \text{in discrete time} \qquad (7.31)$$

$$\mathbb{E}\big(Z(t)\big) = \lambda \mathbb{E}^0(T_1^2) \qquad (7.32)$$

Note that in discrete time, the theorem means that

$$\mathbb{P}\big(X(t) = s\big) = \mathbb{P}\big(Y(t) = s\big) = \lambda \mathbb{P}^0(T_1 \geq s) \ \text{ and } \ \mathbb{P}(Z(t) = s) = \lambda s \mathbb{P}^0(T_1 = s)$$

Example 7.8 Poisson Process
Assume that T_n is a Poisson process (see Section 7.6). We have $f_T^0(t) = \lambda e^{-\lambda s}$ and $\mathbb{P}^0(T_1 > s) = \mathbb{P}^0(T_1 \geq s) = e^{-\lambda s}$ thus $f_X(s) = f_Y(s) = f_T^0(s)$.

This is expected, by the memoriless property of the Poisson process: we imagine that at every time slot, of duration dt, the Poisson process flips a coin and, with probability $\lambda\, dt$, decides that there is an arrival, independent of the past. Thus, the time $X(t)$ until the next arrival is independent of whether there is an arrival or not at time t, and the Palm distribution of $X(t)$ is the same as its time-average distribution. Note that this is specific to the Poisson process; processes without the memoriless property do not have this feature.
The distribution of $Z(t)$ has the density

$$f_T^0(s) = \lambda^2 s\, e^{-\lambda s}$$

i.e. it is an Erlang-2 distribution.[1] Note here that it differs from the Palm distribution, which is exponential with rate λ. In particular, the average duration of the current interval, sampled at an arbitrary point in time, is $\frac{2}{\lambda}$, i.e. twice the average inter-arrival time $\frac{1}{\lambda}$ (this is an instance of Feller's paradox, see later in this section). A simple interpretation for this formula is as follows: $Z(t) = X(t) + Y(t)$, where both $X(t)$ and $Y(t)$ are exponentially distributed with the rate λ and are independent.

Example 7.9 At the Bus Stop

T_n is the sequence of bus arrival instants at a bus stop. We do *not* assume here that the bus interarrival times $T_n - T_{n-1}$ are iid. $\mathbb{E}^0(T_1) = \frac{1}{\lambda}$ is the average time between buses, seen by an inspector standing at the bus stop, spending the hour counting intervals from bus to bus. $\mathbb{E}(T_1) = \mathbb{E}(X(0))$ is the average waiting time experienced by you and me.

Based on (7.30),

$$\mathbb{E}(X(t)) = \mathbb{E}(X(0)) = \frac{1}{2}\left(\frac{1}{\lambda} + \lambda \mathrm{var}^0(T_1 - T_0)\right) \tag{7.33}$$

where $\mathrm{var}^0(T_1 - T_0)$ is the variance, under Palm, of the time between buses, i.e. the variance estimated by the inspector. The expectation $\mathbb{E}(X(t))$ is the minimum waiting time, equal to $\frac{1}{2\lambda}$, when the buses are absolutely regular ($T_n - T_{n-1}$ is constant). The larger the variance, the larger is the waiting time perceived by you and me. In the limit, if the

---

[1] For $k = 1, 2, 3, \ldots$, the **Erlang-k** distribution with parameter λ is the distribution of the sum of k independent exponential distributions with rate λ.

interval between buses seen by the inspector is heavy-tailed, $\mathbb{E}(X(t))$ is infinite. Thus, the inspector should report not only the mean time between buses, but also its variance.

Feller's Paradox

We continue to consider Example 7.9 and assume that Joe would like to verify the inspector's reports by sampling one bus inter-arrival time. Joe arrives at time t and measures $Z(t) =$ (time until next bus $-$ time since last bus). By employing (7.32)

$$\mathbb{E}\big(Z(t)\big) = \frac{1}{\lambda} + \lambda \mathrm{var}^0(T_1 - T_0)$$

where $\mathrm{var}^0(T_1 - T_0)$ is the variance of the inter-arrival time $(= \int_0^\infty s^2 f_T^0(s)\,ds - \frac{1}{\lambda^2})$. Thus, the average of Joe's estimate is *always larger* than the inspector's (which is equal to $\frac{1}{\lambda}$) by a term corresponding to $\lambda \mathrm{var}^0(T_1 - T_0)$. This is the case despite that both observers sample the same system (however with differing viewpoints). This systematic bias is known as ***Feller's paradox***. Intuitively, it occurs because a stationary observer (Joe) is more likely to fall in a large time interval.

In this example, no other assumptions apart from stationarity were made for the process of bus arrivals. Thus, Feller's paradox is true for any stationary point process.

7.3.2   The Rate Conservation Law and Little's Formula

Miyazawa's Rate Conservation Law

This is a fundamental result in queuing systems, but it applies to a large variety of systems, well beyond queuing theory. It is best expressed in continuous time.

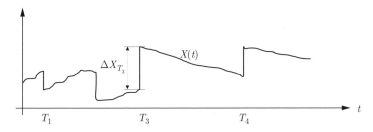

Figure 7.6   Rate conservation law.

Consider a random, real valued stochastic process $X(t)$ with the following properties (Figure 7.6):

- $X(t)$ is continuous everywhere except perhaps at instants of a stationary point process T_n;
- $X(t)$ is continuous to the right;
- $X(t)$ has a right-handside derivative $X'(t)$ for all values of t.

Define ΔX_t by $\Delta X_t = 0$ if t is not a point of the point process T_n and $\Delta X_{T_n} = X(T_n) - X(T_n^-)$, i.e. ΔX_t is the amplitude of the discontinuity at time t. Note that it follows that

$$X(t) = X(0) + \int_0^t X'(s)\,ds + \sum_{n \in \mathbb{N}} \Delta_{T_n} 1_{\{t \leq T_n\}} \qquad (7.34)$$

Theorem 7.4 (Rate Conservation Law [69])
Assume that the point process T_n and $X(t)$ are jointly stationary. If $\mathbb{E}^0\,|\Delta_0| < \infty$ and $\mathbb{E}\,|X'(0)| < \infty$ then

$$\mathbb{E}\big(X'(0)\big) + \lambda \mathbb{E}^0(\Delta_0) = 0$$

where λ is the intensity of the point process T_n and E^0 is the Palm expectation.

The proof in continuous time can be found for example in [70]. We can interpret the theorem as follows.

- $\mathbb{E}\big(X'(0)\big)$ (also equal to $\mathbb{E}\big(X'(t)\big)$ for all t) is the average rate of increase of the process $X(t)$, excluding jumps.
- $\mathbb{E}^0(\Delta_0)$ is the expected amplitude of one arbitrary jump. Thus, $\lambda \mathbb{E}^0(\Delta_0)$ is the expected rate of increase due to jumps.
- The theorem states that, if the system is stationary, the sum of all jumps is canceled out, in average.

Remark. The theorem can be extended somewhat to the cases where certains expectations are infinite, as follows [70]. Assume that the point process T_n can be decomposed as the superposition of the stationary point processes T_n^j, $j = 1, \ldots, J$, and that these point processes have no points in common. Let Δ_t^j be the jump of $X(t)$ when t is an instant of the point process T_n^j, i.e.

$$X(t) = X(0) + \int_0^t X'(s)\,ds + \sum_{j=1}^J \sum_{n \in \mathbb{N}} \Delta_{T_n}^j 1_{\{t \leq T_n^j\}} \qquad (7.35)$$

and $\Delta_t^j = 0$ whenever t is not an instant of the point process T_n^j.

Assume that $X'(t) \geq 0$ and the jumps of a point process are all positive or all negative. More precisely, assume that $\Delta_t^j \geq 0$ for $j = 1, \ldots, I$ and $\Delta_t^j \leq 0$ for $j = I+1, \ldots, J$. Finally, assume that $X(t)$ and the point processes T_n^j are jointly stationary. Then

$$\mathbb{E}\big(X'(0)\big) + \sum_{j=1}^I \lambda_j \mathbb{E}_j^0(\Delta_0^j) = -\sum_{j=I+1}^J \lambda_j \mathbb{E}_j^0(\Delta_0^j) \qquad (7.36)$$

where $\mathbb{E}_j^0$ is the Palm expectation with respect to the point process T_j^n and the equality holds even if some of the expectations are infinite.

Example 7.10 M/GI/1 Queue and Pollaczek-Khinchine Formula

Consider the M/GI/1 queue, i.e. the single server queue with Poisson arrivals of rate λ and independent service times, with mean $\bar{S}$ and variance σ_S^2. Assume $\rho = \lambda\bar{S} < 1$ so that there is a stationary regime (Theorem 8.6). Apply the rate conservation law to $X(t) = W(t)^2$, where $W(t)$ is the amount of unfinished work at time t.

The jumps occur at arrival instants, and when there is an arrival at time t, the jump is

$$\Delta X = \big(W(t) + S\big)^2 - W(t)^2 = 2SW(t) + S^2$$

where S is the service time of the arriving customer. By hypothesis, S is independent of $W(t)$ thus the expectation of a jump is $2\mathbb{E}^0\big(W(t)\big)\bar{S} + \bar{S}^2 + \sigma_S^2$. By the PASTA property (Example 7.19), $\mathbb{E}^0\big(W(t)\big) = \mathbb{E}\big(W(t)\big)$. Thus, the rate conservation law gives

$$\mathbb{E}\big(X'(t)\big) + 2\rho\mathbb{E}\big(W(t)\big) + \lambda\big(\bar{S}^2 + \sigma_S^2\big) = 0$$

Between jumps, $W(t)$ decreases at rate 1 if $W(t) > 0$, thus the derivative of X is $X'(t) = 2W(t)1_{\{W(t)>0\}}$ and $\mathbb{E}\big(X'(t)\big) = -2\mathbb{E}\big(W(t)\big)$. Putting things together, we get

$$\mathbb{E}\big(W(t)\big) = \frac{\lambda\big(\bar{S}^2 + \sigma_S^2\big)}{2(1 - \rho)}$$

By the PASTA property again, $\mathbb{E}\big(W(t)\big)$ is the average workload seen by an arriving customer, i.e. the average waiting time. Consequently, the average response time (waiting time + service time) is (***Pollaczek-Khinchine formula for means***)

$$\bar{R} = \frac{\bar{S}\big(1 - \rho(1 - \kappa)\big)}{1 - \rho} \tag{7.37}$$

with $\kappa = \frac{1}{2}\big(1 + \frac{\sigma_S^2}{\bar{S}^2}\big)$.

Similarly, applying the rate conservation law to $X(t) = e^{-sW(t)}$ for some arbitrary $s \geq 0$ gives the Laplace Stieltjes transform of the distribution of $W(t)$ (see (8.5)).

Campbell's Shot Noise Formula

Consider the following system, assumed to be described by the state of a stationary simulation $S(t)$. Assume that we can observe arrivals of jobs, also called customers, or "shots", and that the the arrival times T_n form a stationary point process.

The nth customer also has an "attribute", Z_n, which may be drawn according to the specific rules of the system. As usual in this chapter, we do not assume any form of iid-ness, but we do assume stationarity; more precisely the attribute Z_n is obtained by sampling the simulation state at time T_n (this is quite general as we do not specify what we put in the simulation state). If the attributes have this property, we say that they are ***marks*** of the point process

T_n and that the process (T_n, Z_n) is a **stationary marked point process**. We do not specify the nature of the attribute, it can take values in any arbitrary space.

When the nth customer arrives, he/she generates a load on the system, in the form of work to be done. Formally, we assume that there is a function $h(s, z) \geq 0$ (the "shot") such that $h(s, z)$ is the load at time s, due to a hypothetical customer having arrived at time 0, and would have mark z. The total load in the system at time t, is

$$X'(t) = \sum_{n \in \mathbb{Z}} 1_{\{T_n \leq t\}} h(t - T_n, Z_n)$$

and the total amount of work to be performed, as a result of customers already being present in the system is

$$X(t) = \sum_{n \in \mathbb{Z}} 1_{\{T_n \leq t\}} \int_t^\infty h(s - T_n, Z_n)\, ds$$

For example, in [7], a customer is an internet flow, its mark is its size in bytes, and the total system load is the aggregate bit rate (Example 7.7). The average load $\bar{L}$, at an arbitrary point in time, is

$$\bar{L} = \mathbb{E}\left(\sum_{n \in \mathbb{Z}} 1_{\{T_n \leq t\}} h(t - T_n, Z_n) \right) = \mathbb{E}\left(\sum_{n \leq 0} h(-T_n, Z_n) \right)$$

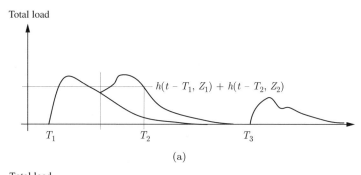

(a)

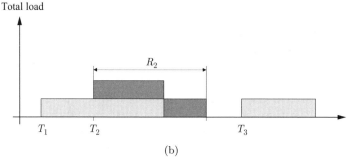

(b)

Figure 7.7 Shot Noise (a) and Little's formula (b).

where the latter is obtained by taking $t = 0$. The work generated during its lifetime by one customer, given that his/her mark is z, is $\int_0^\infty h(t,z)\,dt$. The average load generated by one arbitrary customer can be expressed as a Palm expectation, relative to the point process of customer arrivals, namely as

$$\text{work per customer} = \mathbb{E}^0 \left(\int_0^\infty h(t, Z_0)\,dt \right) \tag{7.38}$$

(Z_0 in the formula stands for the attribute of an arbitrary customer). Let λ be the intensity of the point process T_n, i.e. the customer arrival rate.

The total work decreases at the rate $X'(t)$ and when a customer arrives at time T_n, it jumps by $\Delta_t = \int_0^\infty h(t, Z_0)\,dt$. The jumps are nonnegative and the derivative is nonpositive; we can thus apply Theorem 7.4, or more precisely, the remark after it to $-X(t)$, with $J = 1$ and $I = 0$. We have thus shown the following theorem.

Theorem 7.5 (Shot Noise)
The average load at an arbitrary point in time is

$$\bar{L} = \lambda \times work\ per\ customer \tag{7.39}$$

where equality also holds if either $\bar{L}$ or the work per customer is infinite.

Equation (7.39) is also known as ***Campbell's formula***.

Example 7.11 TCP Flows

In [7], a customer is a TCP flow, $h(t, z)$ is the bit rate generated at time t by a TCP flow that starts at time 0 and has a size parameter $z \in \mathbb{R}^+$. Thus $\bar{V} = \mathbb{E}^0\left(\int_0^\infty h(t, Z_0)\,dt\right)$ is the average volume of data, counted in bits, generated by a flow during its entire lifetime. Campbell's formula says that the average bit rate on the system $\bar{L}$, measured in b/s, is equal to $\lambda \bar{V}$, where λ is the flow arrival rate.

The $H = \lambda G$ Formula

This is an interpretation of the rate conservation law that is quite useful in applications. Consider some arbitrary system where we can observe the arrival and departure of jobs (also called customers). Let T_n be the point process of arrivals times, with intensity λ (not necessarily Poisson, as usual in this chapter). Also assume that when a job is present in the system, it employs some amount of resource, per time unit (for example, electrical power or CPU cycles). Assume the system to be stationary.

Let G_n be the total amount of system resource consumed by job n during its presence in the system; and let $\bar{G}$ be the average resource consumption per job, i.e. the expectation of G_n when n is an arbitrary customer. Furthermore, let $\bar{H}$ be the average rate at which the resource is allocated to jobs, i.e. the expectation of $H(t)$ at any time t. (7.39) can be re-formulated as follows.

Shot Noise (Variant formulation)
The $H = \lambda G$ **Formula**, or **extended little formula** is equivalent
to
$$\bar{H} = \lambda \bar{G} \qquad (7.40)$$

Example 7.12 Power Consumption per Job

A system serves jobs and consumes in average $\bar{P}$ watts. Assume that
we allocate the energy consumption to jobs, for example by measuring
the current when a job is active. Let $\bar{E}$ be the total energy consumed
by a job, during its lifetime, in average per job, measured in Joules.
According to (7.40) we get

$$\bar{P} = \lambda \bar{E}$$

where λ is the number of jobs per second, served by the system.

Little' s Formula

Consider again some arbitrary system where we can observe the arrival and
departure of jobs (also called customers), where T_n is the point process of
arrivals times, with intensity λ. Let R_n be the residence time of the nth
customer, $n \in \mathbb{Z}$ (thus the departure time is $T_n + R_n$). Let $N(t)$ be the number
of customers present in the system at time t. Assume that the mean residence
time $\bar{R}$ (i.e. the expectation of R_n) is finite (according to the stationarity
assumption, it is independent of n).

COMMENT: We have not exactly defined what a customer and the system are, and
we therefore need, formally, to be more precise. This can be done as follows. We are
given a sequence $(T_n \in \mathbb{R}, R_n \in \mathbb{R}^+)_{n \in \mathbb{Z}}$ that is stationary with respect to index n.
Assume that T_n can be viewed as a stationary point process, with intensity λ (i.e.
the expectation of $T_n - T_{n-1}$ is finite, Theorem 7.9). The number of customers in the
system at time t is then defined by

$$N(t) = \sum_{n \in \mathbb{Z}} 1_{\{T_n \leq t < R_n + T_n\}} \qquad \square$$

Note that, by stationarity, λ is also equal to the departure rate. Define
$R(t)$ by $R(t) = R_n$ if and only if $T_n \leq t < T_{n+1}$, i.e. $R(t)$ is the residence time
of the most recently arrived customer at time t. Also let

$$\mathbb{E}^t(R(t)) = \mathbb{E}^0(R(0)) = \bar{R}$$
$$\mathbb{E}(N(t)) = \mathbb{E}(N(0)) = \bar{N}$$

We can apply Campbell's formula by letting $Z_n = R_n$ and $h(t,z) = 1_{\{0 \leq t < z\}}$,
i.e. the load generated by one customer is 1 as long as this customer is present in
the system. Equivalently, we can apply the rate conservation law with $X(t) =$

residual time to be spent by customers present in the system. This gives the celebrated theorem.

Theorem 7.6 (*Little's Formula*)

The mean number of customers in the system at time t, $\bar{N} := \mathbb{E}\big(N(t)\big)$, is independent of t and satisfies

$$\bar{N} = \lambda\bar{R}$$

where λ is the arrival rate and $\bar{R}$ is the average response time, experienced by an arbitrary customer.

Little's formula makes no assumption other than stationarity. In particular, we do not assume that the residence times are independent of the state of the system, and *neighter do* we assume that the arrival process is Poisson. We should also note that the formula holds even if neither $\bar{N}$ or $\bar{R}$ is infinite.

Little's formula is very versatile, since it does not define what can be we called a system and a customer. The next section is an example of this versatility.

Distributional Little Formula

Assume that we are interested not only in the average number of customers in a system, but also in the distribution of ages within it. More precisely, fix $r_0 > 0$; we would like to know $\bar{N}(r_0)$, defined as the average number of customers in the system with an age $\geq r$. Call $f_R(\cdot)$ the PDF of customer residence time. Consider the virtual system, defined such that we count only customers that have been present in the system for at least r_0 time units:

Original System. The nth customer arrives at time T_n and stays for a duration R_n.

Virtual System. The nth customer arrives at time $T_n + r_0$. If $T_n < r_0$, this customer leaves immediately. Otherwise, the customer stays for a duration $R_n - r_0$.

Apply Little's formula to the virtual system. The average customer residence time in the virtual system is

$$\int_{r_0}^{\infty} (r - r_0) f_R(r)\, dr = \int_{r_0}^{\infty} \left[\int_{r_0}^{r} ds \right] f_R(r)\, dr = \int_{r_0}^{\infty} \int_{r_0}^{r} f_R(r)\, ds\, dr$$

$$= \int_{r_0}^{\infty} \left[\int_{s}^{\infty} f_R(r)\, dr \right] ds = \int_{r_0}^{\infty} F_R^c(s)\, ds$$

where $F_R^c(\cdot)$ is the complementary CDF of the residence time, i.e. $F_R^c(r) = \int_r^{\infty} f_R(r)\, dr$. Thus,

$$\bar{N}(r_0) = \lambda \int_{r_0}^{\infty} F_R^c(r)\, dr$$

Let $f_N(\cdot)$ represent the PDF of the distribution of ages at an arbitrary point in time, i.e. such that $\bar{N}(r_0) = \bar{N} \int_{r_0}^{\infty} f_N(r) \, dr$. It follows that $f_N(r) = \frac{\lambda}{N} F_R^c(r) = \frac{1}{R} F_R^c(r)$, i.e.

$$f_N(r) = \frac{1}{\bar{R}} \int_r^{\infty} f_R(r) \, dr \tag{7.41}$$

Equation (7.41) is called a **Distributional little formula**. It relates the PDF f_N of the age of a customer sampled at an arbitrary point in time to the PDF of residence times f_R. Note that there is an analogy with (7.28) (but that the hypotheses are different).

7.3.3 Two Event Clocks

Assume in this section that we observe two point processes from the same stationary simulation, say A_n, B_n, $n \in \mathbb{Z}$. Let $\lambda(A)$ (resp. $\lambda(B)$) be the intensity of the A (resp. B) point process. Whenever $X(t)$ is some observable output, jointly stationary with the simulation, we can sample $X(t)$ with the two event clocks A, or B, i.e. we can define two Palm probabilities, denoted with $E_A^0(X(0))$ and $E_B^0(X(0))$.

We can also measure the intensity of one point process using the other process's clock. For instance, let $\lambda_A(B)$ be the intensity of the B point process measured with the event clock A. Let $N_B[t_1, t_2)$ be the number of points of process B in the time interval $[t_1, t_2)$. We have

$$\lambda_A(B) = \mathbb{E}_A^0(N_B[A_0, A_1)) \tag{7.42}$$

i.e. it is the average number of B points seen between two A points.

Theorem 7.7 (Neveu's Exchange Formula)

$$\lambda_A(B) = \frac{\lambda(B)}{\lambda(A)} \tag{7.43}$$

$$\mathbb{E}_A^0(X(0)) = \lambda_A(B)\mathbb{E}_B^0\left(\sum_{n \in \mathbb{Z}} X(A_n) 1_{\{B_0 \le A_n < B_1\}} \right) \tag{7.44}$$

Equation (7.44) is the equivalent of the inversion formula (7.23), if we replace the standard clock by clock A and the point process T_n by B_n. Indeed, the last term in (7.44) is the sum of the $X(t)$ values observed at all A points that fall between B_0 and B_1.

It follows from this theorem that

$$\frac{1}{\lambda_A(B)} = \mathbb{E}_B^0(N_A[0, B_1)) = \mathbb{E}_B^0(N_A[B_0, B_1)) \tag{7.45}$$

which is the equivalent of (7.25), namely, the intensity of the point process B, measured with A's clock, is the inverse time between two arbitrary B points, again measured with A's clock (the last term, $N_A[B_0, B_1)$, is the number of ticks of the A clock between two B points).

The following theorem follows immediately from Theorem 7.7 and (7.45).

Theorem 7.8 (Wald's Identity)

$$\mathbb{E}_A^0\big(X(0)\big) = \frac{\mathbb{E}_B^0\left(\sum_{n\in\mathbb{Z}} X(A_n)1_{\{B_0\leq A_n < B_1\}}\right)}{\mathbb{E}_B^0\big(N_A[B_0, B_1)\big)} \qquad (7.46)$$

Equation (7.46) is called **Wald's identity**. It is often presented in the context of renewal processes, but this need not be the case: like all Palm calculus formulas, it requires only stationarity, and no independence assumption.

Example 7.13 The Stop-and-Go protocol

We re-visit the computation of the stop and go protocol given in Example 7.3. The A point process consists of the emission times of successful transmissions, and the B point process consists of all transmission and retransmission attempts. Apply (7.45):

$$\frac{1}{\lambda_A(B)} = \mathbb{E}_B^0\big(N_A[B_0, B_1)\big)$$

Note that $N_A[B_0, B_1)$ is 1 if the attempt at B_0 is successful and 0 otherwise. Consequently, the right-handside of the equation is the probability that an arbitrary transmission or retransmission attempt is successful. By definition of α, this is $1 - \alpha$. Thus, $\frac{\lambda(A)}{\lambda(B)} = 1 - \alpha$. Compute $\lambda(B)$ from (7.25): $\frac{1}{\lambda(B)} = (1 - \alpha)t_0 + \alpha t_1$. Combining the two gives

$$\lambda(A) = \frac{1}{\dfrac{\alpha}{1-\alpha}t_1 + t_0}$$

as already found.

Comment: All formulas in this section continue to hold if we replace the semi-closed intervals that span one tick of an event clock to the next, such as $[A_0, A_1)$ (resp. $[B_0, B_1)$), by the semi-closed intervals $(A_0, A_1]$ (resp. $(B_0, B_1]$). However, they do not hold if we replace them by closed or open intervals (such as $[A_0, A_1]$ or (A_0, A_1)).

One can even replace them by the so-called **Voronoi** cells, which are the intervals that are bounded by the middle of two successive points; one can for instance replace $[A_0, A_1)$ by $[\frac{A_{-1}+A_0}{2}, \frac{A_0+A_1}{2})$ or $(\frac{A_{-1}+A_0}{2}, \frac{A_0+A_1}{2}]$. Thus,

$$\lambda_A(B) = \mathbb{E}_A^0\big(N_B[A_0, A_1)\big) = \mathbb{E}_A^0\big(N_B(A_0, A_1]\big)$$

$$= \mathbb{E}_A^0\left(N_B\left[\frac{A_{-1}+A_0}{2}, \frac{A_0+A_1}{2}\right)\right) = \mathbb{E}_A^0\left(N_B\left(\frac{A_{-1}+A_0}{2}, \frac{A_0+A_1}{2}\right]\right)$$

and (7.44) can be generalized to

$$
\mathbb{E}_A^0\big(X(0)\big) = \lambda_A(B)\mathbb{E}_B^0\left(\sum_{n\in\mathbb{Z}} X(A_n)1_{\{B_0\le A_n<B_1\}}\right)
$$

$$
= \lambda_A(B)\mathbb{E}_B^0\left(\sum_{n\in\mathbb{Z}} X(A_n)1_{\{B_0<A_n\le B_1\}}\right)
$$

$$
= \lambda_A(B)\mathbb{E}_B^0\left(\sum_{n\in\mathbb{Z}} X(A_n)1_{\{\frac{B_{-1}+B_0}{2}\le A_n<\frac{B_1+B_2}{2}\}}\right)
$$

$$
= \lambda_A(B)\mathbb{E}_B^0\left(\sum_{n\in\mathbb{Z}} X(A_n)1_{\{\frac{B_{-1}+B_0}{2}< A_n\le\frac{B_1+B_2}{2}\}}\right) \qquad \square
$$

7.4 Simulation Defined as Stochastic Recurrence

7.4.1 Stochastic Recurrence, Modulated Process

Recall (Chapter 6) that a stochastic recurrence is defined by a sequence Z_n, $n \in \mathbb{Z}$, (also called the modulator state at the nth epoch) and a sequence $S_n > 0$, interpreted as the duration of the nth epoch. The state space for Z_n is arbitrary, and not necessarily finite or even enumerable. We assume that (Z_n, S_n) is random, but stationary[2] with respect to the index n. As usual, we do not assume any form of independence.

We are interested in the **modulated process** $\big(Z(t), S(t)\big)$ defined by $Z(t) = Z_n$, $S(t) = S_n$ whenever t belongs to the nth epoch (i.e. when $T_n \le t < T_{n+1}$). We would like to apply Palm calculus to $\big(Z(t), S(t)\big)$.

Example 7.14 Loss Channel Model
A path on the internet is modeled as a loss system, where the packet loss ratio at time t, $p(t)$ depends on a hidden state $Z(t) \in \{1, \ldots, I\}$ (called the modulator state). During one epoch, the modulator remains in some fixed state, say i, and the packet loss ratio is constant, say p_i. At the end of an epoch, the modulator changes state and a new epoch starts.
Once in a while, we send a probe packet on this path, and we thus measure the time average loss ratio $\bar{p}$. How does it relate to p_i? Apply the inversion formula

$$
\bar{p} = \frac{\displaystyle\sum_i \pi_i^0 p_i \bar{S}_i}{\displaystyle\sum_i \pi_i^0 \bar{S}_i}
$$

---

[2] This means that the joint distribution of $(Z_n, S_n \ldots, Z_{n+m}, S_{n+m})$ is independent of m.

where π_i^0 is the probability that the modulator is in state i at an arbitrary epoch (proportion of i epochs) and $\bar{S}_i$ is the average duration of an i-epoch.

For example, assume that Z_n is the **Gilbert loss model** shown in Figure 7.8, i.e. a discrete time two state Markov chain, and S_n is equal to one round trip time. We have $\pi_i^0 = \frac{q_{1-i}}{q_0+q_1}$, for $i = 0, 1$. It follows that

$$\bar{p} = \frac{q_0 p_1}{q_0 + q_1}$$

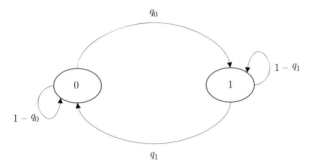

Figure 7.8 The Gilbert Loss Model. When the channel is in state 0 the packet loss ratio is 0, whereas in state 1 it is p_1. The average number of consecutive periods in state i is $\frac{1}{q_i}$ ($i = 0, 2$).

7.4.2 Freezing Simulations

In the previous example, we implicitly assumed that we can apply Palm calculus, i.e. that the process $Z(t)$ is stationary. In the rest of this section we give conditions for this assumption to be valid.

We first make a technical assumption, i.e. that the number of epochs per time unit does not explode. More precisely, for any fixed $t_0 > 0$, define:

$$D(t_0) = \sum_{n=1}^{\infty} 1_{\{S_0 + \cdots + S_{n-1} \leq t_0\}}$$

We interpret $D(t_0)$ as the number of epochs that are entirely included in the interval $(0, t_0]$, given that we start the first epoch at time 0. The technical assumption is

$$\text{For every } t_0, \text{ the expectation of } D(t_0) \text{ is finite} \qquad \text{(H1)}$$

Surprisingly, though (Z_n, S_n) is stationary with respect to n, this is not enough to guarantee the stationarity of $Z(t)$. To see why, assume that $Z(t)$ is stationary and that there exists a stationary point process T_n such that $T_{n+1} - T_n = S_n$.

Apply the inversion formula

$$\lambda = \frac{1}{\displaystyle\int_0^\infty t f_S^0(t)\, dt} \tag{7.47}$$

where $f_S^0(t)$ is the probability density function of S_n (it does not depend on n by hypothesis). Thus, we need to assume that the expectation of S_n is finite. The next theorem states that, essentially, this is also sufficient.

Theorem 7.9

Assume that the sequence S_n satisfies (H1) and has a finite expectation. There exists a stationary process $Z(t)$ and a stationary point process T_n such that

(1) $T_{n+1} - T_n = S_n$;

(2) $Z_n = Z(T_n)$.

The theorem says that we can apply Palm calculus, and in particular treat Z_n as the state of a stationary simulation sampled with the event clock derived from S_n. The proof can be found in [4], where it is called "inverse construction".

Condition (H1) is often intuitively obvious, but may be hard to verify in some cases. In the simple case where S_n are independent (thus iid since we assume stationarity with respect to n), the condition always holds:

Theorem 7.10 (Renewal Case)

If the S_n are iid and $S_n > 0$, then condition (H1) holds

The next example shows a non iid case.

Example 7.15 Random Waypoint, Continuation of Example 7.7

For the random waypoint model, the sequence of modulator states is

$$Z_n = (M_n, M_{n+1}, V_n)$$

and the duration of the nth epoch is

$$S_n = \frac{d(M_n, M_{n+1})}{V_n} \tag{7.48}$$

where $d(M_n, M_{n+1})$ is the distance from M_n to M_{n+1}.

Can this be assumed to come from a stationary process? We apply Theorem 7.9. The average epoch time is

$$\mathbb{E}(S_0) = \mathbb{E}\left(\frac{d(M_n, M_{n+1})}{V_n}\right) = \mathbb{E}\big(d(M_n, M_{n+1})\big)\mathbb{E}\left(\frac{1}{V_n}\right)$$

since the waypoints and the speed are chosen independently. Thus, it is essential that $\mathbb{E}(\frac{1}{V_n}) < \infty$, or in other words that $v_{\min} > 0$.

We also need to verify (H1). We cannot apply Theorem 7.10 since the epoch times are not independent (two consecutive epoch times depend on one common waypoint). However, S_m and S_n are independent if $n - m \geq 2$, and one can show that (H1) holds by using arguments similar to the proof of Theorem 7.10 [52].

What happens if the expectation of S_n is infinite? It can be shown (and verified by simulation) that the model *freezes*: as you run the simulation longer and longer, it becomes more likely to draw a very long interval S_n, and the simulation state stays there for long. This is an interesting case where non-stationarity is not due to explosion, but to **aging** (Figure 7.9). In the random waypoint example above, this happens if we choose $v_{\min} = 0$.

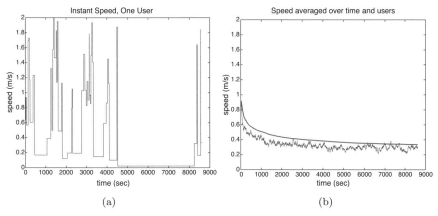

(a)   (b)

Figure 7.9 Freezing simulation: random waypoint with $v_{\min} = 0$. The model does not have a stationary regime and the simulation becomes slower and slower. (a) sample of instant speed versus time for one mobile. (b) speed averaged over $[0; t]$ for one mobile (zig zag curve) or for 30 mobiles (smoother curve). The average speed slowly tends to 0.

7.4.3 Perfect Simulation of Stochastic Recurrence

Assume that we are interested in simulating the modulator process $\big(Z(t), S(t)\big)$. A simple method consists in drawing a sample of (Z_0, S_0) from the joint distribution with PDF $f^0_{Z,S}(z, s)$, then deciding that the simulation remains in this state for a duration S_0, followed by drawing Z_1, S_1 from its conditional distribution given (Z_0, S_0) and so on. For a stochastic recurrence satisfying the hypotheses of Theorem 7.9, as the simulation will time increases, the simulation enter its stationary regime and its state will be distributed according to the stationary distribution of $\big(Z(t), S(t)\big)$.

It is possible to do better, and start the simulation directly in the stationary regime, i.e. avoid transients entirely. This is called **perfect simulation**. It is based on Palm's inversion formula, which provides a means of sampling from the stationary distribution, as we explain now.

We want to start a simulation of the modulator process $(Z(t), S(t))$, in the stationary regime. We need to draw a sample from the stationary distribution of $(Z(t), S(t))$, but this is not sufficient. We also need to sample the time until the next change of modulator state. It is thus useful to consider the joint process $(Z(t), S(t), T^+(t))$, where $T^+(t)$ is the residual time, defined in Section 7.3.1 as the time to run until the next change in modulator state, i.e.

$$\text{if } T_n \le t < T_{n+1} \quad \text{then} \quad T^+(t) = T_{n+1} - t$$

Theorem 7.11 (Stationary Distribution of Modulated Process)
Let $(Z_n, S_n)_{n \in \mathbb{Z}}$ satisfy the hypotheses of Theorem 7.9 and let $f^0_{Z,S}(z, s)$ be the joint PDF of (Z_n, S_n), independent of n by hypothesis. The stationary distribution of $(Z(t), S(t), T^+(t))$ (defined above) is entirely characterized by the following properties:

(1) The joint PDF of $(Z(t), S(t))$ is

$$f_{Z,S}(z, s) = \eta s f^0_{Z,S}(z, s) \tag{7.49}$$

where η is a normalizing constant, equal to the inverse of the expectation of S_n;

(2) The conditional distribution of $T^+(t)$, given that $Z(t) = z$ and $S(t) = s$, is uniform on $[0, s]$.

Recall that Z_n takes values in any arbitrary space, but you may think of it as an element of $\mathbb{R}^k$ for some integer k.[3]

Note that the theorem does not directly give a formula for the joint PDF of $(Z(t), S(t), T^+(t))$, though this can be derived, at least in theory, from the combination of items (1) and (2) (see [57] for an example).

Also, do not confuse item (2) with the unconditional distribution of the residual time $T^+(t)$. From Theorem 7.3, we know that the distribution of $T^+(t)$ has PDF proportional to $1 - F^0_S(t)$, where $F^0_S(\cdot)$ is the CDF of S_n. In other words, it is not uniform.

COMMENT: We can recover this result from the above theorem, as follows. Consider a test function $\phi(\cdot)$ of the residual time $T^+(t)$. The theorem states that

$$\mathbb{E}\left(\phi(T^+(t)) \mid Z(t) = s, \, S(t) = s\right) = \frac{1}{s} \int_0^s \phi(t) \, dt$$

---

[3] Formally, Z_n may take on values in some arbitrary space $\mathcal{Z}$, and S_n is a positive number. We assume that there is a measure μ on $\mathcal{Z}$ and the PDF $f^0_{Z,S}(z, s)$ is defined with respect to the measure product of μ and of the Lebesgue measure on $(0, \infty)$.

thus

$$
\begin{aligned}
\mathbb{E}\left(\phi(T^+(t))\right) &= \eta \int_{z \in Z} \int_0^\infty \left(\frac{1}{s} \int_0^s \phi(t)\, dt\right) s f_{Z,S}^0(z,s)\, dz\, ds \\
&= \eta \int_{z \in Z} \int_0^\infty \left(\int_0^s \phi(t)\, dt\right) f_{Z,S}^0(z,s)\, dz\, ds \\
&= \eta \int_0^\infty \left(\int_0^s \phi(t)\, dt\right) f_S^0(s)\, ds = \eta \int_0^\infty \left(\int_t^\infty f_S^0(s)\, ds\right) \phi(t)\, dt \\
&= \eta \int_0^\infty \left(1 - F_S^0(t)\right)\phi(t)\, dt
\end{aligned}
$$

which shows that the PDF of $T^+(t)$ is $\eta\left(1 - F_S^0(t)\right)$, as given in Theorem 7.3.   □

We obtain a perfect simulation algorithm by immediate application of the above theorem, see Algorithm 7.1. Note the use of the factor s during sampling of the initial time interval: we can interpret this by stating that the probability, for an observer who sees the system in its stationary regime, of falling in an interval of duration s is proportional to s. This is the same argument as in Feller's paradox (Section 7.3.1).

Algorithm 7.1 Perfect simulation of a modulated process

1: Sample (z, s) from the joint distribution with PDF $\eta s f_{Z,S}^0(z,s)$ (Eq. (7.49))
2: Sample t uniformly in $[0, s]$
3: Start the simulation with $Z(0) = z$, $S(0) = s$, $T^+(0) = T$

Example 7.16 Perfect Simulation of Random Waypoint
We assume that the model in Example 7.15 has a stationary regime, i.e. that $v_{\min} > 0$. The modulator process is here

$$
Z(t) = \left(P(t), N(t), V(t), S(t)\right)
$$

where $P(t)$ ($N(t)$) is the previous (next) waypoint, $V(t)$ is the instant speed and $S(t)$ is the duration of the current trip. Note that $S(t)$ is determined by (7.48), i.e.

$$
S(t) = \frac{d\left(P(t), N(t)\right)}{V(t)}
$$

It is thus a deterministic function of $\left(P(t), N(t), V(t)\right)$ and can be omitted from the description of the modulator process.
Note that by a standard change of variable arguments,

$$
f_{P,N,V}(p, n, v) = \frac{d(p, n)}{v^2} f_{P,N,S}(p, n, s)
$$

$$
f_{P,N,V}^0(p, n, v) = \frac{d(p, n)}{v^2} f_{P,N,S}^0(p, n, s)
$$

A direct application of Theorem 7.11(1), gives the joint PDF of $\big(P(t), N(t), V(t)\big)$:

$$f_{P,N,V}(p, n, v) = \frac{d(p, n)}{v^2}\, \eta s f_{P,N,S}^0(p, n, s) = \eta s f_{P,N,V}^0(p, n, v)$$

$$= \eta f_{P,N,V}^0(p, n, v)\frac{d(p, n)}{v}$$

Now, by definition of the random waypoint model, speed and waypoints are chosen independently at a waypoint, i.e.

$$f_{P,N,V}^0(p, n, v) = f_{P,N}^0(p, n) f_V^0(v)$$

Thus

$$f_{P,N,V}(p, n, v) = \eta\, d(p, n) f_{P,N}^0(p, n)\frac{1}{v} f_V^0(v) \qquad (7.50)$$

Since the joint PDF is the product of the PDFs of (P, N) on the one hand, and V on the other hand, it follows that these two are independentIn the other words, when sampled at an arbitrary point in time, the trip endpoints on the one hand, and the chosen speed on the other hand, are independent. Furthermore, by marginalization, the joint PDF of $\big(P(t), N(t)\big)$ is

$$f_{P,N}(p, n) = \eta_1\, d(p, n) \qquad (7.51)$$

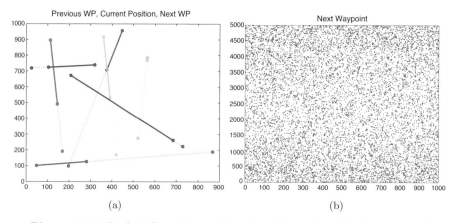

Figure 7.10 Perfect Simulation of Random Waypoint. (a) 7 samples of previous waypoint (P), current mobile location (M), and next waypoint (N) sampled at an arbitrary point in time. P and N are not independent; their joint PDF is proportional to their distance. (Compare to the distribution obtained when sampling an arbitrary waypoint: there, by construction, P and N are independent and uniformly distributed. They are thus independent, by definition of the model.) Given P and N, M is uniformly distributed on $[P, N]$. (b) $10,000$ samples of the next waypoint, sampled at an arbitrary point in time. The distribution is not uniform, with a larger density towards the edges.

for p, n in the area of interest, and 0 otherwise, and where η is a normalizing constant. Thus, the joint PDF of trip endpoints is proportional to their distance, i.e. we are more likely to see long trips in average (this is reminiscent of Feller's paradox in Section 7.3.1; though in space, not in time). It also follows that the distribution of a trip endpoint is not uniform, and that the two endpoints are *not* independent (though they are so when sampled at waypoints). Figure 7.10 shows samples from the marginal distribution of $P(t)$ (which is the same as that of $N(t)$). We used rejection sampling (Theorem 6.3), which does not require knowing the normalizing constant η_1.

We also obtain that the distribution of speed at an arbitrary point in time is proportional to $\frac{1}{v} f_V^0(v)$, which we had already found in Example 7.7. After some algebra, one finds that the CDF of $V(t)$ is

$$F_V(v) = \frac{\ln v - \ln v_{\min}}{\ln v_{\max} - \ln v_{\min}} \tag{7.52}$$

for $v_{\min} \leq v \leq v_{\max}$, 0 if $v \leq v_{\min}$ and 1 if $v \geq v_{\max}$.

Let $M(t)$ be the mobile location at time t. The residual time is related to $M(t)$ by

$$N(t) - M(t) = \frac{T^+(t)V(t)}{d\big(P(t), N(t)\big)} \big(N(t) - P(t)\big)$$

so that adding either $T^+(t)$ or $M(t)$ to the modulator process is equivalent. We can thus take as process state $\big(P(t), N(t), V(t), M(t)\big)$. A direct application of Theorem 7.11(2), together with the change of variable arguments as above, lead to the conditional distribution of $M(t)$, given that $P(t) = p$, $N(t) = n$, $V(t) = v$, being uniform on the segment $[p, n]$. In particular, it is independent of the speed $V(t)$.

We summarize these findings in Algorithm 7.2.

Algorithm 7.2 Perfect simulation of random waypoint.

1: Sample the speed v from the distribution with CDF F_V in (7.52) (e.g. using CDF inversion, Theorem 6.1).

2: Sample the previous waypoint p and next waypoint n from the distribution with PDF proportional to the distance from p to n (e.g. using rejection sampling Theorem 6.3).

3: Sample m uniformly on the segment that joins p and n, e.g. by sampling u uniformly in $[0, 1]$ and letting $m = (1 - u)p + un$.

4: Start the simulation with $P(0) = p$, $N(0) = n$, $V(0) = v$, $M(0) = m$.

7.5 Application to Markov Chain Models and the PASTA Property

In this section, we consider a stochastic process $S(t)$ (the state of the simulation) that can be expressed as a Markov chain, in discrete or continuous time. Formally, this means that the state at time t contains all information for advancing the simulation. Most simulations that we perform in a computer fall within this framework, since the simulation program uses only information available in memory. This does not mean that Markov models are always the best models for analyzing a problem, as the state space may be prohibitively large. But it does provide a convenient framework for reasoning about what we are doing, e.g. to understand what the PASTA property means (Section 7.5.2). In this section, we limit ourselves to Markov chains over a finite state space, as this provides considerable simplifications.

In an appendix of this chapter (Section 7.6), we give a quick review of Markov chains. There are also many very good books on the topic; see for example [21], [108] and [17].

7.5.1 Embedded Sub-Chain

If we observe a Markov chain just after some selected transitions, we obtain an *embedded sub-chain*, which is itself a discrete time Markov chain, clocked by the selected transitions. We explain in this section how to compute all elements of the embedded subchain, in particular the Palm probabilities for events observed with the clock of the embedded subchain.

Consider first discrete time. $S(t)$ is a stationary Markov chain with enumerable state space $\mathcal{S}$. We are interested in observing the transitions of $S(t)$, which is equivalent to observing the process $\big(S(t-1), S(t)\big)$. Note that this is also a Markov chain. Let $\mathcal{F}_0 \subset \mathcal{S}^2$ be a subset of the set of possible transitions, and call T_n, $n = 1, 2, \ldots$, the time instants at which the chain makes a transition in $\mathcal{F}_0$, i.e.

$$T_1 \stackrel{\text{def}}{=} \inf\big\{t \geq 1 : \big(S(t-1), S(t)\big) \in \mathcal{F}_0\big\}$$

$$T_n \stackrel{\text{def}}{=} \inf\big\{t > T_{n-1} : \big(S(t-1), S(t)\big) \in \mathcal{F}_0\big\}$$

We assume that there is an infinity of such times, i.e. $T_n < \infty$ with probability 1, and further, that the expected time between visits is also finite.[4] Then, by Theorem 7.9, we can treat T_n as a stationary point process associated with the stationary process $S(t)$.

The sequence of states observed just after a transition, $S(T_n)$, is itself a discrete time Markov chain, since the knowledge of the state at the nth transition is sufficient to compute the probabilities of future events (this is the strong

---

[4] This is true in cases where $\mathcal{F}_0$ consists of only recurrent non-null states of the chain $\big(S(t-1), S(t)\big)$.

Markov property). The sequence $Y_n = S(T_n)$ is called the **embedded sub-chain**. We call **matrix of selected transitions** the matrix of probabilities C defined by

$$C_{i,j} = Q_{i,j} 1_{\{(i,j) \in \mathcal{F}_0\}}$$

for all (i,j) and where Q is the transition matrix of S (see (7.57)). The matrix C is simply derived by inspection. We also define the matrix $J_{i,j}$ by

$$J_{i,j} \overset{\text{def}}{=} \mathbb{P}\big(S(T_1) = j \mid S(0) = i\big)$$

so that $J_{i,j}$ is the transition probability of the chain Y_n if i is a reachable state of Y_n. Note that J is not equal to C, as the next theorem shows.

In continuous time, the definitions are similar. (Recall that we assume right-continuous sample paths, so a selected transition occurs at time t if $\big(S(t^-), S(t)\big) \in \mathcal{F}_0$.) The matrix of selected transitions is now a rate matrix, given by

$$C_{i,j} = A_{i,j} 1_{\{(i,j) \in \mathcal{F}_0\}}$$

for all (i,j), and where A is the transition rate matrix of S (with $A_{i,i} = -\sum_{j \neq i} A_{i,j}$). Here, we assume that looping transitions are not possible, i.e. $(i,i) \notin \mathcal{F}_0$ for all i. Note that Y_n is a discrete time Markov chain even if $S(t)$ is in continuous time.

Theorem 7.12

Consider a stationary Markov chain in discrete or continuous time $S(t)$ with $t \in \mathbb{Z}$ or $t \in \mathbb{R}$, with stationary probability π, defined over some enumerable state space. Consider an embedded sub-chain Y_n, $n \in \mathbb{N}$, with the assumptions above, and with a matrix of selected transitions C.

(1) The transition matrix J of the embedded sub-chain Y_n satisfies $(\text{Id} - Q + C)J = C$ (discrete time) or $(C - A)J = C$ (continuous time).

(2) The intensity of the point process of selected transitions is $\lambda = \sum_{i,j} \pi_i C_{i,j}$.

(3) The probability that an arbitrary selected transition is (i,j) is $\frac{1}{\lambda} \pi_i C_{i,j}$ (in discrete time this is defined as $\mathbb{P}^0(S_{-1} = i, S_0 = j)$; in continuous time as $\mathbb{P}^0(S_{0-} = i, S_0 = j)$).

(4) The probability of being in state j just after an arbitrary selected transition is $\frac{1}{\lambda} \sum_i \pi_i C_{i,j}$. The probability of being in state i just before an arbitrary selected transition is $\frac{1}{\lambda} \pi_i \sum_j C_{i,j}$.

Example 7.17   Queuing Network in Figure 8.24

There are two stations, called "Gate" and "Think Time", and one class of customers. In order to simplify we assume that the service times in both stations are exponentially distributed with parameters μ (at "Gate") and ν (at "Think Time"). The system can be described as a continuous-time Markov chain where the state is the number of customers at station "Gate", so that $n \in \{0, \ldots, K\}$, where K is the total population size.

This is a single-class productform network, and from Theorem 8.7, the stationary probability is

$$p(n \mid K) = \frac{1}{\eta(K)} \frac{1}{\mu^n} \frac{1}{(K-n)! \nu^{K-n}}$$

where we explicitly write the dependency on the total population size and $\eta(K)$ is a normalizing constant.

Consider the arrivals at station "Gate" to be selected transitions. The matrix of selected transitions is given by

$$C_{n,n+1} = (K-n)\nu \quad \text{and} \quad C_{n,n'} = 0 \quad \text{if } n' \neq n+1$$

The probability that the number of customers is n just after an arrival is, by item (4) of Theorem 7.12,

$$p^0(n) = \frac{1}{\lambda} p(n-1)C(n-1,n) = \frac{1}{\lambda\eta(K)} \frac{1}{\mu^{n-1}} \frac{1}{(K-n)! \nu^{K-n}}$$

This is the same as $p(n-1 \mid K-1)$, if we ignore the normalizing constants. More precisely,

$$p^0(n) = \frac{\eta(K-1)}{\lambda\eta(K)} p(n-1 \mid K-1) \qquad (7.53)$$

Since $\sum_{n=1}^{K} p^0(n) = \sum_{n=1}^{K} p(n-1 \mid K-1) = 1$, the constant $\frac{\eta(K-1)}{\lambda\eta(K)}$ is 1. In other words,

$$p^0(n) = p(n-1 \mid K-1) \qquad (7.54)$$

An arriving customer thus samples the network in the same way as if this customer would be removed (this is an instance of the Arrival Theorem 8.16). It also follows that

$$\lambda = \frac{\eta(K-1)}{\eta(K)} \qquad (7.55)$$

which is an instance of the Throughput Theorem 8.12.

7.5.2 PASTA

Consider a system that can be modeled by a stationary Markov chain $S(t)$ in discrete or continuous time (in practice any simulation that has a stationary regime and is run long enough). We are interested in a matrix of $C \geq 0$ of selected transitions such that

Independence. For any state i of $S(t)$, $\sum_j C_{i,j} \overset{\text{def}}{=} \lambda$ is independent of i.

In other words, the rate of occurrence of a selected transition is independent of the global simulation state. Further, this assumption implies that the point process of selected transitions is a Bernoulli process (discrete time) or a Poisson process (continuous time) with intensity λ (see Section 7.6 for the definition of Poisson and Bernoulli processes).

Theorem 7.13 (PASTA)
Consider a point process of selected transitions as defined above. The Palm probability just before a transition is the stationary probability.

The theorem says that, in the stationary regime, the Bernoulli or Poisson clock of selected transitions sees the system in the same way as the standard clock.

Interpret C as external arrivals into a queuing system. The theorem is known as "Poisson Arrivals See Time Averages", hence the acronym. Note however that this denomination is misleading: Poisson alone is not sufficient. It is essential for the point process of the selected transition to have a rate that is independent of the state (see Example 7.20).

Example 7.18   ARP Requests without Refreshes

IP packets delivered by a host are produced according to a Poisson process with λ packets per second in average. When a packet is delivered, if an ARP request was emitted no more than t_a seconds ago, no ARP request is generated. Otherwise, an ARP request is generated. What is the rate of generation of ARP requests?

Call T_n the point process of ARP request generations, μ its intensity and p the probability that an arriving packet causes the sending of an ARP request. First, we have $\mu = p\lambda$ (to see why, assume that time is discrete and apply the definition of intensity).

Second, let $Z(t) = 1$ if the ARP timer is running, and 0 if it has expired. Thus, p is the probability that an arriving packet sees $Z(t) = 0$. The PASTA property applies, as the IP packet generation process is independent of the state of the ARP timer. (You may establish a formal link with Theorem 7.13 as follows. Think in discrete time. The system can be modeled by a Markov chain with $X(t) = i = $ the residual value of the timer. We have $Q_{i,i-1} = 1$ for $i > 0$, $Q_{0,t_a} = \lambda$, $Q_{0,0} = 1 - \lambda$. The selected transitions are IP packet deliveries, and the probability that one IP packet is delivered in one slot is λ, and does not depend on the state i.)

By the inversion formula

$$p = \mathbb{P}\big(Z(t) = 0\big) = \mu\mathbb{E}^0(T_1 - t_a) = \mu\left(\frac{1}{\mu} - t_a\right) = 1 - \mu t_a \qquad (7.56)$$

Combining with $\mu = p\lambda$ gives $p = \frac{1}{\lambda t_a + 1}$, and the rate of generation of ARP requests is $\mu = \frac{\lambda}{1 + \lambda t_a}$.

Example 7.19 M/GI/1 Queue

A similar reasoning shows that for a queuing system with Poisson arrivals and independent service times, an arriving customer sees the system (just before his/her own arrival) in the same way as an external observer arriving at an arbitrary instant.

Example 7.20 A Poisson Process that does not satisfy PASTA

The PASTA theorem requires the event process to be Poisson or Bernoulli *and* independence on the current state. Here is an example of a Poisson process that does not satisfy this assumption, and thus does not enjoy the PASTA property.

Construct a simulation as follows. Requests arrive as a Poisson process of rate λ, into a single server queue. Let T_n be the arrival time of the nth request. The service time of the nth request is assumed to be $\frac{1}{2}(T_{n+1} - T_n)$. The service times are thus exponential with the mean $\frac{1}{2\lambda}$, but not independent of the arrival process. Assuming that the system is initially empty, there is exactly 1 customer during half of the time, and 0 customers otherwise. Thus, the time-average distribution of the queue length $X(t)$ is given by $\mathbb{P}(X(t) = 0) = \mathbb{P}(X(t) = 1) = 0.5$ and $\mathbb{P}(X(t) = k) = 0$ for $k \geq 2$. In contrast, the queue is always empty when a customer arrives. Thus the Palm distribution of the queue length just before an arrival is different from the time average distribution of the queue length.

The arrival process does not satisfy the independence assumption: at a time t when the queue is not empty, we know that there cannot be an arrival. The probability that an arrival occurs during a short time slot thus depends on the global state of the system.

Application to measurements

The PASTA property shows that sampling a system at random observation instants, distributed like a Poisson or Bernoulli process, independent of the system state, provides an unbiased estimator of the time average distribution.

7.6   Appendix: Quick Review of Markov Chains

7.6.1   Markov Chain in Discrete Time

Let $\mathcal{S}$ be a *finite* set. A discrete time stochastic process $S(t)$ is a Markov chain on $\mathcal{S}$ if the future evolution of S given the entire past up to time t is entirely determined by $S(t)$. The **transition matrix** is the matrix of probabilities $Q_{i,j}$ defined by

$$Q_{i,j} = \mathbb{P}(S(t+1) = j \mid S(t) = i) \tag{7.57}$$

for all i and j in $\mathcal{S}$.

The state space can be partitioned in **communication classes** as follows: two states i and j are in the same communication class if $i = j$ or if the chain $S(t)$ can go from i to j in a finite number of transitions (each transition must have a positive probability), and vice-versa, from j to i. A communication class is either **recurrent** (once the chain $S(t)$ has entered the class, it will remain in the class forever) or not, also called **transient**. If a class is transient, with probability 1, the chain will leave it and never return. States that belong to a transient class are also called transient.

Let $\pi(t)$ be the row vector of probabilities at time t, i.e $\pi_i(t) = \mathbb{P}\big(S(t) = i\big)$. Then, for all $t \in \mathbb{N}$

$$\pi(t) = \pi(0)Q^t \tag{7.58}$$

For the chain $S(t)$ to be stationary, we need $\pi(t)$ to be independent of t, which implies that π satisfies the linear system

$$\begin{cases} \pi = \pi Q \\ \displaystyle\sum_{i \in \mathcal{S}} \pi_i = 1 \end{cases} \tag{7.59}$$

It turns out that this is also sufficient, i.e if $\pi(0)$ is a solution to (7.59), then $S(t)$ is stationary. A solution to (7.59) is called a **stationary probability** of the Markov chain.

Note that, since Q is a stochastic matrix, any solution $\pi \in \mathbb{R}^{\mathcal{S}}$ of (7.59) is necessarily non-negative. Since $\mathcal{S}$ is finite, the situation is simple: stationary probabilities correspond to recurrent classes. More precisely,

- There is at least one recurrent class.
- For every recurrent class c there is one stationary probability vector π^c, such that $\pi_i^c > 0$ if $i \in c$, and $\pi_i^c = 0$ otherwise; any stationary probability is a weighted average of the π^c's.
- If there is only one recurrent class, the chain is called **irreducible**. If the chain is irreducible, there is exactly one stationary probability, and vice-versa, i.e. if (7.59) has only one solution, the chain is irreducible.
- The chain is **ergodic** in the wide sense[5] if it is irreducible, and vice-versa.
- If there is more than one recurrent class, the chain will eventually enter one recurrent class and remain there forever. The probability that the chain enters recurrent class c depends on the initial condition.
- If π is a stationary probability vector and i is a transient state, $\pi_i = 0$.

Thus, when $\mathcal{S}$ is finite, there is always at least one stationary regime. If the chain $S(t)$ is not irreducible (i.e. not ergodic) there may be several stationary regimes, and the stationary regime that the chain eventually enters may be

---

[5] Some authors use a more restrictive definition and say that a finite-space Markov chain is "ergodic" if it is irreducible and aperiodic, see later. We prefer to use the general definition, which is that time averages tend to expectations.

random. This happens for example for systems that may have several failure modes.

Consider an ergodic chain (with finite state space). It is stationary if the initial distribution of state is the stationary probability. Otherwise, it becomes stationary as $t \to \infty$, but there is a technicality due to periodicity. A recurrent class c is called **periodic** with period d if all cycles in the class have a length multiple of some $d \geq 2$ (i.e. whenever $X(t) = i, X(t + s) = i$ for $i \in c$ and $s > 0$, s must be a multiple of d); otherwise, the class is aperiodic. A chain with a single recurrent class is said to be periodic (resp. aperiodic) if its unique recurrent class is periodic (resp. aperiodic).

If the chain is ergodic and aperiodic then

$$\lim_{t \to \infty} \pi(t) = \pi$$

where π is the unique stationary probability and thus the chain becomes stationary for large t. Otherwise, if the chain is periodic with period d

$$\lim_{t \to \infty} \frac{1}{d} \left(\pi(t) + \pi(t + 1) + \cdots + \pi(t + d - 1) \right) = \pi$$

which can be interpreted as follows. Change the time origin randomly uniformly in $\{0, 1, \ldots, d - 1\}$. Then as $t \to \infty$, the chain becomes stationary.

If the state space is enumerable but infinite, the situation is more complex; there may not exist a recurrent class, and even if there does, there may not exist a stationary probability (the chain "escapes to infinity"). However, there is a simple result. If the chain is irreducible, then (7.59) has a 0 or 1 solution. If it has the 1 solution, then it is ergodic and all statements above for an ergodic chain over a finite space continue to hold.

7.6.2   Markov Chain in Continuous Time

In continuous-time, the definition of the Markov Chain is similar, i.e. $\mathcal{S}$ is an enumerable set and the continuous time stochastic process $S(t)$ is a Markov chain on $\mathcal{S}$ if the future evolution of S, given that the entire past up to time t is entirely determined by $S(t)$. We assume as usual that $S(t)$ is right-continuous, i.e. that $S(t^+) = S(t)$, so that if there is a transition at time t, $S(t)$ is the state just after the transition.[6] Note that some authors reserve the term Markov *chain* to discrete time, whereas others reserve it to discrete or continuous time processes over a discrete state space (as we do).

The transition matrix is replaced by a matrix of rates, called the **rate transition matrix**, or **generator matrix**, A. It has the property that

$$\mathbb{P}\big(S(t + dt) = j \mid S(t) = i\big) = A_{i,j} \, dt + o(dt) \tag{7.60}$$

for $i \neq j$. Thus $A_{i,j}$ is interpreted as the rate of transition from state i to j and is necessarily nonnegative. If the state space is infinite, we need to assume

---

[6] Transitions in continuous time are often called "jumps".

that the process is not explosive, which means here that, for all $i \in \mathcal{S}$,

$$\sum_{j \neq i} A_{i,j} < \infty \qquad (7.61)$$

It is customary to pose

$$A_{i,i} = -\sum_{j \neq i} A_{i,j} \qquad (7.62)$$

so that A has non-negative entries everywhere except on the diagonal and $\sum_j A_{i,j} = 0$. It can be shown that the time until the next jump, given that $S(t) = i$, is an exponential random variable with parameter $-A_{i,i}$.

Let $\pi(t)$ be the row vector of probabilities at time t, i.e. $\pi_i(t) = \mathbb{P}(S(t) = i)$. Then for all $t \geq 0$,

$$\pi(t) = \pi(0)\, e^{tA} \qquad (7.63)$$

(the exponential of a matrix is, as for complex numbers, defined by $e^A = \sum_{n=0}^{\infty} \frac{A^n}{n!}$).

A stationary probability is a row vector π that satisfies

$$\begin{cases} \pi A = 0 \\ \sum_{i \in \mathcal{S}} \pi_i = 1 \end{cases} \qquad (7.64)$$

which is the replacement for (7.59). Otherwise, the rest of Section 7.6.1 applies, mutatis mutandi, with one simplification: there is no issue of periodicity. Thus, in particular, a continuous time Markov chain over a finite state space becomes stationary as $t \to \infty$.

For more details about Markov chains in continuous time, see [94].

7.6.3   Poisson and Bernoulli

These are the two memoriless stationary point processes.

A **_Bernoulli process_** with intensity $q \in [0, 1]$ is a point process $T_n \in \mathbb{Z}$ in discrete time, such that the points are independently drawn. In other words, at every time t, toss a coin and decide with the probability q that there is a point; and that otherwise, there is not. With the terminology of Section 7.2, the sequence $N(t)$ is iid. The time intervals between points, $S_n = T_{n+1} - T_n$, are independent and such that $S_n - 1$ has a geometric distribution with parameter q. The same holds for the time from now to the next point.

A **_Poisson process_** $T_n \in \mathbb{R}$ with intensity $\lambda > 0$ is the continuous time equivalent of a Bernoulli process. We do not define it formally here; rather, we give its main properties:

- The probability that there is a point in $[t, t + dt]$ is $\lambda\, dt + o(dt)$
- The number of points in disjoint time intervals are independent random variables.

- The number of points in an interval of duration t is a random variable with a Poisson(λt) distribution.
- The time intervals between points, $S_n = T_{n+1} - T_n$, are independent and have an exponential distribution with parameter λ. The time from now to the next point has the same distribution (but see also Example 7.8).

It can be shown that the Poisson process with intensity λ is the limit, in various senses, when $dt \to 0$, of the Bernoulli process with intensity $q = \lambda \, dt$. This is the case when we map the time slot of the Bernoulli process to a continuous time interval of duration dt.

7.7   Proofs

Except for Theorem 7.10 and Theorem 7.12, we give the proofs in discrete time, as they are simple and require only a first course on probability. The proofs in continuous time that are not given can be found in [4], [88] or [70].

Theorem 7.1

Let $N(t) = 1$ if the point process has a point at time t, and 0 otherwise. We show only that $\mathbb{E}(X(0)) = \lambda \mathbb{E}^0 \left(\sum_{s=1}^{T_1} X(s) \right)$, as the second equality is similar. By definition of a conditional probability and of λ:

$$\lambda \mathbb{E}^0 \left(\sum_{s=1}^{T_1} X(s) \right) = \mathbb{E} \left(\sum_{s=1}^{T_1} X(s) N(0) \right)$$

Now for $s > 0$, the event "$s \le T_1$" is equivalent to "$N(1, s-1) = 0$" thus

$$\lambda \mathbb{E}^0 \left(\sum_{s=1}^{T_1} X(s) \right) = \mathbb{E} \left(\sum_{s=1}^{\infty} X(s) N(0) 1_{\{N(1,s-1)=0\}} \right)$$

$$= \mathbb{E} \left(\sum_{s=1}^{\infty} X(0) N(-s) 1_{\{N(1-s,1)=0\}} \right)$$

$$= \mathbb{E} \left(X(0) \sum_{s=1}^{\infty} N(-s) 1_{\{N(1-s,1)=0\}} \right)$$

where the last line is by stationarity. Let $T^-(-1)$ be the most recent time at which a selected event occured before or at time -1. This time is finite with probability 1, by stationarity. We have $N(-s) 1_{\{N(1-s,1)=0\}} = 1$ if and only if $T^-(-1) = -s$, thus, with probability 1:

$$1 = \sum_{s=1}^{\infty} N(-s) 1_{\{N(1-s,1)=0\}}$$

which demonstrates the formula.

Theorem 7.3

$X(t)$ is jointly stationary with T_n, thus its distribution is independent of t, and we can apply the inversion formula. For any $s \geq 0$, we have

$$\mathbb{P}\big(X(0) = s\big) = \mathbb{E}\big(1_{\{X(0)=s\}}\big) = \lambda\mathbb{E}^0\left(\sum_{u=0}^{T_1-1} 1_{\{X(u)=s\}}\right)$$

Given that there is a point at 0 and $0 \leq u \leq T_1 - 1$, we have $X(u) = T_1 - u$, thus

$$\mathbb{P}\big(X(0) = s\big) = \lambda\mathbb{E}^0\left(\sum_{u=0}^{T_1-1} 1_{\{T_1=u+s\}}\right)$$

Now the sum in the formula is 1 if $T_1 > s$ and 0 otherwise. Thus

$$\mathbb{P}\big(X(0) = \tau\big) = \lambda\mathbb{E}^0\left(1_{\{T_1>s\}}\right) = \lambda\mathbb{P}^0(T_1 > s)$$

which demonstrates the formula for $X(t)$. The formula for $Y(t)$ is similar, using $Y_u = u$ for $0 \leq u \leq T_1 - 1$.

For $Z(t)$, we apply the inversion formula and obtain

$$\mathbb{P}(Z_0 = s) = \lambda\mathbb{E}^0\left(\sum_{u=0}^{T_1-1} 1_{\{Z_u=s\}}\right)$$

Now under P^0, $Z_u = T_1$ does not depend on u for $0 \leq u \leq T_1 - 1$ thus

$$\mathbb{P}(Z_0 = s) = \lambda\mathbb{E}^0\left(1_{\{T_1=s\}} \sum_{u=0}^{T_1-1} 1\right) = \lambda\mathbb{E}^0\left(T_1 1_{\{T_1=s\}}\right) = \lambda s\mathbb{P}^0(T_1 = s)$$

Theorem 7.7

Apply the inversion formula to the B point process and to $X(t)N^A(t)$, where $N^A(t)$ is 1 if there is an A point at t, and 0 otherwise. Note that

$$\sum_{n\in\mathbb{Z}} X(A_n)1_{\{B_0\leq A_n<B_1\}} = \sum_{s=B_0}^{B_1-1} X_s N^A(s)$$

thus

$$\lambda(B)\mathbb{E}\big(X(0)N^A(0)\big) = \mathbb{E}_B^0\left(\sum_{n\in\mathbb{Z}} X\left(A_n\left(1_{\{B_0\leq A_n<B_1\}}\right)\right)\right)$$

$$\lambda(B)\frac{\mathbb{E}_A^0\big(X(0)\big)}{\lambda(A)} = \mathbb{E}_B^0\left(\sum_{n\in\mathbb{Z}} X(A_n)1_{\{B_0\leq A_n<B_1\}}\right)$$

$$\lambda(B)\mathbb{E}_A^0\big(X(0)\big) = \lambda(A)\mathbb{E}_B^0\left(\sum_{n\in\mathbb{Z}} X(A_n)1_{\{B_0\leq A_n<B_1\}}\right) \qquad (7.65)$$

Apply the last equation to $X(t) = 1$ and obtain (7.43). Combine (7.65) with (7.43) and obtain (7.44).

Theorem 7.10

First note that the expectation of $N(t_0)$ is

$$\sum_{n \geq 1} \mathbb{P}(S_0 + \cdots + S_{n-1} \leq t) \tag{7.66}$$

Pick some arbitrary, fixed $s > 0$. By Markov's inequality,

$$\mathbb{P}(S_0 + \cdots + S_{n-1} \leq t_0) \leq e^{st_0} \mathbb{E}\left(e^{-s(S_0 + \cdots + S_{n-1})}\right)$$
$$= e^{st_0} G(s)^n$$

where $G(s) := \mathbb{E}(e^{-sS_0})$ is the Laplace-Transform of S_0. We have $G(s) = 1$ if and only if $sS_0 = 0$ with probability 1. Thus, by hypothesis, $G(s) < 1$ since $s > 0$. By (7.66),

$$E(N(t_0)) \leq e^{st} \sum_{n \geq 1} (G(s))^n < \infty$$

Theorem 7.11

Let ϕ be an arbitrary bounded test function of $Z(t), S(t)$. Apply Palm's inversion formula:

$$\mathbb{E}\left(\phi(Z(t), S(t))\right) = \lambda \mathbb{E}^0\left(\int_0^{T_1} \phi(Z_0, T_1)\, dt\right)$$
$$= \lambda \mathbb{E}^0\left(T_1 \phi(Z_0, T_1)\right) = \lambda \mathbb{E}^0\left(S_0 \phi(Z_0, S_0)\right)$$
$$= \lambda \int_{\mathcal{Z} \times (0, \infty)} \phi(z, s) s f_{Z,S}^0(z, s)\, d\mu(z)\, ds$$

from where item (1) follows, with $\eta = \lambda$.

Since the knowledge of $\mathbb{E}\left(\phi(Z(t), S(t)) \psi(T^+(t))\right)$ for any ϕ, ψ determines the joint distribution of $(Z(t), S(t), T^+(t))$, to show item (2), it is sufficient to demonstrate that for any bounded, test function ψ of $T^+(t)$ and any bounded test function of $Z(t), S(t)$, we have

$$\mathbb{E}\left(\phi(Z(t), S(t)) \psi(T^+(t))\right) = \int_{z \in \mathcal{Z}, s > 0} \phi(z, s) s f_{Z,S}^0(z, s) \left(\int_0^s \frac{1}{s} \psi(t)\, dt\right) d\mu(z)\, ds$$

which is equivalent to

$$\mathbb{E}\left(\phi(Z(t), S(t)) \psi(T^+(t))\right) = \int_{z \in \mathcal{Z}, s > 0} \phi(z, s) f_{Z,S}^0(z, s) \left(\int_0^s \psi(t)\, dt\right) d\mu(z)\, ds \tag{7.67}$$

Apply Palm's inversion formula again:

$$\mathbb{E}\left(\phi(Z(t), S(t)) \psi(T^+(t))\right) = \lambda \mathbb{E}^0\left(\int_0^{S_0} \phi(Z_0, S_0) \psi(S_0 - u)\, du\right)$$
$$= \lambda \mathbb{E}^0\left(s\phi(Z_0, S_0) \frac{1}{s} \int_0^{S_0} \psi(S_0 - u)\, du\right)$$
$$= \lambda \int_{z \in \mathcal{Z}, s > 0} \phi(z, s) f_{Z,S}^0(z, s) \left(\int_0^s \psi(s - u)\, du\right) d\mu(z)\, ds$$

which, after the change of variable $t = s - u$ in the inner integral, is the same as (7.67).

Theorem 7.12

Based on the strong Markov property,

$$J_{i,j} = \mathbb{P}^0\big(X_{T_1} = j \mid X_{T_0} = i\big) = \mathbb{P}\big(X_{T^+(0)} = j \mid X_0 = i\big)$$

Condition with respect to the next transition, selected or not,

$$J_{i,j} = \sum_{k:(i,k)\in F} Q_{i,k} + \sum_{k:(i,k)\notin F} Q_{i,k}\mathbb{P}\big(X_{T^+(0)} = j \mid X_1 = k \text{ and } X_0 = i\big)$$

Now, for $(i,k) \notin F$, given that $X_0 = i, X_1 = k$, we have $T^+(0) = T^+(1)$. Thus, the last term in the previous equation is

$$\sum_{k:(i,k)\notin F} Q_{i,k}\mathbb{P}\big(X_{T^+(1)} = j \mid X_1 = k \text{ and } X_0 = i\big) = \sum_{k:(i,k)\notin F} Q_{i,k}J_{k,i}$$

Combining the two gives $J = C + (Q - C)J$ which demonstrates item (1).

Now, by definition of an intensity, $\lambda = \sum_{(i,j)\in F} \mathbb{P}(X_0 = j, X_{-1} = i)$ and $\mathbb{P}(X_0 = j, X_{-1} = i) = \pi_i Q_{i,j}$, which shows item (2).

By definition of the Palm probability,

$$\mathbb{P}^0(X_{-1} = i, X_0 = j) = \frac{1}{\lambda} \mathbb{E}\left(1_{\{X_{-1}=j\}} 1_{\{X_0=i\}} 1_{\{(i,j)\in F\}}\right)$$
$$= \frac{1}{\lambda} \mathbb{P}(X_{-1} = j, X_0 = i)1_{\{(i,j)\in F\}}$$

which shows item (3). Item (4) follows immediately.

Theorem 7.13

The probability that there is a transition at time 1, given that $X_0 = i$, is λ, independent of i. Thus $N(1)$ is independent of the state at time 0. Since we have a Markov chain, the state at time 1 depends on the past only through the state at time 0. Thus, $N(1)$ is independent of $N(t0)$ for all $t \geq 0$. By stationarity, it follows that $N(t)$ is iid, i.e. it is a Bernoulli process.

The relation between Palm and stationary probabilities follows from Theorem 7.12(4) The Palm probability to be in state i just before a transition is

$$\frac{1}{\lambda_0} \pi_i \sum_i C(i,j) = \frac{\lambda}{\lambda_0} \pi_i$$

where λ_0 is the λ of Theorem 7.12. The sum of probabilities is 1, thus necessarily $\frac{\lambda}{\lambda_0} = 1$.

7.8   Review Questions

7.1 Consider the SURGE model with one user equivalent in Section 3.5.5. Assume that the average inactive off period is Z, that the average active off period is Z', that the average number of URLs requested per active period is V, and that the average response time for a URL request is R. What is the throughput of requests λ?[7]

7.2 A distributed protocol establishes consensus by periodically having one host send a message to n other hosts and waiting for an acknowledgement [5]. Assume that the times to send and receive an acknowledgement are iid, with the distribution $F(t)$. What is the number of consensus per time unit achieved by the protocol? Give an approximation using the fact that the mean of the kth order statistic in a sample of n is approximated by $F^{-1}(\frac{k}{n+1})$.[8]

7.3 (ARP protocol *with* refreshes) IP packets delivered by a host are produced according to a stationary point process with λ packets per second in average. Every packet causes the emission of an ARP if the previous packet arrived more than t_a seconds ago (t_a is the ARP timer). What is the average number of ARP requests generated per second?[9]

7.4 Consider the notation of Theorem 7.3. Is the distribution of $Z(t)$ equal to the convolution of those of $X(t)$ and $Y(t)$?[10]

---

[7] Using the large time heuristic, one finds $\lambda = \frac{1}{V(R+Z')+Z}$.

[8] Call T_n the point process of the starting points for consensus rounds. The required answer is the intensity λ of T_n. We have $\lambda = \mathbb{E}^0(T_1)$. Assuming now that a round starts at time 0, we have $T_1 = \max_{i=1,\dots,n} S_i$ where $S_i \sim$ iid with distribution $F(\cdot)$. Thus

$$\mathbb{P}^0(T_1 < t) = \mathbb{P}^0(S_1 < t \text{ and } \dots \text{ and } S_n < t) = F(t)^n$$

and

$$\mathbb{E}^0(T_1) = \int_0^{+\infty} \left(1 - F(t)^n\right) dt$$

$$\lambda = \frac{1}{\int_0^{+\infty} \left(1 - F(t)^n\right) dt}$$

The Palm distribution of T_1 is that of the maximum of n iid random variables, thus $\mathbb{E}^0(T_1) \approx F^{-1}(\frac{n}{n+1})$.

[9] Apply Neveu's exchange formula to: first process = ARP request emissions (intensity λ_1); second process = all packet arrivals (intensity λ) and $X_s = 1$. This gives $\lambda_1 = \lambda \mathbb{E}^0(N_1(0,_1^T])$, where $\mathbb{E}^0$ is the Palm probability for the second point process and N_1 is the number of ARP requests. Given that there is a packet arrival at time 0, $N_1(0,_1^T] = 1_{\{T_1-T_0>t_a\}}$. Thus, the required throughput is $\lambda_1 = \lambda \mathbb{P}^0(T_1 > t_a)$. It depends only on the tail of the packet inter-arrival time.

[10] On the one hand, $Z(t) = X(t) + Y(t)$, so it seems tempting to say yes. It is true for a Poisson process. However, consider the case where $T_{n+1} - T_n$ is constant equal to some T under Palm. Then, $X(t)$ and $Y(t)$ are uniform on $[0,T]$, the convolution has a positive density on $(0, 2T)$, whereas $Z(t)$ is constant equal to T. The answer is no; $X(t)$ and $Y(t)$ are not independent, in general.

CHAPTER 8

Queuing Theory for Those who cannot Wait

Queuing phenomena are very frequent in computer and communication systems, and explain a vast number of performance patterns. There exists a large body of available results in queuing theory; in this chapter, we focus on results and concepts that are very broadly applicable, some of which are not very known. We present four topics, which constitute a good coverage of all the techniques required in practice.

First, we start with simple, *deterministic* results; they provide results on transient phenomenona, and also some worst-case bounds. These are often overlooked, but give a first, sometimes sufficient, insight. Second, we present *operational laws* for queuing systems; in some sense they are the "physical laws" of queuing: Little's formula, the DASSA property, network and forced flows law. Here, we make frequent use of Palm calculus (Chapter 7). These results also provide tools and bounds for fast analysis. Third, we give a series of simple, albeit important, results for *single queues* with one or several servers and for the processor sharing queue; these can be taken as models for systems without feedback. Fourth, we discuss a *network of queues*, which can be used to model systems with feedback, and also complex interactions. Here, we render the topic as simple as possible, but the result is rather complex, as there exists some description complexity.

We give a unified treatment of queuing networks; we discuss items such as the MSCCC station, a powerful model for concurrency in hardware or software, or Whittle networks, which are used to model bandwidth sharing in the Internet. This latter type of network is traditionally presented as a type of its own, a non product form queuing network. We demonstrate that it must not be so: all of these are instances of the general theory of multi-class product form queuing networks. Presenting the results in this way simplifies the student's job, as there is only a single framework to learn, instead of several disparate results. It is also more powerful as it provides new ways of combining existing building blocks.

Finally, we illustrate in an example how the four separate topics can be articulated and provide different insights in the same performance question.

8.1   Deterministic Analysis

8.1.1   Description of a Queuing System with Cumulative Functions

A deterministic analysis is often very simple, and provides first insights in a queuing system. Perhaps the simplest, and most efficient tool in this toolbox is the use of cumulative functions for arrival and departure counts, which we explain now. For a deeper treatment, see [51] and [23].

Consider a system that is viewed as a black box. We make no specific assumptions about its operation; it may be a network node, an information system, etc. The cumulative functions are

- $A(t)$ (***input function***): amount of work that arrives into the system in the time interval $[0, t]$,

- $D(t)$ (***output function***): amount of work done in the time interval $[0, t]$.

Assume that there is some time $t_0 \leq 0$ at which $A(t_0) = D(t_0) = 0$. We interpret t_0 as an instant at which the system is empty. The main observations are the following:

- $Q(t) := A(t) - D(t)$ is the backlog (unfinished work) at time t.
- Define $d(t) = \min\{u \geq 0 : A(t) \leq D(t + u)\}$ (horizontal deviation on Figure 8.1). If there is no loss of work (no incoming item is rejected) and if the system is first in, first out (***FIFO***), then $d(t)$ is the response time for a hypothetical atom of work that would arrive at time t.

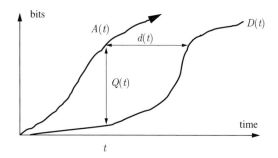

Figure 8.1 The use of cumulative functions to describe a queuing system.

The next example shows how this can be used for worst-case analysis.

Example 8.1 Playout Buffer

Consider a packet switched network that carries bits of information from a source with a constant bit rate r (Figure 8.2), as is the case, for example, with circuit emulation. We have a first system $\mathcal{S}$, the network, with input function $A(t) = rt$. The network imposes some variable delay, because of queuing points, for which reason the output $A'(\cdot)$ does not have a constant rate r. What can be done to re-create a constant bit stream? A standard mechanism is to smooth the delay variation in a playout buffer. It operates as follows. When the first bit of data arrives, at time $d(0)$, it is stored in the buffer until some initial delay has elapsed. Then, the buffer is served at a constant rate r whenever it is not empty. This gives us a second system $\mathcal{S}'$, with input $A'(\cdot)$ and output $D(\cdot)$. What initial delay should we take? We give an intuitive, graphical solution. For a formal development, see [51, Section 1.1.1].

The second part of Figure 8.2 shows that if the variable part of the network delay (called **delay jitter**) is bounded by some number Δ, then the output $A'(t)$ is bounded by the two lines (D1) and (D2). Let the output $D(t)$ of the playout buffer be the function represented by (D2), namely $D(t) = rt - d(0) - \Delta$. This means that we read data from the playout buffer at a constant rate r, starting at time $d(0) + \Delta$. The

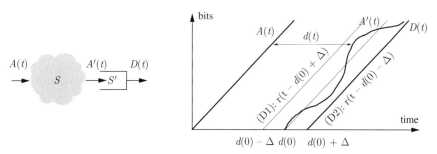

Figure 8.2 A Simple Playout Buffer Example.

fact that $A'(t)$ lies above (D2) signifies that there is never underflow. Thus, the playout buffer should delay the first bit of data by an amount equal to Δ, a bound on delay jitter.

QUESTION 8.1 What is the required playout buffer size?[1]

8.1.2 Reich's Formula

This is a formula for describing the backlog in a single server queue. Consider a lossless, FIFO, system, with a constant service rate c, and with an unlimited buffer size.

Theorem 8.1 (Reich)
The backlog at time t in the system defined above is

$$Q(t) = \max_{s \le t}\big(A(t) - A(s) - c(t - s)\big)$$

Example 8.2 Scaling of Internet Delay

We are interested in knowing whether queuing delays are going to disappear when the Internet grows to broadband. The following analysis is due to Norros [74] and Kelly [45].

Assume that traffic on an internet link grows according to three scale parameters: the volume (v), speedup (s) and number of users (u). This is captured by the relation

$$A(t) = v \sum_{i=1}^{u} A_i(st) \tag{8.1}$$

We are interested in the delay. Assuming that the link is a constant rate server with rate c, this is the backlog divided by c. We also assume that the capacity of the link is scaled with the increase in volume: $c = c_0 v s u$. The question is now: how does the delay depend on v, s, u?
The maximum delay, $D(v, s, u)$ is derived from Reich's formula:

$$D(v, s, u) = \max_{t \ge 0}\left(\frac{A(t)}{c} - t\right)$$

The dependence on v and s is simple to analyze. We obtain

$$D(v, s, 1) = \max_{t \ge 0}\left(\frac{vA_1(st)}{c} - t\right) = \max_{t \ge 0}\left(\frac{A_1(t)}{c_0 s} - \frac{t}{s}\right) = \frac{1}{s}D(1,1,1)$$

and similarly, for $u \ne 1$, we have $D(v, s, u) = \frac{1}{s}D(1,1,u)$. The delay is thus independent of the volume scaling, and inversely proportional to

---

[1] A bound on buffer size is the vertical distance between $A(t)$ and $A'(t)$; from Figure 8.2, we see that it is equal to $2r\,\Delta$.

the speedup factor s. The dependence on u requires more assumptions. To go further, we assume a stochastic model, such that the queue length process $Q(t)$ is stationary ergodic. We can use Reich's formula

$$Q(0) = \max_{t \geq 0} \big(A(-t) - ct \big)$$

where $A(-t)$ is now the amount of work that has arrived in the interval $[-t, 0]$. We assume that (8.1) continues to hold. Further, we model $A_i(-t)$ by a ***fractional Brownian traffic*** [74]. This is a simplified model that captures long range dependence, i.e. the often observed property of an auto-correlation function not decaying exponentially. This means that

$$A_i(-t) = \lambda t + \sqrt{\lambda a}\, B_H^i(t)$$

where B_H^i is fractional Brownian motion, λ the traffic intensity, and a a variance parameter. Fractional Brownian motion is a Gaussian process, with mean λt and variance $\lambda a t^{2H}$. $B_H(t)$ is self-similar in the sense that the process $B_H(kt)$ has the same distribution as $k^H B_H(t)$. Assume that the A_is are independent. It follows from the properties of fractional Brownian motion that $A(-t)$ is also fractional Brownian traffic. Its mean is $u\lambda$ and its variance is $u\lambda a t^{2H}$, thus it has the intensity $u\lambda$ and the same variance parameter a.

According to Reich's formula, we have

$$D(1, 1, u) = \max_{t \geq 0} \left(\frac{A(t)}{c_0 u} - t \right) = \max_{t \geq 0} \left(\left(\frac{\lambda}{c_0} - 1 \right) t + \sqrt{\lambda a}\, B_H(t) \frac{1}{c_0 \sqrt{u}} \right)$$

Changing of the variable $t = k\tau$, gives us

$$D(1, 1, u) \sim \max_{\tau \geq 0} \left(\left(\frac{\lambda}{c_0} - 1 \right) k\tau + \sqrt{\lambda a}\, k^H B_H(\tau) \frac{1}{c_0 \sqrt{u}} \right)$$

where $\sim$ means same distribution. Take k such that $k = \frac{k^H}{\sqrt{u}}$, i.e. $k = u^{-1/2(1-H)}$. We then have

$$D(1, 1, u) \sim u^{-\frac{1}{2(1-H)}} D(1, 1, 1)$$

In summary, the delay scales according to

$$D(v, s, u) = \frac{1}{s u^b} D(1, 1, 1)$$

with $b = \frac{1}{2-2H}$. In practice, we expect H, the Hurst parameter, to lie in the range $[0.67, 0.83]$, thus $1.5 \leq b \leq 3$. In summary, the delay decreases with speedup, and more rapidly with the number of users.

8.2   Operational Laws for Queuing Systems

These are robust results, i.e. they are true with very few assumptions on the queuing system other than stability. Many of them directly derive from Chapter 7, such as the celebrated Little's law. The laws apply to a stationary system; for a single queue, they are true if the utilization is less than 1. This type of analysis was pioneered in [34]; an original, stand-alone treatment can be found in [35].

8.2.1   Departures and Arrivals See Same Averages (DASSA)

Theorem 8.2 (DASSA)

Consider a system where individual customers come in and out. Assume that the arrival process A_n and the departure process D_n are stationary point processes, and that they have no point in common (there are thus no simultaneous arrivals or departures).

Let $N(t) \in \mathbb{N}$ be the number of customers present in the system at time t. Assume that $N(t)$, A_n and D_n are jointly stationary (see Section 7.2).

The probability distribution of $N(t)$ sampled just before an arrival is then equal to the probability distribution of $N(t)$ sampled just after a departure.

The proof is given in Section 8.10; it is a direct application of the Rate Conservation law in Theorem 7.4.

Example 8.3   Inter-Departure Time in M/GI/1 Queue

We want to compute the distribution of the inter-departure time in the stable M/GI/1 queue defined in Section 8.3 (i.e. the single server queue, with Poisson arrival and general service time distribution), and we would like to know in which case it is the same as the inter-arrival distribution.

First note that the time between two departures is equal to one service time if the first departing customer leaves the system non-empty, and, that otherwise, it is the same plus the time until the next arrival. The time until the next arrival is independent of the state of the system and is exponentially distributed, with the parameter of the arrival rate λ. Thus, the **Laplace-Stieltjes transform**[2] of the inter-departure time is

$$\mathcal{L}_D(s) = (1-p)\mathcal{L}_S(s) + p\mathcal{L}_S(s)\frac{\lambda}{\lambda+s}$$

where $\mathcal{L}_S$ is the Laplace-Stieltjes transform of the service time and p is the probability that a departing customer leaves the system empty.

---

[2] The Laplace-Stieltjes transform of a non-negative random variable X is defined by $\mathcal{L}_X(s) = \mathbb{E}(e^{-sX})$. If X and Y are independent, $\mathcal{L}_{X+Y}(s) = \mathcal{L}_X(s)\mathcal{L}_Y(s)$; X is exponentially distributed with parameter λ if and only if $\mathcal{L}_X(s) = \frac{\lambda}{\lambda+s}$.

By DASSA, p is also the probability that an arriving customer sees an empty system. By PASTA (Example 7.19), it is equal to the probability that the queue is empty at an arbitrary point in time, which is also equal to $1 - \rho$, with $\rho = \lambda \bar{S}$ and $\bar{S}$ = mean service time. Thus

$$\mathcal{L}_D(s) = \mathcal{L}_S(s) \left(\rho + \frac{(1-\rho)\lambda}{\lambda + s} \right)$$

which entirely defines the probability distribution of inter-departure times.

The inter-departure times have the same distribution as the inter-arrival times if and only if $\mathcal{L}_D(s) = \frac{\lambda}{\lambda + s}$. Solving for $\mathcal{L}_S$ gives $\mathcal{L}_S(s) = \frac{\lambda/\rho}{\lambda/\rho + s}$, i.e. the service time must be exponentially distributed and the M/GI/1 queue must be an M/M/1 queue.

8.2.2 Little's Law and Applications

Theorem 8.3 (Operational Law)
Consider a stationary system that is visited by a flow of customers (for a formal definition, see Theorem 7.6).

- **Throughput.** *The throughput, defined as the expected number of arrivals per second, is also equal to the inverse of the expected time between arrivals.*

- **Little.** $\lambda \bar{R} = \bar{N}$, *where λ is the expected number of customers arriving per second, $\bar{R}$ is the expected response time seen by an arbitrary customer and $\bar{N}$ is the expected number of customers observed in the system at an arbitrary time.*

- **Utilization Law.** *If the system is a single server queue with the arrival rate λ and the expected service time $\bar{S}$,*

$$\mathbb{P}(server\ busy) = \rho := \lambda \bar{S}$$

If it is a B-server queue,

$$\mathbb{E}(number\ of\ busy\ servers) = s\rho$$

with $\rho := \frac{\lambda \bar{S}}{s}$.

QUESTION 8.2 Consider a single server queue that serves only one customer at a time. What is the average number of customers not in service (i.e. in the waiting room)?[3]

---

[3] $\bar{N}_w = \bar{N} - \rho$, which follows from items (2) and (3) in Theorem 8.3.

The Interactive User Model

The interactive user model is illustrated in Figure 8.3. n users send jobs to a service center. The ***think time*** is defined as the time between jobs sent by one user. Call $\bar{R}$ the expected response time for an arbitrary job at the service center, $\bar{Z}$ the expected think time and λ the throughput of the system. A direct application of little's law to the entire system gives

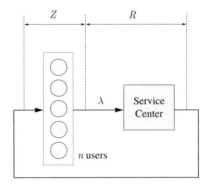

Figure 8.3 The interactive user model.

Theorem 8.4 (Interactive User)

$$\lambda(\bar{Z} + \bar{R}) = n$$

Example 8.4 Service Desk

A car rental company in a large airport has 10 service attendants. Each attendant prepares transactions on its PC and, once completed, sends them to the database server. The software monitor finds the following averages: one transaction every 5 seconds, response time = 2 s. Thus the average think time is 48 s.

8.2.3 Networks and Forced Flows

We often find systems that can be modeled as a directed graph, called a network. We consider models of the form illustrated in Figure 8.4. If the total number of customers is constant, the network is called "closed", and otherwise "open". In Section 8.4, we study such networks in more detail.

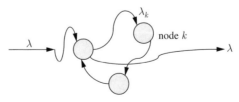

Figure 8.4 Network model.

Theorem 8.5 (Network Laws)

Consider a stationary network model where λ is the total arrival rate.

- **Forced Flows.** $\lambda_k = \lambda V_k$, *where λ_k is the expected number of customers arriving per second at node k and V_k is the expected number of visits to node k by an arbitrary customer during its stay in the network.*

- **Total Response Time.** *Let $\bar{R}$ (resp. $\bar{R}_k$) be the expected total response time $\bar{R}$ seen by an arbitrary customer (resp. by an arbitrary visit to node k)*

$$\bar{R} = \sum_k \bar{R}_k V_k$$

Example 8.5

Transactions on a database server access the CPU, disk A and disk B (Figure 8.5). The statistics are: $V_{\mathrm{CPU}} = 102$, $V_A = 30$, $V_B = 68$ and $\bar{R}_{\mathrm{CPU}} = 0.192$ s, $\bar{R}_A = 0.101$ s, $\bar{R}_B = 0.016$ s.

The average response time for a transaction is 23.7 s.

8.2.4   Bottleneck Analysis

Common sense and the guidelines in Chapter 1 tell us to analyze bottlenecks first. Beyond this, simple performance bounds in the stationary regime can be found by using the so-called bottleneck analysis. It is based on the following two observations:

(1) the waiting time is ≥ 0,

(2) a server utilization is bounded by 1.

We illustrate the method in Figure 8.5. The network is a combination of Figure 8.3 and Figure 8.4. Transactions are issued by a pool of n customers

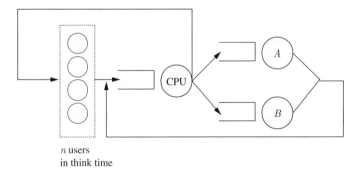

n users
in think time

Figure 8.5 A network example used to illustrate bottleneck analysis. n attendants serve customers. Each transaction uses CPU, disk A or disk B. Av. numbers of visits per transaction: $V_{\mathrm{CPU}} = 102$, $V_A = 30$, $V_B = 17$; av. service time per transaction: $\bar{S}_{\mathrm{CPU}} = 0.004$ s, $\bar{S}_A = 0.011$ s, $\bar{S}_B = 0.013$ s; think time $Z = 1$ s.

which are either idle (in think time) or using the network. In addition, assume that every network node is a single server queue, and let $\bar{S}_k$ be the average service time per visit at node k. Thus, $\bar{R}_k - \bar{S}_k$ is the average waiting time per visit at node k. The throughput λ is given by the interactive user model:

$$\lambda = \frac{n}{Z + \sum_k V_k \bar{R}_k} \tag{8.2}$$

Furthermore, by forced flows, the utilization of the server at node k is $\rho_k = \lambda V_k \bar{S}_k$. Applying the two principles above gives the constraints on λ:

$$\begin{cases} \lambda \leq \dfrac{n}{\bar{Z} + \sum_k V_k \bar{S}_k} \\ \lambda \leq \dfrac{1}{\max_k V_k \bar{S}_k} \end{cases} \tag{8.3}$$

Similarly, using (8.2) and (8.3), we find the following constraints on the response time $\bar{R} = \sum_k V_k \bar{R}_k$:

$$\begin{cases} \bar{R} \geq \displaystyle\sum_k V_k \bar{S}_k \\ \bar{R} \geq n \left(\displaystyle\max_k V_k \bar{S}_k \right) - \bar{Z} \end{cases} \tag{8.4}$$

Figure 8.6 illustrates the bounds. See also Figure 8.15.

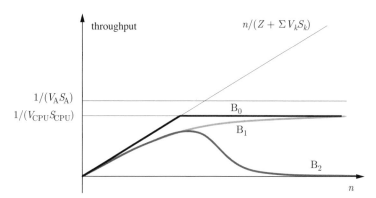

Figure 8.6 Throughput bound (B_0) obtained by bottleneck analysis for the system in Figure 8.5, as a function of the number of users n. B_1, B_2: typical throughput values for a system without (resp. with) congestion collapse.

A node k that maximizes $V_k \bar{S}_k$ is, in this model, called a **bottleneck**. To see why a bottleneck determines the performance, consider improving the system by decreasing the value of $V_k \bar{S}_k$ (by reducing the number of times the resource is used, or by replacing the resource by a faster one). If k is not a bottleneck, this does not affect the asymptote in Figure 8.6, and only marginally increases the slope of the bound at the origin, unlike if k is a bottleneck. In Figure 8.6, we see that the bottleneck is the CPU.

Among the two bounds in (8.3), the former is accurate at low load (when there is no queuing), and the latter is expected to be true at high load (when the bottleneck is saturated). This is what makes bottleneck analysis appealing, as the two bounds cover both ends of the spectrum. Note however that, at high loads, congestion collapse might occur, after which the performance would be worse than predicted by the bound.

QUESTION 8.3 What happens to the example of Figure 8.5 if the CPU processing time is reduced from 0.004 to 0.003? to 0.002?[4]

8.3 Classical Results for a Single Queue

The single queue has received much attention, and there are analytical results available for a large class of systems with random arrivals and service. We give here a minimal, but useful set of results. For more details on certain topics, the classical reference is [46] and [47]; a more compact and up-to-date textbook is [71]. We start with some notation and a generic result.

8.3.1 Kendall's Notation

The classical notation for a queue, in its simplest form, is of the type $A/S/B/K$ where:

- A (character string) describes the type of arrival process: G stands for the most general arrival process, $A =$GI signifies that the arrival process is a point process with iid interarrival times, and M represents a Poisson arrival process.

- S (character string) describes the type of service process: G for the most general service process, $S =$ GI means that the service times are iid and independent of the arrival process, $S =$ M is the special case of GI with exponential service times, and $S =$ D correspond to constant service times.

- B and K are integers representing the number of servers and the capacity (maximum number of customers allowed in the system, queued + in service). When $K = \infty$, it may be omitted.

- Let A_n be the arrival time and S_n the service time of the nth customer, labeled in order of arrival. We assume that the sequence (A_n, S_n) is stationary with respect to the index n and that it can be interpreted as a stationary marked point process (i.e. the expectation of $A_{n+1} - A_n$ is finite, see Theorem 7.9).

- The service discipline is by default FIFO, otherwise it is mentioned explicitly.

---

[4] The disk A becomes the bottleneck. Decreasing the CPU processing time to 0.002 does not improve the bound significantly.

8.3.2   The Single Server Queue

Stability

We consider the most general queue with one single server and with infinite capacity. Note that we do not assume Poisson arrivals, and we allow service times to depend on the state of the system. We assume that the system is work conserving. More precisely, let $W(t)$ be the backlog process, i.e. the sum of the service times of all customers that are present in the system at time t. When a customer arrives, $W(t)$ increases by the (future) service time of this customer. The work conserving assumption means that $W(t)$ decreases at rate 1 over any time interval such that $W(t) > 0$.

An important issue in the analysis of the single server queue is stability. In mathematical terms, it is a measure of whether the backlog $W(t)$ is stationary. When the system is unstable, a typical behavior is that the backlog grows to infinity.

The following is the general stability condition for the single server queue. Let $\bar{S}$ be the expectation of the service time, λ the intensity of the arrival process (expected number of arrivals per second) and $\rho = \lambda \bar{S}$ is the utilization factor.

> **Theorem 8.6 (Loynes [3, Thm 2.1.1])**
>
> If $\rho < 1$, the backlog process has a unique stationary regime. In the stationary regime, the queue empties infinitely often.
>
> Furthermore, for any initial condition, the waiting time of the nth customer converges in distribution as $n \to \infty$ to the waiting time for an arbitrary customer computed in the stationary regime.
>
> If $\rho > 1$, the backlog process has no stationary regime.

A heuristic explanation for the necessary condition is that, if the system is stable, all customers eventually enter the service, and thus the mean number of beginnings of service per second is λ. From Little's law applied to the server (see Section 8.2), we have $\rho =$ the probability of the server being busy, which is ≤ 1. For $\rho = 1$, there may or may not be stability, depending on the specific queue. Be careful that this intuitive stability result holds only for a single queue. For networks of interconnected queues, there is no such general result, as discussed in Section 8.4. The theorem holds for a queue with infinite capacity. For a finite capacity queue, there is, in general, stability for any value of ρ (but for $\rho > 1$, there must be losses).

QUESTION 8.4   Consider a queuing system of the form G/G/1 where the service time S_n of customer n is equal to the inter-arrival time $A_{n+1} - A_n$. What are the values of ρ and of the expected number of customers $\bar{N}$?[5]

---

[5] $\lambda = \frac{1}{\bar{S}}$ thus $\rho = 1$. There is always exactly one customer in the queue. Thus $\bar{N} = 1$.

QUESTION 8.5 Give an example of a stable and an unstable single server queue with $\rho = 1$.[6]

M/GI/1 Queue

The arrival process is Poisson with parameter λ. Moreover, the service times are independent of each other and of the arrival process, with a general distribution. For $\rho < 1$ the queue is stable and for $\rho \geq 1$ it is unstable. Using the rate conservation law as in Example 7.10, we obtain the Laplace-Stieltjes transform of the waiting time (***Pollaczek-Khinchine formula for transforms***):

$$\mathcal{L}_W(s) = \frac{s(1-\rho)}{s - \lambda + \mathcal{L}_S(s)} \tag{8.5}$$

where $\mathcal{L}_S$ is the Laplace-Stieltjes transform of the service time. Note that, by PASTA, the waiting time has the same distribution as the workload sampled at an arbitrary point in time.

QUESTION 8.6 Give the Laplace-Stieltjes transform $\mathcal{L}_R$ of the response time.[7]

The distribution of the number of customers $N(t)$, at an arbitrary point in time, is obtained by first computing the distribution of the number of customers seen at a departure time, and then using DASSA [46, Section 5.6]. The distribution is known via its ***z-transform***[8]

$$G_{N(t)}(z) = (1-\rho)(1-z)\frac{\mathcal{L}_S(\lambda - \lambda z)}{\mathcal{L}_S(\lambda - \lambda z) - z} \tag{8.6}$$

(This formula is also called a *Pollaczek-Khinchine formula for transforms*). The mean values of number of customers in the system or in the waiting room as well as the mean response times and waiting times are easily derived and are given below.

$$\begin{cases} \bar{N} = \dfrac{\rho^2 \kappa}{1 - \rho} + \rho & \text{with } \kappa = \dfrac{1}{2}\left(1 + \dfrac{\sigma_S^2}{\bar{S}^2}\right) = \dfrac{1}{2}(1 + \mathrm{CoV}_S) \\[2mm] \bar{N}_w = \dfrac{\rho^2 \kappa}{1 - \rho} \\[2mm] \bar{R} = \dfrac{\bar{S}\big(1 - \rho(1 - \kappa)\big)}{1 - \rho} \\[2mm] \bar{W} = \dfrac{\rho \bar{S} \kappa}{1 - \rho} \end{cases} \tag{8.7}$$

Note the importance of the coefficient of variation (CoV) of the service time.

QUESTION 8.7 Which of the quantities $\bar{N}$, $\bar{N}_w$, $\bar{R}$, $\bar{W}$ are Palm expectations?[9]

---

[6] The example in Question 8.4 is stable with $\rho = 1$. The M/M/1 queue with $\rho = 1$ is unstable.

[7] The response time is the sum of the service time and the waiting time, and they are independent. Thus, $\mathcal{L}_R(s) = \mathcal{L}_S(s)\mathcal{L}_W(s)$.

[8] The z-transform, $G_N(z)$ of an integer random variable N, is defined by $G_N(z) = E(z^N)$.

[9] $\bar{R}$, $\bar{W}$.

M/M/1 Queue

This is a special case of the M/GI/1 queue where, the service times are exponentially distributed. Here it is possible to obtain all stationary probabilities in explicit (and simple) form, by directly solving the equilibrium equations of the Markov process. One finds that the distribution of the number of customers at an arbitrary point in time, when $\rho < 1$, is

$$\mathbb{P}\big(N(t) = k\big) = (1 - \rho)\rho^k \qquad\qquad (8.8)$$

and the distribution of the service time of an arbitrary customer is given by

$$\mathbb{P}^0(R_0 \leq x) = 1 - e^{-(1-\rho)x/\bar{S}} \qquad\qquad (8.9)$$

Furthermore, (8.7) applies with $\kappa = 1$.

M/M/1/K Queue

This is a modification of the M/M/1 queue where the total number of customers is limited to K. If a customer arrives when the queue is full, this customer is dropped. The M/GI/1 formulas cannot be applied, but, instead, one can directly solve the equilibrium equations of the Markov process.

The system has a stationary regime for *any* value of ρ. The distribution of the number of customers at an arbitrary point in time is

$$\mathbb{P}(N = k) = \eta\rho^k \mathbf{1}_{\{0 \leq k \leq K\}} \qquad \text{with } \eta = \begin{cases} \dfrac{1 - \rho}{1 - \rho^{K+1}} & \text{if } \rho \neq 1 \\[2mm] \dfrac{1}{K + 1} & \text{if } \rho = 1 \end{cases}$$

By PASTA, the probability that the system is full is equal to the loss probability, i.e.

$$\mathbb{P}^0(\text{arriving customer is discarded}) = \mathbb{P}\big(N(t) = K\big) = \frac{(1 - \rho)\rho^K}{1 - \rho^{K+1}}$$

GI/GI/1 Queue

This is the general single server queue where inter-arrival and service times are independent of each other as well as iid. In general, no closed form solution exists, but numerical procedures are available.

One approach is based on a the following equation, which is a stochastic recurrence:

$$W_n = \big(W_{n-1} + S_{n-1} - A_n + A_{n-1}\big)^+$$

where the notation $(x)^+$ means $\max(x, 0)$ and $W_n = W(A_n^-)$ is the workload in the system just before the nth arrival, i.e. the waiting time for the nth customer. (Here, A_n is the arrival time and S_n the service time of the nth customer.) Let $C_n = A_n - A_{n-1} + S_n$. Note that C_n is iid and independent of W_{n-1}, thus

$$W_n \overset{\text{distrib}}{=} \big(W_{n-1} - C_n\big)^+ \qquad\qquad (8.10)$$

If $\rho < 1$, the system has a stationary regime, and the stationary distribution of the waiting time W must satisfy

$$W \stackrel{\text{distrib}}{=} (W - C)^+ \tag{8.11}$$

where C is a random variable with the same distribution as $A_n - A_{n-1} + S_n$. This expression is called **Lindley's equation**. It is classical to use CDFs, which gives the following equivalent form of (8.11):

$$F_W(x) = \begin{cases} 0 & \text{if } x < 0 \\ \displaystyle\int_{-\infty}^{x} F_W(x - y) f_C(y)\, dy \end{cases} \tag{8.12}$$

where F_W is the CDF of waiting times and f_C is the PDF of $A_n - A_{n-1} + S_n$. Equation (8.11) is an equation of the Wiener-Hopf type and can be solved, at least in many cases, using the theory of analytical functions; see [46, Section 8.2].

A second approach consists in solving (8.10) directly by discretization. Pick a time step δ and let, for $n \in \mathbb{N}$ and $k \in \mathbb{Z}$,

$$w_k^n = \mathbb{P}\left(W^n \in \big(k\delta, (k+1)\big)\delta\right) \tag{8.13}$$

$$s_k = P\left(S_n \in \big(k\delta, (k+1)\delta\big)\right) \tag{8.14}$$

$$a_k = \mathbb{P}\left(-A_n + A_{n-1} \in \big(k\delta, (k+1)\delta\big)\right) \tag{8.15}$$

Note that $w_k = s_k = 0$ for $k < 0$ and $a_k = 0$ for $k > 0$. Moreover, the arrays s and a are independent of n. Equation (8.10) can be approximated by

$$\begin{cases} w_k^n = \left(w^{n-1} * s * a\right)_k & \text{if } k > 0 \\ w_0^n = \displaystyle\sum_{i \leq 0} \left(w^{n-1} * s * a\right)_i \\ w_k^n = 0 & \text{if } k < 0 \end{cases} \tag{8.16}$$

where $*$ is the discrete convolution. The error we are making is due to discretization and should decrease with δ. In fact, (8.16) is exact for the modified system where we replaced the service times and inter-arrival times by approximations that are multiples of δ; such an approximation is used by default for the service time (Eq.(8.14)) and by excess for the inter-arrival time (Eq. (8.15)); thus the approximating system has a smaller ρ value than the original system. If the original system is stable, so is the approximating one, and by Loynes' theorem, the iteration converges to the stationary distribution of the waiting time. The method thus consists in numerically evaluating (8.16) until the norm of the difference $w^n - w^{n-1}$ becomes small; the convolution can be computed using the fast Fourier transform. See [39] for an example where this method is used.

A third type of method uses mixtures of exponentials to approximate the distributions of inter-arrival and service times as in Section 8.8.1. The stationary distributions can then be computed explicitly; see [55] and [72].

What this tells us

Though most practical systems are unlikely to exactly fit the assumptions of any of the models in this section, the analytical formulas do explain patterns that are observed in practice. The models here are valid for systems without feedback, since the arrival process is not influenced by the state of the queuing system. Important features of such systems include:

- *Non Linearity of Response Time.* At low values of the utilization factor ρ, the response time tends to increase slowly, and linearly with ρ. In contrast, as ρ approaches 1, the response time grows to ∞ (Figure 8.7). Consequently, the impact of a small traffic increase is dramatically different, depending on the initial value of the utilization factor.

  QUESTION 8.8 What happens to the system in Figure 8.7 if the traffic volume increases by 20%?[10]

- *Variability Considered Harmful.* The Pollacezk-Khinchine formula for the mean in (8.7) shows that the response time and queue sizes increase with the variability of the service time. See also Figure 8.8.

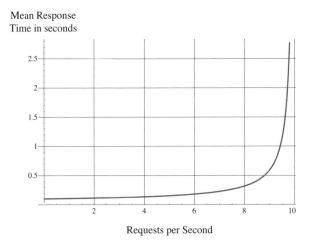

Figure 8.7 The average response time versus requests per second for a database server modeled as an M/GI/1 queue. The time needed to process a request is 0.1 s and its standard deviation is estimated to 0.03. The maximum load that can be served if an average response time of 0.5 s is considered acceptable is 8.8 requests per second. If the traffic volume increases by 10%, the response time becomes 1.75; i.e. it is multiplied by a factor of 3.5.

---

[10] The system becomes unstable $\rho > 1$; in practice, it will lose requests, or enter congestion collapse.

Mean Response Time

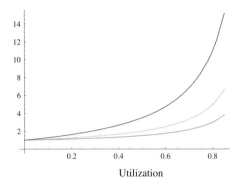

Utilization

Figure 8.8 The mean response time for an M/GI/1 queue, relative to the service time, for different values of the coefficient of variation $\mathrm{CoV}_S = \frac{\sigma_S}{\bar{S}}$: from top to bottom: $\mathrm{CoV}_S = 1.4$, $\mathrm{CoV}_S = 1$ (M/M/1 queue) and $\mathrm{CoV}_S = 0$ (M/D/1 queue).

8.3.3 The Processor Sharing Queue, M/GI/1/PS

This is a special case of the single server queue, with the **Processor Sharing (PS)** service discipline instead of FIFO. We assume there that the server divides itself equally into all present customers; this is an idealization when $\delta \to 0$ of the **round robin** service discipline, where the server allocates times slices of duration δ in turn to each present customer. If there are N customers in the queue, the residual service time for each of them decreases at a rate $\frac{1}{N}$. This is also called **egalitarian processor sharing**. Loynes's theorem applies and the system is stable when $\rho < 1$.

The workload process $W(t)$ is the same as for FIFO queues, but the distribution of waiting times and of customers is not equivalent. We give results for the simple case where the arrivals are Poisson and service times are iid and independent of the arrival process. They are both simple and striking. We assume $\rho < 1$. First, the stationary probability is [92]

$$\mathbb{P}\big(N(t) = k\big) = (1 - \rho)\rho^k \tag{8.17}$$

which shows in particular that it depends on the service time distribution only through its mean (this *insensitivity* property is common to many queues in the theory of networks presented in Section 8.4). It follows that

$$\begin{cases} \bar{N} = \dfrac{\rho}{1 - \rho} \\[2mm] \bar{R} = \dfrac{\bar{S}}{1 - \rho} \end{cases} \tag{8.18}$$

Second, the average response time R_0 of an arbitrary customer, conditional to its service time S_0 satisfies [47]

$$\mathbb{E}^0\big(R_0 \mid S_0 = x\big) = \frac{x}{1 - \rho} \tag{8.19}$$

i.e. it is as if an arbitrary customers sees a server for him/herself alone, but with a rate reduced a the factor $\frac{1}{1-\rho}$. Equations (8.18) and (8.19) can be simply deduced by from results in Section 8.4 if the distribution of service times can be decomposed as a mixture of exponentials; see [100]. Equation (8.17) is a special case of results for product form queuing networks, see Section 8.4.

What this tells us

Compare the M/M/1 and M/M/1/PS queues, where it is implicit that the M/M/1 queue is FIFO. The stationary distribution of numbers of customers are identical, therefore (by Little's law) the mean response times are identical, too. However, the conditional mean response time, given the service time, is very different. For M/M/1/PS, it is given by (8.19). For the M/M/1 queue, the response time is the sum of the waiting time plus the service time, and the former is independent of the latter. The mean waiting time is given in (8.7) with $\kappa = 1$. Therefore, for the FIFO queue,

$$\mathbb{E}^0\left(R_0 \mid S_0 = x\right) = x + \frac{\rho\bar{S}}{1-\rho} \tag{8.20}$$

Figure 8.9 plots the conditional response time for both FIFO and PS queues, and several values of x.

PS and FIFO have the same capacity and the same mean response time. However, the PS queue penalizes customers with a large service time, and the

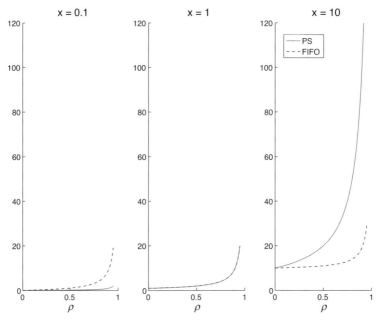

Figure 8.9 The expected response time given that the service time of this customer is x versus the utilization ρ, for M/M/1 queues with FIFO (dashed) and PS (plain) service disciplines, for various values of x. The mean service time $\bar{S}$ is 1 time unit.

penalty is proportional to the service time. This is often considered as a *fairness* property of the PS service discipline.

QUESTION 8.9 For which value of the service time x are the expected response times for M/M/1 and M/M/1/PS equal?[11]

8.3.4 Single Queue with B Servers

The multiple server queue is defined by the fact that a maximum of B customers can be served in parallel. Thus, the workload process decreases at a rate equal to $\min(N(t), B)$ where $N(t)$ is the number of customers present in the queue. The utilization ρ is now defined by $\rho = \frac{\lambda \bar{S}}{B}$. The stability condition is less simple than for single server queues. When $\rho < 1$, there is a stationary regime but it many not be unique [3, 2.3]. When $\rho > 1$ there is no stationary regime.

M/M/B Queue

For a more specific system, there is more to be said. A frequently used system is the M/M/B queue, i.e. the system with Poisson arrivals, B servers, exponential service times and FIFO discipline. The system can be studied directly by solving for the stationary probability. Here, when $\rho < 1$ there is a unique stationary regime, which is also reached asymptotically when we start from arbitrary initial conditions; for $\rho \geq 1$, there is no stationary regime.

When $\rho < 1$, the stationary probability is given by

$$\mathbb{P}\big(N(t) = k\big) = \begin{cases} \eta \dfrac{(B\rho)^k}{k!} & \text{if } 0 \leq k \leq B \\[2mm] \eta \dfrac{B^B \rho^k}{B!} & \text{if } k > B \end{cases} \tag{8.21}$$

with

$$\eta^{-1} = \sum_{i=0}^{B-1} \frac{(B\rho)^i}{i!} + \frac{(B\rho)^B}{B!\,(1-\rho)}$$

and the stationary CDF of the waiting time for an arbitrary customer is

$$\mathbb{P}^0(W_0 \leq x) = 1 - p\,e^{-B(1-\rho)x/\bar{S}}$$

with

$$p = \frac{1-u}{1-\rho u} \qquad \text{and} \qquad u = \frac{\displaystyle\sum_{i=0}^{B-1} \frac{(B\rho)^i}{i!}}{\displaystyle\sum_{i=0}^{B} \frac{(B\rho)^i}{i!}}$$

The probability of finding all servers busy at an arbitrary point in time or at a customer is arrival is (***Erlang-C*** formula):

$$\mathbb{P}(\text{all servers busy}) = \mathbb{P}\big(N(t) \geq B\big) = p \tag{8.22}$$

---

[11] When the service time x is equal to the mean service time $\bar{S}$.

Average quantities can easily be derived:

$$\begin{cases} \bar{N} = \dfrac{p\rho}{1-\rho} + B\rho \\[2mm] \bar{N}_w = \dfrac{p\rho}{1-\rho} \\[2mm] \bar{R} = \dfrac{p\bar{S}}{B(1-\rho)} + \bar{S} \\[2mm] \bar{W} = \dfrac{p\bar{S}}{B(1-\rho)} \end{cases}$$

M/GI/B/B Queue

This is the system with Poisson arrivals, B servers, arbitrary (but independent) service times and no waiting room. An arriving customer that finds all B servers busy is dropped.

The system is stable for any value of ρ and the stationary probability of the number of customers is given by

$$\mathbb{P}\big(N(t) = k\big) = \eta 1_{\{0 \le k \le B\}} \frac{(B\rho)^k}{k!} \quad \text{with } \eta^{-1} = \sum_{k=0}^{B} \frac{(B\rho)^k}{k!}$$

The probability that an arriving customer is dropped is (***Erlang-Loss formula***, or ***Erlang-B formula***)

$$\mathbb{P}^0(\text{arriving customer is dropped}) = \mathbb{P}\big(N(t) = B\big) = \eta \frac{(B\rho)^B}{B!} \qquad (8.23)$$

What this tells us

The simple M/M/B model can be used to understand the benefit of load sharing. Consider the systems illustrated in Figure 8.10.

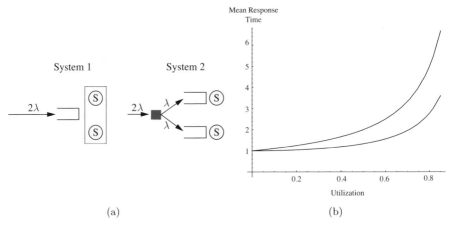

(a)   (b)

Figure 8.10 The mean response time over service time for systems 1 (bottom) and 2 (top), versus the utilization factor ρ.

Assume that processing times and job inter-arrival times can be modeled as independent iid exponential sequences. Thus, the first (resp. second) case is modeled as one M/M/2 queue (resp. a collection of two parallel M/M/1 queues). Assume the load to be balanced evenly between the two processors. Both systems have the same utilization ρ. The mean response for the first system is obtained from Section 8.3.4; we find $\frac{\bar{S}}{1-\rho^2}$. For the second system, it is simply $\frac{\bar{S}}{1-\rho}$ (Figure 8.10).

We see that for very small loads, the systems are similar, as expected. In contrast, for large loads, the response time for the first system is much better, with a ratio equal to $1 + \rho$. For example, for $\rho = 0.5$, the second system has a response time that is 1.5 times larger. However, the capacity is the same for both systems: the benefit of load sharing may be important in terms of response time, but does not change the system's capacity.

8.4   Definitions for Queuing Networks

Realistic models of information and communications systems involve interconnected systems, which can be captured by queuing networks. In general, not much can be said about a queuing network. Even the stability conditions are generally unknow, and there is no equivalent of Loynes's theorem for networks. Indeed, the natural condition that the utilization factor is less than 1 is necessary for stability but may not be sufficient – see [16] for an example of a multi-class queuing network, with FIFO queues, Poisson arrivals and exponential service times, which is unstable with an arbitrarily small utilization factor.

Fortunately, there is a broad class of queuing networks, the so called **multi-class product form queuing networks** for which there are simple and exhaustive results, given in this and the following sections. These networks have the property that their stationary probability has product form. They were developed as **BCMP networks** in reference to the authors of [10] or **Kelly networks** in reference to [44]. When there is only one class of customers, they are also called **Jackson** networks in the open case [42], and Gordon and Newell networks in the closed case [37]. For a broader perspective on this topic, see the recent books [94] and [24]. The latter reference presents, in particular, extensions to other concepts, including the "negative customers" introduced in [36]. A broad treatment, including approximate analysis for non-product form queuing networks can also be found in [101].

We now give the common assumptions required by multi-class product form queuing networks (we defer a formal definition of the complete process describing the network to Section 8.8).

8.4.1   Classes, Chains and Markov Routing

We consider a network of queues, labeled $s = 1, \ldots, S$, also called **stations**. Customers visit stations and queue or receive service according to the particular station service discipline. Once served, they move to another station or leave the network. Transfers are instantaneous (delays must be modeled explicitly by means of delay stations, as shown below).

Each customer has an attribute called **class**, in a finite set $\{1, \ldots, C\}$. A customer may change classes in transit between stations, according to the following procedure (called **Markov routing** in [103]). There is a fixed non-negative **routing matrix**

$$Q = \left(q_{c,c'}^{s,s'}\right)_{s,s',c,c'} \qquad \text{such that for all } s, c \quad \sum_{s',c'} q_{c,c'}^{s,s'} \leq 1$$

When a class-c customer leaves station s (due to a completed service time), the customer performs a random experiment such that: with probability $q_{c,c'}^{s,s'}$ he/she joins station s' with class c'; with probability $1 - \sum_{s',c'} q_{c,c'}^{s,s'}$ he/she leaves the network. This random experiment is performed independently of all the past and present states of the network. In addition, there are fresh independent Poisson arrivals, also independent of the past and present states of the network; ν_c^s is the intensity of the Poisson process of arrivals of class-c customers at station s. We allow $\nu_c^s = 0$ for some or all s and c.

We say that two classes c, c' are **chain equivalent** if $c = c'$ or if it is possible for a class-c customer to eventually become a class-c' customer, or vice-versa. This defines an equivalence relation between classes, and the equivalence classes are called **chains**. It follows that a customer may change classes but will always remain in the same chain.

A chain $\mathcal{C}$ is called **closed** if the total arrival rate of customers $\sum_{c \in \mathcal{C}, s} \lambda_c^s$ is 0. In such a case we require the probability for a customer of this chain to leave the network to also be 0, i.e. $\sum_{c',s'} q_{c,c'}^{s,s'} = 1$ for all $c \in \mathcal{C}$ and all s. The number of customers in a closed chain is constant.

A chain that is not closed is called **open**. We assume that customers of an open chain cannot cycle forever in the network, i.e. every customer of this chain eventually leaves the network.

A network where all chains are closed is called a **closed network**, one where all chains are open is called an **open network** and all others are denoted **mixed networks**.

We define the numbers θ_c^s (**visit rates**) as one solution to

$$\theta_c^s = \sum_{s',c'} \theta_{c'}^{s'} q_{c',c}^{s',s} + \nu_c^s \tag{8.24}$$

If the network is open, this solution is unique and θ_c^s can be interpreted[12] as the number of arrivals per time unit of class-c customers at station s. If c belongs to a closed chain, θ_c^s is determined only up to one multiplicative

---

[12] This interpretation is valid when the network satisfies the stability condition in Theorem 8.7

constant per chain. We assume that the array $\left(\theta_c^s\right)_{s,c}$ is one non-identically zero, non-negative solution of (8.24).

Chains can be used to model different customer populations while a class attribute may be used to model some state information, as illustrated in Figure 8.11.

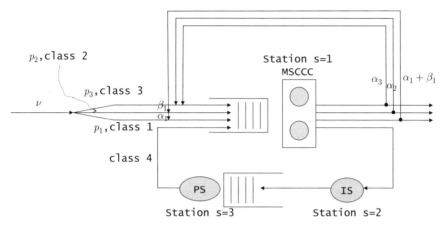

Figure 8.11 A simple product form queuing network with 2 chains of customers, representing a machine with a dual-core processor. Chain 1 consists of classes 1, 2 and 3. Chain 2 consists of class 4 (see Example 8.6).

It is possible to extend Markov routing to state-dependent routing, e.g. to allow for some forms of capacity limitations; see Section 8.8.6.

8.4.2   Catalog of Service Stations

There are certain constraints on the type of service stations allowed in multiclass product form queuing networks. Formally, the service stations must satisfy the property called "local balance in isolation" defined in Section 8.8, i.e. the stationary probability of the station in the configuration of Section 8.4.3 must satisfy (8.96) and (8.97).

In this section, we give a catalog of station types that are known to satisfy this property. There are only two categories of stations in our list ("insensitive", and "MSCCC"), but these are fairly general categories, which contain many examples such as Processor Sharing, Delay, FIFO, Last Come First Serve etc. Thus, in practice, if you have to determine whether a given station type is allowed in multi-class product form queuing networks, a simple solution is to look up the following catalog.

We use the definitions below. Every station type is defined by:

- A **discipline**: this specifies how arriving customers are queued, and which customers receive service at any time. We also assume that there is a **station buffer**: this is where customers are placed while waiting or receiving service, represented by some form of data structure such that every position in the station buffer can be addressed by an index $i \in \mathcal{I}$ where $\mathcal{I}$ is some enumerable set. If $\mathcal{B}$ is the state of the station buffer at a given time, $\mathcal{B}_i$ is the class of the customer present at position i (equal to -1 if there is no customer present). Further, we will make use of two operations. $\mathcal{B}' = \text{add}(\mathcal{B}, i, c)$ describes the effect of adding a customer of class c at a position indexed by i into the station buffer described by $\mathcal{B}$. $\mathcal{B}' = \text{remove}(\mathcal{B}, i)$ describes the effect of removing the customer present at a position i, if any (if there is no customer at position i, $\text{remove}(\mathcal{B}, i) = \mathcal{B}$). For example, if the service discipline is FIFO: the data structure is a linear list such as $\mathcal{B} = (c_1, c_2, \ldots, c_n)$ where c_i is the class of the ith customer (labeled in arrival order); the index set is $\mathcal{I} = \mathbb{N}$; $\text{add}(\mathcal{B}, i, c) = (c_1, \ldots, c_{i-1}, c, c_i, \ldots, c_n)$ and $\text{remove}(\mathcal{B}, i) = (c_1, \ldots, c_{i-1}, c_{i+1}, \ldots, c_n)$. We call $|\mathcal{B}|$ the number of customers present in the buffer, and assume that it is always finite (but unbounded).

- A **service requirement**, also called **service time**. For example, if a customer is a job, the service requirement may be the number of CPU cycles required; if it is a packet or a block of data, it may be the time to transmit it on a link. We assume that service requirements are random and drawn independently from anything else when a customer joins the service station. Unless otherwise specified, the distribution of service requirements may depend on the station and the class. Allowing service requirements to depend on the class is very powerful: it renders it possible to for example model service times that are correlated from one visit to the next.

- A **service rate**: this is the speed at which the server operates, which may depend on the customer class. If the service rate is 1, the service duration is equal to the service requirement (but the response time may be larger, as it includes waiting time). The service rate may be used to model how resources are shared between classes at a station.

Category 1: Insensitive Station or Kelly-Whittle Stations

This category of stations is called "insensitive" or "Kelly-Whittle", for reasons that become clear below. We first give a formal, theoretical definition, then list the most frequent instances.

Formal Definition

(1) The service requirement may be any phase-type distribution; in practice, this may approximate any distribution, see Section 8.8.1. The service distribution may be dependent on the class.

(2) **Insertion Probability** There is an array of numbers $\gamma(i, \mathcal{B}) \geq 0$ defined for any index $i \in \mathcal{I}$ and any station buffer state $\mathcal{B}$, such that: when a class-c customer arrives and finds the station buffer in state $\mathcal{B}$ just before the arrival, the position at which this customer is added is drawn at random, and the probability that he/she is added at a position indexed by i is

$$\gamma\big(i, \text{add}(\mathcal{B}, i, c)\big) \tag{8.25}$$

The same happens whenever a customer finishes a service phase (from the phase-type service distribution), at which time he/she is treated as a new arrival.

We assume to avoid inconsistencies that $\sum_{i \in \mathcal{I}} \gamma(i, \mathrm{add}(\mathcal{B}, i, c)) = 1$ and $\gamma(i, \mathcal{B}) = 0$ if there is no customer at position i in $\mathcal{B}$.

(3) **Whittle Function**. There is a function $\Psi(\cdot)$, called the Whittle Function, defined over the set of feasible station buffer states, such that $\Psi(\mathcal{B}) > 0$ and the service rate allocated to a user in position i of the station buffer is

$$\gamma(i, \mathcal{B}) \frac{\Psi(\mathrm{remove}(\mathcal{B}, i))}{\Psi(\mathcal{B})} \tag{8.26}$$

if there is a customer present at position i, and 0 otherwise. Note that any positive function may be taken as a Whittle function; the converse is not true, i.e. any rate allocation algorithm does not necessarily derive from a Whittle function.

One frequently considers the case of

$$\Psi(\mathcal{B}) = \Phi(\vec{n}) \tag{8.27}$$

where $\vec{n} = (n_1, \ldots, n_C)$ with n_c the number of class-c customers in $\mathcal{B}$, and $\Phi(\cdot)$ is an arbitrary positive function defined on $\mathbb{N}^C$. In other words, the Whittle function in such cases depends on the state of the station only through the numbers of customers (not their position in the buffer). The function Φ is called the **balance function**; the quantity $\frac{\Phi(\vec{n} - \vec{1}_c)}{\Phi(\vec{n})}$ is the rate allocated to class c. As with the Whittle function, any positive Φ may be taken as a balance function, but the converse is not true. In other words, any rate allocation does not necessarily derive from a balance function.

(4) We assume that for any index i, class c and station buffer state $\mathcal{B}$

$$\begin{cases} \mathrm{remove}(\mathrm{add}(\mathcal{B}, i, c), i) = \mathcal{B} \\ \text{if } \mathcal{B}_i \text{ is not empty: } \mathrm{add}(\mathrm{remove}(\mathcal{B}, i), i, \mathcal{B}_i) = \mathcal{B} \end{cases} \tag{8.28}$$

i.e. a state remains unchanged if one adds a customer and immediately removes him/her, or vice-versa.

This formal definition may seem fairly appalling, but, as we demonstrate next, it is rarely necessary to make use of the formal definition. Instead, it may be easier to look up the next list of examples.

Examples of Insensitive Stations

For each of these examples, the service requirement distribution may be any phase-type distribution, and may be class dependent.

Global PS (Processor Sharing). The station is as in the Processor Sharing queue of Section 8.3.3. All customers present in the station receive service, at a rate equal to $\frac{1}{n}$ when there are n customers of any class present at the station.

This is a Kelly-Whittle station, by taking the ordered list of customer classes $\mathcal{B} = (c_1, \ldots, c_n)$ as station buffer. Adding a customer at position i has the effect that existing customers at positions $\geq i$ are shifted by one position, thus (8.28) holds. When a customer arrives, he/she is added at any position 1 to $n+1$ with equal probability $\frac{1}{n+1}$, i.e. $\gamma(i, \mathcal{B}) = \frac{1}{|\mathcal{B}|}$ (recall that $|\mathcal{B}|$ is the total number of customers when the buffer state is $\mathcal{B}$). The Whittle function is simply $\Psi(\mathcal{B}) = 1$ for every $\mathcal{B}$. Thus, the service rate allocated to a customer is $\frac{1}{n}$, as required.

Global LCFSPR. This service station is **Last Come First Serve, Preemptive Resume (LCFSPR)**. There is one global queue; an arriving customer is inserted at the head of the queue, and only this customer receives service. When an arrival occurs, the customer in service is preempted (service is suspended); preempted customers resume service where they left it, when they eventually return to service.

This is a Kelly-Whittle station by taking as station buffer the ordered list of customer classes $\mathcal{B} = (c_1, \ldots, c_n)$ as in the previous example. When a customer arrives, it is added at position 1, i.e. $\gamma(i, \mathcal{B}) = 1_{\{i=1\}}$. The Whittle function is also $\Psi(\mathcal{B}) = 1$ for every $\mathcal{B}$. Thus the service rate allocated to a customer is 1 to the customer at the head of the queue, and 0 to all others, as required.

Per-Class Processor Sharing. This is a variant of the Processor Sharing station, where the service rate is divided between customers of the same class, i.e. a customer receives service at rate $\frac{1}{n_c}$, where n_c is the number of class-c customers present in the system.

This is a Kelly-Whittle station by taking a collection of C lists as station buffer; one per class. Only customers of class c may be present in the cth list. An index is a couple $i = (c, j)$, where c is a class index and j is an integer. Adding a customer at position $i = (c, j)$ has the effect that existing customers in the cth list at positions $\geq j$ are shifted by one position, and others do not move. Thus, (8.28) holds.

When a class-c customer arrives, he/she is inserted into the cth list, at any position 1 to $n_c + 1$, with equal probability. Thus, $\gamma((c, j), \mathcal{B}) = 0$ if the customer at position (c, j) is not of class c, and $\frac{1}{n_c}$ otherwise. We take as Whittle function $\Psi(\mathcal{B}) = 1$ for every $\mathcal{B}$. It follows that the service rate allocated to a customer of class c is $\frac{1}{n_c}$ as claimed above.

Per-Class LCFSPR. This is a variant of the LCFSPR station, where one customer per class may be served, and this customer is the last arrived in this class.

This is a Kelly-Whittle station by taking a collection of C lists as station buffer; one per class as for per-class PS. When a class-c customer arrives, he/she is added at the head of the cth queue, thus $\gamma(i, \mathcal{B}) = 1$ if $i = (c, 1)$ and the class at the head of the cth queue in $\mathcal{B}$ is c, otherwise 0. It follows that the service rate allocated to a customer is 0 unless he/she is at the head of a queue, i.e. this customer is the last arrived in his/her class. We take $\Psi(\mathcal{B}) = 1$ for every $\mathcal{B}$ as Whittle function. It follows that this station is equivalent to a collection of C independent LCFSPR service stations, one per class, with a unit service rate in each.

Infinite Server (IS) or Delay station. There is no queuing, customers start service immediately. This is a Kelly-Whittle station by taking the same station buffer and insertion probability as for Global PS, but with the Whittle function $\Psi(\mathcal{B}) = \frac{1}{n!}$ where $n = |\mathcal{B}|$ is the total number of customers present in the station. It follows that the service rate allocated to any customer present in the station is 1, as required.

PS, LCFSPR and IS with class dependent service rate.   Consider any of the previous examples, but assume that the service rate is class-dependent, and depends on the number of customers of this class present in the station (call $r_c(n_c)$ the service rate for class c).

Thus, for Global PS, the service rate allocated to a class-c customer is $\frac{r_c(n_c)}{n}$; for Per-Class PS, it is $\frac{r_c(n_c)}{n_c}$. For Global LCFSPR, the service rate allocated to the unique customer in service is $r_c(n_c)$; for Per Class LCFSPR, the service rate allocated to the class-c customer in service is $r_c(n_c)$. For IS, the rate allocated to every class-c customer is $r_c(n_c)$.

This fits in the framework of Kelly-Whittle stations as follows. For PS and LCFSPR (per-class or global) replace the Whittle function by

$$\Psi(\mathcal{B}) = \prod_{c=1}^{C} \frac{1}{r_c(1)r_c(2)\cdots r_c(n_c)}$$

so that

$$\frac{\Psi\big(\text{remove}(\mathcal{B}, i)\big)}{\Psi(\mathcal{B})} = r_c(n_c)$$

as required. For IS, replace Ψ by

$$\Psi(\mathcal{B}) = \frac{1}{n!} \prod_{c=1}^{C} \frac{1}{r_c(1)r_c(2)\cdots r_c(n_c)}$$

in order to obtain the required service rate.

PS, LCFSPR and IS with queue-size-dependent service rate.   Consider any of the first five previous examples, but assume that the service rate is class-independent, and depends on the total number of customers n present in the station (call $r(n)$ the service rate). Thus for Global PS, the service rate allocated to one customer is $\frac{r(n)}{n}$ if this customer is of class c; for Per-Class PS, it is $\frac{r(n)}{n_c}$. For Global LCFSPR, the service rate allocated to the unique customer in service is $r(n)$; for Per Class LCFSPR, the service rate allocated to every customer ahead of its queue is $r(n)$. For IS, the service rate for every customer is $r(n)$.

This fits in the framework of Kelly-Whittle stations as follows. For PS and LCFSPR (per-class or global), replace the Whittle function by

$$\Psi(\mathcal{B}) = \frac{1}{r(1)r(2)\cdots r(n)}$$

so that

$$\frac{\Psi\big(\text{remove}(\mathcal{B}, i)\big)}{\Psi(\mathcal{B})} = r(n)$$

as required. For IS, replace Ψ by

$$\Psi(\mathcal{B}) = \frac{1}{n!} \frac{1}{r(1)r(2)\cdots r(n)}$$

in order to obtain the required service rate.

Symmetric Station, also called Kelly station.   This is a generic type introduced by Kelly in [44] under the name of "symmetric" service discipline. The station buffer is an ordered list as in the first example above. For an arriving customer who finds n customers present in the station, the probability to join position i is $p(n+1, i)$, where $\sum_{i=1}^{n+1} p(n+1, i) = 1$ (thus $\gamma(\mathcal{B}, i) = p(|\mathcal{B}|, i)$). The rate allocated to a customer in position i is $p(n, i)$ when there are n customers present. The name "symmetric" comes from the fact that the same function is used to define the insertion probability and the rate.

This fits in the framework of Kelly-Whittle stations, with a Whittle function equal to 1. The global PS and global LCFSPR stations are special cases of Kelly stations.

Whittle Network.   This is a Per-Class Processor Sharing station where the Whittle function is a balance function, i.e. $\Psi(\mathcal{B}) = \Phi(\vec{n})$. It follows that the service rate for a class-c customer is

$$\frac{1}{n_c} \frac{\Phi(\vec{n} - \vec{1}_c)}{\Phi(\vec{n})} \tag{8.29}$$

where $\vec{1}_c = (0, \ldots, 1, \ldots, 0)$ with a 1 in position c. This type of station is used in [13] to model resource sharing among several classes.

A network consisting of a single chain of classes and one single Whittle Station is called a Whittle Network. In such a network, customers of class c that have finished service may return to the station, perhaps under a different class.

A Whittle network can also be interpreted as a single class, multi-station network, as follows. There is one station per class, and customers may join only the station of their class. However, class switching is possible. Since knowledge of the station in which a customer resides entirely defines its class, there is no need for a customer to carry a class attribute, and we have a single class network.

In other words, a Whittle Network is a single class network with PS service stations, where the rate allocated to station c is $\frac{\Phi(\vec{n} - \vec{1}_c)}{\Phi(\vec{n})}$. The product form network in Theorem 8.7 implies that the stationary probability of there being n_c customers in station c for all c is

$$P(\vec{n}) = \frac{1}{\eta} \Phi(\vec{n}) \prod_{c=1}^{C} \bar{S}_c^{n_c} \theta_c^{n_c} \tag{8.30}$$

where $\bar{S}_c$ is the expected service requirement at station c, θ_c is the visit rate and η is a normalizing constant.

Note that the stationary probability in (8.30) depends only on the traffic intensity $\rho_c = \bar{S}_c \theta_c$, and not on the distribution of service times. This is the *insensitivity* property; it applies not only to Whittle networks, but more generally to all service stations of category 1, hence the name.

Category 2: MSCCC Station

This second category of stations contains, as a special case, the FIFO stations with one or any fixed number of servers. It is called *Multiple Server with Concurrent Classes of Customers* in reference to [26], [53] and [11]. A slightly more general form than that presented here can be found in [2].

The service requirement *must be* exponentially distributed with the same parameter for all classes at this station (but the parameter may be different at different stations). If we relax this assumption, this station is no longer admissible for multi-class product form queuing networks. Thus, unlike for category 1, this station type is *sensitive* to the distribution of service requirements.

The service discipline is as follows. There are B servers and G *token pools*. Every class is associated with exactly one token pool, but there can be several classes associated with the same token pool. The size of token pool g is an integer $T_g \geq 1$.

A customer is "eligible for service" when one of the B servers becomes available *and* there is a free token in the pool g to which this customer's class is associated. There is a single queue in which customers are queued in order of arrival; when a server becomes idle, the first eligible customer in the queue, or to arrive, starts service, and busies both one server and one token of the corresponding pool. The parameters such as G, B and the mapping $\mathcal{G}$ of classes to token pools may be different at every station.

The FIFO queue with B servers is a special case with $G = 1$ token pool, and $T_1 = B$.

In addition, this station may have a variable service rate that depends on the total number of customers in the station. The rate must be the same for all classes (rates that depend on the population vector are not allowed, unlike for category 1 stations).

Example 8.6 A Dual-Core Machine

Figure 8.11 illustrates a simple model of a dual-core processor. Classes 1, 2 or 3 represent internal jobs and class 4 internal jobs. All jobs use the dual-core processor, represented by station 1. External jobs can cycle through the system more than once. Internal jobs undergo a random delay and a variable delay due to communication.

The processor can serve up to 2 jobs in parallel, but some jobs require exclusive access to a critical section and cannot be served together. This is represented by an MSCCC station with 2 servers and 2 token pools, of sizes 1 and 2. Jobs requiring access to the critical section use a token of the first pool; other jobs use tokens of the second pool (the second pool has no effect since its size is as large as the number of servers, but it is required to fit in the general framework of multi-class product form queuing networks).

The delay of internal jobs is represented by station 2 (an "infinite server" station) and the communication delay is represented by station 3 (a "processor sharing" station, with a constant rate server).

Internal jobs always use the critical section, whereas external jobs may employ the critical section at most once. This is modeled by means of the following routing rules.

- Jobs of classes 1, 2 or 3 are internal jobs. Jobs of class 1 have never used the critical section in the past and do not use it; jobs of class 2 use the critical section; jobs of class 3 have utilized the critical section in the past but do not use it any more.

  After service, a job of class 1 may either leave or return immediately as class 1 or 2. A job of class 2 may either leave or return immediately as class 3. A job of class 3 may either leave or return immediately as class 3.

- Jobs of class 4 represent internal jobs. They go in cycles through stations 1, 2, 3 forever.

- At station 1, classes 2 and 4 are associated with token pool 1, whereas classes 1 and 3 are associated with token pool 2, i.e. $\mathcal{G}(1) = 2$, $\mathcal{G}(2) = 1$, $\mathcal{G}(3) = 2$ and $\mathcal{G}(4) = 1$. The constraints at station 1 are thus the following: there can be up to 2 jobs in service, with at most one job of classes 2 or 4.

The routing matrix is

$$
\begin{cases}
q_{1,1}^{1,1} = \alpha_1 \quad q_{1,2}^{1,1} = \beta_1 \\
q_{2,3}^{1,1} = \alpha_2 \\
q_{3,3}^{1,1} = \alpha_3 \\
q_{4,4}^{1,2} = 1 \quad q_{4,4}^{2,3} = 1 \quad q_{4,4}^{3,1} = 1 \\
q_{c,c'}^{s,s'} = 0 \quad \text{otherwise}
\end{cases}
$$

where all numbers are positive, $\alpha_i \leq 1$ and $\alpha_1 + \beta_1 \leq 1$.

There are two chains: $\{1,2,3\}$ and $\{4\}$. The first chain is open, the second is closed, so we have a mixed network.

Let ν be the arrival rate of external jobs and p_i the probability that an arriving job is of class i. The visit rates are

Class 1: $\theta_1^1 = \nu \dfrac{p_1}{1 - \alpha_1}$; $\theta_1^2 = 0; \quad \theta_1^3 = 0;$

Class 2: $\theta_2^1 = \nu \left(p_2 + \beta_1 \dfrac{p_1}{1 - \alpha_1} \right)$; $\theta_2^2 = 0; \quad \theta_2^3 = 0;$

Class 3: $\theta_3^1 = \nu \dfrac{1}{1 - \alpha_3} \left(p_3 + \alpha_2 p_2 + \alpha_2 \beta_1 \dfrac{p_1}{1 - \alpha_1} \right)$; $\theta_3^2 = 0; \quad \theta_3^3 = 0;$

Class 4: $\theta_4^1 = 1;$ $\theta_4^2 = 1; \quad \theta_4^3 = 1.$

Note that the visit rates are uniquely defined for the classes in the open chain (1, 2 and 3). In contrast, for class 4, any constant can be used (instead of the constant 1).

8.4.3 The Station Function

Station in Isolation

The expression of the product form theorem uses the ***station function***, which depends on the parameter of the station as indicated below, and takes, as an argument, the vector $\vec{n} = (n_1, \ldots, n_C)$, where n_c is the number of class-c customers at this station. It can be interpreted as the stationary distribution of numbers of customers in the station in isolation, up to a multiplicative constant.

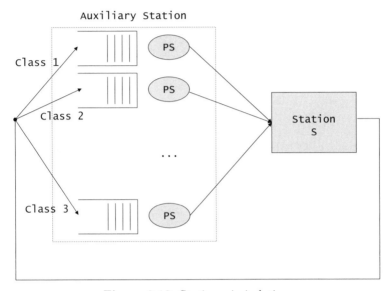

Figure 8.12 Station s in isolation.

More precisely, imagine a (virtual) closed network, made of this station and one external, auxiliary Per Class PS station with mean service time 1 and service rate 1 for all classes, as in Figure 8.12. In this virtual network, there is one chain per class and every class c has a constant number of customers K_c. The product form theorem implies that, for any values of the vector $\vec{K} = (K_1, \ldots, K_C)$, this network has a stationary regime, and the stationary probability that there are n_1 customers of class $1, \ldots, n_C$ customers of class C is

$$P^{\text{isol}}(\vec{n}) = \begin{cases} 0 & \text{if } n_c > K_c \text{ for some } c \\ f(\vec{n}) \dfrac{1}{\eta(\vec{K})} & \text{otherwise} \end{cases} \tag{8.31}$$

where $\eta(\vec{K})$ is a normalizing constant (independent of $\vec{n}$).

It is often useful to consider the ***generating function*** $G(\cdot)$ of the station function, defined as the ***Z-transform*** of the station function. In other words, for $\vec{Z} = (Z_1, \ldots, Z_C)$,

$$G(\vec{Z}) = \sum_{\vec{n} \geq 0} f(\vec{n}) \prod_{c=1}^{C} Z_c^{n_c} \tag{8.32}$$

(Note that, in signal processing, one often uses Z^{-1} instead of Z; we utilize the direct convention, called the "mathematician's z-transform".) The following interpretation of the generating function is quite useful. According to Theorem 8.8, $G(\vec{Z})$ is the normalizing constant for the open network made of this station alone, fed by independent external Poisson processes of rates Z_c, one for each class c. Upon finishing the service at this station, customers leave the network and disappear.

In the rest of this section, we give the station functions for the different stations introduced earlier.

Station Function for Category 1

Let $\mathrm{pop}(\mathcal{B}) \overset{\text{def}}{=} (n_1, \dots, n_C)$, where n_c is the number of class-c customers at this station when the station buffer is in state $\mathcal{B}$ (i.e. $n_c = \sum_{i \in \mathcal{I}} 1_{\{\mathcal{B}_i = c\}}$). The station function is

$$f(\vec{n}) = \sum_{\mathrm{pop}(\mathcal{B}) = \vec{n}} \Psi(\mathcal{B}) \prod_{c=1}^{C} \bar{S}_c^{n_c} \qquad (8.33)$$

where the summation runs $\mathcal{B}$ over all station buffer states $\mathcal{B}$ for which the vector of populations is $\vec{n}$. $\bar{S}_c$ is the mean service time for class c at this station, and Ψ is the Whittle function of this station.

Note that the station function is *independent of the insertion probabilities* γ. For example, the stationary probability is the same whether the station is PS or LCFSPR, since they differ only by the insertion probabilities.

In the case where the Whittle function is a balance function, i.e. $\Psi(\mathcal{B}) = \Phi(\vec{n})$, the summation may sometimes be computed.

(1) If the station uses global queuing as in the Global PS and Global LCFSPR examples, there are $\frac{n!}{n_1! \cdots n_C!}$ station buffer states for a given population vector, with $n = |\vec{n}| = \sum_{c=1}^{C} n_c$. The station function is

$$f(\vec{n}) = \frac{n!}{\prod_{c=1}^{C} n_c!} \Phi(\vec{n}) \prod_{c=1}^{C} \bar{S}_c^{n_c} \qquad (8.34)$$

(2) If the station uses per class queuing as in the Per Class PS and Per Class LCFSPR examples, there is one station buffer state for one population vector and the station function is

$$f(\vec{n}) = \Phi(\vec{n}) \prod_{c=1}^{C} \bar{S}_c^{n_c} \qquad (8.35)$$

Global PS/Global LCFSPR/Kelly Station with constant rate. In these cases we can assume that the service rate is 1; for all of these disciplines the station function is given by (8.34) with $\Phi(\vec{n}) = 1$. The generating function is

$$G(\vec{Z}) = \frac{1}{1 - \displaystyle\sum_{c=1}^{C} \bar{S}_c Z_c} \qquad (8.36)$$

Per Class PS/Per Class LCFSPR with constant rate. Here too, we can assume that the service rate is 1; the station function is given by (8.35) with $\Phi(\vec{n}) = 1$. The generating function is

$$G(\vec{Z}) = \prod_{c=1}^{C} \frac{1}{1 - \bar{S}_c Z_c} \tag{8.37}$$

IS with constant rate. Also in this case we can assume that the service rate is 1; the station function is given by (8.34) with $\Phi(\vec{n}) = \frac{1}{n!}$. The generating function is

$$G(\vec{Z}) = \exp\left(\sum_{c=1}^{C} \bar{S}_c Z_c\right) \tag{8.38}$$

Station Function for Category 2

For the general station in this category, the station function is somewhat complex. However, for the special case of FIFO stations with one or more servers, it has a simple closed form, given at the end of this section.

General MSCCC Station. Recall that the station parameters are:

- $r(i)$: the service rate when the total number of customers is i,
- $\bar{S}$: the mean service time (independent of the class),
- B: the number of servers,
- G: the number of token pools; T_g: the size of token pool g; $\mathcal{G}$: the mapping of the class to the token pool, i.e. $\mathcal{G}(c) = g$ when class c is associated with token pool g.

The station function is

$$f(\vec{n}) = d(\vec{x}) \frac{\bar{S}^{|\vec{n}|}}{|\vec{n}|} \frac{\displaystyle\prod_{g=1}^{G} x_g!}{\displaystyle\prod_{i=1}^{|\vec{n}|} r(i) \prod_{c=1}^{C} n_c!} \tag{8.39}$$

with $|\vec{n}| = \sum_{c=1}^{C} n_c$, $\vec{x} = (x_1, \ldots, x_G)$ and $x_g = \sum_{c:\mathcal{G}(c)=g} n_c$ (the number of customers associated with token pool g). The function d is a combinatorial function of $\vec{x} \in \mathbb{Z}^G$, recursively defined by $d(\vec{x}) = 0$ if $x_g \leq 0$ for some g, $d(0, \ldots, 0) = 1$ and

$$d(\vec{x}) \times bs(\vec{x}) = \sum_{g=1}^{G} d(\vec{x} - \vec{1}_g) \tag{8.40}$$

where $bs(\vec{x}) \overset{\text{def}}{=} \min\left(B, \sum_{g=1}^{G} \min(x_g, T_g)\right)$ is the number of busy servers and $\vec{1}_g = (0, \ldots 1 \ldots 0)$ with a 1 in position g. Note that

$$\text{if } \sum_{g} \min(x_g, T_g) \leq B \qquad \text{then} \qquad d(\vec{x}) = \prod_{g=1}^{G} \frac{1}{\displaystyle\prod_{i=1}^{x_g} \min(i, T_g)}$$

In general, though, there does not appear to be a closed form for d, except when the station is a FIFO station (see below).

For the MSCCC station, the generating function can generally not be explicitly computed. However, when the service rate is constant, i.e. $r(i) = 1$ for all i, one may use the following algorithm. Let D be the generating function of d, i.e.

$$D(\vec{X}) = \sum_{\vec{x} \in \mathbb{N}^G} d(\vec{x}) \prod_{g=1}^{G} X_g^{x_g} \tag{8.41}$$

with $\vec{X} = (X_1, \ldots, X_G)$. For $\vec{\tau} \in \{0 \ldots T_1\} \times \cdots \times \{0 \ldots T_G\}$, let

$$D_{\vec{\tau}}(\vec{X}) \stackrel{\text{def}}{=} \sum_{\vec{x} \geq 0,\, \min(x_g, T_g) = \tau_g,\, \forall g} d(\vec{x}) \prod_{g=1}^{G} X_g^{x_g}$$

so that $D(\vec{X}) = \sum_{\vec{\tau} \in \{0 \ldots T_1\} \times \cdots \times \{0 \ldots T_G\}} D_{\vec{\tau}}(\vec{X})$. One can compute $D_{\vec{\tau}}(\cdot)$ iteratively, using $D_{\vec{0}}(\vec{X}) = 1$, $D_{\vec{\tau}}(\vec{X}) = 0$ if $\tau_g < 0$ for some g and the following, which follows from (8.40),

$$D_{\vec{\tau}}(\vec{X}) = \frac{1}{\text{bs}(\vec{\tau}) - \sum_{g:\tau_g = T_g} X_g} \sum_{g:\tau_g > 0} X_g D_{\vec{\tau} - \vec{1}_g}(\vec{X}) \tag{8.42}$$

It is sometimes useful to note that

$$D_{\vec{\tau}}(\vec{X}) = \prod_{g=1}^{G} \frac{X_g^{\tau_g}}{T_g! \left(1 - \frac{X_g}{T_g} 1_{\{\tau_g = T_g\}}\right)} \qquad \text{if } \vec{\tau} \geq 0 \text{ and } \text{bs}(\vec{\tau}) < B \tag{8.43}$$

The generating function of the MSCCC station with a constant service rate is then given by

$$G(\vec{Z}) = D(X_1, \ldots, X_G) \tag{8.44}$$

with $X_g = \bar{S}\left(\sum_{c \text{ such that } \mathcal{G}(c) = g} Z_c\right)$ for all token pool g.

FIFO with B servers. This is a special case of MSCCC, with much simpler formulas than in the general case. Here, the parameters are

- $r(i)$: the service rate when the total number of customers is i,
- $\bar{S}$: the mean service time (independent of the class),
- B: the number of servers

The station function is derived from (8.39) with $G = 1$. One finds $\vec{x} = (|\vec{n}|)$ and $d(j) = \frac{1}{\prod_{i=1}^{j} \min(B,i)}$ for $j \geq 1$. Thus,

$$f(\vec{n}) = \frac{\bar{S}^{|\vec{n}|}}{\prod_{i=1}^{|\vec{n}|} [r(i) \min(B,i)]} \frac{|\vec{n}|!}{\prod_{c=1}^{C} n_c!} \tag{8.45}$$

In the constant rate case, the generating function follows from (8.43):

$$G(\vec{Z}) = 1 + X + \frac{X^2}{2!} + \cdots + \frac{X^{B-1}}{(B-1)!} + \frac{X^B}{B!\left(1 - \dfrac{X}{B}\right)} \tag{8.46}$$

with $X = \bar{S} \sum_{c=1}^{C} Z_c$.

In particular, for the *FIFO station with one server and constant rate*, the station function is

$$f(\vec{n}) = \frac{\bar{S}^{|\vec{n}|}|\vec{n}|!}{\displaystyle\prod_{c=1}^{C} n_c!} \tag{8.47}$$

and the generating function is

$$G(\vec{Z}) = \frac{1}{1 - \bar{S} \displaystyle\sum_{c=1}^{C} Z_c} \tag{8.48}$$

Example 8.7 Dual-Core Processor in Figure 8.11

The station functions are (we use the notation n_i instead of n_i^1)

$$f^1(n_1, n_2, n_3, n_4) = d(n_2 + n_4, n_1 + n_3)$$
$$\times \frac{(n_1 + n_3)!\,(n_2 + n_4)!}{n_1!\,n_2!\,n_3!\,n_4!}\,(\bar{S}^1)^{n_1+n_2+n_3+n_4}$$
$$f^2(n_4^2) = \left(\bar{S}^2\right)^{n_4^2}\frac{1}{n_4^2!}$$
$$f^3(n_4^3) = \left(\bar{S}^3\right)^{n_4^3}$$

In the equation, d corresponds to the MSCCC station and is defined by (8.40). The generating functions for stations 2 and 3 follow immediately from (8.38) and (8.37):

$$G^2(Z_1, Z_2, Z_3, Z_4) = e^{\bar{S}^2 Z_4}$$
$$G^3(Z_1, Z_2, Z_3, Z_4) = \frac{1}{1 - \bar{S}^3 Z_4}$$

For station 1, more work is required.
First, we compute the generating function

$$D(X, Y) \stackrel{\text{def}}{=} \sum_{m \geq 0, n \geq 0} d(m, n) X^m Y^n$$

Using (8.40), one finds

$$D_{0,0}(X,Y) = 1$$

$$D_{1,0}(X,Y) = \frac{X}{1-X}$$

$$D_{0,1}(X,Y) = Y$$

$$D_{1,1}(X,Y) = \frac{1}{2-Y}\left(XD_{0,1} + YD_{1,0}\right) = \frac{XY}{1-X}$$

$$D_{0,2}(X,Y) = \frac{1}{2-X}YD_{0,1} = \frac{Y^2}{2-Y}$$

$$D_{1,2}(X,Y) = \frac{1}{2-X-Y}\left(XD_{0,2} + YD_{1,1}\right)$$

$$= \frac{XY^2(3-X-Y)}{(2-X-Y)(2-Y)(1-X)}$$

and D is the sum of these 6 functions. After some algebra, we get

$$D(X,Y) = \frac{1}{1-X}\left(1 + Y + \frac{Y^2}{2-X-Y}\right) \qquad (8.49)$$

Using (8.44), it follows that the generating functions of station 1 is

$$G^1(Z_1, Z_2, Z_3, Z_4) = D\big(\bar{S}^1(Z_2 + Z_4), \bar{S}^1(Z_1 + Z_3)\big) \qquad (8.50)$$

QUESTION 8.10 Compare the station function for an IS station with a constant service rate and equal mean service time for all classes with a FIFO station with a constant rate and $B \to \infty$.[13]

QUESTION 8.11 What is the station function $f^{\mathrm{aux}}(\cdot)$ for the auxiliary station used in the definition of the station in isolation?[14]

QUESTION 8.12 Verify that $D(X,0)$ (resp. $D(0,Y)$) is the generating function of a FIFO station with one server (resp. 2 servers) (where $D(\cdot)$ is given by (8.49)); explain why.[15]

---

[13] Both are the same: (8.45) and (8.34) with $\Phi(\vec{n}) = \frac{1}{n!}$ give the same result: $f(\vec{n}) = \frac{\bar{s}^{|\vec{n}|}}{\prod_{c=1}^{C} n_c!}$.

[14] It is a Per Class PS station with $\bar{S}_c = 1$ for all c thus $f^{\mathrm{aux}}(\vec{n}) = 1$. The product form theorem implies that the stationary probability of seeing n_c customers in the station of interest is $\eta f(\vec{n})$.

[15] We find $\frac{1}{1-X}$ and $1 + Y + \frac{Y^2}{2-Y}$ as given by (8.46).

The generating function $D(X,Y)$ is the z-transform of the station function with one class per token group, and is also equal to the normalizing constant for the station fed by a Poisson process with rate X for group 1 and Y for group 2. If $Y = 0$, we have only group 1 customers, and therefore the station is the same as a single server FIFO station with arrival rate X. If $X = 0$, the station is equivalent to a FIFO station with 2 servers and the arrival rate Y.

8.5 The Product-Form Theorem

8.5.1 Product Form

The following theorem gives the stationary probability of the number of customers in explicit form; it is the main available result for queuing networks. The original proof is in [10], and extension to any service stations that satisfies the local balance property can be found in [78] and [44]. The proof that MSCCC stations satisfy the local balance property is given in [53] and [11]. The proof that all Kelly-Whittle stations satisfy the local balance property is novel and is provided in Section 8.10 (see Section 8.8 for more details).

Theorem 8.7

Consider a multi-class network as defined above. In particular, it uses Markov routing and all stations are Kelly-Whittle or MSCCC. Assume that the aggregation condition in Section 8.8.3 holds.

Let n_c^s be the number of class-c customers present in station s and $\vec{n}^s = (n_1^s, \ldots, n_C^s)$. The stationary probability distribution of the number of customers, if it exists, is given by

$$P(\vec{n}^1, \ldots, \vec{n}^S) = \frac{1}{\eta} \prod_{s=1}^{S} \left(f^s(\vec{n}^s) \prod_{c=1}^{C} (\theta_c^s)^{n_c^s} \right) \tag{8.51}$$

where θ_c^s is the visit rate in (8.24), $f^s(\cdot)$ is the station function and η is a positive normalizing constant.

Conversely, let $\mathcal{E}$ be the set of all feasible population vectors $\vec{n} = (\vec{n}^1, \ldots, \vec{n}^S)$. If

$$\sum_{\vec{n} \in \mathcal{E}} \prod_{s=1}^{S} \left(f^s(\vec{n}^s) \prod_{c=1}^{C} (\theta_c^s)^{n_c^s} \right) < \infty \tag{8.52}$$

there exists a stationary probability.

In the open network case, any vector $(\vec{n}^1, \ldots, \vec{n}^S)$ is feasible, whereas in the closed or mixed case, the set of feasible population vectors $\mathcal{E}$ is defined by the constraints on populations of closed chains, i.e.

$$\sum_{c \in \mathcal{C}} \sum_{s=1}^{S} n_c^s = K_{\mathcal{C}}$$

for any closed chain $\mathcal{C}$, where $K_{\mathcal{C}}$ is the (constant) number of customers in this chain.

Note that the station function depends only on the traffic intensities. In particular, the stationary distribution is not affected by the variance of the service requirement, for stations of Category 1 (recall that stations of Category 2 must have exponential service requirement distributions).

QUESTION 8.13 What is the relationship between the sum in (8.52) and η?[16]

8.5.2   Stability Conditions

In the open case, stability is not guaranteed and may depend on conditions on arrival rates. However, the next theorem states that the stability can be verified at every station in isolation, and correspond to the natural conditions. In particular, pathological instabilities as discussed in the introduction of Section 8.4, cannot occur for multi-class product form queuing networks.

Theorem 8.8 (Open Case)
Consider a multi-class product form queuing network as defined above. Assume that it is open. For every station s, $\vec{\theta}^s = (\theta_1^s, \dots, \theta_C^s)$ is the vector of visit rates, f^s is the station function and $G^s(\cdot)$ is its generating function, given in (8.36), (8.38), (8.44), and (8.46).

The network has a stationary distribution if and only if for every station s

$$G^s(\vec{\theta}^s) < \infty \tag{8.53}$$

If this condition holds, the normalizing constant of Theorem 8.7 is $\eta = \prod_{s=1}^{S} G^s(\vec{\theta}^s)$. Further, let $P^s(\vec{n}^s)$ be the stationary probability of the number of customers in station s. Then

$$P(\vec{n}^1, \dots, \vec{n}^S) = \prod_{s=1}^{S} P^s(\vec{n}^s) \tag{8.54}$$

i.e. the numbers of customers in different stations are independent. The marginal stationary probability for station s is

$$P^s(\vec{n}^s) = \frac{1}{G^s(\vec{\theta}^s)} f^s(\vec{n}^s) \tag{8.55}$$

The proof follows from the fact that the existence of an invariant probability is sufficient for stability (as we assume that the state space is fully connected, by the aggregation condition). If the network is closed or mixed, the corollary does not hold, i.e. the states in different stations are *not independent*, though there is product-form. Closed networks are always stable, but it may not be simple to compute the normalizing constant; efficient algorithms exist, as discussed in Section 8.6.

For mixed networks, containing both closed and open chains, stability conditions depend on the rate functions, and since they can be arbitrary, not much can be said in general. In practice, though, the following sufficient conditions are quite useful. The proof is similar to that of the previous theorem.

---

[16] They are equal.

Theorem 8.9 (Sufficient Stability Condition for Mixed Networks)

Consider a multi-class product form queuing network as defined above. Assume that the network is mixed, with C_c classes in closed chains and C_o classes in open chains. Let $\vec{m} = (m_1, \ldots, m_{C_c})$ be the population vector of classes in closed chains, and $\vec{n} = (n_1, \ldots, n_{C_o})$ the population vector of classes in open chains. For every station s and $\vec{m}$, define

$$L^s(\theta \mid \vec{m}) = \sum_{\vec{n} \in \mathbb{N}^{C_o}} f^s(\vec{m}, \vec{n}) \prod_{c=1}^{C_o} (\theta_c^s)^{n_c^s} \qquad (8.56)$$

where $f^s(\vec{m}, \vec{n})$ is the station function.

If

$$L^s(\theta \mid \vec{m}) < \infty \qquad \forall \vec{m}, \; \forall s$$

the network has a stationary distribution.

In simple cases, a direct examination of (8.52) leads to simple, natural conditions, as in the next theorem. Essentially, it states that for the networks considered there, stability is obtained when server utilizations are less than 1.

Theorem 8.10 (Stability of a Simple Mixed Network)

Consider a mixed multi-class product form queuing network and assume that all stations are either Kelly stations (such as Global PS or Global LCFS), IS or MSCCC with constant rates.

Let $\mathcal{C}$ be the set of classes belonging to open chains. Define the utilization factor ρ^s at station s by

$$\rho^s = \begin{cases} \dfrac{\bar{S}^s}{B^s} \displaystyle\sum_{c \in \mathcal{C}} \theta_c^s & \begin{array}{l} \text{if station } s \text{ is MSCCC with } B^s \text{ servers,} \\ \text{and a mean service time } \bar{S}^s \end{array} \\[2em] \displaystyle\sum_{c \in \mathcal{C}} \theta_c^s \bar{S}_c^s & \begin{array}{l} \text{if station } s \text{ is a Kelly station} \\ \text{with a mean service time } \bar{S}_c^s \text{ for class } c. \end{array} \end{cases}$$

The network has a stationary distribution if and only if $\rho^s < 1$ for every Kelly station or MSCCC station s. There is no condition on IS stations.

Example 8.8 Dual-Core Processor in Figure 8.11

Let $q \in (0, 1]$ be the probability that an external job uses the critical section and let $r > 0$ be the average number of uses of the processor outside the critical section by an external job. Thus, $\theta_1^1 + \theta_3^1 = \nu r$ and $\theta_2^1 = \nu q$. Based on Theorem 8.10, the stability conditions are

$$\nu(r + q)\bar{S}^1 \leq 2$$
$$\nu q \bar{S}^1 \leq 1$$

where $\bar{S}^1$ is the average job processing time at the dual-core processor. Note that we need to assume that the processing time is independent of whether it uses the critical section, and of whether it corresponds to an internal or external job. The system is thus stable (has a stationary regime) for $\nu < \frac{2}{\bar{S}^1(q+\max(r,q))}$. Note that the condition for stability bears only on external jobs.

Let K be the total number of class 4 jobs; it is constant since class 4 constitutes a closed chain. A state of the network is entirely defined by the population vector $(n_1, n_2, n_3, n_4, n_4^2)$; the number of jobs of class 4 in station 3 is $K - n_4 - n_4^2$, and $n_c^s = 0$ for other classes. The set of feasible states is

$$\mathcal{E} = \left\{ (n_1, n_2, n_3, n_4, n_4^2) \in \mathbb{N}^5 \text{ such that } n_4 + n_4^2 \leq K \right\}$$

The joint stationary probability is

$$P(n_1, n_2, n_3, n_4, n_4^2)$$
$$= \frac{1}{\eta(K)} d(n_2 + n_4, n_1 + n_3) \frac{(n_1 + n_3)! \, (n_2 + n_4)!}{n_1! \, n_2! \, n_3! \, n_4!}$$
$$\times \left(\left(\theta_1^1\right)^{n_1} \left(\theta_2^1\right)^{n_2} \left(\theta_3^1\right)^{n_3} \left(\bar{S}^1\right)^{n_1+n_2+n_3+n_4} \left(\bar{S}^2\right)^{n_4^2} \frac{1}{n_4^2!} \left(\bar{S}^3\right)^{K-n_4-n_4^2} \right)$$

where we made explicit the dependency on K in the normalizing constant. This expression, while explicit, is too complicated to be of practical use. In Example 8.9, we continue with this example and compute the throughput, using the methods in the next section.

8.6   Computational Aspects

As illustrated in Example 8.8, the product form theorem, although it provides an explicit form, may require much work since enumerating all states is subject to combinatorial explosion, and the normalizing constant has no explicit form when there are closed chains. A large amount of research has been performed on providing efficient algorithms for computing metrics of interest for multi-class product form queuing networks. They are based on a number of interesting properties, which we now derive. In the rest of this section, we give the fundamental ideas used in practical algorithms; these ideas are not just algorithmic, they are also based on special properties of the networks which are of independent interest.

In the remainder of this section, we assume that the multi-class product form queuing network satisfies the hypotheses of the product form Theorem 8.7 as described in Section 8.4, and has a stationary distribution (i.e. if there are open chains, the stability condition must hold – if the network is closed there is no condition).

8.6.1 Convolution

> **Theorem 8.11 (Convolution Theorem)**
>
> *Consider a multi-class product form queuing network with closed and perhaps some open chains, and let $\vec{K}$ be the **chain population vector** of the closed chains (i.e. $\vec{K}_C$ is the number of customers of chain C; it is constant for a given network).*
>
> *Let $\eta(\vec{K})$ be the normalizing constant given in the product form theorem 8.7. Further, let $\vec{Y}$ be a formal variable with one component per chain, and define*
>
> $$F_\eta(\vec{Y}) \overset{\text{def}}{=} \sum_{\vec{K} \geq \vec{0}} \eta(\vec{K}) \prod_C Y_C^{K_C}$$
>
> *Then*
>
> $$F_\eta(\vec{Y}) = \prod_{s=1}^{S} G^s(\vec{Z}^s) \qquad (8.57)$$
>
> *where G^s is the generating function of the station function for station s, and $\vec{Z}^s$ is a vector with one component per class, such that*
>
> $$Z_c^s = \begin{cases} Y_C \theta_c^s & \text{whenever } c \in C \text{ and } C \text{ is closed} \\ \theta_c^s & \text{whenever } c \text{ is in an open chain} \end{cases}$$

The proof is a direct application of the product form theorem, using generating functions. (8.57) is in fact a **convolution equation**, since convolution translates into a product of generating functions. It is the basis for the **convolution algorithm**, which consists in adding stations one by one, see for example [6] for a general discussion and [56] for networks with MSCCC stations other than FIFO. We illustrate the method in Example 8.9 below.

8.6.2 Throughput

Once the normalizing constants are computed, one may derive throughputs for class c at station s, defined as the mean number of class c arrivals at (or departures from) station s:

> **Theorem 8.12 (Throughput Theorem)**
>
> *(See [20]) The throughput for class-c of the closed chain C at station s is*
>
> $$\lambda_c^s(\vec{K}) = \theta_c^s \frac{\eta(\vec{K} - \vec{1}_c)}{\eta(\vec{K})} \qquad (8.58)$$

It follows in particular that, for closed chains, the throughputs at some station *depend only on the throughput per class and the visit rates*. Formally, for every closed chain C, choose a station $s_0(C)$ effectively visited by this chain (i.e. $\sum_{c \in \mathcal{C}} \theta_c^{s_0} > 0$); define the **per chain throughput** $\mathcal{C}$ as the throughput at this station $\lambda_\mathcal{C}(\vec{K}) \overset{\text{def}}{=} \sum_{c \in \mathcal{C}} \lambda_c^{s_0(\mathcal{C})}(\vec{K})$. Since for closed chains the visit rates θ_c^s are determined up to a constant, we may decide to let $\sum_{c \in \mathcal{C}} \theta_c^{s_0(\mathcal{C})} = 1$, and then for all class $c \in \mathcal{C}$ and station s,

$$\lambda_c^s(\vec{K}) = \lambda_\mathcal{C}(\vec{K})\theta_c^s \tag{8.59}$$

Also, the equivalent of (8.58) for the per chain throughput is

$$\lambda_\mathcal{C}(\vec{K}) = \frac{\eta(\vec{K} - \vec{1}_c)}{\eta(\vec{K})} \tag{8.60}$$

(which follows immediately by summation on $c \in \mathcal{C}$).

Note that the throughput for a class c of an *open* chain is simply the visit rate θ_c^s.

Last but not least, the throughput depends only on the normalizing constants and not on other details of the stations. In particular, stations that are different but have the same station function (such as FIFO with one server and constant-rate Kelly function with class-independent service time), give the same throughputs.

The next example illustrates the use of the above theorems in the study of a general case (a mixed network with an MSCCC station). There are many optimizations of this method, see [22] and references therein.

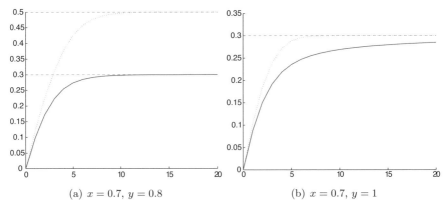

(a) $x = 0.7, y = 0.8$ (b) $x = 0.7, y = 1$

Figure 8.13 The throughput λ of internal jobs for the dual-core processor in Figure 8.11, in jobs per millisecond, as a function of the number of internal jobs. Dotted curve: the throughput that would be achieved if the internal jobs would not use the critical section, i.e. any job could use a processor when one is idle. x is the intensity of external traffic employing the critical section and y of other external traffic. There are two constraints : $x + \lambda \leq 1$ (critical section) and $x + y + \lambda \leq 2$ (total processor utilization). For the dotted line only the second constraint applies. In the first panel, the first constraint is limiting and the difference in performance is noticeable. In the last panel, the second constraint is limiting and there is little difference. In the middle panel, both constraints are equally limiting. $\bar{S}^1 = 1$, $\bar{S}^2 = 5$, $\bar{S}^3 = 1$ ms.

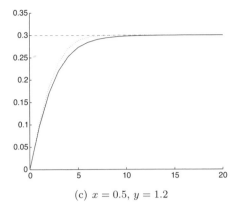

(c) $x = 0.5$, $y = 1.2$

Figure 8.13 (Continuation.)

Example 8.9 Dual-Core Processor in Figure 8.11 Algorithmic Aspect

We continue Example 8.8. Assume now that we let all parameters be fixed except the arrival rate ν of external jobs and the number K of internal jobs; we would like to evaluate the throughput λ of internal jobs as a function of ν and K as well as the distribution of state of internal jobs.

We can use the throughput theorem and we obtain that the throughput $\lambda(K)$ for class 4 is (we drop the dependency on λ from the notation)

$$\lambda(K) = \frac{\eta(K-1)}{\eta(K)} \tag{8.61}$$

We now have to compute the normalizing constant $\eta(K)$ as a function of K. To this end, we use the convolution equation (8.57) to obtain

$$F_\eta(Y) = G^1(\vec{Z}^1) G^2(\vec{Z}^2) G^3(\vec{Z}^3) \tag{8.62}$$

with

$$\vec{Z}^1 = (\theta_1^1, \theta_2^1, \theta_3^1, Y)$$
$$\vec{Z}^2 = (0, 0, 0, Y)$$
$$\vec{Z}^3 = (0, 0, 0, Y)$$

The generating functions G^1, G^2, G^3 are given in Example 8.7. We get

$$F_\eta(Y) = D(Y\bar{S}^1 + x, y) \, e^{\bar{S}^2 Y} \frac{1}{1 - \bar{S}^3 Y} \tag{8.63}$$

with $x = \nu q \bar{S}^1$, $y = \nu r \bar{S}^1$ and $D(\cdot)$ defined in (8.49).

We can compute $\eta(K)$ by performing a power series expansion (recall that $F_\eta(Y) = \sum_{K \in \mathbb{N}} \eta(K) Y^K$) and find $\eta(K)$ numerically. Alternatively, one can interpret (8.63) as a convolution equation $\eta = \eta_1 \star \eta_2 \star \eta_3$

with $F_{\eta_1}(Y) = \sum_{k\in\mathbb{N}} \eta_1(k)Y^k \overset{\text{def}}{=} D(Y\bar{S}^1 + x, y)$, $F_{\eta_2}(Y) = e^{\bar{S}^2 Y}$, $F_{\eta_3}(Y) = \frac{1}{1-\bar{S}^3 Y}$ and use fast convolution algorithms or the `filter` function as in Example 8.11. The throughput for internal jobs follows from (8.61) and is plotted in Figure 8.13.

8.6.3 Equivalent Service Rate

This is a useful concept, which hides away the details of a station and, as we show in the next section, can be used to aggregate network portions. Consider some arbitrary station s, of any category, with station function $f^s(\cdot)$. We call **equivalent service rate** for class c at station s the quantity

$$\mu_c^{*s}(\vec{n}^s) \overset{\text{def}}{=} \frac{f^s(\vec{n}^s - \vec{1}_c)}{f^s(\vec{n}^s)} \tag{8.64}$$

It can be shown that $\mu_c^{*s}(\vec{n}^s)$ is indeed the average rate at which customers of class c depart from station s when the latter is imbedded in a multi-class queuing network and given that the number of customers at station s is $\vec{n}^s$, i.e.

$$\mu_c^{*s}(\vec{n}^s) = \sum_{\vec{e}\in\mathcal{E}(s,\vec{n}^s)} \sum_{\vec{f}\in\mathcal{E}'(s,\vec{e})} P(\vec{e})\mu(\vec{e},\vec{f})$$

Here, $\vec{e}$ is a global micro-state of the network (see Section 8.8.2 for a definition), $\mathcal{E}(s,\vec{n}^s)$ is the set of global micro-states for which the population vector at station s is $\vec{n}^s$, $\mathcal{E}'(s,\vec{e})$ is the set of global micro-states such that the transition $\vec{e} \rightarrow \vec{f}$ is a departure from station s, $P(\cdot)$ is the stationary probability of the network and $\mu(\vec{e},\vec{f})$ is the transition rate. This is true as long as the network satisfies the hypotheses of the product form theorem, and is a direct consequence of the local balance property.

To s we associate a *per class PS* station with a unit service requirement for all classes and with the balance function $f^s(\vec{n}^s)$. This virtual station is called the **equivalent station** of station s. By construction, it is a category-1 station and, according to (8.35), the station functions of this virtual station and of s are identical. Further, the rate of service allocated to customers of class c is also $\mu_c^{*s}(\vec{n}^s)$. Thus, as far as the stationary probability of customers is concerned, it makes no difference whether we use the original station or the equivalent station inside a network. We obtain an even stronger result.

> **Theorem 8.13 (Equivalent Station Theorem)**
> *(See [78]) In a multi-class product form queuing network, any station can be replaced by its equivalent station, with an equivalent service rate as in (8.64), so that the stationary probability and the throughput for any class at any station are unchanged.*

Note that the equivalent station and the equivalent service rate depend only on the station, not on the network in which the station is imbedded. It is remarkable that it thus becomes possible to replace *any* station by a per class

PS station. Note however that the equivalence is only valid for distributions of numbers of customers and for throughputs, not for delay distributions; indeed, delays depend on the details of the station, and stations with the same station function may have differing delay distributions.

The equivalent service rates for a few frequently used stations are given in Table 8.1. For some stations such as the general MSCCC station, there does not appear to be a closed form for the equivalent service rate.

Table 8.1 Equivalent service rates for frequently used stations. Notation: $\vec{n}^s = (n_1^s, \ldots, n_C^s)$ with n^s = number of class c customers at station s; $\bar{S}_c^s$ is the mean service requirement; $r_c^s(n_c^s)$ is the rate allocated to a class-c customer when the service rate is class-dependent; $r^s(|\vec{n}^s|)$ is the rate allocated to any customer when the service rate depends on the queue size; $|\vec{n}^s|$ is the total number of customers in station s. For a constant rate station, take $r_c^s(\cdot) = 1$ or $r^s(\cdot) = 1$.

Station s	Equivalent Service Rate $\mu_c^{*s}(\vec{n}^s)$
Kelly Stations with a Class-Dependent Service Rate. Recall that this contains, as special cases, Global PS and Global LCF-SPR stations with a constant rate.	$r_c^s(n_c^s)\dfrac{r_c^s}{|\vec{n}^s|}\dfrac{1}{\bar{S}_c^s}$
Kelly Stations with a Queue-Size-Dependent Service Rate.	$r^s(|\vec{n}^s|)\dfrac{n_c^s}{|\vec{n}^s|}\dfrac{1}{\bar{S}_c^s}$
IS station with a Class-Dependent Service Rate.	$r_c^s(n_c^s)n_c^s\dfrac{1}{\bar{S}_c^s}$
IS station with a Queue-Size-Dependent Service Rate.	$r^s(|\vec{n}^s|)n_c^s\dfrac{1}{\bar{S}_c^s}$
FIFO station with B servers and a Queue-Size-Dependent Service Rate. Recall that this is a station of Category 2, hence the service requirement is exponentially distributed and has the same mean $\bar{S}^s$ for all classes.	$\dfrac{1}{\bar{S}^s}\min\left(B, |\vec{n}^s|\right)r(|\vec{n}^s|)$

The equivalent service rate is used in the following theorem.

Theorem 8.14

*(See [85]) Consider a multi-class product form queuing network with closed and perhaps some open chains, and let $\vec{K}$ be the **chain population vector** of the closed chains. For any class c of the closed chain $\mathcal{C}$ and any station s, if $n_c^s \geq 1$,*

$$P^s\left(\vec{n}^s \mid \vec{K}\right) = P^s\left(\vec{n}^s - \vec{1}_c \mid \vec{K} - \vec{1}_c\right)\frac{1}{\mu_c^{*s}(\vec{n}^s)}\lambda_c^s(\vec{K}) \qquad (8.65)$$

where $P^s(\cdot \mid \vec{K})$ is the marginal probability at station s and $\lambda_c^s(\vec{K})$ is the throughput for class c at station s.

This theorem is useful if the equivalent service rate is tractable or numerically known. It can be used if one is interested in the marginal distribution of one station; it requires computing the throughputs $\lambda(\vec{K})$, for example by means of convolution or MVA. Equation (8.65) can be employed to compute $P^s(\vec{n}^s \mid \vec{K})$ iteratively by increasing the populations of closed chains [84]. Note that it does not give the probability of an empty station; the latter can be computed based on the fact that the sum of probabilities is 1.

Example 8.10 Dual-Core Processor in Figure 8.11, continued

We now compute the stationary probability that there are n jobs in station 2, given that there are K internal jobs in total. According to (8.65),

$$P^2(n \mid K) = P^2(n-1 \mid K-1)\lambda(K)\frac{\bar{S}^2}{n} \qquad (8.66)$$

since the equivalent service rate for station 2 (which is an IS station) is $\frac{n}{\bar{S}^2}$ when there are n customers in the station. This gives $P^2(n \mid K)$ for $1 \le 1 \le K$ if we know $P^2(\cdot \mid K-1)$; $P(0 \mid K)$ is obtained by the normalizing condition

$$\sum_{n=0}^{K} P^2(n \mid K) = 1$$

We compute $P^2(\cdot \mid K)$ by iteration on K, starting from $P^2(0 \mid 0) = 1$ and using the previous two equations. The mean number of jobs in station 2 follows as

$$\bar{N}^2(K) = \sum_{n=0}^{K} nP(n \mid K) \qquad (8.67)$$

Similarly, for station 3, we have

$$P^3(n \mid K) = P^3(n-1 \mid K-1)\lambda(K)\bar{S}^3 \qquad (8.68)$$

since the equivalent service rate for station 3 (which is a PS station) is $\frac{1}{\bar{S}^3}$. The mean number of internal jobs in station 1 is thus $\bar{N}_4^1(K) = K - \bar{N}^2(K) - \bar{N}^3(K)$.

We derive the mean response times for internal jobs in stations 1 to 3 by using Little's law: $\bar{R}_4^s(K) = \frac{\bar{N}^s(K)}{\lambda(K)}$ for $s = 1, 2, 3$.

From Little's law, $(R_4^1 + R_4^2 + R_4^3)\lambda = K$; for large K, $\lambda \approx \theta_{\max} = \min(1-x, 2-x-y)$ and $R_4^2 \approx \bar{S}^2$, $R_4^3 \approx \bar{S}^3$ (most of the queuing is at station 1), thus $\bar{R}_4^1(K) \approx \frac{K}{\theta_{\max}} - \bar{S}^2 - \bar{S}^3$ for large K. The results are shown in Figure 8.14.

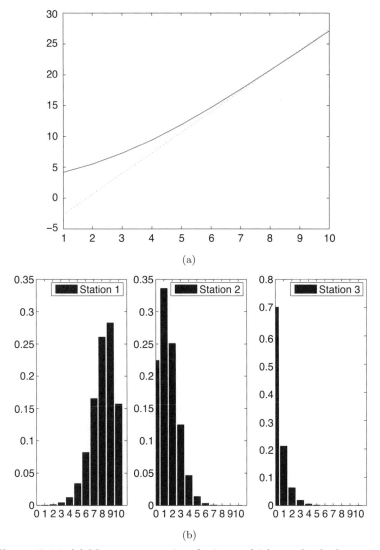

Figure 8.14 (a) Mean response time for internal jobs at the dual-core processor, in millisecond, as a function of the number K of internal jobs. (b) Stationary probability distribution of the number of internal jobs at stations 1 to 3, for $K = 10$. (Details of the computations are given in Examples 8.10 and 8.11; $\bar{S}^1 = 1$, $\bar{S}^2 = 5$, $\bar{S}^3 = 1$ ms, $x = 0.7$, $y = 0.8$.)

8.6.4 Suppression of Open Chains

In an open network, the product form theorem implies that all stations are independent in the stationary regime, and the network is thus equivalent to a collection of stations in isolation. In the mixed or closed case, this does not hold anymore, and station states are mutually dependent.

It is possible to simplify mixed networks by removing open chains. In the modified network, there are only closed chain customers, with the same routing matrix $q_{c,c'}^{s,s'}$ for all c, c' in closed-chains; the stations are the same, but with a modified station function. Let $G^s(\vec{Z})$ be the z transform of the station function and θ_c^s the visit rates in the original network with open chains. In the modified network, the z transform of the station function is

$$G'^s(\vec{Z}) = G^s(\vec{Z'}) \quad \text{with} \quad \begin{cases} Z_c' = Z_c & \text{if } c \text{ is in a closed chain} \\ Z_c' = \theta_c^s & \text{if } c \text{ is in an open chain} \end{cases} \tag{8.69}$$

In the above, $\vec{Z}$ is a vector with one component per class in a closed chain, whereas $\vec{Z'}$ has one component per class, in any open or closed chain.

Theorem 8.15 (Suppression of Open Chains)
Consider a mixed multi-class network that satisfies the hypotheses of the product form Theorem 8.7. Consider the network obtained by removing the open chains as described above. In the modified network, the stationary probability and the throughputs for classes of closed chains are the same as in the original network.

The proof is obtained by inspection of the generating functions. Note that the modified stations may not be of the same type as the original ones; they are fictitious stations as in the equivalent station theorem. Also, the equivalent service rates of the modified stations depend on the visit rates of the open chains that were removed, as illustrated in the next example.

Example 8.11 Dual-Core Processor in Figure 8.11, continued
We now compute the stationary probability at station 1. We suppress the open chains and compute the equivalent service rate at station 1. We have here a single-chain, single-class network, with only customers of class 4. Stations 2 and 3 are unchanged; station 1 is replaced by the station with generating function:

$$G'^1(Z) = G^1(\theta_1^1, \theta_2^1, \theta_3^1, Z)$$

where G^1 is given in (8.50). With the same notation as in Example 8.9, $G'^1(z) = D(Z\bar{S}^1 + x, y)$ with D given by (8.49), and thus

$$G'^1(Z) = \frac{1}{1 - x - Z\bar{S}^1} \left(1 + y + \frac{y^2}{2 - x - y - Z\bar{S}^1} \right) \tag{8.70}$$

The station function $f'^1(n)$ of the modified station 1 is obtained by power series expansion $G'^1(Z) = \sum_{n \geq 0} f'^1(n)Z^n$. modified as follows. Since G'^1 is a rational function (quotient of two polynomials), its power series expansion can be obtained as the impulse response of a filter with rational z transform (Section D.1.8). Consider the filter

$$\frac{1}{1 - x - B\bar{S}^1} \left(1 + y + \frac{y^2}{2 - x - y - B\bar{S}^1} \right) \tag{8.71}$$

where B is the backshift operator. The sequence $\left(f'^1(0), f'^1(1), f'^1(2), \ldots \right)$ is the impulse response of this filter, and can be obtained easily with the `filter` function of Matlab. The equivalent service rate of station 1 for internal jobs is

$$\mu'^1(n) = \frac{f'^1(n-1)}{f'^1(n)} \tag{8.72}$$

Since we know the equivalent service rate, we can determine the probability distribution $P'^1(n)$ of internal jobs at station 1 using Theorem 8.14 as in Example 8.10. The results are shown in Figure 8.14.

8.6.5   Arrival Theorem and MVA Version 1

Mean Value Analysis (MVA) is a method, developed in [86], that does not compute the normalizing constant and thus avoids potential overflow problems. There are many variants of it, see the discussion in [6].

In this chapter, we give two versions. The first, described in this section, is very simple, but applies only to some station types, as it requires the ability to derive the response time from the Palm distribution of the queue size upon customer arrival. The second, described in Section 8.6.7, is more general and applies to all stations for which the equivalent service rate can be easily computed.

MVA version 1 is based on the following theorem, which is a consequence of the product form theorem and the embedded subchain theorem of Palm calculus (Theorem 7.12).

Theorem 8.16 (Arrival Theorem)
Consider a multi-class product form queuing network. The probability distribution of the number of customers seen by a customer just before arriving at station s is the stationary distribution of

- *the same network if the customer belongs to an open chain;*
- *the network, with one customer less in its chain, if the customer belongs to a closed chain.*

Consider now a *closed* network where all stations are FIFO or IS with a constant rate, or are equivalent in the sense that they have the same station function as one of these (thus have the same equivalent service rate). Indeed, recall that stationary probabilities and throughput depend only on the station function. For example, a station may also be a global PS station with class-independent service requirements of any phase type distribution, with the same station function as a FIFO station with one server and exponential service time. In the rest of this section, we call "FIFO" (resp. IS) station one that has the same station function as a single server, constant rate FIFO (resp. IS) station. Recall that at a FIFO station, we need to assume that the mean service requirements are equivalent for all classes at the same station, whereas for the IS station, it may be class-dependent.

We first assume that the FIFO (resp. IS) stations are truly FIFO (resp. IS), and not merely equivalent stations as defined above. We will remove this restriction later. Let $\bar{N}_c^s(\vec{K})$ be the mean number of class-c customers at station s when the chain population vector is $\vec{K}$. The mean response time for a class-c customer at a FIFO station s when the population vector is $\vec{K}$ is

$$\bar{R}_c^s(\vec{K}) = \left[1 + \sum_c \bar{N}_c^s(\vec{K} - \vec{1}_c)\right] \bar{S}^s$$

where $\mathcal{C}$ is the chain of class c. This is due to the exponential service requirement assumption: an arriving customer has to wait for $\bar{S}^s$ multiplied by the number of customers present upon arrival; in average, this latter number is $\sum_c \bar{N}_c^s(\vec{K} - \vec{1}_c)$ according to the arrival theorem. Based on Little's formula,

$$\bar{R}_c^s(\vec{K})\lambda_c^s(\vec{K}) = \bar{N}_c^s(\vec{K})$$

Combining the two gives

$$\bar{N}_c^s(\vec{K}) = \lambda_c^s(\vec{K})\left(1 + \sum_c \bar{N}_c^s(\vec{K} - \vec{1}_c)\right) \bar{S}^s \qquad (8.73)$$

which is valid for FIFO stations. For a delay station, one finds

$$\bar{N}_c^s(\vec{K}) = \lambda_c^s(\vec{K})\bar{S}_c^s \qquad (8.74)$$

This gives a recursion for $\bar{N}_c^s(\vec{K})$ if one can determine $\lambda_c^s(\vec{K})$. The next observation is (8.59), which states that if we know the throughput at one station visited by a chain, then we know the throughputs for all stations and all classes of the same chain. The last observation involves the sum of the numbers of customers across all stations and all classes of chain $\mathcal{C}$ being equal to $K_{\mathcal{C}}$. Combining all this gives, for every chain $\mathcal{C}$, if $K_{\mathcal{C}} > 0$,

$$\frac{K_{\mathcal{C}}}{\lambda_{\mathcal{C}}(\vec{K})} = \sum_{c \in \mathcal{C}} \left[\sum_{s:\text{FIFO}} \theta_c^s \left(1 + \sum_{c'} \bar{N}_{c'}^s(\vec{K} - \vec{1}_c)\right) \bar{S}^s + \sum_{s:\text{IS}} \theta_c^s \bar{S}_c^s \right] \qquad (8.75)$$

and

$$\lambda_{\mathcal{C}}(\vec{K}) = 0 \quad \text{if } K_{\mathcal{C}} = 0 \qquad (8.76)$$

For every FIFO station s and class c,

$$\bar{N}_c^s(\vec{K}) = \theta_c^s \lambda_{\mathcal{C}(c)}(\vec{K}) \left(1 + \sum_{c'} \bar{N}_{c'}^s(\vec{K} - \vec{1}_{\mathcal{C}(c)})\right) \bar{S}^s \quad \text{if } K_{\mathcal{C}(c)} > 0 \quad (8.77)$$

$$= 0 \qquad\qquad\qquad\qquad\qquad\qquad \text{if } K_{\mathcal{C}(c)} = 0 \quad (8.78)$$

Second, we observe that the resulting equations depend only on the station function, for which reason they also apply to equivalent stations.

The **MVA algorithm version 1** iterates on the total population, adding customers one by one. At every step, the throughput is computed using (8.75). Then, the mean queue sizes at FIFO queues are computed using (8.77), which closes the loop. We give the algorithm in the case of a single chain. For the multi-chain case, the algorithm is similar, but there are many optimizations to reduce the storage requirement, see [6].

Algorithm 8.1 MVA Version 1: Mean Value Analysis for a single-chain closed multi-class product form queuing network containing only constant-rate FIFO and IS stations, or stations with equal station functions.

1: K = population size
2: $\lambda = 0$ ▷ throughput
3: $Q^s = 0$ for all station $s \in$ FIFO ▷ total number of customers at station s,
4:   ▷ $Q^s = \sum_c \bar{N}_c^s$
5: Compute the visit rates θ_c^s using (8.24) and $\sum_{c=1}^{C} \theta_c^1 = 1$
6: $\theta^s = \sum_c \theta_c^s$ for every $s \in$ FIFO
7: $h = \sum_{s \in \text{IS}} \sum_c \theta_c^s \bar{S}_c^s + \sum_{s \in \text{FIFO}} \theta^s \bar{S}^s$ ▷ constant term in (8.75)
8: **for** $k = 1 : K$ **do**
9:      $\lambda = \dfrac{k}{h + \sum_{s \in \text{FIFO}} \theta^s Q^s \bar{S}^s}$ ▷ Eq. (8.75)
10:     $Q^s = \lambda \theta^s \bar{S}^s (1 + Q^s)$ for all $s \in$ FIFO
11: **end for**
12: The throughput at station 1 is λ
13: The throughput of class c at station s is $\lambda \theta_c^s$
14: The mean number of customers of class c at FIFO station s is $Q^s \theta_c^s / \theta^s$
15: The mean number of customers of class c at IS station s is $\lambda \theta_c^s \bar{S}_c^s$

Example 8.12 Mean Value Analysis of Figure 8.5
We model the system as a single-class, closed network. The CPU is modeled as a PS station, disks A and B as FIFO single servers, and think time as an IS station. We fix the visit rate $\theta^{\text{think time}}$ to 1 so that $\theta^{\text{CPU}} = V_{\text{CPU}}$, $\theta^{\text{A}} = V_{\text{A}}$ and $\theta^{\text{B}} = V_{\text{B}}$. Note that the routing probabilities need not be specified in detail; only the visit rates are required.

The CPU station is not a FIFO station, but it has the same station function. Consequently, we may apply MVA and treat it as if it were FIFO.

Figure 8.15 shows the results, which are essentially as predicted by the bottleneck analysis in Figure 8.6.

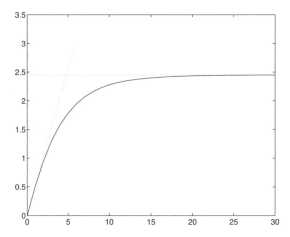

Figure 8.15 The throughput in transactions per second versus the number of users, computed with MVA for the network in Figure 8.5. The dotted lines represent the bounds of the bottleneck analysis in Figure 8.6.

8.6.6 Network Decomposition

A key consequence of the product form theorem is the possibility of replacing an entire subnetwork by an equivalent single station. This can be done recursively and is the basis for numerous algorithms, such as MVA version 2.

Consider a multi-class product form network $\mathcal{N}$ and a subnetwork $\mathcal{S}$. The stations in $\mathcal{S}$ need not be directly connected and the network can be closed, mixed or open. If the network is mixed or open, we consider that outside arrivals occur from some fictitious station 0, and $0 \notin \mathcal{S}$. We create two virtual networks: $\tilde{\mathcal{N}}$ and $\tilde{\mathcal{N}}_{\mathcal{S}}$ and a virtual station $\tilde{\mathcal{S}}$ as follows (Figure 8.16).

The virtual station $\tilde{\mathcal{S}}$, called the **equivalent station** of $\mathcal{S}$, is obtained by isolating the set of stations $\mathcal{S}$ from the network $\mathcal{N}$ and collapsing classes to chains. Inside $\tilde{\mathcal{S}}$, there is only one class per chain, i.e. a customer's attribute is its chain $\mathcal{C}$. Furthermore, the station is a "per class PS" station, with a service rate to be defined later.[17]

$\tilde{\mathcal{N}}$, called the **simplified network**, is obtained by replacing all stations in $\mathcal{S}$ by the equivalent station $\tilde{\mathcal{S}}$. In $\tilde{\mathcal{N}}$, routing is defined by the corresponding

---

[17]Observe that within one service station, customers cannot change class. Therefore, if we aggregate a subnetwork into a single station, we also need to aggregate classes of the same chain.

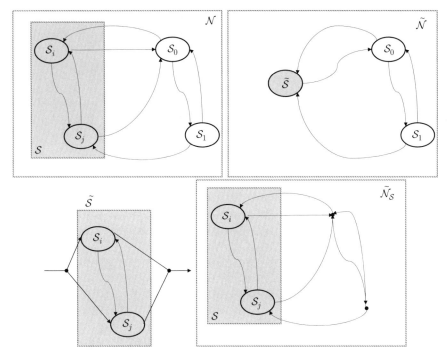

Figure 8.16 Decomposition procedure: original network $\mathcal{N}$, with subnetwork $\mathcal{S}$; simplified network $\tilde{\mathcal{N}}$; equivalent station $\tilde{\mathcal{S}}$; subnetwork in short-circuit $\tilde{\mathcal{N}}_\mathcal{S}$.

natural aggregation, i.e. it is the same as if the stations in $\mathcal{S}$ were still present but not individually observable. Thus, the routing matrix $\tilde{q}$ is

$$\tilde{q}_{c,c'}^{s,s'} = q_{c,c'}^{s,s'} \quad \text{if } s \notin \mathcal{S} \text{ and } s' \notin \mathcal{S}$$

$$\tilde{q}_{\mathcal{C},c'}^{\mathcal{S},s'} = \begin{cases} 0 & \text{if } c' \notin \mathcal{C} \\ \dfrac{1}{\tilde{\theta}_\mathcal{C}} \displaystyle\sum_{s\in\mathcal{S},c\in\mathcal{C}} \theta_c^s q_{c,c'}^{s,s'} & \text{if } c \in \mathcal{C} \end{cases}$$

$$\tilde{q}_{c,\mathcal{C}}^{s,\mathcal{S}} = \begin{cases} 0 & \text{if } c \notin \mathcal{C} \\ \displaystyle\sum_{s'\in\mathcal{S},\,c'\in\mathcal{C}} q_{c,c'}^{s,s'} & \text{if } c \in \mathcal{C} \end{cases}$$

$$\tilde{q}_{\mathcal{C},\mathcal{C}'}^{\mathcal{S},\mathcal{S}} = \begin{cases} 0 & \text{if } \mathcal{C} \neq \mathcal{C}' \\ \dfrac{1}{\tilde{\theta}_\mathcal{C}} \displaystyle\sum_{s,s'\in\mathcal{S},\,c,c'\in\mathcal{C}} \theta_c^s q_{c,c'}^{s,s'} & \text{if } \mathcal{C} = \mathcal{C}' \end{cases}$$

$$\tilde{\theta}_\mathcal{C} = \sum_{s\in\mathcal{S},\,c\in\mathcal{C}} \theta_c^s$$

where, for example, $\tilde{q}_{\mathcal{C},c'}^{\mathcal{S},s'}$ is the probability that a chain-$\mathcal{C}$ customer leaving station $\tilde{\mathcal{S}}$ joins station s' with class c'. If there are some open chains, recall that $s = 0$ represents arrivals and departures and that we assumed that $0 \notin \mathcal{S}$; in such cases, the external arrival rate of chain-$\mathcal{C}$ customers to the virtual station $\tilde{\mathcal{S}}$ is

$$\lambda_{\mathcal{C}}^{\mathcal{S}} = \sum_{s \in \mathcal{S}, c \in \mathcal{C}} \lambda_c^s$$

and the probability that a chain-$\mathcal{C}$ customer leaves the network after visiting $\tilde{\mathcal{S}}$ is

$$\frac{1}{\tilde{\theta}_{\mathcal{C}}} \sum_{s \in \mathcal{S}, c \in \mathcal{C}} \theta_c^s q_c^{s,0}$$

where $q_c^{s,0} \overset{\text{def}}{=} 1 - \sum_{s',c'} q_{c,c'}^{s,s'}$ is the probability that a class-c customer leaves the network after visiting station s.

The visit rates in $\tilde{\mathcal{N}}$ are the same as in $\mathcal{N}$ for stations not in $\mathcal{S}$; for the equivalent station $\tilde{\mathcal{S}}$, the visit rate for chain $\mathcal{C}$ is $\tilde{\theta}_{\mathcal{C}}$ given above. The station function of the equivalent station $\tilde{\mathcal{S}}$ is computed in such a way that replacing all stations in $\mathcal{S}$ by $\tilde{\mathcal{S}}$ makes no difference to the stationary probability of the network. It follows, after some algebra, from the product form theorem (the precise formulation is somewhat heavy), that

$$f^{\mathcal{S}}(\vec{k}) = \sum_{\substack{(\vec{n}^s)_{s \in \mathcal{S}} \text{ such that} \\ \sum_{s \in \mathcal{S}, c \in \mathcal{C}} n_c^s = k_c}} \prod_{s \in \mathcal{S}} \left[f^s(\vec{n}^s) \prod_c \left(\frac{\theta_c^s}{\theta_c^{\mathcal{S}}} \right)^{n_c^s} \right] \qquad (8.79)$$

where $\vec{k}$ is a population vector of closed or open chains. Note that some chain $\mathcal{C}_0$ may be "trapped" in $\mathcal{S}$, i.e. customers of this chain never leave $\mathcal{S}$. The generating function of the virtual station $\mathcal{S}$ has a simple expression

$$G^{\mathcal{S}}(\vec{Z}) = \prod_{s \in \mathcal{S}} G^s(\vec{X}^s) \qquad \text{with } X_c^s = Z_{\mathcal{C}(c)} \frac{\theta_c^s}{\tilde{\theta}_{\mathcal{C}}} \qquad (8.80)$$

where $\mathcal{C}(c)$ is the chain of class c. Here, $\mathcal{C}$ spans the set of all chains, closed or open. Thus, the equivalent station $\tilde{\mathcal{S}}$ is a per-class PS station, with one class per chain, and with the balance function $f^{\mathcal{S}}(\vec{k})$. In the next theorem, we provide an equivalent statement that is easier to use in practice.

The second virtual network $\tilde{\mathcal{N}}_{\mathcal{S}}$ is called the **subnetwork in short-circuit**. It consists in replacing anything that is not in $\mathcal{S}$ by a short-circuit. In $\tilde{\mathcal{N}}_{\mathcal{S}}$, the service times at stations not in $\mathcal{S}$ are 0 and customers instantly traverse the complement of $\mathcal{S}$. This includes the virtual station 0 which represents the outside, and $\tilde{\mathcal{N}}_{\mathcal{S}}$ is thus a closed network.[18] The population vector $\vec{k}$ remains constant in $\tilde{\mathcal{N}}_{\mathcal{S}}$; the visit rates at stations in $\mathcal{S}$ are the same as in the original network for closed chains. For classes that belong to a chain that is open in the original network, we obtain the visit rates by setting the arrival rates to 1.

---

[18] Make sure that this is different from the procedure used when defining the station in isolation. In $\tilde{\mathcal{N}}_{\mathcal{S}}$, $\mathcal{S}$ is connected to a short-circuit, i.e. a station where the service requirement is 0. In contrast, in the configuration called "$\mathcal{S}$ in isolation", $\mathcal{S}$ is connected to a station with unit rate and unit service requirement.

Theorem 8.17 (Decomposition Theorem)

(See [78]) Consider a multi-class network satisfying the hypotheses of the product form theorem 8.7. Any subnetwork S can be replaced by its equivalent station $\tilde{S}$, with one class per chain and station function defined by (8.80). In the resulting equivalent network $\tilde{N}$, the stationary probability and the throughputs that are observable are the same as in the original network.

Furthermore, if C effectively visits S, the equivalent service rate to chain C (closed or open) at the equivalent station $\tilde{S}$ is

$$\mu_C^{*S}(\vec{k}) = \lambda_C^{*S}(\vec{k}) \tag{8.81}$$

where $\lambda_C^{*S}(\vec{k})$ is the throughput of chain C for the subnetwork in short-circuit $\tilde{N}_S$ when the population vector for all chains (closed or open) is $\vec{k}$.

The phrase "that are observable" means: the number of customers of any class at any station not in S; the total number of customers of chain C that are present in any station of S; the throughputs of all classes at all stations not in S; the throughputs of all chains. Recall that the per chain throughput $\lambda_C(\vec{K})$ (defined in (8.59)) is the throughput measured at some station s_C effectively visited by chain C. The station s_C is assumed to be the same in the original and the virtual networks, which is possible since the visit rates are equivalent.

If C does not effectively visit S (i.e. if $\tilde{\theta}_C \overset{\text{def}}{=} \sum_{s \in S, c \in C} \theta_c^s = 0$), then the equivalent service rate μ_C^{*S} is undefined. This is not a problem since we do not need it.

By the throughput theorem, (8.81) can also be written $\mu_C^{*S}(\vec{k}) = \frac{\eta^*(\vec{k}-\vec{1}_C)}{\eta^*(\vec{k})}$, where $\eta^*(\vec{k})$ is the normalizing constant for the subnetwork in short-circuit $\tilde{N}_S$.

If S consists of a single station with one class per chain at this station, then the equivalent station is, as expected, the same as the original station. Also, the theorem implies, as a byproduct, that the equivalent service rate for class c at a station s, as defined in (8.64), is equal to the throughput for class c at the network made of this station and a short circuit for every class (i.e. every class-c customer immediately returns to the station upon service completion, with the same class).

Example 8.13 Dual-Core Processor in Figure 8.11, continued

We replace stations 2 and 3 by one aggregated station $\tilde{S}$ as in Figure 8.17. This station receives only customers of class 4 (internal jobs). Its equivalent service rate is

$$\mu^*(n_4) = \frac{\eta^*(n_4 - 1)}{\eta^*(n_4)} \tag{8.82}$$

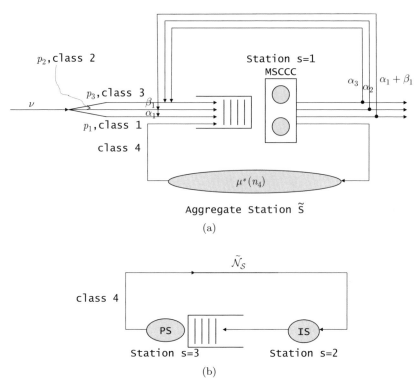

Figure 8.17 Aggregation of stations applied to the dual-core processor example of Figure 8.11. (a) Stations 2 and 3 are replaced by $\tilde{S}$. (b) The network in short-circuit $\tilde{\mathcal{N}}_S$ used to compute the equivalent service rate $\mu^*(n_4)$ of $\tilde{S}$.

where $\eta^*(n_4)$ is the normalizing constant for the network $\tilde{\mathcal{N}}_S$, obtained when replacing station 1 by a short-circuit as in Figure 8.17. The z transform of η^* is given by the convolution theorem 8.11:

$$F_{\eta^*}(Y) = e^{\bar{S}^2 Y} \frac{1}{1 - \bar{S}^3 Y} \qquad (8.83)$$

One can compute a Taylor expansion and deduce $\eta^*(n)$ or use `filter` as in the other examples, but here one can also find a closed form

$$\eta^*(n) = \left(\bar{S}^3\right)^n \sum_{k=0}^{n} \left(\frac{\bar{S}^2}{\bar{S}^3}\right)^k \frac{1}{k!} \qquad (8.84)$$

Note that for large n, $\eta^*(n) \approx \left(\bar{S}^3\right)^n \exp\left(\frac{\bar{S}^2}{\bar{S}^3}\right)$ and thus $\mu^*(n) \approx \frac{1}{\bar{S}^3}$, i.e. it is equivalent to station 3 (but this is true only for large n). We can deduce the equivalent service rate $\mu^*(n)$ and obtain the probability distribution $P^*(n)$ of internal jobs at stations 2 or 3 using Theorem 8.14 as in Example 8.10.

Note that internal jobs are either at station 1, or at stations 2 or 3. We should thus have

$$P^*(n \mid K) = P'^1(K - n \mid K) \qquad (8.85)$$

where $P'^1(\cdot \mid K)$ is the probability distribution for internal jobs at station 1, already obtained in Example 8.11. This can be verified numerically.

8.6.7   MVA Version 2

This is an algorithm which, like MVA version 1, avoids computing the normalizing constant, but which applies to fairly general station types [84]. We give a version for single chain (but multi-class) networks. For networks with several chains, the complexity of this method is exponential in the number of chains, and more elaborate optimizations have been proposed; see [27] and [28] as well as [6] and the discussion therein.

The starting point is the decomposition theorem, which states that one can replace a subnetwork by a single station if one manages to compute its throughputs in short circuit. For example, using MVA version 1, one can compute the throughputs of a subnetwork made of single-server FIFO or IS stations (or equivalent). Therefore, one can replace the set of all such stations in a network by a single station.

MVA version 2 does the same thing for general stations in closed networks. This can be reduced to the simpler problem of how to compute the throughput of a network of 2 stations, with numerically known service rates. If we can solve this problem, we can replace the 2 stations by a new one. The service rate is then equal to the throughput (according to Theorem 8.17), and we can iterate. This problem is solved by the next theorem. It uses the concept of networks in short-circuit.

Theorem 8.18 (Complement Network Theorem)
Consider a closed multi-class product form queuing network $\mathcal{N}$. Let $\mathcal{S}^1, \mathcal{S}^2$ be partitions of $\mathcal{N}$ in two subnetworks and let $\mathcal{N}_{\mathcal{S}^1}, \mathcal{N}_{\mathcal{S}^2}$ be the corresponding subnetworks in short circuit (in $\mathcal{N}_{\mathcal{S}^1}$, all stations in $\mathcal{S}^2$ are short-circuited). Define

- *$P^1(\vec{k} \mid \vec{K})$ as the stationary probability that the number of customers of chain $\mathcal{C}$ present in $\mathcal{S}^1$ is $k_{\mathcal{C}}$ for all $\mathcal{C}$ when the total network population vector is $\vec{K}$; $\vec{k}$ is the vector with generic component k ;*
- *$\eta^1(\vec{K})$ (resp. $\eta^2(\vec{K})$, $\eta(\vec{K})$) as the normalizing constant of $\mathcal{N}_{\mathcal{S}^1}$ (resp. $\mathcal{N}_{\mathcal{S}^2}$, $\mathcal{N}$) when the total network population vector is $\vec{K}$;*
- *$\lambda_{\mathcal{C}}^{*1}(\vec{K})$ (resp. $\lambda_{\mathcal{C}}^{*2}(\vec{K})$, $\lambda_{\mathcal{C}}(\vec{K})$) as the per-chain throughput of chain $\mathcal{C}$ in $\mathcal{N}_{\mathcal{S}^1}$ (resp. $\mathcal{N}_{\mathcal{S}^2}$, $\mathcal{N}$) when the total network population vector is $\vec{K}$.*

Then, for $\vec{0} \leq \vec{k} \leq \vec{K}$,

$$P^1(\vec{k} \mid \vec{K}) = \frac{\eta^1(\vec{k})\eta^2(\vec{K} - \vec{k})}{\eta(\vec{K})} \tag{8.86}$$

and for any chain C such that $k_C > 0$,

$$P^1(\vec{k} \mid \vec{K}) = P^1(\vec{k} - \vec{1}_C \mid (\vec{K} - \vec{1}_C)) \frac{\lambda_C(\vec{K})}{\lambda_C^{*1}(\vec{k})} \qquad (8.87)$$

$$P^1(\vec{k} \mid \vec{K}) = P^1(\vec{k} \mid (\vec{K} - \vec{1}_C)) \frac{\lambda_C(\vec{K})}{\lambda_C^{*2}(\vec{K} - \vec{k})} \qquad (8.88)$$

The inequalities $\vec{0} \leq \vec{k} \leq \vec{K}$ are componentwise. The proof is by direct inspection: recognize in (8.86) the convolution theorem; (8.87) and (8.88) follow from (8.86) and the throughput theorem.

Note that (8.87) is an instance of the equivalent service rate formula (8.65), since $\lambda_C^{*1}(\vec{k}) = \mu_C^{*1}(\vec{k})$ is also equal to the equivalent service rate of $\mathcal{S}^1$. Equation (8.88) is the symmetric of (8.87) when we exchange the roles of $\mathcal{S}^1$ and $\mathcal{S}^2$ since $P^1(\vec{k} \mid \vec{K}) = P^2(\vec{K} - \vec{k} \mid \vec{K})$.

$\mathcal{S}^2$ is called the complement network of $\mathcal{S}^1$ in the original work [84], hence the name.

The MVA Composition Step

In the rest of this section, we consider there to be only one chain, and we drop the index C. Assume that we know the throughputs of the two subnetworks $\lambda^{*1}(K), \lambda^{*2}(K)$; the goal of the composition step is to compute $\lambda(K)$. We compute the distribution $P^1(\cdot \mid K)$ by iteration on K, starting with $P^1(0 \mid 0) = 1$, $P^1(n \mid 0) = 0$, $n \geq 1$. Equations (8.87) and (8.88) become

for $k = 1, \ldots, K$: $P^1(k \mid K) = P^1(k - 1 \mid (K - 1)) \dfrac{\lambda(K)}{\lambda^{*1}(k)}$ (8.89)

for $k = 0, \ldots, K - 1$: $P^1(k \mid K) = P^1(k \mid (K - 1)) \dfrac{\lambda(K)}{\lambda^{*2}(K - k)}$ (8.90)

Neither of the two equations alone is sufficient to advance one iteration step, but the combination of the two is. For example, use the former for $k = 1, \ldots, K$ and the latter for $k = 0$. $\lambda(K)$ is then obtained by the condition $\sum_{n=0}^{K} P^1(k \mid K) = 1$.

MVA Version 2

The algorithm works in two phases. In phase 1, the throughput is computed. The starting point is a network $\mathcal{N}_0$; first, we compute the throughput of the subnetwork $\mathcal{S}^0$ made of all stations to which MVA version 1 applies, as this is faster than MVA version 2. We replace $\mathcal{S}^0$ by its equivalent station; let $\mathcal{N}_1$ be the resulting network.

In one step, we match stations 2 by 2, possibly leaving one station alone. For every pair of matched stations, we apply the MVA Composition Step to the network made of both stations in short circuit (all stations except the two of the pair are short-circuited); we thus obtain the throughput of the pair in short-circuit. We then replace the pair by a single station, whose service rate is the throughput just computed. This is repeated until there is only one aggregate station left, at which time the phase 1 terminates and we have computed the throughput $\lambda(K)$ of the original network.

In phase 2, the distributions of states at all stations of interest can be determined using the equivalent service rate theorem ((8.65)) and normalization to obtain the probability of an empty station; there is no need to use the complement network in this phase.

The number of steps in Phase 1 is on the order of $\log_2(N)$, where N is the number of stations; the MVA Composition Step is applied, in total, on the order of N times (and not 2^N as wrongly assumed in [6]). The complexity of one MVA Composition Step is linear in K, the population size.

In Algorithm 8.2 in Section 8.9.4, we give a concrete implementation.

8.7   What This Tells Us

8.7.1   Insensitivity

Multi-class product form queuing networks are *insensitive* to a number of properties:

- The distribution of service times is irrelevant for all insensitive stations; the stationary distributions of numbers of customers and the throughput depend only on traffic intensities (by means of the visit rates θ_c^s) and on the station functions, which express how rates are shared between classes. The service distribution depends on the class, and classes may be used to introduce correlations in service times. The details of such correlations need not be explicitly modeled, since only traffic intensities matter.
  According to Little's law, the mean response times are also insensitive (but not the distribution of the response time, see Section 8.3.3).

- The nature of the service station plays a role only through its station function. Very different queuing disciplines such as FIFO or global PS, or global LCFSPR with class-independent service times have the same station function. Hence, the same stationary distributions of the number of customers, throughputs and mean response times are also irrelevant.

- The details of routings are also irrelevant, only the visit rates matter. For example, in Figure 8.11, it makes no difference if we assume that external jobs visit station 1 only once, without feedback.

Example 8.14 Internet Model

(See [13]) Internet users, as seen by an internet provider, are modeled by Bonald and Proutière in [13] as follows (they use a slightly different terminology since they do not interpret a Whittle network as a product form station as we do).

User sessions arrive as Poisson processes. A session alternates between active and think time. When active, a session becomes a flow and acquires a class, which corresponds to the network path followed by the session (there is one class per possible path). A flow of class c has a service requirement drawn from any distribution with finite mean $\bar{S}_c$. The network shares its resources between paths according to some "bandwidth" allocation strategy. Let $\mu_c(\vec{n})$ be the rate allocated to class-c flows, where $\vec{n} = (n_1, \ldots, n_C)$ and n_c is the number of class c flows present in the network. We assume that it is derived from a balance function Φ, i.e.

$$\mu_c(\vec{n}) = \frac{\Phi(\vec{n} - \vec{1}_c)}{\Phi(\vec{n})} \qquad (8.91)$$

All flows in the same class share the bandwidth allocated to this class fairly, i.e. according to processor sharing.

When a flow completes, it either leaves the network, or mutates and becomes a session in think time. The think time duration has any distribution with a finite mean S_0. At the end of its think time, a session becomes a flow.

This can be modeled as a single chain open network with two stations: a Per-Class PS station for flow transfers and an IS station for think time, as in Figure 8.18.

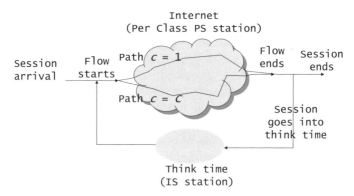

Figure 8.18 The product form queuing network used to model the Internet in [13].

A session in think time may keep the class it inherited from the flow. This means that we allow the classes taken by successive flows to be non-iid, as is probably the case in reality (for example, the next flow of this session might be more likely to take the same path). In fact, we may imagine any dependence, it does not matter as long as the above assumptions hold. This is due to us having a product form queuing network; only the traffic intensities on each flow path matter, as we see next.

With the assumption in (8.91), flow transfers are represented by means of a per-class processor sharing station with Whittle function $\Phi(\vec{n})$ (this is also called a Whittle network); think times are represented by a constant rate infinite server station; both are category 1 stations, thus the network has product form.

More precisely, let θ_c be the visit rate at the Per-Class PS station, class c; it is equal to the number of class-c flow arrivals per time unit. Similarly, θ_0 is the number of arrivals of sessions in think time per time unit. Let n_0 be the number of flows in think time; the stationary probability distribution of $(n_0, \vec{n})$ is, according to the product form theorem,

$$P(n_0, \vec{n}) = \eta \Phi(\vec{n}) \prod_{c=1}^{C} \left(\bar{S}_c \theta_c \right)^{n_c} \left(\theta_0 \bar{S}_0 \right)^{n_0}$$

$$= \eta \Phi(\vec{n}) \prod_{c=1}^{C} \rho_c^{n_c} \rho_0^{n_0} \qquad (8.92)$$

where η is a normalizing constant and $\rho_c = \theta_c \bar{S}_c$, $\rho_0 = \theta_0 \bar{S}_0$ are the traffic intensities.

Equation (8.92) is a remarkably simple formula. It depends only on the traffic intensities, and not on any other property of the session think times or flow transfer times. It holds as long as bandwidth sharing (i.e. the rates $\mu_c(\vec{n})$) derives from a balance function. In [13], it is shown that this is also a necessary condition.

The above is used by the authors in [13] to advocate that bandwidth sharing be performed using a balance function. Bandwidth sharing is the function, implemented by a network, which decides the values of $\mu_c(\vec{n})$ for every c and $\vec{n}$. The set $\mathcal{R}$ of feasible rate vectors $\left(\mu_c(\vec{n}) \right)_{c=1,\ldots,C}$ is defined by the network constraints. For instance, in a wired network with fixed capacities, $\mathcal{R}$ is defined by the constraints $\sum_{c \in \ell} \mu_c < R_l$ where ℓ is a network link, R_l its rate, and "$c \in \ell$" means that a class-c flow uses link ℓ. The authors define **balanced fairness** as the unique allocation of rates to classes which (1) derives from a balance function and (2) is optimal in the sense that for any $\vec{n}$, the rate vector $\left(\mu_c(\vec{n}) \right)_{c=1,\ldots,C}$ is at the boundary of the set of feasible rate vectors $\mathcal{R}$. They show that such an allocation is unique; algorithms to compute the balance function are given in [14].

8.7.2 The Importance of Modeling Closed Populations

Closed chains give a means of accounting for feedback in the system, which may provide a different insight as opposed to that of the single-queue models in Section 8.3. This is illustrated in Section 8.9, where we see that the conclusion (regarding the impact of capacity doubling) is radically different depending on if we assume an infinite or a finite population.

Another useful example is the Engset formula, which we now describe. The Erlang loss formula gives the blocking probability for a system with B servers, a general service time and Poisson external arrivals. If the population of tasks using the system is small, there is a feedback loop between the system and the arrival process, since a job that is accepted cannot create an arrival. An alternative to the Erlang loss formula is the model in Figure 8.19, with a finite population of K jobs, a single class of customers, and two stations. Both stations are IS; station 1 represents the service center with B resources, and station 2 represents the user think time. If station 1 has B customers present, arriving customers are rejected and instantly return to station 2 where they resume service. Service requirements are exponentially distributed. This is equivalent to the form of blocking called partial blocking in Section 8.8.6; a form that requires that routing be reversible. Since there are only two stations, the topology is a bus and the routing is reversible, thus the network has product form.

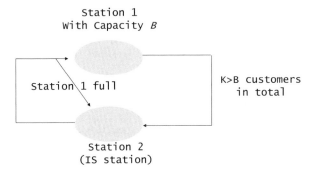

Figure 8.19 The model used to derive the Engset formula.

It follows that the probability $P(n \mid K)$ of there being n customers in service, given that the total population is $K \geq B$, is obtained by the product form theorem and the station functions for IS:

$$P(n \mid K) = \frac{1}{\eta} \frac{\left(\bar{S}^1\right)^n}{n!} \frac{\left(\bar{S}^2\right)^{K-n}}{(K-n)!} \tag{8.93}$$

Here, η is a normalizing constant, $\bar{S}^1$ is the average processing time and $\bar{S}^2$ the average think time. Let $\rho = \frac{\bar{S}^1}{\bar{S}^2}$; we then have:

$$\eta = \sum_{n=0}^{B} \frac{\rho^n}{n!\,(K-n)!}$$

The blocking probability $P^0(B \mid K)$ is equal to the Palm probability for an arriving customer to find B customers in station 1. By the arrival theorem, it is equal to $P(B \mid K-1)$. Thus, for $K > B$,

$$P^0(B \mid K) = \frac{\dfrac{\rho^B}{B!\,(K-B-1)!}}{\displaystyle\sum_{n=0}^{B} \frac{\rho^n}{n!\,(K-n-1)!}} \tag{8.94}$$

and $P^0(B \mid K) = 0$ for $K \leq B$. Equation (8.94) is called the **Engset formula** and gives the blocking probability for a system with B resources and a population of K. Just as the Erlang-loss formula, the expression is valid for any distribution of the service time (and of the think time). When $K \to \infty$, the Engset formula is equivalent to the Erlang-loss formula.

8.8 Mathematical Details about Product-Form Queuing Networks

8.8.1 Phase-Type Distributions

For insensitive stations, the service time distribution is assumed to be a **phase-type** distribution; also called a **mixture of exponentials** or a **mixture of gamma** distribution. It is defined next. Note that the product form theorem implies that the stationary distribution of the network is insensitive to any property of the distribution of service requirement other than its mean. Thus, it seems plausible to conjecture that the product form network continues to apply if we relax the phase type assumption. This is indeed shown for networks made of Kelly stations and of "Whittle network" stations in [8].

A non-negative random variable X is said to have a phase-type distribution if there exists a continuous time Markov chain with finite state space $\{0, 1, \ldots, I\}$ such that X is the time until arrival into state 0, given some initial probability distribution.

Formally, a phase type distribution with n stages is defined by the non-negative sequence $(\alpha_j)_{j=1\ldots,n}$ with $\sum_j \alpha_j = 1$ and the non-negative matrix $(\mu_{j,j'})_{j=1,\ldots,n, \, j'=0,\ldots,n}$. α_j is the probability that, initially, the chain is in state j and $\mu_{j,j'} \geq 0$ is the transition rate from state j to j', for $j \neq j'$. Let $F_j(s)$ be the Laplace-Stieltjes transform of the time from now to the next visit to state 0, given that the chain is in state j now. Based on the Markov property, the Laplace-Stieltjes transform of the distribution we are interested in is $\mathbb{E}\left(e^{-sX}\right) = \sum_{j \neq 0} \alpha_j F_j(s)$ for all $s > 0$. To compute $F_j(s)$, we use the following equations, which also follow from the Markov property:

$$\forall j \in \{0, 1, \ldots, J\} :$$

$$\left(s + \sum_{j' \neq j} \mu_{j,j'}\right) F_j(s) = \mu_{j,0} + \sum_{j' \neq j, \, j' \neq 0} \mu_{j,j'} F_{j'}(s) \qquad (8.95)$$

Consider for example the **Erlang-n** and **hyper-exponential** distributions, which correspond to the Markov chains illustrated in Figure 8.20. The

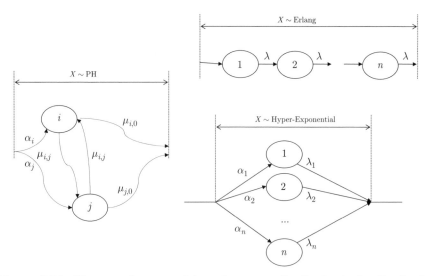

Figure 8.20 Mixtures of exponential: a phase-type distribution is the distribution of the time until absorption into state 0 (state 0 represents the exit and is not shown). The Erlang and Hyperexponential distributions are special cases.

Laplace-Stieltjes transform of the Erlang-n distribution is $F_1(s)$, which is derived from (8.95):

$$(\lambda + s)F_1(s) = \lambda F_2(s)$$

$$\vdots$$

$$(\lambda + s)F_{n-1}(s) = \lambda F_n(s)$$
$$(\lambda + s)F_n(s) = \lambda$$

and is thus $\left(\frac{\lambda}{\lambda+s}\right)^n$. This could also be obtained by noting that it is the convolution of n exponentials. (Note that this represents a special case of Gamma distribution). The PDF is $f(x) = \lambda^n \frac{x^{n-1}}{(n-1)!} e^{-\lambda x}$. The mean is $\bar{S} = \frac{n}{\lambda}$; if we set the mean to a constant and let $n \to \infty$, the Laplace-Stieltjes transform converges, for every $s > 0$, to $e^{-s\bar{S}}$, which is the Laplace-Stieltjes transform of the constant concentrated at $\bar{S}$. In other words, the Erlang-n distribution can be used to approximate a constant service time.

Similarly, the Laplace-Stieltjes transform of the Hyper-Exponential distribution follows immediately from (8.95) and is $\sum_{j=1^n} \frac{\alpha_j \lambda_j}{\lambda_j + s}$. Moreover, the PDF is $f(x) = \sum_{j=1^n} \alpha_j e^{-\lambda_{j'} x}$. This can be used to fit any arbitrary PDF.

8.8.2 Micro and Macro States

The state of every station is defined by a ***micro-state***, as follows.

Insensitive Station. The micro-state is $(\mathcal{B}, \mathcal{J})$, where $\mathcal{B}$ is the state of the station buffer introduced in Section 8.4.2 and $\mathcal{J}$ is a data structure with the same indexing mechanism, which holds the service phase for the customer at this position. In other words, for every index i in the index set of the buffer, $\mathcal{B}_i$ is the class of the customer present at this position, and $\mathcal{J}_i$ is the service phase of the same customer (if there is no customer present at this position, both are 0). A customer at position i receives a service rate $\rho_i(\mathcal{B})$ given by (8.26). This means that the probability that this customer moves from the service phase $j = \mathcal{J}_i$ to a next phase j' in a time interval of duration dt is $\rho_i(\mathcal{B})\mu^c_{j,j'}dt + o(dt)$ where $c = \mathcal{B}_i$ is this customer's class and $\mu^c_{j,j'}$ is the matrix of transition rates at this station for class-c customers, in the phase type representation of service requirement. If the next service phase is $j' = 0$, this customer will leave the station. When a class-c customer arrives at this station, he/she is inserted at position i in the buffer with the probability given in (8.25); the initial stage is set to j with the probability α^c_j, the initial stage distribution probability for customers of this class at this station, and $\mathcal{J}_i$ is set to j.

MSCCC Station. The micro-state is an ordered sequence of classes $(c_1, c_2, \ldots, c_M)$, where M is the number of customers present in the station. When a customer arrives, he/she is added at the end of the sequence. The customers in service are the first B *eligible* customers; a customer in position m is eligible if and only if there is a token available (i.e. $\sum_{m'=0}^{m-1} 1_{\{\mathcal{G}(c_{m'})=g\}} < T_g$ with $g = \mathcal{G}(c_m)$) and there is a server available (i.e. $\sum_g \min(T_g, \sum_{m'=0}^{m-1} 1_{\{\mathcal{G}(c_{m'})=g\}}) < B$). There is no state information about the service stage, since this category of station requires that the service times be exponentially distributed, hence memoryless. The probability that an eligible customer leaves the station in a time interval of duration dt is $\frac{1}{\bar{S}}r(M)\,dt + o(dt)$, where $r(M)$ is the rate of this station when M customers are present and $\bar{S}$ is the mean service time (both independent of the class). Non-eligible customers may not leave the station.

The *global micro-state* of the network is the sequence $(e_1, e_2, \ldots, e_S)$, where e_s is the micro-state of station s. With the assumptions above, this defines a continuous-time Markov chain. A network is defined by the population in closed chains, $K_\mathcal{C}$. The **global micro-state space**, $\mathcal{M}$, is the set of all $(e_1, e_2, \ldots, e_S)$ that are possible, given the rules of each station and provided that

(1) the total number of customers in chain $\mathcal{C}$ present anywhere in the network is $K_\mathcal{C}$, if $\mathcal{C}$ is a closed chain, and any non-negative integer otherwise;

(2) if the visit rate θ^s_c is 0 for some station s and class c, then there may not be any customer of class c at station s.

The **macro-state** of station s is the vector $\vec{n}^s = (n^s_1, \ldots, n^s_C)$, where n^s_c is the number of class-c customers present at this station. The global macro-state is the collection $(\vec{n}^s)_{s=1,\ldots,S}$; the global macro state does not define a Markov chain due to too much information being lost (for MSCCC stations, we lost the order of customers; for insensitive stations, we lost the service phase). The micro-state description is required to prove theorems, but most formulas of interest are expressed in terms of macro-states. The **global macro-state space**, $\mathcal{L}$, is the set of all $(\vec{n}^s)_{s=1,\ldots,S} \geq \vec{0}$ such that

(1) $\sum_{c \in \mathcal{C},s} n^s_c = K_\mathcal{C}$ for every closed chain $\mathcal{C}$;

(2) if the visit rate θ^s_c is 0 for some station s and class c, then $n^s_c = 0$.

8.8.3   Micro to Macro: Aggregation Condition

All results in the previous sections apply to the macro-state description of the network. In the given form, they require that the aggregation condition holds, which states that

aggregation of state from micro to macro

does not introduce non-feasible micro-states

This is equivalent to saying that the set $\mathcal{M}$ is fully connected, i.e. that any global micro-state can be reached from any initial condition in a finite number of transitions of the underlying Markov chain. This is generally true except in pathological cases where the order of customers is preserved throughout the network lifetime. Consider for example a cyclic network with only FIFO stations and one customer per class. The initial order of customers cannot be changed and only states in $\mathcal{M}$ that preserve the initial ordering are feasible. In such a network, the product form does hold, but formulas for macro states are different than those given in this chapter as the number of micro-states providing one specific macro-state is smaller.

8.8.4   Local Balance in Isolation

The station function can be defined both at the micro and macro levels. Formally, the **station function at the micro level** is a function $F(e)$, if it exists, of the micro state e of the function in isolation, such that $F(\emptyset) = 1$, where $\emptyset$ is the empty state. Moreover, the stationary probability of state e in the station in isolation is $\eta(\vec{K})F(e)$, where $\eta(\vec{K})$ is a normalizing constant that depends on the total populations of customers K_c for every class c, in the station in isolation.

We say that a station satisfies the property of **local balance in isolation** if the following holds. For every micro-state e and class c,

the departure rate out of state e due to a class-c arrival

$=$ the arrival rate into state e due to a class-c departure

$$(8.96)$$

In this formula, the rates are given with respect to the stationary probability of the station in isolation, as defined earlier. It follows that one must also have

the departure rate out of state e

due to a departure or an internal transfer, of any class

$=$ the arrival rate into state e

due to an arrival or an internal transfer, of any class

$$(8.97)$$

where an internal transfer is a change of state without arrival nor departure (this is valid for insensitive stations, and is a change of phase for one customer in service). The collection of all these equations is the local balance in isolation. If one finds a station function such that local balance in isolation holds, then this must be the stationary probability of the station in isolation, up to a multiplicative constant.

For example, consider a FIFO station with 1 server and assume that there is one class per chain in the network (i.e. customers do not change class). Let $F(c_1, \ldots, c_M)$ be the stationary probability for the station in isolation. Local balance here writes

$$F(c_1, \ldots, c_M) 1_{\{\sum_{m=1}^{M} 1_{\{c_m = c\}} < K_c\}} = F(c, c_1, \ldots, c_M) \mu \quad \text{for all class } c$$

$$F(c_1, \ldots, c_M) \mu = F(c_1, \ldots, c_{M-1}) 1_{\{\sum_{m=1}^{M-1} 1_{\{c_m = c_M\}} < K_{c_M}\}}$$

where K_c is the number of class-c customers in the system and $\mu = \frac{1}{S}$. The function $F(c_1, \ldots, c_M) = \bar{S}^M$ satisfies both of these types of equations, for which reason it is equal to the stationary probability of the station in isolation, up to a multiplicative constant. $F(c_1, \ldots, c_M) = \bar{S}^M$ is the microscopic station function. The station function $f(\vec{n})$ given earlier follows by aggregation; indeed, let $\mathcal{E}(n_1, \ldots, n_C)$ be the set of micro-states of the FIFO station with n_c customers of class c, for every c.

$$f(n_1, \ldots, n_C) = \sum_{e \in \mathcal{E}(n_1, \ldots, n_C)} \bar{S}^{(n_1 + \cdots + n_C)} = \frac{(n_1 + \cdots + n_C)!}{n_1! \cdots n_C!} \bar{S}^{(n_1 + \cdots + n_C)}$$

since $\frac{(n_1 + \cdots + n_C)!}{n_1! \cdots n_C!}$ is the number of elements of $\mathcal{E}(n_1, \ldots, n_C)$. This is exactly the station function for the FIFO station described in (8.47).

8.8.5   The Product Form Theorem

The product form theorem in 8.7 is a direct consequence of the following main result.

Theorem 8.19

Consider a multi-class network with Markov routing and S stations. Assume that all S stations satisfy local balance in isolation, and let $F^s(e^s)$ be the station function at the micro level for station s, where e^s is the micro state of station s. Then

$$p(e^1, e^2, \ldots, e^S) \stackrel{\text{def}}{=} \prod_{s=1}^{S} F^s(e^s) \tag{8.98}$$

is an invariant measure for the network.

The theorem implies that, if appropriate stability conditions hold, the product $p(e^1, e^2, \ldots, e^S)$ must be equal to a stationary probability, up to a normalizing constant. The proof can be found in [78]; see also [44] and [10]. It consists in a direct verification of the balance equation. More precisely, one shows that, in the network,

> the departure rate out of state e due to a departure of any class
> = the arrival rate into state e due to an arrival of any class   (8.99)

In this formula, the rates are given with respect to the joint network probability of all stations at the micro level, obtained by re-normalizing $p(\cdot)$. Note that the local balance property, as defined in (8.96), generally does not hold inside the network at the micro level.

If the aggregation condition holds, then one can sum up (8.98) over all micro-states for which the network population vector is $\vec{n}$ and obtain (8.51), which is the macro-level product form result. Note that, at the macro-level, one has, in the network, and for any class c,

$$
\begin{aligned}
&\text{the departure rate out of state } e \text{ due to a class-}c \text{ departure} \\
&= \text{the arrival rate into state } e \text{ due to a class-}c \text{ arrival}
\end{aligned}
\tag{8.100}
$$

In this formula, the rates are given with respect to the joint network probability of all stations at the macro-level. Note the inversion with respect to local balance.

The resulting independence for the open case in Theorem 8.8 therefore also holds for micro-states: in an open network, the micro-states at different stations are independent.

The proof of the product form Theorem 8.7 follows immediately from Theorem 8.19 and the fact that all stations in our catalog satisfy the property of local balance in isolation. The proof that MSCCC stations satisfy the local balance property is presented in [53], [11]. For Kelly-Whittle stations, the result was priorly known for some specific cases. For the general case, however it is new.

> **Theorem 8.20**
> *Kelly-Whittle stations satisfy local balance in isolation.*

The proof is given in Section 8.10.

8.8.6 Networks with Blocking

It is possible to extend Markov routing to state-dependent routing, In particular, one can allow for some (limited) forms of blocking, as follows. Assume that there are some constraints on the network state. There may for instance be an upper limit to the number of customers in one station. A customer finishing a service, or, for an open chain, a customer arriving from the outside, is denied access to a station if accepting this customer would violate any of the constraints. Consider the following two cases:

Transparent Stations with Capacity Limitations. The constraints on the network state are expressed by L capacity limitations of the form

$$
\sum_{(s,c)\in\mathcal{H}_\ell} n_c^s \leq \Gamma_\ell \qquad \ell = 1,\ldots,L
\tag{8.101}
$$

where n_c^s is the number of class c customers present at station c, $\mathcal{H}_\ell$ is a subset of $\{1,\ldots,S\} \times \{1,\ldots,C\}$ and $\Gamma_\ell \in \mathbb{N}$. In other words, some stations or groups of stations may put limits on the number of customers of some classes or groups of classes.

If a customer is denied access to station s, she continues her journey through the network, using Markov routing with the fixed matrix Q, until she finds a station that accepts her or until she leaves the network.

Partial Blocking with Arbitrary Constraints. The constraints can be of any type. Further, if a customer finishes the service and is denied access to station s, he/she stays blocked in service. More precisely, we assume that service distributions are of phase-type, and the customer resumes the last completed service stage. If the customer arrived from the outside, he/she is dropped.

Further, we need to assume that Markov routing is **reversible**, which means that

$$\theta_c^s q_{c,c'}^{s,s'} = \theta_{c'}^{s'} q_{c',c}^{s',s} \tag{8.102}$$

for all s, s', c, c'. Reversibility is a constraint on the topology; bus and star networks give reversible routing, but ring networks do not.

Assume, in addition, that the service requirements are exponentially distributed (but may be class-dependent at insensitive stations). The product form theorem then continues to apply for these two forms of blocking ([80], [58] and [44]). There are other cases, too, see [6] and references therein.

There is a more general result: if the service distributions are exponential and the Markov routing is reversible, then the Markov process of global microstates is also reversible [54]. Let X_t be a continuous time Markov chain with stationary probability $p(\cdot)$ and state space $\mathcal{E}$. The process is called **reversible** if $p(e)\mu(e, e') = p(e')\mu(e', e)$ for any two states $e, e' \in \mathcal{E}$, where $\mu(e, e')$ is the rate of transition from e to e'. Reversible Markov chains enjoy the following **truncation property** [44]. Let $\mathcal{E}' \subset \mathcal{E}$ and define the process X_t' by forcing the process to stay within $\mathcal{E}'$; this is done by taking some initial state space $e \in \mathcal{E}'$ and setting to 0 the rate of any transition from $e \in \mathcal{E}$ to $e' \in \mathcal{E}'$. Then the restriction of p to $\mathcal{E}'$ is an invariant probability; in particular, if $\mathcal{E}'$ is finite and fully connected, the stationary probability of the truncated process is the restriction of p to $\mathcal{E}'$, up to a normalizing constant.

Note that setting to 0 the rates of transitions from $e \in \mathcal{E}$ to $e' \in \mathcal{E}'$ is equivalent to stating that we allow the transition from e to e' but then force an immediate, instantaneous return to e. This explains why we have product form for networks with partial blocking with arbitrary constraints.

8.9   Case Study

In this section, we show how the four topics in the previous section can be combined to address a queuing issue. Recently, one could read on the walls of the city where I live the following advertisement for a ski resort: "capacity doubled, waiting time halved". Does this statement hold? I was intrigued by this sweeping statement, and realized that it can be found repeatedly in many different situations: doubling the processor speed or doubling the number of cores in a computer, doubling the web front end in a server farm, etc. In the rest of this section we focus on the ski resort example.

First, we apply the principles in Chapter 1 and define the goals and factors.

- Goal: evaluate the impact of doubling the capacity of a skilift on the response time.
- Factors: c = capacity of skilift in people per second.
- Metrics: response time. A more detailed reflection leads to considering the waiting time, as this is the parameter that affects a customer's perception.
- Load: we consider two load models,
  (1) a heavy burst of arrival (after a train or a bus arrives at the skilift),
  (2) peak hour stationary regime.

8.9.1   Deterministic Analysis

We can model the skilift as the queuing system illustrated in Figure 8.21. The first queue models the gate; it is a single server queue. Its service time is the time between two passages through the gate when there is no idle period. It is equal to $\frac{1}{c}$. The second queue represents the transportation time. It is an infinite server queue, with no waiting time. Since our performance metric is the waiting time, we may ignore the second queue in the rest of the analysis.

Figure 8.21 Queuing model of a skilift.

Assume that the arrival of skiers is one single burst (they all arrive at the same time). Also assume that all skiers spend the same time going through the gate, which is roughly true in this scenario. The model in Section 8.1.1 applies, with $A(t) = $ the number of skiers arriving in $[0, t]$ and $D(t) = $ the number of skiers entering the skilift in $[0, t]$. Thus, the delay $d(t)$ is the waiting time, excluding the time spent on the skilift. We also have $\beta(t) = ct$, where $c = $ the capacity of the skilift, in skiers per second. We have $A(t) = B$ for $t \geq 0$. Figure 8.22 shows that doubling the capacity does indeed divide the worst-case waiting time by two.

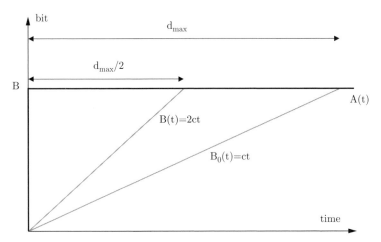

Figure 8.22 Transient Analysis: A burst of skiers arrives at time 0. The impact of doubling the capacity of the skilift.

However, is the average waiting time also divided by 2? To answer this question, we take the viewpoint of an arbitrary customer. We see that the waiting time seen by a customer arriving as number y $(0 \leq y \leq B)$ is linear in y, thus the average waiting time is equal to the worst-case response time divided by 2. Here too, a doubling of the capacity divides the average waiting time by 2.

QUESTION 8.14   In reality, even if the arrival of skiers is bursty, it may not be as simultaneous as we just described. We can account for this by taking $A(t) = kct$ for $0 \leq t \leq t_0$ and $A(t) = A(t_0)$ for $t \geq t_0$, with $k \geq 1$. What is the conclusion now?[19]

8.9.2 Single Queue Analysis

Assume now that we observe the system in the middle of the peak hour. We can model the gate as a single queue, with one or perhaps several servers. It is difficult to give a more accurate statement of the arrival process without performing actual measurements. Whatever the details, doubling the capacity

---

[19] The response time is reduced by a factor higher than 2.

halves the utilization factor ρ. A major pattern of single queue systems is the non-linearity of the response time, as in Figure 8.7.

In fact, the effect on the response time depends on where we are positioned on the curve. If the system is close to saturation, as is probably the case, the effect is a large reduction of the average waiting time, probably much larger than 2. Thus with this model, doubling the capacity decreases the waiting time by more than two.

8.9.3   Operational Analysis

It is probably unrealistic to assume that a reduction in waiting time has no effect on the arrival rate. A better, though simplified, model is illustrated in Figure 8.23. It is a variant of the interactive user model in Figure 8.3. Here, we assume that the mean number $\bar{N}$ of skiers in the system is independent of c.

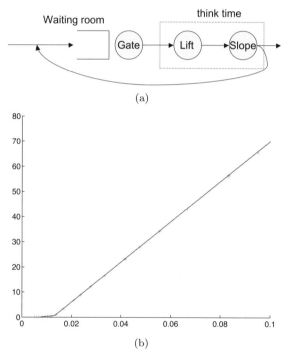

Figure 8.23 (a) A model that accounts for the dependency of the arrival rate and waiting time. (b) The waiting time in minutes for this model versus $\frac{1}{c}$, where c is the skilift capacity (in people per minute). The solid line is the approximation by bottleneck analysis. The crosses are obtained by analytical solution of the queuing network model in Figure 8.24, with the following parameters: population size $K = 800$ skiers; number of servers at gate $B \in \{1, 2, \ldots, 7, 8\}$; service time at gate $\bar{S} \in \{2.5, 5, 10, 20\}$ s; time between visits to the gate $\bar{Z} = 10$ min.

We apply bottleneck analysis. Let λ be the throughput of the skilift, $\bar{S}$ the time spent serving one customer at the lift, $\bar{Z}$ the time spent going up on the lift or down on the slope and $\bar{W}$ the average waiting time at the lift. We have

$$\begin{cases} \lambda(\bar{W} + \bar{S} + \bar{Z}) = \bar{N} \\ \lambda \le c \end{cases}$$

and $\bar{S}$ is assumed to be negligible as compared to $\bar{Z}$. Consequently,

$$\bar{W} \gtrsim \max\left(\frac{\bar{N}}{c} - \bar{Z}, 0\right)$$

Figure 8.23 shows the approximate bound as a function of $\frac{1}{c}$ for the sake of comparison with Figure 8.7. Points obtained by mean value analysis are also plotted and we see that the bound is in fact a very good approximation.

This strongly suggests that the function f that maps $\frac{1}{c}$ to the average response time is convex; the graph of a convex function is below its chords, thus

$$f\left(\frac{1}{2c}\right) < \frac{1}{2} f\left(\frac{1}{c}\right)$$

and doubling the capacity *reduces the waiting time by more than* 2.

We also see that a key value is $c^* = \frac{\bar{N}}{\bar{Z}}$. Note that $\frac{1}{\bar{Z}}$ is the rate at which one customer would arrive at the gate if there was no queue, thus c^* is the rate of customers under the condition that the gate would not delay them. If c is much larger than c^*, the waiting time is small, and doubling of the capacity would have little effect. For c much smaller than c^*, the waiting time increases at an almost constant rate. Thus we should target c on the order of c^*. In other words, we should match the capacity of the gate to the "natural" rate c^*.

QUESTION 8.15 Assume that the system is highly congested before doubling the capacity. What is the reduction in waiting time after doubling the capacity?[20]

8.9.4 Queuing Network Analysis

We can model the network in Figure 8.23 as a single class, closed product form queuing network as in Figure 8.24. There is no specific assumption on the time spent on the slopes ("think time"); in contrast we need to assume that the service time at the gate is exponentially distributed. Let $\bar{S}$ be the mean service time at the gate and B the number of servers, so that $c = \frac{B}{\bar{S}}$. The mean service time at the IS station is $\bar{Z}$.

---

[20] For a highly congested system ($2c$ much smaller than c^*) the offset at 0 becomes negligible and the response time is almost linear in $\frac{1}{c}$. Thus, doubling the capacity reduces the waiting time by 2, roughly speaking – but the system remains congested after doubling the capacity.

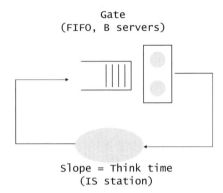

Figure 8.24 A Queuing Network model of Figure 8.23.

The total number of customers is fixed and equal to K. Let $\lambda(K)$ and $\bar{W}(K)$ be the throughput and the average waiting time at the gate. According to Little's law

$$\lambda(K)\big(\bar{W}(K) + \bar{S} + \bar{Z}\big) = K$$

thus

$$\bar{W}(K) = \frac{K}{\lambda(K)} - \bar{S} - \bar{Z} \tag{8.103}$$

We compute $\lambda(K)$ by mean value analysis, which avoids computing the normalizing constants and the resulting overflow problems. Let $P(n \mid K)$ be the stationary probability that there are n customers present (in service or waiting) at the FIFO station, when the total number of customers is K. The mean value analysis equations are (Section 8.6.5)

$$P(n \mid K) = P(n - 1 \mid K - 1)\frac{\lambda(K)}{\mu^*(n)} \qquad \text{if } n \geq 1 \tag{8.104}$$

$$P(0 \mid K) = P(0 \mid K - 1)\frac{\lambda(K)}{\lambda^{[1]}(K)} \tag{8.105}$$

$$\sum_{n=0}^{K} P(n \mid K) = 1 \tag{8.106}$$

where $\mu^*(n)$ is the equivalent service rate of the FIFO station and $\lambda^{[1]}(K)$ is the throughput of the complement of this station. Based on Table 8.1,

$$\mu^*(n) = \frac{\min(n, B)}{\bar{S}}$$

The complement network is obtained by short circuiting the FIFO station; it consists of the IS station alone. Thus

$$\lambda^{[1]}(K) = \frac{K}{\bar{Z}}$$

The mean value algorithm is given in Algorithm 8.2. Figure 8.23 and Figure 8.25 show a few numerical results. The capacity $c = \frac{B}{\bar{S}}$ depends on both the number of FIFO servers B and the service time at the gate $\bar{S}$. The points in Figure 8.23 are obtained by varying both B and $\bar{S}$. The figure shows that the bottleneck analysis provides an excellent approximation. Thus this section confirms the conclusions obtained by operational analysis.

Algorithm 8.2 Implementation of MVA Version 2 to the network in Figure 8.24.

1: $K =$: population size

2: $p(n)$, $n = 0...K$: probability that there are n customers at the FIFO station

3: λ: throughput

4: $p(0) = 1$, $p(n) = 0$, $n = 1...K$

5: **for** $k = 1 : K$ **do**

6:     $p^*(n) = p(n-1)\bar{Z}/\min(pn, B)$, $n = 1...k$ ▷ Unnormalized $p(n \mid k)$,

7:   ▷ (8.104)

8:     $p^*(0) = p(0)\bar{Z}/k$ ▷ Unnormalized $p(0 \mid k)$, (8.105)

9:     $\lambda = 1/\sum_{n=0}^{k} p^*(n)$

10:     $p(n) = p^*(n)/\lambda$, $n = 0...k$

11: **end for**

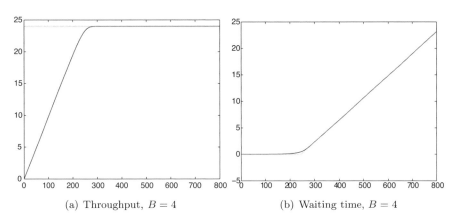

(a) Throughput, $B = 4$ (b) Waiting time, $B = 4$

Figure 8.25 Throughput $\lambda(K)$ in customers per minute and waiting times $W(K)$ in minutes for the skilift example in Figure 8.24 with B servers at the gate, versus the number of customers K. The results are obtained by analytical solution of the queuing network model (using the MVA algorithm). The dotted lines correspond to the maximum throughput $\frac{B}{\bar{S}}$ and the waiting times predicted by bottleneck analysis. $\bar{S} = 10$ s and $\bar{Z} = 10$ min.

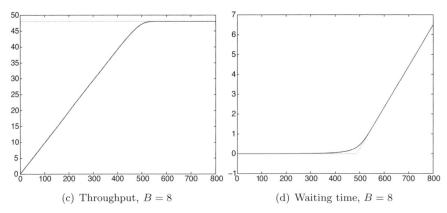

(c) Throughput, $B = 8$ (d) Waiting time, $B = 8$

Figure 8.25 (Continuation.)

8.9.5 Conclusions

Doubling the capacity does indeed reduce the waiting time by a factor of 2 during bursts of arrivals, and by a factor of 2 or more during the stationary regime. This is independent of whether the increase in capacity is obtained by increasing the number of servers or by reducing the service time at the gate.

These findings assume that the arrival rate is not impacted by the capacity increase and does not account for long-term effects. In the long run, a reduction in waiting time might attract more customers and this will in turn increase the waiting time.

There is an optimal capacity c^*, for any target customer population size K^* (maximum number of customers that the ski resort can accommodate on the slopes), given by $c^* \approx \frac{K^*}{\bar{Z}}$ where $\bar{Z}$ is the mean time between visits to the gate. If the capacity is below c^*, the waiting time is large; increasing c beyond c^* brings little benefit to waiting time.

8.10   Proofs

Theorem 8.2

Apply Theorem 7.4 to $X(t) = N(t)$ and $T_n =$ the superposition of arrivals and departures. The derivative of $N(t)$ is 0, and the jumps are $+1$ at instants of arrival, and -1 at instants of departures. Thus, $\mathbb{E}^0(\Delta N_0) = 0$. Now $\mathbb{E}^0(\Delta N_0) = +1 p_a^0 - 1 p_d^0$, where p_a^0 is the probability that an arbitrary point is an arrival (resp. departure). It follows that $p_a^0 = p_d^0$ and since $p_a^0 + p_d^0 = 1$, it follows that $p_a^0 = p_d^0 = 0.5$, which is not so surprising since there should be, in average, as many departures as arrivals.

Apply again the theorem to $X(t) = \frac{1 - z^{N(t)}}{1 - z}$ where z is some arbitrary number in $(0, 1)$. $X(t)$ is constant except at arrival or departure times, thus

$X'(t) = 0$. Further, $\Delta X_t = z^{N(t)-1}$ if t is an arrival instant and $\Delta X_t = -z^{N(t)}$ if t is a departure instant. Thus

$$0 = \mathbb{E}\big(z^{N(t)-1} \mid t \text{ is an arrival instant}\big)p_a^0$$
$$- \mathbb{E}\big(z^{N(t)} \mid t \text{ is a departure instant}\big)p_d^0$$

Now $N(t)$ is right-handside continuous, so $N(t) - 1$ is the number of customers just before t when t is an arrival epoch. Since $p_a^0 = p_d^0$, the distributions of the number of customers just before an arrival and just after a departure are equal.

Theorem 8.5

Forced Flows. We apply Campbell's formula. Let $F(s,t)$ be the random function which returns 1 if $t \geq s$ and the last customer who arrived before or at $-t$ is in node k at time s, else returns 0. By definition of intensity,

$$\lambda_k = \mathbb{E}\left(\sum_{n \in \mathbb{Z}} F(-A_n, 0)\right)$$

where A_n is the point process of customer arrivals. Campbell's formula applied to $F(-t, 0)$ gives

$$\mathbb{E}\left(\sum_{n \in \mathbb{Z}} F(-A_n, 0)\right) = \lambda \sum_{t \in \mathbb{N}} \mathbb{E}^{-t}\big(F(t, 0)\big) = \lambda \sum_{t \in \mathbb{N}} \mathbb{E}^0\big(F(0, t)\big)$$

where the last part is based on stationarity. Thus

$$\lambda_k = \lambda \mathbb{E}^0\left(\sum_{t \in \mathbb{N}} F(0, t)\right) = \lambda V_k$$

Total Response Time. Let $\bar{N}$ (resp. $\bar{N}_k$) be the expected number of customers in the service system (resp. in node k). We have $\bar{N} = \sum_k \bar{N}_k$. Apply Little's and the Forced Flows laws.

Theorem 8.20

We consider a Kelly-Whittle station in isolation, i.e. connected to a unit rate per class station, with K_c customers of class c in total. We want to show that local balance holds at the micro-level ((8.96), (8.97)). The micro-state of the station is $(\mathcal{B}, \mathcal{J})$, where $\mathcal{B}_i$ is the class of the customer in position $i \in \mathcal{I}$ of the station buffer and $\mathcal{J}_i$ is the phase for this customer, in the phase-type representation of service times. If there is no customer in position i, we let $\mathcal{B}_i = \mathcal{J}_i = -1$. We assume that the index set $\mathcal{I}$ is enumerable, and that the initial number of occupied positions is finite, so that it remains finite for ever.

Let α_j^c and $\mu_{j,j'}^c$ be the matrices of initial probabilities and transition rates in the phase type representation of service rates for class c, with $j = 1, \ldots, J^c$ and $j' = 0, \ldots, J^c$. Without loss of generality, we assume $J^C = J$. Recall that $j' = 0$ corresponds to an end of service. For every c, let the array θ_j^c, $j = 1, \ldots, J$, be a solution of

$$1 = \sum_{j=1}^{J} \theta_j^c \frac{\mu_{j,0}^c}{\bar{\mu}_j^c}$$

$$\theta_j^c = \alpha_j^c + \sum_{j'=1}^{J} \theta_{j'}^c \frac{\mu_{j',j}^c}{\bar{\mu}_{j'}^c}$$

with

$$\bar{\mu}_j^c = \sum_{j'=0}^{J} \mu_{j,j'}$$

so that θ_j^c is the mean number of visits to stage j during one class c customer's service time. Note that the mean service requirement for class c is

$$\bar{S}^c = \sum_{j=1}^{J} \frac{\theta_j^c}{\bar{\mu}_j^c} \tag{8.107}$$

We will show that the stationary probability of the station in isolation is proportional to

$$F(\mathcal{B}, \mathcal{J}) \stackrel{\text{def}}{=} \Psi(\mathcal{B}) \prod_{\substack{i \in \mathcal{I} \\ \mathcal{B}_i \neq -1}} \frac{\theta_{\mathcal{J}_i}^{\mathcal{B}_i}}{\bar{\mu}_{\mathcal{J}_i}^{\mathcal{B}_i}} \tag{8.108}$$

where Ψ is the Whittle function. Clearly, this will imply that F is the station function. Note that the product is always finite. We now show that the equations of local balance, (8.96) and (8.97), hold. Consider first (8.96). The departure rate due to a class-c arrival is simply $F(\mathcal{B}, \mathcal{J})1_{\{n_c(\mathcal{B}) < K_c\}}$, by definition of the station in isolation, where $n_c(\mathcal{B}) \stackrel{\text{def}}{=} \sum_{i \in \mathcal{I}} 1_{\{\mathcal{B}_i = c\}}$ is the number of class-c customers. The arrival rate due to a class-c departure is 0 if $n_c(\mathcal{B}) < K_c$ (one cannot reach a state where all class-c customers are in the station by a departure) and otherwise, by definition of the service rate,

$$\sum_{i \in \mathcal{I}, j=1, \ldots, J} F\big(\text{add}(\mathcal{B}, i, c), \text{add}(\mathcal{J}, j, c)\big) \gamma\big(i, \text{add}(\mathcal{B}, i, c)\big)$$

$$\times \frac{\Psi\big(\text{remove}(\text{add}(\mathcal{B}, i, c), i)\big)}{\Psi\big(\text{add}(\mathcal{B}, i, c)\big)} \mu_{j,0}^c$$

$$= F(\mathcal{B}, \mathcal{J}) \sum_{i \in \mathcal{I}, j=1, \ldots, J} \frac{\theta_j^c}{\bar{\mu}_j^c} \gamma\big(i, \text{add}(\mathcal{B}, i, c)\big) \mu_{j,0}^c$$

$$= F(\mathcal{B}, \mathcal{J}) \left(\sum_{i \in \mathcal{I}} \gamma\big(i, \text{add}(\mathcal{B}, i, c)\big) \right) \left(\sum_{i \in \mathcal{I}, j=1, \ldots, J} \frac{\theta_j^c}{\bar{\mu}_j^c} \mu_{j,0}^c \right) = F(\mathcal{B}, \mathcal{J})$$

Consequently, (8.96) holds. We now show (8.97). The left-hand side is

$$F(\mathcal{B},\mathcal{J})\sum_{i\in\mathcal{B}}\sum_{c=1}^{C}\sum_{j=1}^{J}\gamma(i,\mathcal{B})\frac{\Psi\big(\mathrm{remove}(\mathcal{B},i)\big)}{\Psi(\mathcal{B})}\,\bar{\mu}_{j}^{c}1_{\{\mathcal{B}_{i}=c\}}1_{\{\mathcal{J}_{i}=j\}}$$

and the right-hand side is $\mathrm{RHS}_{a}+\mathrm{RHS}_{t}$, where the former term corresponds to an arrival, and the latter to an internal transfer:

$$\mathrm{RHS}_{a}=\sum_{i\in\mathcal{I}}\sum_{c=1}^{C}\sum_{j=1}^{J}F\Big(\mathrm{remove}(\mathcal{B},i),\mathrm{remove}(\mathcal{J},i)\Big)\gamma(i,\mathcal{B})\alpha_{j}^{c}1_{\{\mathcal{B}_{i}=c\}}1_{\{\mathcal{J}_{i}=j\}}$$

$$=F(\mathcal{B},\mathcal{J})\sum_{i\in\mathcal{I}}\sum_{c=1}^{C}\sum_{j=1}^{J}\frac{\Psi\big(\mathrm{remove}(\mathcal{B},i)\big)}{\Psi(\mathcal{B})}\frac{\bar{\mu}_{j}^{c}}{\theta_{j}^{c}}\gamma(i,\mathcal{B})\alpha_{j}^{c}1_{\{\mathcal{B}_{i}=c\}}1_{\{\mathcal{J}_{i}=j\}}$$

We use the notation $\mathcal{B}^{i',i}\overset{\mathrm{def}}{=}\mathrm{add}\big(\mathrm{remove}(\mathcal{B},i),i',\mathcal{B}_{i}\big)$. By hypothesis, $\mathcal{B}^{i,i}=\mathcal{B}$ and $\mathcal{B}^{i',i}$ is the only buffer state $\mathcal{B}'$ such that $\mathrm{remove}(\mathcal{B}',i')=\mathrm{remove}(\mathcal{B},i)$ and $\mathcal{B}'_{i'}=c$. Also note that $\mathrm{add}\big(\mathrm{remove}(\mathcal{B},i),i,\mathcal{B}_{i}\big)=\mathcal{B}$. Thus,

$$\mathrm{RHS}_{t}=\sum_{i,i'\in\mathcal{I}}\sum_{c=1}^{C}\sum_{j,j'=1}^{J}F\Big(\mathcal{B}^{i',i},\mathrm{add}\big(\mathrm{remove}(\mathcal{J},i),i',j'\big)\Big)$$

$$\times\gamma(i',\mathcal{B}^{i',i})\frac{\Psi\big(\mathrm{remove}(\mathcal{B}^{i',i},i')\big)}{\Psi(\mathcal{B}^{i',i})}\mu_{j',j}^{c}$$

$$\times\gamma\Big(i,\mathrm{add}\big(\mathrm{remove}(\mathcal{B}^{i',i},i'),i,c\big)\Big)1_{\{\mathcal{B}_{i}=c\}}1_{\{\mathcal{J}_{i}=j\}}$$

$$=\sum_{i,i'\in\mathcal{I}}\sum_{c=1}^{C}\sum_{j,j'=1}^{J}F\Big(\mathcal{B}^{i',i},\mathrm{add}\big(\mathrm{remove}(\mathcal{J},i),i',j'\big)\Big)$$

$$\times\gamma(i',\mathcal{B}^{i',i})\frac{\Psi\big(\mathrm{remove}(\mathcal{B},i)\big)}{\Psi(\mathcal{B}^{i',i})}\mu_{j',j}^{c}$$

$$\times\gamma\Big(i,\mathrm{add}\big(\mathrm{remove}(\mathcal{B},i),i,c\big)\Big)1_{\{\mathcal{B}_{i}=c\}}1_{\{\mathcal{J}_{i}=j\}}$$

$$=F(\mathcal{B},\mathcal{J})\sum_{i,i'\in\mathcal{I}}\sum_{c=1}^{C}\sum_{j,j'=1}^{J}\frac{\theta_{j'}^{c}\bar{\mu}_{j}}{\theta_{j}^{c}\bar{\mu}_{j'}}$$

$$\times\gamma\Big(i',\mathrm{add}\big(\mathrm{remove}(\mathcal{B},i),i',\mathcal{B}_{i}\big)\Big)\frac{\Psi\big(\mathrm{remove}(\mathcal{B},i)\big)}{\Psi(\mathcal{B})}\mu_{j',j}^{c}$$

$$\times\gamma(i,\mathcal{B})1_{\{\mathcal{B}_{i}=c\}}1_{\{\mathcal{J}_{i}=j\}}$$

$$=F(\mathcal{B},\mathcal{J})\sum_{i\in\mathcal{I}}\sum_{c=1}^{C}\sum_{j,j'=1}^{J}\frac{\theta_{j'}^{c}\bar{\mu}_{j}}{\theta_{j}^{c}\bar{\mu}_{j'}}\frac{\Psi\big(\mathrm{remove}(\mathcal{B},i)\big)}{\Psi(\mathcal{B})}\mu_{j',j}^{c}1_{\{\mathcal{B}_{i}=c\}}1_{\{\mathcal{J}_{i}=j\}}\gamma(i,\mathcal{B})$$

$$\times\sum_{i'\in\mathcal{I}}\gamma\Big(i',\mathrm{add}\big(\mathrm{remove}(\mathcal{B},i),i',c\big)\Big)$$

$$\mathrm{RHS}_t = F(\mathcal{B}, \mathcal{J}) \sum_{i \in \mathcal{I}} \sum_{c=1}^{C} \sum_{j,j'=1}^{J} \frac{\theta_{j'}^c \bar{\mu}_j}{\theta_j^c \bar{\mu}_{j'}} \frac{\Psi\big(\mathrm{remove}(\mathcal{B}, i)\big)}{\Psi(\mathcal{B})} \mu_{j',j}^c 1_{\{\mathcal{B}_i=c\}} 1_{\{\mathcal{J}_i=j\}} \gamma(i, \mathcal{B})$$

$$= F(\mathcal{B}, \mathcal{J}) \sum_{i \in \mathcal{I}} \sum_{c=1}^{C} \sum_{j=1}^{J} \frac{\bar{\mu}_j}{\theta_j^c} \frac{\Psi\big(\mathrm{remove}(\mathcal{B}, i)\big)}{\Psi(\mathcal{B})} 1_{\{\mathcal{B}_i=c\}} 1_{\{\mathcal{J}_i=j\}}$$

$$\times \gamma(i, \mathcal{B}) \sum_{j'=1}^{J} \frac{\theta_{j'}^c}{\bar{\mu}_{j'}} \mu_{j',j}^c$$

$$= F(\mathcal{B}, \mathcal{J}) \sum_{i \in \mathcal{I}} \sum_{c=1}^{C} \sum_{j=1}^{J} \frac{\bar{\mu}_j}{\theta_j^c} \frac{\Psi\big(\mathrm{remove}(\mathcal{B}, i)\big)}{\Psi(\mathcal{B})} 1_{\{\mathcal{B}_i=c\}} 1_{\{\mathcal{J}_i=j\}} \gamma(i, \mathcal{B}) \big(\theta_j^c - \alpha_j^c\big)$$

Thus, combining the two gives us

$$\mathrm{RHS}_a + \mathrm{RHS}_t = F(\mathcal{B}, \mathcal{J}) \sum_{i \in \mathcal{I}} \sum_{c=1}^{C} \sum_{j=1}^{J} \bar{\mu}_j \frac{\Psi\big(\mathrm{remove}(\mathcal{B}, i)\big)}{\Psi(\mathcal{B})} 1_{\{\mathcal{B}_i=c\}} 1_{\{\mathcal{J}_i=j\}} \gamma(i, \mathcal{B})$$

which is equal to the right-hand side as required.

8.11   Review

8.11.1   Review Questions

8.1 Why are stations of category 1 called "insensitive"?[21]

8.2 Consider a multi-class queuing network, with FIFO queues, Poisson arrivals and exponential service times; under which condition does it satisfy the hypotheses of the product form theorem?[22]

8.3 Explain (8.17) and (8.21) by the product form theorem.[23]

8.4 Consider the network in Figure 8.24 and assume that there is only one class of customers. Assume that the service requirement at the bottom station is exponential (ν). State which category each station is from. Write the station functions for both functions and verify the product-form theorem when the

---

[21] Their station function depends on the distribution of service time only through the mean.

[22] The service time distributions must be independent of the class.

[23] The M/GI/1/PS queue is an open queuing network with one class of customers and one station, with a visit rate equal to λ. The station function for a constant rate PS station is $f(n) = \bar{S}^n$, thus the stationary probability of the M/GI/1/PS queue is $\eta \rho^n$. By normalization, $\eta = \frac{1}{1-\rho}$, which is (8.17). Similarly for (8.21), using the station function of the FIFO station with B servers.

number of servers is $B = 1$. Compute the throughput and verify the throughput theorem.[24]

8.5 In Section 8.4, we mention the existence of a network in [16] which is unstable with an utilization factor of less than 1. Can it be a product-form multi-class queuing network? Why or why not?[25]

8.11.2 Summary of Notation

Single Server Queue

Notation	Definition
A/S/B/K	Kendall notation: arrival process/service process/ number of servers/ capacity of queue including customers in service
λ	arrival rate
B	number of servers
$\bar{S}, \sigma_S, \mathcal{L}_S$	mean, standard deviation and Laplace Stieltjes transform of service time
$\rho = \frac{\lambda \bar{S}}{B}$	server utilization
$N, \bar{N}, \sigma_N$	number of customers in system, its mean and standard deviation
$N_w, \bar{N}_w, \sigma_{N_w}$	number of customers waiting, its mean and standard deviation
$R, \bar{R}, \sigma_R$	time spent in system (residence time), its mean and standard deviation
V_k	mean number of visits per customer to node k
$W, \bar{W}, \sigma_W$	waiting time, its mean and standard deviation
$\bar{Z}$	av. think time in interactive user model

Queuing Networks

Notation	Definition
$\mathcal{B}$	State of buffer in insensitive station, containing the list of customer classes
c	customer class

---

[24] The 'Gate" station is a FIFO station, and thus a station of Category 2. Its station function is $f^1(n) = \frac{1}{\mu^n}$ where $\frac{1}{\mu}$ is its mean service time. The second station is a station of category 1 and its station function is $f^2(n) = \frac{1}{n!\nu^n}$. The stationary probability is $p(n) = \frac{f^1(n)f^2(K-n)}{\eta(K)}$ when there are K customers. The balance equations are

$$p(n)\big(\mu + (K-n)\nu\big) = (K - n + 1)\nu p(n - 1)1_{\{n \geq 1\}} + \mu p(n + 1)1_{\{n \leq K-1\}}$$

The verification is by direct computation (the terms match by pair). For the throughput, see Example 7.17.

[25] It cannot be a product-form multi-class queuing network because these are stable when the utilization is less than 1. It violates the assumptions because of FIFO stations with class-dependent service rates.

Notation	Definition
$\mathcal{C}$	customer chain; does not change for a given customer
$d(\vec{n})$	combinatorial function used by MSCCC station, (8.40)
$D(\vec{Z})$	Z-transform of δ, computed by (8.42)
$f^s(\vec{n}^s)$	station function, (8.31)
$G^s(\vec{z})$	generating function of station function, (8.32)
$\mathcal{G}(c)$	token group of class c at an MSCCC station
$\lambda_c^s(\vec{K})$	throughput of class c observed at station s
$\lambda_{\mathcal{C}}(\vec{K})$	throughput of chain $\mathcal{C}$, Section 8.6.2
$\vec{K}$	network population vector; $K_{\mathcal{C}}$: number of chain $\mathcal{C}$ customers in network
ν_c^s	external arrival rate of class c at station s
$\Phi(\vec{n})$	balance function at some Kelly-Whittle stations
$\Psi(\mathcal{B})$	Whittle function at Kelly-Whittle station
$q_{c,c'}^{s,s'}$	routing probability, Section 8.4.1
$\bar{S}_c^s$	mean service requirement at station s for class-c customers
T_g	size of token pool g at MSCCC station
θ_c^s	visit rate to station s, class c ((8.24))

Tables

The following tables can be used to determine confidence intervals for quantiles (including the median), according to Theorem 2.1. For a sample of n iid data points $x_1, \ldots, x_n$, the tables give a confidence interval at the confidence level $\gamma = 0.95$ or 0.99 for the q-quantile with $q = 0.5$ (median), $q = 0.75$ (quartile) and $q = 0.95$. The confidence interval is $[x_{(j)}, x_{(k)}]$, where $x_{(j)}$ is the jth data point sorted in increasing order.

The confidence intervals for $q = 0.05$ and $q = 0.25$ are not given in the tables. They can be deduced by the following rule. Let $[x_{(j)}, x_{(k)}]$ be the confidence interval for the q-quantile given by the table. A confidence interval for the $1 - q$-quantile is $[x_{(j')}, x_{(k')}]$ with

$$j' = n + 1 - k$$
$$k' = n + 1 - j$$

For example, with $n = 50$, a confidence interval for the third quartile ($q = 0.75$) at confidence level 0.99 is $[x_{(29)}, x_{(45)}]$, thus a confidence interval for the first quartile ($q = 0.25$) at confidence level 0.99 is $[x_{(6)}, x_{(22)}]$.

For small values of n no confidence interval is possible. For large n, an approximate value is given, based on a normal approximation of the binomial distribution.

Note

The tables give p, the actual confidence level obtained, as it is not possible to obtain a confidence interval at exactly the required confidence levels. For example, for $n = 10$ and $\gamma = 0.95$, the confidence interval given by the table is $[X_{(2)}, X_{(9)}]$; the table states that it is in fact a confidence interval at level 0.979.

The values of j and k are chosen such that j and k are as symmetric as possible around $\frac{n+1}{2}$. For example, for $n = 31$ the table gives the interval $[X_{(10)}, X_{(22)}]$. Note that this is not the only interval that can be obtained from the theorem. Indeed, we have

346

j	k	$\mathbb{P}\left(X_{(j)} < m_{0.5} < X_{(k)}\right)$
9	21	0.959
10	22	0.971
10	23	0.959

Thus we have *several* possible confidence intervals. The table simply picked one for which the indices were the closest to being symmetrical around the estimated median, i.e. the indices j and k are equally spaced around $\frac{n+1}{2}$, which is used for estimating the median. In some cases, e.g. $n = 32$, we do not find such an interval exactly; we have for instance:

j	k	$\mathbb{P}\left(X_{(j)} < m_{0.5} < X_{(k)}\right)$
10	22	0.965
11	23	0.965

Here, the table arbitrarily picked the former.

Table A.1 Quantile $q = 50\%$, Confidence Levels $\gamma = 95\%$ (left) and 0.99% (right).

n	j	k	p	n	j	k	p
$n \leq 5$: no confidence interval possible				$n \leq 7$: no confidence interval possible			
6	1	6	0.969	8	1	8	0.992
7	1	7	0.984	9	1	9	0.996
8	1	7	0.961	10	1	10	0.998
9	2	8	0.961	11	1	11	0.999
10	2	9	0.979	12	2	11	0.994
11	2	10	0.988	13	2	12	0.997
12	3	10	0.961	14	2	12	0.993
13	3	11	0.978	15	3	13	0.993
14	3	11	0.965	16	3	14	0.996
15	4	12	0.965	17	3	15	0.998
16	4	12	0.951	18	4	15	0.992
17	5	13	0.951	19	4	16	0.996
18	5	14	0.969	20	4	16	0.993
19	5	15	0.981	21	5	17	0.993
20	6	15	0.959	22	5	18	0.996
21	6	16	0.973	23	5	19	0.997
22	6	16	0.965	24	6	19	0.993
23	7	17	0.965	25	6	20	0.996
24	7	17	0.957	26	7	20	0.991
25	8	18	0.957	27	7	21	0.994
26	8	19	0.971	28	7	21	0.992
27	8	20	0.981	29	8	22	0.992
28	9	20	0.964	30	8	23	0.995
29	9	21	0.976	31	8	24	0.997
30	10	21	0.957	32	9	24	0.993
31	10	22	0.971	33	9	25	0.995
32	10	22	0.965	34	10	25	0.991
33	11	23	0.965	35	10	26	0.994
34	11	23	0.959	36	10	26	0.992
35	12	24	0.959	37	11	27	0.992
36	12	24	0.953	38	11	27	0.991
37	13	25	0.953	39	12	28	0.991
38	13	26	0.966	40	12	29	0.994
39	13	27	0.976	41	12	30	0.996
40	14	27	0.962	42	13	30	0.992
41	14	28	0.972	43	13	31	0.995
42	15	28	0.956	44	14	31	0.990
43	15	29	0.968	45	14	32	0.993
44	16	29	0.951	46	15	33	0.992
45	16	30	0.964	47	15	33	0.992
46	16	30	0.960	48	15	33	0.991
47	17	31	0.960	49	16	34	0.991
48	17	31	0.956	50	16	35	0.993
49	18	32	0.956	51	16	36	0.995
50	18	32	0.951	52	17	36	0.992
51	19	33	0.951	53	17	37	0.995
52	19	34	0.964	54	18	37	0.991
53	19	35	0.973	55	18	38	0.994
54	20	35	0.960	56	18	38	0.992
55	20	36	0.970	57	19	39	0.992
56	21	36	0.956	58	20	40	0.991
57	21	37	0.967	59	20	40	0.991
58	22	37	0.952	60	20	40	0.990
59	22	38	0.964	61	21	41	0.990
60	23	39	0.960	62	21	42	0.993
61	23	39	0.960	63	21	43	0.995
62	24	40	0.957	64	22	43	0.992
63	24	40	0.957	65	22	44	0.994
64	24	40	0.954	66	23	44	0.991
65	25	41	0.954	67	23	45	0.993
66	25	41	0.950	68	23	45	0.992
67	26	42	0.950	69	24	46	0.992
68	26	43	0.962	70	24	46	0.991
69	26	44	0.971	71	25	47	0.991
70	27	44	0.959	72	25	47	0.990
$n \geq 71$	$\approx \lfloor 0.50n - 0.980\sqrt{n}\rfloor$	$\approx \lceil 0.50n+1 + 0.980\sqrt{n}\rceil$	0.950	$n \geq 73$	$\approx \lfloor 0.50n - 1.288\sqrt{n}\rfloor$	$\approx \lceil 0.50n+1 + 1.288\sqrt{n}\rceil$	0.990

Table A.2 Quantile $q = 75\%$, Confidence Levels $\gamma = 95\%$ (left) and 0.99% (right).

n	j	k	p	n	j	k	p
$n \leq 10$: no confidence interval possible.				$n \leq 16$: no confidence interval possible.			
11	5	11	0.950	17	7	17	0.992
12	6	12	0.954	18	8	18	0.993
13	7	13	0.952	19	9	19	0.993
14	7	14	0.972	20	10	20	0.993
15	8	15	0.969	21	11	21	0.991
16	9	16	0.963	22	11	22	0.995
17	9	17	0.980	23	12	23	0.994
18	9	17	0.955	24	13	24	0.992
19	10	18	0.960	25	13	25	0.996
20	12	20	0.956	26	13	25	0.993
21	12	20	0.960	27	15	27	0.992
22	13	21	0.956	28	15	27	0.993
23	13	22	0.974	29	16	28	0.992
24	14	23	0.970	30	16	29	0.995
25	14	24	0.982	31	17	30	0.994
26	15	24	0.959	32	18	31	0.993
27	16	25	0.958	33	18	32	0.996
28	17	26	0.954	34	19	32	0.991
29	17	27	0.971	35	20	33	0.990
30	17	27	0.954	36	21	35	0.991
31	18	28	0.958	37	21	35	0.993
32	20	30	0.956	38	21	35	0.990
33	20	30	0.958	39	23	37	0.990
34	21	31	0.955	40	23	37	0.991
35	22	32	0.950	41	23	39	0.997
36	22	33	0.968	42	24	39	0.994
37	22	34	0.979	43	25	40	0.993
38	23	34	0.961	44	26	41	0.992
39	24	35	0.960	45	26	42	0.995
40	25	36	0.958	46	27	42	0.990
41	25	37	0.972	47	28	44	0.993
42	25	37	0.961	48	29	45	0.991
43	26	38	0.963	49	29	45	0.993
44	28	40	0.961	50	29	45	0.990
45	28	40	0.963	51	31	47	0.990
46	28	40	0.951	52	31	47	0.991
47	29	41	0.953	53	31	49	0.996
48	31	43	0.952	54	32	49	0.993
49	31	43	0.954	55	33	50	0.993
50	32	44	0.952	56	34	51	0.992
51	32	45	0.966	57	34	52	0.995
52	33	46	0.964	58	35	52	0.991
53	33	47	0.975	59	36	53	0.990
54	34	47	0.959	60	37	55	0.992
55	35	48	0.959	61	37	55	0.993
56	36	49	0.957	62	37	55	0.991
57	36	50	0.969	63	39	57	0.991
58	37	50	0.951	64	39	57	0.991
59	38	51	0.951	65	40	58	0.991
60	39	53	0.961	66	41	59	0.990
61	39	53	0.963	67	41	60	0.993
62	39	53	0.954	68	42	61	0.993
63	40	54	0.956	69	42	62	0.995
64	42	56	0.955	70	43	62	0.992
65	42	56	0.956	71	44	63	0.991
66	43	57	0.955	72	45	64	0.991
67	44	58	0.952	73	45	65	0.994
68	44	59	0.966	74	45	65	0.992
69	44	60	0.975	75	47	67	0.992
70	45	60	0.962	76	48	68	0.991
71	46	61	0.961	77	48	68	0.992
72	47	62	0.960	78	48	68	0.991
73	47	63	0.971	79	50	70	0.991
74	48	63	0.956	80	50	70	0.991
75	49	64	0.956	81	51	71	0.990
$n \geq 76$	$\approx \lfloor 0.75n - 0.849\sqrt{n} \rfloor$	$\approx \lceil 0.75n+1 + 0.849\sqrt{n} \rceil$	0.950	$n \geq 82$	$\approx \lfloor 0.75n - 1.115\sqrt{n} \rfloor$	$\approx \lceil 0.75n+1 + 1.115\sqrt{n} \rceil$	0.990

Table A.3 Quantile $q = 95\%$, confidence levels $\gamma = 95\%$ (left) and 0.99% (right).

n	j	k	p	n	j	k	p
$n \leq 58$: no confidence interval possible				$n \leq 89$: no confidence interval possible			
59	50	59	0.951	90	76	90	0.990
60	52	60	0.951	91	79	91	0.990
61	53	61	0.953	92	80	92	0.990
62	54	62	0.955	93	81	93	0.991
63	55	63	0.957	94	82	94	0.991
64	56	64	0.958	95	83	95	0.991
65	57	65	0.959	96	84	96	0.992
66	58	66	0.961	97	85	97	0.992
67	59	67	0.962	98	86	98	0.992
68	60	68	0.963	99	87	99	0.992
69	61	69	0.964	100	88	100	0.993
70	62	70	0.964	101	89	101	0.993
71	63	71	0.965	102	90	102	0.993
72	64	72	0.965	103	91	103	0.993
73	65	73	0.966	104	92	104	0.993
74	66	74	0.966	105	93	105	0.993
75	67	75	0.966	106	94	106	0.993
76	68	76	0.966	107	95	107	0.993
77	69	77	0.966	108	96	108	0.993
78	70	78	0.966	109	97	109	0.993
79	71	79	0.966	110	98	110	0.993
80	72	80	0.965	111	99	111	0.993
81	73	81	0.964	112	100	112	0.993
82	74	82	0.964	113	101	113	0.993
83	75	83	0.963	114	102	114	0.992
84	76	84	0.962	115	103	115	0.992
85	77	85	0.961	116	104	116	0.992
86	78	86	0.960	117	105	117	0.992
87	79	87	0.959	118	106	118	0.991
88	80	88	0.957	119	107	119	0.991
89	81	89	0.956	120	108	120	0.991
90	82	90	0.954	121	109	121	0.990
91	83	91	0.952	122	109	122	0.995
92	84	92	0.950	123	110	123	0.995
93	84	93	0.974	124	111	124	0.995
94	85	94	0.973	125	112	125	0.994
95	86	95	0.972	126	113	126	0.994
96	87	96	0.971	127	114	127	0.994
97	88	97	0.970	128	115	128	0.994
98	89	98	0.969	129	116	129	0.993
99	90	99	0.967	130	117	130	0.993
100	91	100	0.966	131	118	131	0.993
101	91	100	0.952	132	119	132	0.992
102	92	101	0.953	133	120	133	0.992
103	93	102	0.953	134	121	134	0.992
104	94	103	0.954	135	122	135	0.991
105	95	104	0.954	136	123	136	0.991
106	96	105	0.954	137	124	137	0.990
107	97	106	0.954	138	124	138	0.995
108	98	107	0.954	139	125	139	0.995
109	99	108	0.954	140	126	140	0.995
110	100	109	0.954	141	127	141	0.994
111	101	110	0.954	142	127	141	0.992
112	102	111	0.953	143	128	142	0.992
113	103	112	0.953	144	129	143	0.992
114	104	113	0.952	145	130	144	0.992
115	105	114	0.951	146	131	145	0.992
116	106	115	0.950	147	133	147	0.992
117	107	117	0.965	148	134	148	0.992
118	108	118	0.963	149	135	149	0.992
119	109	119	0.961	150	136	150	0.991
120	110	120	0.959	151	137	151	0.991
121	110	120	0.967	152	138	152	0.990
122	111	121	0.966	153	138	152	0.992
123	112	122	0.966	154	139	153	0.992
$n \geq 124$	$\approx \lfloor 0.95n - 0.427\sqrt{n} \rfloor$	$\approx \lceil 0.95n+1 + 0.427\sqrt{n} \rceil$	0.950	$n \geq 155$	$\approx \lfloor 0.95n - 0.561\sqrt{n} \rfloor$	$\approx \lceil 0.95n+1 + 0.561\sqrt{n} \rceil$	0.990

Parametric Estimation, Large Sample Theory

B.1 Parametric Estimation Theory

In this appendix, we give a large sample theory that is used for some asymptotic confidence interval computations in Chapter 2 and for the general framework of likelihood ratio tests in Chapter 4.

B.1.1 The Parametric Estimation Framework

Consider a data set x_i, $i = 1, \ldots, n$, which we view as the realization of a stochastic system (in other words, the output of a simulator). The framework of parametric estimation theory consists in assuming that the parameters of the stochastic system are well-defined, but unknown to the observer, who tries to estimate the system as well as possible, using the data set.

We assume here that the model has a density of probability, denoted $f(x_1, \ldots, x_n \mid \theta)$, where θ is the parameter. It is also called the **likelihood** of the observed data. An **estimator** of θ is any function $T(\cdot)$ of the observed data. A good estimator is one such that, in average, $T(x_1, \ldots, x_n)$ is "close" to the true value θ.

Example B.1 iid Normal Data
Assume that we can believe that our data is iid and normal with the mean μ and variance σ^2. The likelihood is

$$\frac{1}{\left(\sqrt{2\pi}\sigma\right)^n} \exp\left(-\frac{1}{2}\sum_{i=1}^{n}\frac{(x_i-\mu)^2}{\sigma^2}\right) \tag{B.1}$$

and $\theta = (\mu, \sigma)$. An estimator of θ is $\hat{\theta} = (\hat{\mu}_n, \hat{\sigma}_n)$ given by Theorem 2.3. Another, slightly different estimator is $\hat{\theta}_1 = (\hat{\mu}_n, s_n)$ given by Theorem 2.2.

An estimator provides a random result: for every realization of the data set, a different estimation is produced. The "goodness" of an estimator is captured by the following definitions. Here, $\vec{X}$ is the random data set, $T(\vec{X})$ is the estimator and $\mathbb{E}_\theta$ corresponds to the expectation when the unknown but fixed parameter value is θ.

- **Unbiased estimator**: $\mathbb{E}_\theta\big(T(\vec{X})\big) = \theta$. For example, the estimator $\hat{\sigma}_n^2$ of variance of a normal iid sample given by Theorem 2.3 is unbiased.

- **Consistent family of estimators**: $\mathbb{P}_\theta\big(\big|T(\vec{X})\big| - \theta\big) > \epsilon \to 0$ when the sample size n goes to ∞. For example, the estimator $(\hat{\mu}_n, \hat{\sigma}_n)$ of Theorem 2.3 is consistent. This follows from the weak law of large numbers.

B.1.2   Maximum Likelihood Estimator (MLE)

A commonly used method for deriving estimators is that of **maximum likelihood**. The maximum likelihood estimator is the value of θ that maximizes the likelihood $f(x_1, \ldots, x_n \mid \theta)$. This definition makes sense if the maximum exists and is unique, which is often true in practice. A formal set of conditions is the regularity condition in Definition B.1.

In Section B.2, we give a result that shows that the MLE for an iid sample with finite variance is asymptotically unbiased, i.e. the bias tends to 0 as the sample size increases. It is also consistent.

Example B.2   MLE for iid normal data

Consider a sample $(x_1, \ldots, x_n)$ obtained from a normal iid random vector $(X_1, \ldots, X_n)$. The likelihood is given by (B.1). We want to maximize it, where $x_1, \ldots, x_n$ are given and $\mu, v = \sigma^2$ are the variables. For a given v, the maximum is reached when $\mu = \hat{\mu}_n = \frac{1}{n}\sum_{i=1}^n x_i$. Let μ have this value and find the value of v that maximizes the resulting expression, or to simplify, the log of it. We thus have to maximize

$$-\frac{n}{2}\ln v - \frac{1}{2v}S_{x,x} + C \qquad (B.2)$$

where $S_{x,x} \overset{\text{def}}{=} \sum_{i=1}^n (x - \hat{\mu}_n)^2$ and C is a constant with respect to v. This is a simple maximization problem in one variable v, which can be solved by computing the derivative. We find that there is a maximum for $v = \frac{S_{x,x}}{n}$. The maximum likelihood estimator of (μ, v) is thus precisely the estimator in Theorem 2.2.

We say that an estimation method is **invariant by re-parametrization** if a different parametrization gives essentially the same estimator. More precisely, assume that we have a method that produces some estimator $T(\vec{X})$ for θ. Assume that we re-parametrize the problem by considering that the parameter is $\phi(\theta)$, where ϕ is some invertible mapping. For example, a normal iid sample can be parametrized by $\theta = (\mu, v)$ or by $\phi(\theta) = (\mu, \sigma)$, with $v = \sigma^2$. The method is called invariant by re-parametrization if the estimator of $\phi(\theta)$ is precisely $\phi\big(T(\vec{X})\big)$.

The maximum likelihood method *is* invariant by re-parametrization. This is because the property of being a maximum is invariant by re-parametrization. It is an important property in our context, since the model is usually not given a priori, but has to be invented by the performance analyst.

A method that provides an unbiased estimator can generally not be invariant by re-parametrization. For example, $(\hat{\mu}_n, \hat{\sigma}_n^2)$ of Theorem 2.3 is an unbiased estimator of (μ, σ^2), but $(\hat{\mu}_n, \hat{\sigma}_n)$ is a *biased* estimator of (μ, σ) (because usually $\mathbb{E}(S)^2 \neq \mathbb{E}(S^2)$, except if S is non-random). Thus, the property of being unbiased is incompatible with invariance by re-parametrization, and may thus be seen as an inadequate requirement for an estimator.

Furthermore, the maximum likelihood is also ***invariant by reversible data transformation***, i.e. the MLE of θ is the same, whether we look at the data or at a one-to-one transform, independent of θ. More precisely, assume that $\vec{X} = (X_i)_{i=1,\ldots,n}$ has a joint PDF $f_{\vec{X}}(\vec{x} \mid \theta)$, and let $\vec{Y} = \varphi(\vec{X})$, where φ is a one-to-one, differentiable mapping independent of θ.

Take $\vec{X}$ as data and estimate θ; we have to maximize $f_{\vec{X}}(\vec{x} \mid \theta)$ with respect to θ, where $\vec{x} = (x_i)_{i=1\ldots,n}$ is the available data. If, instead, we observe $y_i = \varphi(x_i)$ for all i, we have to maximize

$$f_{\vec{Y}}(\vec{y} \mid \theta) = \frac{1}{|\varphi'(\vec{x})|} f_{\vec{X}}(\vec{x} \mid \theta)$$

where $|\varphi'(\vec{x})|$ is the absolute value of the determinant of the differential of φ (i.e. the Jacobian matrix).

In particular, the MLE is invariant by *re-scaling* of the data. For example, if Y_i is a log-normal sample (i.e. if $Y_i = e^{X_i}$ and $X_i \sim$ iid N_{μ,σ^2}), then the MLE of the parameters μ, θ can be obtained by estimating the mean and standard deviation of $\ln(Y_i)$.

B.1.3   Efficiency and Fisher Information

The ***efficiency*** of an estimator $T(\vec{X})$ of the parameter θ is defined as the expected square error $\mathbb{E}_\theta \left(\left\| T(\vec{X}) - \theta \right\|^2 \right)$ (here, we assume that θ takes values in some space Θ where the norm is defined). The efficiency that can be reached by an estimator is captured by the concept of Fisher information, which we now define. For the sake of simplifying, assume first that $\theta \in \mathbb{R}$. The ***observed information*** is defined by

$$J(\theta) = -\frac{\partial^2 l(\theta)}{\partial \theta^2}$$

where $l(\theta)$ is the ***log-likelihood***, defined by

$$l(\theta) = \ln \mathrm{lik}(\theta) = \ln f(x_1, \ldots, x_n \mid \theta)$$

The ***Fisher information***, or ***expected information*** is defined by

$$I(\theta) = \mathbb{E}_\theta \big(J(\theta) \big) = \mathbb{E}_\theta \left(-\frac{\partial^2 l(\theta)}{\partial \theta^2} \right)$$

For an iid model, $X_1, \ldots, X_n$, $l(\theta) = \sum_i \ln f_1(x_i \mid \theta)$ and thus $I(\theta) = nI_1(\theta)$, where $I_1(\theta)$ is the Fisher information for a one-point sample X_1. The Cramer-Rao Theorem states that the efficiency of any *unbiased* estimator is lower bounded by $\frac{1}{I(\theta)}$. Further, under the conditions in Definition B.1, the MLE for an iid sample is asymptotically maximally efficient, i.e. $\mathbb{E}\left(\left\| T(\vec{X}) - \theta \right\|^2 \right) I(\theta)$ tends to 1 as the sample size goes to infinity.

In general, the parameter θ is multi-dimensional, i.e. it varies in an open subset Θ of $\mathbb{R}^k$. Consequently, J and I are symmetric matrices defined by

$$\left[J(\theta) \right]_{i,j} = -\frac{\partial^2 l(\theta)}{\partial \theta_i \partial \theta_j}$$

and

$$\left[I(\theta) \right]_{i,j} = -\mathbb{E}_\theta \left(\frac{\partial^2 l(\theta)}{\partial \theta_i \partial \theta_j} \right)$$

The Cramer-Rao lower bound justifies the name of "information". The variance of the MLE is of the order of the Fisher information: the higher the information, the more the sample tells us about the unknown parameter θ. The Fisher information is not the same as entropy, used in information theory. There are some (complicated) relations – see [30, Chapter 16].

In the next section, we give a more accurate result, which can be used to provide approximate confidence intervals for large sample sizes.

B.2   Asymptotic Confidence Intervals

Here, we need to assume some regularity conditions. Assume that the sample comes from an iid sequence of length n and further, that the following regularity conditions are met.

Definition B.1

The regularity conditions for maximum likelihood asymptotics are [32]:

(1) The set Θ of values of θ is compact (closed and bounded) and the true value θ_0 is not on the boundary.

(2) (identifiability) For varying values of θ, the densities $f(\vec{x} \mid \theta)$ differ.

(3) (regularity of derivatives) There exist a neighborhood B of θ_0 and a constant K such that for $\theta \in B$ and for all i, j, k, n:

$$\frac{1}{n} \mathbb{E}_\theta \left(\left| \frac{\partial^3 l_{\vec{X}}(\theta)}{\partial \theta_i \partial \theta_j \partial \theta_k} \right| \right) \leq K$$

(4) For $\theta \in B$, the Fisher information has full rank.

---

(5) For $\theta \in B$, the interchanges of integration and derivation in

$$\int \frac{\partial f(\vec{x} \mid \theta)}{\partial \theta_i} \, dx = \frac{\partial}{\partial \theta_i} \int f(\vec{x} \mid \theta) \, dx$$

$$\int \frac{\partial^2 f(x \mid \theta)}{\partial \theta_i \partial \theta_j} \, dx = \frac{\partial}{\partial \theta_i} \int \frac{\partial f(\vec{x} \mid \theta)}{\partial \theta_j} \, dx$$

are valid.

The following theorem is proven in [32].

Theorem B.1

Under the conditions in Definition B.1, the MLE exists, converges almost surely to the true value. Further $I(\theta)^{1/2}(\hat{\theta} - \theta)$ converges in distribution towards a standard normal distribution, as n goes to infinity. It follows that, asymptotically:

(1) the distribution of $\hat{\theta} - \theta$ can be approximated by

$$N\left(0, I(\hat{\theta})^{-1}\right) \quad or \quad N\left(0, J(\hat{\theta})^{-1}\right)$$

(2) the distribution of $2\big(l(\hat{\theta}) - l(\theta)\big)$ can be approximated by χ_k^2 (where k is the dimension of Θ).

The quantity $2\big(l(\hat{\theta}) - l(\theta)\big)$ is called the **likelihood ratio statistic**.

In the examples seen in this book, the regularity conditions are always satisfied, as long as: the true value θ lies within the interior of its domain, the derivatives of $l(\theta)$ are smooth (e.g. if the density $f(\vec{x} \mid \theta)$ has derivatives at all orders) and the matrices $J(\theta)$ and $I(\theta)$ have full rank. If the regularity conditions hold, we have an equivalent definition of Fisher information:

$$\big[I(\theta)\big]_{i,j} \stackrel{\text{def}}{=} -\mathbb{E}_\theta\left(\frac{\partial^2 l(\theta)}{\partial \theta_i \partial \theta_j}\right) = \mathbb{E}_\theta\left(\frac{\partial l(\theta)}{\partial \theta_i} \frac{\partial l(\theta)}{\partial \theta_j}\right)$$

This follows from differentiating, with respect to θ, the identity $\int f(x\theta) \, dx = 1$.

Item (2) is more approximate than item (1), but does not require the second derivative of the likelihood to be computed.

Theorem B.1 also holds for non-iid cases, as long as the Fisher information goes to infinity with the sample size.

Example B.3 Fisher Information of Normal iid Model

Assume that $(X_i)_{i=1...n}$ is iid normal with the mean μ and the variance σ^2. The observed information matrix is computed from the likelihood function; we obtain

$$J = \begin{pmatrix} \dfrac{n}{\sigma^2} & \dfrac{2n}{\sigma^3}(\hat{\mu}_n - \mu) \\[3mm] \dfrac{2n}{\sigma^3}(\hat{\mu}_n - \mu) & \dfrac{-n}{\sigma^2} + \dfrac{3}{\sigma^4}\big(S_{xx} + n(\hat{\mu}_n - \mu)^2\big) \end{pmatrix}$$

and the expected information matrix (Fisher's information) is

$$I = \begin{pmatrix} \dfrac{n}{\sigma^2} & 0 \\ 0 & \dfrac{2n}{\sigma^2} \end{pmatrix}$$

The following corollary is used in practice. It follows immediately from the theorem.

Corollary B.1 (Asymptotic Confidence Intervals) *When n is large, approximate confidence intervals can be obtained as follows:*

(1) For the ith coordinate of θ, the interval is

$$\hat{\theta}_i \pm \eta \sqrt{\left[I(\hat{\theta})^{-1}\right]_{i,i}} \qquad or \qquad \hat{\theta} \pm \eta \sqrt{\left[J(\hat{\theta})^{-1}\right]_{i,i}}$$

where $N_{0,1}(\eta) = \frac{1+\gamma}{2}$ (e.g. with $\gamma = 0.95$, $\eta = 1.96$).

(2) If θ is in $\mathbb{R}$, the interval can be defined implicitly as $\{\theta : l(\hat{\theta}) - \frac{\xi}{2} \le l(\theta) \le l(\hat{\theta})\}$, where $\chi_1^2(\xi) = \gamma$. For example, with $\gamma = 0.95$, $\xi = 3.84$.

Example B.4 Lazy Normal iid

Assume that our data comes from an iid normal model X_i, $i = 1, \dots, n$. We compare the exact confidence interval for the mean (from Theorem 2.3) to the approximate ones given by the corollary.
The MLE of (μ, σ) is $(\hat{\mu}_n, s_n)$. The exact confidence interval is

$$\hat{\mu}_n \pm \eta' \frac{\hat{\sigma}_n}{\sqrt{n}}$$

with $\hat{\sigma}_n^2 = \frac{S_{x,x}}{n-1}$ and $t_{n-1}(\eta') = \frac{1+\gamma}{2}$.
We now compute the approximate confidence interval obtained from the Fisher information. We have

$$I(\mu, \sigma)^{-1} = \begin{pmatrix} \dfrac{\sigma^2}{n} & 0 \\ 0 & \dfrac{\sigma^2}{2n} \end{pmatrix}$$

thus the distribution of $(\mu - \hat{\mu}_n, \sigma - s_n)$ is approximately normal with a 0 mean and covariance matrix $\begin{pmatrix} \sigma^2/n & 0 \\ 0 & \sigma^2/2n \end{pmatrix}$. It follows that $\mu - \hat{\mu}_n$ is approximately $N\left(0, \frac{s_n^2}{n}\right)$, and an approximate confidence interval is

$$\hat{\mu}_n \pm \eta \frac{s_n}{\sqrt{n}}$$

with $s_n = \frac{S_{x,x}}{n}$ and $N_{0,1}(\eta) = \frac{1+\gamma}{2}$.

Table B.1 Confidence Interval for σ for an iid, normal sample of n data points by an exact method and an asymptotic result with Fisher information (Corollary B.1). The values represent the confidence bounds for the ratio $\frac{\sigma}{\hat{\sigma}_n}$, where σ is the true value and $\hat{\sigma}_n$ is the estimated standard deviation as in Theorem 2.3.

n	30	60	120
Exact	$0.7964 - 1.3443$	$0.8476 - 1.2197$	$0.8875 - 1.1454$
Fisher	$0.7847 - 1.3162$	$0.8411 - 1.2077$	$0.8840 - 1.1401$

Thus the use of Fisher information gives the same asymptotic interval for the mean as Theorem 2.2. This is quite general: the use of Fisher information is the generalization of the large sample asymptotic of Theorem 2.2.

We can also compare the approximate confidence interval for σ. The exact interval is given by Theorem 2.3: with probability γ, we have

$$\frac{\xi_2}{n-1} \leq \frac{\hat{\sigma}_2^n}{\sigma^2} \leq \frac{\xi_1}{n-1}$$

with $\chi_{n-1}^2(\xi_2) = \frac{1-\gamma}{2}$ and $\chi_{n-1}^2(\xi_1) = \frac{1+\gamma}{2}$. Thus, an exact confidence interval for σ is

$$\hat{\sigma}_n \left[\sqrt{\frac{n-1}{\xi_1}}, \sqrt{\frac{n-1}{\xi_2}} \right] \tag{B.3}$$

With Fisher information, we obtain that $\sigma - s_n$ is approximately $N_{0,\,\sigma^2/2n}$. Consequently, with probability γ,

$$|\sigma - s_n| \leq \eta \frac{\sigma}{\sqrt{2n}}$$

with $N_{0,1}(\eta) = \frac{1+\gamma}{2}$.

Divide by σ and obtain, after some algebra, that with probability γ

$$\frac{1}{1 + \dfrac{\eta}{\sqrt{2n}}} \leq \frac{\sigma}{s_n} \leq \frac{1}{1 - \dfrac{\eta}{\sqrt{2n}}}$$

Taking into account that $s_n = \sqrt{\frac{n-1}{n}} \hat{\sigma}_n$, we obtain the approximate confidence interval for σ

$$\hat{\sigma}_n \left[\sqrt{\frac{n-1}{n}} \frac{1}{1 + \dfrac{\eta}{\sqrt{2n}}}, \sqrt{\frac{n-1}{n}} \frac{1}{1 - \dfrac{\eta}{\sqrt{2n}}} \right] \tag{B.4}$$

For $n = 30, 60, 120$ and $\gamma = 0.95$, the confidence intervals are as shown in Table B.1, where we compare to exact values; the difference is negligible already for $n = 30$.

QUESTION 2.1 Which of the following are random variables: $\hat{\theta}$, θ, $l(\theta)$, $l(\hat{\theta})$, $J(\theta)$, $I(\theta)$, $J(\hat{\theta})$, $I(\hat{\theta})$?[1]

B.3   Confidence Interval in Presence of Nuisance Parameters

In many cases, the parameter has the form $\theta = (\mu, \nu)$, and we are interested only in μ (e.g. for a normal model: the mean) while the remaining element ν, which still needs to be estimated, is considered a nuisance (e.g. the variance). In such cases, we can use the following theorem to find confidence intervals.

Theorem B.2 ([32])

Under the conditions in Definition B.1, assume that $\Theta = M \times N$, where M, N are open subsets of $\mathbb{R}^p, \mathbb{R}^q$. Thus the parameter is $\theta = (\mu, \nu)$ with $\mu \in M$ and $\nu \in N$ (p is the "dimension", or number of degrees of freedom, of μ).

For any μ, let $\hat{\nu}_\mu$ be the solution to

$$l(\mu, \hat{\nu}_\mu) = \max_\nu l(\mu, \nu)$$

*and define the **profile log likelihood** pl by*

$$\mathrm{pl}(\mu) \stackrel{\text{def}}{=} \max_\nu l(\mu, \nu) = l(\mu, \hat{\nu}_\mu)$$

Let $(\hat{\mu}, \hat{\nu})$ be the MLE If (μ, ν) is the true value of the parameter, the distribution of $2\big(\mathrm{pl}(\hat{\mu}) - \mathrm{pl}(\mu)\big)$ tends to χ_p^2.

An approximate confidence region for μ at level γ is

$$\left\{ \mu \in M : \mathrm{pl}(\mu) \geq \mathrm{pl}(\hat{\mu}) - \frac{1}{2}\xi \right\}$$

where $\chi_p^2(\xi) = \gamma$.

   The theorem essentially states that we can find an approximate confidence interval for the parameter of interest μ by computing the profile log-likelihood for all values of μ around the estimated value. The estimated value is the one that maximizes the profile log-likelihood. The profile log likelihood is obtained by fixing the parameter of interest μ to some arbitrary value and computing the MLE for the other parameters. A confidence interval is obtained implicitly as the set of values of μ for which the profile log likelihood is close to the maximum. In practice, all of this is done numerically.

---

[1]In the classical, non-Bayesian framework: $\hat{\theta}$, $l(\theta)$, $l(\hat{\theta})$, $J(\theta)$, $J(\hat{\theta})$, $I(\hat{\theta})$ are random variables; θ and $I(\theta)$ are non-random but unknown.

Example B.5 Lazy Normal iid Revisited

Consider the log of the data in Figure 2.12, which appears to be normal. The model is $Y_i \sim$ iid N_{μ,σ^2}, where Y_i is the log of the data. Assume that we would like to compute a confidence interval for μ but that we are too lazy to apply the exact Student statistic in Theorem 2.3.

For any μ, we estimate the nuisance parameter σ, by maximizing the log-likelihood:

$$l(\mu, \sigma) = -\frac{1}{2}\left(n \ln \sigma^2 + \frac{1}{\sigma^2}\sum_i (Y_i - \mu)^2\right)$$

We obtain

$$\hat{\sigma}_\mu^2 = \frac{1}{n}\sum_i (Y_i - \mu)^2 = \frac{1}{n}S_{YY} + (\bar{Y} - \mu)^2$$

and thus

$$\mathrm{pl}(\mu) \stackrel{\text{def}}{=} l(\mu, \hat{\sigma}_\mu) = -\frac{n}{2}\left(\ln \hat{\sigma}_\mu^2 + 1\right)$$

In Figure B.1, we plot $\mathrm{pl}(\mu)$. We find $\hat{\mu} = 1.510$ as the point that maximizes $\mathrm{pl}(\mu)$. A 95%-confidence interval is obtained as the set $\left\{\mathrm{pl}(\mu) \geq \mathrm{pl}(\hat{\mu}) - \frac{1}{2}3.84\right\}$. We obtain the interval $[1.106, 1.915]$. Compare to the exact confidence interval obtained with Theorem 2.3, which is equal to $[1.103, 1.918]$: the difference is negligible.

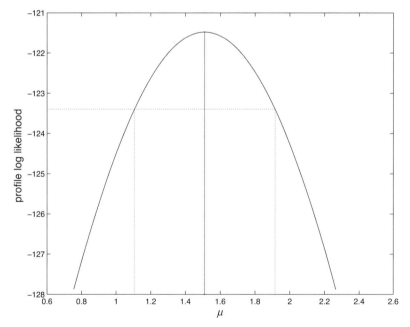

Figure B.1 The profile log-likelihood for parameter μ of the log of the data in Figure 2.12. The confidence interval for μ is obtained by application of Theorem B.2.

QUESTION 2.2 Find an analytical expression of the confidence interval obtained with the profile log likelihood for this example and compare to the exact interval.[2]

Example B.6 Re-Scaling

Consider the data in Figure 2.12, which does not appear to be normal in natural scale, and for which we would like to perform a Box-Cox transformation. We would like a confidence interval for the exponent of the transformation.

The transformed data is $Y_i = b_s(X_i)$, and the model now assumes that Y_i is iid $\sim N_{\mu,\sigma^2}$. We take the unknown parameter to be $\theta = (\mu, \sigma, s)$. The distribution of X_i, under θ, is

$$f_{X_i}(x \mid \theta) = b_s'(x)f_{Y_i}\big(b_s(x) \mid \mu, \sigma\big) = x^{s-1}h\big(b_s(x) \mid \mu, \sigma^2\big)$$

where $h(x \mid \mu, \sigma^2)$ is the density of the normal distribution with mean μ and variance σ^2.

The log-likelihood is

$$l(\mu, \sigma, s) = C - n\ln\sigma + \sum_i \left((s-1)\ln x_i - \frac{\big(b_s(x_i) - \mu\big)^2}{2\sigma^2} \right)$$

where C is some constant (independent of the parameter). For a fixed s, it is maximized by the MLE for a Gaussian sample

$$\hat{\mu}_s = \frac{1}{n}\sum_i b_s(x_i)$$

$$\hat{\sigma}_s^2 = \frac{1}{n}\sum_i \big(b_s(x_i) - \hat{\mu}\big)^2$$

We can use a numerical estimation to find the value of s that maximizes $l(\hat{\mu}_s, \hat{\sigma}_s, s)$; see Figure B.2 for a plot. The estimated value is $\hat{s} = 0.0041$, which gives $\hat{\mu} = 1.5236$ and $\hat{\sigma} = 2.0563$.

We now give a confidence interval for s, using the asymptotic result in Theorem B.2. A 95% confidence interval is readily obtained from Figure B.2, which gives the interval $[-0.0782, 0.0841]$.

---

[2] The profile log likelihood method gives a confidence interval defined by

$$\frac{(\hat{\mu} - \mu)^2}{S_{YY}/n} \le e^{\eta/n} - 1 \approx \frac{\eta}{n}$$

Let $t \stackrel{\text{def}}{=} \frac{\hat{\mu} - \mu}{\sqrt{S_{YY}/n(n-1)}}$ be the Student statistic. The asymptotic confidence interval can be rewritten as

$$t^2 \le (n-1)(e^{\eta/n} - 1) \approx \frac{\eta(n-1)}{n}$$

An exact confidence interval is $t^2 \le \xi^2$, where $\xi = t_{n-1}\frac{1-\alpha}{2}$. For large n, $\xi^2 \approx \eta$ and $\frac{n-1}{n} \approx 1$ so the two intervals are equivalent.

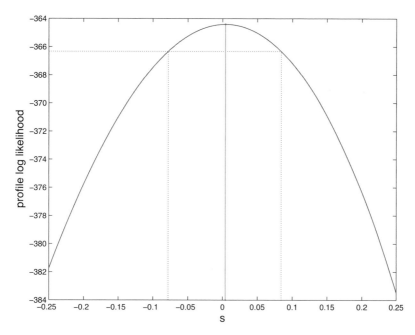

Figure B.2 Profile log-likelihood for Example B.6, as a function of the Box-Cox exponent s. The maximum likelihood estimator of s is the value that maximizes the profile log likelihood: a confidence interval for s is the set of s for which the profile log-likelihood is below the horizontal dashed line.

QUESTION 2.3 Does the confidence interval justify the log transformation?[3]

Alternatively, by Theorem B.1, we can approximate the distribution of $\hat{\theta} - \theta$ by a centered normal distribution with covariance matrix $J(\hat{\theta})^{-1}$. After some algebra, we compute the Fisher information matrix. We compute the second derivative of the log-likelihood, and estimate the Fisher information by the observed information (i.e. the value of the second derivative at $\theta = \hat{\theta}$). We find

$$
J = \begin{pmatrix} 23.7 & 0 & -77.1 \\ 0 & 47.3 & -146.9 \\ 77.1 & -146.9 & 1291.1 \end{pmatrix}
$$

and

$$
J^{-1} = \begin{pmatrix} 0.0605 & 0.0173 & 0.0056 \\ 0.0173 & 0.0377 & 0.0053 \\ 0.0056 & 0.0053 & 0.0017 \end{pmatrix}
$$

---

[3]Yes, since 0 lies within the interval.

The last term of the matrix is an estimate of the variance of $\hat{s} - s$. The 0.95 confidence interval obtained from a normal approximation is $\hat{s} \pm 1.96 \sqrt{0.0017} = [-0.0770, 0.0852]$.

Gaussian Random Vectors in $\mathbb{R}^n$

C.1 Notation and a Few Results of Linear Algebra

C.1.1 Notation

Unless otherwise specified, we view a vector in $\mathbb{R}^n$ as a column vector, and denote identifiers of vectors with an arrow, as in

$$\vec{X} = \begin{pmatrix} X_1 \\ \vdots \\ X_n \end{pmatrix}$$

The identity matrix is denoted with Id.

Matrix transposition is denoted with ^{T}, giving, for example, $\vec{X}^T = (X_1, \ldots, X_n)$ and $\vec{X} = (X_1, \ldots, X_n)^T$.

The **inner product** of $\vec{u}, \vec{v} \in \mathbb{R}^n$ is

$$\vec{u}^T \vec{v} = \vec{v}^T \vec{u} = \sum_{i=1}^{n} u_i v_i$$

The **norm** of $\vec{u}$ is, otherwise specified, the Euclidian norm, i.e.

$$\|\vec{u}\| = \sqrt{\vec{u}^T \vec{u}}$$

An **orthogonal matrix** U is one that satisfies any one of the following equivalent properties:

(1) its columns have unit norm and are orthogonal;
(2) its rows have unit norm and are orthogonal;
(3) $UU^T = \text{Id}$;
(4) $U^T U = \text{Id}$;
(5) U has an inverse and $U^{-1} = U^T$.

C.1.2 Linear Algebra

If M is a linear subspace of $\mathbb{R}^n$, the **orthogonal projection** on M is the linear mapping, Π_M, from $\mathbb{R}^n$ to itself such that $\Pi_M(\vec{x})$ is the element of M that minimizes the distance to $\vec{x}$:

$$\Pi_M(\vec{x}) = \arg\min_{\vec{y} \in M} \|\vec{y} - \vec{x}\| \tag{C.1}$$

$\Pi_M(\vec{x})$ is also the unique element $\vec{y} \in M$ such that $\vec{y} - \vec{x}$ is orthogonal to M. Π_M is symmetric $(\Pi_M = \Pi_M^T)$ and idempotent $(\Pi_M^2 = \Pi_M)$.

Π_M can always be put in diagonal form as follows:

$$\Pi_M = U^T D U$$

with

$$D = \begin{pmatrix} 1 & 0 & \cdots & & & & \\ 0 & 1 & \cdots & & & & \\ \vdots & \vdots & \ddots & & & & \\ & & & 1 & 0 & \cdots & \\ & & & 0 & \cdots & & 0 \\ & & & \vdots & & \ddots & \\ & & & 0 & \cdots & & 0 \end{pmatrix} \tag{C.2}$$

where the number of 1s on the diagonal is the dimension of M, and U is an orthogonal matrix.

Let H be an $n \times p$ matrix, with $p \leq n$, and M the linear space spanned by the columns of the matrix H, i.e.

$$M = \left\{ \vec{y} \in \mathbb{R}^n : \vec{y} = H\vec{z} \text{ for some } \vec{z} \in \mathbb{R}^p \right\}$$

If H has full rank (i.e. rank p), then $H^T H$ has an inverse and

$$\Pi_M = H\left(H^T H\right)^{-1} H^T \tag{C.3}$$

C.2 Covariance Matrix of a Random Vector in $\mathbb{R}^n$

C.2.1 Definitions

Let $\vec{X}$ be a random vector with values in $\mathbb{R}^n$. If each of the components $X_1, \ldots, X_n$ has a well-defined expectation, then $\mathbb{E}(\vec{X})$ is defined as

$$\mathbb{E}(\vec{X}) = \begin{pmatrix} \mathbb{E}(X_1) \\ \vdots \\ \mathbb{E}(X_n) \end{pmatrix}$$

For any non-random matrices H and K (with appropriate dimensions such that the matrix products are valid)

$$\mathbb{E}(H\vec{X}K) = H\mathbb{E}(\vec{X})K \tag{C.4}$$

Further, if $\mathbb{E}(X_i^2) < \infty$ for each $i = 1, \ldots, n$, the **covariance matrix** of $\vec{X}$ is defined by

$$\Omega = E\left((\vec{X} - \vec{\mu})(\vec{X} - \vec{\mu})^T\right) \tag{C.5}$$

with $\vec{\mu} = \mathbb{E}(\vec{X})$. This is equivalent to

$$\Omega_{i,j} = \text{cov}(X_i, X_j) \overset{\text{def}}{=} \mathbb{E}\left((X_i - \mathbb{E}(X_i))(X_j - \mathbb{E}(X_j))\right) \tag{C.6}$$

for all $i, j \in \{1, \ldots, n\}$.

Further, for any $\vec{u}, \vec{v} \in \mathbb{R}^n$

$$\mathbb{E}\left((\vec{u}^T(\vec{X} - \vec{\mu}))(\vec{v}^T(\vec{X} - \vec{\mu}))\right) = \vec{u}^T \Omega \vec{v} \tag{C.7}$$

Also

$$\Omega_{i,i} = \text{var}(X_i) \tag{C.8}$$

If $\vec{X}$ and $\vec{Y}$ are random vectors in $\mathbb{R}^n$ and $\mathbb{R}^p$ with well defined covariance matrices, the **cross covariance matrix** of X and Y is the $n \times p$ matrix defined by

$$\Gamma = E\left((\vec{X} - \vec{\mu})(\vec{Y} - \vec{\nu})^T\right) \tag{C.9}$$

with $\vec{\mu} = \mathbb{E}(\vec{X})$ and $\vec{\nu} = \mathbb{E}(\vec{Y})$.

C.2.2 Properties of Covariance Matrix

The covariance matrix is symmetric ($\Omega = \Omega^T$) and **positive semi-definite**. The latter means that $u^T \Omega u \geq 0$ for all $u \in \mathbb{R}^n$, which follows immediately from (C.7).

If $\vec{X}' = \vec{X} + \nu$, where $\nu \in \mathbb{R}^n$ is a non-random vector, then the covariance matrices of $\vec{X}'$ and $\vec{X}$ are identical.

If $\vec{X}' = AX$, where $\vec{X}'$ is a random vector in $\mathbb{R}^{n'}$ and A is a non-random $n' \times n$ matrix, the covariance matrix Ω' of $\vec{X}'$ is

$$\Omega' = A\Omega A^T \tag{C.10}$$

Any covariance matrix can be put in standard diagonal form as follows:

$$\Omega = U^T \begin{pmatrix} \lambda_1 & 0 & \cdots & & & & \\ 0 & \lambda_2 & \cdots & & & & \\ \vdots & \vdots & \ddots & & & & \\ & & & \lambda_r & 0 & \cdots & \\ & & & 0 & \cdots & 0 & \\ & & & \vdots & \ddots & & \\ & & & 0 & \cdots & 0 & \end{pmatrix} U \tag{C.11}$$

where U is an orthogonal matrix $(U^T = U^{-1})$, r is the rank of Ω and $\lambda_1 \geq \ldots \geq \lambda_r > 0$.

It follows from this representation that the equation $\vec{x}^T \Omega \vec{x} = 0$ has a non-zero solution $(\vec{x} \neq \vec{0})$ if, and only if, Ω has full rank.

C.2.3   Choleski's Factorization

Equation (C.11) can be replaced by a computationally much less expensive reduction, called **Choleski's factorization**. This is a polynomial time algorithm for finding a lower triangular matrix L such that $\Omega = LL^T$. Choleski's factorization applies to positive semi-definite matrices and is readily available in many software packages.

C.2.4   Degrees of Freedom

Let $V = \mathrm{span}(\Omega)$ be the linear sub-space of $\mathbb{R}^n$ spanned by the columns (or rows, since Ω is symmetric) of Ω. Recall that $\vec{X}$ is not necessarily Gaussian.

Proposition C.1 $\vec{X}$ *is constrained to the affine sub-space parallel to V that contains $\vec{\mu} = \mathbb{E}(\vec{X})$, i.e. $\vec{X} - \vec{\mu} \in V$ with probability 1.*

It follows that the number of **degrees of freedom** of $\vec{X}$ (defined in this case as the smallest dimension of an affine space that $\vec{X}$ can be imbedded in) is equal to the dimension of V, namely, the rank of Ω. In particular, if Ω does not have full rank, V has zero mass (its Lebesgue measure is 0) and the integral of any function on V is 0. Thus, it is impossible that $\vec{X}$ has a probability density function. Conversely,

Corollary C.1 *If $\vec{X}$ has a probability density function (PDF) then its covariance matrix Ω is invertible.*

Example C.1

In $\mathbb{R}^3$, let the covariance matrix of $\vec{X}$ to be

$$\Omega = \begin{pmatrix} a & 0 & a \\ 0 & b & b \\ a & b & a+b \end{pmatrix} \qquad (C.12)$$

where a, b are positive constants. The rank is $r = 2$. The linear space generated by the columns of Ω is the plane defined by $x_1 + x_2 - x_3 = 0$. Thus the random vector $\vec{X} = (X_1, X_2, X_3)^T$ is in the plane defined by $X_1 + X_2 - X_3 = \mu_1 + \mu_2 - \mu_3$, where $\vec{\mu} = (\mu_1, \mu_2, \mu_3)^T$.

C.3   Gaussian Random Vector

C.3.1   Definition and Main Properties

Definition C.1

A random vector $\vec{X}$ with values in $\mathbb{R}^n$ is a **Gaussian vector** if any of the following is true:

(1) For any non-random $u \in \mathbb{R}^n$, $u^T \vec{X}$ is a normal random variable.

(2) $\vec{X}$ is a non-random linear combination of p iid normal random variables, for some $p \in \mathbb{N}$

(3) The expectation $\vec{\mu}$ and covariance matrix Ω of $\vec{X}$ are well-defined and its **characteristic function** is

$$\phi_{\vec{X}}(\vec{\omega}) \overset{\text{def}}{=} \mathbb{E}\left(e^{j\vec{\omega}^T \vec{X}}\right) = e^{j\vec{\omega}^T \vec{\mu} - \frac{1}{2}\vec{\omega}^T \Omega \vec{\omega}} \qquad (\text{C.13})$$

for all $\vec{\omega} \in \mathbb{R}^n$

Example C.2

The vector $(\epsilon_1, \dots, \epsilon_n)^T$ with $\epsilon_i \sim N_{0,\sigma^2}$, and $\sigma \neq 0$ is a Gaussian cvector, called **white Gaussian noise**. It has $\vec{\mu} = 0$ and $\Omega = \sigma^2 Id$. The vector

$$\vec{X} = \begin{pmatrix} \sqrt{a}\,\epsilon_1 \\ \sqrt{b}\,\epsilon_2 \\ \sqrt{a}\,\epsilon_1 + \sqrt{b}\,\epsilon_2 \end{pmatrix}$$

is Gaussian with $\vec{\mu} = 0$ and Ω as in (C.12).
The constant (non-random) vector $\vec{X} = \vec{\mu}$ is Gaussian with covariance matrix $\Omega = 0$.

It follows immediately that any (non-random) linear combination of Gaussian vectors is Gaussian. In particular, if $\vec{X}$ is Gaussian and A is a non-random matrix, then $A\vec{X}$ is Gaussian.

Gaussian vectors are entirely defined by their first and second order properties. In particular,

Theorem C.2 (Independence Equals Non-Correlation)
Let $\vec{X}$ (resp. $\vec{Y}$) be a Gaussian random vector in $\mathbb{R}^n$ (resp. $\mathbb{R}^p$). $\vec{X}$ and $\vec{Y}$ are independent if and only if their cross-covariance matrix is 0, i.e.

$$\text{cov}(X_i, Y_j) = 0 \quad \text{for all} \quad i = 1, \dots, n, \ j = 1, \dots, p$$

Note that this is specific to Gaussian vectors. For non-Gaussian random vectors, independence implies non-correlation, but the converse may not be true.

Theorem C.3 (Density)

If Ω is invertible, $\vec{X}$ has a density, given by

$$f_{\vec{X}}(\vec{x}) = \frac{1}{\sqrt{(2\pi)^n \det \Omega}}\, e^{-\frac{1}{2}(\vec{x}-\vec{\mu})^T \Omega^{-1}(\vec{x}-\vec{\mu})}$$

Conversely, we know from Corollary C.1 that if Ω is not invertible (as in the previous example), $\vec{X}$ cannot have a density. A frequent situation where Ω is invertible is the following.

Proposition C.4 *Let $\vec{X} = L\vec{\epsilon}$ where $\vec{X} = (X_1, \ldots, X_p)^T$, $\epsilon = (\epsilon_1, \ldots, \epsilon_n)^T$ is white Gaussian noise and L is a non-random $p \times n$ matrix. The vector $\vec{X}$ is Gaussian with covariance matrix $\Omega = LL^T$. The rank of Ω is equal to the rank of L.*

We use these properties in the following case, which arises in the analysis of ARMA and ARIMA processes.

Corollary C.2 *Let ϵ_i, $i = 1, \ldots, n$ be white Gaussian noise. Let $m \leq n$ and $X_{n-m+1}, \ldots, X_n$ be defined by*

$$X_i = \sum_{j=1}^{i} c_{i,j}\epsilon_j \qquad \text{for } i = m+1, \ldots, n \tag{C.14}$$

with $c_{i,i} \neq 0$. The covariance matrix of $\vec{X} = (X_{n-m+1}, \ldots, X_n)$ is invertible.

C.3.2 Diagonal Form

Let U be the orthogonal transformation in (C.11) and define $\vec{X}' = U\vec{X}$. The covariance matrix of $\vec{X}'$ is

$$\Omega' = \begin{pmatrix} \lambda_1 & 0 & \cdots & & & & \\ 0 & \lambda_2 & \cdots & & & & \\ \vdots & \vdots & \ddots & & & & \\ & & & \lambda_r & 0 & \cdots & \\ & & & 0 & \cdots & 0 & \\ & & & \vdots & & \ddots & \\ & & & 0 & \cdots & & 0 \end{pmatrix} \tag{C.15}$$

Consequently, $X'_{r+1}, \ldots, X'_n$ have 0 variance and are thus non-random, and X'_i, X'_j are independent (as $\mathrm{cov}(X'_i, X'_j) = 0$ for $i \neq j$).

Since $\vec{X} = U^T X'$, it follows that any Gaussian random vector is a linear combination of exactly r independent normal random variables, where r is the rank of its covariance matrix. In practice, one obtains such a representation by means of Choleski's factorization. Let $\vec{\epsilon}$ be a Gaussian white noise sequence with unit variance and let $\vec{Y} = L\vec{\epsilon}$. Then $\vec{Y}$ is a Gaussian vector with covariance matrix Ω and 0 expectation (and $\vec{Y} + \vec{\mu}$ is a Gaussian vector with expectation $\vec{\mu}$, for any non-random vector $\vec{\mu}$). This is used to simulate a random vector with any desired covariance matrix.

Example C.3

One Choleski fatorization of Ω in (C.12) is $\Omega = LL^T$ with

$$L = \begin{pmatrix} \sqrt{a} & 0 & 0 \\ 0 & \sqrt{b} & 0 \\ \sqrt{a} & \sqrt{b} & 0 \end{pmatrix}$$

Let $\epsilon = (\epsilon_1, \epsilon_2, \epsilon_3)$ be Gaussian white noise with unit variance, i.e. such that the covariance matrix of ϵ is equal to Id. Let $\vec{Y} = L\vec{\epsilon} + \vec{\mu}$, i.e.

$$Y_1 = \mu_1 + \sqrt{a}\,\epsilon_1$$
$$Y_2 = \mu_2 + \sqrt{b}\,\epsilon_2$$
$$Y_3 = \mu_3 + \sqrt{a}\,\epsilon_1 + \sqrt{b}\,\epsilon_2$$

In this case, $\vec{Y}$ has a covariance matrix Ω and an expectation $\vec{\mu}$. This gives a means to simulate a Gaussian vector with expectation $\vec{\mu}$ and covariance matrix Ω.

Note that we find, as seen in Example C.12, that $Y_1 + Y_2 - Y_3$ is a (non-random) constant.

C.4   Foundations of ANOVA

C.4.1   Homoscedastic Gaussian Vector

Definition C.2

A Gaussian vector is called **homoscedastic** with variance σ^2 if its covariance matrix is $\sigma^2\text{Id}$ for some $\sigma > 0$. The expectation $\vec{\mu}$ is not necessarily 0.

Let $\vec{X} = (X_1, X_2, \ldots, X_n)^T$. This definition is equivalent to claiming that $X_i = \mu_i + \epsilon_i$, with μ_i non-random and $\epsilon_i \sim$ iid N_{0,σ^2}.

A homoscedastic Gaussian vector always has a density (since its covariance matrix is invertible) given by

$$f_{\vec{X}}(\vec{x}) = \frac{1}{(2\pi)^{n/2} \sigma^n} e^{-\frac{1}{2\sigma^2}\|\vec{x}-\vec{\mu}\|^2} \tag{C.16}$$

Homoscedasticity is preserved by orthogonal transformations.

Theorem C.5

Let U be an orthogonal matrix (i.e. $U^{-1} = U^T$). If $\vec{X}$ is homoscedastic Gaussian and $\vec{Y} = U\vec{X}$, then $\vec{Y}$ is also homoscedastic Gaussian with the same variance.

The following theorem underlies the ANOVA theory.

Theorem C.6

Let $\vec{X}$ be homoscedastic Gaussian in $\mathbb{R}^n$, $\vec{\mu} = \mathbb{E}(\vec{X})$ and M some linear subspace of $\mathbb{R}^n$, of dimension k. Let Π_M be the orthogonal projection on M.

(1) $\Pi_M \vec{X}$ and $\vec{Y} = \vec{X} - \Pi_M \vec{X}$ are independent,

(2) $\left\|\Pi_M \vec{X} - \Pi_M \vec{\mu}\right\|^2 \sim \chi_k^2$,

(3) $\left\|\vec{Y} - \vec{\mu} + \Pi_M \vec{\mu}\right\|^2 \sim \chi_{n-k}^2$,

where χ_n^2 is the χ-square distribution with n degrees of freeedom.

C.4.2   Maximum Likelihood Estimation for Homoscedastic Gaussian Vectors

---

Theorem C.7 (ANOVA)

Let $\vec{X}$ be homoscedastic Gaussian in $\mathbb{R}^n$ with variance σ^2 and expectation $\vec{\mu}$. Assume that $\vec{\mu}$ is restricted to a linear subspace M of $\mathbb{R}^n$; let $k = \dim M$. We are interested in estimating the true values of $\vec{\mu}$ and σ^2.

(1) The MLE of $(\vec{\mu}, \sigma^2)$ is $\hat{\mu} = \Pi_M \vec{X}$, $\hat{\sigma}^2 = \frac{1}{n}\left\|\vec{X} - \hat{\mu}\right\|^2$.

(2) $\mathbb{E}(\hat{\mu}) = \vec{\mu} = \mathbb{E}(\vec{X})$.

(3) $\vec{X} - \hat{\mu}$ and $\hat{\mu}$ are independent Gaussian random vectors and $\left\|\vec{X} - \vec{\mu}\right\|^2 = \left\|\vec{X} - \hat{\mu}\right\|^2 + \left\|\vec{\mu} - \hat{\mu}\right\|^2$.

(4) $\left\|\vec{X} - \hat{\mu}\right\|^2 \sim \chi_{n-k}^2 \sigma^2$ and $\left\|\hat{\mu} - \vec{\mu}\right\|^2 \sim \chi_k^2 \sigma^2$.

(5) (Fisher distribution)

$$\frac{\dfrac{\left\|\hat{\mu} - \vec{\mu}\right\|^2}{k}}{\dfrac{\left\|\vec{X} - \hat{\mu}\right\|^2}{n-k}} \sim F_{k,n-k}$$

A special case is the well-known estimation for iid normal random variables, used in Theorem 2.3

Corollary C.3 *Let* $\left(X_i\right)_{i=1...n} \sim N(\mu, \sigma^2)$.

(1) The MLE of (μ, σ) *is*

$$\hat{\mu} = \bar{X} \stackrel{\text{def}}{=} \frac{1}{n} \sum_{i=1}^{n} X_i \qquad \hat{\sigma}^2 = \frac{1}{n} S_{XX}$$

with $S_{XX} \stackrel{\text{def}}{=} \sum_{i=1}^{n} \left(X_i - \bar{X}\right)^2$.

(2) S_{XX} *and* $\bar{X}$ *are independent and*

$$\sum_i \left(X_i - \mu\right)^2 = S_{XX} + n(\bar{X} - \mu)^2$$

(3) $S_{XX} \sim \chi_{n-1}^2 \sigma^2$ *and* $\bar{X} \sim N(\mu, \frac{\sigma^2}{n})$.

(4) (Student distribution):

$$\frac{\sqrt{n}\,(\bar{X} - \mu)}{\sqrt{\dfrac{S_{XX}}{n-1}}} \sim t_{n-1}$$

C.5   Conditional Gaussian Distribution

C.5.1   Schur Complement

Let M be a square matrix, decomposed in blocks as $M = \left(\begin{smallmatrix} A & B \\ C & D \end{smallmatrix}\right)$, where A and D are square matrices (but B and C need not be square) and A is invertible. The **Schur complement** of A in M is defined as

$$S = D - CA^{-1}B$$

It has the following properties.

(1) $\det(M) = \det(A)\det(S)$;
(2) If either M or S is invertible then so is the other and M^{-1} has the form $\left(\begin{smallmatrix} \star & \star \\ \star & S^{-1} \end{smallmatrix}\right)$, where $\star$ stands for unspecified blocks of appropriate dimensions;
(3) If M is symmetrical (resp. positive definite, positive semi-definite), then so is S.

C.5.2   Distribution of $\vec{X}_1$ given $\vec{X}_2$

Let $\vec{X}$ be a random vector in $\mathbb{R}^{n_1+n_2}$ and let $\vec{X} = \left(\begin{smallmatrix} \vec{X}_1 \\ \vec{X}_2 \end{smallmatrix}\right)$, with $\vec{X}_i$ in $\mathbb{R}^{n_i}$, $i = 1, 2$. We are interested in the conditional distribution of $\vec{X}_2$ given that $\vec{X}_1 = \vec{x}_1$ (this is typically for prediction purposes). By general results of the probability theory, this conditional distribution is well defined; if $\vec{X}$ is Gaussian, it turns out that this conditional distribution is also Gaussian, as explained next.

Let $\vec{\mu}_2 = \mathbb{E}(\vec{X}_2)$, $\vec{\mu}_1 = \mathbb{E}(\vec{X}_1)$ and decompose the covariance matrix of $\vec{X}$ into blocks as follows.

$$\Omega = \begin{pmatrix} \Omega_{1,1} & \Omega_{1,2} \\ \Omega_{2,1} & \Omega_{2,2} \end{pmatrix}$$

with $\Omega_{i,j}$ (cross-covariance matrix) defined by

$$\Omega_{i,j} = \mathbb{E}\big((\vec{X}_i - \vec{\mu}_i)(\vec{X}_j - \vec{\mu}_j)^T\big) \qquad i,j = 1,2$$

Note that $\Omega_{2,1} = \Omega_{1,2}^T$ and $\vec{X}_2$ and $\vec{X}_1$ are independent if and only if $\Omega_{2,1} = 0$.

Theorem C.8 ([32])

Let $\vec{X}$ be a Gaussian random vector in $\mathbb{R}^{n_1+n_2}$. The conditional distribution of $\vec{X}_2$, given that $\vec{X}_1 = \vec{x}_1$, is Gaussian. If $\Omega_{1,1}$ is invertible, its expectation is $\vec{\mu}_2 + \Omega_{2,1}\Omega_{1,1}^{-1}(\vec{x}_1 - \vec{\mu}_1)$ and its covariance matrix is the Schur complement of the covariance matrix $\Omega_{1,1}$ of $\vec{X}_1$ in the covariance matrix Ω of $(\vec{X}_1, \vec{X}_2)$. In particular, the conditional covariance of $\vec{X}_2$, given that $\vec{X}_1 = \vec{x}_1$, does not depend on $\vec{x}_1$.

The property that the conditional covariance matrix is independent of $\vec{x}_1$ generally holds true only for Gaussian vectors. By the properties of covariance matrices, if Ω is invertible, then this is also the case for $\Omega_{1,1}$ also (this follows from the last sentence in Section C.2.2). In this case, by the properties of the Schur complement, the conditional covariance matrix also has full rank.

C.5.3   Partial Correlation

Theorem C.8 provides a formula for the conditional covariance. Though it is valid only for Gaussian vectors, it is used as the basis for the definition of *partial covariance* and *partial correlation*, employed in time series analysis. Informally, these parameters quantify the residual correlation between X_1 and X_n when we know the values of $X_2, \ldots, X_{n-1}$.

Definition C.3 (Partial Covariance and Correlation, Gaussian case)

Let $\vec{X} = (X_1, X_2, \ldots, X_{n-1}, X_n)^T$ be a Gaussian vector such that its covariance matrix is invertible. Let

$$\Gamma = \begin{pmatrix} \gamma_{1,1} & \gamma_{1,n} \\ \gamma_{1,n} & \gamma_{n,n} \end{pmatrix}$$

be the covariance matrix of the conditional distribution of (X_1, X_n) given $(X_2 = x_2, \ldots, X_{n-1} = x_{n-1})$. By Theorem C.8, Γ is independent of $x_2, \ldots, x_{n-1}$. The **partial covariance** of X_1 and X_n is $\gamma_{1,n}$ and the **partial correlation** of X_1 and X_n is

$$r_{1,n} = \frac{\gamma_{1,n}}{\sqrt{\gamma_{1,1}\gamma_{n,n}}}$$

If $X_1, \ldots, X_n$ is a Markov chain, and $n > 1$, then X_n is independent of X_1, given $X_2, \ldots, X_{n-1}$. In such a case, the partial correlation of X_1 and X_n is 0 (but the covariance of X_1 and X_n is not 0). Partial correlation can be used to test if a Markov chain model is adequate. The following theorem gives a simple way to compute partial correlation.

Theorem C.9 ([32])

Let $\vec{X} = (X_1, X_2, \ldots, X_{n-1}, X_n)^T$ be a Gaussian vector such that its covariance matrix Ω is invertible. The partial correlation of X_1 and X_n is given by

$$r_{1,n} = \frac{-\tau_{1,n}}{\sqrt{\tau_{1,1}\tau_{n,n}}}$$

where $\tau_{i,j}$ is the (i,j)th term of Ω^{-1}.

The classical definition of partial correlation consists in extending Theorem C.9:

Definition C.4 (Partial Correlation)

Let $\vec{X} = (X_1, X_2, \ldots, X_{n-1}, X_n)^T$ be a random vector such that its covariance matrix Ω is well-defined and invertible. The **partial correlation** of X_1 and X_n is defined as

$$r_{1,n} = \frac{-\tau_{1,n}}{\sqrt{\tau_{1,1}\tau_{n,n}}}$$

where $\tau_{i,j}$ is the (i,j)th term of Ω^{-1}.

C.6   Proofs

Proposition C.1

Let $v \in \mathbb{R}^n$ be in the kernel of Ω, i.e. $\Omega v = 0$ and let $Z = v^T(X - \mu)$. We have

$$\mathbb{E}(Z^2) = \mathbb{E}(v^T(X - \mu)(X - \mu)^T v) = v^T \Omega v = 0$$

thus $Z = 0$ w.p. 1, i.e. $X - \mu$ is orthogonal to the kernel of Ω.

Since Ω is symmetric, the set of vectors that are orthogonal to its kernel is V, thus $X - \mu \in V$.

Proposition C.4

X is Gaussian with covariance matrix LL^T by (C.10). We now show that the rank of LL^T is equal to the rank of L^T, by demonstrating that LL^T and L^T have the same null space. Indeed, if $L^T x = 0$, then $LL^T x = 0$. Conversely, if $LL^T x = 0$ then $x^T LL^T x = \left\| L^T x \right\|^2 = 0$ and thus $L^T x = 0$. Finally, the rank of a matrix is equal to that of its transpose.

Theorem C.5

The covariance matrix of $U\vec{X}$ is $U(\sigma^2 \mathrm{Id}) U^T = \sigma^2 \mathrm{Id}$.

Theorem C.6

Let $\vec{X}' = \vec{x} - \mu$ and $\vec{Y}' = \vec{X}' - \Pi_M \vec{X}'$. By linearity of Π_M, $\Pi_M \vec{X}'$ and $\Pi_M \vec{X}$ (resp. $\vec{Y}'$ and $\vec{Y}$) differ by a constant (non-random) vector, thus the cross-covariance Γ of $\vec{X}$ and $\vec{Y}$ is that of $\vec{X}'$ and $\vec{Y}'$. Consequently,

$$
\begin{aligned}
\Gamma &= \mathbb{E}\left(\Pi_M \vec{X}' \vec{Y}'^T \right) = \mathbb{E}\left(\Pi_M \vec{X}' (\vec{X}' - \Pi_M \vec{X}')^T \right) \\
&= \mathbb{E}\left(\Pi_M \vec{X}' \vec{X}'^T - \Pi_M \vec{X}' \vec{X}'^T \Pi_M^T \right) \\
&= \Pi_M \mathbb{E}\left(\vec{X}' \vec{X}'^T \right) - \Pi_M \, E\left(\vec{X}' \vec{X}'^T \right) \Pi_M^T
\end{aligned}
$$

Now, $\mathbb{E}\left(\vec{X}' \vec{X}'^T \right) = \sigma^2 \mathrm{Id}$ and thus

$$
\Gamma = \sigma^2 \Pi_M - \sigma^2 \Pi_M \Pi_M^T = 0
$$

since $\Pi_M = \Pi_M^T$ and $\Pi_M^2 = \Pi_M$. By Theorem C.2, $\Pi_M \vec{X}$ and $\vec{Y}$ are independent. This proves item (1).

Let $Z = \Pi_M X - \Pi_M \mu$. Put Π_M in diagonal form as in (C.2) and let $\tilde{X} = U^T(\vec{x} - \mu)$ and $\tilde{Z} = U^T Z$, so that

$$
\tilde{Z} = D\tilde{X}
$$

thus

$$
\tilde{Z}_i = \begin{cases} \tilde{X}_i & \text{for } i = 1, \ldots, m \\ 0 & \text{for } i = m+1, \ldots, n \end{cases}
$$

Note that

$$
\left\| \tilde{Z} \right\| = \left\| \Pi_M \vec{X} - \Pi_M \vec{\mu} \right\| \tag{C.17}
$$

since U is orthogonal. Now $\tilde{X}$ is homoscedastic Gaussian with 0 expectation and variance σ^2 (Theorem C.5), thus $\tilde{X}_i \sim \mathrm{iid} N_{0,\sigma^2}$, and finally

$$
\left\| \Pi_M \vec{X} - \Pi_M \vec{\mu} \right\|^2 = \sum_{i=1}^{m} \tilde{X}_i^2
$$

This proves item (2), and similarly, item (3).

Theorem C.7

The log likelihood of an observation $\vec{x} = (x_1, \ldots, x_n)^T$ is

$$l_{\vec{x}}(\vec{\mu}, \sigma) = -\frac{N}{2} \ln(2\pi) - N \ln(\sigma) - \frac{1}{2\sigma^2} \sum_{i=1}^{n} (x_r - \mu_r)^2$$

$$= -\frac{N}{2} \ln(2\pi) - N \ln(\sigma) - \frac{1}{2\sigma^2} \left\| \vec{x} - \vec{\mu} \right\|^2 \qquad (C.18)$$

For a given σ, by (C.1), the log-likelihood is maximized for $\vec{\mu} = \hat{\mu} = \Pi_M(\vec{x})$, which is independent of σ. Let $\vec{\mu} = \hat{\mu}$ in (C.18) and maximize with respect to σ, this gives the first item in the theorem. The rest follows from Theorem C.6.

Digital Filters

Here, we review all we need to know for Chapter 5 regarding causal digital filters. It is a very small subset of signal processing, without any Fourier transform. See for example [83] or [75] for a complete and traditional course.

D.1 Calculus of Digital Filters

D.1.1 Backshift Operator

We consider data sequences of finite, but arbitrary length and call $\mathcal{S}$ the set of all such sequences (i.e. $\mathcal{S} = \bigcup_{n=1}^{\infty} \mathbb{R}^n$). We denote with $\text{length}(X)$ the number of elements in the sequence X.

The **backshift** operator is the mapping B from $\mathcal{S}$ to itself defined by

$$\text{length}(BX) = \text{length}(X)$$
$$(BX)_1 = 0$$
$$(BX)_t = X_{t-1} \qquad t = 2, \ldots, \text{length}(X)$$

We usually view a sequence $X \in \mathcal{S}$ as a column vector, so that we can write

$$B \begin{pmatrix} X_1 \\ X_2 \\ \vdots \\ X_n \end{pmatrix} = \begin{pmatrix} 0 \\ X_1 \\ \vdots \\ X_{n-1} \end{pmatrix} \tag{D.1}$$

when $\text{length}(X) = n$.

If we know that $\text{length}(X) \leq n$, we can express the backshift operator as a matrix multiplication:

$$BX = B_n X \tag{D.2}$$

Here, B_n is the $n \times n$ matrix

$$B_n = \begin{pmatrix} 0 & 0 & 0 & \cdots & & \\ 1 & 0 & 0 & \cdots & & \\ 0 & 1 & 0 & \cdots & & \\ \vdots & \vdots & \vdots & \ddots & & \\ & & & & 0 & 0 \\ & & & & 1 & 0 \end{pmatrix}$$

Obviously, if $n = \text{length}(X)$, then applying B n times to X gives a sequence of 0s; in matrix form:

$$(B_n)^n = 0 \tag{D.3}$$

D.1.2   Filters

Definition D.1

A **filter** (also called "causal filter", or "realizable filter") is any mapping, say F, from $\mathcal{S}$ to itself that has the following properties.

(1) A sequence of length n is mapped to a sequence of the same length.

(2) There exists an infinite sequence of numbers h_m, $m = 0, 1, 2, \ldots$ (called the filter's **impulse response**) such that, for any $X \in \mathcal{S}$,

$$\left(FX\right)_t = h_0 X_t + h_1 X_{t-1} + \cdots + h_{t-1} X_1 \qquad t = 1, \ldots, \text{length}(X) \quad \text{(D.4)}$$

Example D.1

The backshift operator B is the filter with $h_0 = 0$, $h_1 = 1$, $h_2 = h_3 = \cdots = 0$.

The identical mapping, Id, is the filter with $h_0 = 1$, $h_1 = h_2 = \cdots = 0$.

The de-seasonalizing filter of order s, R_s, is the filter with $h_0 = \cdots = h_{s-1} = 1$, $h_m = 0$ for $m \geq s$.

The differencing filter at lag s, Δ_s, is the filter with $h_0 = 1$, $h_s = -1$ and $h_m = 0$ for $m \neq 0$ and $m \neq s$.

Equation (D.4) can also be expressed as

$$F = \sum_{m=0}^{\infty} h_m B^m \tag{D.5}$$

where $B^0 = \text{Id}$. Note that the summation is only apparently infinite, since for a sequence X in $\mathcal{S}$ of length n, we have $FX = \sum_{m=0}^{n-1} h_m B^m X$.

In matrix form, if we know that $\text{length}(X) \leq n$ we can write (D.4) as

$$FX = \begin{pmatrix} h_0 & 0 & 0 & \cdots & & & \\ h_1 & h_0 & 0 & \cdots & & & \\ h_2 & h_1 & h_0 & \cdots & & & \\ \vdots & \vdots & \vdots & \ddots & & & \\ & & & & h_0 & 0 \\ h_{n-1} & h_{n-2} & \cdots & \cdots & h_1 & h_0 \end{pmatrix} X \qquad (D.6)$$

A filter is called **Finite Impulse Response (FIR)** if $h_n = 0$ for n large enough. Otherwise, it is called **Infinite Impulse Response**.

D.1.3 Impulse response and Dirac Sequence

Define the **Dirac sequence** of length n

$$\delta_n = \begin{pmatrix} 1 \\ 0 \\ \vdots \\ 0 \end{pmatrix} \qquad (D.7)$$

The impulse response of a filter satisfies

$$\begin{pmatrix} h_0 \\ h_1 \\ \vdots \\ h_{n-1} \end{pmatrix} = F\delta_n \qquad (D.8)$$

This is used to compute the impulse response if we know some algorithm to compute FX for any X.

D.1.4 Composition of Filters, Commutativity

Let F and F' be filters. The composition of F and F', denoted with FF', is defined as the mapping from $\mathcal{S}$ to $\mathcal{S}$ obtained by applying F' first, then F, i.e. such that for any sequence X

$$\left(FF'\right)(X) = F\left(F'(X)\right) \qquad (D.9)$$

It can easily be seen that FF' is a filter. Furthermore, *the composition of filters commute*, i.e.

$$FF' = F'F \qquad (D.10)$$

The first n terms of the impulse response of FF' can be obtained by

$$\begin{pmatrix} g_0 \\ g_1 \\ \vdots \\ g_{n-1} \end{pmatrix} = \left(FF' \right) \delta_n = F(F'\delta_n) = \left(F'F \right) \delta_n = F'(F\delta_n) \qquad \text{(D.11)}$$

Example D.2

Let us compute the impulse response of FF' when $F = \text{Id} - B$ (differencing at lag 1) and $F' = \text{Id} - B^5$ (differencing at lag 5). Let n be large:

$$F'\delta_n = \left(1, 0, 0, 0, 0, -1, 0, 0, 0, 0, 0, \ldots \right)^T$$
$$F(F'\delta_n) = \left(1, -1, 0, 0, 0, -1, 1, 0, 0, 0, 0, \ldots \right)^T$$

thus the impulse response g of FF' is given by

$$\begin{cases} g_0 = g_6 = 1 \\ g_1 = g_5 = -1 \\ \text{else } g_m = 0 \end{cases} \qquad \text{(D.12)}$$

Alternatively, we can carry out the computations in reverse order and obtain the same result:

$$F\delta_n = \left(1, -1, 0, 0, 0, 0, 0, 0, 0, 0, 0, \ldots \right)^T$$
$$F'(F\delta_n) = \left(1, -1, 0, 0, 0, -1, 1, 0, 0, 0, 0, \ldots \right)^T$$

D.1.5   Inverse of Filter

Since the matrix in (D.6) is triangular, it is invertible if and only if its diagonal terms are non-zero, i.e. if $h_0 \neq 0$, where h_0 is the first term of the impulse response. If this holds, it can also be seen that the reverse mapping F^{-1} is a filter, i.e it satisfies the conditions in Definition D.1. Thus, *a filter F is invertible if and only if $h_0 \neq 0$.*

For example, the inverse filter of the filter with impulse response $h_m = 1$ for $m \geq 0$ (integration filter) is that with the impulse response $h_0 = 1$, $h_1 = -1$, $h_m = 0$ for $m \geq 2$ (differencing filter). This can also be written as

$$\left(\sum_{n=0}^{\infty} B^n \right)^{-1} = \text{Id} - B \qquad \text{(D.13)}$$

D.1.6   AR(∞) Representation of Invertible Filter

Let F be an invertible filter and $Y = FX$. Let $g_0, g_1, \ldots$ be the impulse response of F^{-1}. We have $X = F^{-1}Y$ thus for $t \geq 1$

$$X_t = g_0 Y_t + g_1 Y_{t-1} + \cdots + g_{t-1} Y_1 \tag{D.14}$$

Note that $g_0 = \frac{1}{h_0}$, thus

$$Y_t = c_0 X_t + c_1 Y_{t-1} + \cdots + c_{t-1} Y_1 \tag{D.15}$$

with

$$\begin{cases} c_0 = \dfrac{1}{g_0} = h_0 \\[2mm] c_m = -\dfrac{g_m}{g_0} = -g_m h_0 \quad \text{for } m = 1, 2, \ldots \end{cases} \tag{D.16}$$

The sequence $c_0, c_1, c_2, \ldots$ used in (D.15) is called the AR(∞)[1] representation of F. It can be used to compute the output Y_t as a function of the past output and the current input X_t. This applies to any invertible filter.

If F^{-1} is FIR, then there exists a certain q such that $c_m = 0$ for $m \geq q$. The filter F is called **auto-regressive** of order q: (AR(q)).

D.1.7   Calculus of Filters

When the filter F' is invertible, the composition $F(F'^{-1})$ is also denoted $\frac{F}{F'}$. There is no ambiguity since composition is commutative, namely

$$\frac{F}{F'} = F(F'^{-1}) = (F'^{-1})F \tag{D.17}$$

We have thus defined the product and division of filters. It is straightforward to see that the addition and subtraction of filters are also filters. For example, the filter $F + F'$ has the impulse response $h_m + h'_m$ and the filter $-F$ has the impulse response $-h_m$.

It is customary to denote the identity filter with 1. With this convention, we can write the differencing filters as

$$\Delta_s = 1 - B^s \tag{D.18}$$

and the de-seasonalizing filter as

$$R_s = 1 + B + \cdots + B^{s-1} \tag{D.19}$$

We can also rewrite (D.13) as

$$\frac{1}{\sum_{n=0}^{\infty} B^n} = 1 - B$$

---

[1] AR stands for "Auto-Regressive".

or

$$\frac{1}{1-B} = \sum_{n=0}^{\infty} B^n \tag{D.20}$$

The usual manipulations of fractions work as expected, and can be combined with the usual rules for addition, subtraction, multiplication and division (as long as the division is valid, i.e. the filter at the denominator is invertible). Thus, if F and F' are invertible, the inverse of $\frac{F}{F'}$ is $\frac{F'}{F}$:

$$\frac{1}{\frac{F}{F'}} = \frac{F'}{F}$$

Example D.3

We can recover (D.12) as follows:

$$FF' = (1-B)(1-B^5) = 1 - B - B^5 + B^6$$

Example D.4

$$\frac{\Delta_5}{\Delta_1} = \frac{1-B^5}{1-B} = \frac{(1-B)(1+B+B^2+B^3+B^4)}{1-B} \tag{D.21}$$
$$= 1 + B + B^2 + B^3 + B^4 = R_5$$

If F and G are FIR, then FG, $F+G$ and $F-G$ are also FIR, but $\frac{F}{G}$ is (generally) not.

D.1.8 z Transform

It is customary in signal processing to manipulate transforms rather than the filters themselves. By definition, the **transfer function** of the filter with impulse response h is the power series

$$H(z) = h_0 z + h_1 z^{-1} + h_1 z^{-2} + \cdots \tag{D.22}$$

i.e. it is the z transform of the impulse response. This is considered as a formal series, i.e. there is no worry about its convergence for any value of z. Note the use of z^{-1} (customary in signal processing) rather than z (customary in maths).

It follows from the rules on the calculus of filters that using transfer functions is the same as replacing B by z^{-1} everywhere.

Example D.5

The transfer function of the filter

$$F = \frac{Q_0 + Q_1 B + \cdots + Q_q B^q}{P_0 + P_1 B + \cdots + P_p B^p} \tag{D.23}$$

with $P_0 \neq 0$ is precisely

$$H(z) = \frac{Q_0 + Q_1 z^{-1} + \cdots + Q_q z^{-q}}{P_0 + P_1 z^{-1} + \cdots + P_p z^{-p}} \qquad (D.24)$$

You may find it more convenient to use z-transforms and thus transfer functions if you do not feel comfortable manipulating the backshift operator B (and vice-versa: if you do not like transfer functions, use the backshift operator instead).

D.2 Stability

A filter F with impulse response h_n is called **stable**[2] if and only if

$$\sum_{n=0}^{\infty} |h_n| < +\infty \qquad (D.25)$$

For a sequence $X \in \mathcal{S}$, let $\|X\|_\infty = \max_{t=1,\ldots,\text{length}(X)} |X_t|$. If F is stable and $Y = FX$ then

$$\|Y\|_\infty \leq M \|X\|_\infty \qquad (D.26)$$

where $M = \sum_{n=0}^{\infty} |h_n|$. In other words, if the input to the filter has a bounded magnitude, so does the output. In contrast, if F is not stable, the output of the filter may become infinitely large as the length of the input increases. A stable filter has an impulse response h_n that decays quickly as $n \to \infty$.

For example, the filter in (D.21) is stable (as is any FIR filter) and the filter in (D.20) is not stable.

In practice, if a filter is not stable, we may experience numerical problems when computing its output (Figure D.1).

D.3 Filters with Rational Transfer Function

D.3.1 Definition

Filters with Rational Transfer Function are filters of the form in (D.23), or, equivalently, whose transfer function has the form in (D.24), with $P_0 \neq 0$. Many filters used in practice are of this type. Note that

$$\frac{Q_0 + Q_1 B + \cdots + Q_q B^q}{P_0 + P_1 B + \cdots + P_p B^p} = \frac{Q_0' + Q_1' B + \cdots + Q_q' B^q}{1 + P_1' B + \cdots + P_p' B^p}$$

with $Q_m' = \frac{Q_m}{P_0}$ and $P_m' = \frac{P_m}{P_0}$, so we can always assume that $P_0 = 1$.

---

[2]or Bounded Input, Bounded Output (BIBO)-stable.

384   Digital Filters

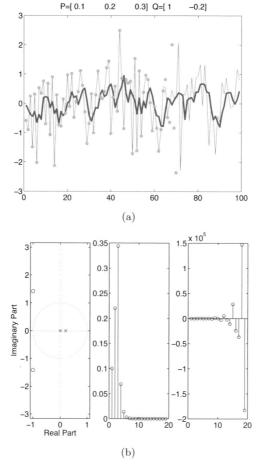

(a)

(b)

Figure D.1 A numerical illustration of the filter $F = \frac{0.1 + 0.2\,B + 0.3\,B^2}{1 - 0.2\,B}$. (a) A random input sequence X (thin line), the corresponding output $Y = FX$ (thick line), obtained by the Matlab command `Y=filter([0.1 0.2 0.3],[1 -0.2],X)` and the reconstructed input $F^{-1}Y$ obtained by `filter([1 -0.2],[0.1 0.2 0.3],Y)` (small disks). (b) left: Poles (x) and zeroes (o) of F, obtained by `zplane([0.1 0.2 0.3],[1 -0.2])`. The filter F is stable (poles within unit disk) but F^{-1} is not (at least one zero outside the unit disk). (b) middle and right: impulse response of F (`h=filter([0.1 0.2 0.3],[1 -0.2],D)`, where D is a dirac sequence) and F^{-1} (`h=filter([1 -0.2],[0.1 0.2 0.3],D)`). Reconstruction of X as $F^{-1}Y$ fails for $t \geq 60$; this is a symptom of F^{-1} being unstable.

A filter with a rational transfer function can always be expressed as a ***linear constant-coefficient difference*** equation. Indeed, consider F as in (D.23) with $P_0 \neq 0$ and let $Y = FX$. Recall that this is equivalent to

$$Y = \left(P_0 + P_1 B + \cdots + P_p B^p\right)^{-1}\left(Q_0 + Q_1 B + \cdots + Q_q B^q\right)X$$

i.e.

$$\left(P_0 + P_1 B + \cdots + P_p B^p\right)Y = \left(Q_0 + Q_1 B + \cdots + Q_q B^q\right)X$$

Thus for $t = 1, \ldots, \text{length}(X)$:

$$P_0 Y_t + P_1 Y_{t-1} + \cdots + P_p Y_{t-p} = Q_0 X_t + Q_1 X_{t-1} + \cdots + Q_q X_{t-q} \quad \text{(D.27)}$$

with the usual convention $Y_t = X_t = 0$ for $t \leq 0$. Since $P_0 \neq 0$, this equation can be used to iteratively compute $Y_1 = \frac{Q_0 X_1}{P_0}$, $Y_2 = \frac{Q_0 X_2 + Q_1 X_1}{P_0}$, etc.

The *impulse response* of F is usually computed by applying `filter` to a Dirac sequence. It may also be computed by Taylor series expansion, using classical rules for Taylor series of functions of one real variable.

Example D.6

The impulse response of the filter $G = \frac{1-2B}{1-B^2}$ is obtained as follows. We use the rule $\frac{1}{1-x} = 1 + x + x^2 + \cdots$ and obtain

$$
\begin{aligned}
\frac{1 - 2B}{1 - B^2} &= (1 - 2B)\bigl(1 + B^2 + B^4 + \cdots\bigr) \\
&= 1 + B^2 + B^4 + B^6 + \cdots - 2B - 2B^3 - 2B^5 - \cdots \\
&= 1 - 2B + B^2 - 2B^3 + B^4 - 2B^5 \ldots
\end{aligned}
$$

Thus, the impulse response of G is $(1, -2, 1, -2, 1, -2, \ldots)$.

Note that, in general, a filter with a rational transfer function has an infinite impulse response.

The *inverse* of the filter F exists if $Q_0 \neq 0$ and is

$$F^{-1} = \frac{P_0 + P_1 B + \cdots + P_p B^p}{Q_0 + Q_1 B + \cdots + Q_q B^q} \quad \text{(D.28)}$$

i.e. it is obtained by exchanging numerator and denominator.

D.3.2   Poles and Zeroes

By definition, the **Poles** of a filter with rational transfer functions are the values of z, other than 0, for which the transfer function is not defined. If the transfer function is in a form that cannot be simplified,[3] the poles are the zeroes of the denominator. Similarly, the **Zeroes** of the filter are the values of $z \neq 0$ such that $H(z) = 0$.

A filter with a rational transfer function is stable if it has no pole or its *poles are all inside the unit disk*, i.e. they have a modulus of less than 1. This follows from the definition of stability and standard results on the theory of Taylor series of rational fractions in one variable.

The location of zeroes is useful to assess the stability of the reverse filter. Indeed, if the filter is invertible (i.e. $Q_0 \neq 0$), then the inverse filter is stable if all zeroes of the original filter are within the unit disk.

---

[3] i.e. of the form $\frac{p(z^{-1})}{q(z^{-1})}$, where p, q are polynomials with no common root

Example D.7   Numerical Stability of Inverse Filter

Consider the filter

$$F = \frac{0.1 + 0.2\,B + 0.3\,B^2}{1 - 0.2\,B} \tag{D.29}$$

We apply the filter to an input sequence X (thin line in Figure D.1) and obtain the output sequence Y (thick line). F is a filter with a

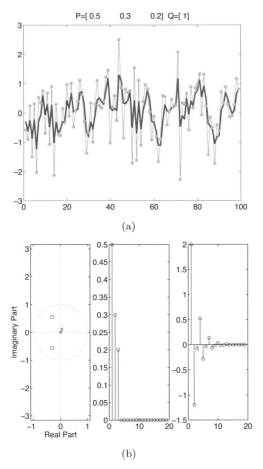

(a)

(b)

Figure D.2 A numerical illustration of the filter $G = G = 0.5 + 0.3\,B + 0.2\,B^2$. (a) A random input sequence X (thin line), the corresponding output $Z = GX$ (thick line) and the reconstructed input $G^{-1}Z$ (small disks). (b) left: Poles ($\times$) and zeroes ($\circ$) of G. Depending on the conventions, the origin may or may not be considered as a pole. With our conversion, there is no pole but the employed software shows a pole of multiplicity 2 at 0. The filter G and its inverse are stable (poles and zeroes are within the unit disk). (b) middle and right: Impulse response of G and G^{-1}. Reconstruction works perfectly.

rational transfer function, equivalent to the linear constant-coefficient difference equation

$$Y_t = 0.1\,X_t + 0.2\,X_{t-1} + 0.3\,X_{t-2} + 0.2\,Y_{t-1}$$

The poles are the zeroes of $1 - 0.2\,z^{-1}$, which are the same as the zeroes of $z - 0.2$ (i.e $z = 0.2$).

The poles lie inside the unit disk, and the filter is thus stable. Its impulse response quickly decays to 0. The filter is invertible but the inverse is not stable as the zeroes are not all inside the unit disk. The impulse response of the inverse filter does not decay. We also compute $F^{-1}(Y)$ which, in theory, should be equal to X (small disks). However, the inverse filter in not stable and can be difficult to apply in practice; we see indeed that rounding errors become significant for $t \geq 60$.

If we consider instead $G = 0.5 + 0.3\,B + 0.2\,B^2$, then both the filter and its inverse are stable, and there are no numerical errors in the reconstruction (Figure D.2).

D.4 Predictions

We use the filter to model time series and perform predictions. Many formulas in Chapter 5 are based on the following result.

D.4.1 Conditional Distribution Lemma

Lemme D.1 *Let* (X_1, X_2), (Y_1, Y_2) *be two random vectors, both with values in the space* $\mathbb{R}^{n_1} \times \mathbb{R}^{n_2}$*, and such that*

$$Y_1 = F_1 X_1$$
$$Y_2 = F_{21} X_1 + F_{22} X_2$$

where F_1, F_{21}, F_{22} *are non-random linear operators and* F_1 *is invertible.*

Let X_2' *be a random sample drawn from the conditional distribution of* X_2*, given that* $X_1 = x_1$ *and*

$$y_1 = F_1 x_1$$
$$Y_2' = F_{21} x_1 + F_{22} X_2'$$

The law of Y_2' *is the conditional distribution of* Y_2 *given that* $Y_1 = y_1$*.*

D.4.2 Predictions

Let X_t, Y_t be two real-valued random sequences (not necessarily iid), defined for $t \geq 1$. Assume that $Y = FX$, where F is an invertible filter with impulse response $h_0, h_1, h_2, \ldots$ and $AR(\infty)$ representation $c_0, c_1, c_2, \ldots$. The following theorem claims that making a prediction for X is equivalent to making a prediction for Y. It is a direct consequence of Lemma D.1.

Theorem D.2 (Conditional Distribution of Futures)

Assume that $(y_1, \ldots, y_t)^T = F(x_1, \ldots, x_t)^T$ *and let* $\ell \geq 1$.

Assume that $(X'_{t+1}, \ldots, X'_{t+\ell})$ *is a random sample drawn from the conditional distribution of* $(X_{t+1}, \ldots, X_{t+\ell})$ *given that* $X_1 = x_1, \ldots, X_t = x_t$. *Let*

$$\left(y_1, \ldots, y_t, Y'_{t+1}, \ldots, Y'_{t+\ell}\right)^T = F\left(x_1, \ldots, x_t, X'_{t+1}, \ldots, X'_{t+\ell}\right)^T$$

Then $(Y'_{t+1}, \ldots, Y'_{t+\ell})$ *is distributed according to the conditional distribution of* $(Y_{t+1}, \ldots, Y_{t+\ell})$ *given that* $Y_1 = y_1, \ldots, Y_t = y_t$.

We can derive explicit formulas for point predictions.

Corollary D.1 (Point Prediction) *Define the ℓ-point-ahead predictions by*

$$\hat{X}_t(\ell) = \mathbb{E}\left(X_{t+\ell} \mid X_1 = x_1, \ldots, X_t = x_t\right)$$
$$\hat{Y}_t(\ell) = \mathbb{E}\left(Y_{t+\ell} \mid Y_1 = y_1, \ldots, Y_t = y_t\right)$$

then

$$\left(y_1, \ldots, y_t, \hat{Y}_t(1), \ldots, \hat{Y}_t(\ell)\right)^T = F\left(x_1, \ldots, x_t, \hat{X}_t(1), \ldots, \hat{X}_t(\ell)\right)^T \quad (D.30)$$

In particular,

$$\hat{Y}_t(\ell) = h_0 \hat{X}_t(\ell) + h_1 \hat{X}_t(\ell-1) + \cdots + h_{\ell-1} \hat{X}_t(1) + h_{\ell-1} x_t + \cdots + h_{t-1} x_1 \quad (D.31)$$

and

$$\hat{Y}_t(\ell) = c_0 \hat{X}_t(\ell) + c_1 \hat{Y}_t(\ell-1) + \cdots + c_{\ell-1} \hat{Y}_t(1) + c_\ell y_t + \cdots + c_{t-1} y_1 \quad (D.32)$$

In the frequent case where X_t is assumed to be iid, we can deduce more explicit results for the point prediction and mean square prediction errors:

Corollary D.2 *Also assume that X_t is iid with mean $\mu = \mathbb{E}(X_t)$ and variance $\sigma^2 = \mathrm{var} X_t$. Then*

(1) (Point predictions)

$$\left(y_1, \ldots, y_t, \hat{Y}_t(1), \ldots, \hat{Y}_t(\ell)\right)^T = F\left(x_1, \ldots, x_t, \mu, \ldots, \mu\right)^T \quad (D.33)$$

In particular

$$\hat{Y}_t(\ell) = (h_0 + h_1 + \cdots + h_{\ell-1})\mu + h_{\ell-1} x_t + \cdots + h_{t-1} x_1 \quad (D.34)$$

and

$$\hat{Y}_t(\ell) = c_0 \mu + c_1 \hat{Y}_t(\ell-1) + \cdots + c_{\ell-1} \hat{Y}_t(1) + c_\ell y_t + \cdots + c_{t-1} y_1 \quad (D.35)$$

(2) (Mean square prediction error) Define

$$\text{MSE}_t^2(\ell) \overset{\text{def}}{=} \text{var}\big(Y_{t+\ell} \mid Y_1 = y_1, \ldots, Y_t = y_t\big)$$
$$= \mathbb{E}\left(\big(Y_{t+\ell} - \hat{Y}_t(\ell)\big)^2 \;\Big|\; Y_1 = y_1, \ldots, Y_t = y_t\right)$$

then

$$\text{MSE}_t^2(\ell) = \sigma^2\big(h_0^2 + \cdots + h_{\ell-1}^2\big) \tag{D.36}$$

Corollary D.3 (Innovation Formula) *For $t \geq 2$:*

$$Y_t - \hat{Y}_{t-1}(1) = h_0(X_t - \mu) \tag{D.37}$$

This is called an innovation formula as it can be used to relate X_t (the "innovation") to the prediction error.

D.5   Log Likelihood of Innovation

Let X_t, Y_t be two real-valued random sequences (not necessarily iid), defined for $t \geq 1$. Assume that $Y = FX$ where F is an invertible filter with impulse response $h_0, h_1, h_2, \ldots$. Also assume that for any n, the random vector $(X_1, \ldots, X_n)$ has a PDF $f_{\vec{X}_n}(x_1, \ldots, x_n)$.

***

Theorem D.3
Assume that the impulse response of F is such that $h_0 = 1$. Then for all n the random vector $(Y_1, \ldots, Y_n)$ has a PDF equal to

$$f_{\vec{Y}_n}(y_1, \ldots, y_n) = f_{\vec{X}_n}(x_1, \ldots, x_n)$$

with $(y_1, \ldots, y_n)^T = F(x_1, \ldots, x_n)^T$.

***

Theorem D.3 can be used for estimations in the context of ARMA models, where X_t is the non observed innovation, assumed to be iid. The theorem states that the log-likelihood of the model is the same as if we had observed the innovation; estimation methods for iid sequences can then be applied, as in Example 2.5.

D.6   Matlab Commands

filter. $Y = \texttt{filter}\big([Q_0\ Q_1\ \cdots\ Q_q], [P_0\ P_1\ \cdots\ P_p], X\big)$ with $P_0 \neq 0$ applies the filter

$$\frac{Q_0 + Q_1 B + \cdots + Q_q B^q}{P_0 + P_1 B + \cdots + P_p B^p} \tag{D.38}$$

to the input sequence X and produces an output sequence Y of the same length as X.

poles and zeroes can be obtained with `zplane`

de-seasonalizing. The de-seasonalizing filter with period s is $R_s = \sum_{i=1}^{s-1} B^i$; $X = R_s Y$ can be obtained using

```
R = ones(1,s)
X = filter(R,1,Y)
```

differencing filter. $X = \Delta_s Y$ can be obtained by

```
X = filter([1,0,...,0,-1],[1],Y)
```

where `-1` is at position $s + 1$. The inverse filter is obtained by exchanging the first two arguments:

```
Y = filter([1],[1,0,...,0,-1],X)
```

and the terms $h_0, h_1, \ldots, h_\ell$ of the impulse response of Δ_s^{-1} are obtained by the command:

```
h = filter([1],[1,0,...,0,-1],[1,0,...,0])
```

where the last vector has ℓ zeroes.

  The command `Y=diff(X,s)` also applies the differencing filter Δ_s to X but it removes the first s entries instead of setting them to 0 as `filter` does

impulse response. `impz([P0 P1 ... Pp], [Q0 Q1 ... Qq], n)` gives the first n terms of the impulse response of the filter in (D.38). It is equivalent to using `filter([P0 P1 ... Pp], [Q0 Q1 ... Qq], deltan)` with `deltan` equal to the sequence `[1 0 ... 0]` (with $n - 1$ zeroes).

parameter estimation of an ARMA model can be done by direct application of Theorem 5.4 and `lsqnonlin` for the solution of the non-linear optimization problem. For simple ARMA models, it can be done in one step with `armax`.

convolution. `c=conv(a,b)` computes the sequence of length $\text{length}(a)$ $+\text{length}(b) - 1$ such that $c_k = \sum_i a_i b_{k-i}$, where the sum is for i such that a_i and b_{k-i} are defined. The command `Y=filter(P1,Q1,filter(P2,Q2,X))` is equivalent to

```
P = conv(P1,P2)
Q = conv(Q1,Q2)
X = filter(P,Q,X)
```

simulation of an ARMA process as defined in Definition 5.1 can be done with

```
e = sigma * randn(n,1)
x = mu + filter(A,C,e)
```

D.7 Proofs

Lemma D.1

The characteristic function of Y_2' is

$$
\begin{aligned}
\phi_{Y_2'}(\omega_2) &= \mathbb{E}\big(e^{-j(\langle \omega_2, F_{21}x_1\rangle + \langle \omega_2, F_{22}X_2'\rangle)}\big) = e^{-j\langle \omega_2, F_{21}x_1\rangle}\mathbb{E}\big(e^{-j\langle \omega_2, F_{22}X_2'\rangle}\big) \\
&= e^{-j\langle \omega_2, F_{21}x_1\rangle}\mathbb{E}\big(e^{-j\langle \omega_2, F_{22}X_2\rangle} \mid X_1 = x_1\big) \\
&:= e^{-j\langle \omega_2, F_{21}x_1\rangle}h(x_1) := f(x_1)
\end{aligned} \tag{D.39}
$$

where $\langle \cdot, \cdot \rangle$ is the inner product. Now let $g(y_1) := f(F_1^{-1}y_1)$. We want to show that

$$
g(y_1) = \mathbb{E}\big(e^{-j\langle \omega_2, Y_2\rangle} \mid Y_1 = y_1\big) \tag{D.40}
$$

By definition of a conditional probability, this is equivalent to showing that for any $\omega_1 \in \mathbb{R}^{n_1}$

$$
\mathbb{E}\big(e^{-j\langle \omega_1, Y_1\rangle}g(Y_1)\big) = \mathbb{E}\big(e^{-j\langle \omega_1, Y_1\rangle}\, e^{-j\langle \omega_2, Y_2\rangle}\big) \tag{D.41}
$$

Now, by the definition of $g(\cdot)$

$$
\begin{aligned}
\mathbb{E}\big(e^{-j\langle \omega_1, Y_1\rangle}g(Y_1)\big) &= \mathbb{E}\big(e^{-j\langle \omega_1, Y_1\rangle}\, e^{-j\langle \omega_2, F_{21}F_1^{-1}Y_1\rangle}h(F_1^{-1}Y_1)\big) \\
&= \mathbb{E}\big(e^{-j\langle \omega_1, F_1X_1\rangle}\, e^{-j\langle \omega_2, F_{21}X_1\rangle}h(X_1)\big) \\
&= \mathbb{E}\big(e^{-j\langle \omega_1, F_1X_1\rangle}\, e^{-j\langle \omega_2, F_{21}X_1\rangle}\, e^{-j\langle \omega_2, F_{22}X_2\rangle}\big)
\end{aligned}
$$

where the last equality is, by definition of $h(\cdot)$, a conditional expectation in (D.39). This shows (D.41) as desired.

Note that the proof is simpler if X_1, X_2 have a density, but this may not always hold, even for Gaussian processes.

Theorem D.3

The random vector $\vec{Y}_n = (Y_1, \ldots, Y_n)^T$ is derived from the random vector $\vec{X}_n = (X_1, \ldots, X_n)^T$ by $\vec{Y}_n = H_n\vec{X}_n$ where H_n is the matrix in (D.6), with $h_0 = 1$. Based on the formula of change of variable, we have

$$
f_{\vec{X}_n}(x_1, \ldots, x_n) = \big|\det(H_n)\big|f_{\vec{Y}_n}(y)
$$

and $\det(H_n) = 1$.

Bibliography

[1] The ns-3 Network Simulator. http://www.nsnam.org/.

[2] I. Adan, J. Visschers and J. Wessels. Sum of Product Forms Solutions to MSCCC Queues with Job Type Dependent Processing Times. *Memorandum COSOR 98-19*, 1998.

[3] F. Baccelli and P. Bremaud. *Elements of Queueing Theory: Palm Martingale Calculus and Stochastic Recurrences*. Springer Verlag, 2003.

[4] François Baccelli and Pierre Brémaud. *Palm Probabilities and Stationary Queues*. Springer LNS, 1987.

[5] O. Bakr and I. Keidar. Evaluating the Running Time of a Communication Round over the Internet. In *Proceedings of the twenty-first annual symposium on Principles of Distributed Computing*, pages 243–252. ACM New York, NY, USA, 2002.

[6] S. Balsamo. Product Form Queueing Networks. *Lecture Notes in Computer Science*, pages 377–402, 2000.

[7] C. Barakat, P. Thiran, G. Iannaccone, C. Diot and P. Owezarski. Modeling Internet Backbone Traffic at the Flow Level. *IEEE Transactions on Signal Processing*, 51(8):2111–2124, 2003.

[8] A. D. Barbour. Networks of Queues and the Method of Stages. *Advances in Applied Probability*, 8(3):584–591, 1976.

[9] P. Barford and M. Crovella. Generating Representative Web Workloads for Network and Server Performance Evaluation. *SIGMETRICS Perform. Eval. Rev.*, 26(1):151–160, 1998.

[10] F. Baskett, K. M. Chandy, R. R. Muntz, and F. G. Palacios. Open, Closed, and Mixed Networks of Queues with Different Classes of Customers. *Journal of the ACM (JACM)*, 22(2):260, 1975.

[11] S. A. Berezner, C. F. Kriel and A. E. Krzesinski. Quasi-Reversible Multiclass Queues with Order Independent Departure Rates. *Queueing Systems*, 19(4):345–359, 1995.

[12] C. R. Blyth and H. A. Still. Binomial Confidence Intervals. *Journal of the American Statistical Association*, pages 108–116, 1983.

[13] T. Bonald and A. Proutiere. Insensitive Bandwidth Sharing in Data Networks. *Queueing Systems*, 44(1):69–100, 2003.

[14] T. Bonald and J. Virtamo. Calculating the Flow Level Performance of Balanced Fairness in Tree Networks. *Performance Evaluation*, 58(1):1–14, 2004.

[15] G. E. P. Box and G. M. Jenkins. *Time Series Analysis, Forecasting and Control*. Holden-Day, San Francisco, 1970.

[16] M. Bramson. Instability of FIFO Queueing Networks with Quick Service Times. *The Annals of Applied Probability*, 4(3):693–718, 1994.

[17] P. Brémaud. *Markov Chains: Gibbs Fields, Monte Carlo Simulation and Queues*. Springer, 1999.

[18] P. J. Brockwell and R. A. Davis. *Introduction to Time Series and Forecasting*. Springer Verlag, 2002.

[19] P. J. Brockwell and R.A. Davis. *Introduction to Time Series and Forecasting, second edition*. Springer-Verlag, New York, 2002.

[20] J. P. Buzen. Computational Algorithms for Closed Queueing Networks with Exponential Servers. *Commun. ACM*, 16(9):527, 1973.

[21] E. Çinlar. *Introduction to Stochastic Processes*. Prentice Hall, 1975.

[22] K. Mani Chandy and Charles H. Sauer. Computational Algorithms for Product Form Queueing Networks. *Commun. ACM*, 23(10):573–583, 1980.

[23] C. S. Chang. *Performance Guarantees in Communication Networks*. Springer-Verlag, New York, 2000.

[24] X. Chao, M. Miyazawa and M. Pinedo. *Queueing Networks: Customers, Signals and Product Form Solutions*. Wiley, 1999.

[25] J. B. Chen, E. Yasuhiro and C. Kee. The Measured Performance of Personal Computer Operating Systems, 15 thACM SOSP. *Colorado, United States: Copper Mountain*, pages 169–173, 1995.

[26] G. Chiola, M. A. Marsan and G. Balbo. Product-Form Solution Techniques for the Performance Analysis of Multiple-Bus Multiprocessor Systems with Nonuniform Memory References. *IEEE Transactions on Computers*, 37(5):532–540, 1988.

[27] A. E. Conway and N. D. Georganas. RECAL New Efficient Algorithm for the Exact Analysis of Multiple-Chain Closed Queuing Networks. *Journal of the ACM (JACM)*, 33(4):768–791, 1986.

[28] A. E. Conway, E. S. Silva and S. S. Lavenberg. Mean Value Analysis by Chain of Product Form Queueing Networks. *IEEE Transactions on Computers*, 38(3):432–442, 1989.

[29] Verizon Corporation. Verizon NEBS(TM) Compliance: Energy Efficiency Requirements for Telecommunications Equipment. Technical Report VZ.TPR.9205, September 2008.

[30] T. M. Cover and J. A. Thomas. *Elements of Information Theory*. Wiley, 1991.

[31] M. E. Crovella and M. S. Taqqu. Estimating the Heavy Tail Index from Scaling Properties. *Methodology and computing in applied probability*, 1(1):55–79, 1999.

[32] A. C. Davison. *Statistical Models*. Cambridge University Press, 2003.

[33] A. C. Davison and D. V. Hinkley. *Bootstrap Methods and their Application*. Cambridge Univ Pr, 1997.

[34] P. J. Denning and J. P. Buzen. The Operational Analysis of Queueing Network Models. *ACM Computing Surveys (CSUR)*, 10(3):225–261, 1978.

[35] M. El-Taha and Shaler Jr. Stidham. *Sample-Path Analysis of Queueing Systems*. Kluwer Academic, 1998.

[36] E. Gelenbe. Product-Form Queueing Networks with Negative and Positive customers. *Journal of Applied Probability*, pages 656–663, 1991.

[37] W. J. Gordon and G. F. Newell. Closed Queuing Systems with Exponential Servers. *Operations Research*, 15(2):254–265, 1967.

[38] G. Grimmett and D. Stirzaker. *Probability and Random Processes*. Oxford University Press, USA, 2001.

[39] M. Grossglauser and J. C. Bolot. On the Relevance of Long-Range Dependence in Network Traffic. *IEEE/ACM Transactions on Networking (TON)*, 7(5):629–640, 1999.

[40] B. Hechenleitner and K. Entacher. On Shortcomings of the ns-2 Random Number Generator. *Proceedings of Communication Networks and Distributed Systems Modeling and Simulation* (CNDS 2002), 2002.

[41] C. C. Holt. Forecasting Seasonal and Trends by Exponentially Weighted Moving Averages. Carnegie Institute of Technology, Pittsburgh, Pennsylvania, 1957.

[42] J. R. Jackson. Jobshop-like Queueing Systems. *Management Science*, 50(12):1796–1802, 1963.

[43] N. L. Johnson, S. Kotz and A. W. Kemp. *Univariate Discrete Distributions*. Wiley-Interscience, 2005.

[44] F. P. Kelly. *Reversibility and Stochastic Networks*. Wiley, 1979.

[45] F. P. Kelly. Models for a self-managed Internet. *Philosophical Transactions: Mathematical, Physical and Engineering Sciences*, pages 2335–2348, 2000.

[46] L. Kleinrock. *Queueing Systems Volume I: Theory*, volume 1. John-Wiley & Sons, 1975.

[47] L. Kleinrock. *Queueing Systems Volume II: Computer Applications*, volume 2. John-Wiley & Sons, 1976.

[48] A. B. Koehler, R. D. Snyder and O. J. Keith. Forecasting Models and Prediction Intervals for the Multiplicative Holt-Winters Method. *International Journal of Forecasting*, 17:269–286, April-June 2001.

[49] M. A. Law and W. D. Kelton. *Simulation Modeling and Analysis*. McGraw-Hill, 2000.

[50] J.-Y. Le Boudec. Rate Adaptation, Congestion Control and Fairness: a Tutorial. http://ica1www.epfl.ch/PS_files/LEB3132.pdf.

[51] J.-Y. Le Boudec and P. Thiran. *Network Calculus*. Springer Verlag Lecture Notes in Computer Science volume 2050 (available online at http://lcawww.epfl.ch), July 2001.

[52] J.-Y. Le Boudec and M. Vojnovic. The Random Trip Model: Stability, Stationary Regime, and Perfect Simulation. *IEEE/ACM Transactions on Networking*, 14(6):1153–1166, 2006.

[53] J.-Y. Le Boudec. A BCMP Extension to Multiserver Stations with Concurrent Classes of Customers. *ACM SIGMETRICS Perform. Eval. Rev.*, 14(1):78–91, 1986.

[54] J.-Y. Le Boudec. Interinput and Interoutput Time Distribution in Classical Product-Form Networks. *IEEE Transactions on Software Engineering*, pages 756–759, 1987.

[55] J.-Y. Le Boudec. Steady-State Probabilities of the PH/PH/1 Queue. *Queueing Systems*, 3(1):73–87, 1988.

[56] J.-Y. Le Boudec. The MULTIBUS Algorithm. *Performance Evaluation*, 8(1):1–18, 1988.

[57] J.-Y. Le Boudec. Understanding the Simulation of Mobility Models with Palm Calculus. *Performance Evaluation*, 64(2):126–147, 2007.

[58] L. M. Le Ny. Étude analytique de reseaux de files d'attende multiclasses à routage variable. *RAIRO Recherche Operationnelle/Oper. Res*, 14:331–347, 1980.

[59] P. L'Ecuyer. Random number generation. *Handbook of Simulation: Principles, Methodology, Advances, Applications, and Practice*, 1998.

[60] P. L'Ecuyer. Software for Uniform Random Number Generation: Distinguishing the Good and the Bad. In *Proceedings of the 33nd Conference on Winter Simulation*, pages 95–105. IEEE Computer Society Washington, DC, USA, 2001.

[61] E. L. Lehmann. On Likelihood Ratio Tests. In *IMS Lecture Notes- 2nd Lehmann Symposium*, volume 49, pages 1–8, 2006.

[62] E. L. Lehmann and J. P. Romano. *Testing Statistical Hypotheses*. Springer, 2005.

[63] T. Leighton. Improving Performance on the Internet. *Commun. ACM*, 52(2):44–51, 2009.

[64] W. E. Leland, M. S. Taqqu, W. Willinger, D. V. Wilson, and M. Bellcore. On the Self-Similar Nature of Ethernet Traffic (extended version). *IEEE/ACM Transactions on networking*, 2(1):1–15, 1994.

[65] G. Malinas and J. Bigelow. Simpson's Paradox. *Stanford Encyclopedia of Philosophy*, online.

[66] S. Manthorpe and J.-Y. Le Boudec. A Comparison of ABR and UBR to Support TCP Traffic. *Networking and Information Systems Journal*, 2(5-6):764–793, 1999.

[67] M. Matsumoto and T. Nishimura. Mersenne Twister: a 623-Dimensionally Equidistributed Uniform Pseudo-Random Number Generator. *ACM Transactions on Modeling and Computer Simulation (TOMACS)*, 8(1):3–30, 1998.

[68] R. Merz and J.-Y. Le Boudec. Conditional Bit Error Rate for an Impulse Radio UWB Channel with Interfering Users. In *2005 IEEE International Conference on Ultra-Wideband, 2005. ICU 2005*, pages 130–135, 2005.

[69] M. Miyazawa. The Derivation of Invariance Relations in Complex Queueing Systems with Stationary Inputs. *Advances in Applied Probability*, 15(4):874–885, 1983.

[70] M. Miyazawa. Rate Conservation Laws: A Survey. *Queueing Systems*, 15(1-4):1–58, 1994.

[71] P. Nain. Basic Elements of Queueing Theory: Application to the Modelling of Computer Systems. *Course notes*.

[72] M. F. Neuts. Stationary Waiting-Time Distributions in the GI/PH/1 Queue. *Journal of Applied Probability*, 18(4):901–912, 1981.

[73] J. P. Nolan. Stable Distributions. *Math/Stat Department, American University*, 2009.

[74] I. Norros. A Storage Model with Self-Similar Input. *Queueing systems*, 16(3):387–396, 1994.

[75] A. V. Oppenheim, R. W. Schafer and J. R. Buck. *Discrete-Time Signal Processing (2nd ed.)*. Prentice-Hall, Inc., 1999.

[76] A. Papoulis and S. U. Pillai. *Probability, Random Variables, and Stochastic Processes*. McGraw-Hill New York, 1965.

[77] J. Pearl. *Probabilistic Reasoning in Intelligent Systems: Networks of Plausible Inference*. Morgan Kaufmann Publishers, 1988.

[78] J. Pellaumail. Formule du produit et décomposition de réseaux de files d'attente. *Ann. Inst. H. Poincaré Sect. B (N.S.)*, 15(3):261–286, 1979.

[79] M. D. Perlman and L. Wu. The Emperor's New Tests. *Statistical Science*, pages 355–369, 1999.

[80] B. Pittel. Closed Exponential Networks of Queues with Saturation: The Jackson-Type Stationary Distribution and its Asymptotic Analysis. *Mathematics of Operations Research*, 4(4):357–378, 1979.

[81] H. V. Poor. *An Introduction to Signal Detection and Estimation*. Springer, 1994.

[82] K. R. Popper. *Logik der Forschung: Zur Erkenntnistheorie der modernen Naturwissenschaft*. J. Springer, 1935.

[83] P. Prandoni and M Vetterli. *Signal Processing for Communications*. EPFL Press, Communication and Information Sciences, 2008.

[84] M. Reiser. Mean-Value Analysis and Convolution Method for Queue-Dependent Servers in Closed Queueing Networks. *Performance Evaluation*, 1(1):7–18, 1981.

[85] M. Reiser and H. Kobayashi. Queuing Networks with Multiple Closed Chains: Theory and Computational Algorithms. *IBM Journal of Research and Development*, 19(3):283–294, 1975.

[86] M. Reiser and S. S. Lavenberg. Mean-Value Analysis of Closed Multichain Queuing Networks. *Journal of the ACM (JACM)*, 27(2):313–322, 1980.

[87] H. Rinne. *The Weibull Distribution: A Handbook*. Chapman & Hall/CRC, 2008.

[88] Ph. Robert. *Stochastic Networks and Queues*. Stochastic Modelling and Applied Probability Series. Springer-Verlag, 2003.

[89] S. A. Roberts. A General Class of Holt-Winters Type Forecasting Models. *Management Science*, 28(7):808–820, July 1982.

[90] S. M. Ross. *Simulation.* Academic Press, 2006.

[91] W. Rudin. *Real and Complex Analysis.* McGraw-Hill Series in Mathematics, 1987.

[92] M. Sakata, S. Noguchi and J. Oizumi. Analysis of a Processor Shared Queueing Model for Time Sharing Systems. In *Proc. 2nd Hawaii International Conference on System Sciences*, volume 625628, 1969.

[93] G. Samorodnitsky and M. S. Taqqu. *Stable Non-Gaussian Random Processes: Stochastic Models with Infinite Variance.* Chapman & Hall/CRC, 1994.

[94] R. Serfozo. *Introduction to Stochastic Networks.* Springer Verlag, 1999.

[95] R. Serfozo. *Basics of Applied Stochastic Processes.* Springer Verlag, 2009.

[96] A. Shaikh, J. Rexford and K. G. Shin. Load-Sensitive Routing of Long-Lived IP Flows. In *Proceedings of the Conference on Applications, Technologies, Architectures, and Protocols for Computer Communication*, pages 215–226. ACM New York, NY, USA, 1999.

[97] R. H. Shumway and D. S. Stoffer. *Time Series Analysis and its Applications with R Examples.* Springer-Verlag, New York, 2006.

[98] P. J. Smith, M. Shafi and H. Gao. Quick Simulation: a Review of Importance Sampling Techniques incommunications systems. *IEEE Journal on Selected Areas in Communications*, 15(4):597–613, 1997.

[99] S. Souders. High-Performance Web Sites. *Commun. ACM*, 51(12):36–41, 2008.

[100] J. L. Van den Berg and O. J. Boxma. The M/G/1 Queue with Processor Sharing and its Relation to a Feedback Queue. *Queueing Systems*, 9(4):365–401, 1991.

[101] N. M. Van Dijk. *Queueing Networks and Product Forms: a Systems Approach.* John Wiley & Sons, 1993.

[102] S. Verrill. Confidence Bounds for Normal and Lognormal Distribution Coefficients of Variation. Technical Report Research Paper 609, USDA Forest Products Laboratory, Madison, Wisconsin, 2003.

[103] J. Walrand. *An Introduction to Queueing Networks.* Prentice Hall, 1988.

[104] R. Weber. C11: Statisics, online lecture notes, http://www.statslab.cam.ac.uk.

[105] R. Weber. Time Series, online lecture notes, http://www.statslab.cam.ac.uk.

[106] Wikipedia. Harmonic Mean. http://en.wikipedia.org.

[107] P. R. Winters. Forecasting Sales by Exponentially Weighted Moving Averages. *Management Science*, 6(60):324–342, 1960.

[108] B. Ycart. *Modèles et algorithmes markoviens*, volume 39. Springer Verlag, 2002.

Index

crete-Time Signals.

3 Signals and Hilbert Spaces – Euclidean Geometry: A Review – From Vector Spaces to Hilbert Spaces – Subspaces, Bases, Projections – Signal Spaces Revisited.

4 Fourier Analysis – Preliminaries – The DFT (Discrete Fourier Transform) – The DFS (Discrete Fourier Series) – The DTFT (Discrete-Time Fourier Transform) – Relationships Between Transforms – Fourier Transform Properties – Fourier Analysis in Practice – Time-Frequency Analysis – Digital Frequency vs. Real Frequency.

5 Discrete-Time Filters – Linear Time-Invariant Systems – Filtering in the Time Domain – Filtering by Example (Time Domain) – Filtering in the Frequency Domain – Filtering by Example (Frequency Domain) – Ideal Filters – Realizable Filters.

8 Stochastic Signal Processing – Random Variables – Random Vectors – Random Processes – Spectral Representation of Stationary Random Processes – Stochastic Signal Processing.

9 Interpolation and Sampling – Preliminaries and Notation – Continuous-Time Signals – Bandlimited Signals – Interpolation – The Sampling Theorem – Aliasing – Discrete-Time Processing of Analog Signals.

10 A/D and D/A Conversions – Quantization – A/D Conversion – D/A Conversion.

11 Multirate Signal Processing – Downsampling – Upsampling – Rational Sampling Rate Changes – Oversampling.

12 Design of a Digital Communication System – The Communication Channel – Modem Design: The Transmitter – Modem Design: The Receiver – Adaptive Synchronization.

ORDER FORM

You may order our books through your bookshop

I wish to order:	Switzerland (CHF incl. VAT)	France, Belgium (€ excl. VAT):
_____copies «**Signal Processing for Communications**»	79.–	49.50
		(prices may be subject to modification)

Company / Institute: _____

Name / First name: _____

Delivery address: _____ E-mail: _____

Zip code: _____ City: _____ Land: _____

Date: _____ Signature: _____

SIGNAL PROCESSING FOR COMMUNICATIONS

Paolo Prandoni and Martin Vetterli

With a novel, less classical approach to the subject, the authors have written a book with the conviction that signal processing should be taught to be fun. The treatment is therefore less focused on the mathematics and more on the conceptual aspects, the idea being to allow the readers to think about the subject at a higher conceptual level, thus building the foundations for more advanced topics.

The book remains an engineering text, with the goal of helping students solve real-world problems. In this vein, the last chapter pulls together the individual topics as discussed throughout the book into an in-depth look at the development of an end-to-end communication system, namely, a modem for communicating digital information over an analog channel.

Richly illustrated with examples and exercises in each chapter, the book offers a fresh approach to the teaching of signal processing to upper-level undergraduates.

After studies in Padua and Berkeley, PAOLO PRANDONI received his Doctorate from the EPFL in the Audiovisual Communications Laboratory in 1999. His interests have included musical timbre, audio modelling and compression, communication system design and image analysis. He is now the founder and Director of Quividi, a company based in Paris, France, and is a visiting lecturer in signal processing at the EPFL.

MARTIN VETTERLI works at the Swiss Federal Institute of Technology in Lausanne (EPFL) on signal processing and communications, with an emphasis on wavelet theory and applications, image and video compression, joint source-channel coding, self-organized communication systems and sensor networks. He has won many prizes including the Swiss National Latsis Prize in 1996, the SPIE Presidential award in 1999, and the IEEE Signal Processing Technical Achievement Award in 2001. He is a fellow of the IEEE, a member of SIAM, and has held numerous editorial roles. He is the author of two other books and more than 150 research articles.

2008, 392 pages, 16 x 24 cm, hardcover
EPFL Press ISBN: 978-2-940222-20-9
CRC Press ISBN: 978-1-4200-7046-0